Transformative Change in Western Thought
A History of Metamorphosis from Homer to Hollywood

LEGENDA

LEGENDA, founded in 1995 by the European Humanities Research Centre of the University of Oxford, is now a joint imprint of the Modern Humanities Research Association and Maney Publishing. Titles range from medieval texts to contemporary cinema and form a widely comparative view of the modern humanities, including works on Arabic, Catalan, English, French, German, Greek, Italian, Portuguese, Russian, Spanish, and Yiddish literature. An Editorial Board of distinguished academic specialists works in collaboration with leading scholarly bodies such as the Society for French Studies and the British Comparative Literature Association.

MHRA

The Modern Humanities Research Association (MHRA) encourages and promotes advanced study and research in the field of the modern humanities, especially modern European languages and literature, including English, and also cinema. It also aims to break down the barriers between scholars working in different disciplines and to maintain the unity of humanistic scholarship in the face of increasing specialization. The Association fulfils this purpose primarily through the publication of journals, bibliographies, monographs and other aids to research.

Maney Publishing is one of the few remaining independent British academic publishers. Founded in 1900 the company has offices both in the UK, in Leeds and London, and in North America, in Philadelphia. Since 1945 Maney Publishing has worked closely with learned societies, their editors, authors, and members, in publishing academic books and journals to the highest traditional standards of materials and production.

Transformative Change in Western Thought

A History of Metamorphosis from Homer to Hollywood

EDITED BY
INGO GILDENHARD AND ANDREW ZISSOS

LEGENDA

Modern Humanities Research Association and Maney Publishing
2013

Published by the
Modern Humanities Research Association and Maney Publishing
1 Carlton House Terrace
London SW1Y 5AF
United Kingdom

LEGENDA is an imprint of the
Modern Humanities Research Association and Maney Publishing

Maney Publishing is the trading name of W. S. Maney & Son Ltd,
whose registered office is at Suite 1C, Joseph's Well, Hanover Walk, Leeds LS3 1AB

ISBN 978-1-907975-01-1

First published 2013

Printed in Great Britain

Cover: 875 Design

Copy-Editor: Richard Correll

CONTENTS

ACKNOWLEDGEMENTS

This volume has its origins in an international workshop on 'Myths of Transform-ation' that we, the editors, co-organized in September 2008. The workshop took place under the auspices of the Durham Institute of Advanced Study, whose theme for 2008–09 was 'Being Human'. We are grateful to the Institute (and its nonpareil director at the time, Professor Ash Amin) for a conference grant that enabled us to run the workshop, together with additional funds from the Faculty of Arts & Humanities of Durham University, via the Durham Centre for the Study of the Classical Tradition. Less tangible, but equally crucial support from the Institute came in the form of a highly stimulating environment throughout the year of the 'Being Human' theme, in which we could develop our ideas on transformative change. In particular, we greatly benefited from the first-hand encounter with artworks by Jane Alexander (and the artist herself), on the occasion of an exhibition of her work in Durham Cathedral ('On Being Human', 3–22 March 2009). First thoughts on Alexander's art as well as on the theme of metamorphosis more generally have appeared in the exhibition catalogue *Jane Alexander on Being Human*, ed. by Pep Subirós (Durham: Institute of Advanced Study and Durham University) and the Institute's on-line journal *Insights* <http://www.dur.ac.uk/ias/insights/beinghuman/>.

It took some time for a selection of the workshop papers, additionally recruited pieces, and our own thinking to evolve into the present volume, and we are deeply grateful to our contributors, who responded to endless requests for adjustments and alterations with remarkable and much appreciated grace and patience: our search for the right kind of focus, something approximating coherence, and at least a semblance of balanced coverage has not always been quick and easy, to say the least, and we feel privileged to have been able to work with such a fine group of scholars. After first sounding out more conventional options, we decided to approach Legenda as a possible venue for publication; it turned out to be a serendipitous choice: ever since, we have enjoyed, and benefited from, the vision, care, and encouragement of their editorial team, notably Graham Nelson. The timely appearance of this volume is in no small part due to his vision and support, including just the right amount of gentle pressure to get on with it, a patience with missed deadlines that qualifies for sainthood, and the willingness to proceed with publishing a text that ultimately weighed in at more than twice the contractually agreed length. Likewise, we are much indebted to Richard Correll, who copy-edited our extremely demanding manuscript with critical acumen and good grace.

We would further like to record our profound gratitude to Jane Heath, Viviane Dutaut, and Andreas Pečar for bibliographical pointers and helpful feedback on drafts of our Introductions; to the Durham Institute of Advanced Study for a publication subvention that helped to offset parts of the costs associated with securing the cover images and illustrations; to the Leverhulme Trust for the award of a research fellowship to Ingo Gildenhard that at an early stage much assisted work on the volume; and the Humanities Center of the University of California at Irvine, which awarded Andrew Zissos a generous grant towards the cost of publication in a time of severe financial crisis.

PREFACE

This book contains original scholarship at the cutting edge of various disciplines in the humanities, including classics, history, and various modern literatures and cultures, in particular English, French, and Italian, but also German and American. We hope that, in addition to specialist audiences, our volume will also appeal to the general reader, within as well as beyond academia. Both our chosen theme and the range of our historical coverage are designed to capture the imagination. The composite whole that we hope will emerge out of the individual parts is a profile of sorts of Western culture, from an unexpected point of view: transformative change. And in its endeavour to delineate 'a history of metamorphosis from Homer to Hollywood', *Transformative Change in Western Thought* explores, not least, the imbrication of three core constituents of Western cultural experience across a span of time that covers close to three millennia — from the first instances of metamorphosis in our literary record to the rise of the mutant in our post-Darwinian age: the classical tradition, Judeo-Christian religion, and modern science. Such an undertaking (to quote the anonymous reader of our initial proposal) is, of course, 'impossibly ambitious' — and not just 'on the face it'. No one is more aware than we are that any attempt 'to plot' Western culture *tout court*, from however partial a perspective, risks the charge of hubris, as does the effort to correlate and interlink the three domains of the classical, the biblical, and the scientific. In the modern academy, at least, they tend to be kept well apart.

Why, then, design a volume that defies the principles of disciplinary coherence and specialist focus, principles which underwrite not only the modern knowledge industry, but also the commissioning policy of commercial presses? Apart from the intellectual exhilaration involved in trying to get — and to convey — a sense of 'the big picture', we are in fact convinced that there is a broad readership for a volume such as ours, quite beyond the specialist scholar. One constituency that we have had very much in mind are students at the undergraduate level who are in the process of acquiring an overview of Western culture and its historical foundations in classical antiquity through courses in 'Greek and Roman Mythology' or 'Western Civilization'. The teaching materials available for such modules tend to adopt a survey approach, with an emphasis on facts, figures, and systems of thought, but offer rather limited intellectual stimulus to think through, and with, the formative influences of the Western cultural tradition on a large scale. With its — we hope provocative — focus on the slippery phenomenon of transformation (and how it is tied up with changing conceptions of reality), our volume narrates an alternative history of European culture that brings into view evolved and evolving continuities as well as sedimentations and ruptures, and makes a special point of drawing attention to the implicit and explicit frictions in the Western cultural imaginary from archaic Greece to the present. Even if the results are anything but conclusive and the coverage necessarily selective, we hope that this book will intrigue readers from various backgrounds to think further — as well as outside conventional frames of reference.

From a generic point of view, *Transformative Change in Western Thought* is a hybrid between a monograph and an edited collection. The General Introduction ('Metamorphosis: A Phenomenology') and the three internal introductions ('Antiquity and Archetypes', 'Christianity and Classicizing', 'Science: From the "Post-Metamorphic" to the Posthuman') account for roughly one-quarter of the volume and are designed to provide a theoretical and historical matrix for the individual case studies, which, arranged as they are in rough (but not strict) chronological order, offer representative soundings in both the theoretical issues to do with transformative change identified in the introductions and the three millennia of cultural history explored in the course of this volume. Whereas the introductions aim at sketching broader patterns, the case studies explore specific themes or authors. The objective throughout has been to achieve some sort of coverage and cohesion, without sacrificing depth and sophistication: each case study both constitutes one chapter in a larger story and aims at breaking new ground in its area of specialization.

Our selection of papers has been made with an eye to the volume's overall coherence. This also explains the decision to limit coverage to the Western cultural tradition: while one could imagine a comparative study of conceptions of transformative change from across the globe, a systematic treatment of the material would have resulted in a loss of focus, and at least doubled the size of the volume. That said, we wish to register our profound gratitude to Evan Killick, who presented a paper on Amazonian myths of transformation at the Durham workshop, drawing on his fieldwork in Peruvian Amazonia. Evan's paper was one of the highlights of the event, not least in how it put all the others in a wider, comparative perspective. The next step towards a truly global study of metamorphosis would indeed be to compare and contrast the ways in which this phenomenon has figured in Western culture with its place and function in other cultural traditions; unfortunately, in the present volume we are unable to do more than gesture towards such a project here, again in the spirit of inviting the reader to explore the topic further, beyond our own, self-imposed remit.

LIST OF CONTRIBUTORS

Manuel Baumbach is Professor of Ancient Greek at the University of Bochum

Sarah Annes Brown is Professor of English and Media Studies, Anglia Ruskin University

Carlo Caruso is Professor of Italian in the School of Modern Languages and Cultures, Durham University

Robert Carver is Senior Lecturer in the English Department, Durham University

Guido Giglioni is Cassamarca Lecturer in Neo-Latin Cultural and Intellectual History 1400–1700, The Warburg Institute

Ingo Gildenhard was Professor of Classics & the Classical Tradition in the Department of Classics & Ancient History, Durham University, and is now a Fellow of King's College, Cambridge, and Lecturer in the Faculty of Classics, Cambridge University

Zoe Jaques is Lecturer in English at Anglia Ruskin University and Homerton College, Cambridge

Christopher Lloyd is Professor of French in the School of Modern Languages and Cultures, Durham University

Sonia Macrì is Assistant Professor at the Università degli Studi di Enna 'Kore'

Luke Pitcher is Fellow of Somerville College and University Lecturer in Classics, Oxford University

Francesca Spiegel received her BA degree from King's College London in 2006 and an MA degree from Yale University in 2007, since when she has been a freelance writer and researcher.

Andrew Zissos is Professor of Classics at the University of California, Irvine

LIST OF ILLUSTRATIONS

Cover Illustrations:

Pelike. Attributed to the Ethiop Painter. *c.* 460 BC Dresden, Staatliche Kunstsammlungen Dr. 323. © Skulpturensammlung, Staatliche Kunstsammlungen Dresden Photographer: Hans-Peter Klut, 1999

Grosz, George (1893–1959): *Circe*, 1927.
New York, Museum of Modern Art (MoMA).
Watercolour, pen and ink, and pencil on paper, 26 × 19 1/4″ (66 × 48.6 cm).
Gift of Mr and Mrs Walter Bareiss and an anonymous donor (by exchange) 73.1981 © 2011.
Digital image, The Museum of Modern Art, New York/Scala, Florence
© Photo SCALA, Florence, and DACS 2012

Interior:

Fig. 1, General Introduction: Quinten Massys, *An Old Woman* ('The Ugly Duchess')
Bequeathed by Miss Jenny Louisa Roberta Blaker, 1947
Credit: © The National Gallery, London

Fig. 2, Chapter 1: *Medea's Flight Map*

Fig. 3, Chapter 4: J. W. Waterhouse, *Hamadryade*, 1893
Credit: © akg-images

Fig. 4, Introduction to Part II: Frontispiece of John Bulwer, *Anthropometamorphosis*, 1654
Credit: © The British Library

Fig. 5, Chapter 5: Sieder, *Meroe and her Metamorphosed Victims*, 1538, fol. 2^r (= sig. A2^r)

Fig. 6, Chapter 5: Sieder, *Byrrhena's Statuary of Diana and Actaeon*, 1538, fol. 7^r (= sig. B3^r)

Fig. 7, Chapter 5: Sieder, *Lucius becomes an Ass*, 1538, fol. 17^v (= sig. E1^v)

Fig. 8, Chapter 7: *Lucius and the Matron of Corinth*, Sala dell'Asino d'oro, Rocca dei Rossi di San Secondo
Photograph by Dr C. Torelli, Comune di San Secondo
Reproduced by kind permission of Dr M. Baccaro, Comune di San Secondo.

Fig. 9, Introduction to Part III: Grosz, George (1893–1959), *Circe*, 1927. See *Cover* above.

Fig. 10, Introduction to Part III: Füssli, Johann Heinrich, 'Nachtmahr', 1790
Credit: © akg-images

Fig. 11, Introduction to Part III: Jane Alexander, 'Butcher Boys' (1985–86)
Reinforced plaster, oil paint, animal bones, horns, wood; 128.5 × 213.5 × 88.5 cm
Collection of the South African National Gallery, Cape Town
Photograph: Mark Lewis
© Jane Alexander, reproduced by kind permission of the artist

Fig. 12, Introduction to Part III: *The Fly*, 1958, dir. Kurt Neumann (Movie Still)

Metamorphosis:
A Phenomenology[1]

Ingo Gildenhard & Andrew Zissos

Avant Propos

In the Western cultural tradition, prejudices against marvellous transformation (and its treatment in literature and art) run deep, and metamorphosis has routinely functioned as the alien other of various norms and systems of belief. Evidence of aversion ranges from Servius, the late fourth-century commentator on the *Aeneid*, who rebuked Virgil (70–19 BC) for the scattered myths of metamorphosis included in his epic, to the church father Augustine (354–430), who considered empirically inexplicable change the work of demons, from Christianity's belief in the devil as the shape-shifter par excellence and the modern contempt for alchemy, which, for its practitioners, counted as 'a science of transformation', to Johann Joachim Winckelmann (1717–1768), who expressed his displeasure at what he considered the baroque mannerism of *Apollo and Daphne* by Gian Lorenzo Bernini (1598–1680).[2] In the light of the epistemic and aesthetic protocols associated with the Bible, scientific rationality, classicism, naturalism, and realism, stories involving marvellous change would seem to belong into the realms of the abnormal or the fantastic, the grotesque or the irrational, the monstrous, obscene, or occult, the pagan or the primitive, the surreal, non-western or zany — in short, the exact opposite of the qualities that underwrite essentialist notions of identity, realist protocols of representation, regulatory ideals of beauty, and rational conceptions of reality in occidental thought. The following quotation sums up Western strictures against (the possibility of) metamorphosis:[3]

> One ought here to take into consideration that transformations *stricto sensu* are not permitted in modern western society, at least not officially, and at most fit into its world-picture as fraud, metaphor, or pathological delusion. As goes without saying, in sociology's conception of reality the transformation of persons is impossible, which of course does not preclude the analysis of societies, in which humans transform themselves into ghosts and vice versa. In our society it is rather the case that one can undergo drastic change, up to becoming unrecognizable; but even the most determined alteration in form or status is often, against appearances, construed as change, but not as transformation, which is to say that it does not affect the permanent core of one's identity, Heidegger's 'Jemeinigkeit'.

In laying some important theoretical groundwork, while also serving as a welcome 'reality check', Hahn's hard-nosed dismissal of transformative change offers an excellent 'degree-zero' point of departure for our forays into the domain of the metamorphic. To begin with, he helpfully insists on the (crucial) distinction between change and transformation: while every transformation involves change, not every change amounts to a transformation.[4] Not everyone honours this distinction: the tendency to use 'metamorphosis' as a mere synonym for 'change' is quite widespread. And while the interface between *Wandel* and *Verwandlung*, or change and transformation, is less clear-cut than Hahn allows, it remains of heuristic value to think of transformation as a distinct type of change. Secondly, with his ethnographic gesture to other societies, in which the transformation of humans into different categories of being is considered possible, Hahn draws attention to the diversity of world-views that human cultures have brought forth and the varying status accorded to phenomena of transformative change within them: what the contemporary sociologist regards as a fiction could well be accorded the status of fact in another cultural system.[5] Finally, his claim that transformative change figures in modern western society at best as 'fraud, metaphor, or pathological delusion' invites considered disagreement. Transubstantiation — the mysterious transformation of bread and wine into the body and blood of Christ during the celebration of the Eucharist — remains a fundamental tenet of the Catholic creed. Contemporary cultural production — from Hollywood to artistic traditions across the globe — is obsessed with the phenomenon of transformative change, as betokened, for instance, by the *Terminator* or *Transformers* film series or the sculptures of Jane Alexander or Patricia Piccinini.[6] And one of the reasons for this enduring interest in metamorphic creatures (human or otherwise) is, surely, the fact that science is gradually catching up with fiction: the stunning progress in genetic engineering and the production of cybernetic organisms over the last half century has started to render the mythic plots of Pygmalion and Frankenstein, in which humans acquire divine powers of transformative creation, eerily (or alluringly, as the case may be) plausible. None of this affects Hahn's point that for the modern social scientist supernaturally induced traffic across ontological boundaries has to be considered an impossibility; but these examples, which could easily be multiplied, point to the fact that modes of the metamorphic, both as a phenomenon in its own right and as a figure of thought, have a significant presence in (modern) western society, quite beyond the categories of 'fraud', 'metaphor', or 'pathological delusion'.

Contemporary engagements with the metamorphic continue and rework in complex ways a millennia-old tradition that has its origins in classical antiquity and Judeo-Christian religion. From a broadly historical point of view, metamorphosis has proven an exceptionally malleable and persistent figure of thought for negotiating our 'selves' and our world throughout history and across a wide range of texts, discourses, and media. The habit of thinking with (and against) transformative change is thus co-extensive with our cultural memory: it begins with ancient Greek myths of metamorphosis (and their Near Eastern antecedents), including the occasional instance recorded in the Old Testament; and it continues today in science fiction and other genres that explore such topical issues as gene mutation and hybridization. It is, not least, the pronounced hostility within the Western cultural imaginary towards certain types of transformative change, and the hopeful investment in others, that renders metamorphosis such a complex and fascinating topic. Depending on the perspective, the possibility of substantive transformation frightens or inspires hope; and the history of tussles over its potential and plausibility — as well as the strategies of subversion and containment it has inspired over the centuries — furnishes privileged insights into the contested nature of 'reality' and diverse conceptions thereof. In short, transformative change, despite habitual dismissals, has a continuing presence within Western culture — from, as it were, Homer to Hollywood.[7] This volume tries to profile this presence, by means of theorizing, historical surveys, and a series of case studies that range from antiquity to the present, paying particular attention to how metamorphosis figures, in often conflicting ways, in three formative configurations in the Western tradition: the classical, the biblical, and the scientific.[8]

The challenge to generate a story out of two millennia and a half of cultural history, though, appears nothing short of overwhelming. Traversing such a span of time is bound to induce disorientation, especially when the theme supposed to provide coherence happens to be flux. Before we set out on the long march down the centuries an exploratory canvassing of the territory may hence prove useful, and this is what this General Introduction is intended to supply. It tries to get some theoretical purchase on metamorphosis and to identify a few of the principal themes and issues that will — *mutatis mutandis* — recur along the way by visiting the elusive phenomenon from the point of view of Semantics, Ontology, Anthropology, and Ethics.

Our initial focus will be on the semantics of metamorphosis, as we survey the range of meanings that the term has accrued over time. We then move on to, broadly speaking, 'ontological considerations', in an effort to locate transformative change within the domain of change more generally: as we already had occasion to note, metamorphosis involves change, but not every change qualifies as a metamorphosis. To do this, we map the domain of change from one extreme (chaos) to the other (immutable being), before exploring various modes of *transformative* change, with special attention to the (supernatural) agent taken to be responsible for the transformation. Our third section offers some comments of an 'anthropological' kind, to do with our species-specific ability to conceive of the phenomenon in the first place and to undergo various modes of auto-metamorphosis. The ability to enact transformative change, whether in nature or rhetorically, raises issues in ethics, which is the topic of our fourth and final section. As the focus shifts from semantics to ontology, from anthropology to ethics, what ought to emerge is something akin to a 'phenomenology', or, perhaps, 'pathology', of metamorphosis, as a point of reference and departure for the historical case studies to follow. In order to give the theoretical discussion some life we have chosen to develop the argument on the basis of textual passages taken, wherever possible, from Ovid and the Bible. They have been chosen mainly as means of bringing theoretical issues into focus, even though they also ought to help prefigure and facilitate the subsequent historical sweep.

Semantics

'Meta-morphosis' is a compound of the prefix μετα-, which here signifies change,[9] and the noun μόρφωσις ('shaping', 'bringing into shape', from the verb μορφόω, 'to give shape or form to'). It thus denotes the process of changing shape or the outcome of such a process, that is, a transformation. The term metamorphosis does its meaning justice: it is a protean term or principle. Gaston Bachelard, for instance, 'makes metamorphosis through identification with animals virtually synonymous with the imagination itself'.[10] Charles Tomlinson coalesces metamorphosis and translation.[11] For Hans Blumenberg, metamorphosis is the principle behind the emergence of myth as such, a basic figure of thought that enables previously formless divinities to assume a recognizable shape.[12] And Leonard Barkan deems metamorphosis 'an essential metonym for the classical civilization that gave it birth' — 'from St. Augustine to the seventeenth century (at least)'.[13] Quite apart from the aesthetic pleasure to be derived from such neat rhetorical turns, these universalizing formulas, by which metamorphosis gets equated with, or subsumed under, a wide range of other phenomena (imagination, translation, myth, classical civilization) are a real stimulus to thought. But in their very originality, these gestures tend to be indifferent to, or indeed blur, the fine distinctions of historical semantics.

The same is true of efforts to turn metamorphosis into a sound critical concept by delimiting its meaning, either by creating a definition by *fiat*, or through the attempt to pin down its 'original' essence. An example of the former is Peter Kuon's proposal to confine use of the term to 'nicht-lineare historische, kulturelle und ästhetische Prozesse' ['non-linear historical, cultural, and aesthetic processes'] — in contrast to other variants of change or development that manifest a more predictable pattern or logic.[14] An example of the latter is Christian Zgoll's *Phänomenologie der Metamorphose*, which offers an ambitious taxonomy in the endeavour to come up with a precise definition of the notion in Augustan poetry (though excluding Ovid's *Metamorphoses*).[15] Zgoll restricts the label 'metamorphosis' to changes of a human being into another shape found in nature, such as flora, fauna, stones, water, or mythical creatures and involving suddenness, supernatural intervention and irreversibility; conversely, he carefully distinguishes such 'hard-core' from peripheral transformation (such as sex-change) and a range of related phenomena such as allophany (i.e. the appearance of a god in disguise), magical transformations achieved through witchcraft, genesis and growth, apotheosis, and catasterism (i.e. the transformation of a human being into a star).

One of the problems with this quest for the original, authentic meaning of metamorphosis, which a reviewer has likened to the 'pinning of corpses of swarms of gaily coloured butterflies in neatly arranged display cabinets' is that in Ovid's *Metamorphoses* all of these neat distinctions break down.[16] Despite the fact that Ovid himself, in his proem to the *Metamorphoses* and retrospectively in his exile poetry,[17] places the emphasis on the transformation of *human* beings, a refusal to relate (say) Jupiter's 'allophany' to Europa in the form of a bull that Ovid recounts in the second book of his *Metamorphoses* to the title of the epic requires a rather compartmentalized reading of the poem. In Ovid's epic — a work *sui generis* —

metamorphosis functions as an umbrella term for a ragbag of items. Most of the transformations recounted in the poem constitute instances of what scholars like to call a 'proper' or 'significant' metamorphosis — though Ovid is also not beyond reversing the usual direction of change: if most stories start with humans and end up with a piece of flora or fauna or an inanimate object, a certain number of his tales of human regeneration are about the miraculous emergence of humans from stones (Deucalion and Pyrrha), dragon's teeth (the inhabitants of Thebes), or ants (the replenished population of Aegina, after a plague ravaged the island). Likewise, the poem also comprises any other conceivable form of change, shape-shifting, or transformation, be it allophany or apotheosis, anthropogenesis or catasterism, cosmic creation or destruction, magic or metempsychosis, miraculous sex-changes or womanufacturing. Moreover, Ovid extends the remit of the term to the realm of poetics, again broadly conceived. In this category we may mention translation — beginning with the translation of the Greek *Metamorphoses* of the title into the Latin *mutatas formas* in the opening line of the poem; the mutation of mythic material in the process of rewriting; and, more specifically, Ovid's handling of his predecessors in acts of intertextual transformation. In the light of the encyclopaedic remit that metamorphosis acquires in Ovid, it arguably stands to reason that 'the poem offers no clear prescription for understanding the phenomenon'.[18] Rather, Ovid, both in his poem and for Western culture ever after, configured metamorphosis as an expansive and hence fuzzy category that subsumes various conceptions and modalities of change. And while Ovid is far and away the worst culprit in blurring the semantics of metamorphosis, the ancient evidence simply does not bear out any fine semantic distinction: from the archaic age to late antiquity, Greek and Roman authors used metamorphosis (or related terms) to refer to every conceivable kind of (reversible) transformative change, involving an animal turning into a human (Aesop), a human into an animal (Apuleius), or a god into whatever shape best suited his sexual exploits.[19]

Efforts in definition and taxonomy such as those of Kuon and Zgoll, then, are heuristically valuable insofar as they force us to think about what 'the essence' of the term (or of the phenomenon it denotes) might be — and to situate it within a set of related ideas. But from a historical point of view, they inevitably result in splitting uses of metamorphosis and related words — both in the ancient Greek and as loanwords in Latin and the European vernaculars — into 'proper' and 'improper'. As long as three decades ago, the futility of fixing the precise essence of metamorphosis motivated I. Massey to suggest a somewhat different approach: 'what may be somewhat easier than identifying a single principle in metamorphosis is establishing a set of categories under which the problems of metamorphosis can be studied.'[20] Perhaps, then, a compromise is called for: if one refrains from trying to turn metamorphosis itself into a technical term but properly theorizes its various 'signifieds' according to a typology of modes of change, one would not lose sight of any of the relevant data domains in relation to which metamorphosis has been brought into play. Such abstention from turning metamorphosis into a sharply defined concept might be deemed a lost opportunity, but it enables us to appreciate the richness of historical semantics without sacrificing theoretical precision. Put differently, as long as we are clear about *what*, precisely, metamorphosis is meant to signify in each instance, we can embrace the protean existence that the signifier has led. Both, attention to historical usage and investment in conceptual exactness, are prerequisites to bringing into view the fascinating story of thinking with and against the reality or possibility of transformative change in the Western cultural tradition.

As a first orientation in the prodigious variety of meanings that have accrued around the term, one could do worse than consult — however banal the move may appear — that archive of historical semantics, the *Oxford English Dictionary*. In its entry for 'metamorphosis', the *OED* recognizes three basic senses of the term. Sense 1 and Sense 3 both refer to types of change (or instances thereof) that are 'truly' transformative; yet they differ with respect to the principle or power that causes the transformation. Sense 1 ('the action or process of changing in form, shape, or substance; esp. transformation by supernatural means') captures types of transformation that defy empirical plausibility; it presupposes, in its most pregnant use, a *supernatural* catalyst, that is, some factor or force sufficiently powerful to enable an otherwise *un-natural* event to occur — in contradistinction to the kinds of metamorphosis the *OED* has registered under Sense 3. These result from biological or chemical processes, in particular the 'change of form in an animal, or its part, during post-embryonic development' that many insects and invertebrates, as well as some vertebrates such as frogs, undergo in the course of maturing. These processes have *natural* causes (one now knows) and can thus be fully accounted for in scientific terms. Instances of Sense 1 are at home in such spheres as theology, magic, or classical mythology; Ovid and his epic *Metamorphoses* — the title of which is the earliest surviving instance of the noun in Latin[21] — exercise a notable influence here, from John Gower (*c.* 1330–1408) and Geoffrey Chaucer (*c.* 1343–1400) onwards. The earliest use of Sense 3 recorded by the *Oxford English Dictionary* comes from the 1665 *Philosophical Transactions* of the Royal Society.

Under Sense 2, defined as 'a complete change in the appearance, circumstances, condition, or character of a person, a state of affairs, etc.', the *OED* catalogues such phenomena as the alteration of personal identity by means of disguise, the changes in appearance caused by ageing, modes of perceiving that give the impression *as if* a miraculous transformation takes place in front of our eyes, or a radical shift in social position — from private man to prince, for instance, or from silent onlooker to judge. If one were to insist on a pregnant meaning of metamorphosis, Sense 1 and Sense 3 both refer to *actual*, substantive transformations of one type or another, whereas Sense 2 is a mere synonym, emphatic or pretentious as the case may be, of 'conventional' change. From this point of view, calling such change a 'metamorphosis' becomes a hyperbole designed to underscore the radical nature of the change that has occurred by associating it with the miraculous transformations in substance recognized by Sense 1 or the biological and chemical processes of change captured by Sense 3. (Though historically speaking, Sense 3, too, may be understood as a belated, metaphorical application to natural phenomena that *appear* miraculous; yet in contemporary parlance, and certainly in scientific discourse, the metaphorical force in this usage is all but dead.)

Such rhetorical-metaphorical deployment of metamorphosis in Sense 2 has tradition — as betokened by some verses of Ovid's 'autobiography' *de vetula* ('On the Crone'), a delightful, thirteen-century piece of pseudo-epigraphy.[22] In the second book the erotomaniac author reacts to the appearance of his aged beloved, whom he has not seen for some years, with a visceral horror that would do today's anti-ageing industry proud (II. 495–99):[23]

> In nova formas
> corpora mutatas cecini, mirabiliorque
> non reperitur ibi mutatio quam fuit ista,
> scilicet, ut fuerit tam parvo tempore talis
> taliter in talem vetulam mutata puella.

> [I have sung of forms changed into new bodies, but no more miraculous a transformation can be found there [i.e. in the *Metamorphoses*] than was this one, *sc.* that such a (beautiful) girl had been transformed in so short a time in such fashion into such a hag.]

In nova formas | *corpora mutatas cecini* ['I have sung of forms changed into new bodies'] reworks the opening two lines of the *Metamorphoses*, inclusive of the enjambment (*In nova fert animus mutatas dicere formas* | *corpora*: ['my mind carries me to sing of forms changed into new bodies']). Yet the author notes in horror that the appalling changes caused by the process of ageing outdo the marvellous transformations he recounted in his famous epic: the speed (cf. *parvo tempore*), by which the beautiful young girl (*puella*) he loved has turned into a 'disfigured' old hag (*vetula*) whom he cannot help but abhor, surpasses the miraculous changes in substance of which he sang in the *Metamorphoses*.

The Antwerp painter Quinten Massys (1465–1530) aims for a similar effect in his grotesque depiction of an (imaginary?) old woman, in the picture 'The Ugly Duchess' (*c.* 1513), which has been linked to Margaret, Duchess of Tyrol (see Fig. 1). Recent research has suggested that the sitter suffers from a rare form of Paget's disease, or *osteodystrophia deformans*, which caused enlargement and deformation of the skeletal structure of her face, hands, and collarbones.[24] Be that as it may, the painting represents the transformative power of time in a spirit akin to the passage from the *de vetula* we just considered. As art historians note, the partially open rose bud that the duchess gingerly holds in her right hand hints at virginity, youth, and the promise of great beauty — qualities that the old woman still claims for herself, as betokened by her choice of clothing, in particular the tight gown and headset, yet her efforts to arrest time are defied by the quasi-metamorphosis she has undergone since her youth. As Al Johnson points out, Massys achieves an unsettling ambiguity in gender and has endowed his sitter with a 'monkey-like expression', with her 'huge ears, snub nose, and tiny little piggy eyes'.[25] Or, as Susan Foister puts it, the duchess, in her age-inappropriate pursuit of love or lust, comes across as 'more an animal than a human being'.[26] Yet even though commentators have tended to spot a dehumanizing effect, we are dealing with metamorphosis in Sense 2, where significant change *appears* to amount to a transformation; and a natural response to Massys's painting surely involves embarrassment for the evident obliviousness of the sitter to the transformative powers of time (and the apparently non-transformative

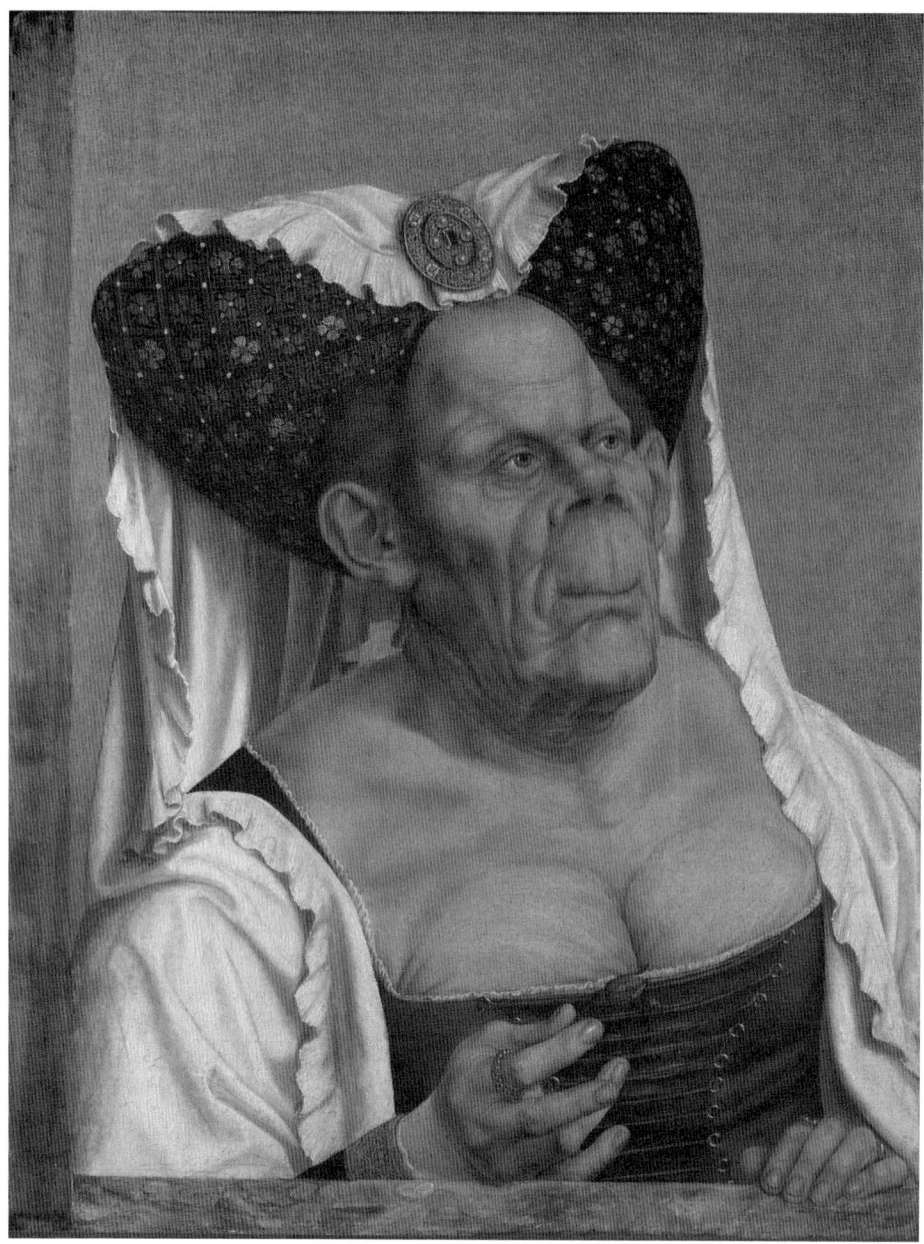

FIG. 1. Quinten Massys, *An Old Woman* ('The Ugly Duchess'), *c.*1513
© The National Gallery, London
Bequeathed by Miss Jenny Louisa Roberta Blaker, 1947

gaze and brush of the artist), that allows her to retain the sense of pride and hope that comes with the misplaced belief in her own desirability against the unfortunate flaws of her appearance.

On the premise that every 'genuine' metamorphosis of either the supernatural or the natural kind involves change, but not every change constitutes a 'genuine' metamorphosis, Sense 1 and Sense 3 can be called literal — they refer to *substantive* transformations that *actually* happened by whatever means and in whatever discursive domain. In contrast, Sense 2, as already noted, is metaphorical: it recognizes the habit of applying a term that elsewhere signifies an extraordinary kind of change to changes that are ultimately ordinary or a mere matter of misapprehension. The distinction between a 'literal' and a 'metaphorical' use of metamorphosis, however, says nothing about the ontological status of the instance of transformative change under discussion. Many of the 'metaphorical' metamorphoses (such as ageing) are quite 'real', while some would argue that all metamorphoses that fall under the literal Sense 1 are mere figments of the imagination (or, to recall the stronger language of Hahn, 'frauds' and 'pathological delusions') — even though within the discursive worlds in which they feature or have been 'recorded', they figure as facts and may be accepted as such by interpretive communities. To those who believe in a literal reading of the Bible, for instance, God, once upon a time, *really* turned Lot's wife into a pillar of salt: on their flight from Sodom and Gomorrah, she had violated the injunction of the angels that had set them on their path not to look behind and was accordingly visited with transformative punishment (Genesis 19. 15–26). An instance of transformative change recounted in a text may for some be a motif or a metaphor, but for others a historical record of an actual event: it all depends on the conception of reality and the representational value that respective readers bring to bear upon the text. Likewise, one ought not to underestimate the real consequences of figurative transformations even though they are the result of rhetoric (verbal or visual) or reside in the eye of the beholder. Both in literary and political discourse, there exists a long tradition of using the animal kingdom as a (metaphorical) point of reference to discuss fellow human beings, often to deny them full participation in humanity. The tradition of transformative dehumanization stretches from Semonides, who correlates different types of women with different animals, to medieval bestiaries,[27] to contemporary artists, such as Jane Alexander, who explores the dehumanizing impact of the South African apartheid regime in her works,[28] to what Eduardo Mendieta has called 'the modern political bestiary', populated by 'terrorists, Islamo-fascists, narco-traffickers, pederasts', which operates according to the logic that 'the bestialized other has to be exterminated, and in order to do so, we ourselves must become like beasts.'[29]

Before leaving the realm of the dictionary, with its neat and tidy distinctions, we ought to acknowledge that, in practice, the various meanings may blur into one another in complex and unpredictable ways. Consider the following passage from *The Government of the Tongue* (1674) by Richard Allestree, which, just like the verses from the *de vetula*, seems to have lost none of its relevance during the intervening centuries (Preface to Section 12: 'Of Obscene Talk'):

> There is another vice of the Tongue which I cannot but mention, [...] obscene,
> and immodest talk, which is offensive to the purity of God, damageable and
> infectious to the innocence of our Neighbors, and most pernicious to ourselves:
> and yet is now grown a thing so common, that one would think we were fallen
> into an Age of Metamorphosis, and that the Brutes did (not only poetically
> and in fiction) but really speak. For the talk of many is so bestial, that it seems
> to be but the conceptions of the more libidinous Animals clothed in human
> Language.

The notion of metamorphosis, which is acknowledged as belonging into the
domains of 'poetry and fiction', is here employed to comment critically on everyday
experience. The passage underscores the importance of language as an expression
of our humanity — or lack thereof: Allestree posits the possibility of, indeed
diagnoses, a process of decline in civilized manners that amounts to a full-scale
dehumanization of the kind one finds in the literature of metamorphosis. In his
version of the 'myth of the ages', he suggests that we have now reached a stage of
decline at which traditional stabilities and certainties no longer apply. Tellingly, the
current age is not an 'Age of Fable', a genre, that is, in which animals routinely
display the capacity for human speech; rather, Allestree suggests that the current
era be called one of transformative change, which manifests itself on two levels,
one explicit, the other implicit. He maintains that uttering obscenities constitutes
animal speech couched in human language — but those who spew forth such filth
(so the intimation) are nothing but libidinous beasts transformed into humans, who
have retained the outlook and ethos of their previous, bestial existence.[30] Allestree
refrains from spelling this out, though in places he deliberately blurs the boundary
between appearance ('one would think', 'it seems to be') and reality ('that the
Brutes did [...] but really speak'). The playful oscillation between a literal and a
metaphorical understanding of metamorphosis rests on a peculiar merging of the
classical and the biblical. The possibility of ontological slippage Allestree found
prefigured in pagan myths of metamorphoses (here turned into a proper 'Age'),
but he validates the idea that the boundaries between animal and human are fluid
within a decidedly Christian framework: the obscenities he witnesses in free and
abundant circulation are acts of blasphemy, the causes and consequences of moral
pollution that re-enacts the primordial fall ('we were fallen into').

The discussion so far should have illustrated the wide semantic and thematic
compass of 'metamorphosis' and its presence in diverse systems of thought, traditions, and undertakings. Indeed, one could argue that the critical value of metamorphosis as a concept (especially, again, from the point of its history) would
seem to lie, at least in part, precisely in its fluidity and fuzziness, arising from its
application to a miscellaneous set of ultimately incongruous ideas and phenomena
and enabling authors and thinkers to use the term for interconnecting diverse
domains of nature and culture and establishing some measure of contact or affinity
between different world views, such as pagan myths and their reception in the
classical tradition, Judeo-Christian theology, and modern science. Apart from its
occurrence in diverse spheres of cultural endeavour, transformative change also
raises problems of considerable complexity: the challenge to situate modes of
transformation within the realm of change more generally; the distinction between

literal and metaphorical uses of metamorphosis (and the blurring thereof); the need to define and differentiate between the factors responsible for causing changes that can be labelled transformative; and the conceptions of reality that underwrite the classification of a metamorphosis as 'real' or 'imaginary'.

Ontology

Imagine a world in total flux — a world, that is, in which everything and anything can arise and disintegrate without a moment's notice. We could label such a state of rampant contingency with a loanword from ancient Greek (via Latin) 'chaos' (χάος). While it originally meant something akin to 'chasm' or 'abyss', in time it began to signify the formless, primordial matter out of which our world originated.[31] In Ovid's *Metamorphoses*, for instance, Chaos represents both the enabling matrix and the other of the world we inhabit: it is an anarchic agglomerate of elements hostile to any form of life, indeed hostile to form as such, that, however, contains within itself the seeds or building blocks of our ordered universe, or — to use the common antithesis to chaos — cosmos (*Met.* I. 5–9):[32]

> Ante mare et terras et, quod tegit omnia, caelum
> unus erat toto naturae vultus in orbe,
> quem dixere Chaos, rudis indigestaque moles
> nec quicquam nisi pondus iners congestaque eodem
> non bene iunctarum discordia semina rerum.

> [Before there were sea, earth, and all-covering sky,
> the outlook of physical matter was identical everywhere,
> which they called *Chaos*,[33] a shapeless, disorderly bulk,
> nothing but motionless mass and amassed within
> the warring seeds of entities ill-connected.]

Ovid here explores the paradox that identity presupposes difference, that *one* form (*unus vultus*) is *no* form.[34] In such circumstances, a trans-formation, that is, a shift from one form to another, is strictly speaking impossible. It is a situation well captured by Baudrillard's notion of 'change without becoming', a condition of endless morphism that never results in the (renewed) stability of form required for a genuine metamorphosis.[35] In Ovid, style enacts theme: the two and a half lines in apposition after Chaos, which is placed right in the middle of the passage, are designed to explicate the notion of disorganized topsy-turvydom and do so, not least, on the level of syntax. The three principal nouns 'bulk' (*moles*), 'mass' (*pondus*), and 'seeds' (*semina*) — all in contradistinction to the distinct things or entities (*rerum*) yet to come — are awkwardly linked by way of the connectives *nec* and *-que* and endowed with conflicting attributes such as 'motionless' (*iners*) and 'warring' (*discordia*).[36] In a chaotic condition, items that belong together are linked only loosely, if at all. Yet Ovid has also scripted the solution to the problem into his text, in the form of the etymologically related participles *indigesta* (from *in* + *di-gero*) and *congesta* (from *con* + *gero*): if the latter signifies the collapse or absence of distinction and ensuing disorder, the former contains the promise of differentiation and order: *digero* means 'to divide, separate, distribute', in this case, above all, the various elements (aether, air, earth, water) that, once properly set out, constitute our universe.[37]

In counterpoint to chaos, thinkers of a philosophical or religious bent have long hankered after absolute order and stability. The desire for a reality immune to change manifests itself in 'the old dream which Western metaphysics has dreamed from Parmenides to Hegel of a timeless, space-less, supra-sensuous realm as the proper region of thought.'[38] In this dream, the absence of change is tantamount to perfection: witness the Platonic Forms or the divinity of Christian theology, as imagined (for instance) by Augustine in his *Confessions*. Their shared attributes include eternity and immutability. The same principles of stability, though less perfectly enacted, also inform influential, pre-modern conceptions of the universe at large. One of the most striking notions, which has had a career that stretches from Aristotle via Stoicism and Christian theology to early-modern times and still resonates, if mostly negatively, today, is the so-called *scala naturae*, the ladder of nature or 'the great chain of being' — the notion, in other words, that from the pits of Hell to the summit of Heaven, the world is made up of different ontological layers.[39] Such a view of the world reassures by means of affirming stability, hierarchy and ultimate justice, as it assigns each element a fixed place in the larger order of things.

Still, that things change — however much they also continue to remain the same — is undeniable. Any change, including transformation, plays itself out between inchoate flux and inflexible being. Types of change are legion; and the phenomenon has received various forms of taxonomic treatment according to diverse criteria such as 'direction' (some change is cyclical — 'a man may fish with the worm that hath eat of a king, and eat of the fish that hath fed of that worm' as Shakespeare puts it in *Hamlet* 4.3 — while other is uni-directional); the object undergoing change (nature, an individual, a collective, an entire civilization, or humanity as such); or the degree of determinism with which alterations occur (ranging from random to preordained). The challenge to capture change in historical time has brought forth models of progress, decline, or (negative) dialectics, notions of successive ages or cosmic cycles, and schemes of causation or teleology, though in the course of the twentieth-century endeavours to sum up human history in comprehensive 'meta-narratives' have fallen into disrepute and conceptions of change that emphasize contingent reconfigurations are on the rise, both in social and cultural theory and the natural sciences.

In the contemporary life sciences, the dominant paradigm of change operates with principles of mutation, that is, an unpredictable yet permanent change in the DNA sequence of a gene, and evolution.[40] In this context, less can be more — as a recent study in *Nature* has shown: it argues that what constitutes our humanity within the larger chimpanzee family to which we belong is a result of loss of DNA that regulated (in the sense of inhibited) brain growth and induced the growth of small hard spines on the male reproductive organ. Bigger brains and smoother penises, so the argument goes, enhanced our capacity for thought, social and physical bonding, owing to longer copulation times, and the adoption of a monogamous reproduction strategy.[41] More generally, evolution constitutes a significant break within the tradition of Western metaphysics and its extreme resistance to the world of becoming. After Darwin, the so-called ladder of nature, which symbolized distinct ontological layers and qualitative differences, morphed into an infinite series of gradations, or, indeed, a continuum. And, as Lovejoy notes, 'a qualitative continuum [...] is a contradiction in terms.'[42] The insights of evolutionary theory and genetics join those of quantum physics in moving scientific conceptions of change towards the chaotic end of the spectrum, away from essentialist notions of the universe grounded in basic principles of order and stability.[43] Perhaps not coincidentally, the age that has produced these insights has frequently been thought of as marked by a pronounced fluidity. Hannah Arendt, for instance, identified as a hallmark of a modern, post-traditional condition, 'the loss of the groundwork of the world, which indeed since then has begun to shift, to change and transform itself with ever-increasing rapidity form one shape into another, as though we were living and struggling with a Protean universe where everything at any moment can become almost anything else.'[44]

Change, then, is all around us. But what within this sea of change meaningfully amounts to (a type of) *transformative* change? As our section on Semantics has already demonstrated, any attempt to draw a clear-cut line between change and transformation, or, in German, *Wandel* and *Verwandlung*, will, to some degree, always be countervailed by the historical meanings that the term metamorphosis has accrued over time. One way of getting a better purchase on the factors that turn change into transformative change — and to show that the problem has a history — is by means of a comparison between the conceptions of the world developed in Lucretius's *De Rerum Natura* ['On the Nature of Things'], a didactic poem about the philosophy of Epicurus, who endorsed an atomistic physics, and Ovid's *Metamorphoses*.[45] Ovid himself invites such a comparison by strategically alluding to his predecessor in his account of chaos. The phrase *semina rerum* ['the seeds of things'] in particular is an unmistakable catchphrase of Lucretius, who uses it as one of his terms for atoms. But the relation is far from straightforward. Lucretius gives a materialist account of the universe, in which transformation *stricto sensu* is impossible. Instead, there is incessant flux: entities come into, and go out of, existence through the agglomeration, reconfiguration, and dispersal of atoms — the minuscule building blocks of matter that remain always the same. To cite one representative passage (*De Rerum Natura*, I. 498–502; trans. by Melville):

> sed quia vera tamen ratio naturaque rerum
> cogit, ades, paucis dum versibus expediamus
> esse ea quae solido atque aeterno corpore constent,
> semina quae rerum primordiaque esse docemus,
> unde omnis rerum nunc constet summa creata.

> [But yet, because true reason and nature itself
> Compel, be with me, while I demonstrate
> In a few verses that there do exist
> Bodies that are both solid and everlasting,
> Which we teach are seeds or primal atoms of things
> From which now all creation has been made.]

Lucretius' account of the universe combines eternal stability at the level of elementary particles with constant mutability at the supra–atomic level. While the nature of the constituent elements never changes (*certissima corpora quaedam | sunt quae conservant naturam semper eandem*), through their coming and going and their shifting order, things change their nature and bodies are altered (*quorum abitu aut aditu mutatoque ordine mutant | naturam res et convertunt corpora sese*).[46] In a world made up of atoms, there is then a significant amount of change; yet even though Lucretius employs the same lexicon as metamorphic poets such as Ovid (*mutare, convertere*), his conception of change does not seem to allow for a 'transformation' in any pregnant sense of the term. The constant agglomeration and dispersal of atoms implies the absence of any meaningful continuity between one thing and another even if the atoms involved are, and remain, the same. Lucretius makes the point explicitly at various moments in the poem (*De Rerum Natura*, I. 670–71; trans. by Melville):[47]

> nam quodcumque suis mutatum finibus exit,
> continuo hoc mors est illius quod fuit ante.
>
> [For things have limits fixed; if they by change
> Transgress them, then death follows instantly.]

As Bailey comments: 'It was just here that the Atomists claimed their fundamental superiority to their predecessors. All the theories of Monists and Pluralists alike postulated creation through the change of one element into another: the Atomists alone explained how the unchanging could give rise to all the variety of things.'[48] In deploying Lucretian idiom and imagery at the start of his own literary world, Ovid hints at a suggestive affinity between the conception of the universe developed by his Epicurean predecessor and his own. For metamorphosis, too, hints at an underlying, invisible link that enables the transformation of bodies into new forms. 'This kinship of all creation prior to the emergence of distinct forms, which enables the transformation of human beings into animals, trees, flowers, and other aspects of the woods, is the ever returning materialist theme of the *Metamorphoses*.'[49] On inspection, however, there are significant differences between a 'changed configuration' (*ordo mutatus*) of Lucretius and the 'forms changed into new bodies' (*formae in nova corpora mutatae*) of Ovid. Ovid, to be sure, subsumes reconfiguration of matter under his encyclopaedic conception of metamorphosis: after all, the narrative part of his epic opens with the transformation of chaos into cosmos, a process that involves, among other things, the separation of the primordial elements of air, earth, and water out of their chaotic commingling. But already the shift in semantics in the phrase 'the seeds of things' (*semina rerum*), which means 'atoms' in Lucretius but primordial elements in Ovid constitutes a significant difference between the nuclear materialism of the former and the metamorphic materialism of the latter, even though Ovid employs Lucretian language to develop his point.[50] Ovid, then, playfully integrates a warped conception of nuclear physics in the tradition of the atomists and Epicurus/Lucretius into his epic, as the enabling condition for a decidedly anti-Lucretian universe that features the transformation of human beings into other items in nature (flora, fauna, or features of landscape such as stones, wells, or mountains).[51]

For our concerns two further differences are of particular importance. First, Ovidian metamorphosis, and metamorphosis more generally, frequently implies or even foregrounds an element of continuity between pre- and post-transformation that is absent from Lucretius's conception of bodies and their forms arising and disappearing as the result of atomic motion. And second, the identification of an agent responsible for the constitution of (the) cosmos is a major departure from, indeed rebuttal, of Lucretian physics: Ovid's formulation *deus et melior natura* ('demiurgic god and better nature': *Met.* I. 21) acknowledges precisely the kind of purposeful, divine force that is conspicuously absent from the Epicurean universe.[52] Transformation, unlike change, does not simply happen; rather, it requires a code of nature, a supernatural (or human) agent, or another catalyst of sorts. Change tends to be random; a metamorphosis never is. These two aspects, that is, the element of continuity in transformative change and agency, merit further elaboration.

For some scholars it is indeed a special type of 'continuity in transformation' that sets metamorphoses apart from other kinds of change: 'It is not mutability as such, but a change in form, that constitutes the core of metamorphosis, which acquires renewed stability in its new articulation and retains within itself the memory of its previous shape [...]. The new shape has to build in some fashion on the old.'[53] As with other attempts at definition, insistence on stability in change is unable to account for all instances of change that have figured under the label 'metamorphosis', but the definition does capture something important about many metamorphic moments in our cultural record. Ovid, for instance, while flirting with the chaotic mutability as both the other of metamorphosis and, on a smaller scale, an underlying principle of his metamorphic cosmos (his keynote at *Met.* I. 17: *nulli sua forma manebat* –'nothing retained its form' is picked up by Pythagoras at *Met.* XV. 178: *cuncta fluunt* — 'everything flows'), also recognizes variants of stability (once transformed, always transformed), continuity of identity (especially in the case of divinities undergoing countless self-transformations) and the endurance of consciousness throughout and after the process of transformation. The first human–animal metamorphosis recorded in his epic, the change of the ferocious blasphemer Lycaon into a wolf by an irate Jupiter, is a good illustration of the point (*Met.* I. 237–39):

> fit lupus et veteris servat vestigia formae;
> canities eadem est, eadem violentia vultus,
> idem oculi lucent, eadem feritatis imago est.

> [He becomes a wolf and yet preserves traces of his former shape. The grey hair is the same, the fierce expression is the same, the same eyes glint, the overall image of savagery is the same.]

The example deftly illustrates that in the case of stories involving the transformation of human beings the author can demonstrate ingenuity by choosing two states, pre- and post-transformation that eloquently speak to one another: a correlation that underscores continuity reveals an inherent logic in the metamorphosis that compels rhetorically, much like a well-chosen and insightful metaphor. At the same time it bears stressing that in some cases meaningful correspondences between the *mutandum* and the *mutatum* are notional or non-existent.[54] A similar contrast between Ovid and Lucretius emerges if one considers the disquisition on the transmigration of the soul (conceived as immortal) delivered by the philosopher Pythagoras in the final book of the *Metamorphoses*. This concluding perspective again highlights the distinction between atomistic reconfiguration, which implies the death of the disintegrated entity (it simply ceases to exist), and the continuity in consciousness implied in virtually all metamorphoses involving humanoid creatures, even those in which the end result is an apparently inanimate object, such as a stone. (Niobe, even after having undergone petrifaction, continues to weep.) In this respect, there is greater affinity between Ovidian metamorphosis and Pythagorean metempsychosis than between either of these systems of thought and Epicurean physics.

Another exercise in comparison and contrast, this time between Ovid and St Paul, will further help to profile possibilities of continuity in transformation. If in Ovid metamorphosis usually implies a change in form and continuity in material substance, Christian thought posits the possibility of transformative change that involves change in material substance and continuity in form. Thus Paul, in 1 Corinthians 15, in addressing the question of what happens at the moment of resurrection ('How do the dead rise again? Or with what manner of body shall they come?') prefaces his theological disquisition on bodies with a reference to seeds, καὶ ὃ σπείρεις, οὐ τὸ σῶμα τὸ γενησόμενον σπείρεις ἀλλὰ γυμνὸν κόκκον; ['And that which thou sowest, thou sowest not that body that shall be, but bare grain'] (15. 37), before using seed imagery to visualize the alteration of the terrestrial bodies into celestial bodies at the moment of resurrection.[55] This serves as background for the promise of transformation in resurrection: σαλπίσει γάρ, καὶ οἱ νεκροὶ ἐγερθήσονται ἄφθαρτοι, καὶ ἡμεῖς ἀλλαγησόμεθα ['for the trumpet shall sound, and the dead shall be raised incorruptible, and we shall be changed']. This Christian mode of metamorphosis does not necessarily involve a change in form, which is so typical of the transformations we encounter in pagan authors: in calibrating continuity and difference before and after the moment of transformative resurrection, the shape of our bodies seems irrelevant. Rather, it is the quality of our material substance that has changed — in other words, exactly what tends to remain the same in Ovidian metamorphoses, both in human transformations and divine allophanies. Lycaon and the wolf are two different *formal* instantiations of what is, essentially, the same underlying matter, just as the anthropomorphic Jupiter and the various appearances he assumes while on the prowl for sex present different forms of the same divine being. The same is true of human shape-shifters, such as Erysichthon's daughter Mestra, to whom Neptune granted the wish of a Protean body.[56]

Both pagan and Christian thought explore (or, indeed, insist on) continuity of consciousness before and after the transformation. In Ovid, this continuity comes in various degrees. Reversible metamorphosis implies that full human consciousness continues to reside within the altered shape of the body. Thus when Mestra, gifted as we have just had occasion to note with *transformia corpora* (*Met.* VIII. 871: 'a Protean body'), easily and cyclically oscillates between her human and various animal shapes, her essentially human core and consciousness remain unaffected by her cross-species transformations. The same is the case with Io, who regains her human shape, and occasionally also applies to characters who undergo irreversible metamorphosis such as Actaeon or Callisto: in all three of these episodes, Ovid explores the consequences of a human mind trapped in the body of an alien species, not least in the inability to communicate verbally. In other episodes the underlying identity pre- and post-transformation is minimal, but nevertheless present.[57] Paul, too, emphasizes continuity of identity. Bynum summarizes the essential points as follows: 'first, to Paul, the image of the seed is an image of radical transformation'; and second: 'the image asserts (perhaps without any intention on its author's part) some kind of continuity, although it does not explicitly lodge identity in either a material or a formal principle.' 'Thus, when Paul says "the trumpet shall sound [...] and we shall be changed," he means, with all the force of our everyday assumptions, both "we" and "changed".'[58] Paul, then, manages to square the circle of positing transformative change while upholding Heidegger's identity principle of 'Jemeinigkeit':[59] in resurrection, we undergo a transformation that includes an alternation in corporeal substance while still retaining our specific identities. To emphasize this element of continuity Paul employs a lexicon of 'dressing up' that Ovid uses for gods appearing in disguise, who also remain essentially the same, quite irrespective of the shape they assume.[60]

The second factor to consider in distinguishing between change (plain and simple) and transformative change is the presence of an agent or a code of nature responsible for the metamorphosis. From Ovid's Pythagoras to Johann Wolfgang von Goethe and beyond, philosophers, natural historians, and scientists have identified metamorphosis as a (or, indeed, the) principle of nature or have used the term to describe the transition from one developmental stage to another in certain animals.[61] But the earliest instances of transformative change recorded in Western literature all point to supernatural involvement. This is self-evident in the Greek material where the agents of miraculous transformations are various divinities. But it is also the case in the Bible: the (rare) incidents of metamorphosis recorded in the Old Testament all bear testimony to divine omnipotence. We already had occasion to mention Lot's wife at Genesis 19. 15–26: her transformation into a pillar of salt constitutes a miraculous sign from God and a form of punishment. It is an event of the same order as Zeus's transformation of a snake into a stone as a portent of the fall of Troy (*Iliad*, II. 319) or Poseidon's petrifaction of the Phaeacian ship that returned Odysseus to Ithaca (*Odyssey*, XIII. 163–64).[62] At Exodus 7. 1–12, which recounts the 'sticks made snakes' competition between Aaron and Moses on the one hand and the wise men and sorcerers of Egypt on the other, the ability to transform inanimate objects into formidable living creatures demonstrates the superior 'magic' power that resides in the Lord: while both parties succeed in turning their sticks into serpents, the creature created by Aaron and Moses swallows up all the others.[63] In this passage, the fact that God engages in 'magic' and causes miraculous transformations does not seem to be cause for concern.[64] More strikingly still, the fact that Moses' rivals also possess magical abilities suggests a universe in which more than one supernatural power is at work. In Greek and Roman literature, too, metamorphosis tends to register as an index of supernatural power — whether the gods transform themselves or impose transformations on others, be it as a reward or punishment. (For those who undergo metamorphosis at the whim of others, of course, the flipside of transformative omnipotence is an acute sense of inexplicable contingency, which explains why the motif frequently features in myths that involve moments of crisis or liminality, and in particular unforeseen encounters with the divine.)

A privileged context in which the metamorphic powers of supernatural beings manifest themselves is creation, broadly conceived as the endowment of matter with form (or the creation of material shapes out of nothing). Some scholars, it is true, would not subsume (all acts of) creation under the rubric of transformative change. But historical semantics again suggests otherwise. Thus in the second biblical account of anthropogenesis, God fashions Eve out of the rib of Adam.[65] As tends to be the case in other instances of metamorphosis, the passage underscores the aetiological affinity between the primordial material (Adam's rib) and the final product. Or, as Adam puts it, 'This is now bone of my bones, and flesh of my flesh: she shall be called Woman, because she was taken out of Man.' The configuration of material origins, aetiology, and relational identity also informs anthropogenesis in other traditions, notably those that occur at the beginning of Ovid's *Metamorphoses*. In Genesis the mythic underpinnings are of course pared down to bare essentials; still, instances of reception illustrate that the metamorphic subtext of the second account has continued to resonate. Thus a mischievous writer from the eighteenth century, who is sometimes identified with David Garrick, works out the underlying logic in his verse satire *Adam's tail; or, the first metamorphosis*. It begins as follows:

> When Jove, as learned *Rabbins* say,
> Had form'd our common Sire of Clay,
> Had spun the Nerves, sublim'd the Juices,
> And giv'n each Part its various Uses;
> To grace the Monarch's princely Thighs,   5
> And guard his royal Side from Flies
> That might his tender Flesh assail,
> He furnish'd Adam with a *Tail*.

After providing examples from the animal kingdom (the peacock, the steed) in support of his point that 'from the greatest to the least | The *Tail's* the Pride of ev'ry *Beast*', the author notes that the human being is the exception, for: '*Woman* is the *Pride* of *Man*.' This rhetorical turn points to an equivalence, or even identity between 'tail' and 'woman', and it is precisely this that the rest of the poem sets out to illustrate. As it happens, Adam took rather less care of his tail then he should have, and God, checking up on his creature and its accoutrements, finds his 'Tail so scrubb'd and ragged | With filth, that Adam scarce could wag it'. Almost mistaking man for monkey, He bemoans 'the cruel metamorphosis' and begins to fret that the ontological hierarchies of his cosmic order will come tumbling down 'because a King b-----s his *Tail*'. Off comes the tail; but despite its sorry state God is disinclined to let it go to waste:

> The Scheme is fix'd, the Nod is given,
> That powerful Nod that shakes the Heaven.
> The *Tail*, obedient to the Nod
> Arose a *Woman* from the Sod.   155

The author continues to assert that this is the story told by Moses in the original Hebrew and that the fib with the rib is a mistranslation of the Septuagint; the rest of the poem is then devoted to render the aetiology empirically plausible as well.

The metamorphic aspects of natural creation remain prominent in those (legendary) efforts, in which humans (partially) acquire the quasi-divine power of bringing new creatures into being, in the spirit of Prometheus, the titan credited with anthropogenesis in Greek myth. The most famous instance of this phenomenon in classical myth is the sculptor Pygmalion, who falls in love with one of his own female statues. In Ovid's *Metamorphoses*, Venus, responding to Pygmalion's prayers, turns the ivory object into a human being of flesh and blood.[66] In this story, animation remains a divine prerogative. In contrast, the myth-making of modernity ponders the implications of humanity exercising control over the spark of life and being able to undertake the transformation of inert matter into living creatures thanks to scientific advances. Immanuel Kant called Benjamin Franklin 'the modern Prometheus' on account of his experiments with electricity, and Mary Shelley then created the modern archetype of the hubristic scientist who transforms inanimate into living matter in her novel *Frankenstein; or, The Modern Prometheus* (1818).

Efforts to assert Promethean control over the boundary between life and death, and indeed to create new beings, have particular resonance in the modern age. Advances in science have already signalled our entry into a new age of metamorphosis, in which the dominant agents of transformative change are not the supernatural forces of pre-modern times, nor even natural evolution, but a technologically empowered humanity that has gained control over the building blocks of life. The scientific decoding of these building blocks has resulted in an ever-increasing capacity to intervene and manipulate creation and reproduction through genetic engineering, putting 'real' transformative change on the agenda of modern civilization.

Recent experiments with animal species are indicative of the burgeoning possibilities. 'GM monkey passes jellyfish gene to offspring' ran a recent *New Scientist* headline, reporting on the fact that marmoset monkeys, which Erika Sasaki of the Central Institute for Experimental Animals in Kawasaki, Japan, had genetically altered by introducing a jellyfish gene designed to make them glow in a fluorescent green under UV light, had transmitted the mutation to their children.[67] Both the scientifically inexplicable, supernaturally caused transformations and the transformations that result from scientific knowledge and technological expertise, are ultimately grounded in special powers to shape and alter reality through transformative interventions, beyond 'mere' change.

Likewise, the ability of the human race to self-transform has increased dramatically over the last few decades through advances in cybernetics.[68] The broad project of cybernetics is the merging of organic (normally human) and artificial (usually electronic and mechanical) components with the aim of improving the functionality of the original organic life form. Cybernetics thus holds out the prospect of the improvement, even the 'perfectibility', of the human body. The resulting compound form is a collage, a mixture of organic and replaceable mechanical components, with the latter offering greater control over life and death, even raising the spectre of quasi-immortality. As the human body increasingly acquires inorganic components, the prospect arises of transcending the human condition by means of 'converging technologies', that is, 'the integration of cutting-edge research in nano-, bio-, info- and cogno-sciences for purposes of extending power and control of human beings over their own bodies and their environments.'[69] The result promises to be a humanity variously transcended and enhanced — a 'Humanity 2.0' as it were.[70]

Anthropology

Despite the modern scientist's quest for transformative powers, belief in the reality of certain types of transformative change (as we had occasion to note at the outset of this introduction) figures in other contexts as a sign of delusion or of an undeveloped or immature brain. The ontology that underwrites the possibility of magical or miraculous transformation has often been characterized as 'childlike' — or, if one sees fit to transfer, in the tradition of Piaget, the notion of developmental stages from the individual human being to whole cultures, 'primitive'. As Gottwald has recently put it: 'Metamorphosis as a mythic figure of thought (not as literary motif) is therefore an articulation of cognitively deficient stages of consciousness, in particular of mythic conceptions of causality.'[71] If the world of children in particular features seemingly 'inchoate possibilities', which frequently include a willingness to believe in magic and various modes of miraculous metamorphosis, the 'modern' (Western, scientific) mind reduces such inchoate possibilities to those that conform to the strict causalities of science.

We of course do not wish to deny that many stories that feature certain modalities of change fail to meet contemporary, scientific criteria of plausibility — though note at the same time that one ought not to assume that in pre-modern or 'primitive' cultures people routinely swallowed tales of transformation lock, stock and barrel. Already Penelope in Homer's *Odyssey* shrewdly warns her husband in disguise not to try her patience with a cock-and-bull story of metamorphic anthropogenesis.[72] And there is, indeed, another way of looking at the status and function of metamorphosis in the human imaginary. If one foregrounds the ability to conceive of transformative change, rather than the credibility of such conceptions, metamorphosis emerges as a paradigmatic index of what Mithen has recently called a species-specific 'cognitive fluidity' (a positive variant, as it were, to Gottwald's 'cognitive deficiency'): 'By cognitive fluidity I mean the capacity — indeed the compulsion — to integrate ways of thinking and bodies of knowledge that had evolved/developed independently to come up with completely novel ideas. This is the essence of the creative mind and was evidently lacking from non-*Homo sapiens* hominins.' For Mithen, this cognitive fluidity is primarily the source of religion: 'For *Homo sapiens* these worlds [of people, artefacts and animals] flow into each other and create ideas about supernatural entities whenever they overlap.'[73] But we can generalize, recalling Bachelard, who identifies metamorphosis with our imagination:[74] the creativity that our cognitive fluidity enables is essentially metamorphic; it generates supernatural agents out of empirical objects and experiences and conceives of humans turning into animals, inanimate objects, or, indeed, quasi-divine creatures.

Cognitive fluidity also informs the potential of human language for figurative speech. Just like metamorphosis, metaphor brings together two seemingly disparate elements and asserts their identity ('Achilles is a lion'). Or, put differently, each metaphor enacts a rhetorical metamorphosis, and, conversely, 'each metamorphosis is a change of shape that in its most general form can be defined as the literalization of a metaphor.'[75] The slippage from rhetoric (metaphor) to ontology (metamorphosis), as well as vice versa, is easy, insofar as both metaphorical and metamorphic thought (or mythic thought more generally) betoken a special kind of creativity.[76] Such rhetorical world-making, however fictitious, is anything but inconsequential.

The creative ability to turn 'x' into 'y', then, allows us to reinvent the world or entities therein. As such it bears witness to our 'world-openness': as Peter Berger and Thomas Luckmann argue in their classic study *The Social Construction of Reality*, the human being is biologically underdetermined. Our terms of existence, they maintain, include an 'open' relationship to the environment that is not fixed by nature — in comparison to other creatures that live in 'closed worlds' insofar as they are 'predetermined by [their] biological equipment'. From one point of view, this is a deficiency: continuing a tradition of thought that dates back to Plato's *Protagoras*, Berger and Luckmann note that our 'instinctual organization may be described as underdeveloped, compared with that of the other higher mammals' and argue that 'important organismic developments, which in the animal are completed in the mother's body, take place in the human infant after its separation from the womb'. But as a result, culture is built into our nature: 'From the moment of birth, man's organismic development, and indeed a large part of his biological being as such, are subjected to continuing socially determined interference.'[77] What Berger and Luckmann cast in terms of 'socially *determined* interference' also opens the door for *creative* opportunities in a situation of contingency. Humanity has a species-specific potential to engage in the metamorphic reconfiguration (or evolution) of culture and, as a result, has been acquiring an ever-expanding capacity for transformative interventions into nature as well.

A modern philosopher who in particular stressed the link between metamorphosis, childlike creativity, and creative transgression was Nietzsche, who paradoxically saw in the transformative potential of ludic play a means of transcending the limits of humanity. In *Also sprach Zarathustra*, he has his protagonist detail three stages of transformative change necessary to overcome man and create the superman: 'Drei Verwandlungen nenne ich euch des Geistes: wie der Geist zum Kamele wird, und zum Löwen das Kamel, und zum Kinde zuletzt der Löwe.'[78] Here is Richard Perkins' commentary on the identification of the superman with the child:[79]

> Here is the winding staircase to the superman, ascending through three alternating flights to what Nietzsche prizes most among all our inchoate possibilities. Through its circulating exercise in transformative negation and double negation, preserving, destroying, and recreating our most basic human aspirations and so overcoming ourselves in the process, we might yet emerge

as playing children, innocent, free, and strong in our new attitudes, embracing
our earthly destinies, and transgressing, violating, surpassing all absolute,
exclusive dichotomies that oppose good to evil, truth to illusion, and being to
becoming.

Nietzsche, in short, argues for a like-mindedness of child and superman on the
grounds of their shared potential for playful creativity; but whereas this creativity
comes naturally to the child, an adult has to undergo various stages of mental
transformation in order to regain the productive disposition of his youth.[80]

Given our species-specific ability to conceive of metamorphosis, it is perhaps
unsurprising that in one tradition of anthropological reflection, the human being
also figures as the metamorphic creature par excellence. Humanity has frequently
defied straightforward classification, owing to our problematic position within
the order of things and our perceived ability to move up and down the 'ladder
of nature' in acts of transformative self-fashioning.[81] Already in Genesis, the
position of the human being is imagined as precarious: we are made both out
of earth and in God's image.[82] And New Testament authors, in particular Paul,
develop this inherent duality of our nature further.[83] In later centuries, the biblical
heritage began to interact with classical variants of dualism, notably the Platonic
distinction between mortal body and immortal soul. As creatures who partake both
in the terrestrial and the spiritual we are particularly susceptible to undergoing
transformative change, in one of two directions: conformity with God results in
an upward transformation that comes close to deification; a life of sin results in
a deforming, downward metamorphosis. The classic articulation of the human
being as quintessentially metamorphic comes from Pico della Mirandola's *Oration
on the Dignity of the Human Being*. As God puts it in his speech to Adam (*de Hominis
Dignitate*, § 5):

> 'Nec certam sedem nec propriam faciem nec munus ullum peculiare tibi
> dedimus, o Adam, ut, quam sedem, quam faciem, quae munera tute optaveris,
> ea pro voto, pro tua sententia habeas et possideas. Definita ceteris natura
> intra praescriptas a nobis leges coercetur. Tu nullis angustiis coercitus pro tuo
> arbitrio, in cuius manu te posui, tibi illam praefinies. Medium te mundi posui,
> ut circumspiceres inde commodius, quicquid est in mundo. Nec te caelestem
> neque terrenum neque mortalem neque immortalem fecimus, ut tui ipsius
> quasi arbitrarius honorariusque plastes et fictor, in quam malueris tute formam
> effingas. Poteris in inferiora, quae sunt bruta, degenerare, poteris in superiora,
> quae sunt divina, ex tui animi sententia regenerari.'

> ['I have not given you a specific location or particular appearance or any
> talent that is yours alone, Adam, so that you can have and own whatever
> location, appearance, and talent you yourself desire, according to your will
> and judgement. The fixed nature of all other living beings is confined within
> parameters prescribed by myself. You are confined by no limitations and,
> according to your own free will, in whose power I have put you, you shall
> define your nature for yourself. I have put you in the middle of the universe, so
> that from there you can inspect more easily whatever there is in the universe.
> I have created you neither as a creature of heaven nor a creature of the earth,
> neither mortal nor immortal, so that you — like a free and honorary moulder
> and shaper of yourself — fashion yourself securely in the form that you prefer.

You will be able to degenerate towards the lower levels of the animals, you will be able to recreate yourself through your own will-power into the higher levels of the divine.']

In his insouciant rewriting of Genesis, Pico here gives the biblical account of creation an anthropological spin that in certain ways prefigures the argument of Berger and Luckmann about the world-openness of humanity (even though he puts the emphasis on individual will, whereas they foreground the shaping power of socio-cultural configurations). In his commentary on God's utterance, Pico corroborates the philosophical anthropology of the Lord, in which the human features as the metamorphic animal. We are, in essence, 'chameleons', who can transform ourselves into divine beings — or, as the case may be, lowly brutes.[84]

In the western cultural imaginary the possibility of transformative change in both directions features prominently: ascent to the divine and descent into Hell, spiritual assimilation to God and downward mutation into a beast. Variants of 'upward' transformation include the post-mortem deification of Roman emperors or the road to sainthood open to those who have distinguished themselves in the service of the Catholic creed. After their life on earth, so church doctrine holds, such individuals may assume a privileged position within the hierarchy of being that enables them to intervene beneficially in human affairs. Thus the former Pope John Paul II (1920–2005) recently reached out from the beyond to cure the French nun Marie Simon-Pierre from Parkinson's disease in response to her prayer. After rigorous testing, the Catholic Church decreed the convalescence to be scientifically inexplicable and, on the basis of this miracle, recognized his heroic degree of virtue and quasi-divine status by declaring John Paul II 'Blessed' (*Beatus*), the penultimate stage before sainthood.[85]

A striking illustration of 'degenerative self-transformation' can be gleaned from Plato, *Republic* VIII, 565d–66a (trans. by Shorey):

> 'What, then, is the starting-point of the transformation [ἀρχὴ ... μεταβολῆς] of a protector into a tyrant? Is it not obviously when the protector's acts begin to reproduce the legend that is told of the shrine of Lycaean Zeus in Arcadia?' 'What is that?' he said. 'The story goes that he who tastes of the one bit of human entrails minced up with those of other victims is inevitably transformed into a wolf [Ὡς ἄρα ὁ γευσάμενος τοῦ ἀνθρωπίνου σπλάγχνου, ἐν ἄλλοις ἄλλων ἱερείων ἑνὸς ἐγκατατετμημένου, ἀνάγκη δὴ τούτῳ λύκῳ γενέσθαι]. Have you not heard the tale?' 'I have.' 'And is it not true that in like manner a leader of the people who, getting control of a docile mob, does not withhold his hand from the shedding of tribal blood, but by the customary unjust accusations brings a citizen into court and assassinates him, blotting out a human life, and with unhallowed tongue and lips that have tasted kindred blood, banishes and slays and hints at the abolition of debts and the partition of lands — is it not the inevitable consequence and a decree of fate that such a one be either slain by his enemies or become a tyrant and be transformed from a man into a wolf? [ἆρα τῷ τοιούτῳ ἀνάγκη δὴ τὸ μετὰ τοῦτο καὶ εἵμαρται ἢ ἀπολωλέναι ὑπὸ τῶν ἐχθρῶν ἢ τυραννεῖν καὶ λύκῳ ἐξ ἀνθρώπου γενέσθαι;]' 'It is quite inevitable', he said.

The shock value of the passage derives from the interlocutors' willingness to grant reality to what could have been a fairly unremarkable metaphor or simile: according to Socrates, the tyrant not only exhibits features of, or behaves like, a wolf; he actually *becomes* one. On the basis of the notorious story about the androphagy of the mythic figure Lycaon and his subsequent change into a wolf, everyone agrees that a similar transformation overtakes the tyrant. To turn into such a creature is to lose one's humanity — the tyrant is, quite literally, a savage animal. Socrates does not specify what precisely triggers the metamorphosis, but the way his argument unfolds suggests that the physical transformation into a wolf is thought to follow hot on the heels of a shift to a wolf-like mental disposition, put into gruesome practice. Unlike the myth from which it derives, where Zeus plays the role of transforming agent, Socrates appeals to some sort of divine necessity (ἀνάγκη δὴ [...] καὶ εἵμαρται), a general law of nature or a metaphysically grounded rule of political science, that inexorably kicks in when a human being begins to abuse his power in tyrannical fashion.

The possibility of sliding actually or figuratively into a beast-like state also preoccupies late-antique and medieval exegetes when commenting on those Psalms that (figuratively) speak of changes of humans into animals or the story of Nebuchadnezzar in the book of Daniel.[86] Hugh of St Cher, for instance, diagnosed a bestialization of the mind as a result of an alienation from God and noted how this internal moral transformation caused him to become beast-like also in external appearance.[87] One of the most haunting explorations of downward transformation comes from the twentieth century: Franz Kafka's novella *Metamorphosis*. Much of its power derives from its disquieting demonstration that the social factors which are constitutive of our sense of self may also compel us to alter our self-perception to the point of enforcing a degenerative auto-metamorphosis. Kafka's character Gregor Samsa becomes a monstrous vermin since his family treats him like one: he literally turns into what others think of him, in an unthinking process of auto-metamorphosis. The tale shows, not least, that our humanity depends on its (precarious) recognition by others.[88]

We shall encounter further examples of both upward and downward transformation in the course of this volume. For now, we would like to recognize imaginary human self-transformation as an important mode of metamorphosis, in addition to the types listed by the *Oxford English Dictionary*, that is, metamorphosis as the result of a supernatural intervention, as a figure of speech, and as a technical term in the sciences, especially biology. It is grounded in our distinctively human capacity for cognitive fluidity, our eccentric world-openness, and the figurative, world-making power built into human language.

Ethics

In the hands of humanity, the power to cause transformative change as well as the desire to be transformed tend to be ethically equivocal. The dream of empowerment and control over nature, resulting in the ability to transcend our natural limits, inspires hopes as well as fears. Likewise, metamorphic alterations of human beings, whether by means of bio-engineering or in and through rhetoric, inevitably imply a dehumanization, which, depending on perspective, may appear as either a demotion or a promotion, a loss or a gain; yet even those modes of dehumanization that aim at approximating the divine may turn out to have the opposite effect and reduce us to the level of a beast or monster. Both in Judeo-Christian scripture and in classical myth, the desire to improve upon our natural endowment by assuming quasi-divine attributes tends to come with dire health warnings: it often entails catastrophe. We all know the outcome of Adam and Eve's bites into the apple from the Tree of Knowledge, which gave our ancestors a taste of divine omniscience: access to the Tree of Life blocked, loss of Paradise for humanity, and the onset of *la condition humaine*: pain, suffering, death. When the goddess of dawn (Eos in Greek, Aurora in Latin) requested immortality for her human lover Tithonus, it slipped her mind to ask for eternal youth as well. As the author of the *Homeric Hymn to Aphrodite* illustrates, the results were as grotesque as the aforementioned painting by Quinten Massys (vv. 233–38):

> ἀλλ' ὅτε δὴ πάμπαν στυγερὸν κατὰ γῆρας ἔπειγεν
> οὐδέ τι κινῆσαι μελέων δύνατ' οὐδ' ἀναεῖραι,
> ἥδε δέ οἱ κατὰ θυμὸν ἀρίστη φαίνετο βουλή·   235
> ἐν θαλάμῳ κατέθηκε, θύρας δ' ἐπέθηκε φαεινάς.
> τοῦ δ' ἤ τοι φωνὴ ῥεῖ ἄσπετος, οὐδέ τι κῖκυς
> ἔσθ' οἵη πάρος ἔσκεν ἐνὶ γναμπτοῖσι μέλεσσιν.

[But when loathsome old age pressed full upon him, and he could not move nor lift his limbs, this seemed to her in her heart the best counsel: she laid him in a room and put to the shining doors. There he babbles endlessly, and no more has strength at all, such as once he had in his supple limbs.]

In some versions, Tithonus eventually undergoes a transformation into a cicada.[89] Human endeavours that betoken Promethean hubris also tend to attract disapproving commentary. Shelley's figure of Frankenstein is designed to illustrate the dangers of a human being arrogating to himself the divine prerogative of creation. The myth of Pygmalion and his beloved statue that sprung to life carries a similar message. In Ovid's version, Pygmalion knows full well that his desire to see his artwork animated constitutes a transgression and accordingly formulates his prayer very carefully, requesting as his spouse not the statue itself but a virgin just like her — and is in luck that Venus understands (and grants) his heart's desire (*Met.* x. 270–78). The marriage that ensues is blessed, but the next generation seems to pay for Pygmalion's perverse agalmatophilia, insofar as their son Cinyras becomes the protagonist in a lurid tale of incest with his daughter Myrrha (*Met.* x. 298–518). Similar strictures apply to the figurative use of metamorphosis. Indeed, Miller has interpreted the myths of transformation recounted by Ovid as a meditation on the power of rhetoric to shape reality, with serious ethical consequences: 'Though the gods magically cause the transformation, an unsettling human truth is hidden behind these childish stories of boys turned into flowers, girls into trees. [...] In the cruel justice of the gods we see the terrible performative power that figures of speech may have. Tropes tend to materialize in the real world in ways that are ethical, social, and political. The *Metamorphoses* shows what aberrant figurative language can do. The power of the gods to intervene in human history is the allegorization of this linguistic power.'[90]

Meditations on the ethical ambiguity of metamorphic powers and desires include, not least, J. K. Rowling's *Harry Potter* series. Her heptalogy, which appeared between 1997 and 2007 and has since become the most successful children's series ever, combines a Nietzschean vision of trans-humanism with a decidedly anti-Nietzschean message about the core values of humanity. Rowling's literary world celebrates metamorphic powers and creativity, while also imposing strong ethical strictures on any form of trans-human striving. Since the fantasy-saga brings together various themes of the foregoing pages and has interesting thematic affinities with several of the chapters to follow (not least in illustrating how biblical and classical archetypes of transformative change continue to resonate powerfully today), we want to conclude our General Introduction with a brief look at metamorphosis in *Harry Potter*.

In Rowling's fantasy, Humanity 2.0 has in a sense been realized: her human population falls into wizards and witches on the one hand and so-called 'muggles', that is, ordinary human beings without magical gifts, on the other.[91] The interface between the two groups is porous: intermarriages are possible, not least since muggle parents can give birth to magical children and wizards and witches may produce non-magical offspring (so called 'squibs'); membership in the wizarding community thus depends on a mixture of lineage and luck, as anyone born with the right talents and endowment will receive the chance to enter the world of magic, despite the engrained racism of some of the 'pure-blood' wizards towards colleagues with muggle-background.[92] By and large wizards and muggles live in parallel universes, with the latter being for the most part oblivious to the existence of the magical community (a notable exception being the British prime minister).

In the world of wizards, metamorphosis is omnipresent, and Rowling deftly draws on both biblical and classical modes of transformative change for special effects. Arguably the best example of her puckish play with theological doctrine involves her use of 'transfiguration' or *transfiguratio* in Latin — the term, in other words, which the Latin Bible employs to translate the Greek *metamorphosis* terminology Matthew and Mark draw on to recount the transformation of Jesus on the mountain.[93] At Hogwarts School of Witchcraft and Wizardry transfiguration is a standard subject on the syllabus, if a demanding one: 'Transfiguration is some of the most complex and dangerous magic you will learn at Hogwarts,' announces the resident specialist Minerva McGonagall, before illustrating her skills by turning her desk into a pig and back again.[94] Accomplished magicians can transfigure themselves and become so-called 'animagi', who can take on the shape of a specific animal in an instant.[95] What animagi acquire through strenuous study, so-called 'metamorphmagi' are born with: the ability to alter their shape at will, just like the divinities of Greek myth.[96] Those wizards and witches who have the need to assume temporarily the outward appearance of someone else can brew 'polyjuice potion' according to a recipe that rivals in complexity Medea's rejuvenation draught in Ovid, *Metamorphoses* vii.[97] Among non-human magical creatures, so-called boggarts take on the shape of whatever the person they encounter fears most.[98] Rowling's world also includes such shape-shifters as werewolves, and she explores what happens to human consciousness when an individual undergoes temporary metamorphic dehumanization as a werewolf or animagus.[99]

At the same time, Rowling sets up conspicuous hedges around the metamorphic elements in her literary world. Self-transfiguration into an animal is a rare skill (as rare as human polymorphs in Greek myth, such as Mestra or Periclymenus) and requires government approval: 'the Ministry keeps tabs on witches and wizards who can become animals; there's a register showing what animal they become, and their markings and things'.[100] Metamorphmagi, too, are infrequent: As Nymphadora Tonks, the only metamorphmaga to appear in the series, explains: 'Metamorph-magi are really rare, they're born, not made. Most wizards need to use a wand, or potions, to change their appearance.'[101] At the end of the series the transformers suffer a disproportionately high casualty rate. Among the dead of those fighting on the side of the good are the metamorphmaga Tonks and the werewolf Lupin.[102]

These hedges around the metamorphic fit the Christian humanism at the heart of the series, which manifests itself in an embrace of such values as love, courage, trust, friendship, pity, and self-sacrifice — but above all an acceptance of mortality and the promise of an afterlife. The first volume of the series, which revolves around the so-called 'philosopher's stone', an alchemical object that grants limitless wealth and eternal life, ends with the deliberate destruction of the stone by its owner, Nicholas Flamel, who accepts his death in order to prevent abuse of the stone's power. More generally, in Rowling's Manichean plot, the dividing line between the good and the evil ultimately hinges upon different appraisals of death: whereas the former come to accept it as an inevitable part of the human condition, death is deemed the ultimate evil by the so-called 'death eaters' and their master, the most evil wizard of all time, Harry Potter's great antagonist, Tom Marvolo Riddle, a.k.a. Lord Voldemort, a speaking name based on the French phrase *vol de mort* ('flight of/from death'). Voldemort tries to conquer death through death, at the cost of the wholeness of his soul: in Rowland's world, the quest for immortality paradoxically requires acts of murder that rip the soul apart so that the fragment can be stored separate from the person, in either an object or a living creature (a 'horcrux'). In contrast, two moments of self-sacrifice stand at the beginning and end of Harry Potter's childhood. The narrative starts shortly after Lily Potter died while trying to protect her baby son from Voldemort; and at the end Harry, too, willingly faces death to stop Voldemort and his cohort of monsters and death-eaters from murdering his friends. While he again survives the killing curse, the remarkable decision of a teenager to sacrifice himself is the culminating moment of a meditation on mortality and associated human values that defines the entire heptalogy. Despite the metamorphic capabilities available to her wizards and witches, Rowling represents trans-human striving as profoundly problematic if not evil, whereas those who endorse their human *Jemeinigkeit* and retain their souls intact emerge as the true heroes who simply 'go on' when the time has come.

Notes to the Introduction

1. The General Introduction and the Introductions to the three parts occasionally draw upon and rework material first presented in Gildenhard and Zissos (2010).

2. The work, in capturing the onset of the transformational process of the horrified nymph into a laurel tree, violated his ideal of noble simplicity and calm grandeur ('edle Einfalt, stille Größe'). While he singles out *Apollo and Daphne* as Bernini's best work (with the exception of the *Santa Bibiana*) in a letter from spring 1764, he still objects, among other things, to Daphne's open mouth (which, he feels, generates the impression of a mask), in contrast to the restraint visible in the *Laocoon* group; and he notes that what Daphne lacks in beauty, the artist supplied in form of the miraculous: 'denn an den äußeren Theilen ihres Cörpers fängt schon die bekannte Verwandlung an.' See further Lichtenstern (1992) and Barasch (2000), pp. 99–101.

3. Hahn (2006), p. 47 n. 1 ('Dabei ist allerdings zu bedenken, daß Verwandlungen im strengen Sinne in der modernen westlichen Gesellschaft — zumindest offiziell — nicht erlaubt sind und allenfalls als Betrug, Metapher oder pathologische Selbsttäuschung in ihr Weltbild passen. Auch im Wirklichkeitsverständnis der Soziologie ist selbstverständlich die Verwandlung von Personen etwas Unmögliches, was freilich nicht ausschließt, Gesellschaften zu analysieren, in denen sich Menschen in Geister verwandeln und umgekehrt. Für unsere Gesellschaft gilt aber eher, daß man sich zwar auf drastische Weise, bis zur Unkenntlichkeit, verändern kann. Aber selbst der entschiedenste Gestalt- oder Statuswechsel wird oft gegen den Augenschein als Wandlung, nicht aber als Verwandlung konzipiert, der die 'Jemeinigkeit' (im Sinne Heideggers) nicht berührt.')

4. For this crucial distinction, see also A. and J. Assmann (2006), p. 13, who correlate change, identity, and transformation as follows: 'Man könnte vermuten, daß es von dieser Intensivierung des *Wandels* [*sc.* in modern western society], der als Korrelatbegriff den der Identität wie sein Schatten begleitet, nur noch ein kleiner Schritt ist zum Begriff der *Verwandlung*. Hier soll jedoch die These vertreten werden, daß mit dem Begriff der Verwandlung das Band zu den skizzierten westlichen Identitätskonzepten gekappt und dieser Kulturhorizont verlassen wird. Der Identitätsdiskurs, der Wandel einschließt, schließt Verwandlung als das andere seiner selbst aus' ['One could suppose that the intensification of change [in modern western society], which functions as a correlative concept to the concept of identity, following it like a shadow, is only a small step away from the concept of transformation. Here, however, we wish to champion the thesis that the concept of transformation severs the connection to the western concepts of identity just outlined and leaves behind this particular cultural horizon. The discourse of identity that includes change, excludes transformation as the other of itself'].

5. His choice of example, however, is somewhat infelicitous: human–ghost transformations do not necessarily challenge the 'Jemeinigkeit' of the being or creature that appears at times as human and at times as a ghost. Technically speaking, we are dealing with a subcategory of metamorphosis, that is, polyphany or polymorphism: it presupposes a 'jemeinig' core of the transforming creature and in most instances implies the reversibility of the transformation.

6. For Alexander, see Subirós (2011) and Introduction to Part III below; for Piccinini, <http://www.patriciapiccinini.net/>. Other contemporary artists that explore inter-species mutability include Emilie Clark, Beth Cavener Stichter, Kate Clark: see Bartkowski (2009).

7. Transformation studies have recently received institutional acknowledgement in the form of the IRCM ('Interdisciplinary Research Centre: Metamorphic Changes in the Arts') at the University of Salzburg, directed by Sabine Coelsch-Foisner and Peter Kuon, with its ambitious, six-pronged programme of research, on 'theory of metamorphosis', 'body transformations', 'reception as metamorphosis', 'production as metamorphosis', 'the concept of a work of art', and 'identity and mental transformations'. For results, see Coelsch-Foisner and Schwarzbauer (2005), Gottwald and Klein (2005), Coelsch-Foisner (2006), Stagl (2007), and Allesch and Schwarzbauer (2007).

8. The notion of using the past (kept present in the form of fairy tales and mythic creatures) as a means of envisioning the future informed the recent exhibition 'Fairy Tales, Monsters, and the Genetic Imagination' at the Frist Center for the Visual Arts in Nashville, Tennessee, which features many metamorphic moments. See <http://fristcenter.org/calendar-exhibitions/detail/fairy-tales-monsters-and-the-genetic-imagination>.

9. Liddell and Scott (1968), p. 1109, s.v. μετά G VIII.

10. Bachelard (1939), p. 65 ('le besoin d'animaliser [...] est à l'origine de l'imagination. La fonction première de l'imagination est de faire des formes animales'), cited and discussed by Massey (1976), p. 2.

11. Tomlinson (1983).

12. Blumenberg (1979) p. 384: '*Metamorphosen* ist kein bloßer Sammeltitel für Mythen, sondern das Ausformungsprinzip des Mythos selbst, die Grundform einer noch unzuverlässigen Identität der aus der Formlosigkeit zur Erscheinung herausdrängenden Götter.'

13. Barkan (1986), p. 18.

14. Kuon (2005), p. 1.

15. Zgoll (2004).

16. Hardie (2008), p. 176.

17. At *Tristia*, 1. 7. 13, Ovid retrospectively characterizes the *Metamorphoses* as *carmina mutatas hominum dicentia formas* ['a poem that sings of the changed forms of humans'].

18. Feldherr (2010), p. 35, with a review of suggestions mooted by earlier scholars: 'clarification of some preexisting quality, already present in the old form but more sharply revealed in the new', 'a process of clarification', or the revelation of some 'kind of abiding existence'.

19. For Aesop and Apuleius see Introduction to Part I. For the use of metamorphosis to refer to allophany, see e.g. Ps-Clement, *Homilies*, v. 12, where Jupiter's philandering in various shapes and sizes is referred to as 'sexual encounters concealed by means of metamorphosis' (τὰς διὰ τῆς μεταμορφώσεως λανθανούσας κοινωνίας). The passage is cited and discussed by Klauck (2008), Chapter 7: 'Christus in vielen Gestalten: Die Polymorphie des Erlösers in apokryphen Texten', pp. 304–05. For a contemporary use of the term metamorphosis to capture (among other things) certain types of divine epiphanies, both in the Judeo-Christian and the Graeco-Roman tradition, see Kinlaw (2005).

20. Massey (1976), p. 3. He proposes six broad categories: science, philosophy and theories of the self, anthropology (including such phenomena as totemism, possession, shape-shifting, lycanthropy, and vampirism), religion (in particular if metamorphosis is to include metempsychosis), psychology, and aesthetics (pp. 3–15).

21. Classical Latin knows the verbs *transformare* and *transfigurare*; the noun *transfiguratio* occurs once, at Pliny the Elder, *Natural History*, VII. 188, in a discussion of the destiny of the human soul after death.

22. See Klopsch (1967) and Robathan (1968).

23. The author seemingly draws on a range of passages in Ovid's *oeuvre*. See *Heroides*, 1.115–16 (possibly recalling Propertius, II. 9. 8) and *Epistulae ex Ponto*, I. 4. 1–5, where he portrays himself as unrecognizably aged.

24. See Brown, M. (2008). He points out that 'The painting — one of the most popular in the National Gallery [...] — inspired Victorian illustrator John Tenniel to make the Duchess (the unpredictable, Cheshire Cat-owning baby abuser) one of the most grotesque characters in his illustrations of the Lewis Carroll classic [*Alice's Adventures in Wonderland*].'

25. <http://www.youtube.com/watch?v=o-v6hdjmoxI>.

26. <http://www.youtube.com/watch?v=dPOub8X2cqg&feature=relmfu>.

27. Clark and McMunn (1989), Hassig (1995), Verner (2005).

28. For the monstrous and the metamorphic in the art of Jane Alexander see below, Introduction to Part III.

29. Mendieta (2010), p. 2.

30. See Introduction to Part II for a similar approach to metamorphosis in Aesop.

31. Compare Hesiod, *Theogony*, 116–20 (with West (1966), pp. 192–93) and Plato, *Timaeus*, 29e–30b.

32. For a detailed discussion of this passage see Barchiesi (2005), pp. 148–53, with previous bibliography listed on pp. 147–48.

33. 'They' (in Latin the subject of *dixere*) are, of course, Greek thinkers or the Greeks more generally.

34. Ovid makes the point explicitly several lines later when he describes how the disparate elements ceaselessly configure and reconfigure themselves. The result is that no form can ever acquire any meaningful stability: *nulli sua forma manebat (Met.* 1. 17).

35. Baudrillard (1999), as cited and discussed by Maciocco (2008), p. 56. His distinction between morphism and metamorphosis forms part of his efforts to capture the hallmarks of 'virtual reality'.

36. Likewise, in the Latin, the 'warring seeds' (*discordia semina*) keep apart the entities (*rerum*) from their attribute 'ill-connected' (*non bene iunctarum*).

37. For a twentieth-century engagement with Ovid's conception of chaos, including the significance of *indigesta* and *digero*, see Chapter 10 (Luke Pitcher).

38. Arendt (1961/2006a), p. 11.

39. For a famous illustration see the frontispiece of Didacus Valades, *Rhetorica Christiana* (1579), further Lovejoy (1936); for a deconstruction of the notion in contemporary art see Tregunna and Pickeral (2009).

40. Mutation derives from the basic Latin term for (transformative) change, that is, *mutare*.

41. See Corbyn (2011).

42. Lovejoy (1936), p. 332.

43. See e.g. Langton (1990) and Kauffman (1993) cited, among others, by Hayles (1999), p. 286 for the argument that 'chaos accelerates the evolution of biological and artificial life', within the context of a discussion of a general shift away from metaphysical essentialism to a view of nature (including human nature) that foregrounds relations and networks, a dialectic of pattern/randomness, processes, complexity, and recursive loops (pp. 283–91).

44. Arendt (1961/2006b), p. 95.

45. 'Lucretius' poem, *On the Nature of Things*, stands as a powerful representation of classical antiquity's best and most influential effort to speculate on the material universe and the place and condition of human beings in it': Johnson (2000), p. ix. Kennedy (2002) reactivates the dialogue between Lucretian physics and modern science.

46. *De Rerum Natura*, I. 675–76.

47. The couplet recurs at I. 792–93, II. 753–54, III. 519–20.

48. Bailey (1949) p. 719, with reference to Epicurus, *Letter to Herodotus*, 54: Καὶ μὴν καὶ τὰς ἀτόμους νομιστέον μηδεμίαν ποιότητα τῶν φαινομένων προσφέρεσθαι πλὴν σχήματος καὶ βάρους καὶ μεγέθους καὶ ὅσα ἐξ ἀνάγκης σχήματος συμφυῆ ἐστι. ποιότης γὰρ πᾶσα μεταβάλλει· αἱ δὲ ἄτομοι οὐδὲν μεταβάλλουσιν, ἐπειδή περ δεῖ τι ὑπομένειν ἐν ταῖς διαλύσεσι τῶν συγκρίσεων στερεὸν καὶ ἀδιάλυτον, ὃ τὰς μεταβολὰς οὐκ εἰς τὸ μὴ ὂν ποιήσεται οὐδ' ἐκ τοῦ μὴ ὄντος, ἀλλὰ κατὰ μεταθέσεις ἐν πολλοῖς, τινῶν δὲ καὶ προσόδους καὶ ἀφόδους. ὅθεν ἀναγκαῖον τὰ [μὴ] μετατιθέμενα ἄφθαρτα εἶναι καὶ τὴν τοῦ μεταβάλλοντος φύσιν οὐκ ἔχοντα, ὄγκους δὲ καὶ σχηματισμοὺς ἰδίους· ταῦτα γὰρ καὶ ἀναγκαῖον ὑπομένειν ['In addition, one must assume that the atoms do not possess any of the qualities of visible phenomena expect shape, weight, and size and whatever is out of necessity built into shape. For each quality changes; the atoms, however, do not change since something has to remain in the dissolutions of the connections, something hard and indissoluble, which will not undergo changes either into non-existence or out of non-existence, but in most cases through reconfigurations, or through additions and subtractions. Hence the elements that get reconfigured are of necessity indestructible and do not have the natural characteristics of that which undergoes change, but specific mass and shape. For out of necessity these must remain'].

49. Harrison (1992), pp. 105–06 ('Diese präformale Verwandtschaft aller Schöpfung, die es möglich macht, daß menschliche Wesen in Tiere, Bäume, Blumen und andere Waldphänomene verwandelt werden, ist das immer wiederkehrende materialistische Thema der "Metamorphosen".') (Citation and discussion in Scharold (2000), p. 51.) See also allegorical readings of Homer's Proteus 'as the original undifferentiated substance which contained all the forms': Forbes Irving (1990), p. 1.

50. Lucretius explicitly polemicizes against rival philosophical views that argue for primordial elements such as fire as constituent of the universe. See further Barchiesi (2005), p. 153: '*semina rerum*: è particolarmente provocatorio; l'espressione richiama Lucrezio, che la ripete undici volte sempre nella stessa sede metrica, ma che aveva impresso su questo sintagma lo stampo teorico della concezione atomistica epicurea. Ora invece le stesse parole non sono più equivalenti al concetto chiave della fisica materialistica, 'atomi', ma sono applicate alla concezione dei tre elementi primari, un'idea incompatibile con il programma didattico di Lucrezio' ['*The seeds of*

things: especially provocative; the formulation recalls Lucretius who uses it eleven times always in the same metrical position, yet had endowed the phrase with theoretical meaning derived from Epicurus' atomistic physics. Now, however, the same words no longer correspond to the key concept of materialist physics, i.e. "atoms", but are applied to the notion of three primary elements, an idea incompatible with the didactic programme of Lucretius']. He refers to Virgil, *Eclogue* 6, as a precedent for Ovid's approach.

51. Vial (2010) argues that behind each transformation beckons one of the primordial elements, which turns the *Metamorphoses* into a 'pentavalent poem' (with the human being joining fire, air, water, and earth as the 'fifth element').

52. One wonders whether Ovid's formulation *melior natura* is not a sly dig at Lucretius's version of Epicurean physics: Ovid seems to be saying that his *natura*, understood as world, both literary and real, is better than the *natura* Lucretius discusses and tries to represent in his *De Rerum Natura*, precisely because it features as a purposeful divine agent and matrix of transformative change.

53. Nicklas (2002), pp. 11–12 ('Nicht ganz allgemein die Mutabilität ist der Kern des Motives [der Metamorphose], sondern eine Veränderung der Form, die in ihrer neuen Erscheinung wieder zu Ruhe kommt und die Erinnerung an ihre frühere Gestalt in sich trägt. [...] Die neue Gestalt muß an die alte in irgendeiner Weise anknüpfen.') See also Ferzoco and Gill (2005), p. 1: 'Metamorphosis is not simply a synonym for change of any sort, but a distinctive and polyvalent form of transformation. Metamorphic transformation is startling and dramatic, yet never entirely arbitrary or illogical. In this respect this most radical paradigm of change contains within itself ideas of continuity.' Generally speaking, we agree, though with three modifications: the 'most' in 'this most radical paradigm of change' seems inappropriate since the *most* radical paradigm of change is, surely, chaotic formlessness; the 'never' before 'entirely arbitrary or illogical' strikes us as too categorical; and all paradigms of change — with the exception, perhaps, of chaotic formlessness — contain within themselves ideas of continuity, so continuity as such is neither remarkable nor a distinguishing characteristic of 'metamorphic transformation'.

54. At times Ovid is explicit about minimal and seemingly inconsequential continuity. See e.g. *Met.* XIV. 396: *nec quicquam antiquum Pico nisi nomina restat* ['nothing of Picus' former existence remained except the name'], though Ovid in this episode as elsewhere stresses continuity in consciousness.

55. See esp. 1 Corinth. 15. 42: Οὕτως καὶ ἡ ἀνάστασις τῶν νεκρῶν. σπείρεται ἐν φθορᾷ, ἐγείρεται ἐν ἀφθαρσίᾳ· ['So also is the resurrection of the dead. It is sown in corruption; it is raised in incorruption'], 43: σπείρεται ἐν ἀτιμίᾳ, ἐγείρεται ἐν δόξῃ· σπείρεται ἐν ἀσθενείᾳ, ἐγείρεται ἐν δυνάμει· ['It is sown in dishonour; it is raised in glory: it is sown in weakness; it is raised in power'], 44: σπείρεται σῶμα ψυχικόν, ἐγείρεται σῶμα πνευματικόν ['It is sown a natural body; it is raised a spiritual body'].

56. See Ovid, *Met.* VIII. 725–884. Mestra does not enter the scene until the end of the episode (843 onwards), but she is obliquely flagged up as its telos right at the outset: the narrative begins with the internal narrator, the river god Achelous, drawing a programmatic distinction between irreversible transformations of humans and humans endowed with the power of reversible auto-metamorphosis. See 728–31: '*sunt, o fortissime, quorum / forma semel mota est et in hoc renovamine mansit; sunt, quibus in plures ius est transire figuras, / ut tibi, complexi terram maris incola, Proteu*' ['There are those, courageous hero, whose form has been altered once and who have retained their new appearance; others have the right to enter into more than one shape, as you, Proteus, dweller of the sea that embraces the earth']. *Metamorphoses* VIII, the central book of the poem, contains several such programmatic reflections on the nature (and believability) of transformative change: see further Introduction to Part I.

57. The classic treatment of the phenomenon, also within the classical tradition, remains Skulsky (1981). He notes, among other things, 'the edge of cruelty in the comedy of transformation' (p. 30) that psychological continuity in the context of metamorphosis entails. We return to this theme in more detail in Introduction to Part I.

58. Bynum (1995), pp. 5–6. See also Bynum (2001) (on metamorphosis and identity in a Christian context more broadly) and (2011) (on Christian notions of materiality in the Middle Ages).

59. See above, p. 1 and nn. 3, 5.

60. Compare 1 Cor. 15. 52–54: *immutabimur. oportet enim corruptibile hoc <u>induere</u> incorruptelam et mortale hoc <u>induere</u> inmortalitatem. cum autem mortale hoc <u>induerit</u> inmortalitatem tunc fiet sermo qui scriptus est absorta est mors in victoria* ['and we shall be changed. For this corruptible shall have put on incorruption, and this mortal shall have put on immortality, then shall be brought to pass the saying that is written, Death is swallowed up in victory'] with (say) Ovid, *Met.* 11. 850–51 (of Jupiter): *<u>induitur</u> faciem tauri* ['he took on the appearance of a bull'].

61. For more on Goethe's theory of metamorphosis, see Introduction to Part III; for more on Ovid's Pythagoras, see Introduction to Part I.

62. Introduction to Part I contains a detailed discussion of metamorphosis in Homer.

63. See also Numbers 20. 1–13, which recounts the creation of a well from a rock, struck by Moses with his rod at the behest of God.

64. See, though, the prelude at Exodus 4. 1–4, where the Lord 'inducts' Moses, who is initially scared at the sight of a rod turning into a serpent, into the realm of magical transformations.

65. Genesis 2. 21–25; contrast 1. 27: 'So God created man in his *own* image, in the image of God he created him; male and female created he them', where there is no hint of chronology, dependence, or transformation.

66. *Met.* x. 243–97.

67. <http://www.newscientist.com/article/dn17194-gm-monkey-passes-jellyfish-gene-to-offspring.html>.

68. Liveley (2006) discusses the modern figure of the cyborg within the wider context of its classical precedents.

69. Fuller (2011), p. 103. Earlier literature includes Haraway (1991) and Hayles (1999).

70. This is the title of Fuller (2011).

71. Gottwald (2005), p. 86 ('Die Metamorphose als mythische Denkfigur (nicht als literarisches Motiv) ist somit Ausdruck kognitiv defizitärer Bewußtseinsstufen, im besonderen mythischer Kausalitätsauffassungen').

72. For discussion see Introduction to Part I, pp. 43–44.

73. Mithen (2008).

74. See above p. 4.

75. Miller (1990), p. 1. See also Pianezzola (1979), p. 80: 'la metafora è generatrice di metamorfosi', Le Guern (1981), Barkan (1986), p. 23: 'often the business of metamorphosis [...] is to make flesh of metaphor', Perry (1990), pp. 13–14, Schmidt (1991) (2006), Mikkonen (1996).

76. One of the first to comment on the slippage between metaphor and myth, or trope and story, was Giovanni Battista Vico in his *Scienza Nuova* (1744), in his discussion of 'poetic wisdom'. See Buntfuß (2006), who places Vico in a tradition of metaphorological thought that also includes Cassirer and Blumenberg.

77. Berger and Luckmann (1967). The quotations are from p. 65 (first) and p. 66 (second and third).

78. Chapter 12 ('Three transformations of the spirit I mention to you: how the spirit becomes a camel, and the camel a lion, and finally the lion a child').

79. Perkins (1985), p. 472.

80. Cf. Weiss (1999), p. 74: 'Encouraging children to explore the alternative imaginary schemas opened up by changes in bodily morphology is perhaps one of the oldest, and potentially most subversive tactics available for undermining social constraints on what bodies can and can't do. Unfortunately, for those of us who are no longer able (or willing) to believe that such radical bodily transformation is possible, less magical (and less entertaining!) tactics will have to suffice.'

81. At times, of course, the boundary between self-induced and externally induced transformation of the self is difficult to draw, not least in our age, where mental polymorphism through the use of psycho-pharmaceuticals is becoming increasingly widespread. For some comments on identity-altering interventions to manipulate the neuro-chemical basis of our sense of self by means of drugs as well as the wider historical background (starting with medieval alchemy) see Fuller (2011), p. 131.

82. See Scharold (2000), p. 44, who interprets the results as evidence of primitive thought: 'Die Uneinheitlichkeit des Genesisberichts, der den Menschen als Abbild Gottes und als wesensverwandt mit den Tieren bezeichnet, scheint auf einer *noch nicht* konsolidierten Stellung

des Menschen im Kosmos zu basieren' (our italics). But the notion of a 'not yet consolidated position of the human being within the cosmos' poses the question of when precisely this consolidation has since taken place.

83. See the resurrection imagery at 1 Cor. 15, discussed above.

84. We return to this passage in the Introduction to Part II.

85. On miracles in our times, see further Geppert and Kössler (2011).

86. See e.g. Psalm 32. 9: 'Be ye not as the horse, *or* as the mule, *which* have no understanding: whose mouth must be held in with bit and bridle, lest they come near unto thee' and 49. 20: 'Man *that is* in honour, and understandeth not, is like the beasts *that* perish', as well as the Book of Daniel, esp. 4. 28–32 and 5. 21. For discussion see Chapin (1971), pp. 1–25, esp. 5–7, who also comments on the influence of Platonizing philosophy (esp. as regards the duality of body and soul) on Christian thinking about metamorphosis.

87. Chapin (1971), p. 5–7. She notes that 'the external bestiality, though superficial, is literal, so much so that Nebuchadnezzar is often represented as a wild man in medieval illuminations' (p. 7), with reference to Bernheimer (1952), pp. 12–13 and plate 3.

88. See Introduction to Part III for a more detailed discussion of Kafka.

89. Hellanicus, *Fragmente der Griechischen Historiker* 4 F 140 (= Schol. A *ad Iliad* 3.151).

90. Miller (1990), p. 1.

91. Rowling countervails this differentiation of humans into wizards and muggles by endorsing a universal conception of humanity comprising both (see esp. *Harry Potter and the Deathly Hallows*, ch. 22: 'The Deathly Hallows': ' "We're all human, aren't we? Every human life is worth the same, and worth saving." '), as well as a strong sense of cross-species solidarity (including anthropomorphic and zoomorphic creatures).

92. One is reminded of Plato, *Republic*, III, 415a–c, where Socrates also recognizes the possibility of golden-souled parents giving birth to children who have silver or brass mixed into their soul, and parents of lesser natural endowment engendering golden-souled offspring.

93. See Matthew 17. 1–9 (*et transfiguratus est ante eos*), Mark 9. 2–8 (*et transfiguratus est coram ipsis*); cf. Luke 9. 28–36 (*et factum est dum oraret species vultus eius altera*) and II Peter 1. 16–18. We discuss the passages in more detail in Introduction to Part II.

94. *Harry Potter and the Philosopher's Stone*, ch. 8: 'The Potions Master'. Fun with transfiguration occurs throughout the series, including *Harry Potter and the Deathly Hallows*, ch. 33, where we meet Dumbledore reading in what appears to be a scholarly journal with the title *Transfiguration Today*.

95. In *Harry Potter and the Goblet of Fire*, ch. 26: 'The Second Task', we encounter a mid-way variant, with one wizard turning his upper body into a shark in an 'incomplete form of Transfiguration' to carry out an underwater task.

96. See also *Harry Potter and the Half-Blood Prince*, ch. 5: 'An Excess of Phlegm': 'Some idiot's started selling Metamorph-Medals. Just sling them around your neck and you'll be able to change your appearance at will. A hundred thousand disguises, all for ten Galleons!'

97. See e.g. *Harry Potter and the Chamber of Secrets*, ch. 12: 'The Polyjuice Potion'; *Harry Potter and the Goblet of Fire*, ch. 35: 'Veritaserum'; or *Harry Potter and the Deathly Hallows*, ch. 4: 'The Seven Potters', ch 13: 'The Muggle-Born Registration Commission' and ch. 26: 'Gringotts'. In view of Introduction to Part I, we may note the following distinction between wand- and potion-magic, *Harry Potter and the Philosopher's Stone*, ch. 8: 'The Potions Master': 'As there is little foolish wand-waving here, many of you will hardly believe this is magic. I don't expect you will really understand the beauty of the softly simmering cauldron with its shimmering fumes, the delicate power of liquids that creep through human veins, bewitching the mind, ensnaring the senses.'

98. See e.g. *Harry Potter and the Prisoner of Azkaban*, ch. 7: 'The Boggart in the Wardrobe' or *Harry Potter and the Order of the Phoenix*, ch. 9: 'The Woes of Mrs Weasley'.

99. *Harry Potter and the Prisoner of Azkaban*, ch. 18: 'The [Wolfsbane] Potion […] makes me safe, you see. As long as I take it in the week preceding the full moon, I keep my mind when I transform […] I am able to curl up in my office, a harmless wolf, and wait for the moon to wane again' or the animagus Sirius Black about his condition as a dog: 'my feelings were less — less human, less complex'.

100. *Harry Potter and the Prisoner of Azkaban*, ch. 18: 'Moony, Wormtail, Padfoot and Prongs', which

does not prevent certain members of the magical community acquiring the power of self-transformation illegally. A case in point is the investigative reporter Rita Skeeter, who can turn herself into a beetle and in this shape bug places to get information undercover: see esp. *Harry Potter and the Goblet of Fire*, ch. 37: 'The Beginning'.

101. *Harry Potter and the Order of the Phoenix*, ch. 2: 'The Advanced Guard'.
102. *Harry Potter and the Deathly Hallows*, ch. 33: 'The Prince's Tale'.

PART I

Antiquity and Archetypes

Introduction to Part I

Ingo Gildenhard & Andrew Zissos

In the context of the classical tradition, one text above all others has shaped the discourse of transformative change: Ovid's *Metamorphoses*.[1] This is an epic poem of sorts, written in Latin, that postures as a universal history from the beginning of the world down to the poet's own times (*Met.* I. 3–4: *prima ab origina mundi ad mea tempora*). It was composed in the early years of the Roman empire, prior to its author's notorious banishment from Rome by the emperor Augustus in AD 8. Ovid's *Metamorphoses* dominates the tradition, peerless in its influence; if one were to name a runner-up, the next most influential text would be from the high Roman empire, again written in Latin, and, as it happens, sharing the same title. This second *Metamorphoses*, a novel by the 'Latin sophist' Apuleius (second century AD), is perhaps better known today by its alternative title *The Golden Ass*.[2] The two Latin *Metamorphoses* have played a privileged, if unequal, role in defining for post-classical periods — from late antiquity to post-modernity — how Graeco-Roman antiquity understood and imagined metamorphosis. But their cultural standing as classical archetypes within the vernacular cultures of the West ought not to eclipse that Ovid and Apuleius wrote towards the end of a long sequence of literary development that dates back to eighth- or seventh-century BC Greece, when the traditions of oral poetry that stand behind the names of Homer and Hesiod were first fixed in writing. These archaic Greek poems, moreover, were themselves affiliated, at least in part, to a yet more ancient Near Eastern cultural configuration, which also forms the backdrop for the Hebrew scriptures and their Christian codification in the Old Testament.[3]

From its earliest beginnings, Latin literature was decisively and pervasively influenced by the literature of Hellas. That influence is very much evident in the *Metamorphoses* of Ovid and Apuleius, apart from their (programmatic) Greek title: the former conquered and codified, in Latin, the universe of Greek myth; the latter claimed to have translated a Greek source text now lost (I.I: *Fabulam Graecanicam incipimus*).[4] For the story we wish to tell in this volume, namely how Western society and culture has conceived of, thought with, and reacted to the possibility of transformative change across the centuries, we therefore have to reach back in time beyond the Latin classics. Ancient Greek literature constitutes an important, initial chapter in our account, especially since already in our earliest surviving texts tales of metamorphosis coexisted, indeed coincided, with modes of commentary and reflection that subjected the phenomenon to various forms of epistemic pressure, ranging from implicit censorship to attempts at explanation to outright disapproval and dismissal. Just like the texts and authors it turned into objects of critique, this critical tradition, too, has made history in Western thought, with Christian and

Enlightenment critics of myth and marvellous metamorphosis frequently resorting to arguments first formulated by such fourth-century BC figures as Palaephatus or Euhemerus, who engaged in a rationalist vetting of the mythic heritage, in an effort to realign anything monstrous, marvellous, and metamorphic according to quotidian protocols of plausibility.

In our first historical survey, then, we begin with a detailed, if necessarily selective, look at the place and function of metamorphosis in ancient Greek literature and culture, before moving on, in somewhat more cursory fashion, to Rome, and in particular Ovid; we conclude with a brief introduction to the chapters that make up Part I.

I. Metamorphosis in Greek Culture

For a considerable period, two approaches dominated modern scholarly discussion of Greek myths of metamorphosis.[5] One involved speculation about the deeper impulses behind the pre-historical origins of such tales; the other aimed for a synoptic vision of the phenomenon by extracting tales of metamorphosis from the surviving corpus of Greek literature and ordering the data according to thematic criteria. These approaches often occurred in combination, with typologies fuelling attempts to excavate the 'deep causes' of metamorphic myth-making and vice-versa. Thus Jacob Burckhardt (1818–1897), in his *Griechische Kulturgeschichte*, discusses metamorphosis as a primitive aspect of ancient Greek religion and suggests a range of factors that may have induced the Greeks to make up tales of miraculous transformations, such as an animistic notion of nature, belief in magic or metempsychosis, the anthropomorphic appearance of landscape features, or humanoid animal behaviour.[6] In the course of his treatment, oblique typologies emerge of various kinds of transformation (e.g. temporary or permanent, of gods or of humans), of the diverse destinations of human beings subjected to divinely ordained metamorphosis, and of the motivation that was thought to inform the transformative actions undertaken by the gods, such as revenge, pity, protection, or reward.[7] Burckhardt distinguishes sharply between, while underscoring the conceptual and thematic affinity of, the temporary transformations of divine beings and '*die* Metamorphose', which he defines as the 'definitive und totale Wesensverwandlungen von nichtgöttlichen Wesen' ('the definitive and complete transformation of non-divine creatures'). It is also noteworthy that his embrace of the sources for the phenomenon is more expansive than the canonical selectivity (or myopia) of many a contemporary classicist who tend to adopt a more strictly literary focus: he brings into play evidence from natural historians (in particular Aelian's *On Animals* and Plutarch's *On Rivers*), the paradoxographic tradition, fable and folktale, and belief in witchcraft.

Since Burckhardt, other theories about the genesis of tales of transformation have come (and also gone), most prominently, perhaps, the suggestion that their context of origin is ritual, in particular various forms of animal cult.[8] But scholarly efforts to identify, however speculatively, the primordial impulses behind myths of metamorphosis have lessened in the wake of the realization that the origin of a religious practice or a figure of thought does not determine, let alone explain, its meaning and significance in later settings.[9] To be sure, typologically oriented surveys of the available data continue to be both illuminating and expedient — notably Forbes Irving's comprehensive and systematic classification of the kinds of being into which humans are transformed in Greek myth: he covers animals (birds and mammals, as well as the 'minor categories' of insects, reptiles, and sea creatures), plants, stones, landscape formations (springs, rivers, islands) and throws in, for good measure, the related phenomena of sex change and shape shifting.[10] Yet increasing numbers of scholars (including Forbes Irving and, most recently, Buxton) have started to emphasize the importance of literary and cultural context in evaluating Greek thinking with and about transformative change. The understanding of the meaning and function of metamorphosis as an element or motif in a textual universe as well as the appraisal of its epistemic status both in the literary world within which it occurs and for extra-textual (and ever-changing) audiences require close attention to detail and circumstances.

The aim for greater historical specificity is part of our brief as well, but we would like to start with some general considerations, designed to facilitate cross-cultural comparison. If one takes a diachronic view of Greek literary history and enquires where and when myths of metamorphosis rose to prominence, some of the findings appear *prima facie* paradoxical. First, even though the notion that humans may undergo transformation into another form of being has frequently been associated with a primitive mentality — the product, in other words, of an early stage of cultural development in which humanity was still beholden to indistinct ontological categories and an animistic conception of nature — references to metamorphoses of human beings into flora, fauna, or objects are relatively scarce in Homeric epic, our earliest texts;[11] yet the theme evidently went 'viral' centuries later in the sophisticated and erudite literature of the Hellenistic age (conventionally dated 323–31 BC).[12] The second point concerns the equivocal standing of the theme in the Greek literary imagination. The overwhelming majority of myths of transformation that have come down to us from classical antiquity are Greek or Near-Eastern in origin (even though they may have been preserved for us by Latin authors such as Ovid or Hyginus); Rome added only a smattering of tales to the corpus it inherited from Greece. When Antoninus Liberalis, writing more than a century after Ovid, produced a prose compilation of forty-one metamorphosis tales, he did so relying exclusively on Greek poetic sources.[13] It is nonetheless true that no *major surviving* work of Greek literature makes metamorphosis its focal theme, along the lines of Ovid's *Metamorphoses*. Most poets and many prose authors narrate, refer to, and comment on mythic tales of transformative change in one way or another (even if only by way of allusive gestures or dismissive comments); but no writer of the first rank whose work is still extant deemed it sufficiently arresting to give it centre-stage prominence in his literary world.[14] As a result, the resort to the motif in ancient Greek literature as a whole appears at the same time ubiquitous and marginal.

The diffuse and secondary status of metamorphosis in the literary imagination of the ancient Greek world — as well as the uneven popularity of the theme in our corpus, with significant variations across authors, genres, and periods — would seem to indicate that it belonged to a stock of more-or-less *optional* ideas that authors could activate at their discretion, to whatever degree and in whichever way they liked. As such, the cultural standing of transformative change in ancient Greece differed sharply from the cardinal importance of 'metamorphic dogma' in Christian theology, where the theme is anything but gratuitous: belief in the reality of such metamorphic moments and phenomena as the incarnation, the transfiguration of Christ on Mount Tabor, and his resurrection from the dead and eventual apotheosis, as well as the transubstantiation of bread and wine into his body and blood during the celebration of the Eucharist, constitute essential aspects of the Christian faith and its economy of salvation.[15] This difference in outlook should not surprise: theological dogma played little, if any role, in ancient Greek — or, for that matter, Roman — religion. Neither culture developed a key set of compulsory religious truths codified in sacred scripture that laid down principles of divine, and divinely grounded, ontology that communities of believers and their spiritual leaders or, later, a church establishment aligned with secular powers, enforced as binding. As a result, the interface between the literary imagination and conceptions of the supernatural in society at large was much more pliant and opaque in the classical (or 'pagan') civilizations of ancient Greece and Rome than in cultures that derive their dominant understanding of reality from a theological regime of truth.[16]

Overall, then, we can very schematically position the status of metamorphosis in the Greek cultural imaginary as being located this side of the primitive and that side of the dogmatic. Put differently, from the very beginnings of our literary record, the thematic treatment of transformative change constitutes a strategic choice on the part of the author — rather than a thoughtless reflex or accidental remnant of pre-historical superstition, or an obligatory endorsement of a religious script. At the same time, the majority of texts that allude to or narrate tales of metamorphosis present this material as part of history — as a record of what once actually happened, of 'wie', to speak with Ranke, 'es eigentlich gewesen ist'. This point, however counterintuitive it may seem, is of vital importance. It is the assertion of the (supernatural) phenomenon of transformative change as historical and real in literary texts in the absence of contextual support in the form of theological dogma and religious institutions that underwrites the (precarious) ontological status of divinely induced transformative change in the cultural record of ancient Greece.

Many authors who do recount tales of transformation are fully aware of their doubtful plausibility; and the absence of strict religious policing of intellect and imagination enabled powerful discourses of critique to emerge. These discourses could frequently build on the implicit restraint or self-censorship at work in the literary texts they set out to attack or reinterpret, in the effort to eliminate monstrous, marvellous, or metamorphic elements deemed to be in violation of whatever standards of aesthetic decorum, religious ethics, or empirical evidence were held to be normative or true. The result was a constant interplay between strategic rhetorics of authentication adopted by authors (often tongue-in-cheek) and attending techniques of critical deconstruction, all in the context of an evolved and evolving tradition that acquired its own momentum of truth and served as complex matrix and horizon for further intellectual and imaginary efforts. In the remainder of this section, we want to give this skeleton of general considerations some meat by looking at the presence of transformative change in various Greek texts. This survey will proceed neither according to strict chronology nor by generic categories, but will group the works under scrutiny according to their strategies of engagement with the idea of metamorphosis. This will be followed by an account of efforts to rationalize myths of transformation. Finally, the section will conclude with a brief discussion of countervailing tendencies that re-affirmed marvels and miracles as modes of thought and objects of literature in a post-Palaephatian and post-Aristotelian world.

Homeric Epic and Attic Tragedy

We have already alluded to the curious fact that the earliest western literature, Homeric epic, takes a more guarded approach to metamorphosis than many subsequent texts. While certainly having recourse to the phenomenon of transformative change, both the *Iliad* and the *Odyssey* tend to confine it to the narrative margins.[17] If, as was suggested above, the inclusion of transformative change was from the outset a strategic choice in Greek literature, then the Homeric strategy is predominantly one of containment. It is true, of course, that the *Iliad* and *Odyssey* repeatedly feature marvellous transformations of Olympian divinities, who appear to human beings in various shapes, sizes, and disguises. Indeed, the most common form of divine intervention in both the *Iliad* and the *Odyssey* is exhortation of a character by a god assuming the form of a person who might be expected to be present anyway.[18] That the gods circulate among humans in mortal guise is common knowledge among the Homeric characters themselves. So, for example, one of Penelope's suitors warns Antinous not to abuse a beggar (who is in fact Odysseus, as discussed below) lest he be a god in disguise, making trial of human goodness, as deities often do (*Od.* XVII. 483–87). Such allophanic subterfuge can also be found, albeit more rarely, on the divine level — as with the remarkable transmogrification of Hypnos (the personified deity Sleep), who assumes the form of a bird perched on a tree on Mt Ida (*Il.* XIV. 289–91) in order to come upon the post-coital Zeus unawares.[19] As a rule, though, the Homeric narrator treats these effects with a kind of matter-of-fact minimalism, never describing the process of transformation as such, and often maintaining a studied ambiguity about exactly what it is that the internal audiences perceive.[20] In addition to divine allophanies, supernatural intervention at times also changes the human form: thus Athena renders Odysseus unrecognizable by ageing him (in appearance: his physical vigour is unaffected) before his re-entry into Ithacan society in the guise of a beggar (*Od.* XIII. 429–33). More radical are the tales of marvellous transformations reported by two heroes in the *Odyssey* upon their return from far off places: in Book IV, Menelaus relates his Pharian encounter with the shape-shifting sea-god Proteus, who, while being assailed, assumed the shape of a lion, snake, panther, boar, running water, and a tall tree (*Od.* IV. 454–59); and one of the adventures recounted by Odysseus to the Phaeacians in Book X is his stay on the island of Circe, who, notoriously, turned his companions into pigs.[21] In a corpus that manifests a broad aversion to elaboration or reflection upon the actual process of metamorphosis, this last passage is noteworthy for the attention it pays to both Circe's transformative procedure and her victims' experience of it (*Od.* x. 233–43):

εἶσεν δ' εἰσαγαγοῦσα κατὰ κλισμούς τε θρόνους τε,
ἐν δέ σφιν τυρόν τε καὶ ἄλφιτα καὶ μέλι χλωρὸν
οἴνῳ Πραμνείῳ ἐκύκα· ἀνέμισγε δὲ σίτῳ
φάρμακα λύγρ', ἵνα πάγχυ λαθοίατο πατρίδος αἴης.
αὐτὰρ ἐπεὶ δῶκέν τε καὶ ἔκπιον, αὐτίκ' ἔπειτα
ῥάβδῳ πεπληγυῖα κατὰ συφεοῖσιν ἐέργνυ.
οἱ δὲ συῶν μὲν ἔχον κεφαλὰς φωνήν τε τρίχας τε
καὶ δέμας, αὐτὰρ νοῦς ἦν ἔμπεδος ὡς τὸ πάρος περ.
ὣς οἱ μὲν κλαίοντες ἐέρχατο· τοῖσι δὲ Κίρκη
πὰρ ἄκυλον βάλανόν τ' ἔβαλεν καρπόν τε κρανείης
ἔδμεναι, οἷα σύες χαμαιευνάδες αἰὲν ἔδουσιν.

> [She led them in and had them sit on chairs and seats, and gave them cheese and barley meal and yellow honey with Pramnian wine; but in the food she mixed baneful drugs, that they might completely forget their fatherland. After she had given them the potion, and they had drunk it, she struck them with her wand, and penned them in the sties. And they had the heads, and voice, and bristles, and the form of pigs, but their minds remained unchanged. So they were penned there weeping, and before them Circe flung mast and acorns, and the fruit of the cornel tree, to eat, such things as wallowing pigs are accustomed to feed on.]

Circe's transformation evidently differs from those enacted by the major gods in that it is not the instantaneous consequence of divine will, but rather involves a compound procedure utilizing both baneful drugs (φάρμακα) and a magic wand (ῥάβδος).[22] That is to say, administering the drugs does not in itself suffice to enact the transformation; Circe must subsequently touch Odysseus' companions with her wand for the metamorphosis to be realized.[23] Another noteworthy feature of the episode is its insistence on the uninterrupted consciousness of the transformed figures: metamorphosis is here conceived as an affliction suffered by an unaltered, persisting mind (νοῦς). The incorporeality of mind is thus affirmed by the fantasy of its exile — in this instance temporary — in an alien body.[24] This celebrated episode, with its intriguing perspectives on the metamorphic, would be revisited by subsequent writers — including the epicists Apollonius Rhodius and Ovid.[25]

Whatever the vividness and detail of the Proteus and Circe passages, it is not coincidental that the transformations they contain are both reported as secondary narration (i.e. by internal narrators rather than in the *vox poetae*), and that they take place on the conceptual and even geographic margins of the *Odyssey*. They are extreme and fantastical events within the Homeric universe, and are marked as such.[26]

References to other instances of supernatural transformation, especially that involving terminal metamorphosis, are rather rare in both Homeric epics.[27] The possibility of immortalization is broached in Book v of the *Odyssey*. There Calypso mentions her disappointed wish to make Odysseus her eternal consort, contingent upon his willingness to abide with her forever on her exotic but far-flung island. This metamorphic proposition remains unrealized only because it finds favour neither with the epic's eponymous hero nor its more powerful gods (*Od.* v. 135–37).

The episodes of Circe and Calypso, then, respectively raise the possibility of 'downwards' and 'upwards' human metamorphoses. As these episodes are generally viewed as closer to folktale tradition than epic proper, it is worth noting that Calypso's divinizing aspirations are not altogether anomalous in the *Odyssey*, which generally depicts a rather permeable boundary between the categories of mortal and immortal. An important case in point is the report in Book v of the *Odyssey* of the apotheosis of Ino (*Od.* v. 333–35):

> τὸν δὲ ἴδεν Κάδμου θυγάτηρ, καλλίσφυρος Ἰνώ,
> Λευκοθέη, ἣ πρὶν μὲν ἔην βροτὸς αὐδήεσσα,
> νῦν δ' ἁλὸς ἐν πελάγεσσι θεῶν ἐξέμμορε τιμῆς.

> [Him [*sc.* Odysseus] the daughter of Cadmus, fair-ankled Ino, saw, [she who is now known as] Leucothea, who once was mortal of human speech, but now in the sea has won a share of honour from the gods.]

Here, unusually, a metamorphosis is reported on the primary narrative level as an unambiguous statement of fact. As often with this type of transformation, there is a corresponding change in nomenclature, in this case expository: Ino's new name, Leucothea, means 'white goddess'. The passage is one of a number in the *Odyssey* that indicate a less rigidly maintained divide between gods and humans than is found in the *Iliad*. Indeed, it must be granted that, in this respect at least, the theology of the *Odyssey* differs fundamentally from that of the *Iliad*.[28] In addition to the passages just mentioned, Proteus informs Menelaus that he is not destined to die and descend into the Underworld, but will be transported to the Elysian plain to enjoy immortality in the company of other god-favoured heroes (*Od.* IV. 561–65); and whereas Hercules is said not to have escaped death at *Il.* XVIII. 117–18, he is said to feast eternally in the company of the Olympian gods at *Od.* XI. 601–04; even the Dioscuri are said to be dead and buried at *Il.* III. 243–44, whereas their joint share in immortality is mentioned at *Od.* XI. 301–04.[29]

If one sets aside transformations having to do with disguise, the special cases of Proteus and Circe, and the various references to immortalization, only a small number of metamorphoses remain.[30] The most important of these belong to the literary category of aetiological fable, which would remain crucial for many subsequent poetic treatments of metamorphosis. The Homeric narrator keeps such fables at arm's length: they are invariably presented as embedded references, always carefully detached from and alien to the primary narrative; they are, moreover, consigned to a distant past relative to the narrative present and are treated as fables by the characters themselves; and finally, they are invoked in the service of rhetorical ends, so that their 'veracity' as such is not at issue, and does not register as a problem within the world. The last point in particular also underscores that when tales of transformation do appear they are certainly not thoughtless reflexes or accidental remnants of primitive religious thought, but present a strategic choice on the part of the author. Three such cases will illustrate the argument: the metamorphosis tales of Niobe (*Il.* XXIV. 603–17) and Aedon (*Od.* XIX. 512–29), along with a fleeting reference to anthropogenesis (*Od.* XIX. 162–63). All three differ from the passages discussed thus far, in that they feature references to terminal transformations in an aetiological framework.

The legend of Niobe is aired in the culminating scene of the *Iliad*, in which the Trojan king Priam visits Achilles in order to ransom the body of his son Hector. In the context of convincing the Trojan king, despite his paternal grief, to share a meal with him, Achilles cites as an *exemplum* the remarkable demise of Niobe. Her tale thus serves as advice on coping with extremes of grief, a topic of equal relevance to speaker and addressee.[31] In Achilles' account, Niobe's twelve children, slain by Apollo and Artemis because of their mother's hubristic arrogance, remained unburied for nine days, as Zeus had turned the people into stone. (This is a curious detail, not found in subsequent versions independent of Homer and widely believed to be an adaptation to correspond to Priam's circumstances).[32] On the tenth day the gods saw to the burial, whereupon Niobe, spent from weeping, finally took some nourishment. She subsequently resumed her grieving upon Mt Sipylus, eventually undergoing petrifaction (*Il.* xxiv. 603–17). Achilles explicitly returns to the present order of things (νῦν, 614) in his summation: Niobe stills broods over her god-sent troubles, though now as a stone (ἔνθα, λίθος περ ἐοῦσα, θεῶν ἐκ κήδεα πέσσει, 617).[33] Remarkably, the metamorphosis as such, along with the agency behind it, has been elided — remarkably, that is, until we recall that Achilles' rhetorical purpose (and the Homeric narrator's strategic preference) leads him to focus not on the two marvellous transformations, but rather on the mundane interlude between them, Niobe's act of eating, along with the continuity of her grief. Still, inasmuch as it provides a myth of origins for a natural landmark in the speaker's own day, this sequence engages, uncharacteristically for Homeric epic, in the propagation of metamorphosis tales as aetiological lore. The mythographic digression underscores the anomalous status of Achilles, putting on display his ability to evoke places and conceptual domains remote from the battlefield realities that dominate the Homeric narrative.[34]

Whatever its subtleties, Achilles' rhetorical use of metamorphosis tales is simple and forthright in comparison with the resort to such lore by Penelope and her as yet disguised husband Odysseus in Book xix of the *Odyssey*. A particularly pregnant exchange occurs when Penelope seeks to learn the identity of her seemingly humble guest. 'Tell me', she says, 'your lineage and where you are from' — an entirely benign request up to this point, but then she adds 'for you cannot be born of the oak of ancient story or of a rock' (οὐ γὰρ ἀπὸ δρυός ἐσσι παλαιφάτου οὐδ' ἀπὸ πέτρης, *Od.* xix. 163). The remark, which may be proverbial, refers to myths of anthropogenesis from oak trees and rocks. These tales, already ancient to Penelope, are invoked negatively and with an air of detached scepticism.[35] There is a calculated effect to all of this, inasmuch as Penelope, who is beginning to suspect that her interlocutor is not who he appears to be, alludes to an implausible tale of origins to convey the message: 'don't lie to me, I see through you'.

In response to Penelope's request, Odysseus identifies himself as a certain Aethon, the illegitimate son of the Cretan prince Deucalion, son of King Minos of Crete. This false identity constitutes a sly rejoinder: for Odysseus' putative father is the homonym of a considerably more famous mythological personage, Deucalion the husband of Pyrrha. This better known figure had, after the great deluge, famously regenerated the human race from stones. On the level of mythographic allusion, then, Odysseus archly signals a birth from stones, as he defies Penelope's injunction about falsified origins. The passage thus constitutes a superb exploration of the implicit manipulation of truth and plausibility in the context of fantastical myths of anthropogenesis. Both characters subtly exploit incredible tales of metamorphosis in a discursive setting shaped by issues of truth, lies, and false appearances, in the attempt to conceal/obliquely reveal the truth (in the case of Odysseus) or to get to the bottom of it (Penelope). The success of their allusive rhetorical strategies depends upon a sceptical view of the anthropogonic tales they invoke.

A more one-sided discourse between the same two figures occurs somewhat later in Book XIX, when Penelope invokes the story of the nightingale in a simile in order to elucidate her own state of mind (*Od.* XIX. 512–29). Finding herself in increasingly desperate circumstances, Penelope's mind twists and turns indecisively: should she continue to wait for Odysseus or choose a new husband from among her many suitors? Animal similes are of course a familiar element of Homeric epic, which has a penchant for illustrating aspects of human experience via images from nature.[36] But this instance is unusual in that the nightingale, said to have arisen from metamorphosis, has a human prehistory that is elaborated within the frame of the simile. Penelope speaks vaguely of the daughter of Pandareus: according to the scholiasts on the passage this figure was known to Homer as Aedon, wife of Zethus; later versions would identify her as Procne, wife of Tereus.[37] Aedon is said to have slain her son Itylus δι' ἀφραδίας (523), which could mean 'inadvertently' or, perhaps more plausibly, 'through her folly'.[38] Later accounts make this an act of revenge by Procne against her husband. The Homeric scholiasts, by contrast, describe how Aedon, in a fit of jealousy, attempted to kill one of the many sons of her sister-in-law Niobe, but accidentally killed Itylus instead. Thereupon, overwhelmed with grief, Aedon prayed to Zeus to be changed into a bird. Her wish was granted: she was transformed into a nightingale, in which form she has continued to lament her son.

Critical discussion of this passage is bedevilled by a number of uncertainties, none of which can be addressed here. The precise analogy between Penelope and Aedon remains elusive. It seems nonetheless clear that Penelope's purpose is vividly to convey to her disguised husband the peril to which their son Telemachus now stands exposed, a peril to which her own (in)action will contribute decisively. Her choice of imagery thus seems to constitute an implicit warning to Odysseus that *he* must act in order to forestall a disastrous re-enactment of the myth that will destroy their household.

These last three passages, then, show Homeric characters acting as astute proto-mythographers, deftly invoking, as part of a larger rhetorical strategy, paradigmatic tales of transformation attributed to a distant past. In all, then, Homeric epic maintains a studied ambivalence vis-à-vis the miraculous tales of metamorphosis it includes, distinguishing them from the generally less fantastical (albeit often supernaturally driven) episodes featuring the great heroes of the Trojan War. The instances of transformative change caused by divine intervention or magic narrated by Homer himself or by one of his characters, the rhetorical use of Niobe and Aedon by Achilles and Penelope, and the evidence from the Hesiodic tradition indicates that tales involving miraculous metamorphoses were in principle available to Homer and commanded some degree of plausibility within his literary world and, presumably, his audience as well. At the same time, the authorial distancing, the geographical distribution and the rarity of their occurrence evince an implicit censorship that restricts this material to the narrative margins. Their peripheral status in the *Iliad* and the *Odyssey* points to a deliberate decision on the part of the poet (or the Homeric tradition). Random and indiscriminate metamorphosis, of the sort we find in, say, the Hesiodic *Catalogue of Women*, clearly did not fit into the conception of reality, or the understanding of the human condition, that the epics wished to broadcast. The tales of metamorphosis found in Homeric epic have nothing to do with the quintessentially Hesiodic theme of love affairs between gods and mortal women.

ii

The treatment of metamorphosis in Athenian tragedy has something in common with Homeric epic — perhaps unsurprisingly given that Aeschylus, the earliest of its three greatest exponents, is reported to have characterized his dramas as nothing more than 'slices from the great banquets of Homer' (Athenaeus, *Deipnosophistae*, VIII. 347). In the surviving material of the three great tragedians, Forbes Irving counts six transformation stories recounted or alluded to by Aeschylus, five by Sophocles, and eleven by Euripides.[39] This might *prima facie* suggest a more pronounced presence in the universe of tragedy than in Homeric epic; upon closer inspection, however, it emerges that this genre too hedged the phenomenon with artistic, conceptual, and even formal strictures.

To begin with, no transformation ever occurs on stage.[40] This prohibition is not merely attributable to the attendant technical challenges. Attic tragedy held itself aloof from exciting interest through artifices of stagecraft (what we might term 'special effects'). Strictures against the direct depiction of the grotesque or implausible remained in effect through the Roman period. So in the first century BC, Horace could still declare that 'It is not before the audience that [...] Procne should be transformed into a bird or Cadmus into a snake' (*ne [...] coram populo [...] in avem Procne vertatur, [aut] Cadmus in anguem*).[41]

The most common expedient was to have the metamorphosis reported in a messenger's speech. Even the appearance of a human character in a transformed state is comparatively rare — a notable exception being Io in the *Prometheus Bound*. The text of this tragedy, which is uncertainly attributed to Aeschylus, leaves it unclear how the challenge of representation was met, but it probably involved a modest concession to Io's transmogrification. The evidence of vase paintings suggests that the actor playing Io donned a cow-mask featuring horns, but otherwise did not try to disguise his (all actors were male) human shape; the same device appears to have been used in later periods for plays featuring Actaeon (Pollux 4.141).[42] Io's misery in the *Prometheus Bound* is compounded by the relentless irritation of a gadfly sent by her divine persecutor Hera; this unabated torment pushes her to the brink of insanity. Yet in the tragedy — very much in contrast to Ovid's later treatment — Io retains her capacity for human speech. In this case, the metamorphosis happened before the time of the play; in other cases, it is announced as a future event beyond the chronological frame of the play. Such anticipations of the terminal transformations of key characters include the change of Cadmus and Harmonia into snakes in Euripides' *Bacchae* (prophesied at the close by the god Dionysus) and the transmogrification of Hecuba into a bitch in his *Hecuba* (foretold by her tormentor and blinded assault victim Polymestor).[43] As already noted, the usual expedient for a transformation contemporary with the action of the play was to have it reported by one of the characters. This, for example, appears to have been the solution adopted by Sophocles in his renowned and influential *Tereus*, now unfortunately lost.[44] The triple metamorphosis of Tereus, Procne and Philomela into different species of birds, as the Thracian king pursued wife and sister-in-law with murderous intent, was the culminating moment of the developed myth.[45] In the Sophoclean drama this was almost certainly reported in a messenger speech, followed by a display of at least Tereus at the conclusion of the tragedy, with an indicative change of costume to signal the metamorphosis.[46]

In addition to aesthetic and pragmatic considerations having to do with principles of decorum and stagecraft, tragedy also contained moments of rational critique, glossing traditional instances of mythic lore as frankly unbelievable.[47] Overall, then, the evidence from tragedy is complex. Generally speaking, tragedy, to quote Buxton, 'affirms a strong sense of the *ultimate* boundedness, integrity, and centrality of the human form' — though he also concedes that the genre '*could* make room for mortals permanently to abandon their human form, either as a consequence of extreme transgressions of the norms of human behaviour, or in a state of unbearable suffering'. He thereby follows Forbes Irving, who links the theme of transformation to such tragic preoccupations as 'the grotesque and the primitive as an expression of extremes of emotional or social disorder'.[48] Metamorphosis in tragedy thus links up with wider concerns in the genre's ideology as defined by Eagleton and others: 'Tragedy breaks down the barriers between gods, humans and beasts; and the *pharmakos*, a human being thrust down to the depths of animal destitution yet thereby curiously sacred, combines something of all three species.'[49]

The figure that best captures these concerns is again Procne, whose paradoxical terms of existence predestined her for a stellar career on the tragic stage: she is a singer and musician as well as an infanticide. In the figure of the nightingale we thus capture the coincidence of lyric beauty and loathsome brutality, of the sublimation of gruesome outrage into moving art. It is therefore not surprising to find that the tragic playwrights follow Homer's Penelope in resorting to the figure of Procne in programmatic fashion. References to her in the lyric parts of all major playwrights, from Aeschylus to Euripides, from Sophocles to the author of the *Rhesus*, are so frequent that one could almost call this myth and its aftermath a primal scene of tragic horror.[50] In encapsulating the genre, it furnishes both an archetype and a foil for other tragic plots. The motivation behind the eventual transformation of the protagonists into birds — a mixture of divine pity and punishment — constitutes a further facet of the paradigm of tragic suffering since it resolves little: the metamorphosis does not end their mutual hatred (Sophocles, fr. 581.9–10 Radt); and in avian form, Procne begins her eternal lament over Itys. Every nightingale reflects Procne's history: though a part of nature, it renews each spring her lament for her son. In this way, Procne becomes the founder of a genre, namely lyric poetry, specifically lyric as a song of lament.[51]

Hesiod and the Alexandrians

The poetic tradition in which tales of transformation seem to have developed the greatest traction has come down to us under the name of Hesiod. The two main Hesiodic works, the *Theogony* and the *Works and Days*, include various episodes of metamorphosis — at least in the more capacious senses of that designation. The *Theogony* describes the emergence of the cosmos from an initial state in which there is only Chaos. First Gaia (Earth), Tartarus (the underworld) and Eros come into being, and thereafter successive generations of divinities; this amounts to 'an irreversible theogonic sequence of metamorphosis in nature.'[52] The *Theogony* established Hesiod as the first in a tradition of writers of theological cosmogonies, referred to by Aristotle as θεολόγοι (see e.g. *Metaphysics*, 1000^a 9–10). The *Works and Days* is a didactic work on agriculture that makes frequent reflections on the human condition. It explains the presence of evil in the world as the consequence of a quarrel between Zeus and the Titan Prometheus, who champions the cause of the human race. Zeus' retribution entails creation of the first woman, Pandora, as an ineluctable bane for mankind (*Works and Days*, 80–82). The poem also enumerates successive races of human beings that come into existence and then perish, in a declining sequence of mostly metallic ages — Golden, Silver, Bronze, Heroic, Iron — emblematic of a progressive moral decay. Hesiod is concerned not only with the boundary between mortal and divine, but also that between human and animal, which may be breached by immoral conduct.

Because of their predominantly cosmogonic focus and generalizing approaches, the two main Hesiodic works are virtually devoid of metamorphosis in the narrowest sense of individual human beings transformed into flora, fauna, or inanimate objects. This changes in the other major composition ascribed to Hesiod, the *Catalogue of Women*, in which individual humans belonging to the Heroic Age figure prominently. The *Catalogue*, substantial fragments of which are extant, may have constituted a poetic accretion or perhaps a fusion of distinct compositions. Both its origins and date are much disputed: most scholars would place the most complete (i.e. composite, if such it be) version in the sixth century BC.[53]

Much like the *Theogony* with respect to divine origins, the *Catalogue* represents a systematization of a group of stories about heroic genealogies. It was responsible for spawning an alternate tradition to that of Homeric epos.[54] The organizing principle for this collective poem was the genealogy of Greek heroes, and more specifically their begetting through sexual encounters — mostly rapes — involving male gods and mortal women.[55] It was an ambitious poem in both conception and scale (Hellenistic scholars divided it into five books), with a marked aetiological bent; it used the offspring of gods and mortal women as 'the organising principle' to draw up 'a map of the Hellenic world in genealogical terms'.[56] The opening sets the tone by evoking an earlier age of blessedness in which human beings and gods commingled freely at feasts and the best of the mortal women 'loosened their girdles' for various gods under the influence of Aphrodite. These women subsequently gave birth to magnificent children, a race of heroes.[57] In the wider context of cosmogonic poetry, the *Catalogue* fits in chronologically between the *Theogony* and the *Works and Days*: it describes a post-theogonic period of intercourse between mortals and immortals (that, however, came to a close before the poet's own age as described in the *Works and Days*), focusing on marriage and (supernatural) sex, rape and reproduction, and the consequent patterns of mythic lineages from divine origins.[58]

Metamorphosis is not the primary concern of the *Catalogue*, but even in its fragmentary state it is possible to discern that the motif had a significant presence.[59] The work included various tales of mythic characters transformed into animals, such as Alcyone (turned into a kingfisher), Atalanta (a lioness), or Io (a cow).[60] Metamorphosis generally results from divine anger over inappropriate behaviour; but there are also instances of divine munificence, as with, for example, the transformation of ants into Myrmidons.[61] The *Catalogue* further tells of the protean capacities of Neleus' son Periclymenus (who turned himself into such diverse animals as eagle, ant, snake, or bee, in which form he was finally swatted to death by Hercules) and of Erysichthon's shape-shifting daughter Mestra, whom her father, as a means of satisfying a ravenous hunger punitively imposed by Demeter, repeatedly sold as a slave; she would thereupon escape from her new master by assuming animal form and return to her father.[62] The story of Zeus abducting Europa in the shape of a white bull appears, as does the transformation of Caenis into a man (Caeneus) — in fulfilment of the one wish Poseidon granted her in a moment of post-coital generosity.[63]

The presentation of this material is entirely matter of fact: the poem simply records these events as having occurred in the mythic past, with no indication that metamorphosis is in any way a problematic notion — with the important proviso that the *Catalogue* explicitly locates the events it narrates in an era of history that has come to an end.[64] Such marvellous transformations belong to the Hesiodic conception of the heroic age just as much as the easy-going familiarity between mortals and immortals. These are essential aspects of a vanished world, one that has genealogical connections with the present but operated on different ontological principles. Later authors would extend this factual approach to the implausible lore of metamorphoses to mythic transformations that were thought to have occurred *after* the end of the heroic age.

ii

In Book IV of his epic *Argonautica*, Apollonius Rhodius offers an updated and decidedly un-Homeric treatment of one of Homer's metamorphic figures, Circe, whom Medea and Jason visit en route from Colchis to Thessaly. The Apollonian passage manifests an interest in exploring the process of transformative change itself that is characteristic of the Hellenistic Age.[65] Descriptive attention lingers on the victims of Circe's metamorphic magic: these are not merely transformed humans: they are bizarre hybrids, resembling neither human being nor animal (IV. 672–73). Their bodies are composite (674–81), 'like those beings that the earth herself made to grow from the primal mud, composed of varied limbs' (μικτοῖσιν ἀρηρεμένους μελέεσσιν, 677). As Charles Segal observes, the engrafting of cosmogonic elements upon the fabulous elements of the Circe myth 'enhances the *grotesquerie* and divorces the scene even further from the factuality and clarity of the Homeric narrative.'[66]

Apollonius was an epicist whose allegiance to the Homeric tradition is signalled on numerous levels, perhaps most elaborately by the fashioning of the Argonauts' return voyage as a 'rewrite' of Odysseus' journey — whence, of course, the stopover on Circe's island.[67] But here as elsewhere, the Hellenistic poet's probing of and fascination with the process of transformative change is decidedly un-Homeric. In this Apollonius is very much a child of his time. Indeed, metamorphosis came to be, in the words of E. J. Kenney, 'a specifically Alexandrian subject'.[68] This new enthusiasm for and interest in the phenomenon is seen above all in the production of a number of metamorphosis catalogue poems in the Hellenistic Age. This collective movement amounts to the earliest securely identifiable body of poetry dedicated to the theme of metamorphosis. Such literary production, which amounts to a recognizable poetic sub-genre, combines a characteristically Alexandrian taste for the bizarre with a no less characteristic 'penchant for the systematization of inherited cultural experience'.[69]

By comparison with earlier periods, the poetry of the Hellenistic age manifests a heightened interest in aetiological myth. Before the Alexandrian poets, as G. S. Kirk has observed, few Greek myths were explicitly aetiological.[70] Peter Bing has attributed this new predilection in mythography to two forces: a sense of epigonality and artistic disjunction among the poets of the age, and a new desire by Greeks in Alexandria to assert their own cultural identity in the midst of an old and alien civilization.[71] The emblematic figure for this new trend is Callimachus (fourth to third century BC), the most famous of the Alexandrian poets, whose *Aetia*, a collection of elegies in four books which has survived only in fragmentary form, traced out the mythic origins of various cults and rites. This aetiological mode, of course, has much to do with the prominence of metamorphosis tales. For its literary genealogy, Hellenistic catalogue poetry looked back to Hesiod, whose *Theogony* and *Catalogue of Women* amounted to systematizations of groups of stories involving common themes.

Regrettably, the numerous poems dedicated to transformative change from this period are now either completely lost, or are extant only in fragmentary form. Many works have no doubt disappeared without a trace; some few have survived as little more than names and titles — such as Theodorus and Didymarchus (both writers of Μεταμορφώσεις), and Antigonus (author of Ἀλλοιώσεις).[72] A considerable portion of the scant information available is provided by a much later mythographer, Antoninus Liberalis, perhaps datable to the second century AD. His Μεταμορφώσεων Συναγωγή (*Collection of Metamorphoses*) is a prose compilation of forty-one metamorphosis tales, written in Greek.[73] Beyond the tales themselves, what makes this compilation valuable are annotations recorded in the margins of the lone extant manuscript. Though the annotations are unlikely to be the author's own, they usually indicate his putative source for each tale, and occasionally offer more detailed information. An unusually rich marginal annotation, that for Antoninus' twenty-third transformation tale, on Battus, reads as follows:[74]

Ἱστορεῖ Νίκανδρος Ἑτεροιουμένων αʹ καὶ Ἡσίοδος ἐν Μεγάλαις Ἠοίαις καὶ Διδύμαρχος Μεταμορφώσεων γʹ καὶ Ἀντίγονος ἐν ταῖς Ἀλλοιώσεσι καὶ Ἀπολλώνιος ὁ Ῥόδιος ἐν ἐπιγράμμασιν, ὥς φησι Πάμφιλος ἐν αʹ

[The story is told by Nicander in *Heteroeumena* book 1 and Hesiod in the *Great Ehoiai*, and Didymarchus in *Metamorphoses* book 3, and Antigonus (i.e. of Carystus) in *Transformations*, and Apollonius Rhodius in his epigrams, as Pamphilus says in Book 1.]

There are complex levels of documentation at work here: an anonymous author (the annotator) quotes a lost author (Pamphilus) citing five texts that are either entirely lost or only preserved in meagre fragments. But the mere fact that it was possible to cite three works with the titles *Heteroeumena* (Nicander), *Metamorphoses* (Didymarchus), and *Alloioseis* (Antigonus) for this particular tale of transformation is a suggestive index of the popularity of the metamorphosis theme in the Hellenistic period.

Thanks in no small part to Antoninus Liberalis, we are relatively well informed about the work of two Alexandrian poets of transformation: Nicander and Boeus. It will be useful briefly to summarize what can be gleaned about their work, as each is an important representative of the sub-genre of metamorphosis catalogue poetry, whose influence would continue to be felt, among both Greek and Latin writers, well into the Roman period.

Nicander's *Heteroeumena* ('Changed Ones'), datable to the second century BC, is the earliest work dedicated to metamorphosis for which we have reliable attestations.[75] It is by far the most frequently mentioned source in Antoninus Liberalis, being cited fully twenty-two times. The title *Heteroeumena* is a participial form derived from the verb ἑτεροιόω ('make of a different kind, alter'), a synonym in this sense of the now more familiar forms deriving from the verb μεταμορφόω.[76] The *Heteroeumena* was a poem in four or five books, written in dactylic hexameters.[77] It narrated episodes of metamorphosis from disparate myths and legends, brought together in a single collection. The surviving fragments are scant, but, as already noted, precious testimony is preserved in Antoninus Liberalis.[78] An overarching concern of the *Heteroeumena* was evidently to link tales of metamorphosis to the origin of local landmarks, religious rites or other cultural practices: based on the evidence of Antoninus Liberalis, it can be conjectured that 'most of Nicander's stories were aetiological in focus and explained the origins of surviving cults and local cult practices, as well as a few geographical landmarks and features, very much like Callimachus' *Aetia*.'[79]

After Nicander, the next most frequently attested source in Antoninus Liberalis is the *Ornithogonia* (*Origins of Birds*) of Boeus, with ten citations. We know next to nothing about the author, who may predate Nicander: the dearth of secure evidence makes it impossible to say. The *Ornithogonia* was written in two books; as the title suggests, it exclusively featured myths of humans transformed into various species of bird. In his compendious *Deipnosophistai*, the sophist Athenaeus (late second century AD) cites Boeus for the assertion that all birds had once been human beings (καθόλου δὲ ὁ ποιήσας ταῦτα τὰ ἔπη πάντα τὰ ὄρνεα ἀνθρώπους ἱστορεῖ πρότερον γεγονέναι, IX. 393). This pattern of metamorphic reinscription within the natural order held particular significance in the ancient world. For Greeks and Romans alike, the bird was the augural animal par excellence. Birds provided signs to humans not only through complex actions, which required interpretation, but more frequently by the mere appearance of a particular species in a particular position in the sky (thought to betoken divine approval or disapproval of a proposed action). The myths collected by Boeus evidently explained the characteristic features and conduct of particular species from their metamorphic origins, as well as why certain birds were regarded as favourable or unfavourable omens.

The *Ornithogonia* is interesting not least because of its specialization within the 'field' of metamorphosis. There were abundant thematic criteria for such poetic collections — for example *Lithica* (i.e. poems about characters that were transformed into stone, such as Niobe). Other catalogue poems will have gathered metamorphoses from specific regions, or metamorphoses effected by specific deities.

At the close of the Hellenistic period, Greek metamorphosis poetry evidently found its way to Rome, along with its authors. So, for example, Parthenius, the Greek tutor to Virgil, who came to Rome in 65 BC, composed a *Metamorphoses* in elegiacs, about which we unfortunately know next to nothing. Some recent papyrological discoveries tend to confirm the overall picture.[80]

Aesop and Old Comedy

There are a few ancient literary forms in which metamorphosis belongs to a matrix of fantastic possibilities, available to the author in virtually any situation, within a narrative universe that is overtly contrafactual. Aesopic fable and Aristophanic comedy are two cases in point. On the surface, these works share with the Hesiodic corpus (and much of the tradition it spawned) the unproblematic assertion of metamorphoses as a conceptual possibility and a narrative fact, but they differ in various important respects. Hesiod perpetuated the notion that myths of transformation formed part of the historical record. In Aesopic fable and Aristophanic comedy, by contrast, historical claims — and indeed most protocols of empirical plausibility — are simply forsaken. The resort to metamorphosis tends to be situational: there is no consistently aetiological impulse behind it, no imperative to explain or account for features of the broader cosmos. Indeed, these literary forms opt for a wilfully far-fetched narrative approach; they are, in short, self-conscious genres of fantasy in which the rules and patterns of quotidian reality are suspended and fundamental principles of realism no longer operate. Their narrative universes embrace such physical impossibilities as cities built in the sky, and such zoological impossibilities as talking animals. It is, indeed, a characteristic tendency of these genres to blur the distinction between the categories of human and animal. As Asker observes, 'at the heart of the fable (metamorphic or other) lies impossible blendings' — the talking animal above all else.[81] One could make a similar observation about Aristophanic comedy.

And yet both Aesop and Aristophanes are concerned in no small part with illuminating and reflecting upon ethical issues and social forces in their contemporary (human) societies. Here we touch on a noteworthy aspect of marvellous transformations in both authors: metamorphosis proves to be a supple tool for exploring and reflecting upon the human condition. In the fable, of course, metamorphosis is part of a repertoire of fantastical elements that occur within a narrative framework formally endowed with a second, allegorical sense (usually spelled out in a concluding maxim) that aims at moral education; but in Aristophanes as well the theme of transformation is generally a dramatic device that serves the comic poet's broader concern with illuminating 'the social currents running beneath the surface of public and official discourse'.[82]

Aesop appears to have been a historical figure, plausibly dated to the early sixth century BC. Of his life little may be said with confidence, as the ancient *testimonia* offer conflicting biographical details. The best-known variant makes him a slave from Samos, but the balance of evidence suggests that he was Thracian in origin, and later became politically active in Samos.[83] Whatever his origins and other claims to fame, Aesop was already in antiquity regarded as the greatest writer in the literary genre of fable; a number of collections of fables (λόγοι) ascribed to him have come down to us. A citation in Aristophanes' *Birds* attests to the circulation of collections of fables ascribed to Aesop in fifth-century Greece. The passage in question provides a summary of a fable that is not preserved in the Aesopic corpus. The tale is recounted to the chorus by Peisetaerus, one of the principal human characters, in an overtly didactic fashion (Aristophanes, *Birds*, 471–75):

> Πε. ἀμαθὴς γὰρ ἔφυς κοὺ πολυπράγμων, οὐδ᾽ Αἴσωπον πεπάτηκας,
> ὃς ἔφασκε λέγων κορυδὸν πάντων πρώτην ὄρνιθα γενέσθαι,
> προτέραν τῆς γῆς, κἄπειτα νόσῳ τὸν πατέρ᾽ αὐτῆς ἀποθνήσκειν·
> γῆν δ᾽ οὐκ εἶναι, τὸν δὲ προκεῖσθαι πεμπταῖον· τὴν δ᾽ ἀποροῦσαν
> ὑπ᾽ ἀμηχανίας τὸν πατέρ᾽ αὐτῆς ἐν τῇ κεφαλῇ κατορύξαι.

[*Peisetaerus*: You are naturally ignorant and uninquisitive, and haven't thumbed through your Aesop. He says in his fable that the Lark was the first born of all the birds, before the Earth itself. When her father died of a disease, she dutifully laid him out for five days; but she could find no grave since the Earth was not yet in existence, and so she buried him in her head.]

It is a characteristically humorous touch to have a human chide the chorus of birds for not studying their Aesop diligently enough. Aristophanes thereby plays on the anthropomorphism, the impossible blending of human and animal that lies at the heart of the animal fable, while simultaneously subjecting the allegorical function of fable, an intrinsic part of the genre, to comic pressure. The animals of Aesopic fable are endowed with human characteristics, but the didactic citation of animal fables to animals amounts to an anthropomorphic excess that inverts the compositional premise of the corpus.

At any rate, this fable is one of several belonging to an archaic Aesopic tradition. Characterized by a cosmogonic backdrop and aetiological concerns, hardly any of them has been preserved in the standard collection, in which these thematic emphases are largely absent. But a number of fables in the standard collection feature inexplicable phenomena that belong to the realm of the metamorphic. One well-known example is the fable of the goose that lays golden eggs. The owner, overcome by curiosity as to how the miraculous transformation of eggs into precious metal is achieved, kills the goose and inspects its innards. He thereby foolishly forfeits a source of limitless wealth, while discovering nothing that might explain the miracle (Aesop, *Fables*, 87). Such marvels are standard fare; the disinclination of the Aesopic narrator to reflect upon them is also characteristic of the genre. An intriguing exception is a less well-known tale featuring the short-lived transformation of a cat into human form (Aesop, *Fables*, 50):

γαλῆ ἐρασθεῖσα νεανίσκου εὐπρεποῦς ηὔξατο τῇ Ἀφροδίτῃ, ὅπως αὐτὴν μεταμορφώσῃ εἰς γυναῖκα. καὶ ἡ θεὸς ἐλεήσασα αὐτῆς τὸ πάθος μετεποίησεν αὐτὴν εἰς κόρην εὐειδῆ. καὶ οὕτως ὁ νεανίσκος θεασάμενος αὐτὴν καὶ ἐρασθεὶς οἴκαδε ὡς ἑαυτὸν ἀπήγαγε. καθημένων δ’ αὐτῶν ἐν τῷ θαλάμῳ ἡ Ἀφροδίτη γνῶναι βουλομένη, εἰ μεταβαλοῦσα τὸ σῶμα ἡ γαλῆ καὶ τὸν τρόπον ἤλλαξε, μῦν εἰς τὸ μέσον καθῆκεν. ἡ δὲ ἐπιλαθομένη τῶν παρόντων ἐξαναστᾶσα ἀπὸ τῆς κοίτης τὸν μῦν ἐδίωκε καταφαγεῖν ἐθέλουσα. καὶ ἡ θεὸς ἀγανακτήσασα κατ’ αὐτῆς πάλιν αὐτὴν εἰς τὴν ἀρχαίαν φύσιν ἀποκατέστησεν. οὕτω καὶ τῶν ἀνθρώπων οἱ φύσει πονηροί, κἂν φύσιν ἀλλάξωσι, τὸν γοῦν τρόπον οὐ μεταβάλλονται.

[A cat fell in love with a handsome young man and prayed to Aphrodite to be transformed into a woman. The goddess took pity on her passion and changed her into a beautiful maiden. Thus the young man, upon seeing her, fell in love and brought her home. But when they were lying in their marriage chamber, Aphrodite wanted to know whether the cat, having been transformed with respect to her body, also altered her habits and let loose a mouse in the middle of the room. The cat forgot her present condition, jumped from the bed, and pursued the mouse, in the desire to devour it. Irritated, the goddess restored her to her old form. Likewise, those human beings who are wicked by nature, even if they change their appearance, do not change their habits.]

The divinely sponsored metamorphosis belongs to a set of fantastical phenomena that, in the genre of the fable, constitute an entirely unproblematic category. Yet if radical physical transformation is part of this genre's licence, the motif is here pressed into service for an unusually complex examination of intrinsic attributes. To begin with, the initial anthropomorphic qualities of the cat are remarkable, even by the standards of fable. The creature not only speaks; it also prays to a divinity of human form (Aphrodite) and conceives a passion for a human being. It thus boasts excellent credentials for metamorphic 'elevation' to the human realm. The goddess Aphrodite sees to the transformation — but evidently with retained scepticism, as if undertaking an experiment. The matter that comes in for scrutiny is the mind, which, in fable, is an organ of thought in animals as well as in humans. The tale of the cat-bride thus affirms the (partial) survival of the mind and character against any vicissitudes in the experience and career of the body.

The problem that arises echoes the mind–body dualism of Homeric epic, that is to say, the persistence of an abiding consciousness in a transformed body. A cat enclosed in a human frame, even willingly, experiences alienation not unlike that of a human trapped in an animal body. The fable thus offers an exploration of metamorphosis that has something in common with Homer's Circe episode. But whereas in the Homeric tale the transformation affects unwilling victims and involves a bestial descent, here the transformation is requested and entails an apparent ascent from animal to human. At least initially, this results in happiness all around. But the transformed cat is evidently required forever to suppress residual feline instinctual drives, which have not waned with her altered physical form. The Aesopic narrator notes that it was a mental lapse, that she *forgot* her present circumstances (ἐπιλαθομένη τῶν παρόντων), when she pounced upon the mouse that Aphrodite sent to test her. It is easy to overlook how far she proceeds in the human realm — all the way to the embraces of her beloved in their bridal bed — before letting down her guard and succumbing to an inbred aspect of her feline nature.

Once again, the informing idea is the post-metamorphic persistence of identity in the form of an alienated consciousness. Here it appears to be the persistence of instinctual drives (the term τρόπος, 'habit', 'way of life', is notoriously vague) that is at issue, in a broader consideration of a living creature's essence or nature (φύσις, though the term is used in a confusing proliferation of senses in this fable). The concluding maxim (a stock generic feature) seems bland and inadequate to the remarkable tale. In its insistence on the persistence of certain drives or habits of character in a remarkable case of animal-to-human metamorphosis, this fable ends up with a surprisingly supple notion of metamorphosis. The cat-bride experiences alienation in both forms: as a cat she falls in love with a human; as a human, she succumbs to predatory feline impulses.

ii

The most extensive comic treatment of metamorphosis in extant Greek literature is that found in Athenian Old Comedy, of which there are preserved eleven full plays by Aristophanes.[84] Unlike Attic Tragedy, Old Comedy does not derive its plots from traditional myths — though it frequently refers to them, usually parodically, as well as to particular tragic versions of them, which are likewise mocked and parodied via metatheatrical flourishes. Liberated from traditional mythological paradigms, the plots are flights of fancy, products of the playwright's imagination, used as vehicles to explore social and political issues in contemporary Athens, and often involve the deliberate blurring of the boundary between human and animal.[85]

The metamorphic dimension of Aristophanes' comic fantasy is perhaps best illustrated by *Birds*, his longest play, whose initial dramatic performance was in 414 BC. The plot centres around two Athenians citizens, Peisetaerus and Euelpides, who have grown weary of the stresses and irritations of Athenian life, above all its lawsuits and informers. They make their way to the realm of the birds, to the dwelling-place of the hoopoe and the nightingale — formerly the Thracian king Tereus and his Athenian wife Procne — in the hope that the former will be able to point them to some terrestrial utopia, where they can spend their days in happy tranquillity. In the course of the interview, however, Peisetaerus realizes that the place they seek does not exist on earth, but must be established elsewhere, a city in the sky, to be called Νεφελοκοκκυγία ('Cloud-cuckoo-town'). He simultaneously conceives a scheme whereby the birds can become masters of the universe, as they had been before the advent of the Olympian gods (554). The birds approve his project, and under his direction, construct an enormous fortified city in the sky, through the garrisoning of which they cut off all communication and interchange between heaven and earth. The gods, deprived of the nourishment of sacrifice, and simultaneously blocked from sexual congress with mortal women, are quickly forced into submission. The play ends with the wedding of Peisetaerus, now leader of the birds, with Basileia, daughter of Zeus, and embodiment of his power and prerogatives.[86]

Birds abounds in items of bird-lore culled from every quarter — from history, poetry, drama, legend, fable, and proverb (the references to Aesop at 471 and 651 are among the earliest on record). An apropos and explicitly identified target of its humour is Sophocles' influential *Tereus*. In the comedy, as in the earlier tragedy, the actor playing the aporneosized (avian) Tereus wore a mask made to resemble a hoopoe. An equivalence between the two is explicitly declared by none other than the Aristophanic Tereus himself, in his initial encounter with the two human protagonists (Aristophanes, *Birds*, 99–101):[87]

> Πε. τὸ ῥάμφος ἥμιν σου γέλοιον φαίνεται.
> Επ. τοιαῦτα μέντοι Σοφοκλέης λυμαίνεται
> ἐν ταῖς τραγῳδίαισιν ἐμὲ τὸν Τηρέα.

> [*Peisetaerus*: Your beak looks funny to us.
> *Hoopoe*: This is how Sophocles outrages me
>   in his tragedies. I am Tereus.]

By this exchange, as Griffith well observes, Aristophanes' figure makes it clear that 'he is not merely the Tereus familiar from the broad field of myth but, much more precisely, he is the very same character that Sophocles staged in his *Tereus*'.[88] Much of the play's humour resides in lingering on the post-metamorphic Tereus, now a hoopoe and monarch of the bird realm.[89] The traditional mythic tale associated with him — the rape and mutilation of his sister-in-law, his wife Procne's infanticidal revenge, and the triple metamorphosis during his murderous pursuit of both — provides an inescapable subtext to the action, but details are suppressed, filtered, and even changed outright. The Aristophanic Tereus is a banalized, rather bourgeois, version of his tragic incarnation.

Terminal metamorphosis in ancient myth is rarely entirely arbitrary: a principle of continuity tends to be operative. The transmogrified figure typically exhibits a form and disposition appropriate to its former nature, and often retains physical signs of the crisis that gave rise to the transformation. In the case of the aporneosized Tereus, the long down-curved beak of the hoopoe is appropriate not only to the Thracian king's warlike character, but more specifically to his murderous intent at the moment of transformation. Ovid, indeed, explicitly derives it from the sword brandished by Tereus (*prominet immodicum pro longa cuspide rostrum* ['in place of his long sword extends a drawn out beak'], *Met.* VI. 673). But such temperamental or situational appropriateness is evidently lost on Aristophanes' Tereus, who merely expresses sensitivity over his physical appearance.[90] And indeed, he appears to have little need of such a weapon; far from persisting in the homicidal pursuit of his wife, he has evidently settled into a state of domestic harmony with her.[91] Aristophanes does, in fact, establish continuities between Tereus' human and avian phases of existence, but these are invariably amusing departures from his literary predecessors. So, for example, when Euelpides expresses surprise that Tereus has a servant, the servant explains this in terms of socio-cultural imperatives that bridge the metamorphosis (Aristophanes, *Birds*, 71–74):

> Θε. [...] ὅτε περ ὁ δεσπότης
>   ἔποψ ἐγένετο, τότε γενέσθαι μ’ ηὔξατο
>   ὄρνιν, ἵν’ ἀκόλουθον διάκονόν τ’ ἔχῃ.
> Πε. δεῖται γὰρ ὄρνις καὶ διακόνου τινός;
> Θε. οὗτός γ’, ἅτ’, οἶμαι, πρότερον ἄνθρωπός ποτ’ ὤν [...]

> [*Servant*: When my master became a hoopoe, he asked me
>   to become a bird as well, so that he could have a servant and attendant.
> *Euelpides*: Does a bird need a servant too?
> *Servant*: This one does, at any rate, because he was once human.]

Thus, the persistence of conventional human social hierarchies is seen to trump the miraculous transformation itself. Aristophanes' comedic supplement is characteristically devastating: following the metamorphosis, rather than continuing the violent pursuit of Procne and Philomela, now through the air (as he does in Ovid, for example), or at least pausing in wonder at his radical and unexpected transformation, Tereus takes a moment to provide for his domestic needs. The deflationary effect is unmistakable. Metamorphosis in tragedy belongs to the indefinable, the non-representable; it typically arises from divine pity or horror at wrenching human actions or circumstances. Here we see a sly generic transposition: comedy does not focus on the climactic moment of crisis and transformation; instead, it considers the tragic transformation as a matter of fact and puts the spotlight on the unglamorous aftermath. In the case of the Tereus in *Birds*, the metamorphosis coincides with an exit from the highly wrought world of the tragic theatre and the age of heroes into a new age defined by the banalities of a domestic existence: By dragging Sophocles' Tereus in his transmogrified shape back on stage, Aristophanes gives us the comic equivalent of a 'What Happened To...?' column on a faded Hollywood A-lister.

This banalization of heroic myth and tragic transformation is achieved, outrageously, through a figure whose metamorphosis occurred in singularly extreme circumstances. Indeed, in any other genre the transformation of humans into animals requires the efficacious presence of a supernatural force; in old comedy, by contrast, metamorphosis loses its mysterious and involuntary character, becoming instead at least in part a willed human procedure. As Tereus himself explains when Euelpides and Peisetaerus lament the limitations of their human form (Aristophanes, *Birds*, 654–55):

> Επ. μηδὲν φοβηθῇς· ἔστι γάρ τι ῥιζίον,
>   ὃ διατραγόντ’ ἔσεσθον ἐπτερωμένω.

> [*Hoopoe*: Fear not; there is a little root:
>   once you have eaten it, you will be winged.]

Critics have plausibly linked this with Homer's Circe episode, and in particular the root moly that Hermes administers to Odysseus in order to immunize him against the porcine transformation suffered by his companions (*Od.* x. 304–06). Here Aristophanes operates in the realm of magical transformations, but in a decidedly muted way. When Euelpides and Peisetaerus next appear it is not in full avian form, but unchanged save for the addition of wings. Moreover, when ten thousand bird-mad human applicants apply for citizenship to Νεφελοκοκκυγία, the new city in the sky, there is evidently no further need for arcane magic. Peisetaerus simply orders wings to be collected in baskets so that he can distribute them to the human immigrants (1308–12). The source of this prodigious supply of wings is unspecified, as is the procedure for attaching them.[92] This appears to be aporneosis on a truly industrial scale — but, again, the end product is clearly not fully avian. Such impossible blending, and the pervasive blurring of taxonomical distinctions between birds and humans is compounded by Aristophanes' tendency throughout to mix up real birds with collective and individual humans. Particularly ingenious in its rampant category confusion is Tereus' identification of a bird that physically resembles him as his grandson. The creature in question is the son of Philocles, who is 'the son of Epops' (i.e. the Hoopoe/Tereus) — 'so you see', explains Tereus, 'I am his grandfather' (281–82). Philocles was in fact a tragic poet who had written a *Tereus*, regarded as a mere plagiarism of Sophocles. The joke is thus metaliterary: Philocles is identified as the son of Epops, because he drew direct inspiration from Sophocles' *Tereus* (whose title character Aristophanes' Epops has already equated himself to at 100–01, discussed above), and at the same time he is father to another Epops, since he himself produced another *Tereus*.[93] The confusion of literary and biological genealogies, coupled with the blending of the human and the avian, has a richly destabilizing effect.

No less suggestive are the terms in which Euelpides declares his lust for aporneo-sized Procne, when she materializes on stage. The actor playing Procne was equipped with a nightingale's head, but was otherwise ornately dressed as befits an Athenian princess.[94] Euelpides at once conceives a passionate desire to kiss her; and when Peisetaerus points out the attendant dangers of the two sharp mandibles of her beak, he retorts (Aristophanes, *Birds*, 673–74):

> ἀλλ' ὥσπερ ᾠὸν νὴ Δί' ἀπολέψαντα χρὴ
> ἀπὸ τῆς κεφαλῆς τὸ λέμμα κᾆθ' οὕτω φιλεῖν.

> [*Euelpides*: But I would treat her like an egg and peel off the
> shell from her head, and kiss her so.]

Euelpides invokes the metaphor of the eggshell, but of course what he is referring to is the actor's dramatic mask, the removal of which would yield a human head — and mouth — to match the visibly humanoid features. This is, to be sure, a characteristic Aristophanic metatheatrical flourish; but is it *only* a metatheatrical flourish? Perhaps not, if we recall that Euelpides is lusting after a creature that prior to aporneosis had been a beautiful Athenian princess. Which 'shell' (λέμμα) would he be peeling off, and to reveal which human underneath? *Birds* is a play that blurs taxonomical distinctions and promotes category confusion at every turn. And in so doing, in creating this instability, it magnifies the metamorphic character of its dramatic universe, while at the same time sapping (tragic) metamorphosis of much of its mystery.

Modes of Critique

From the sixth century BC onwards, new genres of thought and writing emerged that presupposed conceptions of the natural world, the workings of history, and supernatural reality that were in many ways fundamentally at odds with the mythic world view found in much of the literary tradition. It is unnecessary — though perhaps tempting — to force the evidence into the procrustean polarity *mythos* (myth) versus *logos* (reason). But critical engagements with traditional tales, with myth in general and metamorphosis in particular, certainly involved the re-positioning of mythic material, often in the context of an intellectual *agon*.[95] Natural philosophy, beginning with the Milesians, had made significant inroads by providing naturalistic explanations of phenomena such as thunder and lightning that had been attributed to the gods. But metamorphosis, like the immoral conduct of divinities it often facilitated, belongs to a more intractable category. If a literal understanding of supernaturally induced transformative change or similarly problematic matter no longer compels, two basic options remain. One can discount the tale as false (and perhaps explain how the misapprehension came into being); or one can claim that the offending text or tradition does not mean what it says and offer an interpretation that identifies its true significance. A practitioner of the former approach is Xenophanes of Colophon (*c.* 570–480 BC) who famously inveighed against anthropomorphism in religion, submitting that each human community creates gods in their own image, and so, were they able, would each animal species.[96] And for good measure he embeds these reflections within a novel epistemology grounded in the principle that what can be known is confined by the limits of our experience. An example of the latter are allegorical readings, as developed by the Stoics and others, in which (say) Homer's gods are turned into hypostasized human traits (Ares = violence; Athena = wisdom; Aphrodite = love; etc.) or, more elaborated personification of natural forces (the shape-shifting Proteus, for instance, becomes an allegory for the undifferentiated, primordial matter out of which the ordered universe came into being).[97]

Whereas the former approach inevitably devalues the mythic heritage, allegorical recuperations permit the retention of texts of high cultural standing and authority, despite the fact that they *prima facie* transmit and endorse unsavoury implausibilities or outright falsehoods. This would prove to be crucial for texts like the *Odyssey*, which attracted allegorical exegesis from antiquity onwards. So, for example, Eustathius, a twelfth-century archbishop of Thessalonica, and perhaps the finest Christian exegete of Homeric epic, extracted a moral lesson from Homer's Circe narrative by construing it allegorically as a demonstration of the power of pleasure and sensuality to render men bestial.

Some genres, such as historiography, which operated with novel criteria of rationalism and empiricism (however defined), practiced oblique forms of scepticism vis-à-vis the marvels of myth. At the opening of his monumental *Histories*, written in the fifth century BC, Herodotus programmatically recounts the tales of Io, Europa, Medea, and Helen as part of a larger geopolitical tussle between Asia and Europe, without so much as a hint of the fabulous aspects that the mythic tradition had woven into the fabric of their tales — including the transformation of Io into a cow and of Jupiter into a bull. In his narrative universe, so Herodotus makes apparent by careful omission and re-contextualization, metamorphic marvels have no place, though he recognizes and retains the human personnel of myth as historical figures.[98]

Thucydides (c. 460–400 BC) followed suit. In an unusual digression in the second book of his *Peloponnesian Wars*, the celebrated historian and 'theorist of power' recounts how the Athenians wished to establish diplomatic relations and a possible alliance with Sitalces, the son of Teres and king of the Thracians. To maintain genealogical clarity, and no doubt to correct earlier writers, Thucydides states that this Teres has nothing to do with the Tereus who married Procne, the daughter of the Athenian king Pandion.[99] He provides a body of evidence for this assertion. First of all, Tereus was not Thracian: he lived at Daulia, in the region now called Phocis, which at the time was occupied by Thracians.[100] It was here that Tereus' wife Procne murdered their son Itys — as borne out by the fact that many poets call the nightingale 'bird of Daulia' (Δαυλιὰς ἡ ὄρνις).[101] Moreover, it stands to reason (εἰκός) that Pandion would choose to form a marriage alliance with a king in the vicinity, which would be more advantageous than one with someone far away (II. 29. 3). Thucydides thus accepts the mundane features of the legend as historical (marriage alliance; death of Itys), but he passes over those aspects at variance with empirical plausibility, above all the concluding transformations. Nonetheless he extracts from these mythic data an additional kernel of historical truth. By mentioning the nightingale, Thucydides signals the metamorphic tradition that had Procne transformed into that particular bird — but only because the geographical epithet ('of Daulia') offers important evidence to make his case. The historian thus implicitly polemicizes against the poets, even as he uses their data as evidence for his own purpose; and he introduces the criterion of 'plausibility' in support of his conclusions.[102]

If Herodotus and Thucydides rationalize myth and metamorphosis implicitly in the course of developing their historical narratives, another intellectual movement undertook to scrutinize and rationalize this traditional material explicitly, by reducing anything marvellous to a plausible core and explaining it as a misunderstanding of an aspect of the natural world or a historical event.[103] The earliest known example of this approach is Hecataeus of Miletus (c. 560–480 BC), the first of the so-called 'logographers'. Among his known works is the fragmentary *Genealogies* (Γενεαλογίαι), a rationalizing history of the heroes and demigods, beginning with Hercules. It opens with a famously sceptical declaration: τάδε γράφω, ὥς μοι δοκεῖ ἀληθέα εἶναι· οἱ γὰρ Ἑλλήνων λόγοι πολλοί τε καὶ γελοῖοι, ὡς ἐμοὶ φαίνονται, εἰσίν ['I write these tales, as they appear true to me. For the stories of the Greeks are many and ludicrous — or so they strike me] *Fragmente der Griechischen Historiker*, 1F1a). Hecataeus sought to integrate the disparate mass of legendary tales within a consistent chronological framework, while stripping them of their fantastic and supernatural elements. So, for instance, Cerberus, the many-headed canine guardian of the Underworld, is simply identified as a venomous snake from Taenarum (where popular belief located an entrance to the nether realms) that

Hercules brought to Eurystheus. It was nicknamed the 'Hound of Hades' because death was inescapable for anyone it bit.[104]

The most systematic outcome of this rationalizing approach to have survived from antiquity is the treatise entitled *On Unbelievable Tales* (Περὶ ἀπίστων) by one Palaephatus, perhaps a contemporary of Aristotle, about whom we know next to nothing and whose name (which means 'Spoken Long Ago' or 'Of Ancient Fame') is suspiciously appropriate to his undertaking.[105] His work has come down to us in an epitome that, in all probability, includes some inauthentic material towards the end.[106] At the outset of his treatise, Palaephatus stakes out a middle ground between the gullible, who believe anything that is said, and the incredulous, who dismiss fabulous tales as wholesale fictions. His own approach is to admit some referential basis for mythic fables on the premise that names (and stories about them) presuppose some deed or event.[107] In identifying the real in the fabulous Palaephatus operates adamantly on a principle of ontological stability across time: whatever is impossible now must have been impossible in the past and will remain impossible in future (hence, for instance, no centaurs). Story elements of an empirically implausible nature are explained as the result of fantastical embroideries of ordinary events. In reducing the world of myth according to quotidian protocols of common sense, he simultaneously rescues the material from wholesale dismissal: mythic tales are not mere figments of the imagination — they contain an identifiable *historical* core.[108] Unsurprisingly, one of the principal victims of this remorseless separation of the chaff of fantasy from the wheat of history in the vetting of the mythic heritage, is metamorphosis. Palaephatus (or the school of thought that he represents) seems to have had a considerable impact in educated circles throughout antiquity;[109] and Christian apologists eagerly appropriated his techniques of critical exegesis to reveal the pagan pantheon and its marvellous myth as so much imaginary rubbish.

Just as shadowy a figure as Palaephatus is Euhemerus, author of a utopian novel entitled *Sacred History* (Ἱερὰ ἀναγραφή), datable to the very early third century BC.[110] In Euhemerus' novel, a first-person account of an imaginary voyage to an island utopia, the Olympian divinities feature as human protagonists. In the course of reception, scholars and poets developed Euhemerus' project in two diametrically opposed ways: rationalists took him to endorse the view that gods are simply humans that were wrongly endowed with divine status — their divinity thus being a matter of erroneous belief. In this sense, Euhemerism constitutes a radicalization of Palaephatus, by also subjecting the Olympian divinities to historical reduction. It was in this guise that Euhemerism would become a favourite weapon of the Christian polemicists.[111] The opposite tendency was to regard Euhemerus as theorist of the phenomenon that human beings could undergo apotheosis, not just as a matter of belief, but in actual fact. The distinction between the two positions is clearly crucial.[112] The issue was of contemporary relevance: in the wake of Alexander the Great, ruler cults proliferated in the Greek world, building on the tradition of hero-worship, in which the permeability of the divide between human and divine, and the blurring of the boundary thereof, find their most distinctive articulation.[113]

The two alternatives (deification as a phenomenon of mere belief or ontological fact) are well brought out in a passage from Cicero's treatise *On the Nature of the Gods*, III. 53:

> Dicamus igitur, Balbe, oportet contra illos etiam, qui hos deos ex hominum genere in caelum translatos *non re sed opinione* esse dicunt, quos auguste omnes sancteque veneramur.

> [So, Balbus, I should also speak against those who say that those gods whom we all worship reverently and devoutly have been transferred from the race of mortals into the sky *not in fact but by public opinion*.]

In Ennius' (loose) Latin translation of Euhemerus, *Euhemerus sive Sacra Historia*, the concept of 'deified humans' is resolved in the sense that humans can become gods, in all likelihood to prepare the ground for Scipio Africanus' deification.[114] And Cicero himself constantly oscillates between 'folk-belief' (implying that the apotheosis is merely alleged rather than real) and genuine deification, especially in contexts in which he argues for the immortality of the soul, or at least the souls of the most outstanding statesmen.[115]

Another intellectual endeavour in which the status of myth, including myths of metamorphosis, as a discourse of truth became precarious was natural history. In a section of his *Historia Animalium* concerned with seasonal changes of colour and voice in birds, Aristotle notes the changes in colour and form that the hoopoe undergoes (μεταβάλλει δὲ καὶ ὁ ἔποψ τὸ χρῶμα καὶ τὴν ἰδέαν, *Hist. An.* 633a) and adds corroborating verses he attributes to Aeschylus. The tragic fragment, which most scholars nowadays assign to Sophocles' *Tereus*, maintains that the hoopoe is in fact two birds in one: in spring, it takes the form of a white-feathered hawk; in the autumn, it assumes the shape of the hoopoe.[116] Implicitly, Aristotle's discussion operates with different registers: this is the only change mentioned in the passage that involves form (ἰδέα); the others concern only colour and voice. Aristotle reports the latter straightforwardly, on his own authority. The more remarkable transformation of the hoopoe is marked as anomalous by its different treatment: it is placed at the end of the discussion, and the authority for the claim takes the form of a poetic citation. Aristotle here follows his encyclopedic impulse to collect all pieces of knowledge he could, however outlandish and implausible they might appear; but he uses subtle differences in how he presents this material to establish implicit distinctions in truth value.

Countervailing Tendencies

In various settings, literary records of divinely induced (or practiced) metamorphosis suffered a loss of credibility during the classical and Hellenistic period. But not all literary discourses were keen to adopt newly available standards of empirical plausibility, accept the insights and information offered by scientific studies of the natural world, or endorse a rational, philosophical theology; nor did the attacks on the conception of reality that the phenomenon of metamorphosis presupposes lessen the appeal of this figure of thought. Indeed, the Hellenistic age saw both, the rise of interest in the marvellous and the fantastic (*thaumasia, paradoxa, apista*) alongside more serious studies of the natural world and ethnographic enquiry;

and, as outlined above, a flowering of compositions devoted to the theme of metamorphosis. The foundational text for the ancient discourse on marvels is Homer's *Odyssey*, more specifically Books IX–XII, in which Odysseus recounts his travels at the margins of the known world — and in antiquity Homer was indeed credited with inaugurating the genre of paradoxography as well.[117] The impulses behind the exploration of our empirical world, including items that challenge the explanatory powers of the human brain are the same that fuel philosophy: the ability to wonder and the desire to know.[118] The emblematic figure of *curiositas*, that is, inquisitiveness, the characteristic human tendency not to yield before or accept the boundaries of the known, is again Odysseus — whose *ardore [...] a divenir del mondo esperto* ['ardour to gain experience of the world'] (Dante, Inferno, XXVI. 97–98) has remained the paradigm of exploring and pushing beyond, frontiers of knowledge from antiquity through the Middle Ages and beyond.[119] In the ancient world the quest for scientific knowledge found its first major systematization in Aristotle and the *corpus Aristotelicum*, a collection of technical treatises that cover topics ranging from cosmology (*De Caelo*) and atmospheric phenomena (*Meteorologica*) to zoology (*Historia Animalium*). This encyclopaedic endeavour found a continuation in the 227 books attributed by Diogenes Laertius to Theophrastus, a student of Aristotle. These tomes seem to have covered the range of contemporary knowledge, with a particular emphasis on the field of botany.[120]

But the practice of systematically collecting *mirabilia* came into its own in the Hellenistic age, in a branch of literature called 'paradoxography'. The Alexandrian exponents of this genre were contemporaneous with the production of collections of myths of transformations discussed earlier, and the two literary movements clearly have important affinities and overlaps. At the same time, paradoxography offers intriguing points of contact with the proto-scientific writings of the philosophical tradition.[121] The Hellenistic paradoxographers took as their subject matter the wondrous features of the natural world, ethnographic peculiarities, and curious historical events. They generated collections of marvels from around the world, codified in books and hence available in libraries for consultation and citation. A crucial feature of the genre was its emphasis on documentation and credibility: authorities were cited and sources scrupulously acknowledged; paradoxographic authors assumed a critical posture in evaluating sources or pieces of information in order to enhance the impression of veracity. At the same time, paradoxographic writing differs fundamentally from that of philosophical science in that it offers 'facts' while omitting explanations. Where scientific writing advances rational accounts aimed at the elimination of wonder, the genre of paradoxography strives to retain wonder and a sense of the inexplicable. The 'marvellous' is thus in part a product of the strategic manipulation of data, and the suppression of explanation stands in tension with the impression of factuality and strategies of documentation.

II. Metamorphosis in Roman Culture

As far as can be determined, tales of transformative change were even more marginal in early and mid-republican Rome than in the surviving literature of archaic and classical Greece. This should not surprise: the political culture of the Roman republic, in particular its civic religion, did not provide fertile grounds for a mythic imagination *à la Greque*. Myths and legends were of course not absent from the cultural imaginary of archaic Rome;[122] but mythopoiesis and its media (in particular a literary tradition consisting of a range of genres and performance settings) did not have the same cultural standing and significance that they had in Greece. While we may wish to reckon with a lively culture of dramatic performances at festivals as well as mythic tale-telling in various other social contexts, the evidence for the circulation of literary texts in Rome before the third century BC is scant indeed.[123] A literary tradition of the kind we find in Greece only emerged in Rome from the middle of the third century BC onwards — almost half a millennium after the Homeric epics were codified in written form. The striking disparity between archaic and classical Greece and early and mid-republican Rome concerning (what we would call) 'literary activities' has, in the past, been attributed to such factors as differences in ethnic disposition or climate.[124] Nowadays, scholars tend to favour explanations based on differences in political culture and its evolution over time.[125] Rome did not begin to cultivate activities involving literary texts until fairly late in its development, not because it did not have the technological means (writing is attested already from the seventh century onwards) or because the Romans somehow lacked genius; rather, the Roman elite and the wider populace privileged other genres (and historical material) in negotiating such key issues as time and the past, communal identities, and symbolic prestige, which in Greece often involved literary texts and performances.

Media, settings, and modes of display that played a key role in the political culture of the Roman republic included the representation of historical genealogies by means of *stemmata* (maps of lineage connections) and *tituli* (short inscriptions detailing the record of public achievements of outstanding individuals) in the houses of noble families or the funerary rites accorded to former office-holders, consisting of a *pompa funebris* and a *laudatio funebris*, which were put on by the kinship group of the deceased but took place within the civic spaces of the city, in particular the forum.[126] Claims to mythic lineage and legendary origins in the sphere of the divine, much cultivated in Greece, existed in Rome as well, but paled in import in the aristocratic strife for prestige and recognition when set against a family's historical record of achievement (however 'brushed up'), which consisted of public offices and military feats in the service of the *res publica*.[127] Even those scholars who like to posit, often in the absence of compelling evidence, a lively culture of drama and song in the Rome of the early and mid-republic (if not before) tend to speculate that the material had a historical slant — though clear-cut categorical distinctions are of course impossible to draw.[128]

In the absence of literary genres that featured anthropomorphic divinities inter-mingling with, and transforming, mortals, and their associated settings, metamorphic mythopoiesis long lacked the means and media to flourish. At the same time, Rome had always also been part of the wider Mediterranean *oikoumene*, participating in dynamic processes of cultural exchange with, above all, Greek-speaking communities in southern Italy and elsewhere. The legend of Aeneas, who fled Troy to play a crucial role in the founding of Rome, is only the most obvious example of how imaginative myth-making established or reinforced connections between Italy and the Greek East.[129] Processes of acculturation accelerated when Rome began to expand its imperial reach to southern Italy and beyond.[130] Starting in the middle of the third century BC, the Romans developed a literature in Latin on the basis of Greek models, in the course of which the metamorphic repertory of Greek myth entered Roman culture, significantly enriching the meagre indigenous material that we can discern in such figures as Tages, a seer who comes into being from a clod of Etruscan earth, or Cipus, who grew horns as a sign of his potential to assume the kingship of Rome.[131] In late republican and Augustan poetry, including Virgil's *Aeneid*, myths of transformation are ubiquitous.[132] Nevertheless, Ovid was clearly hard-pressed to find instances of marvellous transformation when the focus of his epic moves from Greece to Italy and, eventually, Rome in books XIV and XV of his *Metamorphoses*.

In representing metamorphoses, Latin authors deployed techniques of authentication or, as the case may be, distancing devices, similar to those practised by their Greek predecessors. But what referential value did Roman readers or listeners accord this material? We know very little of how audiences responded to metamorphic subject matter in the republican and early imperial periods. But it is probably safe to assume that the ontological status of tales of marvellous metamorphosis in the cultural settings within which literary texts circulated (predominantly Rome's upper-class milieu) will have been for the most part that of (Greek) fiction: 'In general by this period metamorphosis seems to have been regarded by most educated people as an utterly fabulous notion.'[133]

Consideration of Roman religion reinforces the likelihood that most Roman readers will have regarded standard tales of metamorphosis as nothing more (or less) than entertaining fictions. Rome's civic religion had no place for gallivanting divinities and their antics.[134] The late-republican orator Cicero (106–43 BC) is quite clear that divine epiphanies of the sort that routinely occur in Greek tragedy (and also on the Roman stage) are figments of the poetic imagination (*fabulae*) and have nothing to do with how the gods of Rome's civic religion conduct themselves.[135] Cicero's contemporary, Varro (116 — 27), conceptualized this cultural configuration, in which different systems of religious ideas coexisted with limited interference, with his notion of *theologia tripartita*, distinguishing the state religion (*genus civicum*) from philosophical speculation about the gods (*genus physicum*) and the mythological treatment of the gods (*genus mythicum*) that was most appropriate to poets.[136] In a sense, a sound awareness of the distinctions between different domains of discourse and practice and their respective conceptions of (supernatural) reality obviates the need for critical debunking. If the Greeks had to 'discover' the notion of fiction, in republican Rome a significant degree of insight into the distinction between fiction and fact evolved as a side effect of how Rome's socio-political community came to organize and conceptualize the religious dimension of its field of power.[137] Some evidence for a sceptical disposition towards marvellous transformations is also available for later periods. It is worth recalling here the disapproving voice of the late-antique grammarian and Virgil-commentator, Servius. Operating with a clear distinction between subject matter that could plausibly be considered historical (*historia*) and material that was obviously made up (*fabula*), he objected to Virgil's inclusion of tales that feature metamorphosis in an epic that purports to recount history. His remarks on Aeneas' encounter with the transformed Polydorus and the transformation of Aeneas' ships into sea-nymphs at *Aeneid*, III. 46 and IX. 81 are scathing.[138]

At the same time, the status of metamorphosis as fiction at Rome requires some nuancing. One variant of transformative change in particular complicates the picture, especially since it gained in cultural import (if perhaps not always in plausibility) over the last two centuries of the republic and certainly in imperial times: apotheosis. Republican Rome did not deify deceased human beings or award them cultic honours. Not even the legendary Romulus, mythic founder of the eternal city, was the recipient of religious worship along the lines of Greek hero cult; and in historical times, any such elevation of an individual was in fundamental violation of the principle of oligarchic equality upon which the senatorial regime of republican government rested.[139] In discourse outside the field of power, however, the notion of deification gained a measure of traction with the rise of literature at Rome. Ennius' *oeuvre*, for example, featured instances of apotheosis (of Romulus in the *Annals*), Pythagorean metempsychosis (the reincarnation of Homer in himself, also reported in the *Annals*), and the ascent of a human being to the stars (Scipio, in the eponymous poem); as we already had occasion to note, the poet also domesticated Euhemerism at Rome.[140] He thereby anticipated developments in the field of power. For in the late republic, the ontological boundary between human and divine became increasingly permeable, as politicians and litterateurs kept knocking at the door to heaven. The threshold was finally crossed by Caesar, and it was his apotheosis, as much as anything, that signalled the death of the republic. Reacting to the demands for cultic honours designed to recognize Caesar's newly divine status, Cicero branded the deification of any human as an act of blasphemy that would no doubt incur the wrath and vengeance of the gods.[141] Yet his last-ditch effort to reassert republican religious principles was in vain. In the course of the transition from republic to principate, Rome's supernatural sphere underwent significant reorganization in line with the new autocratic realities on earth, which meant, in particular, that the reigning emperor acquired special ontological status as semi-divine and a future god. A senatorial fiat tended to countersign the deification.[142] These considerations also highlight the potentially complex and fluid interface between political developments on the one hand and the distinction between (supernatural) facts and (literary) fiction on the other.

Ovid

As the preceding survey will have made clear, in writing his *Metamorphoses*, Ovid was working within a tradition of metamorphic narrative as old as western literature itself. Specifically, he picked up a theme in vogue in Hellenistic literature, not just in Greek, but also in Latin. We have already had occasion to mention the elegiac *Metamorphoses* of Parthenius, Virgil's tutor, written in Greek; likewise, Ovid's friend Aemilius Macer translated the *Ornithogonia* of Boeus (discussed earlier) into Latin.[143] The initial announcement that this would be a poem about 'forms changed into different bodies' (*in nova [...] mutatas formas | corpora*, I. 1–2) might well have suggested to a contemporary reader that Ovid was inscribing himself in a tradition of metamorphosis poetry *tout court* — setting himself up, that is, as the Roman exemplar of the sub-genre of Hellenistic metamorphosis catalogue poetry represented by such works as Boeus' *Ornithogonia* or Nicander's *Heteroeumena*.[144] But Ovid's epic was vastly more ambitious in conception, and proved to be no less revolutionary in design. In what follows, we will be unable to do full justice to either the *Metamorphoses* or the scholarly literature on it; all we can do is to highlight those features of Ovid's *magnum opus* of special relevance to our story.[145]

Ovid's Metamorphic Cosmos

The history of Ovid's reception shows him, more than any other ancient poet, to have been the victim of his own success. Perhaps a majority of readers in all ages have looked upon the *Metamorphoses* as a loose compilation of fantastic, amusing, and occasionally risqué tales of transformation. The refined exuberance of individual passages, often excerpted and published in volumes of selected tales, have inspired countless acts of creative engagement in literature and art; but selective readings and the plethora of re-workings that focus on one myth only have perennially obscured the cumulative effect of the poem and its overall design. In short, in its history of reception the *Metamorphoses* has often been read as if it were a Hellenistic catalogue poem, in which the individual tales are held together by little other than the shared theme of transformation. Nicander's *Heteroeumena*, let us recall, as well as other 'collective' metamorphosis poems from the Hellenistic period, are characterized by a discontinuous narrative structure: each tale included forms a coherent entry, sufficient unto itself, but the individual stories do not add up to an overarching organic whole. The fact of the matter is, however, that Ovid's *Metamorphoses* marks a radical departure from these predecessors: while each individual tale sports the qualities we associate with the refined and sophisticated, as well as small-scale and discontinuous, that Callimachus and other Hellenistic poets (often, like Callimachus, associated with Alexandria) valued and cultivated, the whole is much more than the sum of its parts. Indeed, it is of breath-taking ambition: Ovid gives us nothing less than a comprehensive vision of the world — both in terms of nature and culture (and their interlocking): the *Metamorphoses* opens with a cosmogony and offers a cosmology: built into the poem is an explanation (highly idiosyncratic, to be sure) of how our physical universe works, with special emphasis on its various meta-morphic qualities and possibilities; and it is set up as a universal history that traces time from the moment of creation to the Augustan age — or, indeed, beyond.[146]

In strictly formal terms, it is this chronological framework of the *Metamorphoses* that constitutes Ovid's innovation within the tradition of ancient catalogue poetry.[147] He marshals into a continuous epic narrative a vast assortment of tales of transformation, beginning with the creation of the cosmos from chaos and ending with the apotheosis of Julius Caesar — and an epilogue in which Ovid lays claim to his own immortality in and through his poetry. The poet's teleological commitment to a notional 'present' (the Augustan age in which the epic was composed) *qua* narrative terminus registers in the declared chronological span of his epic, and this is subtly reinforced by frequent appeals to the contemporary reader's observational experience. In mastering the daunting, seemingly impossible, challenge of fashioning from disparate material a continuous narrative, a *perpetuum [...] carmen* ['unbroken song'] (I. 4) in the traditional epic manner, Ovid finally realized his desire, first mooted in *Amores* I. I, to match himself against Virgil, already widely regarded as the greatest Roman poet by the time of his death in 19 BC.[148] In part, the *Metamorphoses* may be seen as a counterblast to the *Aeneid*, 'an imitation with variation, of Virgil's conception of a universal epic.'[149] The cosmological ambitions of Ovid's epic offer 'a thematically and conceptually rich alternative to the worldviews of Virgil and other epic writers'.[150] The result is a cumulatively compelling sequence that postures, more or less convincingly, as a comprehensive chronicle of the cosmos in all its pertinent facets. Leonard Barkan well characterizes the *Metamorphoses* as 'a grandly cosmological work that attempts to bridge all the orders of creation by understanding heaven and earth, animate and inanimate beings, physical laws, and human emotions through a series of parallel explanations'; in essence, it offers 'a metamorphic explanation of the way things are.'[151]

Taken in its totality, Ovid's epic elevates the phenomenon of metamorphosis from its prior status as a mythographic curiosity into an indispensable mechanism of cosmic history, a fundamental causal element in the evolution of the universe and the story of humanity. On the most fundamental level, the *Metamorphoses* is a poem that traces out the origins and progressive articulation of the natural world, picking up on a tradition of cosmogonic poetry that has affinities with myths of transformative change, insofar as it explores the blurring of the divide between human and animal, even though it conceives of this blurring as having occurred in a primordial stage of the evolution of life forms.[152] Ovid picks up and enshrines this tradition of evolutionary thought, which, in Latin, had found its culmination in Lucretius' *De Rerum Natura*, into his *Metamorphoses*, in particular in the cosmogonic sequence that opens the poem. After an initial account of creation reminiscent of Genesis, with a divine demiurge in charge, it also features the Earth bringing forth all sorts of creatures after the Flood or when drenched by the blood of Giants.[153] Crucially, however, transformation continues as a universal principle beyond the cosmogonic section. Ovid's world is populated by divinities that shift their own shape — including the programmatic Proteus (VIII. 730–37) — and also have the power to transform human beings. These aetiological metamorphoses generally involve some form of 're-inscription' of the transformed human within the natural order, and Ovid frequently appeals to the reader's extra-literary experience as a form of corroboration.[154] Together, the record of supernatural powers and transformed human beings that the *Metamorphoses* chronicles adds up to a unique combination of 'natural' and 'universal' history, in which cosmos and culture evolve together and eventually (in the form of a Roman civilization that has acquired global reach under Augustus) coincide.[155] The interlocking of nature and culture under the sign of eternal flux is also a hallmark of the lengthy disquisition that Ovid puts in the mouth of Pythagoras, which dominates the final book of the poem (xv. 75–478):[156] he complements the myth-historical mode that dominates in the rest of the poem with a sustained natural-historical perspective.

The *Metamorphoses*, then, offers not a mere concatenation of marvellous transformations, but a poetic vision of a universe conceived of as fundamentally and comprehensively metamorphic — at all levels. As one critic has it:

> The world of nature is seen as points of stasis in a reality which constantly changes, and stories of these sudden and abrupt changes of form reflect the nature of language itself as it reflects the mind's impulse to understand the living world and human identity.[157]

This kind of 'natural' aetiology is a significant departure from the aetiological modes prevalent in the Greek literature of the Hellenistic age: 'The stories in Callimachus' *Aetia* (mostly) give rise to ritual practices; the stories in Ovid (mostly) involve a person changing into something else.'[158] In linking the aetiological with the universal, Ovid's *Metamorphoses* enacts a shift from the predominantly local preoccupations of Hellenistic treatments of metamorphosis to a global perspective — though Ovid slyly integrates aetiological references to Rome even in the opening books that are set in the Greek world, a practice that gains in prominence when he reaches Italian and Roman subjects in the last two books of the poem.[159] But on the premise, widely accepted among Ovid's Roman readers, that the city of Rome (*urbs*) is co-extensive with the universe (*orbis*) — an equation that still resonates today in the Papal blessing *urbi et orbi* — his Roman aetiologies implicitly lay claim to cosmic significance. This approach finds its complement in an aggressive stance towards the original aetiological import of his Greek material: in a number of cases Ovid provides a 'delocalized' version of a myth, with no precise setting named; in others he deliberately saps Greek tales of their aetiological point.[160]

Ovid's policy of 'uprooting' mythic tales from their context of origin and his erasure of their local significance for a specific community results in versions that carry a more general meaning and message. In contrast to many of his Greek sources, Ovid's stories are neither consistently linked to local cult practices nor do they negotiate civic identities — as did, for instance, the so-called Atthidographers, who inspired Callimachus, but get an oblique pasting in the *Metamorphoses*;[161] instead, his versions foreground 'anthropological' themes, such as love and passion (from the perverse to the sublime), (sexual) violence and revenge, transformation and death, the body and the soul, or humanity and the gods (including the problem of theodicy), within the wider temporal context of universal history.

Ovidian Anthropology

An important conceptual underpinning of metamorphosis is the assumption that all creatures partake in primordial matter; this shared materiality constitutes the ground of transformation, of the reshaping of forms into new bodies.[162] In this sense the metamorphoses of animals, humans, and gods are fundamentally similar:

they differ only with respect to motivation, agency, method, and consequences (especially in cases of irreversibility). But if the declared theme of the *Metamorphoses*, 'forms changed into different bodies' (*in nova [...] mutatas formas | corpora*, I. 1–2), turns out to have an encyclopaedic remit, it should be noted that in the majority of cases this means *human* forms changed into *non-human* bodies.[163] And even in episodes where there is no actual metamorphosis in the strict sense of the term or the metamorphosis does not involve the transformation of a human being, it is the human mind and the human body, and human affairs in general, that are of greatest concern to Ovid.[164] The preoccupation with the human registers instantly in the multiple anthropogenesis at the beginning of Book I. The account of terrestrial creation at I. 32–88 opens with the formation of the (spherical) Earth, and ends climactically with the generation of the human race. This sequence affirms a close relationship between human physiognomy and the cosmos because of their shared constituents.[165] Ovid then offers his version of the Hesiodic 'Ages of Man' and other traditional vicissitudes of the nascent species and, in the context of the iron age, recounts two further stories of human creation: the earth produces additional human beings from the blood of the giants killed during their assault on heaven and, after Jupiter almost wipes out the entire human race in his punitive universal flood, Deucalion and Pyrrha regenerate humanity with the help of their 'ancient mother' (the Earth). This series of accounts of human origins maps out the potential of human nature, covering as it does the full range from quasi-divine and ethically impeccable (divine spark and golden-age bliss) to bestial and blasphemous (blood of giants and iron-age criminality).[166] Likewise, Ovid's multiple versions of and speculations upon human origins establish a particularly mobile relationship between the human and non-human orders. As Feeney puts it:

> Since the appearance of mankind is a metamorphosis of the earth (I. 87–88), a human's transformation into a rock or tree is a reversion to origins; yet, since there may have been divine elements at man's creation, and since the celestial element may have been lingering in the primeval mud (I. 79–81), a human's elevation to deity may also be seen as a return to something cognate.[167]

In other words, the upward and downward potential of human metamorphosis is fundamental to Ovidian 'anthropology': individual figures manifest the capacity to descend to the level of the beasts and to ascend to the level of the gods.[168]

The overall progression in Ovid's early narrative involves a narrowing of focus, a movement from the metamorphosis of the cosmos, to that of the earth, to that of individual human beings, which thereupon becomes the dominant type. This transition is achieved, significantly, via a particularly opprobrious specimen of humanity, Lycaon. It is with this figure that Ovid first recounts the metamorphosis of an individual human being; Lycaon's lupine transformation is, indeed, the first metamorphosis in the more limited sense of a miraculous, more or less instantaneous, transformation of a specific living creature.[169] The episode raises crucial questions about human degeneracy, personal guilt, and divine retribution. Lycaon's punishment is meted out for crude violations of civilized conduct, in particular ritual practice (I. 226–39).[170] Yet, for all the horrific depravity of his actions — which include serving human flesh to his divine guests — Lycaon is seen as an emblematic figure, on whose account Jupiter resolves to obliterate the entire human race. As Ginsberg observes, 'all the degeneracy of the Age of Iron appears embodied in the figure of Lycaon: his transformation is mankind's first epitaph, his lupine howls seal a sad and almost final chapter in human history.'[171] Feeney rightly sees the episode as part of Ovid's broader exploration of 'what is human about being human', a question probed more insistently in the *Metamorphoses* through erotics.[172]

Ovid's epic presents the human being as a metamorphic creature, whose most radical individual experiences are given embodiment in nature through marvellous transformation. No other work in Graeco-Roman literature foregrounds to the same extent the mutability of the human body.[173] In the process, the *Metamorphoses* contributes more than its fair share to an ancient 'aesthetics of the gruesome' and dwells repeatedly on the physical aspects of human existence, a creature of the body, pain, suffering — here tragic intertexts are often particularly important.[174] But transformation generally means something other than mere physical disintegration. Ovid is equally interested in human psychology. In the judgement of Fränkel, for instance, the principal theme of the *Metamorphoses* is that of the individual human being driven to psychological crisis by extraordinary circumstances.[175] In the narrative build-up to metamorphosis, the emotions indeed tend to receive pride of place, and their transformative consequences are a recurring thematic. Ovid, as Ted Hughes observes, was interested in 'passion when it combusts, or levitates, or mutates into an experience of the supernatural.'[176] The transformative power of disappointed love is reflected in the intertwined tales of Narcissus and Echo (III. 339–510): the latter becomes disembodied sound, the former develops a split identity as a new species of flower and as a shade of his former self that is gazing vainly into the Styx. Love is also the metamorphic determinant — and on more than one level — in the epic's first narrative of mutual love between humans, the tale of Pyramus and Thisbe (IV. 55–166).[177] Other emotions prove to be equally transformative. In the case of Niobe, overwhelming grief at the loss of her children prompts a catatonic response that both anticipates and informs her metamorphosis into stone (X. 300–09).[178] Cyparissus' inconsolable grief at slaying a beloved animal prompts his transformation into a cypress (a tree associated with death and mourning) 'that he might mourn for evermore' (*ut tempore lugeat omni*, X. 135). In such cases, unresolved human grief is 'translated' into a feature of the natural world.[179]

The most striking emotional climax of Ovid's epic is that involving Tereus, Procne, and Philomela just prior to their triple aporneosis. Tereus, stricken by the murder of his son and the grim revelation that he has eaten the latter's flesh, is hell-bent on murderous vengeance; the two women, having both anguished over and exulted in their gruesome revenge, flee him in terror. Here no supernatural agency is mentioned in the marvellous transformations: it is as if, to quote Ted Hughes once again, 'mortal passion makes the breakthrough by sheer excess, without divine intervention'.[180] The resulting transformations are properly aetiological: the three human protagonists are, as it were, 'reinscribed' within the natural order as new species of birds — just as, say, Daphne becomes the *Ur*-laurel (I. 548–52), or Arachne the *Ur*-spider (VI. 139–45). In giving rise to new genera of flora or fauna, such metamorphoses effect a concomitant annihilation of the original self, no matter what traces of that human being are preserved in the form or behaviour of the new species.[181] Ovid's accounts of such transformations of individual humans into new species typically involve a crafty manipulation of language, a concatenation of referential slippages that progresses almost imperceptibly from the particular to the general case. Skulsky has delineated this 'subversive' approach in discussing the dénouement of the Tereus and Procne episode:[182]

> The effect is achieved by a grammatical sleight of hand: singular sentences are allowed to merge into general, proper nouns into common, personal history into natural history. Thus, we seem to be learning about Procne and Philomela when we hear that, in the swiftness of their escape from Tereus, 'you would think their bodies were being lifted by wings — they *were* being lifted by wings' (VI. 667–68). Now the narrative abruptly shifts into what at first appears to be the historical present: 'One of the two seeks the woods; the other comes up on the roofs of houses.' But in the next sentence, what seemed to be the present tense of vivid narrative turns out to have been the tenseless present of zoological generalization; we have been hearing about habitats, not events, and are now informed about characteristic plumage: To this day, the marks of gore have not passed out of [the nightingale's] breast, and its feathers are marked with blood (VI. 669–70).

As a consequence of these metaphoric affinities, nature often serves in the *Metamorphoses* as a *luctus monumentum*, a reminder of the human grief and suffering that gave rise to so many of its features.[183]

There are, of course, a number of human transformations in Ovid's epic that are not aetiological. These metamorphoses tend to preserve awareness, so that the self finds itself in exile, as it were, from its proper form. Such is the case for Actaeon, transformed bodily into a deer by the vengeful goddess Diana: his mind alone, Ovid tells us, remained as before (*mens tantum pristina mansit*, III. 203). Attacked by his own hunting dogs, which naturally fail to recognize their master, he wants desperately to declare his human identity, to cry out *Actaeon ego sum* ['I am Actaeon!'] (III. 230), but lacks the human anatomy to do so.[184] A similar alienation is experienced by Io, after Jupiter transforms her into a cow. Upon beholding her bovine form reflected on the water's surface, Ovid tells us, 'she grew frightened and fled in terror from herself' (*pertimuit seque exsternata refugit*, I. 641). In such cases, as noted earlier for the Homeric Circe episode, metamorphosis is conceived as an affliction suffered by an unaltered, persisting awareness; the incorporeality of consciousness is implied by accounts of its relocation — whether ultimately reversible (Io) or not (Actaeon) — in alien bodies.[185]

The principle of a soul–body dualism is strategically revisited in the lengthy speech of Pythagoras in the epic's final book. Among his tenets is the immortality of the soul and its transmigration from one living form to the next — with the free movement between species providing the ethical underpinning for his advocacy of vegetarianism in Ovid's text. 'We are not merely bodies,' the philosopher declares, 'but winged souls too' (*non corpora solum,| verum etiam volucres animae sumus*, *Met.* XV. 456–57). Pythagoras is of course articulating a belief in metempsychosis (cf. XV. 169–72), but this can be taken to corroborate — and, *mutatis mutandis*, theorize — earlier accounts of metamorphosis as a kind of exile of the self from its rightful body.[186] We see here, then, two crucial Ovidian potentialities of human experience: bodily transformation and soul migration. These two phenomena, as Warner nicely observes, would provide an important conceptual foundation for fantastic literature in the modern era.[187] The universal outlook of Ovid's literary world, which explores our embodiment just as much as the nature and destiny of our souls within the wider cosmos and thereby achieves a curious and unique interlocking of cosmic and natural history and anthropology, explains in part why his distinctive interpretation of the Greek mythological heritage has continued to resonate so powerfully with later ages and cultures. It is one of the reasons why the *Metamorphoses* could turn into the 'pagan bible' of transformative change.[188]

Ovidian Historicity

With our brief discussion of the wider literary and cultural context as backdrop, Ovid's decision to compose a hexametric universal history pegged on the recurring motif of transformative change emerges as the outlandish undertaking it was designed to be. The change in format — from catalogue poetry to epic narrative — underwrote an even more outrageous innovation in epistemological posture. For in claiming to be writing a history that takes as its guiding theme instances of supernaturally induced transformative change, Ovid deliberately (mis-)represents fiction as fact — on a scale and with an insouciance quite beyond anything to be found in earlier writers. This is a key point, easily and often missed by those who believe that the ancients did not distinguish sharply between history and fiction. But quite apart from the evidence of Servius and others who refused to suspend their disbelief when encountering tales of transformation in what purported to be a historical narrative, Ovid himself draws attention to the largely fictitious status of his guiding theme in some of his other works, both before and after completion of his epic.

Thus in *Amores* III. 12 Ovid laments the fact that, owing to the success of his poetry, his girlfriend Corinna has become the toast of Rome's would-be Don Giovannis, with everyone wanting to get in on the action; he thus rather wished that people read his love elegies with the same incredulous disposition they routinely bring to bear on mythic *fabulae* — and proceeds to labour the point in what amounts almost to a blueprint of the *Metamorphoses* (*Amores*, III. 12. 19–44). Ovid's catalogue of unbelievable tales includes Scylla, Medusa, Perseus and Pegasus, gigantomachy, the adventures of Odysseus (notably Circe's magical transformation of his comrades and Aeolus' obliging bagging of unfavourable winds), Cerberus, Phaethon, Tantalus, Niobe and Callisto (*de Niobe silicem, de virgine fecimus ursam*), Procne, Philomela, and Itys, the self-transformations of Jupiter that preceded the rapes of Leda, Danae, and Europa (*Iuppiter aut in aves aut se transformat in aurum | aut secat inposita virgine taurus aquas*), Proteus, the Spartoi that rose from the teeth of the dragon that Cadmus killed at the future site of Thebes, the fire-breathing bulls that Jason conquered with the aid of Medea, the sisters of Phaethon transformed into trees and crying ember, ships turning into nymphs (a sly allusion to Virgil, *Aeneid* IX), the sun reversing its course in horror at the crime of Atreus, and Orpheus' magic music moving immobile and inanimate elements of nature. The catalogue culminates in the punchline that just as no one actually believes in the historical authenticity of such tales, so too readers should be disinclined to take anything he says about Corinna at face value (*Amores*, III. 12. 41–44):

> Exit in inmensum fecunda licentia vatum,
>   obligat historica nec sua verba fide.
> et mea debuerat falso laudata videri
>   femina; credulitas nunc mihi vestra nocet.

> [The creative licence of the poets knows no limits, and does not constrain its words with historical faithfulness. My girl ought to have seemed wrongly praised. I am undone by your credulity.]

In *Tristia*, II. 63–64, by contrast, his recognition that what he recounts in the *Metamorphoses* is not to be believed is short and to the point: *Inspice maius opus, quod adhuc sine fine tenetur,* | *in non credendos corpora uersa modos* ['Look at my greater work, which is as of yet unfinished, bodies transformed in ways not to be believed']. As Little puts it, 'a critic could hardly wish for a more explicit denial of the reality of the myth-world of the *Metamorphoses*.'[189]

In the light of how Ovid presents the theme of metamorphosis elsewhere (including moments of auto-exegesis), it comes as no surprise that 'the *Metamorphoses*' challenges to our belief in its fictions are relentless, for Ovid continually confronts us with such reminders of his work's fictional status.'[190] But this feature of his text, so cherished by modern readers, is merely an epiphenomenon of his decision to write *fiction as history*. Put differently, what is so striking about his project is not that Ovid is writing self-conscious fiction — that much is anyway glaringly obvious, and Ovid knows how to give this aspect of his text a constant playful spin. Rather, it is his paradoxical insistence that his fictions are historical facts. Thus, whereas the artistic logic of his narrative prefigures postmodernity's metafictions, the ontological status claimed by Ovid for his *Metamorphoses* has its closest parallel in the Old Testament. Both texts posture as the literary record of historical events shaped, above all, by supernatural interventions that manifest themselves in the form of marvels and miracles. Even if the status of the text within their principal communities of readers has of course differed radically, given that one functions as sacred scripture, the other as literary entertainment, the rhetorical conception of the two texts features striking parallels: both are conceived as histories (of the world, of a religious community) that begin with creation and then trace the story into the present, with particular attention to those moments when the supernatural (in each case elusive, yet all-powerful) intervenes in human affairs by means of miracles or metamorphoses.[191]

From the start, Ovid draws attention to, and confronts, the issue of credibility. A representative instance comes from his account of how Deucalion and Pyrrha replenish the earth with humans after the flood by throwing stones over their shoulder (*Met.* I. 400–01):

> saxa (quis hoc credat, nisi sit pro teste vetustas?)
> ponere duritiem coepere [...]

[The stones (who would believe this if the age of the tale did not function as witness?) began to lose their hardness [...]]

It is tempting to assume that Ovid here deliberately inverts Penelope's dismissal of the Deucalion-and-Pyrrha myth as a hoary fable; but irrespective of whether we posit an allusion to the passage in *Odyssey* XIX, the same old myth of transformation that Penelope in Homer evoked as emblematic of fairy-tale nonsense is here presented as a historical event, precisely on account of its great age! Ovid thus turns *vetustas* ('antiquity') into a criterion for *veritas* ('truth'), slyly counting on, while at the same time subverting, the investment in tradition in Roman culture (as seen most strikingly in the importance attached to *exempla* and *mores maiorum*, that is, 'instances of exemplary conduct and customs of the ancestors'). From the very outset to the very end of his poem, Ovid cheekily challenges his readers to see fictions as facts. Not coincidentally, his most programmatic confrontation with the issue of credibility occurs at the very centre of the poem. His characters here engage in a tussle over the relation of metamorphosis and divine potency, acting out 'two possible audience reactions to the divine stories of the *Metamorphoses*'.[192] In response to a story recounted by the river-god Achelous about the metamorphosis of nymphs into islands all members of the internal audience accept the *factum mirabile* as true — except one, whom Ovid characterizes as a *contemptor* of the gods: Pirithous reacts with derision and denies that the gods have the power to cause miraculous transformations (*Met.* VIII. 612–15):

> [...] inridet credentes, utque deorum
> spretor erat mentisque ferox, Ixione natus
> 'ficta refers nimiumque putas, Acheloe, potentes
> esse deos' dixit 'si dant adimuntque figuras.'

[Ixion's son ridicules those who believed (*sc.* the just recounted story of transformation) and, being contemptuous of the gods and savage in disposition, declared: 'You are relating fairy tales, Achelous, and ascribe too much power to the gods if you have them give and take away shapes.']

In response to radical expression of doubt of the very principle that sustains Ovid's literary world (and is acknowledged as doing so in the proem), Lelex affirms the infinite power of the gods and narrates the story of Philemon and Baucis as a case in point.[193] Paradoxically, Ovid's own metafictional gestures and explicit confrontation of the problem of credibility can be read as strategies of authentication insofar as they signal authorial concern for the truth-value of the material he has adopted in his history.[194] With his rhetoric of truth, Ovid partially pre-empts the audience's unwillingness to suspend disbelief in the face of the marvellous. His authorial posture resembles those of the paradoxographers, who also aim to convince their audience of the veracity of what defies common sense or is, indeed, frankly incredible.

To be sure, the data of interest to paradoxographers belong for the most part in the domain of natural history, whereas Ovid operates primarily in the medium of myth. But very much in a paradoxographical spirit, Ovid also breaks down the distinction between myth and natural history as two discourses that articulate rival claims to provide an explanation of the universe. From the outset of the epic, he draws on the idiom and vision of philosophical physics, as articulated in the works of Empedocles and Lucretius above all, to set up his metamorphic and divinely manipulated universe.[195] And in the final book of the poem, he dramatizes the apparent opposition between a natural historical approach towards the workings of the cosmos and his own choice of mythic aetiology by giving a prominent place to the figure of Pythagoras: the philosopher, who teaches *rerum causas* (XV. 68) in the manner of a natural historian, recapitulates many of the phenomena recorded in the first fourteen books from a proto-scientific point of view. For example: when Lycian peasants muddy the pond from which Latona, nursing her newborn twins Diana and Apollo, wishes to drink, the deity turns them into frogs (*Met.* VI. 313–81). Ovid effectively delays naming the creatures into which the peasants are transformed until after an elaborate description of their characteristics and concludes the episode with the golden punchline *limosoque novae saliunt in gurgite ranae* ['and in the muddy depth new creatures jump about, — frogs!'] (381). To this mythic account, Pythagoras offers his proto-scientific explanation: *semina limus habet virides generantia ranas* ['the mud contains seeds that bring forth the green frogs'] (XV. 375).[196] By means of the lexical correspondences *limoso* ~ *limus* and *ranae* ~ *ranas* (placed each time in the last foot of the line), Ovid encourages his readers to compare and contrast the two accounts, which, upon inspection, emerge as complementary, rather than mutually exclusive, not least since Ovid proleptically subsumes Pythagoras' point of view into his literary world: throughout the poem, he integrates gestures to the proto-scientific recapitulation that his mythic tales will undergo in Pythagoras' disquisition.[197]

A particularly striking example of this technique is the case of coral in *Met.* IV: the curious plant first came into being, so Ovid recounts, when some seaweed upon which Perseus had bedded the head of Medusa to clean himself soaked up its marvellous powers and became rigid. But then something extraordinary happens: sea nymphs who observed this *mirabile factum* try to repeat the experiment with further twigs; to their delight, they succeed and begin to scatter coral seeds all over the waves.[198] At the end of the account, the mythic past merges into a more scientifically-conceived present through a differentiation between the nature of the fully submerged coral and that exposed to air, all prefaced by the aetiological formula *nunc quoque* (IV. 750). As with the frogs, Pythagoras invokes coral in support of his principle of eternal flux.[199] What is the significance of the fact that phenomena that came into being back then are still observable today, when they occur naturally? Klein comments: '*Nunc quoque*, the typical aetiological phraseology, is here the way to transform the marvellous, the *vis monstri*, into a scientific law involving only natural elements (water and air) to explain the seaweed's metamorphosis into coral' and she argues that 'the aetiological tale then exhibits its function of naturalizing the supernatural and toning down the unbelievable marvellous of the epic (IV .750–52).'[200] While a valid observation, this only captures one half of Ovid's strategy: for just as he naturalizes the supernatural, he 'supernaturalizes' the natural and plays up, rather than tones down, the incredible aspects of his universal history. His imbrication of marvellous myth with proto-scientific observation in the context of a world chronicle generates a complex literary world in which regimes of truth that are elsewhere at variance with one another become mutually reinforcing:[201] myth explains the empirically inexplicable; and the empirically inexplicable demonstrates the veracity of myth.[202]

In this context, it is important to note that the figure of Pythagoras and the contents of his disquisition do not resemble so much a natural scientist in the manner of Aristotle as a writer of paradoxography; or rather, he is a philosopher who uses paradoxographical data as evidence for his theory of eternal flux. If Lucretius attempted to eliminate the marvellous from the real — in his treatment of natural wonders at *de Rerum Natura* VI. 608–1137 he offers rational explanations of seemingly inexplicable phenomena on the basis of Epicurean physics — 'Pythagoras' message is that reality is wondrous rather than rational.'[203] Translated into modern terms, in his *Metamorphoses* Ovid integrates the natural sciences (via gestures to Epicurean physics and theories of primordial elements) with the life sciences (human biology in particular) and theology (a discourse concerned with the care of the soul) in his universe of flux.

Ovid's *Metamorphoses*, then, in turning a quirky theme that had previously received exclusive treatment only in minor genres into the principal preoccupation of an epic narrative and in presenting material as historical fact that blatantly defies empirical plausibility as well as common sense, gleefully violates or inverts generic laws and cultural protocols and thereby constitutes an insouciant affront to all sorts of traditional expectations. Against a long tradition of debunking metamorphosis, he co-opts and reactivates the Hesiodic and Hellenistic tradition of metamorphic poetry and turns the motif into the guiding principle of a text that postures as a universal history.[204]

Metamorphosis in the Metamorphoses

In the General Introduction, we had occasion to quote Feldherr for the claim that 'the poem offers no clear prescription for understanding [metamorphosis]'.[205] Ovid's encyclopaedic approach to (transformative) change indeed thwarts attempts at reducing the multiplicity of modes to a simple formula. At the same time, the fact that Ovid over the course of his work offers a systematic and comprehensive airing of virtually every conceivable phenomenon to do with change or transformation in nature or culture is in itself of programmatic importance and points to a unifying, cosmic vision grounded in the principle of flux, which manifests itself in varying ways in every sphere of human experience. Moreover, as the poem unfolds Ovid very deliberately brings into focus diverse paradigms of metamorphosis, from which we would like to single out four.

First, and most pervasively, there are those transformations that happen by divine fiat. Ovid announces this type in the proem, and instances thereof recur throughout the epic, as different divinities move individual human beings down or up the ontological ladder.[206] Secondly, Ovid devotes significant space to magic as an alternative means of causing transformative change, not least in the Medea episode in Book VII. Throughout the tale the emphasis is on the power of spells and potions to achieve magical effects.[207] In theory, the existence of a 'technological' approach to transformation would seem to render humans capable of performing acts of metamorphosis, given that in this paradigm the power to achieve radical change resides in special knowledge, expertise, and skills as well as their felicitous enactment, rather than divine will. While it of course helps to be a witch like Medea, the emphasis on the right ingredients and the correct performance of magical formulae or incantations in principle puts transformative interventions at the disposal of all mortals — a dream that would prove particularly popular in alchemist circles.[208] Thirdly, at the very end of the epic, Ovid devotes considerable space to the long-winded philosopher Pythagoras, who regales us with a lengthy disquisition on (natural) change. That Ovid should spend just about half of his final book on a paradigm of change that has little to do with the types of metamorphosis that dominate the rest of his poem has long puzzled readers.[209] In light of the foregoing analysis, however, it makes perfect sense: after already playing obliquely with a conception of metamorphic nature at various moments in his narrative, he gives this perspective on (transformative) change explicit and systematic consideration, thus rounding off his gradual unfolding of metamorphic possibilities, from divine fiat to magical know-how to natural scripts. Finally, the *Metamorphoses* celebrates throughout the world-generating (and world-changing) powers of the creative imagination. The figure of the visual and verbal artist is a powerful presence in his work, from the divine demiurge to Vulcan, from the Muses to Arachne, from Marsyas to Orpheus and Pygmalion.[210] They all are ultimately subsumed, in the *sphragis* of the epic, under the master artist, *Ovidius ipse* and his claim to immortality through his poetry.[211]

The Chapters

The four chapters that follow in Part I develop the themes and the story of this Introduction. Our first chapter offers a detailed reading of the Medea-episode in Ovid's *Metamorphoses*, not least to illustrate its key role in establishing magic as a source and paradigm of transformative change in the epic — an aspect that has so far received only tangential consideration in the scholarship. The other two papers dedicated to ancient material explore two further types of metamorphosis: in Chapter 2, 'Lynx-stone and Coral: "Liquid Rocks" between Natural History and Myths of Transformation', Sonia Macrì discusses metamorphic phenomena in natural history (including the relation to their treatment in myth, not least in Ovid), and Manuel Baumbach's Chapter 3, 'Proteus and Protean Epic: From Homer to Nonnos', explores the figure of Proteus, the supernatural polymorph par excellence, as a trope for the transformative powers of the creative imagination that operates within a tradition of rival voices and predecessors. Finally, Zoe Jaques, in 'Arboreal Myths: Dryadic Transformations, Children's Literature, and Fantastic Trees' (Chapter 4), returns to where our General Introduction left off: her analysis of how modern children's literature reworks classical and biblical themes to do with trees, sexuality, and transformation opens up our chronological and theoretical horizons, while emphasizing the importance of the classical and biblical heritage in Western thought. Jaques discusses the affinities between her chosen authors and ancient sources (in particular Ovid) in terms of plot patterns, themes, and imagery, not just in terms of direct and indirect influence, but also in terms of archetypal preoccupations with sexual maturation and awakening, transformative desire, destruction of the self, and death.

Notes to the Introduction

1. See Barkan (1986), p. 1.
2. On the original title, see Winkler (1985), pp. 292–98 (who proposes a double title: *Asinus Aureus, peri metamorphoseon*). A good introduction to Apuleius' biography, *oeuvre* and historical background is available in Harrison (2000). For the history of reception see, in addition to Chapters 5 and 7 (Robert Carver) in this volume, Carver (2007) and Gaisser (2008).
3. For our concerns, this applies in particular to accounts of cosmogony and anthropogony, which tend to involve large-scale metamorphic interventions on the part of divine forces. A selective bibliography of sources in translation and discussion includes Dalley (1998), West (1997), and Haubold (2002), who shows that the differences in emphasis between ancient Near Eastern and Greek thought about humanity and its place in the universe are as striking and interesting as the thematic parallels.
4. For Ovid's 'imperial' attitude towards his Greek predecessors, see Gildenhard and Zissos (2004). It perhaps still bears stressing that in neither case did the creative and aggressive reworking of Greek material stymie originality.
5. Throughout this section we are much indebted to the studies by Forbes Irving (1990) and Buxton (2009).
6. For a more recent variant of this approach see Buxton (2009), Part II: 'The Logic of Transformation', in particular Chapter 7 ('The Human Aetiology of Landscape') and Chapter 8 ('Plants, Trees, and Human Form'). For both Burckhardt and Buxton metamorphosis remains almost entirely a religious phenomenon; thus neither considers the impact of (proto-)scientific discourse on Greek understandings of transformative change from (at least) the fourth-century onwards: for this facet of the story, see Chapter 2 (Sonia Macrì) below.
7. Burckhardt (1956), pp. 7–19 and 396–400.
8. For (critical) discussion and some of the secondary literature see Forbes Irving (1990), pp. 38–57.
9. See e.g. Feeney (1998), pp. 115–16, with reference to the work of Versnel.
10. Unlike Burckhardt, Forbes Irving excludes transformations into stars (catasterism) from systematic consideration. From the point of view of the classical tradition in particular, this is an unfortunate omission.
11. See e.g. Burckhardt (1956), p. 7: 'Aber aus den ältesten Zeiten dämmert uns [...] die Metamorphose entgegen.'
12. We use the qualifier 'evidently' because the vast bulk of Hellenistic literature has been lost; much of what we do have has survived only in fragmentary form. Burckhardt (1956) is aware of this distribution, but tries to turn the evidence on its head by claiming it as proof of the profound engagement of Greek culture with metamorphosis in *prehistoric* times: 'sonst hätte sie nicht noch spät [i.e. in the imperial period] eine ganze Reihe von Sammlern und Dichtern begeistern können' (p. 7).
13. In particular Nicander, Boeus, Corinna, Pherecydes, Menecrates, Hermesianax. The first two sources in this list, along with Antoninus himself, are discussed further below.
14. A possible exception is the mammoth *Dionysiaka* of the late-antique author Nonnos. Buxton (2009), p. 135, characterizes the work, which runs to forty-eight books, as 'an extraordinary literary extravaganza which places metamorphosis at the heart of its world'. See further Shorrock (2011) and our Chapter 3 (Manuel Baumbach).
15. We return to this complex of ideas in more detail in the Introduction to Part II.
16. See Burckhardt (1956), pp. 20–206 ('Die Griechen und ihre Götter'), in particular p. 29 ('Mangel schriftlicher Offenbarung und auferlegter Lehre').
17. Bibliography includes Fauth (1975); Forbes Irving (1990), pp. 8–12; Buxton (2009), pp. 29–48.
18. This is one of a number of features that have facilitated reading strategies treating the Homeric divine machinery as a literary device, detachable adornment, vel sim. For such readings, see, e.g., Strauss-Clay (1997), p. 135.

19. A passage that presents difficulties for attempts to explain away allomorphic divine interventions in mortal affairs as reifications of human emotions or psychological tendencies.

20. Buxton (2009), pp. 29–37.

21. The episodes are most recently discussed by Buxton (2009), pp. 37–42. Proteus is also the protagonist of our Chapter 3 (Manuel Baumbach). See further the papers in Rolet (2009).

22. The magic wand is the metamorphic implement par excellence, occasionally employed even by Olympian gods: elsewhere in the *Odyssey*, Athena uses the touch of a wand to transform Odysseus into an old beggar (XIII. 429–33) and back to his customary form again (XVI. 172). But from Homeric epic onwards, it was a characteristic, almost inevitable, accessory of the witch Circe. In Valerius Flaccus' *Argonautica*, a first-century AD Roman epic, the goddess Venus, temporarily assuming the form of Circe, makes sure to equip herself with colourful clothes and a *magica ... virga* (Val. Fl. VII. 210–12). In ancient art Medea is likewise frequently represented with a magic wand.

23. The picture is admittedly confusing, and the respective functions of the two devices are not altogether clear, but attempts exclusively to locate the metamorphic power in either the drugs or the wand are probably misguided. So, for example, Stanford (1945), following up his own annotation on *Od*. X. 238–39, dismisses Circe's wand as a mere stick to manage her menagerie — a view that finds approval with Yarnall (1994), p. 12. Other critics, by contrast, have confined the transformative magic to the wand alone. De Jong (2001), p. 259 ascribes the confusion to Homer's conflation of two distinct motifs: giving food which makes men forgetful (clearly one of the functions of the drugs here as 236 makes clear; cf. the effects of the Lotus fruit at *Od*. IX. 92–97), and the changing of human form through the touch of a magic wand (cf. Athena's transformation of Odysseus at *Od*. XIII. 429–33 and XVI. 172, discussed above n. 22). Be that as it may, the reversion of Odysseus' companions to human form at X. 391–97 is clearly accomplished by the administration of drugs (though, again, the procedure may be compound, as a wand is mentioned earlier at 389).

24. The seminal discussion is Skulsky (1981), pp. 10–23.

25. Apollonius' treatment is discussed below; for Ovid's, see, e.g., Yarnall (1994), 87–91.

26. The endeavour of Buxton (2009) to challenge the view that Proteus and Circe represent 'fringe' phenomena that operate in contrast to 'the poem's magic-free, anthropomorphic centre' does not compel. Adducing Odysseus' Cretan tales (in which he hides his true identity, or, as Buxton would have it, 'can change himself [...] into many different men': p. 43), Athena's alteration of his appearance, and a dream-vision by Penelope in which an eagle speaks in a human voice as evidence for 'the presence of metamorphosis at the heart of Ithaca' (p. 44), on a par, that is, with Proteus and Circe, amounts to special pleading.

27. The relative scarcity of metamorphoses in Homer has, in the past, served classicists as evidence for their belief in the inherent superiority of the Western (literary) imagination over and against the bodies of myth from, say, ancient Mesopotamia and Amazonia, which sport, in the words of Griffin (1980), an 'exuberant and grotesque play of fantasy' (p. 177), in which 'coherence and rationality are frankly abandoned in favour of shape-changing, incest, friendly animals, and a sequence of events which appears arbitrary and inconsequential' (p. 176). Griffin is, admittedly, reacting to the rather more positive endorsement of the non-Greek material by his Hellenist colleague Kirk (1970), who saw it as more creative and imaginative than what Homer offers.

28. On this difference see Kullmann (1985). See also Edwards (1985), p. 217, castigating Griffin (1977) for downplaying the extent of immortalization in the *Odyssey* — a critique that can now be extended to Forbes Irving (1990), p. 10.

29. The lone instance in the *Iliad*, and an obviously exceptional case, is Zeus' immortalized cupbearer Ganymede, mentioned at *Il*. XX. 231–35.

30. It is worth noting in passing two Homeric passages featuring non-human petrification (the case of Niobe is discussed in more detail below). Both transformations — of a snake in *Iliad* II, and of a ship in *Odyssey* XIII — are presented as divine signs by which Zeus and Poseidon respectively send messages to a human constituency. In the *Iliad*, Odysseus recalls to his comrades that, prior to the expedition, Zeus had sent forth and petrified a snake, yet not before the beast had devoured a sparrow and her eight nestlings. The portent was explained by the seer Calchas as indicating that the Greeks would conquer Troy in the tenth year of the siege (*Il*. II. 307–29).

In the *Odyssey* Poseidon petrifies the ship of the Phaeacians, which had, against his wishes, provided his archenemy Odysseus with safe passage to Ithaca. Alcinous, king of the Phaeacians, interprets the startling incident as the fulfilment of an oracle uttered by his father long ago (*Od.* xiii. 125–84).

31. Schmitz (2001).

32. Richardson (1993), p. 340.

33. Indeed, the rock formation on Sipylus was famous in historical times, and is mentioned at Pausanias I. 21. 3. The later text explains Achilles' statement that Niobe's grief finds expression even after petrifaction: see our discussion of the Pausanian passage in the Introduction to Part II.

34. Griffin (1986), p. 53; Richardson (1993), p. 342.

35. Cf. Nagy (1990), pp. 197–98, suggesting, *inter alia*, that the epithet παλαίφατος ('spoken of a long time ago') is 'a self-conscious poetic allusion to a genre other than epic'. On παλαίφατος, see also our discussion of Palaephatus below.

36. Buxton (2009), pp. 46–47.

37. Scholion on Homer, *Od.* xix. 512, citing Pherecydes and other unidentified sources. The name Aedon would be a personification of ἀηδών (nightingale).

38. Nagy (1996), p. 7, puts 'inadvertently' in quotation marks. See the discussion of Russo et al. (1993), p. 100.

39. Forbes Irving (1990), p. 13, with a catalogue of the plays in n. 20.

40. Forbes Irving (1990), p. 16: 'There is a reluctance to present grotesque events on the actual stage, whether in the sense of indecorous or in the sense of fantastic and magical actions' though such an event may have featured in Aeschylus' *Toxotides* and Euripides' *Melanippe* (p. 16 n. 33).

41. *Ars Poetica* 185–88. Horace is here essentially reiterating Aristotle's stricture at *Poetics* 15.2.

42. For discussion, see Griffith (1983), pp. 198–99. The story of Io also receives extensive coverage in Aeschylus' *Suppliants* (see Murray (1958)) and Sophocles' *Inachus*, which was in all likelihood a satyr-play: see Sutton (1979) and, for the surviving fragments, basic discussion, English translation, and more recent bibliography Lloyd-Jones, (1996), pp. 112–35.

43. Dodds (1960), pp. 235–36; Mossman (1995), pp. 194–202.

44. Cf. Scholion on Aristophanes, *Birds*, 100: Ἐν γὰρ τῷ Τηρεῖ Σοφοκλῆς ἐποίησεν αὐτὸν ἀπωρνιθωμένον καὶ τὴν Πρόκνην ('In Sophocles' *Tereus*, he and Procne are turned into birds').

45. In terms of the developed myth, the Homeric version, discussed above, is eccentric in many respects; Sophocles either invents or adheres to the canonical version.

46. See, e.g., Dobrov (1997), p. 128, suggesting that the three figures appeared on the ἐκκύκλημα (theatrical machine). Aristophanes' mention at *Birds*, 100–01 (quoted and discussed below) of the appearance of Tereus' beak in the Sophoclean tragedy is far more likely to come from a physical alteration (to the actor's mask) than from the messenger's description of the transmogrified Thracian king.

47. At times the critique itself may have arisen as a marginal gloss or later addition. See e.g. Euripides, *Helen*, 257–58 (widely considered spurious), where Helen herself flatly denies that any women ever gave birth to a bird's egg; and she rejects the story that this was her mode of birth, arising from the union of Leda and Zeus in the form of a swan.

48. Buxton (2009), p. 63 and p. 62; Forbes Irving (1990), p. 15.

49. Eagleton (2003), p. 280.

50. See e.g. Aeschylus, *Agamemnon*, 1140–45, Sophocles, *Electra*, 103–09 and 145–49, Euripides, *Helen*, 1107–16, and [Euripides], *Rhesus*, 546–50. Note in each case the presence of poetological terminology as well as the emphasis on murder and grief.

51. For the myth's tremendous history of reception, both in later classical literature and beyond, see Gildenhard and Zissos (2007). Only with the Romantics has the bird regained its innocence: see e.g. Samuel Coleridge, who, in 'The Nightingale' (1798), calls up only to reject as untrue and unnatural the mythic aetiology of the tragic songbird: 'And hark! the Nightingale begins its song | "Most musical, most melancholy" bird! | A melancholy bird? Oh! idle thought! | In Nature there is nothing melancholy. [...] My Friend, and thou, our Sister! we have learnt | A different lore: we may not thus profane | Nature's sweet voices, always full of love | And joyance! 'Tis

the merry Nightingale | That crowds and hurries, and precipitates | With fast thick warble his delicious notes.'

52. Bakhtin (1981), p. 113.

53. Cf. Hunter (2005), pp. 2–3.

54. Modern critics sometimes identify the tradition spawned by the *Catalogue*, in contradistinction to that of Homeric epic, as 'feminine' in its focus and concerns; cf. Pausanius' characterization of the *Catalogue* as 'an epic in the honour of women' (Pausanias, I. 43; III. 24).

55. Cf. Barchiesi (2005), pp. cviii–cix, describing it as 'un poema collettivo incentrato sulle genealogie degli eroi greci e sulla loro origine, legata a incontri sessuali fra gli dei e le donne dei tempi antichi'.

56. Hunter (2005), p. 1. As such, the *Catalogue* already features 'the same general principle as Pseudo-Apollodorus' book, with systematic exposition of the great genealogies': West (1985), p. 299.

57. Hesiod, *The Shield, Catalogue of Women, Other Fragments*, ed. and trans. by G. W. Most (Cambridge, MA: Loeb Classical Library, 2007), fr. 1 (pp. 40–43). For text and commentary see also *Fragmenta Hesiodea*, ed. by R. Merkelbach and M. L. West (Oxford: Oxford University Press, 1967) [= MW]; and M. Hirschberger, *Gynaikōn katalogos und Megalai Ēhoiai: ein Kommentar zu den Fragmenten zweier hesiodeischer Epen* (Munich: K. G. Saur, 2004) [= H].

58. In antiquity, the *Catalogue* was regarded as a continuation of the *Theogony* and was evidently transmitted as part of the latter poem until they were separated, perhaps in response to the requirements of an emergent book trade; the identification of the *Catalogue* as a separate poem seems to have occurred no later than the Hellenistic Age: Hunter (2005), p. 1.

59. Haubold (2005), p. 96 well notes the poem's 'fondness for rupturing the chronological fabric of the story by introducing narratives of metamorphosis'.

60. Alcyone: 10 Most = 10a MW = 5 H; Atalanta: 51 Most = 72 MW; Io: 72 Most = 124 MW.

61. 145 Most = 205 MW = 95 H.

62. Periclymenus: 31 Most = 33(a) MW = 25 H; Mestra: Fr. 70 Most = 43(b) MW.

63. Europa: 89 Most = 140 MW; Caenis: 165 Most = 87 MW; another work ascribed to Hesiod, the *Melampodia*, contained the story of Tiresias' sex changes (from man to woman and back again) in the wake of his arbitration of the dispute between Zeus and Hera over which sex experiences the greater amount of pleasure during orgasm: Forbes Irving (1990), pp. 12–13. For transformations involving sex-change in Hellenistic times see O'Hara (1996) and Gärtner (2007).

64. 155 Most = 204 MW.

65. See the influential discussion of Lafaye (1904), pp. 21–22.

66. Segal (1968), p. 429.

67. See conveniently Clare (2002), pp. 9–32 and *passim*.

68. Kenney (1982), p. 433.

69. Buxton (2009), p. 110.

70. Kirk (1970), pp. 227–28.

71. Bing (1988), p. 75.

72. For Theodorus we have the testimony of ps.-Probus on Virgil, *Georgics*, I. 399 that he was a source for one of Ovid's extended account of the Halcyon myth in *Met.* XI: see further Chapter 1 (Gildenhard and Zissos) in this volume.

73. Accessible to Anglophone readers in the translation of F. Celoria, *The Metamorphoses of Antoninus Liberalis: A Translation with Commentary* (London and New York: Routledge, 1992).

74. The text is available in Most's Loeb edition of Hesiod (194b = 256 MW; p. 270), whose translation we cite.

75. On the dubious evidence for earlier collections of metamorphoses, see Lafaye (1904), 24–27.

76. The widespread use of the now inevitable terms deriving from μεταμορφόω (including, of course, μεταμόρφωσις, 'metamorphosis') is not found until well into the Roman period.

77. The *Suda* reports an opus in five books; Gow and Scholfield (1953), p. 206, believe this mistaken, as Antoninus Liberalis cites tales from only Books 1 to 4.

78. The fragments are conveniently gathered in Gow and Scholfield (1953).

79. Myers (1994), p. 23.

80. See e.g. Hutchinson (2008) on P. Oxy. 4711, of anonymous authorship, but potentially pre-Ovidian, which contains fragments of a poem consisting of tales of transformation: the

surviving evidence points to 'fairly short accounts', which are 'formally unjoined' (p. 207). Both characteristics, i.e. brevity of the individual tale and catalogue-like listing, are important to bear in mind as background and foil for Ovid's *Metamorphoses*. On P. Oxy. 4711 see also Bernsdorff (2007).

81. Asker (2001), p. 12.

82. Henderson (1992), pp. 312–13.

83. For a full discussion of the evidence, see Luzzatto (2012).

84. For stimulating discussions see Silk (2000) and Buxton (2009).

85. For the custom of comedy to employ choruses dressed up as animals see Rothwell (2007).

86. In reference to the overall scheme, Bowie (1993), p. 177 well observes that *Birds* 'bases itself on myth-types that promise regeneration and new beginnings: foundation myths, cosmogony, and even Gigantomachy and Zeus' succession. But [...] the basic message of the myths is subverted, and their artificial nature laid bare. The foundation of Νεφελοκοκκυγία is not only a fantastic impossibility for reasons physiological and physical, it is also not a solution to the problems it is supposed to resolve: rather, it becomes a restatement of the problem in a different form.'

87. Sophocles' *Tereus* is again signalled, albeit indirectly, at 281–82, discussed below.

88. Griffith (1987), p. 60.

89. Strictly speaking, of course, Tereus' human personality should not survive the metamorphosis so completely, nor should he still be alive in avian form so many centuries (according to conventional mythological chronologies) after his human existence.

90. Cf. Tereus' apology for his scruffy plumage, attributed to moulting, at 105–06.

91. At 209–23, for example, Procne obediently appears at his bidding and sings.

92. *Birds*, 1330–34 indicates vaguely that the wings are taken from birds (dead or alive?); the verb πτερώσεις (1334) could mean that Peisetaerus attaches them himself.

93. The Scholion on Aristophanes, *Birds*, 281 informs us that Philocles' tragedy, part of a tetralogy known as the Πανδιονίς was entitled Τηρεὺς ἢ Ἔποψ.

94. So the Scholion on Aristophanes, *Birds*, 667: Ἑταιρίδιον πρόσεισι, τὰ ἄλλα μὲν κεκαλλωπισμένον, τὴν δὲ κεφαλὴν ὄρνιθος ἔχον ὡς ἀηδόνος ['The young hetaira advances, beautified all over, and having the head of a bird, like a nightingale'].

95. See the collection of papers edited by Buxton (2002).

96. Fragments B 16 and B 15 Diels-Kranz (*Die Fragmente der Vorsokratiker, griechisch-deutsch*, ed. and trans. by H. Diels and W. Kranz, 6th edn (Berlin: Weidmann, 1951–52)). Convenient access to the fragments of Xenophanes is provided by, e.g., Lesher (1992).

97. Forbes Irving (1990), p. 1.

98. Herodotus, *Histories*, I. 1–5.

99. Patterson (2010), p. 55, points out that the effort Thucydides makes in refuting these arguments 'suggests that he was fighting a well-entrenched position'.

100. Sophocles is the earliest source directly to link Tereus to Thrace; earlier traditions make him a hero from Phocis. His cult was located in Megara (Pausanias I. 41. 8). Pseudo-Apollodorus neatly reconciles the rival traditions by having Tereus rule in Thrace and making Daulis the place where he nearly caught up with the fleeing Procne and Philomela, and so the place of the triple apornesosis (*Library*, III. 14. 8). For a discussion of the various socio-political forces operating on the debate, see Patterson (2010), pp. 55–56.

101. No surviving Greek poet mentions the 'bird of Daulia', but various Latin poets do, beginning with Catullus, 65. 13–14.

102. See further Gomme (1956), p. 90.

103. The currency of such rationalizing procedures is suggested by the reference to them at Plato, *Phaedrus*, 229c–e: Socrates speaks of the revision of mythological tales according to probability (τὸ εἰκός), resulting in 'solutions' (λύσεις) that eliminate the incredible aspects.

104. *Fragmente der Griechischen Historiker*, 1 F 27.

105. On the name and ancient biographical information, see Stern (1996), pp. 1–7.

106. Stern (1996), pp. 1–7, and Santoni (2000), pp. 9–42, discuss the contents, likely date, and the history of transmission. The precise thrust of his treatise remains a matter of controversy. See e.g. Stern (2002) or Brodersen (2005), who argues that Palaephatus attacks secondary figures of myth to enhance believability in the Olympian divinities.

107. For discussion, and the wider intellectual background of musings on the relation of words (or names) and things, see Santoni (2000), pp. 23–24.

108. A recent proponent of such a historicizing ('neo-Palaephatian') approach to myth can be found in Bernal (1987), who also proceeds on the premise that mythic tales retain some traces of real events that can be identified and turned into the basis of history. Critiques include Hall (1996), who points out, among other things, that Bernal is in many ways a throwback to a kind of myth-exegesis in vogue in the nineteenth century (but since archived as naïve) and Morales (2007), pp. 14–18 ('Kernels of Truth').

109. Thus Heraclitus the Paradoxographer, who dates to the late first or early second century AD, wrote a treatise entitled *On Unbelievable Tales* — like Palaephatus, though with a more extensive range of critical techniques. See Stern (2003), which contains an introduction and translation of the text, as well as a commentary.

110. Next to nothing is known about his life; on the basis of the available evidence, it is difficult to be more precise than that he lived around 300 BC: see Winiarczyk (2002), pp. 1–10.

111. Seznec (1953), p. 12, mentioning Clement of Alexandria's citation of Euhemerus (*Patrologia Graeca*, VIII. 152) in declaring to pagans that 'Those to whom you bow were once men like yourself'.

112. Winiarczyk (2002), p. 136.

113. Recent contributions to a vast bibliography on the subject include Burkert (2005), Schmitz and Bettenworth (2009) and Jones (2010). It is worth mentioning that 'hero' (*heros*) is a Greek notion, bridging the divide between mortal and immortal in a way that is culturally quite specific: it has no lexical equivalent in Latin. Winiarczyk (2002) uses the (Euhemeristic) paraphrase *homines pro diis culti* (Appendix 1).

114. For Ennius' *Euhemerus* see Winiarczyk (1994) and (2002), pp. 119–35; for his *Scipio*, Bosworth (1999), pp. 10–11.

115. Gildenhard (2011), pp. 373–84.

116. *Tragicorum Graecorum Fragmenta, Vol. 4: Sophocles*, edited by S. Radt (Göttingen: Vandenhoeck & Ruprecht, 1977), pp. 437–38.

117. Ps.-Plutarch, *De Vita Homeri*, VI. 618.

118. Pinotti (1989).

119. Vanotti (2007), pp. 20–32 ('Il genere paradossografico'), esp. 20–21; Stierle (2003), pp. 25–50 (on Dante's figure of Odysseus and its significance for Petrarch). See more generally Hall (2008).

120. His natural science figures prominently in Chapter 2 (Sonia Macrì).

121. For the intersections, which resulted in works of a paradoxographical nature entering into the Aristotelian *corpus*, see Vanotti (2007). For the (pitiful) surviving remains see the editions by Westermann (1839), Keller (1877), and Giannini (1966). Studies include: Ziegler (1949); Giannini (1963) (1964) and, especially, Schepens and Delcroix (1996), with ample further bibliography.

122. Wiseman (2004).

123. For a survey of the data see Suerbaum (2002) with the reviews by Gildenhard (2003) and Feeney (2005). The apparent absence and the eventual emergence of literary traditions at Rome have been the focus of much debate in recent years. Apart from Suerbaum (2002), contributions include Horsfall (1994), Feeney (1998), Habinek (1998) (2005), Rüpke (2000), Wiseman (2004), Goldberg (2005), and Gildenhard (2010).

124. See e.g. Teuffel (1870), p. 1: 'Den Römern fehlte die Beweglichkeit, Vielseitigkeit und die Phantasie der Hellenen; ihre Vorzüge liegen in der Nüchternheit und Schärfe des Denkens, der Festigkeit und Ausdauer des Willens' ['The Romans lacked the mobility, diversity, and the imagination of the Greeks; their talents lie in the soberness and acuity of thought, the firmness and perseverance of will'] and Simcox (1883), p. 3: 'Other differences less intelligible to us were not less weighty: the volcanic character of the western plain of central Italy, the want of a fall to the coast (which caused some of the water-courses to form marshes, and made the Tiber a terror to the Romans for its floods), told in ways as yet untraced on the character of the inhabitants. For one thing, the ancient worship of Febris and Mefitis indicates a constant liability to fever; then the air of Greece is lighter than the air of Italy, and this may be the reason that it was more inspiring.'

125. See Martin (1979) (1994) (1997), Flaig (1993), and Gotter (2008) for comparative studies of Greek and Roman society and culture in the archaic and classical (or early and middle republican)

periods. Their insights have yet to find the resonance they deserve among scholars of literature and literary history.

126. Flaig (1995) (2003), pp. 49–68, Flower (1996).

127. Gildenhard (2010), pp. 160–64, with further bibliography, in particular Hölkeskamp (1999).

128. See e.g. Wiseman (1998).

129. Gruen (1991), pp. 6–51 ('The Making of the Trojan Legend'); cf. Erskine (2001).

130. For incisive and complementary discussions of this complex phenomenon see Flaig (1999) and Gotter (2000).

131. Ovid includes the myths in *Met.* xv. 547–621, together with the transformation of Romulus' lance into a tree. For this stretch of his epic see Hardie (2002c).

132. For the presence of the motif in Augustan literature outside Ovid's *Metamorphoses*, see Zgoll (2004).

133. Hutchinson (1988), p. 334 with reference to Veyne (1983). We agree, but would distance ourselves from the phrase 'by this period' if it is meant to imply a progressive development from superstitious belief to enlightened scepticism. As our introductions try to show, the credibility of different kinds of transformative change depends on — and varies in accordance with — a variety of factors and cannot be easily mapped onto a story of progress.

134. For this distinction between Roman state religion and Roman religion more generally, see Bendlin (2000), further Gildenhard (2011), pp. 246–54.

135. See e.g. *de Haruspicum Responso* 62 with Gildenhard (2011), pp. 342–43.

136. On Varro and his *Antiquitates Rerum Divinarum* see Cardauns (1976) (1978). It is important to stress that limited interference is not the same as saying that interference was non-existent: see Gildenhard (2009). Cicero notably innovated by importing religious figures of thought prevalent in literary discourse but alien to the protocols and principles of Rome's civic religion into his political rhetoric: Gildenhard (2011), pp. 246–390. But this kind of dialogue is only possible (and comes into view) if one presupposes (or sees) distinctive spheres in the first place. In a world of 'anything goes' every cultural transaction is equally meaningful (or rather meaningless).

137. For the discovery and cultural status of fiction in the ancient world, see Rösler (1980), Feeney (1993), Gildenhard (2010), pp. 166–67.

138. See Feldherr (2002), pp. 167–68 and (2010), p. 30, further Fucecchi (2009) as well as, more generally, Hardie (1992).

139. See the studies by Classen (1962), (1963) and, more recently, Feeney (1998), pp. 108–10.

140. Gildenhard (2011), p. 255.

141. *Philippic* 1.6. For discussion, see Gildenhard (2011), pp. 351–72.

142. For a satirical view of the phenomenon see Seneca's *Apocolocyntosis*.

143. From *Tristia*, IV. 10. 43–44 it is clear that Ovid was at the very least familiar with Macer's Latin translation of Boeus, if not the original Greek text.

144. Wheeler (1999), p. 21.

145. For commentaries on the entire poem see Bömer (1969–1986), Galasso (2000), and, especially, the new Fondazione Lorenzo Valla edition (2005–) curated by Alessandro Barchiesi: it includes R. Tarrant's Oxford Classical Text, an Italian translation by L. Koch (books I–IV) and G. Chiarini (books V–XV), and a detailed and sophisticated commentary by A. Barchiesi (I–II), A. Barchiesi and G. Rosati (III–IV), G. Rosati (V–VI), E. J. Kenney (VII–IX), J. D. Reed (X–XII) and P. Hardie (XIII–XV). Volumes 1–4 (covering *Met.* I–IX) have appeared so far: see Barchiesi (2005), Barchiesi and Rosati (2007), Rosati (2009), and Kenney (2011).

146. Ingleheart (2010), pp. 98–99 points out that Ovid redefines the *ad mea ... tempora* ['down to my own times'] of the proem (1. 4) as eternity in the sphragis: *perque omnia saecula fama | [...] vivam* ['Through all centuries I shall live in fame'] (XV. 878–79). The most insistent probing of *Ovidius Mythistoricus* is Cole (2008), who argues that Ovid's immediate models were both historiographical: the *Chronica* of Castor of Rhodes and the *De Gente Populi Romani* of Marcus Terentius Varro. See also Wheeler (2002), with a survey of earlier scholarship, including a critique of Schmidt (1991), who denies the value of seeing the *Metamorphoses* as a version of universal history.

147. See, e.g., Due (1974), p. 96; Galinsky (1975), pp. 2–3; Wheeler (1999), p. 21.

148. The announcement of a continuous narrative structure does not imply a straightforward

execution; chronology and time come in for much play in the course of the poem: see e.g. Feeney (1999) and Gildenhard and Zissos (1999a).

149. Hardie (1986), p. 380.

150. Tissol (1997), p. 191.

151. Barkan (1986), p. 27.

152. See e.g. Empedocles B 61 Diels-Kranz: πολλὰ μὲν ἀμφιπρόσωπα καὶ ἀμφίστερνα φύεσθαι, | βουγενῆ ἀνδρόπρωιρα, τὰ δ' ἔμπαλιν ἐξανατέλλειν | ἀνδροφυῆ βούκρανα, μεμειγμένα τῆι μὲν ἀπ' ἀνδρῶν | τῆι δὲ γυναικοφυῆ σκιεροῖς ἠσκημένα γυίοις ['Many creatures arose with double faces and double breasts, offspring of oxen with human faces, and again there sprang up children of men with oxen's heads; creatures, too, in which were mixed some parts from men and some of the nature of women, furnished with sterile members'].

153. On Empedoclean epos and its significance for Roman poetry (especially Lucretius and Ovid) see Hardie (2009).

154. Well discussed by Tissol (1997), p. 192.

155. See the analogy between Jupiter and Augustus at *Met.* xv. 858–60: *Iuppiter arces | temperat aetherias et mundi regna triformis, | terra sub Augusto est; pater est et rector uterque* ['Jupiter controls the citadels in the air, the earth is under the control of Augustus; each one is father and governor'].

156. For more on Pythagoras, see below, pp. 71–72, 75–77. For Pythagoras on the rise of Rome (*Met.* xv. 426–36) see Gildenhard and Zissos (2004), pp. 69–71, challenging prevailing orthodoxies.

157. Asker (2001), p. 2.

158. Hutchinson (1988), p. 329. This is not to deny an interplay between the local and the Panhellenic in Hellenistic literature: see most recently the papers in Cingano (2010).

159. Tissol (1997), pp. 209–14, noting that in Book xiv Ovid reconfigures the narrative of Homer's Circe to make it a vehicle for the presentation of Roman legend; for anticipations of Rome's rise to imperial glory in the opening books see the end of the Apollo and Daphne episode (*Met.* i. 557–67) and Gildenhard and Zissos (2004), pp. 52–53, on the seemingly unmotivated reference to the Capitoline geese at *Met.* ii. 536–39.

160. For 'delocalized' versions of myths in Ovid, see Hinds (1987), p. 85; for Ovid's imperialist rewriting of Greek myth, see Gildenhard and Zissos (2004).

161. Gildenhard and Zissos (2004).

162. See General Introduction, above, pp. 11–16.

163. See *Tristia,* i. 7. 13, cited and discussed in the General Introduction.

164. Skulsky (1981), p. 61. See also Vial (2010), who discusses the variety of thematically affiliated substitutes for genuine metamorphosis that Ovid explores in his poem, not least for the sake of variety.

165. Myers (1994), pp. 42–43.

166. See Schmidt (1991). Ovid himself renders the point explicit after the regeneration of humanity by means of stones. See *Met.* i. 414–15: *inde genus durum sumus experiensque laborum | et documenta damus, qua simus origine nati* ['hence we are a hardy race and experienced in toil and give testimony from what source we are born'].

167. Feeney (1991), p. 194.

168. Cf. Pico della Mirandola's *de Hominis Dignitate* § 5, cited in the General Introduction.

169. For discussions, see Barkan (1986), 24–27, Anderson (1989), Forbes-Irving (1990), pp. 90 and 216–18, and Feldherr (2010) pp. 38–39. In the light of our earlier discussion, it is worth noting that the transformation of the Greek character Lycaon into a wolf (*lupus* in Latin) reveals the essence of this particular human being; as Feldherr suggestively points out, in Ovid 'metamorphosis as cosmic clarification depends on the translation of Greek into Latin' (39).

170. Barkan (1986), p. 27.

171. Ginsberg (1989), p. 228.

172. Feeney (1991), p. 195. In this respect should the father–daughter combination Lycaon–Callisto be subjected to analysis? Is it problematic that Jupiter is associated with both?

173. See e.g. Murray (1998) and Segal (2005).

174. Gildenhard and Zissos (1999b).

175. Fränkel (1945), p. 183.

176. Hughes (1997), p. ix. On this crucial Ovidian thematic, see Anderson (1963), pp. 7–17.

177. See Anderson (1963), p. 10.

178. In an earlier variation on petrification, Ovid has Aglauros, overcome by envy (*invidia*) of her sister, turning into a livid-coloured stone: *sua mens infecerat illam* ['her mind stained the stone'] (II. 832).

179. The permanence of the change to the natural world is signalled by formulae such as *nunc quoque*, and verbs such as *manere* and *durare*. See the section on Ovid's aetiological phraseology in Myers (1994), pp. 63–67.

180. Hughes (1997), p. x. In fact, Ovid's imagery invites the reader to understand the supernatural void as being filled by the Furies: see Gildenhard and Zissos (2007), pp. 12–13 and Feldherr (2010) pp. 238–39.

181. The fundamental ambivalence of nearly all such transformations, the death-in-preservation, bubbles to the surface in the account by Aeneas' host Anius of his daughters' fate. About to become war captives, the four daughters are 'helped' by Bacchus by being transformed into doves — 'if,' Anius observes sardonically, 'destroying in some miraculous fashion can be called helping' (*si miro perdere more | ferre vocatur opem*, XIII. 670–71). This is not an aetiological metamorphosis (the daughters are merely added to a pre-existing species) and the focalization through Anius makes it impossible to know if the daughters' consciousness persisted in their new form, but the father experiences their transformation as annihilation.

182. Skulsky (1981), pp. 34–35.

183. Tissol (1997), p. 176. See also Forbes Irving (1990), pp. 36–37, who observes that Ovid, in contrast to the Alexandrian poets, tends to supplement the concluding *aetion*, by offering some reflection on the continuity of individual human traits in the new form of flora or fauna that emerges.

184. Likewise, e.g., Io (I. 744–45) and Hecuba (XIII. 568–69).

185. A particular poignant case is Callisto, who is transformed into a bear by Juno after having been raped by Jupiter, but retains full human consciousness (*mens antiqua manet*). After a number of years in ursine form Callisto is almost killed by her son Arcas, who only sees the wild beast and not the mother within, before Jupiter takes pity and catasterizes both (*Met.* II. 401–507).

186. There is an oblique analogy at the categorical level between the forms (*formae*) and bodies (*corpora*) of Ovid's opening lines (*Met.* I. 1-2) and Pythagoras' key concepts of souls (*animae*) and bodies (*corpora*), though physical metamorphosis and soul-migration of course constitute fundamentally different paradigms of transformative change.

187. Warner (2002). The same principle informs the significant attention Ovid gives to hybridity and hybrid creatures. The papers in Casanova-Robin (2009) consider both the theme in Ovid and the impact of the *Metamorphoses* on treatments of hybridity in later ages.

188. The allusion is to sixteenth-century vernacular versions of Ovid's *Metamorphoses*, suitably abridged and allegorized, that circulated under the title *Bible des poètes*.

189. Little (1970), p. 347.

190. Feeney (1991), p. 229 with reference to earlier literature in n. 152.

191. For a view of the Old Testament that brings out the striking parallels with Ovid's *Metamorphoses*, see Alter (1981).

192. Feeney (1991), p. 230. This portion of the epic has received much discussion: treatments of particular relevance for our concerns include Graf (1988), pp. 67–68 and Fabre-Serris (2009).

193. *Met.* VIII. 618–19: '*immensa est finemque potentia caeli | non habet et, quidquid superi voluere, peractum est.*'

194. Ovid's faux-critical attitude also comes to the fore in passages where that which beggars belief has nothing to do with miraculous transformations. See e.g. *Met.* VI. 561, where Ovid glosses the report (*fertur*) that Tereus continued to abuse Philomela after the glossectomy with *vix ausim credere* ['I hardly dare believe it'].

195. Nelis (2009).

196. For further examples see Little (1970), p. 359 and Myers (1994), esp. pp. 133–35 and 155–57.

197. For a discussion of earlier views (Fränkel, Otis, Zinn, among others) of how the disquisition of Pythagoras fits into the *Metamorphoses* as a whole (is it the key to the whole work or an incongruous inset?) see Little (1970), who argues that Ovid used the speech to generate an 'impression of unity' (p. 360) that is not designed to withstand close philological scrutiny. More

recently, Schmitz-Emans (2006) has used Ovid's Pythagoras as point of departure for exploring metamorphosis and metempsychosis as two rival models of change.

198. This is only one of many places in the poem when nymphs play a key role in Ovid's cosmos. See further Zissos (1999).

199. *Met.* xv. 416–17.

200. Klein (2009), p. 198 and p. 197.

201. Indeed, Klein, too, instantly deconstructs her analysis and points the way to a better appreciation of the Ovidian agenda when she writes (p. 198) that 'while overtly displaying an opposition between the marvellous in epic and its reduction in the aetiological narrative, the Ovidian text invites us to qualify this opposition and to reconsider the latter's relationship with paradoxographic *mirabilia*.' Chapter 2 below (by Sonia Macrì) takes this invitation up, with specific reference to the lynx-stone and the coral.

202. The effect is often enhanced by etymological word play, which generally speaking indicates an allegiance to the Alexandrian poetic tradition and its characteristic erudition, and which can lend a veneer of 'scientific' veracity to a fantastic metamorphic tale: see Tissol (1997), pp. 171–77.

203. Beagon (2009), p. 289.

204. The Hesiodic influence on Ovid's epic has recently started to receive detailed attention from other perspectives as well: see Hardie (2005), Fletcher (2005), and Ziogas (2011).

205. Feldherr (2010), p. 35.

206. Upward metamorphoses via catasterism or deification (or both) occur with particular frequency in the final two books of the poem (Romulus and Hersilia, Aeneas, Caesar, as well as, prospectively, Augustus), but are not unheard of in earlier parts of the narrative: see Callisto and Arcas in *Met.* ii and Hercules in *Met.* ix.

207. Cf. esp. *Met.* vii. 116: *tantum medicamina possunt*, with reference to the herbs Medea uses to protect Jason from the fire-breathing bulls and 167: *quid enim non carmina possunt?* (Jason speaking, pleading with Medea to rejuvenate his father by ageing himself).

208. See Introduction to Part II.

209. Solodow (1988), p. 163 argues that Pythagoras discusses change rather than metamorphosis.

210. For a suggestive discussion in a wider context — the history of the artist from God to Picasso — see Barolsky (2010), ch. 3: 'Ovid's Protean Epic and Artistic Personae'.

211. For Ovid's artistry and the figure of the artist see e.g. Hardie (2002) and Pavlock (2009).

CHAPTER 1

The Transformations of Ovid's Medea
(*Metamorphoses* VII. 1–424)

Ingo Gildenhard & Andrew Zissos

Introduction

Few figures in ancient myth have provoked such abiding fascination as Medea, the Colchian princess and sorceress who betrayed family and nation out of love for the Greek hero Jason, and then exacted horrific vengeance years later when Jason abandoned her for another woman. Already by the Augustan age in which Ovid wrote, Medea had developed into a complex, sometimes contradictory, literary figure whose textual incarnations spanned virtually all poetic genres and time periods. In her lengthy career in Greek literature, she had been Pindar's vatic advisor, Apollonius Rhodius' anguished young lover, and Euripides' infanticidal mother.[1] She also appeared in the epic *Nostoi*, as well as numerous non-Euripidean tragedies, of which we know next to nothing. The vicissitudes of textual survival have left us even less well informed about Ovid's Roman predecessors — including Ennius, Accius, Pacuvius, Varro of Atax, and many others besides — but Medea will have continued to evolve as a literary figure under these writers as well.[2] And she continues to exercise the imagination.[3]

Medea was a figure of particular interest to Ovid. Prior to her dominating role in one of the longest episodes of the *Metamorphoses* (VII. 1–424), she had featured prominently in two of his epistolary *Heroides* as well as an eponymous tragedy, now lost. *Heroides* XII contains Medea's reaction to the report that Jason has abandoned her, through a letter written on the eve of her infanticide. As Verducci has observed, this epistolary appeal to Jason, through its sweeping retrospective treatment, uniquely permits the Medea of Euripides to speak with the same voice as her younger self in Apollonius Rhodius.[4] *Heroides* VI offers a no less suggestive treatment: Medea is refracted through the thoughts of the Lemnian queen Hypsipyle, Jason's earlier mistress. Hypsipyle emphasizes the destructiveness of her powerful 'barbarian' rival, her verbal slings culminating in a striking fantasy: *Medeae Medea forem!* ['I'd like to be a Medea to Medea!'] (*Her.* VI. 151). Only two lines of Ovid's lost tragedy are preserved, one an ominous warning made by Medea to Jason: '*servare potui; perdere an possim rogas?*' ['I was able to save you; do you think I cannot destroy you?']. In this line we again have hints of the Euripidean Medea, a transplanted alien who wreaks havoc in the Greek domestic sphere — not only in Corinth (where she murders her own children by Jason), but also previously in Thessaly (where she tricks the daughters of Pelias into slaying their father) and subsequently in Athens (where she attempts to murder her stepson Theseus).

Prima facie, the fact that Ovid, after already creating an epistolary and a tragic variant of Medea, both of which show a poet self-consciously striving to accommodate the complexities of Medea's literary tradition, should return to this heroine for yet a third time in his epic *Metamorphoses* is curious, not least since she had arguably little to contribute to his chosen theme: the pre-Ovidian Medea was not an especially metamorphic figure. Her conventional biography, though certainly abounding in gruesome murders and attempts thereat, hardly abounded in transformative feats: her lone exploit was the rejuvenation of Jason's father Aeson. And she herself never experienced metamorphosis, unless we count the quasi-apotheosis she seems to undergo at the end of Euripides' tragedy.[5] To be sure, the capacity to engage in transformative change was not altogether wanting: Medea was, after all, a sorceress, and not just any sorceress — she was niece of the witch Circe, whose celebrated exploits included the transformation of Odysseus' men into pigs.[6] But the fact remains that the pre-Ovidian Medea had but one celebrated metamorphic feat to her credit — and, unlike her divine aunt, she was no 'serial transformer'.

Medea's dominance across such an extended narrative stretch (she 'owns' more than half a book, a privilege she shares, not coincidentally, with Pythagoras) thus calls for critical attention. The top billing she receives suggests that, in spite of her modest metamorphic résumé, Medea is a figure of fundamental importance in Ovid's cosmic history. In this chapter, we would like to argue that this importance resides, ultimately and above all, in her status as a watershed figure in the universal history of transformative change that unfolds in the course of the poem. Specifically, Ovid uses her episode to introduce a crucial new paradigm of the metamorphic. Thus far — and we are nearing the mid-point of the fifteen-book epic — the power to transform has been the exclusive province of the gods. Medea, in contrast, is the first, and by far the most prominent, human agent of transformation in the poem.[7] Within the overall scheme of the epic, what we may call 'the human metamorphic' is comparatively limited by comparison with the divine, but its implications are in many respects more profound. Rather than the spontaneous acts of transformation undertaken by the Olympian gods, the human metamorphic is what we might call 'procedural' in nature. Whereas the divinities tend to achieve the desired result instantaneously by some innate power, which is apparently common to all members of the pantheon, the human metamorphic involves a series of steps that must be carefully performed, typically with a combination of herbs or other natural substances that have been prepared in some fashion.[8] This amounts to a veritable 'technology of transformation' entailing special skills and knowledge (including knowledge of how to invoke supernatural support at key moments). And Medea is the 'poster child' for the human metamorphic in Ovid's epic.

Medea's role as the prime representative for a specific type of magical metamorphosis has important implications for how her presence in the *Metamorphoses* relates to earlier literary treatments (including Ovid's own). The phases of her story that Ovid covers in the *Metamorphoses* are traditional: with varying levels of detail, he follows Medea's career and its ever-shifting geographical location, from Colchis (Medea assists Jason in gaining the fleece) to Thessaly (rejuvenation of Aeson, murder of Pelias), Corinth (infanticidal revenge against Jason's infidelity) and Athens (marriage to Aegeus, attempted murder of Theseus). Within this conventional frame, Ovid concentrates on two periods in particular: Medea's initial love for Jason in Colchis, and, following her relocation to Greece as Jason's bride, her increasingly exuberant practice of witchcraft in Thessaly. In contrast to his earlier versions, Ovid here primarily writes *against* the established canon, above all against the conception of Medea as defined by Euripides and Apollonius Rhodius. As one scholar has recently put it, 'Ovid faced the challenge of making new his favorite mythic figure, of magically rejuvenating and transforming both her and her story.'[9] And it is not least the apparently incongruous juxtaposition of the seemingly youthful maiden with the full-blown witch that enables Ovid to open up, in metaliterary as well as thematic terms, a space for a transformative treatment of his heroine and her literary heritage.

Ovid's re-articulation of Medea's mythic biography has two essential aspects. On the one hand, *Metamorphoses* VII ostentatiously reduces the complex storylines of Euripides and Apollonius to a mere handful of verses, thereby creating space for a metamorphic 'rewrite'; on the other hand, Ovid plays up Medea's comparatively modest metamorphic career by offering a detailed elaboration upon and curious 'multiplication' of her one well-known metamorphic feat, the rejuvenation of Aeson. This emphasis enables him to concentrate on the human metamorphic and its implications, a concentration aided by a 'programmatic' elision of the customary epic divine machinery. The marginalization of the traditional *deorum ministeria* is a noteworthy effect: Ovid resolutely sidelines conventional deities from his account, thereby opening up a narrative space in which magic and sorcery seem to hold sway over both the human and natural realms.

The analogies between thematics and poetics in this narrative stretch endow Medea's activity with a strong allegorical force, as her magical activities are seen to move in step with the epic project of the poet. In this metapoetic scheme the rejuvenation of Aeson in particular, but also the other deeds recounted by Ovid, become symbolically associated with both a novel inflection of Medea's literary biography and a new chapter in Ovid's history of transformative change. As elsewhere in the poem, 'metamorphosis' thus operates simultaneously on a metaphorical as well as a literal level: it is Ovid's mythic material, as much as the transformed objects and life forms featured in his narrative, that undergoes transformative renewal. This renewal manifests itself in a variety of ways, both literal and metaphorical: Ovid vitiates and marginalizes the versions of his predecessors; he concentrates on Medea's performance of rejuvenating magic; and he prolongs the textual lifespan of his heroine by a kind of second-order metamorphism, inventing an extended aerial chariot ride that turns into a catalogue of obscure myths of transformation. Throughout, Ovid re-charts the course of Medea's established mythographic biography: in the *Metamorphoses* she is an interstitial character who lives in the gaps of her own tradition, gaps that are used to supply metamorphic feats and evocations.

But this is not all: Ovid uses Medea's aerial chariot ride to generate what amounts to a negative *mise en abîme* of the *Metamorphoses* itself, a distorting refraction of the compositional principles and poetic vision that inform Ovid's sweeping narrative of cosmic history from chaos to Rome. This rival poetic vision, which foregrounds the topographical at the expense of the chronological, and the local at the expense of the global, implicitly sets Ovid's own literary achievement against that of his Greek predecessors. It thereby constitutes yet another enactment of his imperial poetics, in which the Greek cultural heritage is subordinated to and subsumed by Ovid's overarching vision.

The Medea of the *Metamorphoses*, then, is not only unlike her previous Ovidian incarnations, but radically different from all other treatments in ancient literature. Ovid reinvents his heroine as both agent and embodiment of transformation, at various carefully interwoven and mutually implicated levels. The following, detailed re-reading of her episode will attempt to bring out the various aspects of her metamorphic powers and metapoetic status.[10]

Metaliterary Transformation: Model Compression, Model Deflation

The tale of the Argonauts, the Greek heroes who sailed to Colchis in quest of the golden fleece, was among the most widely treated myths in ancient literature. Already in Homer the myth is said to be of interest to all (Ἀργὼ πᾶσι μέλουσα, *Od.* XII. 70), suggesting its prominence from no later than the archaic period, and perhaps indicating the existence of an epic *Argonautica* prior to the *Odyssey*. From no later than Pindar, virtually all writers who treat Medea do so in the context of her relationship with Jason, the Argonauts' leader. That is, Medea became incorporated within the Argonautic legend — and with an increasingly important role. In Pindar's *Pythian* 4, Medea seems to be presented as a goddess, though it is through the machinations of Aphrodite that she falls in love with Jason. She provides a helpful prophecy, instructing him in regard to divine will — an act that entails no familial betrayal, divided loyalties, or similar conflicts. Soon thereafter she became a more active helper, providing the magical means whereby Jason accomplishes the trials set for him by her father Aeetes, as well as helping him take possession of the golden fleece.

Treatments of the tale of Medea and Jason evidently abounded across the generic spectrum in both Greek and Roman literature, but the tradition had coalesced around a composite storyline by Ovid's day. As already noted, two ancient texts in particular defined that storyline for later authors: Euripides' *Medea* and Apollonius Rhodius' *Argonautica*.[11] The latter emphasized Medea's love for Jason and assigned her the decisive role in the Greek heroes' acquisition of the golden fleece.[12] In similar fashion, the Euripidean tragedy decisively defined the post-Argonautic Medea. The horrific revenge plot may not have been entirely original to Euripides, but it was his heroine who became the inevitable point of reference for subsequent treatments.[13] As her tradition developed, and her assistance of Jason became magnified, Medea took on pronounced metaliterary attributes, emerging as a potent embodiment of generic rupture. Above all, her decisive role in Apollonius Rhodius' *Argonautica* turned epic standards on their head, in one of the most extended bouts of generic self-interrogation in all of ancient literature.[14]

Ovid's initial treatment in *Metamorphoses* VII can be seen as responding to Apollonius' epic in particular, and above all the much-admired third book, which recounts Medea's awakening love for Jason, and the latter's performance, with her magical assistance, of the deadly trials set by Aeetes. The Ovidian engagement is characteristically complex, addressing a number of poetic issues raised by the model. In particular, Ovid humorously expands and elaborates upon Apollonius' subtle exploration of deflationary, anti-epic forces, which reaches its effective climax and resolution in his third book. Other parts of the Hellenistic epic are subjected to severe compression. Ovid opens his own 'Argonautica' with an ostentatiously reductive rendering of Apollonius' first two books (*Met.* VII. 1–6):

> Iamque fretum Minyae Pagasaea puppe secabant,
> perpetuaque trahens inopem sub nocte senectam
> Phineus visus erat, iuvenesque Aquilone creati
> virgineas volucres miseri senis ore fugarant,
> multaque perpessi claro sub Iasone tandem
> contigerant rapidas limosi Phasidos undas.

[And now the Minyans [*sc.* the Argonauts] were plowing the sea in their Pagasaean vessel [*sc.* the Argo]. They had seen Phineus, drawing out his helpless old age in perpetual night; the sons of Boreas had driven away the maidenly birds [*sc.* the Harpies] from the mouth of the wretched old man. Having experienced many travails under their illustrious leader Jason, they at last reached the swift waters of the muddy Phasis.]

The narrative opens in the vein of an epic *Argonautica*. But the classic epic material, of adventure on the high seas, which occupies the first two books and 2600 verses of Apollonius Rhodius, is dispatched in a mere handful of lines. Various critics have pointed out the epic resonance of *multa ... perpessi* ['having experienced many travails'] (VII. 5) which harks back to the programmatic opening of the *Odyssey* (πολλὰ δ' ὅ γ' ἐν πόντῳ πάθεν ἄλγεα [...], Hom. *Od.* 1. 4). But the Ovidian phrase, unlike the Homeric, alludes to elided narrative: it signals not a programme but a *praeteritio*. The subtle use of tenses — Ovid unexpectedly switches from imperfect (*secabant*) to pluperfects (*visus erat, fugarant, contigerant*) before continuing in the present tense as he turns to the events in Colchis (VII. 7: *dumque adeunt regem* [...]) — and the adverb *tandem* vault the narrative present beyond the account of the sea-voyage. This is epic storytelling denied.[15]

Before moving on, it is worth pointing to some further suggestive touches in this initial *praeteritio* of an elaborated epic narrative. A central programmatic preoccupation of the *Metamorphoses*, signalled in the exordium, is the aesthetic tension arising from the conflicting demands of a *carmen perpetuum* (referring to large-scale epic composition) and a *carmen deductum* (referring to smaller-scale poetry characterized by Alexandrian refinement). With respect to the present passage, Barchiesi has argued that *perpetua*, the first word of the second verse, is a programmatic echo of the exordium.[16] A second suggestive touch, also noted by Barchiesi, is the muddiness of the Phasis. This is not a quality attributed to this river elsewhere, but the image of the muddy waterway belonged to the system of poetological metaphors that Callimachus bequeathed to Roman poets. It is famously invoked at the end of the *Hymn to Apollo* (108–09), in a derisive reference to large-scale epic composition. At the precise moment Ovid bypasses a detailed epic account, he appears to mark this programmatic choice with appropriate, programmatically charged terminology. Finally, given that the Telchines appear in an unflattering light later in the episode (VII. 365–67), the contours of an overarching allusive strategy begin to come into view: since Callimachus' *Aetia*, the Telchines, mythological sorcerers conventionally located on the island of Rhodes, had been associated with the advocacy of large-scale epic poetry, and this association was extended, at least in the view of ancient critics, to Callimachus' supposed arch-rival Apollonius who hailed from Rhodes. In his Argonautic 'rewrite', then, Ovid recasts Apollonius' epic in a Callimachean key — in what amounts to a brilliant spoof on a heated aesthetic controversy in Hellenistic poetics.

Following the more extended treatment of events recorded in Apollonius' third book at *Met.* VII. 7–148, Ovid reverts to a pattern of radical compression. The fourth and final book of the Hellenistic *Argonautica* is dispensed with almost as efficiently as the first two, with only Medea's quelling of the fleece-guarding dragon with magical herbs treated in any detail (*Met.* VII. 149–58):[17]

> pervigilem superest herbis sopire draconem,
> qui crista linguisque tribus praesignis et uncis
> dentibus horrendus custos erat arboris aureae.
> hunc postquam sparsit Lethaei gramine suci
> verbaque ter dixit placidos facentia somnos,
> quae mare turbatum, quae concita flumina sistunt,
> somnus in ignotos oculos ubi venit, et auro
> heros Aesonius potitur spolioque superbus
> muneris auctorem secum, spolia altera, portans
> victor Iolciacos tetigit cum coniuge portus.

[It remained to put to sleep the ever-wakeful dragon who, conspicuous for his crest, his triple-forked tongue and curving fangs, was the dreadful guardian of the gold-laden tree. After Medea sprinkled upon him the juice of Lethean herbs, and thrice uttered sleep-inducing words, words that calm turbulent seas and fast-flowing rivers, then did unknown sleep steal upon the dragon's eyes; and the Aesonian hero [*sc.* Jason] took possession of the golden fleece, and proud of this booty, and taking with him further spoils in the form of she who was the originator of his success, he returned in victory with his new bride to the Iolchian port.]

Ovid thus provides not so much a retelling as a précis of the greater part of Apollonius' *Argonautica*, signalling *en passant* the three books dealing with the properly epic subject matter of adventure on the high seas. With this compound gesture of compression, Ovid signals a confrontation with the canonical authority of his Hellenistic predecessor. That leaves Book III, which, as already noted, is not scaled back as radically as the others, and indeed is faithfully reproduced in some parts.[18] Apollonius famously made Jason's heroic stature a central concern, in part by making Medea's magical assistance essential to the success of the mission.[19] Even characters within the text express doubt over the heroic credentials of a figure so dependent upon others. But, as Hunter has argued, Jason's heroism seems ultimately to be confirmed.[20] After an initial flirtation with the idea of an inadequate hero, Apollonius redeems Jason in the climactic concluding scenes of the third book, when the Greek hero undertakes the trials set for him by Aeetes. The martial vigour demonstrated by Jason in the course of the trials rings true to his epic pedigree, in spite of Medea's initial assistance. The tone is set by the bravura account of Jason wrestling the deadly, fire-breathing bronze bulls into submission (*Arg.* III. 1305–14).

Ovid's account of Jason's trials clearly harks back to Apollonius' version, as close initial echoes on the level of detail confirm.[21] And, following in the footsteps of his Hellenistic predecessor, Ovid launches an interrogation of Jason's heroic stature. Unlike Apollonius, however, Ovid does not ultimately validate his hero. Indeed, the very scenes in which Jason establishes his epic credentials in the Hellenistic epic are humorously deflated in the *Metamorphoses*. The reworking of Jason's struggle with the fire-breathing bulls (VII. 115–19) is a case in point. The confrontation is prepared emotionally by the horror of Jason's comrades, anxious witnesses to the proceedings, at the sight of the formidable beasts (VII. 115). But the dramatic tension is immediately undermined by a parenthetical reminder that the awesome power of Medea's magic has pre-empted any danger (*tantum medicamina possunt!*, 116). And the nominally heroic confrontation with the bulls unravels into absurdity when Jason pacifies the monstrous creatures by 'stroking their pendulous dewlaps with his daring right hand' (*pendulaque audaci mulcet palearia dextra*, 117). The epic resonance of *audaci ... dextra*, which stands in rather marked contrast to the verb *mulcet* ('strokes') underscores the bathos of the scene. Instead of Apollonius' account of Jason heroically wrestling the ferocious, flame-belching bulls to the ground, Ovid's hero strokes them into docility: the dewlaps, the only 'cuddly' part of a bull's anatomy, are a magnificently deflating touch. Shortly thereafter, when Jason faces combat with the earth-born men, the poet affords Medea an unprecedented 'real-time' magical intervention (*carmen | auxiliare canit*, 'she chanted reinforcing spells', VII. 137–38), a supernatural doubling-down that emphasizes her role while once again undercutting Jason's heroic stature at a critical moment.[22]

Further examples could be adduced, but these should suffice to demonstrate that the very scenes of vigorous epic action by which Apollonius ultimately confirmed Jason's heroic credentials are ruthlessly and humorously deflated by Ovid. The impression of success without heroic toil is reinforced by repeated reminders of Medea's intervention, as well as the ironic deployment of epic language and trivializing similes. At the end of the quest narrative, with the Argonauts returning in triumph to Thessaly, Jason is described as 'glorying in his spoils' (VII. 156: *spolio... superbus*) and as a 'victor' (VII. 158: *victor*). Pride in valiant deeds is intrinsic to heroic psychology in ancient epic, and Ovid specifically recalls Virgil's Hercules;[23] here, though, as Anderson well observes, 'inasmuch as Jason himself has accomplished so little, the adjective *superbus* causes smiles.'[24]

With respect to the tragic literary inheritance, later events in Corinth, made canonical by Euripides' *Medea*, are subjected to the same treatment as Apollonius' first two books. Medea's abandonment by Jason and her consequent revenge, involving the murder of both his new bride and her own children, is likewise radically compressed (*Met.* VII. 394–99):

> sed postquam Colchis arsit nova nupta venenis
> flagrantemque domum regis mare vidit utrumque,
> sanguine natorum perfunditur inpius ensis,
> ultaque se male mater Iasonis effugit arma.
> hinc Titaniacis ablata draconibus intrat
> Palladias arces [...]

[But when the new bride had been consumed by the Colchian's [*sc.* Medea's] poisons, and the sea on either side had seen the king's residence ablaze, and the impious sword had been soaked with her sons' blood, then the mother, having ill-avenged herself, fled from Jason's arms. Borne hence by the Sun-god's dragons, she entered the citadel of Pallas [*sc.* Athens].]

Medea's anguished decision to commit infanticide, her drawn-out and excruciating transition from *dolor* to *nefas*, is reduced to a dispassionate shorthand, robbed of psychological detail and motivation.[25] The initial *sed postquam* instantly vaults the narrative present beyond the events of Euripidean tragedy, which had come to be etched in ancient literary consciousness. Once again, the poet offers a breathless *praeteritio* of well-known material — material that had fascinated Ovid himself in his earlier work, to say nothing of other writers.[26]

To take stock: Ovid compresses and deflates the treatments of his two most prominent literary predecessors, from the two major genres that treated the myth of Jason and Medea, epic and tragedy. All this signals a movement against the inherited tradition. Inasmuch as such strategies open up a space for alternatives, they indicate a striving for novelty within this notoriously over-written literary context.[27] His reductive intertextual engagements permit Ovid to transform Medea's story in line with his principal narrative theme.

Metaphysical Transformation: The Human Metamorphic

Another prominent element in Ovid's transformative strategy is Medea's interior monologue (VII. 11–71), the first of the epic.[28] This is generally read as affording genuine psychological insight into Medea's character. Kenney, for example, sees it as embodying Ovid's characteristic fascination for 'the psychology of love in people who are the victims of their own passions, in particular women faced with the decision whether or not to commit a crime'.[29] A popular critical approach has been to juxtapose the ostensibly naïve and innocent young woman who expresses her feelings in this soliloquy with the apparently more sinister figure, a full-blown witch and infanticide, that emerges after Medea has taken up residence in Greece. This approach takes its cue from scholarship on Apollonius Rhodius, and has at its root the Hellenistic poet's fashioning of the second half of his epic as a 'preparation' for the events of Euripides' *Medea*, which had acquired a canonical status. Over the course of Ovid's episode, so the argument goes, Medea has under-gone a transformation from an innocent, love-struck girl to a wicked sorceress and infanticidal mother. Critical focus has been on psychological exegesis: 'how',

Newlands for one has asked, 'does the trembling maiden become the murderess?'[30] Are these two figures psychologically consistent? Rosner-Siegel detects a progressive 'deterioration' of Medea's character as the episode advances, triggered by specific narrative developments.[31]

Such readings, however, ultimately run into the problem that Medea's monologue does not yield a coherent psychological portrait.[32] Her musings follow a metaliterary rather than a properly psychological logic. Over the course of her soliloquy she undergoes a transformation from a hopelessly naïve young girl, barely able to diagnose her amorous feelings for Jason, to a worldly-wise woman who resolves to insist on a marriage commitment in return for her aid (VII. 46–47), who looks forward to celebrity bordering on apotheosis in Greece (56–59), and who impossibly foresees the idiosyncratic route and attendant perils of the Argonauts' return voyage (61–65).[33] Considered in its totality and remembering that Medea has yet to actually meet or converse with Jason — she refers to him as *quem modo denique vidi* ['whom I just laid eyes on [*sc.* for the first time] moments ago'] (VII. 15) — this progression in her thinking lacks all psychological plausibility. Rather than reflecting the limited perspective of Medea's immediate narrative circumstances, the monologue operates according to an intertextual logic, addressing metaliterary concerns and engaging previous literary versions, which it progressively absorbs and exhausts. Whence comes the remarkable density of allusion in the interior monologue: Medea is in a sense thumbing through and summing up her own literary tradition. She repeatedly quotes previous versions of herself and other characters (Jason above all).[34] And she even cites 'spin-off' figures, such as Virgil's Dido, who was modelled in no small part on Apollonius Rhodius' Medea.[35] Her thoughts are largely *prospective* — she proceeds with remarkable self-assurance to project a future that encompasses a vast poetic tradition.[36] More than merely a character in Ovid's poems, she is a reader of her literary past — a reader who gradually turns into an author, exercising control over and scripting her narrative future. Again, the striking degree of metaliterary competence exhibited by Medea is difficult to reconcile with an 'ingenuous' reading of her monologue.

A more technical impediment to a psychological reading arises from the peculiarities of the narrative treatment in the wake of Medea's monologue. Her subsequent actions are increasingly deprived of the kind of psychological illumination needed properly to motivate them. As the narrative milieu switches from Colchis to Greece, Ovid introduces an abrupt switch in focalization. After being herself the focalizing subject in Colchis, Medea is relegated to the focalized object of a remarkably superficial and psychologically restricted authorial perspective for the remainder of the tale.[37] As Medea becomes more apparently 'monstrous', the reader is progressively distanced from her reasoning and motivation. Ovid thereby effectively short-circuited any meaningful attempt at a psychological reading of Medea's behaviour.[38] Earlier poets, and Euripides in particular, had explored Medea's psychology as the basis for casting her as a figure of disruption and transgression. But this is clearly not where Ovid's thematic or narrative focus lies: as we have just seen, he brazenly effects a banalization of the most shocking moment in her career — her infanticide. If readers are invited to reflect upon their changing perception of the episode's central figure, the basis for such reflection is not psychological insight. By his progressive distancing, achieved not least by his striking switch in focalization, Ovid has 'enacted', through his subtle manipulation of narrative modalities, the impossibility of penetrating the mind of the sorceress. As the narrative advances, he concentrates more on what Medea does, and less on why she does it. Within the context of the *Metamorphoses* this aligns perfectly with her inaugural role as the epic's first practitioner of a new paradigm of transformative change: the human metamorphic. In this regard, the importance of Medea's soliloquy resides principally in its inauguration of a metaphysical reorientation in Ovid's narrative: the ruminations of the Colchian princess mark the beginning of a systematic suppression of the conventional epic divine machinery.

In her monologue Medea initially concedes that Jason's fate, whether he lives or dies, lies in the hands of the gods (*vivat an ille | occidat, in dis est*, VII. 23–24). In the very next breath, however, she exclaims 'but let him live!' (*vivat tamen!*, VII. 24), seemingly arrogating the *ius vitae necisque*, the power over life or death, which she had just acknowledged as a divine prerogative, to herself. Shortly thereafter, upon considering the various threats to Jason's life she once more appeals to the gods with the familiar appeal *di meliora velint* ['May the gods forefend!'] (VII. 37); yet again, she instantly undoes the gesture to the divinities by proclaiming (VII. 37–38):

> [...] quamquam non ista precanda,
> sed facienda mihi.

['Yet these are not things I should pray for, but things I should myself accomplish!']

The brash declaration that actions, not prayers, are required, signals a pivotal moment in the episode. It raises the spectre of a shift in the oversight and management of narrative developments. As a sorceress, Medea can take control of events, essentially bypassing the Olympian gods, who conventionally orchestrate the plot of epic narratives. This is indeed how the episode plays out — in the teeth of earlier versions of the myth. Previous treatments insisted on the active role of the Olympian deities. Pindar featured Aphrodite as his principal divine instigator. Even Apollonius, who offers little of the Homeric *deorum ministeria* elsewhere in his narrative, resuscitates it — albeit in a deliberately eccentric manner — for the story of Medea's love for Jason. In the *Argonautica*, the goddess Hera figures as the primary orchestrator of events. She had arranged with Aphrodite for the latter's son Eros (Roman Cupid) to fire a shaft into Medea's heart in order to incite overwhelming erotic passion for Jason and thereby compel her assistance. Ovid's narrative, in contrast, remains silent about this Olympian master-plot — but can we therefore already assume that it is not operative? Initially, no: indeed, there are strong allusive hints that Ovid wishes us to read Medea's soliloquy with the Apollonian arrangements in mind. But then this intertextual model promptly collapses when Medea's patriotic resolve quickens and she temporarily overcomes her passion (VII. 72–73):

> [...] et ante oculos rectum pietasque pudorque
> constiterant, et victa dabat iam terga Cupido.

[And before her eyes stood right and piety and shame; and Cupid, having been defeated, turned his back in flight.]

This surprising intermezzo, a development that has received little critical attention, breaks away from the love plot of Apollonius Rhodius. Regardless of how we understand *Cupido* here, this development clearly and emphatically distances Ovid's account from the literary world of the Hellenistic *Argonautica* and its all-powerful gods. This puts paid to the implied reader's natural assumption that Ovid's Medea, like her Apollonian incarnation, had fully succumbed to an irresistible intervention by Eros/Cupid. Matters are more complicated, as Medea — quite unlike any of her literary predecessors — manages to fight off the meddlesome divinity. Ovid quickly follows up this precise exclusionary gesture by another. When Medea proceeds to the grove of her patron Hecate, goddess of magic, she comes upon Jason, and her love is rekindled: [...] *cum videt Aesoniden exstinctaque flamma reluxit* (VII. 74–77). One of the reasons is that, *by chance*, Jason happened to look exceptionally handsome (VII. 84–85):

> et casu solito formosior Aesone natus
> illa luce fuit: posses ignoscere amanti.

[and by chance the son of Aeson was even more beautiful than usual that day: you could have forgiven Medea for falling in love.]

With one inconspicuous word — *casu*, i.e. 'by chance' — Ovid jettisons the divine epic machinery of his predecessor. For in Apollonius, Jason's outstanding beauty at the moment of his meeting with Medea was anything but happenstance: Hera herself saw to it that her protégé made the best possible impression by resorting to the familiar divine expedient of beautifying the hero prior to an important encounter (*Arg.* III. 919–23).[39]

Overall, then, Ovid's treatment pointedly and systematically excludes the well-known divine apparatus of the Hellenistic *Argonautica*. Medea's love is rekindled by chance in Hecate's grove. This site suggests a gradual shift into the realm of the magical and the fantastic, which is reflected in the mysterious atmospherics. When Jason makes his oath to Medea, he is made to swear 'by the sacred rites of the three-formed goddess [sc. Hecate], and whatever divine force might be in that grove' (*per sacra triformis [...] deae lucoque foret quod numen in illo*, VII. 94–95). Hecate is, indeed, the (absent) divine authority under whose sign the episode unfolds.[40]

Jason thereupon receives the magical herbs that will protect him during his performance of Aeetes' trials, along with instructions as to how to apply them (*accipit cantatas protinus herbas | edidicitque usum*, VII. 98–99). Here we are approaching the realm of the human metamorphic, and a veritable technology of transformation. These herbs temporarily render Jason immune to the fire-blasts of the bronze bulls (VII. 115–16):

> [...] subit ille nec ignes
> sentit anhelatos (tantum medicamina possunt)

[He enters and does not feel the fiery breaths (such is the power of the herbs!)]

This is not the first mention in Ovid's poem of protective pharmaceutics. The ointment with which Medea treated her hero has similar properties to the cream that Sol applies to the head of his son Phaethon in *Metamorphoses* II to shield him from the heat of the paternal sunbeams — only that this particular *medicamen* comes with the attribute *sacrum* ('holy').[41] Less wholesome are the herbs that Hermes and Aphrodite use to contaminate the well in which their joint offspring Hermaphroditus was compelled to undergo a feminizing merger with the nymph Salmacis: in response to his (or her) prayers, they endow the waters with permanent transformative powers by treating them with an 'unholy' (*incestum*) substance.[42] And Minerva, too, resorts to magical herbs to transform Arachne into a spider (*Met.* VI. 139–42):

> Post ea discedens sucis Hecateidos herbae
> sparsit, et extemplo tristi medicamine tactae
> defluxere comae, cum quis et naris et aures,
> fitque caput minimum; toto quoque corpore parva est
> [...]

> [Turning to leave, [Minerva] sprinkled [on Arachne] juices from a herb of Hecate; and upon being touched by the infernal lotion, her hair fell out, along with her nose and ears, and her head grows tiny; indeed her whole body becomes small [...]]

In this instance, the transformative liquid is explicitly identified as deriving from the domain of Hecate, and we can more generally diagnose a gradual increase in (sinister) potency in how Ovid operates with *medicamen/medicamina* in the *Metamorphoses*. If in Book II it refers to an asbestos-like sun-cream from the medicine cabinet of an Olympian divinity, the *medicamen* in Book IV has the same gender-bending powers as an overdose of oestrogen. Ovid does not cite the provenance of the drug, but the context suggests that Aphrodite could have acted as supplier. And finally, Arachne suffers a dramatic insectile metamorphosis at Minerva's devising, though Ovid never explains why Minerva, in this instance, needed to rely on a *medicamen* (as noted earlier, divinities in the *Metamorphoses* tend to transform both themselves and others by a mere act of will). Perhaps the poet wanted partially to prepare the ground for what happens in the Medea episode. For it is here that the triangular configuration of magic, metamorphosis, and *medicamina* comes fully into its own, together with other devices of the dark arts at the command of Hecate and her disciples, in particular when the action shifts to Thessaly.[43] But Ovid maintains a tight focus on the various techniques and media of procedural magic throughout the account of events in Colchis. If Medea began with a protective ointment, later in the trials, as she begins to worry that Jason may need further help, she secretly makes supplementary magical efforts (VII. 137–38):

> neve parum valeant a se data gramina, carmen
> auxiliare canit secretasque advocat artes.

> [lest the herbs she had given prove insufficiently powerful, she chants reinforcing spells and summons secret arts.]

In the midst of the action, in a moment of acute anxiety, a moment that would typically prompt a prayer for divine aid, Medea bolsters Jason's capacity through a renewed application of her preternatural art, this time by casting supplemental spells in case her herbal prophylactics were insufficient. Once again, the possibility of interventionist gods, and, more broadly, control of events on the divine level, has been circumvented, though it is important to note that what has been suppressed is not so much mention of the Olympian gods as their representation as *dramatis personae*, as fully constituted characters that participate directly in narrative events. The effect resembles (and recalls) the absence of Olympian divinities in the Tereus and Procne episode of the previous book.[44] There, however, the concluding metamorphosis, while unattributed, seems to presuppose some divine agency asserting itself (other than the furies). In contrast, the elided Olympian gods have no jurisdiction over the narrative realm that Medea inhabits: they have, in essence, been supplanted by the young Colchian sorceress. Medea emerges as an alternative figure of narrative control, the witch, a champion not of celestial sublimity but of the macabre, the grotesque, and the chthonic, operating under the tutelage of Hecate. Over the course of Ovid's account of events in Colchis, then, we have a three-fold transition: first, the narrative shifts from upper to lower divine authorities (from Olympian to chthonic/underworld deities); second, this reorientation coincides with a shift from divine to human agency (no gods are shown in action in this episode); and thirdly, Ovid switches the thematic focus from instantaneous to procedural metamorphosis.

Thematic Transformation: Rejuvenation and its Variants

The foregoing suggests a conception of Medea less as a psychological subject than as a metaliterary figure and metamorphic agent. Her actions simultaneously encode an aggressive encounter with an overly prescriptive mythographic tradition and make an important contribution to the titular theme of the epic by establishing transformative change by means of magic as an integral component of Ovid's literary universe. Medea's metaliterary competence might also be said to relate to her magical competence. The play on *carmina* as 'songs' (i.e. poems) and *carmina* as (witches') spells was well established in Latin poetry and is operative in Jason's request to Medea for the rejuvenation of his father when he adds *quid enim non carmina possunt?* (VII. 167).[45] At a moment when Jason is in effect requesting that Ovid's poetic narrative veer away from its models, both senses of *carmina* clearly resonate. Medea's magic reflects an aspect of Ovid's poetic power, his imaginative power to re-imagine, reinvent, and refashion inherited tales.

The focus on Medea as sorceress, and more particularly as an agent of transformation, is an important part of Ovid's re-articulation of her literary persona. Inasmuch as his narrative delves into magical subject matter, it strains the laws of epic propriety. Earlier works certainly deal with the magical, but only with the greatest circumspection.[46] In pre-Ovidian epic, the acknowledgment of magical forces as distinct from the conventional power of the Olympians and the divine hierarchy under them was typically grudging and partial. Even by the Augustan age, the detailed elaboration of magical procedure was still very much the stuff of lower genres. There is a good reason, however, why magic takes centre stage in the *Metamorphoses*, quite beyond any interest Ovid may have had in generic 'contamination'. In choosing to flesh out the story in this rather eccentric manner, he rechannels his epic into the realm of the human metamorphic. This marks a significant moment in the cosmic history of transformation mapped out in his poem. Medea becomes the first and by far the most prominent of the very few human agents of transformation in the *Metamorphoses*.[47]

The subsequent stages of the episode bear out this impression, as Ovid works to break away from the established tradition by focusing on metamorphic feats and evocations — elements either altogether absent from his models or consigned by them to the narrative margins. If Ovid's solution is to explore, elaborate or even invent a career for an interstitial Medea, she is certainly not 'marginal' in the scheme of the *Metamorphoses*: the poet presents her as a figure of singular power, elaborating on the magical procedures she uses to stake out the novel terrain of the human metamorphic.

The first major component of this 'epic reinvention' of Medea is an elaborate account of the magical rejuvenation of Jason's aged father, Aeson. This episode presents an interstitial Medea who is, in terms of the chronology of her career, post-Apollonian and pre-Euripidean. Ovid provides a lengthy and remarkably detailed account of this metamorphic procedure (VII. 159–296). This authorial choice recalibrates earlier preferences: in the mythographic tradition, Medea's slaying of Pelias was her best-known and most widely treated exploit in Thessaly, whereas the rejuvenation of Aeson was a more marginal episode, one that elevated poetic treatments generally kept at arm's length. It did, to be sure, receive mention in the *Nostoi*;[48] but in the classical period it seems to have been mainly the stuff of comic fodder.[49] Ovid is the only major extant poet to provide an account.[50]

Ovid's elaboration of a secondary, frequently suppressed episode is fully committed: the rejuvenation becomes the centrepiece of his narrative. When set against the compression of Euripidean and Apollonian elements, this signals a striving for novelty.[51] A suggestive feature is that Jason's initial request for the rejuvenation of his father prompts a disquisition by Medea on both the possibilities and ethics of magical tampering with human mortality. She notes that Jason's request to alter the allotted span of a mortal life is forbidden by Hecate, who here seems to be invoked as a kind of supreme cosmic authority. In an epic, of course, one would expect Zeus/Jupiter to be authorizing or forbidding such tampering with the mechanics of destiny, and this is precisely what we find at IX. 394-441, when the rejuvenation of Iolaus by Hebe prompts various gods to demand the right to rejuvenate their favourite mortals, compelling Jupiter to step in to forbid such reckless tampering with the mechanisms of fate. The contrast with the later passage underscores that in the Medea episode we are dealing with yet another partial occlusion of the normal *deorum ministeria*. For Medea, this is a pivotal 'Promethean' moment in which she arrogates to herself divine prerogatives. For now Ovid's heroine explicitly places Hecate's authority alongside her own inclination and volition (VII. 172–78):

> [...] ergo ego cuiquam
> posse tuae videor spatium transcribere vitae?
> nec sinat hoc Hecate, nec tu petis aequa; sed isto,
> quod petis, experiar maius dare munus, Iason.
> arte mea soceri longum temptabimus aevum,

> non annis renovare tuis, modo diva triformis
> adiuvet et praesens ingentibus adnuat ausis.

> [So I seem to be able to transfer a portion of your life to someone else? Hecate
> would not allow this, nor do you seek something just; but, Jason, I'll try to give
> you an even greater gift than the one you seek. With my art, and not your years,
> I shall try to renew the old age of my father-in-law, if only the three-formed
> goddess grants her aid and with her presence approves the great undertaking.]

The relation between Hecate and Medea implied in this passage is complex, and
it is not easy to disentangle the lines of authority. Medea has a clear sense of limits
imposed upon the magical activities of mortals. Hecate evidently prohibits the
transference of part of an allotted lifespan from one individual to another — a motif
familiar from the myth of Admetus and Alcestis[52] — but she does not seem to
object to an individual *repeating* part of his lifespan. This is surprising: Medea rightly
claims that what she offers is a 'greater' (*maius*) gift than what Jason has asked for.
His request involves an unselfish zero-sum arrangement, insofar as he would have
lost the years that his father would have gained, whereas Medea's procedure adds
additional years on top.[53] For this feat, Hecate's approval is evidently required, but
Medea does not seem to anticipate any difficulty on that account. Indeed, Medea's
reference to the goddess here is formulaic: she invokes her as a protégé appealing
to a technical authority, and decides to proceed with the experiment on terms that
she is confident will meet with approval.[54]

As Medea begins the rejuvenation of Aeson, Ovid describes her as achieving
a 'more than mortal purpose' (*propositum mortali ... maius*, VII. 276). This is, if
anything, an understatement, for Medea is undertaking something forbidden even
to the gods. It is true that Medea's act of rejuvenation is less dramatic in its transformative effect than the metamorphoses achieved by the gods: rejuvenation is a
comparatively weak and recursive form of metamorphosis, producing not so much
a new form as the reversion to a prior one (made explicit at VII. 293: *se reminiscitur*).
Its ethical implications are, however, rather more profound. The tampering with
an individual's predestined span of life is flagged as problematic, both in the present
episode (e.g. VII. 171–75) and elsewhere in the poem. This is particularly clear in
the aforementioned passage in Book IX, where Jupiter warns off the various gods
clamouring to rejuvenate their favourite mortals. The supreme god declares that
even he is subject to the fates (*me quoque fata regunt*, IX. 434), and points to his
ageing and vulnerable son Minos, whose senescence he is powerless to reverse.[55]
Earlier epic had established that even the gods could not securely extend mortal
lives beyond their allotted span, starting with Homer's Zeus, whose renunciation
of interference to save his son Sarpedon in *Iliad* XVI set the tone for subsequent
treatments (and indeed informs Ovid's treatment at IX. 394–441). At the same time,
inasmuch as the Iliadic Zeus seeks to extend a life cut off in its prime, the Homeric
passage offers something qualitatively different from Medea's intervention, which
seeks to restore an old man to his prime. Rejuvenation reverses the course of nature,
and thereby constitutes, as sorcery often does, an overt violation of natural law.

As already noted, Medea's rejuvenation of Aeson is the epic's first full account of
what we have called a 'procedural' metamorphosis. To this point metamorphosis

has predominantly been the instantaneous product of divine will. In a few earlier episodes, all featuring female deities, there have been hints of something more procedural involving the application of herbs or other ingredients, rather than simple divine fiat. Thus one of the rejected tales of the Minyades features a nymph who used powerful herbs magically to transform human beings into fish (IV. 49–50). And, while not amounting to a metamorphosis as such, Tisiphone blends ingredients in a bronze cauldron (IV. 500–05) to produce a potion that will induce filicidal madness in Ino and Athamas. In transforming Arachne into a spider, as we have already had occasion to note, Minerva sprinkles her with 'the juices of a Hecatean herb', which brings about the metamorphosis (VI. 139–42).[56] Such references to magical procedures evoke a realm of transformative powers and possibilities that, from Homer onwards, enjoyed an uneasy coexistence with the more conventional powers and capacities of the epic gods.[57] Already the *Odyssey* offers an account of Circe transforming Odysseus' men into swine by means of procedural witchcraft (*Od.* x. 233–43) and Apollonius, too, engages with magic in his Medea episode. But in Ovid's predecessors the magical tends to be marginalized, or at least placed under the overarching power of the Olympian divinities. So in the *Odyssey*, Hermes prophylactically provides Odysseus with a kind of anti-metamorphic herbal remedy, moly, a potent antidote that trumps Circe's magic (and notes that it is much easier for gods than for mortals to recognize these powerful herbs). This intervention in essence 'contains' Circe's magic and subordinates it to the power of Zeus and the Olympian order.

In contrast to such treatments, Ovid's Medea episode provides a detailed account of metamorphosis achieved in the human realm via the due application of an arcane herbal elixir whose individual ingredients are meticulously documented by the poet. It is precisely this detailed attention to Medea's 'recipe' that enables Ovid to introduce and explore a new paradigm of transformative change, that of procedural metamorphosis. The magical rejuvenation, which unfolds over an extended period of time — the entire process takes a number of weeks and dozens of verses — proceeds in four distinct phases: in the first (179–91), Medea ritually prepares and purifies herself; in the second (192–219), she prays to the appropriate supernatural forces; in the third (219–37), she embarks on an aerial journey in her dragon-drawn chariot to gather the necessary herbs for the rejuvenating elixir; in the fourth (238–93), the final preparations and the rejuvenation transformation take place.

In her prayer to the nether spirits, Medea offers an extended catalogue of her magical powers (VII. 199–209). As Kenney notes, this enumeration is a significant ratcheting-up vis-à-vis Apollonius' catalogue of Medea's supernatural abilities at *Argonautica*, III. 531–33, to say nothing of Ovid's own earlier treatments at *Heroides*, VI. 83–92, and *Amores*, I. 8. 5–12 and II. 1. 23–28.[58] Then Medea lays out her project: *nunc opus est sucis per quos renovata senectus | in florem redeat primosque recolligat annos* ['now I need medicines by which old age may be renewed, return to the bloom of life, gain back its early years'] (VII. 215–16). It becomes clear from the account of the actual procedure that she means to produce an elixir that will replace the aged blood in Aeson's veins, and by this means he will be rejuvenated (VII. 285–86). Medea's instruments for the rejuvenation procedure itself are a bronze sickle for cutting the herbs she gathers, a capacious bronze cauldron, and a knife for cutting her subjects (to drain their blood). There is a certain sense of the medicinal, insofar as ancient medical theory associated the debilitation of old age with the waning vigour of the body's blood;[59] and the culinary, in that Ovid provides a complex recipe for the rejuvenating elixir. The literary form he uses for this is the epic catalogue, by which he enumerates first the individual locations in which Medea gathers the necessary herbs and then the ingredients, herbal and non-herbal, that she mixes in the cauldron to produce her potion.

There are certainly precedents for this passage.[60] At *Argonautica*, III. 844–68, Medea is described cutting the root of the Promethean plant used to bolster Jason's strength and resistance for the trials set by Aeetes. Even closer may have been a lost Sophoclean drama, the *Rhizotomoi* ('Root cutters'). In this play Sophocles evidently described Medea gathering poisonous herbs in preparation for some injurious act, possibly the murder of Pelias.[61] And of course the distant archetype is Odysseus' harvesting of the herb moly, at the advice of the god Hermes, as an antidote to the metamorphic magic of Circe.[62] On the inclusion of such material in Greek drama, Scarborough observes that

> Athenian playwrights have unwittingly left clear indications that there was an ordinarily accepted 'common knowledge' of drugs and herbal remedies in the fifth century BC, and that such pharmaceutical lore was generally accepted in both magico-legendary and empirical-practical ways. Playwrights, whether of tragedy or comedy, must use allusions readily comprehensible by their audiences, so that mentions of herbs or drugs in the plays can be assumed to be understood by Athenians who sat through the productions.[63]

Ovid taps into this tradition of technical knowledge, with his emphasis on threefold and ninefold iterations, numbers with magical associations, his pseudo-empirical attention to the various ingredients, and his intelligence that Medea's implements of choice were made of bronze, which was thought best for such purposes.[64] At the same time he ratchets up such effects by turning Medea's herb-gathering into an epic event, involving a nine-day aerial excursion in her dragon-drawn chariot that is reported in the form of a catalogue. This is a novelty in itself: Ovid is the earliest extant author to have Medea's dragon-drawn chariot utilized for the gathering of herbs.

This expedition is described in careful geographical detail (222–33). The chariot puts in at various Thessalian locales, including mountains (Pelion, Ossa, Othrys, Pindus, Olympus), banks of rivers (Apidanus, Amphrysus, Enipeus, Peneus), and a lake (Boebe). As noted before, for Medea to perform her metamorphic magic, she must for a time step outside the realm of human civilization. Here, as later, this is connected to her aerial chariot, a vehicle that also detaches her from the human realm and quotidian human experience. This aerial tour of Thessaly is appropriate for Medea insofar as Thessaly was the area of Greece most notorious for witchcraft.[65] So even if Medea is an alien and characterized as the ultimate outsider, the ultimate barbarian, she is very much at home in this region.[66] In fact, the stages of her voyage seem quite deliberate and Ovid implies that this is not Medea's first time harvesting magical herbs in these parts.[67]

As Medea returns from her aerial herb-gathering excursion, the dragons drawing the chariot are rejuvenated from the mere exhalation of the plants that she has harvested (*Met.* VII. 236–37):

> [...] neque erant tacti nisi odore dracones,
> et tamen annosae pellem posuere senectae.

[Though touched by nothing more than the odor [*sc.* of the gathered herbs], the dragons shed their aged skins.]

The sloughing of skin is to be sure a natural process for serpents — though of course flying dragons need not follow standard zoological principles. Nonetheless, it is clear that the potency of these herbs, even in a raw and uncombined form, suffices to trigger a 'natural' metamorphosis — a foretaste of what is to come, the first of several 'rejuvenations' in the passage.[68] Medea's herbal magic is already exhibiting its transformative power.

If the herb-gathering trip by Medea in her dragon-drawn chariot is treated at length, it is followed by a yet more extravagant enumeration of the ingredients of the witch's brew. This is a calculated breach of epic propriety, which typically shunned detailed expositions of magical procedure. After due ritual preliminaries, Medea proceeds with preparation of the rejuvenating elixir, which bubbles away in the cauldron (VII. 262–63). The concoction is described in detail: the poet revels in the pharmocopeia. Ovid's enumeration of magical ingredients takes the form of an epic catalogue, now used in an unprecedented manner (*Met.* VII. 266–76):

> adicit extremo lapides Oriente petitos
> et quas Oceani refluum mare lavit harenas;
> addit et exceptas luna pernocte pruinas
> et strigis infamis ipsis cum carnibus alas
> inque virum soliti vultus mutare ferinos
> ambigui prosecta lupi; nec defuit illis
> squamea Cinyphii tenuis membrana chelydri
> vivacisque iecur cervi; quibus insuper addit
> ova caputque novem cornicis saecula passae.
> his et mille aliis postquam sine nomine rebus
> propositum instruxit mortali barbara maius.

[She adds stones fetched from the farthest Orient, and sands washed by Ocean's ebbing tides, and hoar-frost gathered at night by the moon's light, and the ill-omened wings and flesh of the screech-owl, and the entrails of a shape-shifting wolf that had been accustomed to transform his ferocious appearance into human form. Nor is there lacking the thin and scaly skin of the Cinyphian water-snake, or the liver of the long-lived stag; on top she adds the eggs and head of a crow that has lived through nine ages. With these and a thousand other additional things without name the barbarian woman prepared her more than mortal purpose.]

There is a certain logic to this brew. As befits Medea's purpose, the 'organic' ingredients in this concluding section fall into two main groups, involving body parts taken from animals known for either their longevity (crow, stag) or their meta-morphic nature (werewolf, water-snake). Both are pertinent to Medea's project. The final authorial capitulation before a thousand nameless ingredients (*mille ... aliis*) is an ingenious touch. For Newlands, the hyperbole establishes 'Ovid's segregation as a narrator from Medea': 'The excess of detail is part of the humour of Ovid's portrayal of Medea as witch. When he comes at last to her cauldron and begins to itemize at length its exotic and horrible ingredients [...] he indicates that his patience is exhausted with the length and oddity of the list by mockingly concluding that she added a thousand other nameless items.'[69] There is also, of course, a characteristic mystification on the part of the author in the face of magical procedure. But part of the effect here is to signal a baffling complexity through a proliferation of ingredients, a cataloguing excess. Ovid invokes a topos of inexpressibility to convey his bafflement in the face of Medea's awesome magical power. Indeed, the inexpressibility here is apparently quite literal: these final items are beyond the reach of language because they have not been named (*sine nomine rebus*). Conversely, Medea's alchemical power resides in the knowledge that allows her to gather from the natural world those secret and efficacious items she requires for her magic, which in turn enables her, through her expertise in spells and incantations, to override or supplant the laws of nature. This alchemical power is evidently a complex science, and Ovid characterizes it as such.

If the skin-shedding of the dragons, an effect of the wafting herbs, offered a foretaste of the transformations to come, the effects of the mingled ingredients of Medea's concoction now become overtly supernatural, as the old olivewood branch with which she had been stirring the elixir undergoes a rejuvenating transformation (*Met.* VII. 279–84):

> ecce vetus calido versatus stipes aeno
> fit viridis primo nec longo tempore frondes
> induit et subito gravidis oneratur olivis;
> at quacumque cavo spumas eiecit aeno
> ignis et in terram guttae cecidere calentes,
> vernat humus, floresque et mollia pabula surgunt.

[Behold — the old stick that had stirred the warm cauldron at first grows green and shortly thereafter takes on leaves, and then suddenly is laden with fat olives. And wherever the fire throws out froth from the hollow cauldron, and hot drops fall on the earth, the ground becomes green, and up spring flowers and soft grass.]

After these inadvertent but propitious indications of the efficaciousness of her elixir, Medea proceeds to the task at hand, the rejuvenation of Aeson (*Met.* VII. 285–93):

> [...] stricto Medea recludit
> ense senis iugulum veteremque exire cruorem
> passa replet sucis; quos postquam conbibit Aeson
> aut ore acceptos aut vulnere, barba comaeque
> canitie posita nigrum rapuere colorem,
> pulsa fugit macies, abeunt pallorque situsque,
> adiectoque cavae supplentur corpore rugae,
> membraque luxuriant: Aeson miratur et olim
> ante quater denos hunc se reminiscitur annos.

[...drawing a sword, Medea opened the old man's throat; she let the old blood run out, replacing it with her potion. Once Aeson had imbibed the potion by mouth and wound, his beard and hair, shedding their grey, took on a black hue. His gauntness fled, his wasting pallor vanished, and new flesh closed up his hollow wrinkles; his limbs filled out. Aeson marvelled, and remembered himself from forty years past.]

Following the rejuvenation of Aeson, the narrative continues with a more widely attested exploit, Medea's gruesome and convoluted murder of Pelias (VII. 297–349). The motivation provided for this murderous deception, *neve doli cessent* ['that such tricks might not cease'] (VII. 297), has often been singled out as a curiously vague and inadequate motivation for what is usually described as an act of revenge on Jason's behalf.[70] Translators and critics have generally understood the meagre half-line to betoken a psychological transformation in Medea. To this point, so the argument goes, her actions have been motivated by love and wifely devotion; she now seems to act out of wickedness or, as Newlands puts it, 'purely for malice's sake'.[71] There is certainly a shift from the benign to the destructive application of her magical powers. But *neve doli cessent* is, to say the least, psychologically vague. Indeed, as Kenney points out, it could even be construed impersonally.[72] Rather along these lines, Pavlock detects a bilingual etymological pun on 'Medea' (*doli* being a Latin approximation of μήδεα, 'cunning schemes').[73] No matter how the clause is construed, what *can* be securely affirmed here is the lack of a genuine authorial investment in Medea's psychological motivation. Yet the increasing abstractness of attributed motivation facilitates the alignment of the respective projects of heroine and implied poet: as Medea becomes less particularized on the psychological level, her capacity for metapoetic signification emerges more clearly.

The occlusion of human motivation has an analogy on the divine level. Many of Ovid's predecessors invoke the gods as prime movers and shakers behind the ghastly death of Pelias. In Apollonius Rhodius, for example, Hera schemes to have Medea end up in Greece, in part so that the goddess can avenge herself on the king (*Arg.* III. 1134–36). The two levels of human and divine causality are, of course, fully congruent, and were available as a characteristic epic double motivation. What is crucial is that once again Ovid has elided the barest mention of the goddess whom his Hellenistic predecessor had made the divine mastermind overseeing and controlling the action on the human level. *Neve doli cessent* is therefore in a sense also the marker of an absence, the absence of the Olympian goddess Juno and the exercise of her celebrated epic wrath. Ovid's account is striking for its occlusion of Juno's scheming as much as Jason's. And it is also appropriate, in a general sense, to the essentially amoral realm of magic, which has no ethical imperatives as such or apparent need to follow a specific cultural logic — such as getting even. With *neve doli cessent* Ovid has stripped Medea's conduct of easy intelligibility, while signalling more broadly a transition into a poetic domain or a narrative mode that refuses properly to account for narrated action.[74]

The principal elements in this sequence are trickery and repetition. Medea dupes the princesses into butchering Pelias as the spurious prerequisite to a metamorphic procedure that she has no intention of carrying out. That the tyrant's death is accomplished by the hands of his own daughters was an essential aspect of the inherited tale, achieving Jason's vendetta in a particularly complete form, even though Ovid has made this problematic by suppressing any involvement on Jason's part. A programmatic feature of this narrative section is Medea's further twofold performance of the rejuvenation procedure, first in an authentic and then in a feigned guise. In order to convince Pelias' daughters of the efficacy of her transformative powers — her diabolical scheme requires their implicit trust — Medea rejuvenates in their presence an ageing ram (*Met.* VII. 316–21):

> [...]
> membra simul pecudis validosque venefica sucos
> mergit in aere cavo: minuunt medicamina corpus
> cornuaque exurunt nec non cum cornibus annos,
> et tener auditur medio balatus aeno:
> nec mora, balatum mirantibus exsilit agnus
> lascivitque fuga lactantiaque ubera quaerit.

> [[...] the witch plunged the ram's body and her powerful potions into the hollow bronze cauldron. The potions shrank the body, and burnt away the horns, and with the horns the years. Then from the middle of the cauldron was heard a gentle bleating; and, while they still marvelled at the bleating, out jumped a lamb and skipped about, seeking a mother's milky teats.]

This amounts to a procedural variation on the earlier rejuvenation of Aeson, and one that strengthens the sense of the culinary, inasmuch as the creature to be transformed is thrown wholesale in the cauldron along with the ingredients of the elixir. This procedure resembles a sacrifice performed in reverse: instead of the death of a living creature, it is renewed life that comes out of Medea's cauldron.

As already noted, the rejuvenation of the ram is part of an elaborate scheme of deception whereby the tyrant's daughters are enticed to participate in a supposed rejuvenation of their father along the lines of that which Medea had just performed for Aeson. Because Pelias is not rejuvenated, however, there is, strictly speaking, no physical transformation in this sequence. Instead, Ovid emphasizes the semantic and ethical transformation that Medea's trickery has effected. After drugging the king and his bodyguards, Medea leads the daughters into the royal bedchamber and urges them to take to their father with swords, so as to drain off his blood and make room for its rejuvenating substitute. Ironically, Medea urges them on by invoking them to perform their *officium*, 'moral obligation or duty' (337). The paradoxical inversions are emphatic here (VII. 339–42):

> his, ut quaeque pia est, hortatibus inpia prima est
> et, ne sit scelerata, facit scelus: haud tamen ictus
> ulla suos spectare potest, oculosque reflectunt,
> caecaque dant saevis aversae vulnera dextris.

> [As each daughter was pious, the sooner she became, by Medea's urgings, impious; and in order not to be sinful, she committed a sin. Scarce was any able to watch her own blows: they averted their eyes and struck blindly with savage right hands.]

This contrasts pointedly with the lead-up to the series of rejuvenations, where Ovid identified Jason's filial *pietas* as the compelling motivation for Medea. Even though she, as we have seen, objects to the original terms of Jason's petition, 'she was moved by the devotion of him making the request' (*mota est pietate rogantis*, VII. 169). Now we see the perversion of *pietas* by Medea's beguiling of Pelias' daughters. Medea seems to be operating in an ethical vacuum or, rather, a paradoxical universe in which ethical distinctions (*pius/inpius*) are difficult to uphold. In this sense, her magical activity has affinities with other episodes in the *Metamorphoses* that feature infernal influence or quasi-magical objects, in particular the story of Tereus, Procne, and Philomela in Book VI and Althea's murder of her son Meleager in Book VIII.[75]

In the Pelias sequence, Medea's act of persuasion replaces the moment of transformative change and forms a rhetorical equivalent to her ability to pervert, and often invert or reverse, the proper physical operation of the universe (as she makes clear in her prayer catalogue of her habitual magical powers). Her successful transmutation of the daughters' piety into unspeakable impiety is a striking effect, but it remains strangely uncontextualized — in contrast to earlier versions of the myth, where it serves as the climactic part of a larger revenge plot that has its origins in Pelias' order to Jason to recover the golden fleece, which was designed as an impossible mission and hence an indirect death-sentence. Ovid, by contrast, just serves up unmotivated and amoral slaughter, without even exploring or even signalling the ethics of revenge. Tellingly, when the faltering daughters leave the gruesome preliminaries half-finished, Medea cuts short Pelias' address to his children by polishing him off herself. She slashes his throat (thereby curtailing his speech) and then plunges him in this mangled state into the boiling cauldron. If the throat-cutting 'is elaborated at far greater length and with a conscious sense of the criminality of the act',[76] Medea proceeds to make a characteristic airborne exit, removing herself from accountability. Here, unlike, for example, the Tereus and Procne episode, the issue of punishment or terminal transformation does not figure.

Referential Transformation: Medea and the 'Meta-Metamorphic'

At this point the reader might well pause to take stock. Aeson's metamorphosis was naturally the culminating moment of the episode, to which Ovid had been building up for several dozen verses. But it is worth noting that this rejuvenation was preceded by others — the winged dragons (236–37), the olive wood stick (279–81), and the vegetation around the cauldron (282–84) — and was followed by others. The counterfeit rejuvenation of Pelias would be, were it authentic, the sixth such transformation in the episode. This is an unusual concentration for Ovid, whose normal compositional mode privileges variety over repetition.[77] It allows a detailed exploration of the technology of transformation to be sure, but at the same time, it must be acknowledged that the sense of repetition is becoming overpowering. Medea's rejuvenations are getting a bit old.

The repetitions of the rejuvenation metamorphosis expose a crucial programmatic dynamic. The means by which Medea, despite her conventionally limited meta-morphic career, dominates one of the longest episodes in Ovid's epic of trans-formation are here laid bare. Simply put, for Medea to continue to feature in the *Metamorphoses*, she must be continually associated with transformative change: Ovid's self-imposed poetic programme entails a necessary skewing of inherited material towards the metamorphic. Considered from this angle, then, we might understand this six-fold iteration of rejuvenation metamorphosis as the outlandish textual embodiment of an intrinsic and recurring quandary, namely, how to incorporate important but metamorphically deficient myths and characters in an epic of transformation. In perpetuating her prodigious textual existence of more than 400 lines, Medea must repeatedly enact or evoke metamorphoses.

If the death of Pelias is achieved under the sign of obsessive metamorphic repetition, it is not the most striking such case. We have deferred until now discussion of a curious reiterative coda attached to the account of Aeson's rejuvenation. In this mythographic addendum, the poet reports that the god Bacchus, who has evidently been watching Medea's exploits from on high, takes note of this metamorphic possibility, with the intention of exploiting it to extend the natural lifespan of his nurses (*Met.* VII. 294–96):[78]

> viderat ex alto tanti miracula monstri
> Liber et admonitus, iuvenes nutricibus annos
> posse suis reddi, capit hoc a Colchide munus.

> [Bacchus had beheld this strange miracle from on high, and learning that the years of their youth could be given back to his nurses took this boon from the Colchian.]

Crucially, an Olympian deity finally appears in the Medea narrative. But that deity is entirely passive, a spectator looking on from 'on high' (presumably Olympus) who learns something of value by observing Medea in action. This enacts in striking terms the subordination of the conventional *deorum ministeria*.

We have, moreover, another characteristic blending of Medea's metamorphic and metaliterary modes. One would be hard pressed to make full sense of this passage, were it not for the precious testimony of the hypothesis to Euripides' *Medea*, which mentions, along with the rejuvenation of Aeson, Medea's performance of the same feat for the Nurses of Dionysus. For the latter it cites a now lost drama, the *Trophoi* of Aeschylus, probably a satyr play. Ovid's associative gesture demonstrates his sure-handed control of diverse mythographic materials.[79] But it does something more: it makes of his own narrative a belated myth of origins for Aeschylus' lost play. This trans-generic gesture countervails the tendency of a literary tradition of high seriousness that was accustomed to make the events of Euripides' *Medea* the remote narrative telos of the earlier epic action. The nineteenth-century German scholar Karl Robert was the first to suggest that Ovid drew directly from the Euripidean hypothesis in writing this coda; if so, it would constitute a particularly apposite paratextual gesture.[80] But whatever Ovid's source of inspiration, a crucial point is that Medea is now being associated not merely with metamorphic feats in her own narrative, but with those in other narratives as well. This is a crucial development: the strange coda signals repetition on the metaliterary level, veering into what we might call the 'meta-metamorphic'. As Ovid continues to stretch out the textual lifespan of his heroine, he is obliged to up the ante, affording Medea an associative function, making of her something like a patron saint of metamorphic narrative.

Medea's meta-metamorphic status is developed further in the aftermath of Pelias' death. With the gruesome murder accomplished, Medea makes a hasty airborne departure, thereby inaugurating a particularly odd and seemingly gratuitous section of her eccentric narrative, which looks like nothing so much as an extended bout of aerial tourism (VII. 350–92). Through Euripidean influence, Medea's relocation to Corinth with Jason became the inescapable next step of her mythic biography — usually as a direct consequence of the death of Pelias. Ovid does not omit the move, but innovates in having Medea make the journey alone on her chariot (Jason having evidently made the trip at an earlier stage). This offers scope for further development of Medea's 'interstitial' career, which is fully exploited: she chooses an extraordinarily roundabout route to reach her new home.[81] Rather than proceeding southward to Corinth, as logic would dictate, Medea sets off in a seemingly random manner: the chariot first proceeds northeastward, flying over Mt Pelion (352), then veers off to the southwest and Mt Othrys (353). And this is just the beginning. Medea now turns eastward and proceeds across the Aegean to Asia Minor. Flying over Mt Ida near Troy (359), she heads southward down the coastline to Rhodes (365), before returning back to Greece. Passing over the island of Ceos (368), she then moves about the Corinthian gulf, first overshooting Corinth to the west, then overshooting it to the east, before finally circling back and reaching her destination (see Fig. 2).

The narrative telescoping denies even Corinth the sense of a genuine terminus: Medea's travels are interrupted for a mere four verses, before she takes to the air again, this time en route to Athens for the final phase of her career in Greece. Newlands well notes that accordingly Corinth, 'the focal point of so much suffering in Euripides' play, is simply one stopping point in a long, learned journey'.[82] The sense of continuity between the two chariot rides is achieved through Ovid's radical textual compression of tragic events in Corinth. By introducing the Euripidean plot with an initial *sed postquam* (VII. 394), and following with a single breathless sentence, Medea seems barely to set foot on the tragic *terra firma* of Corinth before resuming her wandering. The effect is not merely to marginalize the tragic material, but also to relegate Euripides' notorious invention of Medea's aerial escape at the end of this play to an appendix of her more extravagant Aegean chariot ride in the *Metamorphoses*.

The narrated itinerary becomes the occasion for a flight of mythographic fantasy, an enumeration of metamorphic tales associated with the landscape over which Medea journeys. It should be acknowledged at once that this series of 'fly-by' metamorphoses, while nicely illustrating the topography of Medea's erratic journey, is entirely gratuitous on the level of plot: it has no direct connection with Medea or the myth of the Argonauts more broadly.[83] If Medea's own transformative career has been exhausted, her textual lifespan is now rather preposterously extended by making her the itinerant witness to the residual effects of more than a dozen, largely obscure tales of metamorphosis.[84]

This eccentric textual sequence has baffled and exasperated critics. Many have simply passed over it in silence; a few, such as Otis, have more bluntly dismissed it as unworthy of discussion; others, following Bardon, write it off as an excess of Ovid's baroque imagination.[85] But scholarship has been gradually coming round, and some ingenious, if unpersuasive, attempts at explanation have been advanced. One scholar

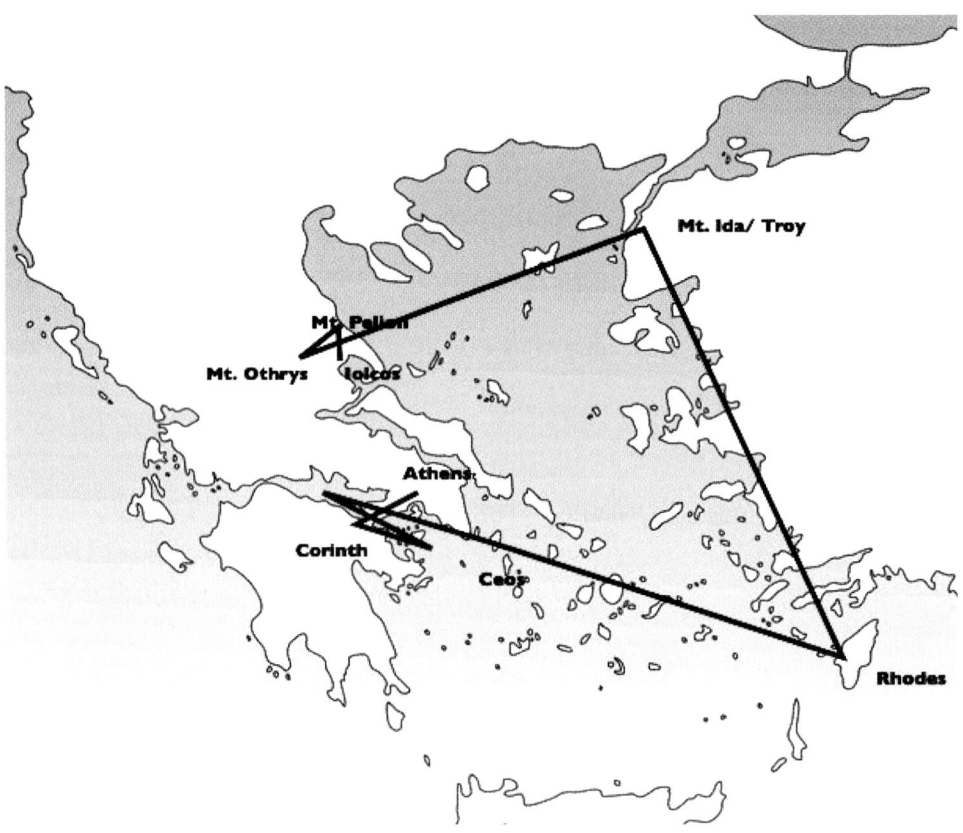

FIG. 2. Medea's Flight Map

has suggested that Medea is tracing out a magic circle around Corinth in order to ensure the efficacy of her spells in this new location; another has suggested that Medea simply cannot control the dragons (which is hard to square with the pinpoint precision of her earlier herb-gathering trip).[86] Our analysis to this point suggests that seeking a motivation on the immediate level of plot may not be the most fruitful approach. In more abstract and metaliterary terms, it is surely suggestive that Medea's route constitutes something like a mini-*Argonautica*. As we have seen, Ovid compressed the Argonauts' celebrated voyage, recounted in Apollonius' first, second and fourth books, into a mere handful of verses. Its schematic 'replacement' here thus stands as an audacious reconception of the inherited mythic material, a striking metaliterary transformation. Medea's departure from Iolcus is marked by initial references to Mt Pelion and Chiron (352 *Philyreia* identifies him by his mother Philyra), both closely associated with the Argo myth.[87] She subsequently proceeds eastward to Asia Minor, and southward down the coast to Rhodes, before heading back to Greece; but, as already observed, she overshoots her destination and has to circle back.

In very schematic terms, this route has obvious similarities with the Argonauts' own voyage as described in Apollonius Rhodius. Newlands well observes that Medea 'has in a sense appropriated the Argonauts' role, but at the wrong time and wrong place in the story.'[88] The fact that, as Lenoir has pointed out, parts of Medea's flight corresponds closely to actual sea-routes reinforces these similarities, and thus the sense of a schematic substitution.[89] These insights nicely round out the metapoetic story we have been piecing together: throughout this episode, Ovid and his heroine have been attempting to escape from the orbit of influential literary predecessors, to tell the myth of Jason, Medea, and the Argonauts in a novel way. Unlike the Argonauts' voyage, of course, and indeed her own earlier herb-gathering expedition, Medea's aerial excursion over the Aegean is utterly gratuitous. The journey has no practical objective: Medea is a sightseer, a tourist, who remains aloft for the duration and performs no concrete task. Previously, she was a figure of action, a metamorphic agent, but that is no longer the case: this part of the narrative is concerned with what she sees rather than what she does. The focus is on her itinerary, on the new vistas and perspectives that it offers. Over the course of the journey, Medea's chariot flies over more than a dozen locations whose history includes (or in some cases will include) a tale of metamorphosis. These are for the most part obscure and inconsequential episodes that contribute nothing of significance to Ovid's larger unfolding history of the universe. They are notable primarily for leaving traces in the local landscape or affecting local culture. They are mentioned in passing, often merely alluded to in the familiar manner of a catalogue. In terms of the poem's requisite thematic, this has every appearance of being a contrivance for extending the textual lifespan of Medea. Her metamorphic career having evidently been exhausted, she is now made a kind of belated witness or internal index to obscure tales of metamorphosis. Through this attenuated, second-order association with the metamorphic, Medea maintains her programmatic relevance to Ovid's epic of transformation. She has become insistently meta–metamorphic: as earlier with the Bacchic coda, Medea is made to evoke narratives of transformation that have nothing whatsoever to do with immediate narrative circumstances. To a large extent this involves Ovid substituting *references* to narratives for narrative as such.

What of the embedded tales of transformation themselves? Medea's travelogue amounts to a metamorphic anthology, a systematic collection of tales of meta-morphosis. It is *a priori* likely that her anthology is not a random collection. In the *Metamorphoses*, embedded or second-order sequences of tales of transformation occur quite frequently, as a convenient platform for articulating Ovid's abiding metapoetic preoccupations. In the Arachne episode (VI. 1–145), for example, the weaving contest between mortal and goddess allows the evocation of the rival poetic visions and competing aesthetic agendas that have informed the *Metamorphoses* from its opening verses. Arachne's and Minerva's weaving have been termed 'poetic tapestries' by Byron Harries, as containing not just pictorial but literary 'threads' that touch upon, *inter alia*, the competing impulses of classicizing versus Hellenistic literary aesthetics.[90] For present purposes, Arachne's tapestry is particularly apposite, for it amounts to an irreverent catalogue of erotically motivated divine metamorphoses, all *caelestia crimina* (VI. 131), that indicate the Hesiodic and Hellenistic affiliations of her artwork, in contrast to the classicizing balance and symmetry of Minerva's composition.[91] Medea's aerial journey works similarly: the Aegean tour allows her to 'map out' a mini-anthology of local tales of metamorphoses in the spirit of Alexandrian poetry.[92] Thus, while the precise textual phenomena in question are somewhat different, the overall effect is quite similar.

The Medea anthology is principally comprised of little-known tales: five of her fifteen tales are otherwise unattested. Five more have only a single parallel; of these, three are from Nicander's *Heteroeumena*, the Hellenistic metamorphosis catalogue poem about which we are best informed, and an important model for Ovid. In general, there is little doubt that a number of the myths invoked in the course of Medea's chariot rides have come from Nicander, including the stories of Cytesylla (368–70) and Cycnus (371–81), which were treated by Nicander (Antonius Liberalis, 1, 12) and probably derive from him.[93] Dietze suggests that at least two additional tales may come from Nicander as well: those of Paris' tomb (361) and the Telchines (365).[94] In the case of the Alcyone tale (400–01), the version here is reported by ps.-Probus (on Virgil, *Georgics*, 1. 399) to have been taken from Nicander. After Nicander's *Heteroeumena*, the Hellenistic metamorphosis catalogue poem about which we are best informed is Boeus' *Ornithogonia*, a poem of humans transformed into birds. It is striking that several of the transformations signalled in this passage are of this type. For Crabbe, 'there is a piquancy to this predominance of birds when Medea herself is aloft'.[95] But the recurring motif also calls to mind specialized Hellenistic catalogue poetry, and that of Boeus in particular. The tales of Botres (388–90) and Periphas (399–401) are likely to have come, whether directly or via Aemilius Macer's translation, from Boeus' *Ornithogonia* (Antonius Liberalis, 18, 6). The poor state of the evidence — we are dealing with fragmentary or lost model texts in all cases — does not allow precision.[96] But it is clear enough that the myths of transformation invoked in the course of Medea's journey hark back to this Alexandrian tradition of metamorphosis catalogue poetry.

Because of the extremely fragmentary survival of these precursors, the precise details of Ovid's intertextual gestures are in many cases irrecoverable, but the contours of the overall strategy may be sketched out. In programmatic terms, what we have here are glimmers of an Alexandrian poetics of transformation — Callimachean, to be sure, but evoking more specifically metamorphosis catalogue poets like Nicander.[97] Critics have pointed out the embeddedness of Nicander's tales in local topography and cult: an overarching concern of the *Heteroeumena* was evidently to link tales of metamorphosis to the origin of local landmarks, religious rites or other cultural practices.[98] Ovid's sequence here exhibits a characteristic Nicandrian blending of geography and mythology as tales of transformation are mapped onto precise geographical locations, with a tight correspondence between literary and geographical *loci*. The Medea anthology is almost exclusively comprised of fringe metamorphoses: such obscure tales, culled from the periphery rather than the mainstream of myth, were the preference of Nicander and his contemporaries, even though, as we shall see, Ovid by no means felt obliged to always stick to the version he found in his Hellenistic models.

Medea's tour — or Ovid's account thereof — recapitulates the essential compositional dynamics of a catalogue poem on the theme of metamorphosis. It brings together within a single textual framework a collection of tales of transformation that exhibit certain common features but otherwise have nothing whatsoever to do with one another. There is no overarching causal or temporal structure to this sequence. The metamorphosis tales evoked by Medea's journey embody a kind of 'Hellenistic' celebration of the idiosyncratic features of local topography and cultural practices in the Hellenic world. All are closely connected to their locales, whether or not the metamorphosis in question results in a concrete monument. Thus, for example, the regions around Othrys are said to have been made famous by the metamorphosis of Cerambus, a human transformed into a beetle (353). More ingeniously, Tempe is said to have been rendered famous by Cycnus' sudden transformation into a swan (371–72), but Ovid's description — *Cycneia Tempe,* | *quae subitus celebravit olor* — could also be taken to mean that Tempe suddenly found itself frequented by swans, thus touching on a local feature of the landscape.[99]

With regard to poetics, Medea's aerial tourism well accords with Ovid's anti-Apollonian agenda in this episode. As we have seen, the route taken by Medea retraces in miniature the voyage of the Argo, displacing the 'muddy' narrative of the epic *Argonautica* in favour of allusive snap-shots of localized significance that require readerly erudition to be properly decoded. The sense of substitution for Apollonius in particular is reinforced by the programmatic mention of the Telchines at Rhodes as one of the vistas (VII. 365–67). The Telchines were a mythical race said to have migrated to Rhodes from Crete. They were sometimes regarded as magicians, and are noteworthy for the metamorphic capacity of their gaze, the so-called 'evil eye': as Ovid himself has it, 'their eyes corrupted all things merely by looking at them' (VII. 366).

In the prologue to the *Aetia*, Callimachus famously sketched out the terms of a contemporary aesthetic debate, pitting the small-scale refinement of his own poetic compositions against the large-scale epic that was favoured by poetic rivals, whom he pseudonymically designated Telchines. In so doing he articulated a kind of manifesto for Alexandrian (or Callimachean) poetics. The Telchines, we are told, rail against the kind of discontinuous narrative structures of catalogue poetry. They insist on 'a single continuous narrative' (ἓν ἄεισμα διηνεκὲς) in thousands of verses, treating the deeds of 'kings or heroes' (ἢ βασιλη ... ἢ ... ἤρωας, 3–5). In short, Callimachus, in one of the most famous poetological passages in all of Greek literature, made the Telchines advocates of large-scale poetry. Whatever the truth of the legendary quarrel between Callimachus and Apollonius Rhodius, these mythic figures can be taken as emblematic of the kind of lengthy epic narrative of which Apollonius' *Argonautica* was a notional representative. Of course his epithet Rhodius indicates that he, like the Telchines, was, if not a native, an inhabitant of Rhodes. The submerging of the Telchines thus sends a suggestive programmatic signal. Together with the reference to the muddy Phasis and Ovid's use of the adjective *perpetuus* at the beginning of the Medea episode, the allusion to the Telchines enacts a suggestive metageneric and stylistic debate.[100] Ovid introduces the Telchines with a notable flourish: *Phoebeamque Rhodon et Ialysios Telchinas* (VII. 365). As Kenney notes, this verse, consisting entirely of Greek names, is a striking instance of Alexandrian preciosity, and quite possibly pays homage to Callimachus in particular.[101] The Argonauts' adventures constituted an epic tale par excellence, and Medea's chariot ride sketches out a substitution, a triumphant Callimachean displacement of a muddy Argonautic epic.

Whereas Apollonius' rendering of the tale maintains a rigorous chronological structure within a continuous narrative (ἓν ἄεισμα διηνεκὲς), Medea's metamorphic 'anthology' shatters any such overarching temporal coherence. It subverts the logic of temporal succession, indeed of logical sequence and the interconnection of narrated events. If Medea's chariot ride is in some sense a 'substitute' *Argonautica*, its content has evidently been refracted through an anti-heroic, Callimachean lens. The only tale from this series of 'fly-by' metamorphoses elaborated in any detail features the love-struck hero Phylius undertaking a series of trials for his beloved Cycnus, trials that culminated in subduing a bull (371–79). As Kenney observes, this seems to replay, in an Alexandrian and homoerotic key, Hercules' servitude to Omphale.[102] Cycnus plays Omphale to Phylius' Hercules, setting a series of tasks for the latter to perform, but this all unfolds in an amatory context, and is decidedly unheroic. When Phylius refuses to hand over the bull as a present, Cycnus petulantly attempts suicide by jumping off a cliff, but undergoes a saving metamorphosis into a swan.[103] The swan was an important poetological symbol in ancient literature, and by the Augustan age it had become an established emblem of Callimachean poetics. The tale of Cycnus and Phylius can thus be seen to both embody and encode the winnowing down of epic heroism into small-scale Alexandrian anti-heroism.

This is the second of three swan metamorphoses in the *Metamorphoses*. Scholars have often argued that the recurring swan imagery signals Ovid's allegiance to the literary tradition of Alexandria.[104] But in the *Metamorphoses*, it is crucial to recall, Ovid pursues the seemingly impossible ambition of realizing Alexandrian sophistication on an epic scale, by weaving together tales of transformation from the beginning of time to the present day in a universal history of Homeric proportions.

As we have discussed in the Introduction to Part I, from the perspective of Hellenistic metamorphosis catalogue poetry, Ovid's crucial innovation was the chronological framework. He aspired to a *carmen perpetuum* (Callimachus' ἓν ἄεισμα διηνεκὲς) that 'transcends' catalogue poetry as the Callimachean Telchines would have it — precisely because of its continuity, its careful temporal unfolding of narrative sequence. Ovid surely succeeded: the *Metamorphoses* dwarfs Apollonius' *Argonautica* and also substantially surpasses the length of its immediate Roman predecessor, Virgil's *Aeneid*.

Considered against this ever-present metaliterary backdrop, Medea's anthology does more than simply displace Apollonius' epic. It also constitutes something like a perverse *mise en abîme* that runs afoul of, and so challenges, Ovid's global artistic choices. The catalogue of tales generated during Medea's chariot ride, while on one level clearly belonging within the thematic remit of the *Metamorphoses*, on another level emerges as a veritable anti-*Metamorphoses*, as it defies the very principles that sustain Ovid's literary universe, including supernatural protagonists, the truth value of mythic variants, chronological coherence, and (Roman) cultural ideology. We will consider each of these categories in turn.

While the Olympian deities, as we had occasion to note, are excluded altogether from the Medea episode proper, they register insistently in the mythic narratives evoked by her chariot ride, not least as metamorphic agents. This is most obvious in the case of those deities that are explicitly named: Bacchus (Liber) transforms a cow stolen by his son into a stag (359–60) in an episode otherwise unknown; Jupiter submerges the Telchines (364–66); and Apollo changes Botres, the unnamed grandson of Cephisos, into a seal (388–89). In other cases, the role of Olympians in the tales can be inferred from elsewhere in Ovid's epic or from other texts. The petrified serpent (357–58) probably refers to the creature that was about to desecrate the head of Orpheus, in which case it was the victim of Apollo's metamorphic intervention (cf. *Met.* XI. 59–60).[105] The unnamed Ctesylla's transformation into a dove (368–70) is probably the work of Apollo and/or Diana (cf. Antonius Liberalis, I); the transformation of Cycnus into a swan (377–79) is elsewhere attested to be the work of Apollo (cf. Antonius Liberalis, 12). For many of the other tales, we have no useful attestations to fill out Ovid's fleeting references; but it is likely that a number of them also involved Olympian deities. So, for instance, Ps.-Lactantius implies that the horns that grew on the Coan women (363–64) were a metamorphic punishment inflicted by Venus.[106] Yet far from signalling a return of the Olympians to epic prominence, the fleeting and allusive manner in which they register here creates a marginalizing effect. In the context of the Medea episode, moreover, the Olympian gods are confined to local aetiological tales bereft of cosmic significance. They are 'bit players' relegated to participation in the kind of obscure local fare favoured by Hellenistic catalogue poets like Callimachus, Nicander and Boeus.

With regard to the truth-value of mythic variants, the version of the Alcyone myth obliquely referred to as Medea completes the brief aerial journey from Corinth to Athens is a particularly interesting case (*Met.* VII. 400–01):

> [intrat Palladias arces, quae] videre [...]
> innixamque novis neptem Polypemonis alis.

[Medea enters the citadel of Pallas, which had seen the granddaughter of
Polypemon rising on new wings.]

This riddling statement requires decoding. Alcyone is here daughter of the Athenian
Sciron, son of Polypemon. Her dissolute conduct provoked her father's wrath, and
so he cast her into the sea; as she was falling, she was transformed into a bird. In the
variant indirectly reported here, then, the halcyon takes its origins from Alcyone,
daughter of the brigand Sciron. Some four books later, however, Ovid provides a
different aetiology for the halcyon, as drawing its origins from a different Alcyone,
wife of Ceyx (XI. 267–748). In this later account, one of the longest and most
celebrated episodes of the *Metamorphoses*, Alcyone's inconsolable grief at the death
of her husband in a shipwreck leads to her transformation into a halcyon. The two
rival, and mutually exclusive, versions are obviously not asserted with equal vigour
by Ovid: here an obscure and fleeting two-verse reference, later a lengthy episode.
But the contradiction is there nonetheless, and was noted by an ancient commentator
(ps.-Probus on Virg. *Georg.* I. 399), who offered the following valuable observation:
*varia est opinio harum volucrum originis. itaque in altera sequitur Ovidius Nicandrum, in
altera Theodorum* ['There is a difference of opinion about the origin of these birds.
Accordingly in one account Ovid follows Nicander; in the other, Theodorus']. In
other words, the earlier of Ovid's two versions of Alcyone, that is the one here
at VII. 400–01, comes from Nicander. And it clearly stands as a 'rival' or alternate
version to the one Ovid elaborates more fully later in the poem. A similar effect
is achieved by the seemingly off-hand reference to a petrified serpent at 357–58,
which clearly asks to be (and has been) identified with the creature that attacked
the head of Orpheus, an event that will occur much later in the *Metamorphoses*
(XI. 56–60). There is, however, a slight discrepancy in geographical location: in
Met. VII, the snake is located at Pitane in Aeolia on the mainland of Asia Minor; in
Met. XI, the attack and subsequent petrifaction occurred at Methymna on the island
of Lesbos. From Medea's point of view, as she flies southwards along the coast, the
two locations all but face each other across the intervening water, the mainland
location on the left, the island location on the right. This produces a suggestive
mirroring effect, with the inset and framing narratives inverting one another. The
two snakes thus both are and are not the same, relating as object and reflection, the
latter an embedded simulacrum of the former.

Even more disconcerting are the chronological distortions that the chariot-ride
enacts within the larger context of the *Metamorphoses*. Medea's mini-catalogue has
an impressively wide temporal span, almost as wide-ranging as Ovid's own. The
earliest chronological reference occurs with Medea's arrival at Corinth. Ovid makes
this city less noteworthy for tragic events à la Euripides than for a peculiar tradition
of anthropogenesis: it was there that, according to one tradition, human beings
initially sprang from mushrooms (*Met.* VII. 392–93):

> [...] hic aevo veteres mortalia primo
> corpora vulgarunt pluvialibus edita fungis.

[It was here, as men of old used to say, that in the earliest age human bodies
were produced from rain-sprung mushrooms.]

Rather than dwelling on the tragic culmination of the story of Medea and Jason, the poet focuses on a decidedly bizarre cosmogonic metamorphosis. This would appear to offer a new account of the genesis of the human race, one that seems to rival Ovid's more elaborate anthropogenesis sequence in the opening book (1. 76–88).[107] Moreover this mention comes near the midpoint of an epic whose stated program is a systematic chronological progression from cosmogony to Ovid's own time (*prima [...] ab origine mundi |ad mea [...] tempora*, 1. 3–4). This is, in other words, a rather curious place to address fundamental developments of cosmogony that were settled in the opening book.

If this belated cosmogonic supplement is an awkward intrusion in Ovid's chronological scheme, more problematic still is the brief account of the metamorphosis of Cerambus, given as Medea travels over Mt Othrys (*Met.* VII. 353–56):

> [fugit ... super ...] eventu veteris loca nota Cerambi:
> hic ope nympharum sublatus in aera pennis
> cum gravis infuso tellus foret obruta ponto
> Deucalioneas effugit inobrutus undas.

> [Medea fled over the region made famous by old Cerambus' fate. By the aid of nymphs he was raised into the air on wings, at the time when the overburdened earth had sunk beneath the advancing sea, and thereby escaped Deucalion's flood unsubmerged.]

Again, this is a decidedly odd textual locale to narrate details from the primordial flood: *Deucalioneas ... undas* makes unambiguous that Ovid is rehashing events narrated at 1. 262–437. Moreover this brief sketch of Cerambus' metamorphosis evidently promulgates a rival version of the flood that contradicts Ovid's earlier account. In particular, the survival of Cerambus contradicts the statement that airborne creatures perished (1. 307–08) along with the other animals, so that all species had to be reproduced after the waters subsided (1. 416–17). Ovid indicated quite clearly that the only survivors of the flood were Pyrrha and Deucalion (1. 325–26). In other words, this reference offers an emended version of cosmic history, one that seems to challenge the veracity of Ovid's earlier account, yet features nymphs, part of the divine hierarchy under Jupiter, as metamorphic agents. A glance at Nicander's account, the only other version of the Cerambus myth that has come down to us, confirms that we are dealing with a deliberate affront. Antoninus Liberalis 22, citing Nicander, reports that Cerambus dwelled at the foot of Mt Othrys; he angered the local nymphs who consequently transformed him into a scarabaeus or winged beetle; Nicander, in short, had nymphs changing Cerambus into a beetle as a punishment in a non-deluvian context. Ovid's treatment is entirely different; and the differences, clearly a conscious choice on Ovid's part, create problems for the framing narrative of the epic.

The backward glances to the cosmogonic sequence in the opening book are matched by prospective glances to the event that brings the Greek part of Ovid's narrative to a close, namely, the Trojan War, recounted in *Met.* XII and XIII. Like the coded reference to Alcyone (Ovid calls her *neptem Polypemonis*, 401), these gestures are not instantly obvious: Paris figures behind *pater Corythi* (361) and Hecuba (probably) behind *Maera* (362).[108] Ovid has every reason to be coy about these allusions to the experiences of two prominent figures of the Trojan War: within the ordered chronological scheme of the poem, they are impossible. Consider the reference to Paris at VII. 361, or more precisely the reference to the unimpressive grave mound (cf. *parva tumulatus harena*) of the 'father of Corythus' (*pater Corythi*). This periphrastic designation identifies Paris, who was father of Corythus by Oenone, his Asian bride whom he forsook for Helen (Oenone is also, of course, the fictional author of *Heroides* v).[109] The necessary implication of a grave is that Paris is already dead — but Ovid features him still alive and well at XII. 598–606, where he accomplishes the crucial feat of killing Achilles. So Medea is here passing over a grave that cannot yet exist in the narrative universe of the *Metamorphoses*. The inconsistency is not merely internal to Ovid's epic: ancient mythographic chronologies invariably date the Trojan War to a period *after* the exploits of the Argonauts.[110] Moreover, the Oenone variant mentioned here does not belong to the conventional epic tradition, which has Paris die on the battlefield.[111] What we have, then, is a humble death monument memorializing a hero not yet born who, consequently, has not yet had the chance to embark upon his epic career. It is no wonder that the grave is small! In its immediate context, the diminutive monument embodies, and neatly serves as a metaphorical image of, Medea's anti-epic programme.[112]

The incongruous retrospective and prospective references to the cosmogony and the Trojan War, respectively, stage a breakdown of the temporal scheme that underwrites the *Metamorphoses*. Medea's chariot ride plunges the poem into a defiantly atemporal mode, distorting narrative time and destroying the temporal sequencing (the ἓν ἄεισμα διηνεκὲς) that, as a formal feature, makes Ovid's epic something 'more' than a catalogue poem. The individual metamorphoses are treated briefly with a high degree of allusivity, rather than *in extenso* (ἐν πολλαῖς ἤνυσα χιλιάσιν) as the Callimachean Telchines preferred and as Ovid does elsewhere in the epic. In previous articles we have examined some of the ways in which Ovid focuses upon and plays with problems of temporality in the early books of the *Metamorphoses*.[113] For the most part, Ovid 'plays with time' in the early books in order to project the poem's triumphant Roman teleology. Something more radical is going on here: a comprehensive, if momentary, rupturing of the poem's chronological framework. Medea's journey maps out a 'Nicandrian' poetic programme, i.e. that of Alexandrian metamorphosis catalogue poetry in the Nicandrian manner. In crucial respects this programme runs counter to that of Ovid's own poem. Medea's aerial voyage gives rise to a sequence of metamorphosis tales that has its own structuring principles and as such suggests an alternate possibility for the unfolding of Ovid's poem. It constitutes a rival aesthetic construction, an embedded poetic scheme that renders precarious the poetic project of the framing epic. Medea's counter-vision contradicts the narrative reality of the *Metamorphoses*; it disrupts the chronological imperative of the principles of causality that are operative elsewhere in the poem. The modal switch from a temporal to a spatial logic is suggestive in itself: as far as can be determined, Hellenistic metamorphosis catalogue poetry was structured according to atemporal schemes, and will have often used geography either as a primary or secondary organizing principle.

Medea's counterworld extends to the level of cultural ideology. To begin with, as we have seen, the episode turns away from tales of 'kings and heroes' (ἢ βασιλη ... ἢ ... ρους ἥρωας), the *sujet* of traditional epic (such as Apollonius Rhodius' *Argonautica*) and the preferred reading matter of the Telchines. More importantly, Medea's aerial tourism enacts a cultural poetics that Ovid excised from the larger epic — a poetics rooted in the countless local cultures of the Greek world. Her catalogue presents a collection of stories involving metamorphosis that privilege the idiosyncratic features of local legends at the expense of global narrative coherence. It thereby fleetingly celebrates a cultural poetics that stands at odds with the imperial, Roman thrust of the *Metamorphoses* as a whole. Indeed it is the opposite of Ovid's *modus operandi* elsewhere in the epic, which consists of disentangling or even uprooting his chosen myths from their original aetiological context, depriving them of their local import, as they become components of a universal history, the telos of which is Rome.[114] As Buxton observes, 'instead of localizing the transformation in a specific part of the Greek world, or relating it to cultic activities which take place "even today", the Ovidian emphasis is generic'.[115] As discussed elsewhere in this volume, Ovid was by no means the first poet to write a poem dedicated to the theme of metamorphosis.[116] The Hellenistic Age saw the production of a great many such works, and Ovid certainly had a number of these at hand.[117] The audacity of Ovid's epic lies not in its programmatic resort to metamorphosis as such, but rather its reconception of cosmic history as a continuous narrative of metamorphosis. This continuity and coherence sets the *Metamorphoses* apart from Hellenistic metamorphosis catalogue poems, which simply grouped transformations by type or other non-continuous criteria. Yet in the Medea episode, Ovid stages a return of the elided and suppressed, in order to show up Hellenistic predecessors like Nicander and Boeus, and thereby set his own poetic achievement in relief.

Conclusion

Medea's final moment in the *Metamorphoses* is a fitting end to her singular career in Ovid's epic, as she yields the narrative stage to a heroic figure, who is, in many ways, her opposite: Theseus, son of her new husband, Aegeus, king of Athens.[118] She tries to poison Theseus, scheming to have the unwitting Aegeus kill his son, as yet unrecognized, in a generational inversion of the murder of Pelias. But at the last moment the Athenian king recognizes Theseus and knocks the poisoned chalice from his lips. Though caught red-handed, Medea once again escapes punishment. This evasion is her last action in Ovid's narrative: *effugit illa necem nebulis per carmina motis* ['she escapes death, after mists have been summoned by spells'] (VII. 424). The text clearly implies that Medea conceals herself by generating mists with her spells, but Ovid chooses an ablative absolute construction — *nebulis per carmina motis* — that occludes agency as Medea finally vanishes from the narrative. It is a programmatically inconclusive exit, and in various ways.

The nature of Medea's disappearance highlights once more her ambiguous status between mortal and immortal, and her ability to arrogate divine privileges for personal use: concealment in mist is a familiar expedient of epic divinities for protecting their mortal favourites, and Medea is here both the generator and the recipient of this device, both god-like and yet vulnerable to harm, though this harm is never realized. How does she get away? Presumably, in her aerial chariot, but Ovid does not say so. Where is she going? Presumably, back to Asia, to live out the Medeian phase of her biography, but Ovid does not tell us this. The conclusion is remarkable for its indeterminacy in other respects as well: critics have noted the unusual lack of a terminal metamorphosis, along with the absence of other signals of closure. The effect of Ovid's treatment is to make her seem perpetually in motion. She is, to be sure, a notoriously itinerant figure: as one critic has well observed: '[f]rom Colchis to Corinth to Athens to Persia she flees, unable to take root in the Greek landscape — a heroine not of foundation, but of annihilation'.[119] Ovid's episode ends with her in motion, but that motion is, paradoxically, an apt resting place for her narrative in the *Metamorphoses*, for it leaves her in precisely that interstitial space in which Ovid reinvented her literary biography. The sense of anti-closure is suggestive in other ways as well. If we read the episode as an allegory of poetic composition, then it is appropriate that it does not so much end as fold back into the framing narrative of the *Metamorphoses* itself.[120] The Medea narrative has no teleology as such. Her magical activities, homicidal schemes, and aerial tours of the Greek world eventually peter out inconsequentially, as Ovid's own narrative resumes, and its programmatic qualities reassert themselves. Yet the manner of her narrative exit reinforces Medea's special status as the metaliterary champion of a rival poetic vision. It is surely no coincidence that Medea takes her exit *per carmina*, a term that encapsulates her double function as a figure who stands out for her metapoetic (*carmen*, in the sense of poetry) and metamorphic (*carmen*, in the sense of transformative spell) significance. Her story in the *Metamorphoses* amounts to a particularly elaborate and sustained allegory. Medea's metaliterary qualities have been well analysed by Gertz, who, however, distinguishes her from other such figures in that she 'focuses her art on continuous narrative action, thereby avoiding creation of an actual metaphor'.[121] But if there is no metaphor for the artistic product, there is one for the artistic process — in the form of Medea's chariot, an aerial vehicle, drawn by winged dragons, connected to her grandfather Sol, the sun god. It is found only once in earlier literature, appearing as a kind of *deus ex machina* during the dénouement of Euripides' *Medea*, to facilitate Medea's escape from Corinth after murdering her children (a scene briefly signalled at *Met.* VII. 398–99). For the Greek playwright, it was emblematic of her supernatural powers and her curious proximity to godhead. In *Metamorphoses* VII, this striking aeronautic vehicle features fully four times, twice in extended episodes. Ovid, then, affords the aerial chariot a new role and a greatly increased importance; as Kenney well notes, it speaks to the controlling power exercised by Medea — not only over nature, but also over narrativity.[122] The vehicle first appears at the conclusion of Medea's initial prayer for magical empowerment, and evidently in response to it (VII. 218–19). The chariot is, of course, a stock poetological metaphor, suggesting Medea's status as a figure of poetic self-reference (much like the fact that she produces *carmina*).[123] The aerial chariot affords Medea a god-like perspective, which is also an authorial perspective, on the world and mortal affairs. The bizarre voyages through the skies, then, represent a specific mode of empowerment. As Pavlock observes, aerial flight in the *Metamorphoses* 'is a form of liberation from normal human constraints that implies common ground with the creative experience of the poet himself'.[124] The chariot rides, in other words, support the overall reading of the episode as an elaborate allegory of poetic composition. They are the embodiment of and narrative 'vehicle' for Ovid's innovative treatment, but also a symbol of his veering off from conventional mythographic accounts. From this perspective, Medea's repeated aerial journeys become at once both the poetological metaphor and the narrative realization of Ovid's quest for a new narrative direction in the treatment of his heroine's biography. As Gertz puts it, 'Medea's journeying becomes a metaphor for the power of poetry to generate new tales, perhaps most obvious when in naming the stations of Medea's flight, Ovid presents loci that concomitantly serve as reminders of various other myths and fictions.'[125]

But Medea's metaliterary status, important and intriguing as it is in its own right, is arguably supplemental to a larger purpose. Within his metamorphic history of the cosmos, Ovid uses the Medea episode to explore alternate transformative modalities, basically juxtaposing two different sources of metamorphic energy. On the one hand, there is the essentially instantaneous ability of the gods to manipulate matter (both organic and inorganic, both self and other) at whim by virtue of an innate supernatural capacity. This is the principal transformational mechanism of Ovid's narrative. On the other hand, there is the magical power of herbs and similar ingredients when manipulated by those possessing the requisite knowledge.[126] This is a rival source that periodically emerges in the course of the epic, but nowhere more forcefully than in the Medea episode. From Homer's Circe episode onwards, the two systems of transformation uneasily coexist in latent forms of rivalry: think of Hermes' intervention to save Odysseus from Circe's magical powers, as he combats her magical herbs with yet another magical herb, known to the Olympians. It was Ovid who made Medea truly metamorphic, a virtual patron saint of transformative change.[127] His reinvention of Medea as a metamorphic character both addresses the programmatic requirements of his epic and constitutes a carefully orchestrated and self-consciously staged authorial encounter with the overly prescriptive tradition he inherited.

Notes to Chapter 1

1. For representations of Medea on Greek vases see e.g. Buxton (2010) or Revermann (2010).
2. See Zissos (2008), pp. xvii–xxv; Cowan (2010).
3. For her classical and post-classical career see the edited collections by Clauss and Iles Johnston (1997), Hall, Macintosh, and Taplin (2000), and Bartel and Simon (2010).
4. Verducci (1985), p. 71.
5. In her prayer to various deities for magical assistance at *Met.* VII. 199–214, Medea provides a catalogue of past and habitual magical feats, which includes no metamorphoses. The same holds for Hypsipyle's enumeration of Medea's powers at Ovid, *Heroides*, VI. 83–92.
6. This, at any rate, is the canonical genealogy attested from Hesiod, *Theogony*, 956–62. A later tradition, attested at Diodorus Siculus, IV, 45, strengthens Medea's ties to sorcery by making her sister (rather than niece) to Circe and daughter (rather than priestess) to Hecate, goddess of witchcraft, whose poetic epithet *triformis* (*Met.* VII. 94, 177) speaks to her regular alternation of form.

7. As we have discussed in the Introduction to Part I, the third metamorphic paradigm appears in the final book of the epic with Pythagoras, who is a spokesperson for what we might call 'natural metamorphosis'.

8. For the distinction, cf. Segal (2002), p. 6: 'Ovid's gods generally act through their own supernatural power rather than by magic'.

9. Liveley (2011), p. 77, though identifying *amor* as the key magical ingredient effecting the transformation.

10. We thereby cover some of the same ground as Pavlock (2009), ch. 2: 'The Metamorphic Medea', though reaching some rather different conclusions, in particular about the role and function of Medea within the *Metamorphoses* as a whole.

11. Cf. Binroth-Bank (1994), p. 150.

12. The canonical status of Apollonius' treatment for Roman poets is indicated by the 'translation' of Varro of Atax in the first century BC; see further Zissos (2008), p. xxii.

13. According to the first hypothesis of the play, Euripides followed the outline of an earlier drama by Neophron; see Boedeker (1997), p. 127.

14. See in particular Hunter (1993), pp. 8–25.

15. Cf. the pertinent, if obtuse, suggestion of Kienzl (1903), p. 40, that Ovid derived these verses from a mythological compendium.

16. Barchiesi (2001), pp. 159–61. It should be added that *perpetuus* is used in reference to Phineus, a pre-eminent prophet in Apollonius' *Argonautica*, and as such a poet-substitute who after his delivery from torment 'charts out' the remainder of the action of the epic for the Argonauts (such disclosure carried to excess being the reason for his torment in the first place).

17. By insisting on the variant in which Medea herself takes care of the dragon — the opening *pervigilem superest herbis sopire draconem* forecloses other possibilities — Ovid elides more heroic versions in which Jason fights the dragon.

18. The basic narrative correspondences are clear enough — Ovid's reworking at *Met.* VII. 106–10 of the simile at *Arg.* III. 1299–1305 signals the close imitation — and will not be enumerated here; but see also n. 21 below.

19. See conveniently Hunter (1993), pp. 15–25.

20. Hunter (1993), p. 31; for opposing views, see Carspecken (1952), pp. 99–140; Lawall (1966), pp. 121–69.

21. The trials take place at dawn in the field of Mars, with the local population sitting on the surrounding hills as spectators (*Met.* VII. 100–02 ~ *Arg.* III. 1191–92, 1270, 1276); Aeetes sits in splendour in the middle (*Met.* VII. 102–03 ~ *Arg.* III. 1275). See further Kienzl (1903), pp. 38–39.

22. For further comments on this important passage see below pp. 99–100.

23. See Virgil, *Aeneid*, VIII, 201–04: *nam maximus ultor | tergemini nece Geryonae spoliisque superbus | Alcides aderat taurosque hac victor agebat | ingentis*. The intertext underscores the shift from Hercules' heroic defeat of the monstrous giant and the victorious abduction of the bulls as spoils to Jason's adventures in the petting zoo and his victorious abduction of the fleece and the maiden.

24. Anderson (1972), p. 261. More recently Kenney (2011), p. 237 has pointed to the ironic force of *heros Aesonius* (156), given the resounding lack of heroism demonstrated by Jason up to this point. Rather similar in spirit, if different in purpose, is Hypsipyle's jibe at *Her.* VI. 103–04 that 'it was not Aeson's son but Aeetes' daughter, the Phasian woman, who removed the golden fleece of Phrixus' ram'.

25. Note that *flagrantem ... domum* makes concrete an imagined detail from Euripides: his Medea considers the possibility of arson (*Med.* 376–79), but dismisses it as too risky an undertaking. Ovid's formidable heroine thus both recapitulates and trumps her predecessor.

26. Cf. Lafaye (1904), p. 91: 'il passe [...] parce qu'il l'a traité dans sa tragédie de *Médée*.' Some critics have suggested that Ovid's compression of the tragic fallout is facilitated by the parallelism between Medea's plight in Corinth and Procne's in Book VI, which allows for the rehearsal of pertinent tragic issues and themes (such as maternal infanticide) elsewhere. See, e.g., Larmour (1990), pp. 132–34 and Newlands (1997), pp. 192–208.

27. Cf. Binroth-Bank (1994), p. 150.

28. The use of such interior monologue is itself indebted to Apollonius Rhodius, who used the technique three times in his epic to illuminate Medea's anguished passion for Jason. For Apollonius' important development of the use of the interior monologue in ancient epic, see Fusillo (2001).

29. Kenney (1986), p. 413; cf. Anderson (1972), p. 243.

30. Newlands (1997), p. 181.

31. Rosner-Siegel (1982), p. 234 (and *passim*).

32. Cf. Auhagen (1999), pp. 137–44, esp. 144, who notes that 'Ovid Medea diesen Monolog nicht zur Illustration ihres Charakters oder als "realistische" Erläuterung ihrer Handlungen in den Mund gelegt hat, sondern als intellektuelle, sprachlich und inhaltlich anspruchsvolle Gedankenspielerei.'

33. Medea's anticipation that, on the voyage to Greece, she and the Argonauts will encounter Scylla and Charybdis, two monsters that infested the strait between Italy and Sicily (*Met.* VII. 62–65) is impossible to explain on the immediate narrative level. This signals the version of Apollonius, who, rather than having the Greek heroes retrace their outward voyage, had opted for a particularly elaborate return route that sees the Argonauts proceed by the rivers of northern Europe to the western coast of Italy, whence they return to Greece passing Scylla and Charybdis. In Apollonius' narrative, the Greek heroes themselves do not consider taking a homeward route different to that by which they came until long after their departure from Colchis (*Arg.* IV. 253–56). Ovid's Medea on the other hand, has evidently managed to map out their return voyage shortly after their arrival. In both contextual and intertextual terms, Medea's informed speculation about the Argonauts' route back to Greece is an absurdity, and rendered even more absurd by the fact that in *Met.* VII Ovid does not bother to specify which route home the Argonauts took (cf. VII. 156–58). For this sort of intertextual play throughout the episode see further Hinds (1994).

34. Previous versions of herself: Medea's epigrammatic declaration *aliudque cupido, | mens aliud suadet; video meliora proboque, | deteriora sequor* ['Passion approves one course, reason another; I see and approve the better course, but I follow the worse'] (VII. 19–21) recalls her stated dilemma at Euripides, *Medea*, 1078–79: καὶ μανθάνω μὲν οἶα δρᾶν μέλλω κακά, | θυμὸς δὲ κρείσσων τῶν ἐμῶν βουλευμάτων ['I realize the wrongs I am about to commit, but my wrath overpowers my reason']. This is a case of transposed self-citation. Ovid's 'Apollonian' Medea, still in her initial pangs of passion, quotes herself from her 'Euripidean' future, from the moment in which she will resolve to murder her children. This transposed citation signals a kind of telescopic transcendence of the inherited tradition, as Medea fuses her epic present with her tragic future. Likewise, Medea 'anticipates' arguments that Euripides' Jason uses at a chronologically subsequent stage, as when, by way of discounting his debt to Medea, Jason remarks 'In return for saving me, you got more than you gave [...] you left a barbarous land (βαρβάρου χθονὸς) to become a resident of Greece' (Euripides, *Medea*, 534–37). Ovid's Medea 'anticipates' this: *nempe est mea barbara tellus [...] non magna linquam, magna sequar* (VII. 53–55). Jason's later rationalization for his act of spousal desertion neatly becomes Medea's rationalization for her act of filial desertion.

35. So, for example, Medea chides herself for thinking of her projected relationship with Jason as a marriage: *coniugiumne putas speciosaque nomina culpae | inponis, Medea, tuae?* ['You think it wedlock, Medea — you apply that respectable term to your offense?'] (*Met.* VII. 69–70). This is a clear echo of Virgil's characterization of Dido's behaviour at *Aeneid*, IV. 172 (*coniugium vocat, hoc praetexit nomine culpam*). The echo is intertextually apt inasmuch as Virgil had in crucial respects modelled the character of Dido on Apollonius' Medea. So on one level, it can be seen as an act of intertextual reclamation, and one endowed with a conspicuous metaliterary competence. In the *Aeneid*, Dido is not fully aware of or willing to own up to her *culpa*: it is the poet himself who, making a rare editorial intervention, suggests that she is deluding herself and others in calling the relationship a marriage. In the *Metamorphoses*, by contrast, Medea recasts the negative judgment of the Virgilian authorial persona in the form of a self-critique.

36. The close connection of Medea's monologue with the sentiments she expresses in *Heroides* XII has been well discussed in modern criticism — see, e.g., Knox (1986) and Hinds (1994). As Wise (1982), observes, though, there is a crucial difference: 'whereas the Medea of the epistles

interprets past events, the Medea of the *Metamorphoses* projects possibilities for the future' (p. 16).

37. This fundamental insight is already made by Binroth-Bank (1994), p. 112, observing that once Ovid's account turns to her magical activity, the reader is no longer afforded access to her thoughts, only to her actions.

38. Cf. the blunt assessment of Kenney (2001): 'Ovid's solution to the problem of accounting for the metamorphosis of bewildered ingénue to "shrewdly calculating woman" of the world is unscrupulous: to burke, to proceed, in effect, as if it did not exist. He [Ovid] makes no attempt to emulate Apollonius' subtle explorations of the paradoxes of Medea's character' (p. 283).

39. Some scholars have found it difficult to accept a radical, literal reading of Ovid's text here. See e.g. Kenney (2011) pp. 226–27, who states that '*casu*' should be placed in quotation marks since Jason is 'obviously' not specially handsome by chance, but because of a strategic intervention by an unnamed divinity (he nominates Cupid as the most likely candidate): put differently, he interprets the passage as if Ovid were repeating, rather than rewriting, Apollonius.

40. As a general rule, it might be said that Hecate, goddess of magic, opens up a provisional realm of female empowerment, often set against male figures or male authority. So, for example, when Virgil's Dido curses Aeneas, she does so with an invocation to Hecate (*Aen.* IV. 609).

41. *Met.* II. 122–23: *tum pater ora sui <u>sacro medicamine</u> nati | contigit et rapidae fecit patientia flammae.*

42. *Met.* IV. 387–88: *motus uterque parens nati rata verba biformis | fecit et <u>incesto</u> fontem <u>medicamine</u> tinxit.*

43. Ovid programmatically uses *medicamen* three times in the Medea episode. Apart from VII. 116, the word occurs also at 262 and 311. There are only two further instances in the rest of the poem: XIV. 285 (*tantum medicamina possunt*, with reference to the potion that Circe uses to turn men into animals) and XV. 533–34 (*nec nisi Apollineae valido medicamine prolis | reddita vita foret*, with reference to the substance Apollo's son Aesculapius used to revive Hippolytus as Virbius).

44. See Gildenhard and Zissos (2007) for the switch from Olympian to chthonic divinities (the Furies) in this episode.

45. Indeed Ovid himself provides the *locus classicus* in his earlier poetry at *Amores* II. 1.

46. Most notably *Odyssey* X and *Argonautica* III and IV. Medea was, to be sure, already a formidable sorceress in Apollonius Rhodius' last book — her destruction of the bronze giant Talos from a distance, for example, provokes an authorial interjection (IV. 1673–77) — but not a practitioner of metamorphic magic as such.

47. See Riddehough (1959), p. 203. We exclude from this category the anthropogenesis of the Pyrrha and Deucalion episode, in which humans merely facilitate a divine act under divine instruction (I. 398–402; cf. 416-17, where Tellus performs a like act *sponte sua* ['of her own accord']), as again with the similarly 'agricultural' generation of the earth-born men at III. 101-10 and the reprise of this feat at VII. 121-30.

48. *Nostoi*, fr. 7 Bernabé: αὐτίκα δ' Αἴσονα θῆκε φίλον κόρον ἡβώοντα | γῆρας ἀποξύσασα ἰδυίῃσι πραπίδεσσι, | φάρμακα πόλλ' ἕψουσ' ἐνὶ χρυσείοισι λέβησιν ['After having boiled many drugs in the golden cauldron, [Medea] turned Aeson into a dear young boy, stripping off his old age through her sagacity'].

49. See below p. 110.

50. The rejuvenation was excluded from elevated poetic accounts and explicitly ruled out in certain versions of the myth (e.g. those in which Pelias murders Aeson before Jason's return from Colchis with Medea). In one variant, reported at Pseudo-Apollodorus, I. 9. 27, Jason himself performed the rejuvenation procedure; see further Bömer (1976), pp. 241–42.

51. The continuing discomfort occasioned by Medea's rejuvenation metamorphosis is evident in Boccaccio's evasive treatment: *Et post longas, secundum quosdam, circumitiones in Thesaliam devenit, ubi precibus Jasonis Esonem patrem annositate decrepitum in robustiorem retraxit etatem* (*Gen. D.* IV. 12.4). By crediting Jason's prayers without naming Medea, Boccaccio almost seems to make divine agency responsible for the transformation.

52. The fullest account of this tale, in which the wife volunteers to have her own lifespan transferred to her husband, is found in Euripides' *Alcestis*. An interesting detail, excluded from the Euripidean account, is found at Aeschylus, *Eumenides* 728, reporting that Apollo got the fates to agree to this unusual transference by first getting them drunk.

53. In this context, it is interesting that we get a hint of ethical relativity: Medea is moved by Jason's

pietas (*mota est pietate rogantis*, VII. 169), but refers to his request as a *scelus* (172). In this case, it is a matter of point of view: a request that is pious from the perspective of Jason as son is also a wicked act from the perspective of Medea as wife: she cannot be particularly pleased by the prospect of having a prematurely aged husband.

54. This is an intriguing anticipation of the ethical qualms of modern science fiction, even if the issue is not followed up in Ovid's subsequent narrative. In the prayer that follows, Medea even adopts a peremptory tone with the nether deities, almost as if she knows that they will (have to) do her bidding: perhaps we capture here a conflation of two models, one in which the divinity in charge retains a certain degree of ethical autonomy (and can refuse to cooperate in acts she deems illicit) and one which assumes that certain magical procedures are sufficiently powerful to enforce supernatural support if correctly performed. This was also the case with certain rituals in Rome's civic religion: for discussion, see Gildenhard (2011), pp. 299–326.

55. The Orpheus and Eurydice episode (X. 1–77) raises similar issues. Likewise Aesculapius incurs Jupiter's wrath for restoring Hippolytus to life (prophesied by his nurse Ocyrhoe at II. 640–48). Ovid does not recount Aesculapius' revivification of Hippolytus in the *Metamorphoses*, but does so at *Fasti*, VI. 753–56: 'Three times [Aesculapius] touched [Hippolytus'] breast, and three times spoke salubrious words; [Hippolytus] raised his head, laid low, from the earth.' It is procedural, and Jupiter is crucially said to slay him because of the dangerous precedent of his excessive use of *artes*: *Iuppiter, exemplum veritus, derexit in ipsum | fulmina qui nimiae artis moverat opem* (*Fasti*, VI. 759–60). See also Virbius' retrospective at *Met.* XV. 533–34 (cited above, n. 43).

56. It is also suggestive that other goddesses use liquids that seem to play a role in metamorphosis: Diana splashes Actaeon as she turns him into a stag (III. 188–97); Ceres throws a drink into the face of a boy she changes into a lizard (V. 446–61); Proserpina throws liquid into the face of an informer (V. 538–45).

57. In terms of the human metamorphic and the miraculous use of herbs, note that at XV. 359–60 Pythagoras mentions, with scepticism, the report that Scythian women, by applying herbs, are able to cover their bodies with feathers. Pythagoras evinces a scientific scepticism towards magic here; he is a spokesperson for 'natural' metamorphosis. Medea's aggressive control over nature (VII. 200–02), which resembles that of her aunt Circe (XIV. 407–09), is in a sense antithetical to Pythagoras' emphasis on natural processes.

58. Kenney (2011), p. 242.

59. In the later, feigned, rejuvenation of Pelias, Medea seems to propose to his daughters something more along the lines of a blood transfusion: *veterem [...] haurite cruorem | ut repleam vacuas iuvenali sanguine venas* ['drain the old blood so that I may fill his empty veins with youthful blood'] (VII. 333–34). Indeed, in the trial demonstration with an old ram, Medea drains the creature's blood and then plunges it into the cauldron bubbling with magical ingredients (314–17); and she follows this procedure with Pelias (348–49), the difference being that the ingredients in the cauldron are powerless and inert (326–27).

60. See Tupet (1986), esp. p. 2635.

61. Details of this lost tragedy are preserved at Macrobius, *Saturnalia*, V. 19. 9–11.

62. Homer, *Odyssey*, X. 275–306.

63. Scarborough (1991), p. 143

64. One could consider appending *Met.* VII. 226–27 ([...] *placitas* [sc. *herbas*] *partim radice revellit, | partim succidit curvamine falcis aenae*) to the allusive dialogue between Sophocles' *Rhizotomoi* and Virgil, *Aeneid*, IV. 513–14 (*falcibus et messae ad lunam quaerentur aënis | pubentes herbae nigri cum lacte veneni*; from the scene of witchcraft Dido performs in anticipation of her suicide) that Macrobius claims to have spotted at *Saturnalia*, V. 19.6–12. He argues that Virgil took at his model for his bronze blades (*falcibus ... aënis*) the Greek phrase χαλκέοις δρεπάνοις, which refers to the bronze instrument Medea uses in the Sophoclean play to cut her roots. Ovid would then be returning the bronze blade that originally belonged to Medea but had temporarily been borrowed by Dido to her rightful owner, while perhaps also 'correcting' the title of Sophocles' drama by stressing that his Medea *pulls out* some herbs *with their roots* and cuts others. Macrobius, of course, weakens his case for direct borrowing by also noting that 'bronze instruments are generally used for sacrifice, and above all in sacrifices that aim either to soothe people, or curse them, or (finally) heal them of illnesses' (V. 19. 11, trans. by Kaster).

65. Indeed, one tradition, attested at the Scholion to Aristophanes, *Clouds*, 74, made Medea directly responsible for the prevalence of magic in Thessaly.
66. Kenney (2011), pp. 244–45 aptly refers to it as a kind of 'spiritual homeland'.
67. With *certis regionibus* (VII. 223), which Melville translates as 'regions she knew of old'.
68. The dragons' skin sloughing may have been suggested by Sophocles' *Rhizotomoi*: cf. Macrobius, *Saturnalia*, V. 19.10–11 [= Soph. fr. 492 Radt]: *Medeam describit maleficas herbas secantem, sed adversam, ne vi noxii odoris ipsa interficeretur* ['in which [Sophocles] describes Medea cutting noxious herbs, but with her head turned away, lest she be killed by the power of the harmful odor '].
69. Newlands (1997), p. 187.
70. So, e.g., Galinsky (1975), p. 65: 'the motivation is relegated to half a line at the beginning of the episode [...] and it comes without any previous development that would explain it.' Nearly all versions of the legend have Medea acting for Jason, getting revenge on his behalf. Ovid himself had signalled this at *Heriodes*, XII. 129–32; and in the *Metamorphoses* the fact that Medea maintains the pretence of a rift with Jason over an extended period would seem to necessitate collusion on his part, even if Ovid does not explicitly report it. Pseudo-Apollodorus (I. 9. 16) and Hyginus (*Fab.* 24) actually state that Jason plotted the murder of Pelias, using Medea as his instrument. Pindar's account likewise projects this future, though without motivating it on any level, by characterizing Medea, as she flees Colchis with Jason, as τὰν Πελίαο φονόν (*Pyth.* IV. 250).
71. Newlands (1997), p. 188.
72. Kenney (2011), p. 254.
73. For such punning on Medea's name, which goes back at least to Pindar, see Hunter (1989), p. 185 on *Arg.* III. 826: μήδεα κούρης.
74. The examination of the rival sources of metamorphic power in the Medea episode provides a crucial precedent for Lucan's witch Erictho in *Bellum Civile* VI. The Neronian poet learned a great deal from Ovid's Medea episode, taking up this opposition between magic and divine fiat. If Medea temporarily supplants the Olympian gods in Ovid and conjures more generally a vision of an inverted poetic universe, in which the conventional Olympian gods (and the associated divine machinery) are excluded from the primary narrative level, marginalized by their relegation to a series of insignificant local aetiological tales, Lucan eclipses the gods programmatically throughout his epic, at the centre of which he places Erictho.
75. See Gildenhard and Zissos (1999b) and (2007). See in particular *Met.* VI. 635 (*scelus est pietas in coniuge Tereo*) and VIII. 477 (*impietate pia est*), which is followed by an invocation of the Furies (480–84).
76. Segal (2002), p. 16.
77. On *varietas* as a compositional principle in the *Metamorphoses*, see now Vial (2010).
78. Bacchus' nurses, called Nyseides, are mentioned taking care of the infant god at III. 314–15. They seem to have had a variety of metamorphic experiences: for other transformations (into panthers and centaurs), see Forbes Irving (1990), p. 221. Bacchus' 'learning by observation' has a precedent in the nymphs' reaction to the impact of Medusa's head on seaweed at *Met.* IV. 740–52, which produces coral: see Chapter 2 (Sonia Macrì) below.
79. So Kenney (2011), p. 253.
80. Mentioned by Lafaye (1904), pp. 60–61 (citing the work *Bild und Lied*, p. 231).
81. Interesting, in this respect at least, is the suggestion of Gertz (2003) that 'Ovid's Medea is depicted, in a sense, as a counterpart to [Homer's] Odysseus, since her movement from locus to locus is emphasized' (p. 33).
82. Newlands (1997), p. 190.
83. We might contrast the aetiology that arises from Medea's later plotting against her stepson Theseus: her selection of aconite as a suitable poison gives rise to an aetiological metamorphosis tale (VII. 406–19) — on how it arose from the spittle of Cerberus, the grim by-product of one of Hercules' labours. This is not only germane to narrative circumstances, but it also gives a general aetiology, not a local one, in contrast to the 'pageant' of local tales.
84. For purposes of analysis, and following the practice of previous scholars, we will group the fifteen metamorphoses of the Aegean tour with the two additional metamorphoses that belong to the flight from Corinth to Athens.

85. Bardon (1958), p. 84.

86. Lenoir (1982), p. 54; Anderson (1972), p. 283.

87. Pelion is both the inevitable source of the timber from which Argo was constructed, as well as the usual point of departure. Chiron conventionally lived in one of its caves, and is closely associated with the Argo myth, particularly as preceptor or mentor to Jason (cf. *Arg.* I. 33).

88. Newlands (1997), p. 191.

89. Lenoir (1982), pp. 52–54 dividing the voyage into four nautical phases (departure from the Gulf of Pagasai, 350–56; across the Aegean to Asia Minor, 357–61; down the coast to Rhodes, 362–67; Rhodes to Ceos, 368–70) and one terrestrial phase (about the Gulf of Corinth, 371–92). He further notes that the places mentioned in the first (Aegean) phase of the journey are either ports, islands, or mountains bordering on the sea (Pelion, Othrys, Ida).

90. Harries (1990), p. 65.

91. For its 'Hesiodic' affiliations, see now Fletcher (2004).

92. Kenney (1986), p. 409.

93. See, e.g., Forbes Irving (1990), p. 257.

94. Dietze (1905), p. 23.

95. Crabbe (1981), p. 2304.

96. Schubert (1989), p. 178 offers some useful cautions about drawing inferences, given our lack of information on these myths.

97. Cf., e.g., Kenney (2011) pp. 54–55 on the series of ornithological metamorphoses beginning at VII. 368–70 in which Ovid 'accenna alla ricchezza di materiale a sua disposizione in fonti come gli *Heteroeumena* di Nicandro, l'*Ornithogonia* di Boio e l'imitazione che ne fece l'amico Emilio Macro (*FLP* 293–94), e di conseguenza, anche alla cernita che ne fa e alla moderazione con cui le usa'.

98. So, e.g., Asquith (2005), p. 269: 'Nicander's stories tend to be peculiar to certain local cults, and often do not involve the major deities'; similarly Buxton (2007), p. 111, also noting, in reference to Nicander, the absence (as far as we can tell) of descriptions of the process of metamorphosis itself.

99. See, e.g., Kenney (2011) on *Met.* VII. 372.

100. See above p. 93.

101. Kenney (2011), p. 55. The transition in Ovid's catalogue from Rhodes to Ceos is suggestive. In the *Aetia*, Callimachus has them start on Rhodes, but they end up perishing on Ceos. Now Ovid has them submerged and perish on Rhodes, but by mentioning Ceos as Medea's next stop, he probably signals an 'acknowledgement of Callimachus' account.'

102. Kenney (2011), p. 262, with reference to *Ars Amatoria*, II. 217–22. Cf. Pavlock (2009), who believes that Cycnus rather 'plays the role of Eurystheus vis-à-vis Hercules as he imposes on Phylius the task of bringing back vultures, a lion, and a bull' (p. 53). For present purposes, all that matters is the recognition that lurking behind the Cycnus and Phylius tale is a properly heroic archetype.

103. The Latin word *cycnus* (like the Greek κύκνος) means 'swan'; the present tale would have important aetiological and zoological implications, were it not for the fact, as disussed below, that this is the second of three swan metamorphoses in the epic. The Cycnus of Book VII thus merely becomes one more member of the species *cycnus* that arose from his namesake in Book II.

104. See, most elaborately, Papaioannou (2007), p. 84.

105. So, e.g., Bömer (1976), p. 288.

106. See Bömer (1976), p. 290.

107. Note that *veteres ... vulgarunt* neatly raises the question of the authority of this tale, as befits a rival version to Ovid's 'official' genesis tale at the beginning of the epic.

108. Maera is the name of the dog of Icarius, who was slain by drunken peasants and then buried for concealment. Icarius' daughter Erigone, searching for her father, was directed to the spot by Maera's howling, and thereupon hanged herself. But since that took place in Attica, Burman and many subsequent scholars have taken this Maera to be a doublet of Hecuba, who underwent canine metamorphosis at the end of the Trojan War.

109. Perhaps significantly, *Heroides*, V does not mention a son: see Gantz (1993), pp. 638–39 for the various versions. Numerous sources attribute to Oenone the unique power to heal Paris, which

she ultimately withheld to her subsequent chagrin, for she leapt to her death on his flaming pyre.

110. Another problematic 'Trojan' reference is achieved via the mention of the Coan women who grew horns, a metamorphosis associated with a stopover by Hercules on his return from sacking Troy (363–64). The Greek hero sacked the city and killed its king Eurypilus (Ps.-Apollod. II. 7.1), but this metamorphosis of the women is an otherwise unattested detail. But the crucial point, once again, is that Hercules' expedition against Troy has yet to occur: Ovid reports it at XI. 212–17.

111. Lightfoot (1990), p. 391.

112. Curiously, the reference to this landmark does not gesture to a metamorphosis.

113. See Gildenhard and Zissos (1999a) and (2004).

114. See Gildenhard and Zissos (2004) for a representative discussion of myths involving the city of Athens.

115. Buxton (2007), p. 112.

116. See Introduction to Part I, above pp. 49–51.

117. See, e.g., Galinsky (1975), p. 2.

118. Intriguingly, the way Theseus features in the *Metamorphoses*, where he appears on and off for the next two books, also contrasts sharply with Ovid's treatment of Medea: Medea dominates the action — she is ubiquitous, controlling and manipulating everything and everyone; other characters connected with her tale barely register or are elided altogether. This is even true of Jason as the narrative develops — for he almost disappears entirely after requesting the rejuvenation of his father Aeson. In contrast, Theseus, far from being a prominent protagonist, remains oddly marginal (and often figures as an onlooker): his heroic legacy never comes properly into focus (see Mack (1988), pp. 136–42 on this 'nonstory' (p. 140)), very much in line with Ovid's programmatic assault on Athenian legendary material elsewhere in the epic: Gildenhard and Zissos (2004).

119. Krevans (1997), p. 82.

120. It is important to note here that Medea's metamorphic play is never teleological in a cosmic sense, nor does it contribute significantly to the unfolding of political or cultural realms. The indecisive closure elides the last part of her biography, which was consequential in that it involved the founding of a new civilization in the east. In the final phase of her career, Medea was said to have settled among the Arioi in the Iranian highlands who have since that time been called 'Medes' (sometimes Medus is their eponym rather than Medea herself, via her son Medus by Aegeus). Ovid offers not even a hint of this — this offspring is never mentioned and the aetiology is suppressed. There is thus no shared code with Ovid's programme. In this sense *neve doli cessent* says it all: one of the longest episodes in the epic contains no *consequential* metamorphosis. Medea is actor and metamorphic agent par excellence: but she takes on these roles out of enthusiasm, rather than programmatic necessity.

121. Gertz (2003), p. 133.

122. Kenney (2011), p. 244.

123. The chariot journey is a frequent Pindaric metaphor for poetic composition. Callimachus used the image in the *Aetia* prologue in speaking of his desire 'to follow tracks not trampled by wagons' (*Aetia*, fr. 1.25–26 Pfeiffer). The flight metaphor itself is an extension of the widespread journey metaphor for poetry.

124. Pavlock (2009), p. 49.

125. Gertz (2003), p. 148.

126. *Mutatis mutandis*, this opposition gets mapped onto God versus the devil during the Christian millennium.

127. It is not by chance that, centuries later, Renaissance practitioners of alchemy would devote special attention to this episode, regarding it as a practical guide, a singularly rich compendium of metamorphic lore, in which many thought to be encoded the secret laws of nature: see Introduction to Part II.

CHAPTER 2

Lynx-stone and Coral: 'Liquid Rocks' between Natural History and Myths of Transformation[1]

Sonia Macrì

Introduction

In the last book of his *Metamorphoses*, Ovid introduces the figure of Pythagoras, who soon launches into a lengthy disquisition designed to illustrate the principle of permanent flux and how it manifests itself in both nature and history. In the course of his talk, Pythagoras touches upon a ragbag of items, such as metempsychosis, vegetarianism, the decline of Greek cities and the rise of Rome, as well as changes in our physical environment that defy easy explanation. His catalogue of natural wonders includes the alterations in colour at the disposal of the chameleon, an animal said to live off winds and the breeze, or the ability of the hyena to change its sex. In addition to such marvellous mutations involving chromaticism and chromosomes, Pythagoras also lists two natural phenomena of transformative change, in which fluid or pliant matter solidifies, seemingly inexplicably, into a rock-like substance: the hardening of the urine of the lynx into a stone of sorts (the so-called 'lynx-stone', τὸ λυγγούριον in ancient Greek and variously spelt *lyngurium* or *lyncurium* in Latin);[2] and the dual nature of coral, a creature that is soft under water, but petrifies upon exposure to air (*Met.* XV. 413–17):

> victa racemifero lyncas dedit India Baccho:
> e quibus, ut memorant, quicquid vesica remisit,
> vertitur in lapides et congelat aere tacto.
> sic et curalium quo primum contigit auras
> tempore, durescit: mollis fuit herba sub undis.

413

[Conquered India gave lynxes to grape-bearing Bacchus: they say that whatever their bladder discharges, turns into stones and congeals upon contact with air. So coral too hardens at the first contact with air; it was a soft plant under water.]

With his titbits of rock-lore Ovid's Pythagoras recalls mythic tales from earlier parts of the poem: we learn of the transformation of King Lyncus into a lynx at *Met.* V. 649–60; and of the origins of coral at *Met.* IV. 740–52, where it is presented, within the story of Perseus and Andromeda, as a consequence of the exposure of sea-plants to the head of Medusa. The philosopher thereby continues Ovid's practice of linking the mytho-historical universe of the *Metamorphoses* and diverse bodies of knowledge about natural phenomena that, to varying degrees, draw on empirical observations, folkloristic beliefs, and philosophical speculations. Outside the *Metamorphoses*, we capture this type of knowledge in the writings of philosophers, natural historians, paradoxographers, and, in the cases of lynx-stone and coral, authors of so-called 'lapidaries', that is, treatises devoted to gems, rocks and rock-like substances (such as metals and minerals, fossils and earths) and their respective qualities.[3] Many writers on the topic shared the assumption that the solid state of their object of interest was by no means a given and offered elaborate explanations of how it came about. Thus in what are the two earliest attempts to devise a theory of rock-formation in ancient Greece, Plato, in the *Timaeus*, posits as cause the extraction of water from earth (60b–c); and Aristotle, in the *Meteorologica*, adduces processes to do with various types of vaporous exhalation and the intervention of heat or cold (III. 378a–b).[4] The example par excellence here is crystal, which authors such as Seneca the Younger and Pliny the Elder deemed to be permanently frozen water or snow.[5] Some types of stones were even deemed to have partaken in the realm of animate nature before acquiring their solid and inert state; their putative past as living objects — or rather vestiges thereof — was then taken to explain their ability to assume the form of herbs or blood, tears or milk, or other organic fluids.[6]

The supposition that rocks, or rock-like substances such as crystal, are the result of a transformative process in the course of which liquid or gaseous matter acquires solidity while retaining some qualities of their previous condition, helped natural historians to explain how these apparently lifeless entities could display characteristics of animate species. The discourses that emerged in antiquity about the world of rocks frequently betoken complex systems of knowledge and belief that posit affinities and correlations between rocks and creatures that belong to other spheres within the natural realm. Reflections on the points of contact between the animate and inanimate world are a ubiquitous theme in the lapidaries, which explore substances with the ability to pass from one state or sphere to the other and thus escape precise classification, seemingly testifying to the existence of an intermediate realm, inhabited by entities that are of a composite nature. Examples include the herb called *lithospermos* on the grounds of its ability to generate 'small white pebbles [...] hard as stones', of which Pliny says that it attests to the difficulty that nature surmounts in giving birth to a stone from a plant;[7] some watery plants such as nettles, which were thought to move and eat meat; or sponges, which Pliny considered to be part of neither the animal nor the vegetal kingdom, but to possess a third nature that shares in both.[8] Considerations such as this one echo an Aristotelian view of nature as defying clear-cut categorical distinctions, in which the transitions — from the animal to the vegetal to the mineral — happen in ways that are impossible to trace.[9] In the course of Pliny's *Natural History*, the idea of this continuum between the spheres is rarely expounded in theoretical terms; yet it emerges clearly enough through the frequent appearance of homologies and the exposition of a dense net of correlations between different types of beings or objects.[10]

This chapter explores how ancient authors thought with and about rocks or rock-like entities and their metamorphic qualities, focusing on the lynx-stone and on coral: as in Ovid, these two entities are frequently discussed together since both are associated with a miraculous transformation from a condition of liquidity, or pliant softness, to solidity.[11] Needless to say, our ancient sources offer accounts that are in many ways incommensurate with mineralogical facts as established by modern science. But my aim here is not primarily to assess their scientific truth-value or, to put it differently, the empirical plausibility or accuracy of the stories under investigation. Rather, I want to use the accounts (or tales) of transformation that concern the lynx-stone and coral as evidence for key coordinates in ancient thought to do with the distinction, but also the porous boundaries and interfaces, between animate and inanimate nature and diverse kinds of knowledge, from the folkloristic to the scientific.

The Lynx and his Stony Treasure

Theophrastus' little work *De Lapidibus* [*On Stones*], 'the oldest scientific treatise dealing expressly with minerals', is marked, in the words of recent editors, 'by a comparative freedom [...] from fable and magic' — a notable quality, 'for many of the works in this field written centuries later, particularly the medieval lapidaries, dwell largely upon the fancied magical or curative powers of precious stones'; indeed, until early-modern times, *On Stones* 'remained the most rational and systematic attempt at a study of mineral substances.'[12] Be that as it may, for our concerns the qualifier 'comparative' in front of 'freedom' proves crucial. For while Theophrastus' outlook on the world of stones for the most part matches what we would recognize as a 'scientific' disposition, occasionally he feels at liberty to include data that we would classify as folklore. One such instance is his treatment of the lynx-stone. Theophrastus begins his entry (*On Stones*, 28) by noting that seals are cut from it, before describing its physical characteristics: it is very hard, like real stone; just like amber, it has the power of attraction (he records the opinion of some that it not only attracts straws and pieces of wood but also, if the stones used are thin, copper and iron); and it is very transparent and cold.[13] Yet when he reaches the question of its genesis, we get the following:[14]

> it is better when it comes from wild animals rather than tame ones and from males rather than females; for there is a difference in their food, in the exercise they take or fail to take, and in general in the nature of their bodies, so that one is drier and the other more moist. Those who are experienced find the stone by digging it up; for when the animal makes water, it conceals this by heaping earth on top.

The transition from mineralogical discussion to animal lore is as stark as it is unmarked; Theophrastus clearly assumed that the origin of the stone from the urine of the lynx was an established fact for his audience, which he could simply presuppose without further explication. He thus instantly launches into an exploration of perceived correlations between the predator and its product: the quality of the stone varies according to the living conditions (food, exercise) and the sex of the animal responsible for the urine. The two criteria yield a spectrum: at one end, we have the high-quality stones of wild, male cats; on the other the low-quality stones of tame, female ones. (Theophrastus does not specify whether a tame, male lynx or a wild, female lynx produces better stones.)

Even in antiquity, opinions diverged widely on what stone Theophrastus had in mind. Some, like Pliny, even questioned whether such a gemstone existed in the first place.[15] W. Watson, writing in the mid-eighteenth century, makes 'no scruple to think it to be exceedingly probable, that what we now call the *Tourmaline was the Lyncurium* of Theophrastus'.[16] His opinion is shared by D. E. Eichholz in a more recent discussion of the problem: 'On balance it seems most probable that the *lyngurium* of Theophrastus was yellow and brown tourmaline.'[17] Others remain aporetic.[18] For Watson and Eichholz, the animal-origin of the substance under consideration is beneath discussion. But throughout antiquity and the Middle Ages, natural historians and authors of bestiaries shared the view of Theophrastus that the urine of the lynx hardens into a precious stone upon contact with air.[19] In what follows, I want to explore a bit further this — from our point of view imaginary — interface between what we would classify as two separate domains in geology and biology, namely mineralogy and zoology.

The lynx-stone manifests a certain hybridity: the substance of which it is made appears both in the form of an organic fluid and as a solid; likewise, variations in the properties of the stone that derive from differences in habitat and sex flag up its ambivalent place midway between the animal kingdom and the world of minerals. The biological processes of the living creature are deemed to have a direct impact on shaping the structure of the stone, according to characteristic patterns: a stone that originates from a comparatively dry body will be superior to one that originates from a comparatively humid body. The discussion that Pliny devotes to the lynx-stone further clarifies how certain variables are taken to affect the final product. While Pliny himself, in the context of his discussion of gems (and more specifically amber) in Book XXXVII of his *Natural History*, adopts a radically sceptical attitude towards the veracity of lynx-stone lore, he reports that according to Demostratus — a Roman senator, historian, and paradoxographer of the early imperial period — the difference between male and dry on the one hand, and female and humid on the other, manifests itself in the respective colour of the stone: following in the tradition of Theophrastus, he too submits that if the urine comes from a male specimen the lynx-stone will sport a red, fiery colour (*fulvum et igneum*), whereas the colour of the stones that originate from the urine of female lynxes is duller and whitish (*languidius atque candidum*).[20] The gendered identity of the stone, then, is taken to manifest itself in its colour and appearance (vivid and luminous or dull and opaque), its properties (dry or humid, hot or cold), and its value (the male product being of greater worth than the female). These hierarchical differentiations reflect ancient modes of thinking about sex and gender: the male tends to get associated with heat, fertility (and the principle of life), and a colourful complexion, the female with coldness, sterility, and a pale complexion. Such a partition recurs as a characteristic of many stones and betokens the application of the 'polarity principle', which G. E. R. Lloyd has identified as a hallmark of ancient Greek thought, that is, the peculiar tendency to impose order upon reality by means of dichotomies.[21] Far from being limited to the sphere of sex and gender, the distinction between male and female has a symbolic significance and corresponds to a strategy of classification that also shapes ancient discussion of minerals and gems, other than the lynx-stone;[22] and it also appears in works of a botanical, alchemical, or mechanical remit.[23]

Other ancient authors extended the interrelation between organic and inorganic nature, between animal and mineral, further by ascribing to the stone therapeutic powers that derive from its peculiar origins. On the grounds that the substance of which the stone was made originated in the urinary apparatus of the lynx, some considered it a medicine for the treatment of various types of stomach ailments if taken with water.[24] We here capture a crucial theme of lapidary lore, namely 'the principle of sympathetic magic or *similia similibus curantur* — like cures like.'[25] In the medieval lapidary conventionally ascribed to Damigeron or Evax, 31, the stone features as an amulet in the household for pregnant women and children and protects the bearer from haemophilia or, mixed with wine and drunk, may serve as medicine against it. Pliny reports, but does not necessarily endorse, a tradition (*tradunt*) that on the island of Karpathos the ashes gained from burning the skin and the claws of the lynx, if taken with water, reduce the sex-drive in both men and women and are, moreover, a good cure to relieve itching of the skin, whereas the urine serves as medicine against difficulties with passing water (*stillicidia vesicae*: 'the reduction of urine flow to a trickle').[26] The *Cyranides*, a collection of writings compiled in the fourth century AD that belongs into the Hermetic tradition of occult knowledge about magic and medicine, also speak of the magical uses of the lynx-stone; the author describes a talisman made from it, designed to cure such ailments as weakening vision and cataracts.[27] Even in the absence of explicit references, there is a striking equivalence between the ophthalmological effects ascribed to the lynx-stone and the lynx's proverbial keenness of sight, which is part of the ancient lore about the animal.[28] The identity of the lynx-stone and its perceived properties thus seem to derive in part from empirical observations about the characteristics of the animal that produces it — a line of enquiry that can be expanded further by taking stock of what ancient authors actually knew about the lynx.

Ancient knowledge of this predator is limited to a few aspects and overlaps with those on other animals. In classical and medieval sources the lynx is often likened to a wolf, leopard, panther or hyena; it is only in the taxonomy of Carl Linnaeus (1707–78) that the *genus lynx* is classified as part of the family of felids. Aelian (*c.* 175–*c.* 235), in his *On Animals*, a work of natural history in seventeen books, assimilates the overall appearance of the lynx to that of a 'πάρδαλις';[29] yet he notes the characteristic tuft of hair on top of the ears. Moreover, his treatment provides some information about its way of hunting that is factually correct: the lynx launches itself from its hiding place with very high leaps and jumps on its prey with extraordinary force.[30] Pliny emphasizes the immense voracity of the animal and relates this to the peculiar anatomical shape of its digestive system.[31] Pliny's familiarity with lynxes, however, is limited; he notes that they come from foreign parts and reports their appearance in the arena during games of Pompey the Great, together with other exotic animals never before seen in Rome.[32] Under the same rubric as the lynx, he includes fabulous, yet monstrous creatures said to inhabit Aethopia that are composite in nature, made up of parts that come from different animals, such as *leucrocotas*, which consist in part of a badger, a lion, and a stag or *mantichoras*, which have a human face, the body of a lion, and the tail of a scorpion — disturbing creatures, in other words, insofar as they manifest the incongruous mixture of familiar elements in unheard-of combinations.[33]

The likely reason why the lynx appears in the vicinity of such monstrous creatures consists in the difficulty of distinguishing the cat clearly from other animals. Pliny testifies to the indeterminate nature of the lynx by classifying it now among the *chama*, now among the *lupi cervarii*, and now among the *pardi*. Other authors emphasize further peculiarities that set this animal apart. Plutarch, for instance, highlights its solitary nature and the impossibility of spotting it.[34] Several authors articulate a marked distrust of the animal, owing to an innate ambiguity that manifests itself both in its outward appearance and its behaviour. Aelian notes the deformed appearance of its face (ἀπρόσωπον), citing a fragment of Euripides, in which the lynx appears as an unsightly creature (ἄμορφον) born for mischief (δύστοκον).[35] Latin sources underline its streaked and mottled (*varius, maculosus*) fur.[36] As far as his behaviour is concerned, authors register tell-tale signs of mental quickness, which point to a polymorphism of the mind. A tragic fragment notes the rapid ability of the cat to think up diverse strategies, in a terminology that elsewhere in Greek literature is applied to the highly prized quality of human shrewdness.[37] Along these lines, Pliny suggestively relates the apparent inability of the lynx to retain focus: 'people say that however hungry this animal happens to be, if it turns its head while eating, it becomes oblivious of the food, and departs to seek further food elsewhere.'[38] The attention deficit disorder that Pliny diagnoses is not borne out by scientific studies of its behaviour. On the contrary, biologists have found the animal to possess a strong sense of orientation, based on an excellent capacity to recall places in the territory it inhabits.[39] The lack of concentration ascribed to the animal should therefore be considered in the context of the difficulties of classification it poses and the symbolic projects (and projections) of ancient authors, in particular their tendency to ascribe human qualities to the lynx.

One aspect of the behaviour of the lynx, namely its habit of covering its urine with earth and thus hiding it from view, has also attracted significant commentary.[40] Whereas Theophrastus (*On Stones*, 28), Plutarch (*On the Intelligence of Animals*, 962f), and Pseudo-Aristotle (*Mirabilium Auscultationes* 835b), refer only to burial, Pliny explains this practice by suggesting that the lynxes, aware of how precious the stones are for humans, envy us their use and deliberately try to hide their treasure, even though the burial accelerates the crystallizing process.[41] He is followed by Isidore in his *Etymologiae* (XII. 2. 20). The projection of the human category of envy upon the lynx by Pliny and others is symptomatic of an approach towards the natural world that does not confine itself to register empirically verifiable information, but brings symbolic aspects into play. As M. Bettini has shown more generally, when ancient authors explore their nature, these animals become 'weak subjects' whose identities often derive from the choices of the authors rather than their natural or objective characteristics.[42]

The figure of thought that brings humanity and data from the natural world into the closest contact is of course metamorphosis, which effects a two-way aetiology by correlating a human individual with a specific animal on the basis of shared characteristics: knowledge of the human character helps to account for the traits of the beast; and the traits of the beast are perceived to derive from the personality of the human character. The myth of King Lyncus, as recounted in Ovid, *Metamorphoses* v, as part of the story of Ceres, offers an excellent illustration of this point. When the goddess decided to spread knowledge of agriculture to parts of the world not yet familiar with the practice, she arrived in Athens on a chariot drawn by two serpents and gave a handful of grain to Triptolemus so that he might scatter it across the entire earth. The young man took over the reins of the chariot from the goddess and flew across the regions of Europa and Asia, eventually reaching Scythia at the end of his journey, where he stopped at the palace of King Lyncus. Then the following happened (*Met.* v. 657–60):

> barbarus invidit tantique ut muneris auctor
> ipse sit, hospitio recipit somnoque gravatum
> adgreditur ferro: conantem figere pectus
> lynca Ceres fecit [...]

> [The barbarian king is struck with envy and, in order to be himself credited with the provision of so great a boon, receives Triptolemus with hospitality and, once his guest was heavy with sleep, attacks him with a sword: just as he was trying to pierce his breast, Ceres transformed him into a lynx.]

It is worth lingering over this remarkable passage: it is our earliest attestation of this particular myth of transformation and there is every indication that Ovid invented it for the occasion;[43] and it has baffled those commentators who do not simply pass it over in silence. Thus G. Rosati notes that the nexus between the metamorphosis into a lynx and the character of King Lyncus remains obscure, before mooting two suggestions: the shared trait could consist either in the feline shrewdness by means of which both king and animal go about stalking their prey; or more likely (according to Rosati), Ovid here humorously plays with an inverse correlation between the blindness of the king, who is unable to see that his guest is on a divine mission, and the proverbial keenness of sight with which the animal is endowed.[44]

It is indeed possible to point to suggestive parallels between the mythic character Lyncus and the lynx: just like the nocturnal predator, which hides itself well, obscures its presence, and attacks unexpectedly, the Scythian king waits for his intended victim to fall asleep before attempting to perpetrate the crime. The design of the plot, which has the king stalk his victim without being seen, has an analogue in the emphasis on keen eyesight in naturalistic accounts of the animal. A further correspondence between King Lyncus and the lynx consists in their ability for mental and physical disguise. A variant of the myth transmitted by Hyginus explicitly relates the untrustworthy and deceptive comportment of the king to the dappled fur of the beast.[45] Likewise, Artemidorus, under the rubric of dreams about wild animals, makes a passing reference to the lynx, assigning to it the same symbolic value as other animals, such as monkeys, foxes, or wolves, which are all well suited to represent humans who are shrewd and deceitful and operate in secret; among the other animals mentioned, the presence of the πάρδαλις is striking, insofar as it is taken to refer to shrewd and malignant persons because of its dappled (ποικίλον) fur.[46] The *mens varia* that Hyginus attributes to Lyncus does not so much refer to his inherent fickleness, but rather to his shrewdly dissimulating conduct: his gesture of hospitality becomes a trap, preparing as it does the attempted murder of his guest at night. This aspect can be placed in a wider context: both king and beast are clearly savage creatures, inhabiting a sphere outside human civilization (Scythia is proverbially situated at the margins of the civilized world), where hunting remains the primary mode of subsistence, in contrast to the civilizing impact of agriculture.[47] The cat of the dappled fur and mutable mind lends itself as animal equivalent of a certain type of human being — one, that is, who exhibits a fickle character and a propensity towards treachery.

The most intriguing link between Lyncus and the lynx, however, has so far been missing from our discussion: envy. This emotion is a key aspect of the myth of the king as well as the lore of the animal. The former undertakes his attempted homicide because he envies Triptolemus his standing as culture hero, acquired on account of disseminating Ceres' gift of agriculture across the world, and plots his murder so that he can step into the vacant role of global benefactor and the glory this entails. The latter is conscious of the fact that his petrified urine is of considerable value to humanity and jealously tries to thwart our exploitation of this natural resource by hiding its precious stone in the earth. That the king is motivated in his attempted murder by envy thus plays off the envy that natural historians project upon the animal, as evinced by its habit of hiding its precious stones. The seeds that King Lyncus tries in vain to steal, bringing down upon himself the irreversible punishment of the goddess, inversely correspond to aspects of natural-historical lore about the lynx-stone. If Triptolemus shares his treasure widely — an approach that, so Ovid implies in *ut ipse sit muneris auctor*, King Lyncus would have continued had he succeeded in his homicidal scheming — the animal tries to retain exclusive possession of his treasure. Likewise, whereas the seeds are life-giving nutrients designed to bear fruits, the stone is the result of a transformation of organic into inorganic matter.[48] In ideological terms, the last inversion recalls the difference between Ovid's age of silver, during which human beings first began to practice agriculture (after the natural and effortless bounty of the age of gold) and his age of iron, in which the earth is exploited not just for nourishment and food, but precious metals and minerals — 'incitements to wickedness' (*inritamenta malorum*).[49] In the passage quoted above, then, Ovid achieves a confrontation of the ages: the spirit of progress that characterizes the dawn of agriculture (here, in Book v, presented as the outcome of divine munificence) encounters the savage outlook of iron-age culture, which he captures in the metonymic phrase *adgreditur ferro* (with 'iron' standing here for 'sword').

If the current state of our evidence is indeed correct in suggesting that Ovid invented this myth, we are dealing with a remarkable instance of mythopoiesis with larger implications for our understanding of the *Metamorphoses* as a whole. For Ovid here employs an element of lynx-lore as his raw material for myth-making:

his King Lyncus is, as it were, fashioned out of the envy that, as natural historians maintain, the animal harbours with regard to his petrified urine. The results are humorous: in the light of Ovid's myth, the animal's endeavour to bury his stone emerges as a sterile caricature of the agricultural bounty and fame that led to the attempted homicide and eventual transformation. It is true of course that this aspect of Ovid's narrative only resonates with those of his readers who are familiar with the presumed habits of the lynx. Yet irrespective of whether 'envy' is to be counted among the traits, Ovid clearly designed the myth of King Lyncus as in part an explanation of certain qualities of the lynx, which the feline predator retained from its previous human existence. As such, the aetiological value of his mythic tale outperforms the explanatory power of Pythagoras' natural history in *Metamorphoses* xv, which simply notes the petrifaction of lynx-urine as a marvellous illustration of his principle of flux.

In all, ancient lore about the lynx and its precious stone interrelates the world of nature (and presumed knowledge thereof) and the world of myth: various types of speculation (including implicit and explicit aetiologies) relate the peculiarities of the animal, its urine, and its fossilized end-product to the human sphere. The elusive identity of the lynx and its polymorphism — of mind, appearance, and even origin, which (Ovidian) myth locates in the transformation of a human being into an animal — turns it into a creature capable of producing a mineral. The stone, in turn, on account of its hybrid nature, reflects the qualities of the animal: the mutable lynx-stone encapsulates the ability of the lynx to alter its shape, to change its mind, to be present without being seen, and to go about under the cover of darkness as if dressed in a cloak that constantly and emblematically changes in appearance.

Through the Looking Glass, Darkly: The Case of Coral

Coral is a peculiar lifeform. Nowadays biologists classify the polyps that form coral among the so-called *antozoaria*, that is, 'flower animals'. These animals have the ability to extract calcium ions from the seawater, which they use to build an exoskeleton by means of depositing the carbonate mineral aragonite; over many generations, this process has resulted in the calciferous structures known as coral reefs. Yet the classification of coral among animals is relatively recent: it dates to the eighteenth century. Until then, these organisms, which remain apparently motionless, were classified as sea plants that somehow had the ability to become hard as stones.[50] This feature secured them a place in the lapidary tradition; and like the lynx and its precious stone, the coral received both mythic and scientific attention, with intriguing reciprocities and interferences between these two modes of thought as ancient writers tried to account for the peculiar nature of the creature, including its origins. A preliminary look at Theophrastus' treatment of aquatic vegetation more generally in his *Enquiry into Plants* will help to establish some of the larger parameters within which classical authors discussed coral.

In his botanical writings, Theophrastus considers various items of flora open to a double classification, depending on whether the respective plant is examined underwater or above the surface. In the fourth book of his *Enquiry into Plants* he writes of forests that follow one another into the abyss; he likens them to bay, olive and thyme, only submerged in water; 'so far as they project above the sea', these sea plants are like stones.[51] Several points are important here. To begin with, while the sea world is to some extent open to observation (through a looking glass, darkly, as it were), humans are unable to enter it for extended periods of time, much less live in it. This explains the curious double vision that ensues: as long as the sea plants remain underwater and out of sight, they are imagined as verdant forests; but viewed from above, through the water, they appear like stone gardens. Second, in his account the aquatic plants figure as duplicates of terrestrial ones. This symmetry enables the use of (inverted) analogy to discuss underwater vegetation, which is by and large inaccessible to prolonged empirical study in its natural habitat. The resemblance, however, only applies to a certain degree: the aquatic dimension is both like and unlike the world human beings inhabit, seemingly within reach but also irretrievably alien and categorically different. Third, Theophratus' formulations imply a hierarchy: his aquatic plants are far inferior to their terrestrial namesakes. Apart from the examples given above, he also mentions palms that have too short a trunk, fig trees without leaves, or fruits similar to almonds, but hopelessly compressed.[52] And fourth, when a transition from one world to the other does occur, it coincides with a drastic transformation. Aquatic bay, olive and thyme trees may be similar in name and aspect to their terrestrial counterparts, but as soon as they leave the water mineralization kicks in: they become salt or stone.[53] These substantive alterations testify to the incommensurability of the sea world and life on land: it is impossible to pass from one to the other without undergoing irreversible change in one's nature — and this is precisely what happens to coral.[54] Theophrastus' treatise, then, amply bears out Vermeule's point that, in ancient thought, the sea surface was a meeting point between reality and imagination, but also life and death.[55] Many Greek texts, including a number of funerary epigrams, found a close relationship between the sea world and the other world: they are both present but unknown and impassable to the living.[56]

Ancient thought about coral fits into these more general reflections about the sea and the life-forms it harbours; and as with the ancient discourse on the lynx and its fossilized urine, classical authors systematically imbricate natural history and myth in their discussion of coral. In the following, I first want to explicate how ancient writings define coral as a hybrid phenomenon that defies a straightforward classification, insofar as it is situated at the interface of animate and inanimate nature, life and death, plant and stone, sea and land, before exploring how this hybridity also manifests itself in the tales of transformation that give mythic accounts of the origins of coral. For this agenda, two texts are of particular importance: Ovid's *Metamorphoses* and the so-called *Orpheus Lapidary*, a late-antique, theurgic poem about the magical powers of stones, written in epic hexameters.[57] In both texts, coral features as a phenomenon of both natural history and myth — and as we shall see, the interfaces each author creates between these two modes of knowledge are as interesting as the striking differences in their respective treatments.

The lengthy discussion of coral in the *Orpheus Lapidary* covers verses 510–609. The passage can be divided into the following sections:

510–16: preface
517–38: phenomenology
539–74: mythic origins
575–609: theurgic properties

In the preface, the poet proleptically signals the mythic genealogy of coral as 'a descendent of Perseus' as well as some of its magical properties as antidote to various kinds of poison, before identifying none other than the god Apollo as the source of his knowledge about the marvellous transformation that the coral undergoes (513–16):

τοῦδε δέ μοι πάντων περιώσιον, ὅσσα φύονται,
Φοῖβος ἀκειρεκόμης φύσιν ἔμμεναι ἐξ ἑτέροιο
μυθεῖτ᾽ εἰς ἕτερον στρωφωμένου εἶδος ὅ τίς τοι
ψεῦδός κεν φαίη, τὸ δ᾽ ἐτήτυμον οἶδα τετύχθαι.

[its wonderful nature, among all things born on land, was revealed to me by long-haired Phoebus: this ability to change its appearance from one aspect to the other. Someone might think it a lie, but I know it is the truth.]

The lapidary itself, at the beginning of the description, identifies the extraordinary quality of coral with the capability to change its appearance, in Greek εἶδος. The preface thus looks forward to the two accounts that the lapidary offers of the curious mineralization that the sea-creature undergoes when exposed to air: a 'scientific' description of what happens to coral in the sea and on land; and an aetiology that traces the ambiguous nature of coral (half plant, half stone) to Perseus' killing of Medusa, her petrifaction of weeds while the hero washed his bloody hands, and the permanence of the dual nature of coral through the intervention of Athena. Both the scientific description and the legendary *aition* are characterized as unbelievable but true and labelled a 'prodigy' (535–41). Indeed, from the outset, the author flags the marvellous nature of the phenomenon he is about to discuss and acknowledges that it may defy belief — a recurrent theme throughout his account of coral.[58] After this appeal to divine authority and the polemical recognition that credibility is an issue, the author continues for some twenty verses with a fairly straightforward description of the creature (verses 517–38).[59] This 'phenomenology', which has many parallels in the treatment of coral in other naturalists, places coral squarely within the ancient imaginary patterns about life in the sea set out above. Thus the *Orpheus Lapidary* notes the counterintuitive fact that coral flourishes in a medium otherwise associated with barrenness (517–19):

χλωρὴ γὰρ βοτάνη πρῶτον φύει οὐδ᾽ ἐνὶ γαίῃ,
ἥν γε φυτῶν ἴσμεν στερεὴν τροφόν, ἀλλ᾽ ἐνὶ πόντῳ
ἀτρυγέτῳ, ἵνα φύκι᾽, ἵνα βρύα γίνετ᾽ ἐλαφρά.

[For to begin with, coral grows as a green plant not on the earth that, we know, is solid nourishment for plants, but in the barren sea, where seaweed and light mosses grow.]

The passage implicitly defines the place of coral in the Greek botanic code, where plants are classified according to their proximity to the sun. Hence lettuce, and even more 'sea lettuce' (βρύον) as well as other seaweeds and mosses find themselves in the last place;[60] and here they appear in the company of coral, which, paradoxically, becomes associated with sterility and death in its condition of green and damp vegetation. In line with its existence in the aquatic realm, coldness, sterility, and decay are hallmarks of sea greenery more generally; and coldness in particular is a noted feature of coral. Both Pliny and Dioscorides report on its refrigerating property and its resistance to fire.[61] Pliny's observation that the berries of coral are white hints at sterility — only ashore they take on the semblance of ripe, reddish fruits, but by then they have become petrified.[62] The coral's petrifaction upon death is a central thematic concern of the *Orpheus Lapidary* as well (520–28):

> αὐτὰρ ἐπεί κ' ἔλθησι μαραινομένη ποτὶ γῆρας,
> ἤτοι μέν οἱ φύλλα περιφθινύθουσιν ὑφ' ἅλμης
> αὐτὴ δ' ἐν βένθεσσιν ὑπὸ φλοίσβοιο θαλάσσης
> νήχεται, ὄφρα ἑ κύματ' ἀποπτύσῃ αἰγιαλόνδε.
> ἔνθα δ' ἄρ' ἐξαπίνης μιν ἀναπλησθεῖσαν ὑπ' αἴθρης
> βάζουσ', οἵ περ ἴδοντο, κρατυνομένην ὁράασθαι.   525
> δηρὸν δ' οὐ μετέπειτα πάγῳ περιπαχνωθεῖσα
> πετροῦται. [...]

[but when it ages and withers, its leaves gradually rot because of the salt; it wanders into the abyss through noisy waves, until the waves wash it ashore. Here, the witnesses say, it suddenly hardens because it fills with air; and very soon it turns into stone because of the cold.]

The mineralization here almost emerges as the natural outcome of the properties of coral in its aquatic state, such as its coldness, sterility and, generally, contiguity with death. The author underscores the connection between death and the sea, eloquently evoking the vast expanse and the bottomless abyss of the ocean, which envelops everything within its reach and rarely delivers what is hidden in its recesses.[63] And death and petrifaction coincide with visibility as the coral is washed ashore where it hardens.[64] Coral thus fluctuates between two states of being: on the one hand, it leads an invisible, cold, sterile underwater life; on the other, it turns into stone when it becomes visible ashore. Ancient taxonomies of coral, which for all intents and purposes start with Pliny the Elder, thus deem coral open to a double classification: a vegetal one and a mineral one (*Natural History*, XXXII. 22):[65]

> forma est ei fruticis, colos viridis. bacae eius candidae sub aqua ac molles, exemptae confestim durantur et rubescunt qua corna sativa specie atque magnitudine; aiunt tactu protinus lapidescere, si vivat.

> [In shape coral is like a shrub, and its colour is green. Its berries are white under the water and soft; when taken out they immediately harden and grow red, being like, in appearance and size, to those of cultivated cornel. It is said that at a touch it immediately petrifies, if it lives.] (trans. by W. H. S. Jones)

Dioscorides gives a scientific explanation of this metamorphosis, and affirms that it is due to the passage from water to air (*De Materia Medica*, V. 121. 1):

> τὸ δὲ κουράλιον, ὅπερ ἔνιοι λιθόδενδρον ἐκάλεσαν, δοκεῖ μὲν εἶναι φυτὸν ἐνάλιον, στερροποιεῖσθαι δέ, ὅταν ἐκ τοῦ βυθοῦ ἑλκυσθῇ τῆς ἁλὸς ἁπτόμενον τοῦ περικεχυμένου ἡμῖν ἀέρος.

[But Coral (which some have called Lithodendron) seems to be a sea plant, but to undergo hardening when it is drawn out of the deep sea and brought into contact with the air flowing all around us.]

In combining two opposing natures, coral emerges as a paradoxical entity: it has botanical features, but is, in essence, a stone, undergoing mineralization as soon as it is removed from its natural habitat. The *Orpheus Lapidary* considers this phenomenon a natural marvel that fascinates, challenges the imagination, and inspires thoughts of the supernatural (533–37):

> [...] ἐγὼ δ᾽ οὐκ οἶδα, τί μοι θέλγητρον ἰδόντι
> αἰὲν ἐπὶ πραπίδας καταλείβεται· οὐδὲ δύνανται
> ὄσσε κορεσθῆναι θηευμένου, ἀλλά με θάμβος
> σεύεται ἐν στέρνοισιν ὀϊόμενον τέρας εἶναι.
> καί οἱ πιστεύων περ ἔολπά μιν εἶναι ἄπιστον.

[When I see it, I do not know what charm pervades my soul; my eyes cannot get enough of that sight. Then I feel mystified and I think I can discern a prodigy and, though I believe it, I think it is incredible.]

Within the *Orpheus Lapidary* the term τέρας ('prodigy') signals a switch in discursive registers, from empirical observation of an inexplicable phenomenon to mythic aetiology. And if we follow suit and move from naturalistic descriptions to mythological lore, we find the persistence of the same motifs mentioned so far, in particular hybridity. The naturalists underline that coral cuts across various *genera* of being, such as living and inanimate, vegetal and mineral, aquatic and terrestrial. And the same confusion of categories characterizes the mythic figure generally credited with bringing coral into being: Medusa (or the Gorgons more generally). This kind of monster itself originated from the superimposition of incompatible parts. As Pseudo-Apollodorus notes, the head of the Gorgons were encased with the scales of dragons; they had great tusks like boars; their hands were brazen; and they sported golden wings that enabled them to fly. And most pertinently for present purposes, they turned anyone who looked at them into stone.[66] The ability to petrify pliant matter sets up an interesting affinity between the monsters and the coral; and one of the names that coral acquired in antiquity was indeed 'Gorgonia', that is, 'stone of the Gorgon': 'the reason for its name', as Pliny points out, 'is that it is transformed into the hardness of stone after having softened in the sea'.[67] And in various Greek and Roman texts, the coral undergoes a transformation from a tree that is green and alive into a 'tree of stone' (λιθόδενδρον). F. Frontisi-Ducroux has explicated the correlation between the name *Gorgonia*, which is given to coral in the lapidary tradition, and the γοργόνειον as a duplicate figure of Medusa: the γοργόνειον is the motionless, visible figure, in Greek εἰκών, of an original living being that is itself inaccessible to sight; coral, in its turn, shows itself when it becomes a stone replica of the invisible sea plant.[68] The transformation that coral undergoes as it hardens into stone thus materializes and visualizes what eludes human sight, and thereby helps to symbolize invisible dimensions of our universe, such as the sea or death.[69] In this context, it is worth mentioning that both coral and the Gorgon come out of the sea-world, insofar as Medusa's birth is connected to the figure of Pontus.[70]

In myth, the story of coral tends to be associated with the fatal encounter between

Perseus and the Gorgon Medusa, which ends in the beheading of the latter. Even in
its state of decapitation the head loses none of its petrifying powers, which, together
with Medusa's gushing blood, enter into action by way of fossilizing weeds while
Perseus washes off the blood. The appearance of coral within the myth as a whole
has a precise function, namely to generate a veritable mirror image of the figure of
Medusa in the world of nature. But in order to decipher this symbolic function of
coral, it is necessary to situate the mythic aetiology within wider frames of ancient
thought. As already noted, two of the most detailed accounts of the relationship
between the mythological figure and the stone come from the *Orpheus Lapidary* and
Ovid's *Metamorphoses*. Both sources connect the birth of coral with the power of
Medusa. But beyond this shared motif, the two accounts differ greatly, notably in
how they explain, within the story of Perseus, the transformation of seaweed into
coral. In the *Orpheus Lapidary*, the mythic tale serves to explain the colour of coral
(558–72):

> ἀλλὰ τότ᾽ αἰλιαλόνδε φόνῳ πεπαλαγμένος ἥρως
> ἐλθών, εἰσόκε λύθρον ἀποπλύνειε θαλάσσῃ,
> θερμὴν ἐξ ὁμάδου κεφαλὴν ἔτι καὶ τρομέουσαν
> Γοργείην κατέθηκεν ἐπὶ χλοεραῖς βοτάνῃσιν.
> [...]
> τόφρα δὲ πορφυρέοιο διαινόμενοι κορέσαντο
> αἵματος, οἵ ῥα κέχυντο χαμαὶ ὑπὸ κράατι θάμνοι.
> ἀμφὶ δ᾽ ἄρα σφίσιν αἶψα θοαὶ πόντοιο θύγατρες
> λύθρον ἐπεσσύμεναι θάμνοις περιπήγνυον αὖραι
> πήγνυτο δ᾽ ὥστε σε πάγχυ λίθον στερεὴν ὀΐσασθαι·
> οὐδ᾽ ἔτ᾽ ἔην ὀΐσασθαι, ἐπεὶ στερεὴ λίθος ἦεν.
> ἐκ δ᾽ ὄλεσεν βοτάνης ὑγρὸν δέμας ἀλλὰ καὶ ἔμπης
> ὀλλυμένης πάμπαν βοτάνης οὐκ ὤλεσεν εἶδος.
> τὴν μὲν ἄρα χροιὴν ἐξ αἵματος ἔσχεν ἐρυθρήν.

[But then the hero went to the shore, he was smeared with blood and before
he washed himself in the waters, he put the Gorgon's head, hot and palpitating
after the fight, on the weeds. [...] The scattered shrubs on the ground under
Medusa's head satisfied themselves with the red blood. At once the breezes, the
swift daughters of the sea, ran to the spot and caused that blood mixed with
dust to congeal all around the bushes. The blood petrified so that you might
have thought that it really was a hard stone: but it was no longer necessary to
imagine that, because it really was a hard stone. It had lost its soft plant essence,
but, though dead, it had not lost its original appearance. It derived its red colour
from blood.]

Descriptions of coral, as we already had occasion to note, distinguish between
the white colour that the creature possesses in the water and the red colour that it
assumes outside the sea. The lapidary ascribes this chromatic variation to the contact
with Medusa's head, right after her decapitation. The weeds drink the blood, which
a few seconds before had given life to the Gorgon, and acquire a new chromatic
quality; at this point the breezes intervene and cause the petrifaction. The sequence
is paradoxical insofar as in ancient natural history metamorphosis into stone is
usually the result of the drying out of organic fluids; here the opposite procedure
prepares the petrifaction: the gorging of the weeds with blood. In this, the coral

features some similarities with the stone called *haimatitis*, which is also the result of the fossilization of blood. Whereas some lapidaries simply note the chromatic correspondence between blood and the stone,[71] others, such as the *Orpheus Lapidary*, include an account of the legendary origins of *haimatitis* from the blood of Uranus in the wake of his castration by his son Kronos: according to this tale, some drops of the immortal blood fell unto the earth and became transformed into the stone when they were dried up and petrified by the horses of Helios (646–59).[72]

Ovid's account also focuses on the phenomenon of mineralization when coral comes into contact with Medusa, though, as already noted, his description is very different from the tale in the lapidary.[73] Towards the end of *Metamorphoses* IV, Perseus is wandering through the air, on his winged boots, when he comes upon the figure of Andromeda, who is chained to some cliffs by the sea. Ovid notes her utter 'rock-like' immobility: if a light breeze had not moved her hair, the hero might have taken the virgin for a statue. In an inverse anticipation of what is about to happen, Perseus touches down and frees her, returning what appears to be stone to mobility and life — whereupon the sea monster to whom Andromeda was to be sacrificed appears. Quickly extracting from Andromeda's anxious parents a promise of marriage in return for her rescue — and as Ovid archly notes, who in his right mind would have hesitated to accept the terms proffered in this situation? — Perseus slaughters the beast, though not without getting the blood that gushes forth from the stricken monster all over his hands. Welcomed by the locals as king's future son-in-law, Perseus proceeds to wash up, and it is at this juncture that Ovid's text veers from the sensational events just described to equally sensational proto-science (*Met.* IV. 740–52):

> ipse manus hausta victrices abluit unda,   740
> anguiferumque caput dura ne laedat harena,
> mollit humum foliis natasque sub aequore virgas
> sternit et inponit Phorcynidos ora Medusae.
> virga recens bibulaque etiamnum viva medulla
> vim rapuit monstri tactuque induruit huius   745
> percepitque novum ramis et fronde rigorem.
> at pelagi nymphae factum mirabile temptant
> pluribus in virgis et idem contingere gaudent
> seminaque ex illis iterant iactata per undas:
> nunc quoque curaliis eadem natura remansit,   750
> duritiam tacto capiant ut ab aere quodque
> vimen in aequore erat, fiat super aequora saxum.

[He himself draws water and washes his victorious hands. So as not to damage the snake-sprouting head through the hard sand, he softens the ground with leaves, spreads out branches of water-plants and lays the head of Medusa, daughter of Phorcys, on top. The sea-greenery, fresh and still alive with a sponge-like marrow, snatched the power of the monster, grew hard through its touch, and took up a novel hardness on branches and leaves. But the nymphs of the sea test out the marvellous phenomenon on ever more branches, take delight in achieving the same results, and repeatedly throw seeds from those plants across the waves. Even now coral has retained the same nature so that it hardens upon contact with air and what was a plant in the sea, becomes a stone above it.]

Ovid's version of the origin of coral inevitably activates some of the thematic patterns that evolved in ancient discourse around this creature, though he manages to give a surprising twist even to conventional elements. First of all, his relocation of the *aition* from the moment of Medusa's decapitation to his victory over the sea-monster includes an oblique commentary on the version his account is designed to eclipse: the gore in the story is not supplied by Medusa, but the sea-monster, and, at any rate, only plays a negligible part in the creation of coral by making Perseus put down the Gorgon's head to wash his hands. And yet Ovid signals obliquely that he is quite aware of the version of the story that ascribes a principal role to the soaking up of blood in bringing coral into being, not least to explain its reddish colour. In his account of the fight between Perseus and the sea-monster, the hero's wings became so drenched in the blood and sea-water spewed forth by the beast that they no longer sustain his flight: *nec bibulis ultra Perseus talaribus ausus | credere*: IV. 730–31; but when Ovid soon afterwards records the soaking performed by the sea-plants, he switches from the concrete to the abstract: by means of their *bibula medulla*, the absorbing capacity of their live inner core, the plants are able to co-opt the petrifying power (*vis*) of Medusa. Several aspects register oddly: first, Ovid underscores that it is precisely the fact that the plants are not yet dead (*virga [...] etiamnunc viva*) that enables their acquisition of the ability to harden into stone; second, rather than being the passive victims of Medusa's capacity to cause a rigor mortis, here the plants are presented as active agents that appropriate the power to petrify for themselves;[74] and finally, Ovid, ingeniously, eliminates not only the Gorgon's blood, but also her paralysing gaze as the cause of the dual nature of coral: in his version of the story, the transforming factor consists in touch.

These features add up to a deliberate policy of erasing the thematics of gore and death that dominate the creation of coral in alternative versions — in accordance with the overall tone of light-hearted playfulness that prevails throughout the *aition*, in deliberate contradistinction to the bloody battle with the sea-monster that precedes the generation of coral. Moreover, by tweaking various details, Ovid also achieves an exact analogue between the inaugural instance of fossilization (contact with the head) and all later repetitions of the phenomenon (contact with air).[75] The proto-scientific aetiology that Ovid offers in the medium of myth thus emerges as, in a sense, far superior to the paradoxical marvel as which coral figures in the discourse of Pythagoras in Book XV (a passage cited at the outset of the chapter): he not only notes the baffling fact that coral seemingly becomes hard upon contact with air, he also 'explains' why that should be the case. In Book IV, we are witnessing the birth of a new species of plants that has somehow managed to internalize the power of Medusa and possesses the capacity of self-petrifaction, with the air functioning as catalyst. Indeed, as it turns out, this process unfolds in the presence of an unexpected group of attentive observers: the sea nymphs (747: *pelagi nymphae*). Ovid concludes his *aition* with two sets of three lines each (747–49, 750–52) that blur the boundary between mythic aetiology and the proto-science of natural history. Remarkably — and quite unlike a standard paradoxographer — the adventurous nymphs do not simply marvel at the *factum mirabile*; like any good scientist, they instantly try to replicate the results by repeating the experiment, more than once (*temptant* | *pluribus in virgis*), and are overjoyed when the outcome always turns out to be exactly the same (*idem contingere gaudent*). What is more, the nymphs do not content themselves with confining their endeavours to a localized laboratory; they disseminate their Medusa-modified crop throughout the world, sowing the plants' seed (*semina*) across the waves, in a spirit of marine agriculture that presupposes acts of sowing, cultivation, and harvest. In the second triplet, Ovid switches from mythic times to the present, insisting in the spirit of aetiology that the phenomenon that came into being back then is still very much with us now (*nunc quoque*). In all, then, we get a story of how, on account of the intervention of humanoid creatures such as nymphs, the natural world underwent an alteration and our natural universe bears the imprint of divine culture.

Throughout, Ovid plays with the binary patterns scripted into the traditional story: he turns concrete gore into the abstract power of petrifaction; he recognizes the key difference between air and water through repeated use of such phrases as *sub aequore* (742), *per undas* (749), *in aequore* (752), *super aequora* (752) — only to render the boundary between these two domains irrelevant by choosing as his protagonists the sea-nymphs who are equally at home in both spheres; he makes fun of the terrifying powers of Medusa by having Perseus worry about damage to her precious head caused by the 'hard sand' — a hilarious malapropism that transfers the effect of Medusa to an item usually known for its softness; and he turns the 'death by petrifaction' that is Medusa's hallmark on its head (as it were) by endowing his new subspecies of coral with the special ability of self-transformation, which presupposes a living entity. As in the case of the lynx, then, we are dealing with highly original mythopoiesis on Ovid's part, which not only shows his ludic imagination at its playful best, but also provides precious insights into the creative principles that inform his literary universe: his myth-historical narrative of how our world came into being simultaneously draws on and trumps the discourses of natural history and paradoxography.

Appendix: Two Early-Modern Discussions of Coral

With a view to the watershed caused by the rise of modern science, when textual authority gradually gave way to empirical observation and the experiment as the privileged source of knowledge about the natural world, it is worth citing two passages that document an early-modern tussle about the nature of the coral. The first comes from Thomas Brown Knight, *Pseudodoxia Epidemica: or, Enquiries Into The Very Many Received Tenents And Commonly Presumed Truth* (London: Printed by T. H. for Edward Dod, 1646), Book 2: Of sundry popular Tenets concerning Mineral, and vegetable bodies, generally held for truth; which examined prove either false, or dubious, Chapter 5: Compendiously of sundry other common Tenents, concerning Mineral and Terreous Bodies, which examined, prove either false or dubious:

> (6). That Corall (which is a Lithophyton or stone-plant, and groweth at the bottom of the Sea) is soft under water, but waxeth hard as soone as it arriveth unto the ayre, although the assertion of Dioscorides, Pliny, and consequently Solinus, Isidore, Rueus, and many others, and stands believed by most, we

have some reason to doubt, not onely from so sudden a petrifaction and strange induration, not easily made out from the qualities of Ayre, but because we finde it rejected by experimentall enquirers. Johannes Beguinus in his Chapter of the tincture of Corall, undertakes to cleere the world of this errour, from the expresse experiment of *John Baptista de Nicole*, who was Overseer of the gathering of Coral upon the Kingdome of Thunis. This Gentleman, saith he, desirous to finde the nature of Corall, and to be resolved how it groweth at the bottome of the Sea, caused a man to goe downe no lesse then a hundred fathom into the Sea, with expresse to take notice whether it were hard or soft in the place where it groweth, who returning brought in each hand a branch of Corall, affirming it was as hard at the bottome, as in the ayre where he delivered it. The same was also confirmed by a triall of his owne, handling it a fathome under water before it felt the ayre. *Boetius de Boote* in his accurate Tract *De Gemmis*, is of the same opinion, not ascribing its concretion unto the ayre, but the coagulating spirits of salt, and lapidificall juyce of the sea, which entring the parts of that plant, overcomes its vegetability, and converts it into a lapideous substance, and this, saith he, doth happen when the plant is ready to decay; for all Corall is not hard, and in many concreted plants some parts remaine unpetrified, that is, the quick and livelier parts remaine as wood, and were never yet converted. Now that plants and ligneous bodies may indurate under water without approachment of ayre, we have experiments in Coralline, with many Coralloidall concretions, and that little stony Plant which Mr. Johnson nameth, *Hippuris coralloides*, and *Gesner foliis mansu Arenosis*; we have our selfe found in fresh water, which is the lesse concretive portion of that Element. We have also with us the visible petrification of wood in many waters, whereof so much as is covered with water converteth into stone, as much as is above it and in the ayre retaineth the forme of wood, and continueth as before.

This account drew the ire of Alexander Ross, who published a rebuttal in *Arcana Microcosmi*: OR, The hid Secrets of MAN's Body discovered; In an Anatomical Duel between Aristotle and Galen concerning the Parts thereof: As also, By a Discovery of the strange and marvellous Diseases, Symptomes & Accidents of MAN's BODY. With A Refutation of Doctor *Brown*'s VULGAR ERRORS, The Lord BACON's NATURAL HISTORY, And Doctor *Harvy*'s Book DE GENERATIONE, *COMENIUS*, and Others (London, Printed by *The Newcomb*, 1652). The relevant passage comes from Book 2 (Of the strange Diseases and Accidents of MANS BODY; Wherein divers of Dr. *Browns* vulgar errors and assertions are refuted, and the ancient Tenents maintained), Chapter 19 (The Navigation of the Ancients by the stars: they knew not the compass. 2. Goats bloud softneth the Adamant. Gold loses its vertue and gravity with its substance. Iron may grow hot with motion. Coral is soft under water, and hardened by the air. Viscum or Mistletoe, how it grows. The shade of the Ash-tree, pernicious to Serpents):

> (4). He will not believe that Coral is soft under water, and hard in the air, because one who went down a hundred fathom into the sea, returned with Coral in each hand, affirming it was as hard at the bottom, as in the air. Answ. Boetius in his second Book of stones and gems, c. 153. tells us, that Coral doth not harden or grow stony till it be dead; it seems then, whilst it is alive, its soft under water, and therefore this Diver lighted upon a dead Coral; but because that was hard, it will not follow that all Coral under water is hard, except all

under water be dead. There is also a difference between old and young plants, the older the plant grows, the harder it is; perhaps this was not only dead but also an old plant: Its no wonder then if Coral petrifie when taken out of the sea, for then it dieth being separated from its matrix and element, in which it had life and vegetation; and it seems by the same Boetius, that the substance of Coral at first is wood, for he saw some which was partly wood and partly stone, not being throughly petrified, which might proceed from some internal impediment it is therefore no more wonder for a sea-plant to petrifie in the air, then for a land-plant to petrifie in the sea, or other waters. This is called in Greek λιθόδενδρον, as you would say stone-tree, or stone-plant, and κωράλιον, quasi χιράλιον, because it petrifieth when it is touched by the hands, and because the Gorgons were turned into stones, therefore in Pliny, Coral is called Gorgonia.

Notes to Chapter 2

1. I would like to express my gratitude to Professors Gabriella Barbier and Donatella Puliga for their help and support in the writing of this chapter.
2. The name λυγγούριον is found in epigraphic documents from the third century BC as a material of seals: see Olivieri (1998), pp. 257–69. Another popular etymology links the name of the stone to the mountain Λυγγὸς: see *Cyranides*, I. 11. 5. For the Greek text, see Kaimakis (1976).
3. For overviews of the genre from antiquity to early-modern times, see e.g. Halleux and Schamp (1985), pp. xiii–xxxiv ('Origines et typologie de la littérature lapidaire') and Duffin (2005). Both pieces offer further bibliographical guidance.
4. For a discussion, see Eichholz (1949).
5. Seneca, *Natural Questions*, III. 25. 12; Pliny the Elder, *Natural History*, XXXVI. 161 and XXXVII. 21–23. See more generally Healy (1999), pp. 173–78 ('Early Theories of the Origin of Minerals').
6. I explore this mode of thought in detail in Macrì (2009).
7. Pliny, *Natural History*, XXVII. 98.
8. Pliny, *Natural History*, IX. 146: *neque animalium neque fruticum, sed terziam quondam ex utroque naturam habent, urticis dico et spongeis.*
9. Conte (1982), pp. xvii–xlvii; Beagon (1992).
10. Voelke-Viscardi (2001).
11. Apart from Ovid's *Metamorphoses*, see e.g. Sextus Empiricus, *Pyrrhoniae Hypotyposes*, I. 119, and see further Olivieri (1998).
12. Caley and Richards (1956), p. 10. Healy (1999), pp. 176–77 concurs with their appraisal, virtually verbatim.
13. διαφανῆ τε σφόδρα καὶ ψυχρά is the text printed in the edition of Caley and Richards (1956). Furlanus, in his edition of the treatise 'On Stones' published in 1605 at Hanover, conjectures πυρρά ('of fiery red colour') for ψυχρά ('cold') on the basis of Pliny the Elder's recapitulation of Theophrastus at *Natural History*, XXXVII. 53, which describes the stone as *colorem igneum*. See the commentary by Caley and Richards (1956), p. 110.
14. I cite the translation by Caley and Richards (1956).
15. *Natural History*, XXXVII. 53.
16. Watson (1759–1760), p. 396.
17. Eichholz (1967), p. 104.
18. See the note in König (1994), p. 156.
19. For a survey of sources, see Walton (2001), pp. 357–79. For the ancient lapidary tradition and its continuation in the Middle Ages more generally, see the bibliography of primary and secondary sources in Mantello and Rigg (1996), pp. 408–10.
20. Pliny, *Natural History*, XXXVII. 34: *Demostratus lyncurium vocat et fieri ex urina lyncum bestiarum, e maribus fulvum et igneum, e feminis languidius atque candidum.*

21. Lloyd (1966); see more recently Sassi (1986).

22. 'Gendered' commentary on precious stones in Pliny's *Natural History* also occurs in his treatment of *carbunculi* (XXXVII. 92), *sandastros* (XXXVII. 100–01) and *sarda* (XXXVII. 105–06). In his treatment of *smaragdos*, Pliny applies another feature of animate nature to the item under scrutiny: he claims that the gem 'ages' (XXXVII. 70). On 'living stones' see further Halleux (1970) and Macrì (2009).

23. See e.g. Tortzen (1991).

24. Dioscorides Pedanius, *De materia medica* 2.81: τὸ δὲ τῆς λυγγός, ὃ δὴ λυγγούριον καλεῖται, ἅμα τῷ ἐξουρηθῆναι λιθοῦσθαι πεπίστευται· διὸ καὶ ματαίαν ἔχει τὴν ἱστορίαν. ἔστι γὰρ τὸ καλούμενον ὑπ' ἐνίων ἤλεκτρον πτερυγοφόρον, ὅπερ ποθὲν σὺν ὕδατι στομάχῳ καὶ ῥευματιζομένῃ κοιλίᾳ ἁρμόζει. ὄνου δὲ οὖρον παραδέδοται πινόμενον νεφριτικοὺς ὑγιάζειν. (*De Materia Medica: Being an Herbal with many other medicinal materials*, translated by Tess Anne Osbaldeston (Ibidis Press: Johannesburg, 2000), 2.100: '*Lyncurium* [urine of a lynx] is thought (as soon as it is pissed out) to grow into a stone, as a result it has only a foolish report. Some call this *succinum pterygophoron* [the wing of accompaniment] because it draws feathers to it. Taken as a drink with water it is good for a stomach and intestines troubled with excessive discharge.')

25. Pliny, *Natural History*, X.203; XX.1; XXXVII.59: *Nunc quod totis voluminibus his docere conati sumus de discordia rerum concordiaque, quam antipathian Graeci vocavere ac sympathian, non aliter clarius intellegi potest.* See Conte (1982), p. XXX; Duffin (2005), p. 59.

26. Pliny, *Natural History*, XXVIII. 122.

27. *Cyranides*, 1.11.20–22: ὠφελεῖ γὰρ πρὸς ἀμβλυωπίαν καὶ ὑποχύσεις ὀφθαλμῶν. ['For it will help against dim-sightedness and cataract.'] For text, translation, and discussion, see Waegeman (1987), pp. 88–93.

28. *Appendix Proverbiorum*, III. 71, ed. by E. L. von Leutsch and F.G. Schneidewin, *Corpus paroemiographorum Graecorum*, vol. 1. Göttingen: Vandenhoeck & Ruprecht, 1839 (repr. Hildesheim: Olms, 1965), pp. 379–467: Λυγκέως ὀξύτερον βλέπει [...] οἱ δέ φασιν ὅτι ὁ λυγκεὺς θηρίον ἐστὶ ὀξυδερκέστατον; Pliny, *Natural History*, XXVIII. 32: *clarissime quadripedum omnium cernunt*; Arrian, *Cynegeticus*, IV. 5; Oppian, *Cynegetica*, III.

29. The Greek word can denote various felines, such as panther, leopard, cheetah: Detienne (1977), p. 93.

30. Aelian, *On Animals*, XIV. 6. On the stalk of the lynx, see Tumlison (1987).

31. Pliny, *Natural History*, XI. 202.

32. Pliny, *Natural History*, VIII. 70–80.

33. Pliny, *Natural History*, VIII. 70–80. For illustrations, see König (1976), pp. 196–201.

34. Plutarch, *De Sollertia Animalium*, 962f.

35. Aelian, *On Animals*, XIV. 6.

36. Virgil, *Georgics*, III. 264 and *Aeneid*, I. 323, with the commentary by Servius; Hyginus, *Fabulae*, 259.

37. *Tragica Adespota*, fragment 349 (Nauck), in *Tragicorum Graecorum Fragmenta* (Leipzig: Teubner, 1889; repr. Hildesheim: Olms, 1964).

38. Pliny, *Natural History*, VIII. 84: *quamvis in fame mandenti, si respexerit, oblivionem cibi subrepere aiunt digressumque quaerere aliud.*

39. Tumlison (1987) with bibliography.

40. Adult lynxes commonly urinate along trails, to mark their territories: Tumlison (1987).

41. Pliny, *Natural History*, VIII. 137; see also XXXVII. 52–53.

42. Bettini (1998), pp. 234–43.

43. The other two authors who recount it, Hyginus (*Fabulae*, 259) and Servius (on Virgil, *Aeneid*, I. 323), both depend on Ovid: Rosati (2009), p. 238. For the argument that we are dealing with an instance of original mythopoiesis on Ovid's part, see Michalopoulos (2001), p. 115 (cited by Rosati).

44. Rosati (2009), pp. 238–39.

45. Hyginus, *Fabulae*, 259: *ob quam rem irata Ceres, eum convertit in lyncem varii coloris, ut ipse variae mentis extiterat.*

46. Artemidorus, *Oneirocritica*, II. 12. 91.

47. Guidorizzi (2000), p. 511, n. 1078.

48. For the inverse correlation of the growing grain that has to be buried first to benefit humankind and the lynx-stone, which is hidden away by the animal to pre-empt any benefit for humanity, see Halna-Klein (1995), p. 120.

49. See Ovid, *Metamorphoses*, I. 113–50, in particular 123–24 (*semina tum primum longis Cerealia sulcis | obruta sunt, pressique iugo gemuere iuvenci*) and 137–40 (*nec tantum segetes alimentaque debita dives | poscebatur humus, sed itum est in viscera terrae, quasque recondiderat Stygiisque admoverat umbris, | effodiuntur opes, inritamenta malorum*).

50. Thompson (1947), pp. 125–27.

51. Theophrastus, *Enquiry into Plants*, IV. 7. 1. See also IV. 7. 3 where Theophrastus reports that the soldiers of Alexander the Great, when they came back from India, saw green, live vegetation, but only in the water. The very same vegetation, when taken out, became similar to salt or stone.

52. Theophrastus, *Enquiry into Plants*, IV. 6. 9–10, IV. 7. 4.

53. Similarly, according to a widespread ancient belief, foam carried by waves turns into pumice-stone when it reaches the shore: see e.g. Pliny, *Natural History*, XIII. 138: *extra Herculis columnas porri fronde nascitur frutex et alius lauri ac thymi, qui ambo eiecti in pumicem transfigurantur* or Isidore, *Etymologiae*, XVI. 4. 7 (Lindsay): *Pumex vocatur eo quod spumae densitate concretus fiat; et est aridus, candore parvus, tantamque naturam refrigerandi habens ut in vas missus musta fervere desinant.*

54. See further Lindenlauf (2003).

55. Vermeule (1979).

56. Georgoudi (1988); Bettini (1986), p. 205. For a pithy formulation of the point, see *Anthologia Palatina*, VII. 630. 3 (Beckby): ἴσος Ἄϊδι πόντος.

57. For an introduction with bibliographical guidance, the Greek text, and a French translation, see *Lapidaire Orphique*, ed. and trans. by R. Halleux and J. Schamp in *Les Lapidaires Grecs* (Paris: Les Belles Lettres), pp. 1–123.

58. See also 536–41, as well as 573–75, where the author records the marvel of both Perseus and Athena at the transformation of the seaweed into coral, with Klein (2009), p. 198: 'In the *Orphica Lithica* [...] the account of coral, which is very close to the Ovidian episode, is said to be the most marvellous thing ever seen and as difficult to believe in as the whole Perseus legend.'

59. Halleux and Schamp (1985), p. 110 n. 2: 'Le poète prétend faire ici une véritable analyse phénoménologique, comme il l'affirme à deux reprises en ouvrant et en fermant le développement (vv. 515–16 et 538).'

60. Detienne (1972).

61. See, for instance, Dioscorides, *De Materia Medica*, V. 121. 3 or Pliny, *Natural History*, XXXII. 24, further Magdelaine (2000), pp. 239–53.

62. Pliny, *Natural History*, XXXII. 22, cited below.

63. Georgoudi (1988).

64. Frontisi-Ducroux (1996), pp. 159–65. This feature is underlined by the word περιφθινύθω, which means 'to vanish in consequence of consumption': see *Dictionnaire étymologique de la langue grecque*, s.v. φθίνω, p. 1200–01: '*se consumer, s'épuiser, languir, se flétrir, (de)perir, mourir d'épuisement*' dit des êtres vivants; dit aussi des choses: 'passer, décliner, disparaître', spécialement à propos de la lune qui décroît (Arist.), donc du mois finissant.

65. The only evidence prior to Pliny is a short notice in Theophrastus, *On Stones*, 38: τὸ γὰρ κουράλιον, καὶ γὰρ τοῦθ' ὥσπερ λίθος, τῇ χρόᾳ μὲν ἐρυθρόν, περιφερὲς δ' ὡς ἂν ῥίζα· φύεται δ' ἐν τῇ θαλάττῃ. ['Coral, which is like a stone, is red in color and rounded like a root, and it grows in the sea.']

66. Pseudo-Apollodorus, *Library*, II. 40. See more generally Vernant (1985) (1991); Clair (1989).

67. Pliny, *Natural History*, XXXVII. 164: *Gorgonia nihil aliud est quam curalium; nominis causa quod in duritiam lapidis mutatur emollitum in mari.*

68. Frontisi-Ducroux (1996).

69. Vernant (1965). On the power of gemstones to symbolize and materialize the invisible world see Macrì (2009), pp. 89–98.

70. Some ancient authors explain the word κωράλιον as a diminutive of κόρη ('girl'). See Eustathius, *Commentary on Dionysius the Periegete*, 1107, Müller: Τὸ δὲ κουράλιον τοῦ τῆς Γοργόνος αἵματος ἀποστάξαι μυθεύεται, ἀφ' ἧς οἷα κόρης οὔσης ἡ κλῆσις τῷ λίθῳ ἐνεκάθισεν ['they say that *coral* grows from the blood oozed from the Gorgon, whence the name was given to the stone, because she was a maiden (*kore*)].

71. *Orphei Lithica Kerygmata*, ed. and trans. by R. Halleux and J. Schamp in *Les Lapidaires Grecs* (Paris: Les Belles Lettres), p. 22.

72. A related phenomenon are correspondences between milk and the stone *galactitis*; see e.g. Pliny, *Natural History*, XXXVII. 162; *Orpheus Lapidary*, 191–229; *Orphei Lithica Kerygmata*, 2; Damigeron-Evax, 34; Dioscorides, *De Materia Medica*, v. 150. The ability of stones to lactate (and hence the power of certain stones to aid in lactation) is still a motif in contemporary Spanish folklore: see Hildburgh (1951). In Christian tradition, the resemblance in colour between the stone and milk gave rise to the legend that at least those stones collected in the Holy Land were milk, more specifically, the milk of Maria, who spilt a drop during her flight to Egypt: see De Mely (1890).

73. This section of the paper has been developed in dialogue with the account of Ovid in the Introduction to Part I.

74. 745: *rapuit*; 746: *percepit* — a point reinforced in 751: *duritiam [...] capiant*.

75. Lexical correspondences reinforce the point: compare *tactuque induruit huius* (745) with *duritiam tacto capiant ut ab aëre* (751).

CHAPTER 3

Proteus and Protean Epic:
From Homer to Nonnos

Manuel Baumbach

As the history of reception shows, the meaning of literary texts is subject to continual change.[1] Once released into the world, texts have no way back into the apparently secure harbour of authorial control over what they signify; as soon as they fall into the hands of recipients, any tutelage exercised by their producers ceases to apply. From the point of view of the author, this phenomenon has been a significant source of anxiety, from antiquity onwards;[2] yet from the point of view of reception, the division of author and text enables the constant and ever-changing re-activation of the signifying potential of a literary work in the act of reading. This process does not (or ought not to) entail utterly arbitrary interpretations: Wolfgang Iser's work on the 'aesthetics of impact' (*Wirkungsästhetik*) as well as contemporary theorizing on the role of interpretative communities that interact with texts according to specific codes have identified the existence of limits to the potential meanings that texts may assume. Certain constraints thus coexist alongside the semantic indeterminacy that inheres in texts, which may be particularly marked through the presence of so-called 'sites of openness and uncertainty' (*Leer- oder Unbestimmtheitsstellen*).

In modern literary theory, the shape-shifting sea god Proteus has become a virtual emblem for such semantic mutability – the iconic godfather, as it were, of 'protean literature'. This chapter examines the figure of Proteus in two ancient texts, Homer's *Odyssey* and Nonnos' *Dionysiaka*. It will be shown that, in contrast to the modern fixation on the mutability of 'meaning', in these epics Proteus is invested with a much more complex symbolism, one that involves poetic inspiration and textual production as much as textual reception. Both in the *Odyssey* and the *Dionysiaka* Proteus undergoes repeated transformation on the level of plot, which enables insights into the fictive character of the epics, and at the same time assumes a 'poetic function' as chiffre for the construction of epic narrative. The metamorphoses of Proteus thus mirror the transformation of the texts in which they occur; and engagement with him turns into a privileged site of poetic reflexion. In addition to representing semantic mutability, the presence of Proteus can be read on at least three different levels: at the level of the text, Proteus is initially a figure as any other and part of the action and the plot of the narrative. From the point of view of composition, he is a figure that can be employed to reflect upon the process of literary production, that is, the *poiesis* of the text, in which he occurs. And thirdly, on a more general metapoetic level, he can turn into a figure connected to broader reflection on the artistry of epic poetry as such. In any particular passage, the first dimension of signification may coincide with either or both of the other two; but as a rule, the history of reception shows that the metapoetic potential of Proteus increases from the archaic period to the imperial age. As a result, Proteus assumes the role of 'generic memory' (*Gattungsgedächtnis*) within the Greek epic tradition.

Figural Metamorphoses and Poetological Reading: Homer's Proteus

The earliest and most elaborate appearance of Proteus in Greek literature occurs in the so-called Telemachy, in the fourth book of the *Odyssey*. In the search for information about the whereabouts of his father, Telemachus comes to Sparta, where he meets Menelaus, who tells him about his own return home. Stuck in Egypt because of a *Windstille*, he is advised by the nymph Eidothea, to capture the ancient sea-god Proteus as someone who would know the reasons for the delay in his journey.[3] Menelaus is told to hide himself together with three companions under seal-skins in a coastal location that Proteus frequents at noon to count his seals. The plan succeeds, and the two quasi-transformations of Menelaus, that is, his disguise as seal and his subsequent revelation as hero, set the stage for the well-known sequence of real metamorphoses of Proteus (*Odyssey*, IV. 450–63):[4]

> ἔνδιος δ' ὁ γέρων ἦλθ' ἐξ ἁλός, εὗρε δὲ φώκας   450
> ζατρεφέας, πάσας δ' ἄρ' ἐπῴχετο, λέκτο δ' ἀριθμόν.
> ἐν δ' ἡμέας πρώτους λέγε κήτεσιν, οὐδέ τι θυμῷ
> ὠΐσθη δόλον εἶναι· ἔπειτα δὲ λέκτο καὶ αὐτός.
> ἡμεῖς δὲ ἰάχοντες ἐπεσσύμεθ', ἀμφὶ δὲ χεῖρας
> βάλλομεν· οὐδ' ὁ γέρων δολίης ἐπελήθετο τέχνης,   455
> ἀλλ' ἦ τοι πρώτιστα λέων γένετ' ἠϋγένειος,
> αὐτὰρ ἔπειτα δράκων καὶ πάρδαλις ἠδὲ μέγας σῦς·
> γίγνετο δ' ὑγρὸν ὕδωρ καὶ δένδρεον ὑψιπέτηλον·
> ἡμεῖς δ' ἀστεμφέως ἔχομεν τετληότι θυμῷ.
> ἀλλ' ὅτε δή ῥ' ἀνίαζ' ὁ γέρων ὀλοφώϊα εἰδώς,   460
> καὶ τότε δή μ' ἐπέεσσιν ἀνειρόμενος προσέειπε·
> τίς νύ τοι, Ἀτρέος υἱέ, θεῶν συμφράσσατο βουλάς,
> ὄφρα μ' ἕλοις ἀέκοντα λοχησάμενος; τέο σε χρή;

['and at noon the old man came forth from the sea and found the fatted seals; and he went over all, and counted their number. Among the creatures he counted us first, nor did his heart guess that there was guile; and then he too laid him down. Threat we rushed upon him with a shout, and [455] threw our arms about him, nor did that old man forget his crafty wiles. Nay, at the first he turned into a bearded lion, and then into a serpent, and a leopard, and a huge boar; then he turned into flowing water, and into a tree, high and leafy; but we held on unflinchingly with steadfast heart. [460] But when at last that old man, skilled in wizard arts, grew weary, then he questioned me, and spoke, and said: "Who of the gods, son of Atreus, took counsel with thee that thou mightest lie in wait for me, and take me against my will? Of what hast thou need?"']

Three approaches have dominated exegesis of this passage, all prefigured in ancient attempts at making sense of the figure of Proteus. First, rationalistic interpretations, which date back to the choral lyric of the archaic poet Stesichorus, have tried to show that Proteus stands in reality for an old Egyptian king, who had acquired secret knowledge and the facility of a seer. The Homeric metamorphoses could thus be explained — as, for instance, by Diodorus Siculus in his world history (1. 62) — by way of the changing headgear of the king that appeared in the shape of a lion, a snake, or even a tree. Second, Proteus was interpreted in an allegorical philosophical mode as demiurge or creator of the universe, who rules the elements: he transforms himself into them, employs them in the formation of the cosmos, and can give birth to new forms with the help of his daughter Eidothea, who is 'in form divine'. Third and finally, the Homeric text is taken as an originary metaphor for the changeability of the human psyche — as seen, for example, in Plato's criticism of a sophist as Proteus, the notorious charlatan Peregrinus Proteus in Lucian, and the deceitful lover Proteus in Shakespeare's *The Two Gentlemen of Verona*.[5]

These interpretations, which are strongly context-oriented and try to identify the meaning with reference to the rootedness of Homeric epic in the archaic period, can be supplemented by a poetological approach. The first point to note is that the Proteus-episode interrupts the narrative as a 'retarding insertion' and therefore invites the extra-diegetic recipients to reflect upon the function of the episode within the plot and the structure of the *Odyssey* as a whole. Four poetological markers are particularly striking.

First, Proteus' ability to transform — into animal, water or tree — signals that the art of metamorphosis itself is turned into a principal theme here, not least since the actual metamorphoses of Proteus are set up by the fake-transformation of Menelaus by means of disguise. The metamorphosis as disguise transforms Proteus: the transformative play-acting forces him to counter with a series of real metamorphoses. This *mise-en-scène* of metamorphosis by Menelaus happens in close dialogue with the text that produces and records it, that is, the art of narrative staging.

Secondly, after his transformations Proteus returns to his original appearance, to the form he had when he first appeared in the text, so that all of his metamorphoses can be read as a commentary on or inflection of his initial appearance, as different readings of the same text that rings the changes of form, in a self-reflexive gesture speaking to the potential multiplicity of meaning.[6] From this point of view, the metamorphoses of Proteus turn into fleeting manifestations of a more fundamental and permanent reality, which constitutes their point of departure as well as return: Proteus' actual form, to which we need to return to understand him and the text.

Thirdly, Proteus does not change his appearance voluntarily; rather, it is an extraneous force that motivates his metamorphoses, or, in other words, triggers the generation of meaning — in perfect analogy to the interaction between text and reader. Menelaus and his companions approach the figure of Proteus because they are in need of information and seek ways to understand the world and their environment differently and better — a very similar interest informs and guides ancient and modern readers of literary texts who can expect, in addition to entertainment, something 'useful' (in Horace's classic formulation). From this point of view, the text-immanent attempt of Menelaus to capture Proteus in Homer mirrors the effort of the reader or audience to engage with the text, whereas the metamorphoses of Proteus could be taken to symbolize the potential alterations of texts 'in the act of reading' as conceptualized by Wolfgang Iser. The comparability of the figure of Proteus with the 'essence' of literature seems fitting not least because texts, as observed at the beginning, thwart any endeavour to fix their meaning — just like Proteus. Each encounter with the sea-god produces a somewhat different result, just as each act of reading alters the semantics of the text and opens up new potential meanings. This aspect is also manifest in the divergence between Eidothea's anticipation of three expected metamorphoses and the six transformations that Menelaus then actually experiences. For during her instructions to Menelaus (IV. 410–24), Eidothea enumerates one type of transformation (into fire), which the hero will in the end not encounter at all (417–18):

> πάντα δὲ γιγνόμενος πειρήσεται, ὅσσ' ἐπὶ γαῖαν
> ἑρπετὰ γίγνονται καὶ ὕδωρ καὶ θεσπιδαὲς πῦρ·

> [For try he will, and will assume all manner of shapes of all things that move upon the earth, and of water, and of wondrous blazing fire.]

For each recipient, so the discrepancy implies, Proteus has in store a new meta-morphosis: just like literary texts, it is impossible to describe him completely, let alone fix his significance once and for all.

Fourth, Proteus' metamorphoses are followed by speech and narration. This is an utterly unusual telos of transformative change since the majority of figures undergoing metamorphosis turn into flora, fauna, or inanimate objects, all without speech; or, in case of other self-transformations by divine figures such as Zeus or Thetis, the metamorphoses are associated with certain actions, not narration. In contrast, Proteus is a means of projecting narration, a means of narrating in a narrative, and a significant one: through his story, Proteus enables not only the return home of Menelaus (and, consequently, Telemachus' visit to Sparta); he also disseminates the status of Odysseus among humankind and, with the information he provides, reinforces Penelope's decision to wait and hope for the return of her husband. Proteus' discourse therefore illuminates the plot and one of the principal themes of the *Odyssey*, while his series of transformations gestures to (and enacts) the fluid narrative structure and position of the narrator within the epic.

A further observation reinforces the poetological function of the figure of Proteus: his episode is situated thematically and narratologically in the centre of the *Odyssey*. The central theme of Proteus' speech is 'return': he recounts three stories of return with specific reference to the destinies of Ajax, Agamemnon, and Odysseus; and his appearance in the epic is of course embedded within, and hence part of, Menelaus' own return narrative. The Proteus-episode is therefore a miniature version of the *nostoi* (stories of homecoming) that underwrite the *Odyssey*, and one could even ascribe to it the function of a *mise en abyme*, not least because in Proteus' speech the successful return of Odysseus is structurally prefigured through its proximity to the successful return of Menelaus. From a narratological point of view, the Proteus-episode orchestrates the representation of movement and travel in the

Odyssey. On the human level, we start out in Ithaca, from where Telemachus sets out on a journey to Menelaus, who in turn brings him and us to Proteus. Proteus' speech 'travels' in the exact opposite direction: he addresses Menelaus, who tells his utterance to Telemachus, who, in turn, returns to Ithaca and reports to his mother (XVII. 138–41):

> ταῦτα δ' ἅ μ' εἰρωτᾷς καὶ λίσσεαι, οὐκ ἂν ἐγώ γε
> ἄλλα παρὲξ εἴποιμι παρακλιδὸν οὐδ' ἀπατήσω·
> ἀλλὰ τὰ μέν μοι ἔειπε γέρων ἅλιος νημερτής,
> τῶν οὐδέν τοι ἐγὼ κρύψω ἔπος οὐδ' ἐπικεύσω.

> [But in this matter of which thou dost ask and entreat me, verily I will not swerve aside to speak of other things, nor will I deceive thee; but of all that the unerring old man of the sea told me, not one thing will I hide from thee or conceal.]

Telemachus subsequently cites four verses from Proteus' speech (XVII. 143–46), which he had heard from Menelaus (IV. 557–60). This citation has a double effect: on the one hand, the reiteration of Proteus' words reinforce their import for the narrative of the *Odyssey* as a whole, not least since the insertion of elements from the fourth book into the seventeenth produces an autopoetic circularity: the audience is encouraged to remember, revisit and, indeed, once the epic circulated in written form, re-read the earlier portion of the narrative.[7] On the other hand, we see a relay of Proteus-like figures as narrators: what Proteus was for Menelaus, that is, a source of information, Menelaus is for Telemachus, who in turn becomes 'Proteus' for Penelope, who enquires about the return of Odysseus and hears part of Proteus' speech as cited by her son in response.[8] All figures within Homer's narrative therefore share a common interest in Proteus' utterance, who indeed seems to address them as a group — an aspect internalized by the characters inasmuch as, in repeating what he learned from Menelaus, it seems as if Telemachus reports to his mother what he had *personally* learned from Proteus (see XVII. 140, cited above).

With Proteus, the narrator of the *Odyssey* chose or created a figure of narration, whose speech contains the key to the overall structure, the central theme, and the narrative telos of the epic.[9] Moreover, Proteus, just like the narrator, is omniscient: he knows the past, is familiar with the cares of the present, and has knowledge of the future: he is cognizant of how everything is going to, or ought to, happen.[10] In other words, Proteus is a narrator who, over and above his role in the plot, addresses the audience of the epic in his significance for the overall design of the epic and, in his omniscience, stands in as an inner-textual representative and mirror-image of the omniscient author or narrator.[11]

Proteus as Metapoetic Figure of Epic Self-Reflection: Nonnos' *Dionysiaka*

The proposed poetological reading of the Homeric Proteus-episode finds support from the point of view of reception through Nonnos' *Dionysiaka* (fifth century AD), which, with its forty-eight books, is the longest epic that has been transmitted from antiquity.[12] The chronologically arranged work about the life and the deeds of the god Dionysus begins in a traditional key with a (Homeric) invocation of the Muse (verse 1: Εἰπέ, θεά), but then breaks with the Homeric tradition in a twofold way: on the one hand, the poet includes himself in his narrative and thereby construes a parallel between *auctor* and *actor* that all but collapses the distinction between the figure of the god and the figure of the poet inasmuch as they share in the same mental and literary processes;[13] on the other hand, the poet now explicitly employs the Homeric Proteus as a kind of surrogate Muse of his work, which entails an even stronger emphasis and further profiling of Proteus' poetological potential (1. 11–33):[14]

> ἄξατέ μοι νάρθηκα, τινάξατε κύμβαλα, Μοῦσαι,
> καὶ παλάμῃ δότε θύρσον ἀειδομένου Διονύσου·
> ἀλλὰ χοροῦ ψαύοντα, Φάρῳ παρὰ γείτονι νήσῳ
> στήσατέ μοι Πρωτῆα πολύτροπον, ὄφρα φανείη
> ποικίλον εἶδος ἔχων, ὅτι ποικίλον ὕμνον ἀράσσω·   15
> εἰ γὰρ ἐφερπύσσειε δράκων κυκλούμενος ὁλκῷ,
> μέλψω θεῖον ἄεθλον, ὅπως κισσώδεϊ θύρσῳ
> φρικτὰ δρακοντοκόμων ἐδαΐζετο φῦλα Γιγάντων·
> εἰ δὲ λέων φρίξειεν ἐπαυχενίην τρίχα σείων,
> Βάκχον ἀνευάζω βλοσυρῆς ἐπὶ πήχεϊ Ῥείης   20
> μαζὸν ὑποκλέπτοντα λεοντοβότοιο θεαίνης·
> εἰ δὲ θυελλήεντι μετάρσιος ἅλματι ταρσῶν
> πόρδαλις ἀίξῃ πολυδαίδαλον εἶδος ἀμείβων,
> ὑμνήσω Διὸς υἷα, πόθεν γένος ἔκτανεν Ἰνδῶν
> πορδαλίων ὀχέεσσι καθιππεύσας ἐλεφάντων·   25
> εἰ δέμας ἰσάζοιτο τύπῳ συός, υἷα Θυώνης
> ἀείσω ποθέοντα συοκτόνον εὔγαμον Αὔρην,
> ὀψιγόνου τριτάτοιο Κυβηλίδα μητέρα Βάκχου·
> εἰ δὲ πέλοι μιμηλὸν ὕδωρ, Διόνυσον ἀείσω
> κόλπον ἁλὸς δύνοντα κορυσσομένοιο Λυκούργου·   30
> εἰ φυτὸν αἰθύσσοιτο νόθον ψιθύρισμα τιταίνων,
> μνήσομαι Ἰκαρίοιο, πόθεν παρὰ θυιάδι ληνῷ
> βότρυς ἀμιλλητῆρι ποδῶν ἐθλίβετο ταρσῷ.

[Bring me the fennel, rattle the cymbals, ye Muses! put in my hand the wand of Dionysus whom I sing: but bring me a partner for your dance in the neighbouring island of Pharos, Proteus of many turns, that he may appear in all his diversity of shapes, since I twang my harp to a diversity of songs. For it, as a serpent, he should glide along his winding trail, I will sing my god's achievement, how with ivy-wreathed wand he destroyed the horrid hosts of Giants serpent-haired. If as a lion he shake his bristling mane, I will cry "Euoi!" to Bacchus on the arm of buxom Rheia, stealthily draining the breast of the lionbreeding goddess. If as a leopard he shoot up into the air with a stormy leap from his pads, changing shape like a master-craftsman, I will hymn the son of Zeus, how he slew the Indian nation, with his team of pards riding down the elephants. If he make his figure like the shape of a boar, I will sing Thyone's son, love-sick for Aura the desirable, boarslayer, daughter of Cybele, mother of the third Bacchus late-born. If he be mimic water, I will sing Dionysus diving into the bosom of the brine, when Lycurgus armed himself. If he become a quivering tree and tune a counterfeit whispering, I will tell of Icarius, how in the jubilant winepress his feet crushed the grape in rivalry.]

Nonnos' epic assumes a protean shape from three points of view. First, whereas in

Homer Menelaus has to go in search of Proteus, the poet of the *Dionysiaka* calls upon the Muses, demoted to the status of helpers, to bring Proteus to him. In contrast to Homer and also Virgil, in Nonnos it is the poet himself who engages with Proteus in this initial dynamic of inspiration.[15] Proteus is the new muse who inspires new poetry by means of his changing forms and their literary manifestations. Secondly, instead of proclaiming Homeric truth, Nonnos' Proteus is now the source of Dionysiac transformations. By means of his Odyssean 'much-turning' essence (see πολύτροπον in line 14, in clear allusion to the first line of the *Odyssey*, but here meant in a metamorphic rather than a psychological sense), the sea-god turns into the creative principle of the *Dionysiaka*, an epic characterized by its protean variety (see ποικίλον in line 15).[16] In Nonnos, Proteus gives the entire epic his form, or, rather, forms, though it is striking that his description of the sea-god's metamorphoses by and large follows the Homeric model. The Homeric transformations of Proteus attained canonical status, gaining stability within flux. Thus, to use the terminology of Renate Lachmann, Proteus has become part of the 'memory' of the epic genre.[17]

A poetological reading of Proteus could see the figure as the symbolic embodiment of the creative remit of poetry, which is in principle infinite and may assume, in terms of both content and form, as many shapes as the mythic character and his potential for transformations. But the reception of Proteus — at least within the epic genre used by Homer and Nonnos — delimits this infinity of options, insofar as the genre creates for itself a 'predictable Proteus' who always manifests the same range of metamorphoses. This type of generic control does not of course eliminate all poetic licence — on the contrary: tradition correlates with, indeed enables, modest innovation. Nonnos, for instance, varies the sequence of the Homeric metamorphoses: in his epic, Proteus first turns into a snake and then becomes a lion. In comparison with Homer, Nonnos thus inverts the first two transformations, which has little import on the level of theme, but carries a programmatic poetological message:[18] the poet has the ability to engage creatively with the material of the tradition, he can change and reconfigure the order and design adopted by his predecessors, and he can do so without breaking with the conventions of his chosen genre.[19]

From a poetological point of view, Proteus amounts to something like the midwife of new poetry, which finds its correspondence on the level of genealogy: what follows the epic invocation of the Muses in Nonnos is initially not a heroic epic narrative, but the announcement of a hymn to Dionysus, which identifies a god, rather than a hero, as protagonist of epic poetry. The combination of Homeric invocation of the Muses with the hymnic convention of establishing at the outset the genealogy of the deity (in our case Dionysus) entails a formal conflation of hymn and heroic epic; and conversely the simultaneous presence of two generic codes (and two sets of generic expectations on the part of the reader) has a symbolic correspondence in the double birth of Dionysus. Also on the level of content, Nonnos employs birth and genealogy to locate his text: the narration of Athena's extraordinary birth from the head of Zeus, right after the double birth of Dionysus, and the emphasis on her military function by means of the epithet 'shining' signals

already in the proem that the overall orientation of the epic is primarily concerned
with the military exploits of Dionysus. And finally, the emphasis on the birth and
genealogy of the god Dionysus also interacts with the cultural background of the
poet. The available evidence suggests that Nonnos hailed from the Egyptian town
of Panopolis;[20] in other words, he belongs to the same geographic region as his
poetic auxiliary Proteus, whom already Homer had situated in Egypt. *Auctor* and
actor share a common origin: for Nonnos, the well of epic song no longer flows out
of Smyrna or other places with Homeric associations,[21] but out of Egypt, which
is ennobled by being the abode of the Muse Proteus.[22] A direct allusion at the
climactic end of the proem renders Nonnos' confrontation with Homer explicit
(34–38):

> ἄξατέ μοι νάρθηκα, Μιμαλλόνες, ὠμαδίην δὲ
> νεβρίδα ποικιλόνωτον ἐθήμονος ἀντὶ χιτῶνος   35
> σφίγξατέ μοι στέρνοισι, Μαρωνίδος ἔμπλεον ὀδμῆς
> νεκταρέης, βυθίῃ δὲ παρ' Εἰδοθέῃ καὶ Ὁμήρῳ
> φωκάων βαρὺ δέρμα φυλασσέσθω Μενελάῳ.

> [Bring me the fennel, Mimallons! On my shoulders in place of the wonted
> kirtle, bind, I pray, tight over my breast a dapple-back fawnskin, full of the
> perfume of Maronian nectar; and let Homer and deep-sea Eidothea keep the
> rank skin of the seals for Menelaus.]

Homer is here introduced by name. In case the reader has so far missed the poetic
agon that Nonnos, in his preface, set up with his predecessor, these verses render
the intertextual emulation explicit. Indeed, the programmatic repetition in verse
34 of the opening segment of verse 11, that is, ἄξατέ μοι νάρθηκα, encourages the
audience to reconsider the entire passage from verse 11 onwards anew, in the light
of the information that Nonnos provides in lines 34–38. The emulative spirit is
now also fully apparent. By leaving behind the seal-skin as disguise, which played
such a vital role in Homer and for Homer's protagonist Menelaus (it ensured the
success of the undertaking) and labelling it negatively with the derogatory epithet
βαρὺ ('rank', verse 38), the narrator implies that he no longer needs Homer's narrative technique. For him, Proteus is not an opponent, to be conquered by means
of a ruse, but an easily available and gladly utilized source of inspiration. Nonnos'
appropriation of the Homeric tradition, with the purpose of outdoing it in the
development of his own poetic style, continues in the internal proem at the beginning of Book xxv. Again, Homer is invoked directly as model (8–10), but only to
announce shortly thereafter the surpassing quality of his own theme: 'for Time
never saw before another struggle like the Eastern War, not after the Indian War
in later days has Enyo seen its equal. No such army came to Ilion, no such host of
men' (22–27).[23]

★　　★　　★　　★　　★

At the outset, I mentioned the tension between the determinate sequence of signs
that constitutes a text and the variety and unpredictability of its reception. Proteus
embodies both sides of this tension by means of his stable identity as a sea-god and
his temporary, and ever changing, metamorphoses as a notorious shape-shifter.[24]

As a text subjected to the act of reading, he is the source of meaning and, again just like a text that has been read, every meaning realized stands in dialogue with, and refers back to, him. This makes Proteus 'readable' from a poetological point of view. He acquires, as in Homer, his self-reflective significance above all in his narrations, which, above and beyond their import for the epic plot, also contain hints and information about the overall conception, structure and message of the poetry in which they occur. In the epic tradition, and especially in the *Dionysiaka*, Proteus becomes a figure of metapoetic significance. Nonnos employs the sea-god and his transformations as a poetic means for the creation of narrative, and transforms Proteus into a Muse of inspiration — a Muse who knows everything and is mutable in form, but also a Muse who escapes in ecstasis and proves difficult to pin down — a difficult, perhaps even intractable Muse as it were, but for that very reason the aesthetics of her, and her metamorphoses in Protean epic, appeal.

Notes to Chapter 3

1. The chapter presupposes a broadly conceived notion of 'text', which includes texts that are orally performed or, rather, derive from a tradition of oral poetry. I would like to thank all participants of the *Transformative Change* conference in Durham for helpful criticism and Ingo Gildenhard for translating my paper.

2. Examples include Plato's critique of writing in the *Phaedrus* and the well-known passage from Horace's *Epistles* (I. 20. I–8), in which the author warns his just-finished first book of letters, which urges the poet to get on with publication, of the potentially negative consequences of such a step.

3. For Egypt as the mythical home of Proteus and variations in the post-Homeric tradition see O'Nolan (1960).

4. All texts and translations of Homer's *Odyssey* are taken from A. T. Murray's Loeb Classical Library edition.

5. Compare also the debtor in Horace's *Satires* who eludes his lenders in Protean fashion (II. 3. 71–73). Clarke (1995), pp. 58–60 offers a psychoanalytic view of Proteus.

6. Cf. Lonsdale (1988), p. 166: 'A god such as Proteus has a finite cycle of transformations. Once he has exhausted his repertoire of magical shifts of shape, the god can be seen in his true form.' For an account of the shape-shifters' 'standard lists of animals and elements' in Homer see Forbes Irving (1990), pp. 171–94.

7. Steinrück (1992), p. 59 observes that the citation contains a small alteration that de-emphasizes the optimistic tenor of the speech of Menelaus and thus conditions a pessimistic interpretation of the episode by Penelope.

8. Cf. Lonsdale (1988), p. 165: 'In particular, it can be shown that in the central episode of the book Proteus and Menelaus exchange aspects of each other's identities. Like Proteus the sea-prophet, Menelaus performs the role of prophet (and by extension bard) for Telemachus in pronouncing an omen about the return of Odysseus. The form his prophetic omen takes is the simile. In using this rhetorical device, Menelaus momentarily resembles the poet, whose means of shifting shape can occur in similes fashioned from words. A certain complicity exists between the poet's own activity and the actions of certain of his characters.'

9. See also Strabo's note (I. 2. 30) that Homer invented the story of Proteus.

10. Among other things, Proteus knows that Menelaus is predestined for Elysium after his death, which constitutes an 'external prolepsis': see De Jong (2001). For the prophetic character of the figure, see Rosenberger (2001).

11. De Jong (2001), pp. 109–10.

12. For the difficulties in dating Nonnos and the classification of his poem as epos, see the studies by Shorrock (2001) (2011), Hopkinson (1994), and Schmitz (2005), pp. 197–200.

13. As a result, the authoritative impartiality of the Homeric narrator gets de-emphasized and

the entire proem illustrates how the poet is transformed into, or consecrated as, a Dionysiac singer (see Shorrock (2001), p. 114). The distance between the poet and the subject of his poetry disappears, insofar as the poet is initiated into the cult of the god — an approximation of narrator and his narrative material that recurs at the end of the proem (34–37) in a framing capacity.

14. Text and translation are taken from W. H. D. Rouse's Loeb Classical Library edition.

15. For poetological implications in Virgil's reception of the Homeric figure of Proteus in the *Eclogues* and *Georgics* see Baumbach (2012).

16. See further Schmitz (2005), p. 207: 'Die Vielgestaltigkeit des Proteus entspricht also der des Dionysos; deshalb steht er Pate für den epischen Text. Zugleich macht der Erzähler im gesamten Proömium deutlich, dass die Darstellung eines solch wandlungsfähigen Gottes auch einen besonders wandlungsfähigen Stil erfordert.'

17. Lachmann (1990), p. 76. Also cf. her observation on the importance of intertextuality as the crucial means of creating *Gedächtnisräume* as well as generic memory: 'Die Intertextualität der Texte zeigt das Immer-Wieder-Sich-Neu- und Umschreiben einer Kultur, einer Kultur als Buchkultur und als Zeichenkultur, die sich über ihre Zeichen immer wieder neu definiert. Das Schreiben ist Gedächtnishandlung und Neuinterpretation der (Buch-)Kultur ineins. [...] So lässt sich — noch einmal — sagen, daß das *Gedächtnis des Textes* die Intertextualität seiner Bezüge ist, die im Schreiben als einem Abschreiten des Raumes zwischen Texten entsteht.'

18. At the most one can speak of a programmatic turning away from the Homeric simile for fighters as such, for which Nonnos substitutes an animal of greater Dionysiac significance. For the lion-simile in the *Odyssey*, see Magrath (1982).

19. On the poetological dimension of the proem and the play with the generic expectations of the recipient see also Schmitz (2005), pp. 202–08.

20. See *Anthologia Palatina*, IX. 198. His name also points to Egypt: since the fourth century BC, Νόννος appears in letters and documents as a popular name in Egypt. It remains unclear, however, whether the name can be securely traced back to Egyptian or Syrian origins or, perhaps, is an artificial name coined with reference to ὁ νέννος, which appears in epigrams and, in poetry, can designate the maternal uncle or grandfather.

21. For the close link between Homer and Smyrna in imperial Greek epic see the internal proem of Quintus of Smyrna's *Posthomerica* and the studies by Bär (2007), pp. 29–64 and (2009).

22. See Hopkinson (1994).

23. See also Shorrock (2001), pp. 170–74 and Schmitz (2005), pp. 208–12.

24. For this type of shape-shifter, see Forbes Irving (1990), pp. 171–94.

CHAPTER 4

Arboreal Myths:
Dryadic Transformations,
Children's Literature, and Fantastic Trees

Zoe Jaques

'Used to be a tree, didn't you?
Glad you're back. I hate it when pretty girls turn into trees'.[1]

When Apollo in Rick Riordan's *Percy Jackson and the Titan's Curse* (2007) welcomes Thalia back from her time as a tree, he alludes to the classical tradition of transforming humans between various states-of-being.[2] In the case of Thalia, her transformation from a semi-divine being (a 'half-blood') into a pine tree occurred in an earlier volume of the series, at a moment of mortal-death, when her father, Zeus, took pity on her and brought about a rapid metamorphosis of her physical body. According to the satyr who witnessed Thalia's final fight against an army of monsters, the young heroine 'was wounded and tired, and she didn't want to live like a hunted animal.'[3] Thalia's metamorphosis thus occurs due to a threat to her mortal body; it is only through being transformed into a pine tree that her spirit is able to live on, continuing to 'protect the borders of the valley'.[4]

Riordan's rendering of Thalia's transformation is clearly a version of the many transformations of girls into trees that occur in classical tradition,[5] and in particular an allusion to, or reworking of, Ovid's story of Apollo and Daphne in his *Metamorphoses*. Wandering 'manless [...] through untrodden woods' and forsaking the pleas of her father to provide him with a son-in-law and grandchildren, the young Daphne implores protection from the unwanted advances of Apollo or any other man (*Met.* 1. 483–87):

> illa velut crimen taedas exosa iugales
> pulchra verecundo suffuderat ora rubore
> inque patris blandis haerens cervice lacertis   485
> 'da mihi perpetua, genitor carissime,' dixit
> 'virginitate frui! [...]'

> [She hated like a crime the bond of wedlock,
> And, bashful blushes tingeing her fair cheeks,
> With coaxing arms embraced him and replied:
> 'My dear, dear father, grant I may enjoy
> Virginity for ever.']

Daphne's flight and Apollo's chase are rendered in highly sexual terms; her body appears with svelte grace and fragile beauty, while his predatory pursuit is as of a hunter bearing down upon his prey.[6] At the point of capture, however, Daphne's plea to her father to be transformed results in a rapid metamorphosis (*Met.* I. 548–52):

> vix prece finita torpor gravis occupat artus,
> mollia cinguntur tenui praecordia libro,
> in frondem crines, in ramos bracchia crescunt,   550
> pes modo tam velox pigris radicibus haeret,
> ora cacumen habet: remanet nitor unus in illa.

> [Scarce had she made her prayer when through her limbs
> A dragging languor spread, her tender bosom
> Was wrapped in thin smooth bark, her slender arms
> Were changed to branches and her hair to leaves;
> Her feet but now so swift were anchored fast
> In numb stiff roots, her face and head became
> The crown of a green tree; all that remained
> Of Daphne was her shining loveliness.]

As with Thalia, Daphne is transformed at the moment her physical body is threatened. Tree transformations move the young girl from a mortal life, categorized by physical vulnerability and temporality, to a state of permanence — the tree offers an impenetrable casement, which classically protects the maiden from corporeal assault. In the case of Daphne, as Mary Barnard explains, the transformation of the nymph into a tree makes her immune to male desire:

> The transformation enables Daphne to leave a body split by opposing forces of beauty and chastity and to acquire the physical shape that conforms to her conception of herself as a virgin free from sexuality; she is converted into a nonhuman form, into tree life incapable of passion. By escaping into her arboreal citadel, within which she will be secure from overzealous males, Daphne achieves the ultimate withdrawal from a world threatening to her identity.[7]

For Thalia too the tree offers protection from mortal peril, yet while Riordan does allude to the sexual element of the tale — Apollo comically laments his experience of 'pretty girls' turning into trees — the story of Thalia's transformation primarily focuses on her heroism as opposed to her sexual vulnerability. Thalia may be susceptible to an attack by monsters, but Riordan avoids making her twelve-year old body a target for male lust.

This transformation of the tale from one of rape-avoidance to one of self-sacrifice is perhaps what we might expect in a work of children's literature; children and sex are a taboo subject generally — as James R. Kincaid calls it, 'monster-talk'.[8] Yet children's literature frequently does tackle the difficult intersection between childhood and adulthood, as epitomized by the development of the sex instinct, often utilising metamorphic or hybrid beings to comment on issues of sexual development. There has been much recent critical interest in the transformations of the classics in modern literature,[9] but the role of children's fiction in this metamorphic process has tended to be overlooked. This chapter will argue that the fantastical plant, wood nymph or dryad[10] operates in a liminal space variously haunted by religious, mythological and ethical implications, and authors of children's literature frequently allude to or transform preceding myths and traditions to comment on issues of sexual identity. Trees and woodlands, which have long been sites of sexual tension,[11] provide an ambiguous site for both legitimising and vilifying sexual development. At a moment when the child is crossing a boundary into an essentially adult, eroticized world — a metamorphic movement itself — such fantastical botanicals conceptualize the experience of growing up, and offer comment on the contrastive models for sexual behaviour open to the human child in the real world.

★   ★   ★   ★   ★

Hans Christian Andersen's fairy tale 'The Dryad' (1868) offers a vivid depiction of fantastical tree life, with a specifically sexual message which inverts the 'girl turned to tree' motif of classical tradition.[12] The tale tells of a young dryad who yearns to escape the confines of a chestnut tree, desiring to experience all the wonders of the world that she discovers from butterflies and dragonflies and from the priest who teaches school children under a nearby oak tree. News of the wonders of the Field of Mars and the Paris Exhibition further exacerbate her state of longing, as the Dryad laments being unable to follow the country-girl Marie who leaves the parish and heads for the delights and dangers of the city streets. The Dryad's wish to be freed is granted when her tree is dug up and moved to Paris, to be planted in a little square surrounded by high houses and bustling streets. Eventually, however, the Dryad's joy at merely watching the crowds from her 'little cramped corner'[13] wanes, and, in a reversal of the Daphne-Apollo myth, she is transformed into a human girl, able for a single night to indulge in the pleasures of the Parisian streets.

Andersen's narrative clearly revels in a range of threats associated with the exotic Paris. From the smog and sewers of the city to its drunkenness and drug-taking, Andersen presents the French capital as a wasteland of moral degradation and the degeneration of nature — the Dryad's chestnut tree only comes to Paris to replace the dead, uprooted one which was killed by 'gas fumes, kitchen-fumes, and all the plant-killing vapours of a town'.[14] Everything in the city is artificial; while the countryside abounds with organic images of growth and renewal, Andersen's cityscape contains machinery and glass walls, throngs of people and tin-plated water-plants. Yet while the ecological trajectory of the narrative is clear, and in keeping with the primary agenda of many talking tree tales,[15] the principal sense of 'knowing' that tempts the Dryad is a sexual one, which builds upon the longstanding associations between trees, knowledge, and sexual guilt. Andersen's tale works to position the female who gives in to sexual temptation as 'ruined'; his transformation of the myth of Apollo and Daphne acts as a warning as to the dangers of human sexual appetite so that 'being human' is perceived as a lesser state than being a plant. The *scala naturae* is thus destabilized; the Dryad's transformation out of her tree should be a progression to a higher state of being but is depicted by Andersen as a false and treacherous movement that necessitates female destruction. As Theodore Ziolkowski has argued, each Ovidian metamorphosis is either a spiritual or physical transformation characterized as 'degradation' or 'ascension'.[16] Where Andersen differs from Ovid, however, is that he depicts an 'upward' change as in itself a degradation, so that vegetative matter becomes more worthy of praise than human flesh.

The Dryad's reverse transformation is depicted in terms that resonate with the myth of Daphne's arboreal metamorphosis. Although her goal could not be more different, her impassioned prayer to be made free from her imprisoning tree clearly resembles Daphne's plea to her father:

> Take my lifetime, and give me the half of the Ephemera's life! Free me from my imprisonment, give me human life, human joy for a short space, only this single night, if it must be so, and punish me thus for my presumptuous spirit, my longing for life! Annihilate me; let the fresh, young tree that encloses me then wither and fall, become ashes, and be scattered to the winds.[17]

These dual desires, one for innocence and one for experience, are also simultaneously quests for death and both have negative connotations. Daphne elects to be immortal, and thus inhuman, changing her being forever into the static form of a tree, while Andersen's Dryad chooses a mortal life — a state that is characterized by its temporality. In both cases, the sexual options open to the female lead to some form of 'ruin' — to avoid passion the young girl must renounce a human life, but to indulge in it necessitates death. Children's fiction generally displays a preference for humanity over immortality; as Sarah Annes Brown notes, in Disney's version of *Hercules* (1997) the hero chooses to renounce immortality in order to pursue a more human (and thus brief) existence, and much other children's fiction follows a similar model.[18] Yet for Andersen, the Dryad's desire to enjoy a human life is shown to be fundamentally flawed and appears predicated on his own distrust of the sexualized female. The 'half-deaths' of both the Dryad and her Ovidian forebear are sites of sexual tension, for while Daphne's transformation spares her from an imminent ravishment by the 'straining muzzle' that 'scrapes her heels',[19] the moment of metamorphosis for Andersen's Dryad is essentially one of sexual awakening:

> A rustling passed through the branches of the tree; there came a *titillating* feeling, a *trembling* in every leaf, as if a fire ran through it or out of it, a blast went through the crown of the tree, and in the midst of it arose a woman's form, the Dryad herself.[20]

Like Daphne, however, the Dryad is exquisitely beautiful after her transformation, shifting from the 'school-child'[21] of the countryside parish to the young woman of the city streets:

> The Dryad sat by the foot of the tree, by the door of the house she had locked and of which she had thrown away the key. So young, so beautiful! The stars saw her and twinkled. The gas-lamps saw her and beamed and beckoned! How slender she was and yet strong, a child and yet a full-grown maiden. Her clothes were fine as silk, and green as the fresh, newly-unfolded leaves in the crown of the tree; in her nut-brown hair hung a half-blown chestnut blossom; she looked like the goddess of spring.[22]

Such a description, as with the pre-metamorphosis and threatened Daphne, positions the Dryad as a highly sexualized being. She is both 'newly-unfolded' and 'half-blown' — organic terms which resonate with a sense of growing sexual awareness. When she takes flight to indulge in the delights of Paris she becomes 'like a gazelle'[23] — an animal as vulnerable to the predatory hunter as the lamb, hind or dove to which Ovid likens Daphne pursued by Apollo. She is also an ephemeron — given just half of the lifetime of a fly to enjoy her dalliances in the city. She functions as both animal and human, child and full-grown maiden, Dryad and the country-born Marie, who like her tree-nymph counterpart 'had the same desire and longing for the great city'.[24] Throughout the narrative laments ring out for both the missing Marie and the transformed Dryad, insisting that for both of them the city 'will be thy ruin!'[25] The Dryad's *choice* moves her from a place of safe asexual permanence to one of dangerous and erotic temporality, just as Daphne's desire to avoid Apollo's advances encases her within a permanent arboreal chamber. Both the journey to tree-like chastity and the movement from tree to sexual woman are fraught with difficulty; while choice is posited as key to these vegetative transformations, both perpetual virgins and deflowered women are shown to be negative.

Andersen's representation of the delights and sights of Paris by night reverberates with the sexual threat implicit to the maiden who seeks out such earthly pleasures. The location for this tale is one that cannot fail to call to mind sexual connotations, and her experiences of Parisian streets, underworld catacombs and garden dance parties resonate with the dangers to which a human girl might fall. Andersen points to the universal Marie in his tale of sexual threat, and throughout her one night of freedom the Dryad continually imagines that she might find this young maiden from the countryside bedazzling in her new Paris lifestyle:

> There shone in her thoughts two bright eyes, and she thought of Marie, poor Marie! The happy, ragged child with the red flower in her black hair. She was in the city of the world, rich, and dazzling, as when she drove past the priest's house, the Dryad's tree and the old oak. She was here, no doubt in the deafening noise; perhaps she had just got out of that magnificent coach waiting yonder; splendid carriages stood here with laced coachmen and silk-stockinged footmen. The grand people alighting were all women, richly dressed ladies. They went through the open lattice-door, up the high, broad stairs, which led to a building with white marble columns. Was this perhaps the 'Wonder of the World'? Then certainly Marie was there![26]

The environment in which Andersen's Dryad initially finds herself, however, is in fact the Church of the Madeleine, and it is the music of 'Sancta Maria' that she finds within its walls. The Dryad is swift to recognize that her desire for a single night of total pleasure belongs outside of this religious space:

> Some of the ladies knelt in silent prayer before the altars, others sought the confessionals. The Dryad felt a restlessness, a fear, as if she had entered a place where she ought not to have set foot. Here was the home of silence, the palace of secrets; all was whispered and confined without a sound being heard. The Dryad saw herself disguised in silk and veil, resembling in form the other rich and high-born ladies; was each of them a child of longing like herself? There

sounded a sigh, so painfully deep; did it come from the confessional corner, or from the breast of the Dryad? She drew her veil closer around her. She breathed the incense and not the fresh air. Here was no place for her longing.[27]

In these dual descriptions of the Parisian church, Andersen suggests an irony regarding the behaviour of the church-going women, which continues throughout his tale. The arrival of the ladies at church is figured like the arrival of Cinderella to a ball; the splendid carriages, diligent servants, and richly dressed ladies are discordant with the nature of their visit to a place of devout worship. Similarly, the Dryad cannot help but recognize her own connection to the women she watches, suggesting that a cloak and veil cannot cloud the passionate, fleshly desires which flutter inside their bodies, just as the chestnut tree could not contain the Dryad's own quest for sexual freedom. Andersen's image of the church women depicts them as silent dryads themselves, each with the same desire to engage in the fleshly pleasures of the world, while attempting to enshroud themselves in the trappings of religious piety.

This contradiction is revisited at the garden to which the Dryad later journeys, where the branches of a weeping-willow, rather than the folds of a well-positioned veil, function to hide the sexual yearnings of the Paris-ensnared female:

> Beautiful weeping-willows, real weeping-willows of the spring-time, drooped their fresh branches like a green transparent but concealing veil. Here, amongst the bushes, blazed a bonfire; its red glow shone over small, half-dark, silent arbours, permeated with tones, with a music thrilling to the ear, captivating, alluring, chasing the blood through the veins. She saw young women, beautiful in festival attire, with trusting smiles, and the light laughing spirit of youth, a 'Marie', with a rose in the hair, but without carriage and footmen. How they floated, how they whirled in the wild dance! As if bitten by the Tarantella, they sprang and laughed and smiled, blissfully happy, ready to embrace the whole world.[28]

The Bacchanalian women of the dance are those of the confessional — each being bitten by the tarantella of sexual desire. The Dryad herself, within this garden, further experiences the rush of sexual knowledge and is described both according to her sensuality and her erotic posturing:

> The Dryad felt herself carried away in the dance [...]. A consuming desire of life thrilled through the Dryad; it was like an opium trance.
> Her eyes spoke, her lips spoke, but the words were not heard for the sound of the flutes and violins. Her partner whispered words in her ear, they trembled in time to the music of the Can-Can; she did not understand them, — we do not understand them either. He stretched his arms out towards her, and only embraced the transparent, gas-filled air.[29]

Just as she became a lady in the confessional, the Dryad here becomes one of the female dancers, entranced by the eroticism of the dance and the heady mixture of popping champagne corks, clapping hands and murmuring water. She reflects and mirrors all of the women of the story, each of whom reveals the dangers of sexual yearning. The fact that there is an inability to 'understand' the words of her male partner highlights the implicit threat of his company.

FIG. 4. J. W. Waterhouse,
Hamadryade, 1893
Credit: © akg-images

The death of the Dryad at the close of the narrative fully implements the message on female fragility. Andersen ensures that his readers are aware of the Dryad's bargain; she has exchanged the protective bower of her tree in order to know the pleasures of human flesh and only truly recognizes her error when it is already too late:

> The Dryad felt a dread, like that of the woman who in the bath has cut her artery and is bleeding to death, but while bleeding wishes still to be live. She raised herself, came some steps forward, and again sank down in front of a little church.[30]

The entanglement of death and sex depicted through the erotic bleeding of the self-harming female morphs onto the form of the Dryad who lies repentantly on the footsteps of the church. While the church could not provide an outlet for her lustful longings earlier in the narrative, it is a fitting site for her death, and she dies to the sounds of the organ playing out a reproachful moral: 'Thy longing and desire uprooted thee from thy God-given place. It became thy ruin, poor Dryad!'[31] The Biblical association of female ruin through desire and trees is clear here, as the Dryad becomes an Eve-figure forever cast out of her 'God-given place'. The fragility of the female is repeatedly stressed in the final lines of the tale, as the Dryad is likened to a soap-bubble or tear-drop and suddenly vanishes with the first beams of the sun. There can be no salvation for the female who leaves her God-given path to indulge in her longings and desires — 'the Church had no power to call' to life the 'withered, broken chestnut flower'[32] that the Dryad leaves behind. As is the case for this last remnant of the Dryad, those females who engage too easily in the heady pleasures of the flesh will be trodden to dust by the devouring 'foot of a man'.[33] Like Daphne, whose laurel tree becomes a site for Apollo's possession once her body is unassailable,[34] the crushing of the chestnut flower under a male foot makes the Dryad a symbol of Andersen's position on female vulnerability. While the choice to be human might be celebrated in much children's fiction, Andersen's transformation of the story of Apollo and Daphne posits a deadly path for human girls who choose sexual proclivity over maidenhood.

The opposing tales of Ovid's Daphne and Andersen's Dryad reflect a double-bind for women, in which both absolute female abstinence and precocious female sexuality are seen as problematic. For Andersen the crime of transformation, of leaving one's 'God-given place', leads resolutely to a young girl's ruin, while in Ovid it is quite literally a divine intervention (the shooting of Apollo and Daphne with hostile arrows) that necessitates such transformation. In both cases, the female body is a site of vulnerability. As I outlined in the earlier part of this chapter, trees classically provide sites for protecting maidens from corporeal assault, but they are also organic beings that are themselves vulnerable to physical attack. For C. S. Lewis, an author who famously limits his female protagonists in *The Chronicles of Narnia*,[35] dryads and their trees are particularly vulnerable to the threats of male violence, rather than their own sexual yearnings, and as such are more faithful to the classical tradition than Andersen's depiction of the sexualized Dryad. In particular, Ovid's tale of the crime of Erysichthon is pertinent to Lewis's dryads. Ovid tells of Erysichthon's wilful destruction of the grove of the dryads and murder of Ceres's favourite nymph at the blow of his axe (*Met.* VIII. 755–64):

> 'non dilecta deae solum, sed et ipsa licebit   755
> sit dea, iam tanget frondente cacumine terram.'
> dixit, et obliquos dum telum librat in ictus,
> contremuit gemitumque dedit Deoia quercus,
> et pariter frondes, pariter pallescere glandes
> coepere ac longi pallorem ducere rami.   760
> cuius ut in trunco fecit manus inpia vulnus,
> haud aliter fluxit discusso cortice sanguis,
> quam solet, ante aras ingens ubi victima taurus
> concidit, abrupta cruor e cervice profundi.

> ['Be this the tree the goddess loves, be this
> The goddess' very self, its leafy crown
> Shall touch the ground today. Thus he spoke, and poised his axe
> To strike a slanting cut. The holy tree
> Shuddered and groaned, and every leaf and acorn
> Grew pale and pallor spread on each long branch.
> And when his impious stroke wounded the trunk,
> Blood issued, flowing from the severed bark,
> As when a mighty bull is sacrificed
> Before the altar and from his riven neck
> The lifeblood pours.]

In *The Last Battle* Lewis depicts the murder of the dryads by a hostile power in terms that resonate with this Ovidian myth:

> 'Woe, woe, woe!' called the voice. 'Woe for my brothers and sisters! Woe for the holy trees! The woods are laid waste. The axe is loosed against us. We are being felled. Great trees are falling, falling, falling.'
>
> With the last 'falling' the speaker came in sight. She was like a woman but so tall that her head was on a level with the Centaur's, yet she was like a tree too [...].
>
> 'A-a-a-h,' gasped the Dryad, shuddering as if in pain — shuddering time after time as if under repeated blows. Then all at once she fell sideways as suddenly as if both her feet had been cut from under her. For a second they saw her lying dead on the grass and then she vanished. They knew what had happened. Her tree, miles away, had been cut down.[36]

As is the case in Andersen's fairy-tale, the death of the tree here carries with it an implicit warning about the dangers of human mistreatment of the environment,[37] the invaded Narnia being akin to the Parisian wasteland of machinery and dying plant life. Even the parallel mythology can be read as an ecological warning. Ceres, the goddess of agriculture, punishes Erysichthon's tree-felling by sending famine to dwell in his entrails, causing him to be forever tormented by insatiable hunger. After selling all of his possessions, including his own daughter, he begins to eat his own limbs and is eventually entirely self-devoured, offering a warning as to the androcentric dangers of felling trees. The environmentally savage deaths of the Erysichthon nymphs and the dryads of *The Last Battle* are due to the coterminous link between their own lives and that of their organic arbours. As the author of the *Homeric Hymn to Aphrodite* explains, hamadryads are mortally dependent upon the trees in which they live (vv. 259–72):

> [...] at their birth pines or high-topped oaks spring up with them upon the
> fruitful earth, beautiful, flourishing tress, towering high upon the lofty
> mountains (and men call them holy places of the immortals, and never mortal
> lops them with the axe); but when the fate of death is near at hand, first those
> lovely trees wither where they stand, and the bark shrivels away about them,
> and the twigs fall down, and at last the life of the Nymph and of the tree leave
> the light of the sun together. (trans. by H. G. Evelyn White)

The hamadryad's death, unlike that of the dryad, is caused by the death of her
tree. Such a fatal connection between tree and human clearly carries ecological
implications; as Nicole M. DuPlessis has argued, 'the anguish of the Dryad at seeing
her "brothers and sisters" murdered and the pain of her own death provide a vividly
human perspective on the horror of deforestation.'[38] But the hamadryad also relates
to her tree the way that the virgin's soul relates to her body. If the body becomes
assaulted, the soul must also perish.

Thus while the horrors of environmental destruction are explicit in this moment
of Narnian genocide, the sexual threat to the vulnerable female is implicit. The
felling of the tree in Ovid and the death of the dryad in Lewis are depicted in
erotic terms, just as the transformations of Andersen's dryad and Ovid's Daphne are
sexualized. Lewis's dryad and Ceres's tree shudder and groan under the repeated
strokes of the axe, their bodies subjected to the violation of being cut open by
masculine aggression and domination. As Simone de Beauvoir points out in *The
Second Sex* (1949), there is a strong connection between female cutting and sexual
penetration.[39] The torture of these dryads is one of unsolicited male advance, as
they are violently stripped of their sacred and innocent status. Erysichthon's threat
of forcing the nymph's leafy head to the ground is realized in the brutal felling
of Lewis's dryad who moves from being a tall, graceful being, to one vulnerably
prostrate. It is her feet, the parts which classically allow the sexually threatened
dryad to flee from male predators, which Lewis pointedly describes as vanishing at
the blow of the axe. Unlike Daphne, Lewis's dryad cannot escape from the assault
by withdrawing into protective bark for she herself withers the moment her organic
bower is violated. The fleeting depiction of the beautiful nymph lying dead on the
grass underscores the deadly violation of her vulnerable body.

Although Lewis concentrates on female dryads in his *Narnia* series, he also
regularly alludes to the presence of male dryads. Such male experience of the forest
is part of a long tradition in classical myth and fairy tale that seeks to re-gender (at
least from the traditional standpoint) the association of woods as places of erotic
danger. Ovid's tale of Venus and Adonis, for instance, warns of the sexual dangers
present in the woods. Adonis's wounded thigh implies a symbolic castration or
penetration suffered in the dangerous forest, and his transformation into the
anemone links him with the fleeing maidens of the *Metamorphoses*. In Shakespeare,
trees can become prisons for unfortunate males; the incarceration of Ariel by the
witch Sycorax in *The Tempest* (1611) repositions the male as vulnerable to female
will. While he is rescued by Prospero's 'art', Ariel still endures a dozen years lodged
inside a cloven pine for failing to yield to Sycorax's command. Similarly the forests

of fairy-tale,[40] which for females can be both savage and reclusive, can also be problematic for males who find themselves there threatened by female appetites.[41] In the Grimm Brothers' story of 'The Old Woman in the Wood', the authors depict a male human-tree, who has been transformed into a dryad by an evil female enchantress. In the tale, a young servant girl, following the murder of the family she serves by a band of robbers, finds herself alone in the dense forest. She is visited by a dove, who beseeches her to travel to a cottage and procure a ring from one of its rooms without speaking to the woman who lives there. This she does, and thereby breaks the spell that compels the prince and all of his servants to exist as trees. On her return from the cottage, she is rewarded with the explicitly sexual transformation of her prince back into his human form:

> [...S]he leant against a tree, determined to wait for the dove. As she thus stood, it seemed just as if the tree was soft and pliant, and was letting its branches down. And suddenly the branches twined around her, and were two arms, and when she looked around her, the tree was a handsome man, who embraced and kissed her heartily.[42]

The prince's transformation is an exact reversal of Daphne's, but akin to that of Andersen's Dryad; he is returned from tree to human form and gains sexual fulfilment as opposed to perpetual chastity. Yet while the Dryad must suffer death, the male is here rewarded.

Although the dangerous female in this fairy-tale is a haggard witch while the younger beautiful woman is the hero (in line with Shakespeare's divide of Sycorax and Miranda), the female dryads of classical legend complicate these distinctions by being both beautiful and vengeful to males who dare cross them. It is the dancing nymphs of Ceres' grove who demand punishment for Erysichthon's unnatural crime, while the story of Rhœcus depicts the hamadryad of an oak tree as an extremely volatile being who blinds her one-time rescuer when he ignores her advances.[43] Such instances point to the classical tensions between vegetative female beauty and male vulnerability, which are alluded to and transformed by writers of children's literature in disparate and intriguing ways.[44] Preventative narratives are thus part of a continuum in which young women are taught to avoid the dangers of rape or seduction, while young men are taught that they might be tricked, if not forced, into prospect-damaging sex.

Following Freud's work on the death drive, which in itself reworks older traditions, critics of desire have tended to focus on the connection of sex with death, absence and danger. As Jonathan Dollimore puts it: '[...T]he strange dynamic which, in Western culture, binds death into desire is not the product of a marginal pathological imagination, but crucial in the formation of that culture.'[45] In other words, the link between sex and death is so ingrained that it makes us who we are. At the level of language this conjunction operates in the French *petit mort*, or as Shakespeare has it 'desire *is* death.'[46] This critical tradition focuses on the perils of desire, and such an emphasis of course becomes amplified when applied to children, who are legally asexual beings. However, an approach to the dangers of desire, whereby sex of any kind leads to potential death, is eschewed in other traditions of children's literature. Even Andersen provides a more positive representation of trees and childhood sexuality in his 'The Elder-Tree Mother'. Two children in the story-within-the-story plant an elder-tree branch that grows alongside their burgeoning sexual love and eventually overlooks the happily married couple on their golden wedding anniversary. In the main plot, the Elder-Tree Mother becomes a 'little girl, with her bright blue eyes, peeping out from behind the petals'[47] and befriends the boy of the story to take him on a similarly sexual (if imaginary) journey, so that he becomes an old man who also celebrates his golden anniversary. In both plots the tree becomes a symbol of appropriate sexual longevity and devotion; as in Ovid's tale of the transformations of the ageing Philemon and Baucis into two trees 'from one twin trunk grown side by side,'[48] the tree in Andersen's story lives as long as true love. The tree's final message is that '[s]ome call me Little Elder-tree Mother; others a Dryad; but my real name is "Remembrance." '[49] The tree here becomes a location of safe sexual expression in a lasting marriage full of happy memories.

Yet as far back as 1885 children's literature has offered less socially conservative examples of sexual exploration in the woods. Frank R. Stockton's critically neglected tale 'Old Pipes and the Dryad' tells of 'Old Pipes', a shepherd who loses his ability to call the village animals down from the mountain with his 'familiar instrument' because '[h]e had grown old, and his breath was feeble.'[50] The combination of old age and failed piping baldly points to issues of impotence, and the entire narrative is shaped around the liberating effects of fulfilled desire through the vivification of a dryad. The process begins when the old man finds a Dryad tree, and sets free the maiden who lives within by using its 'key'. Once he lets her out, the 'beautiful' Dryad declares: 'I am so happy and so thankful that I must kiss you, you dear old man!'[51] The Dryad subsequently kisses him again when he is asleep and thus restores the old man's ability to 'pipe' by removing twenty years from his age. The fulfilment of desire leads to renewed vigour and an ability to earn a living again. Old Pipe's mother, however, disapproves of the liaison, and tries to quash it: '[...T] he old woman became very angry indeed. She did not believe in Dryads; and if they really did exist, she knew they must be witches and sorceresses, and she would have nothing to do with them.'[52] Here the woman takes the traditional stance that female magical creatures offer only sexual threat. But when the Dryad kisses the sleeping mother on her cheeks, she too is given renewed youth and vitality. The familial objection to the sexual development of its younger generation therefore becomes sidelined, and a positive representation of woodland sexuality emerges. Although the story interestingly warns children from attempting to kiss dryads,[53] as they of course would disappear if they became that much younger, the kiss of the magical female is celebrated as being positive both for the individual male and for the community he must work within.

★   ★   ★   ★   ★

Whilst this chapter has principally focused on the methods by which authors of children's literature displace concerns regarding appropriate modes of sexuality onto the figures of fantastical trees, it is also worth briefly considering how the thematic nexus of trees, environmentalism and (a)sexuality are alluded to and configured in the work of authors whose fantasy work, whilst not conceived purely for child audiences, has nonetheless become an important part of the canon of children's and young-adolescent fiction. J. R. R. Tolkien, for example, writes an interesting counterpoint to Stockton's narrative of desire by representing its dangerous *lack*. As he puts it in one of his letters, '[t]he dislocation of sex-instinct is one of the chief symptoms of the Fall.'[54] In terms of his *Lord of the Rings* trilogy, it is through his representation of trees, the classical location of 'the Fall', that his ideas about sex are played out. This trilogy famously suffers from an absence of substantially delineated female (human) characters. At the same time, critics have noticed the importance of homo-social bonding to the character development and narrative.[55] Fellowship becomes the chief virtue, and camaraderie explicitly excludes women.

But the understanding of sexual desire in the *Lord of the Rings* trilogy would be enhanced by considering the apocalyptic narratives associated with the Ents, who impart a moral which explicates the dangers of separating men and women and failing to engage in appropriate sexual union. While the threat of apocalypse is frequently located in the ecological vision of such texts, with Tolkien's trees clearly marching against the destruction of nature enforced by Sauron's regime, apocalypse can also relate to the *inability* to procreate on a more literal level. The Ents have famously lost their Entwives, and Treebeard's desire to save the species from deforestation is set alongside a greater disaster stemming from self-induced extinction:

> There have never been many of us and we have not increased. There have been no Entings — no children, you would say, not for a terrible long count of years. You see, we lost the Entwives.[56]

Later in the trilogy, Treebeard reinforces this point: '"Forests may grow," he said. "Woods may spread. But not Ents. There are no Entings."'[57] Even Treebeard's parting words as he leaves his companions resonate with his desire to recapture the Entwives: '"Well, good-bye!" he said. "And don't forget that if you hear any news of the Entwives in your land, you will send word to me."'[58]

In his recounting of the loss of the Entwives and Entmaidens, Treebeard explains why they departed:

> [...] our hearts did not go on growing in the same way: the Ents gave their love to things that they met in the world, and the Entwives gave their thought to other things, for the Ents loved the great trees; and the wild woods, and the slopes of the high hills; and they drank of the mountain-streams, and ate only such fruit as the trees let fall in their path; and they learned of the Elves and spoke with the Trees. But the Entwives gave their minds to the lesser trees, and to the meads in the sunshine beyond the feet of the forests; and they saw the sloe in the thicket, and the wild apple and the cherry blossoming in spring, and the green herbs in the waterlands in summer, and the seeding grasses in the autumn fields. They did not desire to speak with these things; but they wished them to hear and obey what was said to them. The Entwives ordered them to grow according to their wishes, and bear leaf and fruit to their liking; for the Entwives desired order, and plenty, and peace (by which they meant that things should remain where they had set them). So the Entwives made gardens to live in. But we Ents went on wandering, and we only came to the gardens now and again.[59]

Tolkien here offers a stereotypical view of human masculinity and femininity, whereby the Entwives are homemakers interested in order and domesticity, and the Ents are travellers who take pleasure in wilderness and exoticism. These dislocated modes of living, whilst having endured successfully from at least the period of the Victorian separate spheres and well into the period in which Tolkien was writing, seem to suggest a potential pitfall to the sexual harmony of the species, at least if taken too far. Differing interests and behavioural patterns, optimised by Treebeard's comment that 'our hearts did not go on growing in the same way', leads to a separation that is punctured only by occasional sexual union. As such visits become fewer, and the Entwives make new gardens elsewhere, the threat of enforced separation becomes literalised:

> We crossed over Anduin and came to their land [...]. But the Entwives were not there. Long we called, and long we searched; and we asked all folk that we met which way the Entwives had gone. Some said they had never seen them; and some said that they had seen them walking away west, and some said east, and others south. But nowhere that we went could we find them. Our sorrow was very great.[60]

Tolkien here seems to offer an important corrective to the idea that desire leads to death. The dangers inherent in ignoring desire for the sake of expeditions abroad become apparent and the trees' homo-social modes of interaction ultimately limit, or indeed extinguish, their reproductive choice. Once again there is a focus here on the importance of choosing a mode of existence that either endorses sex or enforces temporality; in the case of the Ents, their choice to limit their reproductive potential is a biological hazard resulting in the extinction of the species. *Lack* of desire here leads to death.

As a final counter-example to the common critical linkage of desire and death in children's literature (and literature in general), I would like to turn to Philip Pullman's recent depiction of fantastical nature in the *His Dark Materials* trilogy and in particular his rejection of the traditional Genesis account of the Fall of man. As I argued earlier in this chapter, Genesis' focus on the Tree of Knowledge and the body of Eve as the locations for original sin have shaped subsequent associations between sex, trees and death. Pullman reworks the Fall into an act of justified rebellion and the Botanic Gardens of the dual Oxfords become his transformative Edenic locations. It is here that Will and Lyra exchange their vows, having tasted of the forbidden fruit and revelling in each other's love:

> 'It is this way,' said Lyra, tugging at Will's hand.
> She led him past a pool with a fountain under a wide-spreading tree, and then struck off to the left between beds of plants towards a huge many-trunked pine. There was a massive stone wall with a doorway in it, and in the further part of the garden the trees were younger and the planting less formal. Lyra led him almost to the end of the garden, over a little bridge, to a wooden seat under a low-branched tree.
> 'Yes!' she said. 'I hoped so much, and here it is, just the same... Will, I used to come here in *my* Oxford and sit on this exact bench whenever I wanted to be alone, just me and Pan. What I thought was that if you — maybe just once a year — if we could come here at the same time, just for an hour or something,

then we could pretend we were close again — because we would be close, if you sat here and I sat just here in my world.'[61]

Their final sexual knowledge is achieved in a strangely platonic scene, although the annual meeting alludes to a sexual history. Certainly Lyra and Will's brief encounter must move from 'erotic love to ethics,'[62] whereby the good of the whole universe justifies the parting of mere individuals, but erotic love is also celebrated in this garden rather than necessitating exile in itself. Pullman does two things of particular importance here. Firstly, he reconfigures a sexualized tree-land setting positively, so that the erotics of nature are not dangerous or even threatening as they have been in much Biblical and classical tradition. Secondly, he offers an equal-opportunities moment of eroticism, whereby male and female children can come together. The garden, as Daphne's 'untrodden woods' and Eve's Eden certainly were not, becomes a space of gender equality, where sex is not about power, but is a natural product of a natural union.

★   ★   ★   ★   ★

This chapter has examined the multitudinous associations of sex and fantastical trees in children's and fantasy literature. It has shown how classical and Biblical traditions have impacted on children's fiction in fairly traditional ways, so that female virtue is subjected to peril through dangerous sexual encounters. Importantly, it has also traced breaks from this tradition, which go back as far as the Victorian period. Little boys are shown to be subject to similar sexual dangers, especially through their relationships with older women. And sex for both girls and boys is depicted as a positive experience in certain works of children's literature, which even move to celebratory takes on childhood sexual development.

Sexual maturation is here posited as the key to transforming children into adults, as one might expect, but alongside this transformation is the correlative danger of making children somehow less human in that journey. Children's writers seem fixated upon the liminality of the space between childhood and adulthood, and the woods serve as a site for delaying, while heightening the danger of, that position. In earlier traditions, to be human is paradoxically to be treelike for young women and un-treelike for young men. Males are here far less likely to be physically transformed, or at least such alterations prove to be reversible, suggesting that sexual union has a less transformative effect on men than it does on women. Yet in later works the sexed binary becomes more confused, so that the development of sexual identity and species identity becomes commingled. At the same time sex in itself, essential for humanness and all complex life forms, becomes denaturalized. The othering of nature here serves to disguise the necessary human links with it. That disconnected tradition becomes subject to scrutiny in twentieth-century writers, with Tolkien being comfortable with the metaphorical and anthropomorphic deployment of fantastical trees as pseudo-humans, and Pullman interested in how children, nature and eroticism can commingle in healthy ways that are antagonistic to both classical and Christian traditions.

Notes to Chapter 4

1. Rick Riordan, *Percy Jackson and the Titan's Curse* (London: Puffin Books, 2007), p. 45.
2. *Percy Jackson and the Titan's Curse* is the third of a series of five books in Riordan's 'Olympians' series. Although set in the United States, the books are based on Greek mythology and focus on the trials of a group of young demi-gods, each of whom has both a mortal and a divine parent.
3. Rick Riordan, *Percy Jackson and the Lightning Thief* (London: Puffin Books, 2006), p. 155.
4. Riordan, *Lightning Thief*, p. 115.
5. The most famous example of a human–plant transformation is the metamorphosis of Daphne into a laurel. There are, however, numerous examples of girls being turned into trees in the classical tradition. Some notable examples from Ovid's *Metamorphoses* include the transformations of the grieving sisters of Phaethon into trees whose tears still flow from their arboreal chambers and harden as amber (II. 343–66); the transformation of the body of Leucothoe into a 'shrub of frankincense' (IV. 251–55) and her sister, Clytie, into a heliotrope (IV. 266–69); the nymph Lotis who was transformed into a lotus tree when fleeing 'Priapus's lechery' (IX. 346–48) and the subsequent metamorphosis of Dryope, who is turned into a black poplar when she picks one of Lotis's blossoms to give to her young son (IX. 350–62). During her transformation, Dryope here offers a rather pointed moral (directed to her son but also to the reader): 'Let him beware of pools and never pick | Blossoms from trees, but fancy every bush | A Goddess in disguise' (IX. 380–81). (English translations of Ovid are taken from A. D. Melville's translation of *Metamorphoses* (Oxford: Oxford University Press, 1986); line numbers refer to the Latin.) Michael Ferber (1999), p. 74 asserts that there is a distinct connection between girls and flowers: '[f]lowers, first of all, are girls. Their beauty, their beauty's brevity, their vulnerability to males who wish to pluck them — these features and others have made flowers, in many cultures, symbolic of maidens, at least to males who have set those cultures' terms.' In terms of myths of plant metamorphosis, however, girls are almost invariably transformed into trees, while young males tend to become flowers: see the metamorphosis of Hyacinth (X. 206–16), Narcissus (III. 510) and Adonis (X. 734–38). In the case of Adonis, the youth is also born of a transformed tree (X. 503–17). His mother, Myrrha, is changed into a tree following incest with her father (X. 490–500). As Rowena Fowler (2006) has observed, the lure of arboreal transformation has a certain appeal to male authors too: 'Male writers turned themselves into trees to find a momentary respite from time and history or to tap for themselves the dryad's mysterious privilege of access: "I stood still and was a tree amid the wood, | Knowing the truth of things unseen before" (Pound, "The Tree")' (p. 382).
6. Artistic interpretations of this Ovidian scene also frequently render the moment of transformation in explicitly sexual terms. Most notoriously, Bernini's enraptured sculpture (1622–25) of the naked Daphne is overtly sexual, her alabaster limbs forever cast at the moment of transformation, her fingers turned to slender branches as Apollo grapples at her nakedness. Antonio del Pollaiuolo's painting 'Apollo and Daphne' (1470–80) similarly captures Daphne in a state of half-change, her arms dense foliage while her body remains in human shape, this time more modestly cloaked from the arms which attempt to ensnare it. Two miniatures from Christine de Pisan's *L'Epître d'Othéa* (*c.* 1450–60), however, are less faithful to the Ovidian scene, illustrating the transformed Daphne as still partially human. In these depictions, Daphne's head has been replaced by the leaves of a tree, her neck being either branch or trunk, but her body, far from being enshrouded in protective bark, remains a naked female human. Such a depiction radically alters the notion that the laurel protects her virginity, leaving Daphne still dangerously, if temporarily, exposed to Apollo's advances. For more on the illustrative traditions of Ovid see, for example, Llewellyn (1988).
7. Barnard (1987), p. 36. Of course, Daphne's original disinterest in Apollo is also guaranteed by Cupid; it is his shooting of a leaden arrow into the young nymph that ensures her rejection of all amorous suitors (*Met.* I. 452–80).
8. Kincaid (1992), p. 3.
9. See, for example, Martindale (1988), Brown (1999) (2005), Ziolkowski (2005). For an anthology of works that have transformed and evolved Ovidian myths see Hofmann and Lasdun (1994).

10. The term 'dryad' derives from the Greek for the oak; thus dryads are specifically the nymphs of oak trees. The word has come to refer more generally to wood nymphs, and thus dryads can be divided into three different categories: (i) semi-divine beings associated with trees and inhabiting woodlands; such beings are strongly associated with the goddess Diana; (ii) nymphs whose lives are coterminous with trees; (iii) nymphs who actually inhabit trees. These categories are here broadly defined, and many dryads partake of the characteristics of more than one grouping. The latter two groups are sometimes called hamadryads, a term which relates to the relationship between a nymph's life and that of her tree. Classical transformations of nymphs and human girls into trees end mortal life, although some residual consciousness of a previous existence tends to remain: see for example the tears of the Heliades (*Met.* II. 364–65) or the labour pains of Myrrha (x. 506–10). Modern authors tend to use these terms fairly loosely, so that a wood nymph, dryad or hamadryad can partake of any, or all, of the above characteristics. John William Waterhouse's painting *Hamadryade* (Fig. 4) suggestively evokes the full range of possibilities.

11. The long and varied history of trees and sex in literature is the topic for an entire book, but some key examples include Shakespeare's *A Midsummer Night's Dream* and *As You Like It* which depict the forest as a space of sexual ambiguation in which desire becomes distorted and interrogated. In chivalric romances, knights are frequently endangered in the trackless forest by the beguiling beauty of fairy enchantresses. The third story of the fifth day in Boccaccio's *Decameron* (1350–53), for instance, depicts the darker side of sexual desire in a woodland space. The Tree of Knowledge, of course, also offered Adam and Eve a specifically sexual kind of knowing whereby their nakedness caused them shame and, eventually, death.

12. As in many fairy-tale collections, Andersen's stories are replete with talking flowers and symbolic trees. His tale 'The Fir-Tree' (1844) follows a similar pattern to that of 'The Dryad', as the tree longs to leave his shady nook. He soon becomes pained by his role as a Christmas tree, however, and laments his untimely fate. Both tales offer an overarching moral message to children that they must be content with their 'God-given' roles but also carry an ecological message regarding the beauty of the natural over the artificial.

13. Hans Christian Andersen, *The Complete Fairy Tales of Hans Christian Andersen* (London: Wordsworth, 1998), p. 992.

14. Ibid., p. 991.

15. The act of giving voice to plants and trees almost always carries with it ecological implications. J. R. R. Tolkien's Treebeard is certainly the most famous talking tree who advocates some form of environmental justice, proclaiming in *The Lord of the Rings: The Two Towers* (1954) that 'nobody cares for the woods' (London: HarperCollins, 1999), p. 83. For an extended consideration of Tolkien's ecology, see Dickenson and Evans (2006). For a more wide-ranging consideration of the ecological agendas of children's fiction, see the recent collection by Dobrin and Kidd (2004) and Whitley (2008).

16. Ziolkowski (2005), p. 78.

17. Andersen, *The Complete Fairy Tales*, p. 992.

18. Some examples include the final volume of the Percy Jackson series, *The Last Olympian* (London: Puffin Books, 2009), where the young hero is offered the choice of immortality but chooses to remain human. In Disney/Pixar's *Toy Story* (dir. by John Lasseter. Pixar Animation Studios/Walt Disney Productions, 1995) Buzz must learn that being a toy has far greater value than believing to be a posthuman spaceman, while in *Toy Story 2* (dir. by John Lasseter. Pixar Animation Studios/Walt Disney Productions, 1999) Woody's ability to last forever in a hermetically sealed museum case is rejected in favour of the wear-and-tear of everyday life with a child. In both cases ontological hierarchies can be mapped on to the human experience — being superhuman or immortal is positioned as less favourable than having a 'real' human life. In Collodi's *Pinocchio* (1881), a similar quest for humanness consumes the tale: in spite of the wooden puppet's posthuman abilities, most notably his superior strength and inability to die, he still desires above all things to be 'a real boy' (Carlo Collodi, *Pinocchio*, trans. by Ann Lawson Lucas (Oxford: Oxford University Press, 2004), ch. 25, p. 92). The creation of the puppet-boy bears some striking similarities to that of the human-statue of Ovid's Pygmalion, for while a godly, or at least supernatural, act imports a soul into both the ivory of Pygmalion's statue

and the wood of Gepetto's puppet, both narratives require a human creator to shape the raw materials into an object of human form.

19. Ovid, *Metamorphoses*, 1. 536. (The imagery is from a simile in which Apollo is compared to a hound and Daphne to a hare.)

20. Andersen, *The Complete Fairy Tales*, p. 992. Italics mine.

21. Ibid., p. 984.

22. Ibid., p. 993.

23. Ibid., p. 993.

24. Ibid., p. 985.

25. Ibid., p. 988.

26. Ibid., p. 994.

27. Ibid., p. 994–95.

28. Ibid., p. 997–98.

29. Ibid., p. 998.

30. Ibid., p. 1002.

31. Ibid., p. 1002.

32. Ibid., p. 1003.

33. Ibid., p. 1003.

34. Once Daphne is transformed Apollo declares that if she shall not be his bride, she will be his tree, and thus her wreathes adorn the heads of Roman generals and stand sentinel at the gates of Augustus. For more on the symbolic nature of this declaration, see Feldherr (2002), pp. 172–73.

35. Consider for example C. S. Lewis's rejection of Susan in *The Last Battle* (1956) for being interested in nothing except 'nylons and lipstick and invitations' (London: HarperCollins, 1998), p. 165. For discussion see Pullman (1998).

36. C. S. Lewis, *The Last Battle*, pp. 28–29.

37. Lewis's depiction of the horrors of deforestation here is in keeping with an early interest in environmental protection which is indicated throughout *The Chronicles of Narnia*. For example, Jadis's control over the seasons in *The Lion, The Witch and The Wardrobe* (1950), an action which sees Narnia in a perpetual winter without ever reaching Christmas, points to Lewis's concerns over man's manipulation of the natural order and seems to predict the type of seasonal disruption more modern readers might associate with climate change. Similarly, Lewis's depictions of Uncle Andrew's joy in *The Magician's Nephew* (1955) on discovering the commercial potential of a world where everything grows, and blatant maltreatment of animals, fantastical creatures and children (who are themselves experimented on by Uncle Andrew like laboratory animals), suggests a negative stance on animal experimentation. For more on environmental awareness in Narnia see DuPlessis (2004). DuPlessis seeks to establish a direct relationship between Lewis's perspectives on issues such as colonialism and vivisection and his use of 'enchanted woods' as a 'metaphor for the human experience of nature' (p. 115). DuPlessis argues that although Lewis would not have allied himself explicitly with proto-environmentalism, his work connects with the movement in its depiction of the ecological consequences of deforestation and exploitation of natural resources (pp. 115–16). See also Patterson (1994) which makes similar claims regarding Lewis's environmentalism but focuses on his writing for adults and its relationship to 'Ecology for Christians' (p. 5). Laurent (1993) explores C. S. Lewis's 'concern over the abuse of animals in scientific experimentation' (p. 46), particularly in relation to evolutionary theory. Like Nancy-Lou Patterson, Laurent focuses particularly on science-fiction work for adult readers.

38. DuPlessis (2004), p. 124.

39. de Beauvoir (1997), p. 377.

40. Fairy-tales frequently allude to the dangers of the enchanted forest — a space that tends to allow magical transformation to occur rather than being enchanted itself. These woodland locations have generally been read as sites of sexual anxiety and provide an interesting comparison to the more animistic plants and trees that appear in other forms of literature. Bottigheimer (1987) dedicates a chapter to the function of forests and trees in fairy tale and although it is principally a summary of instances when a hero(ine) becomes lost in the forest, she does assert that 'the tales in the collection outline very different relationships to forest isolation for male and female protagonists' (pp. 102–03). Other key critical texts which discuss these topics include: Propp

(1968); Zipes (1979 & 1991), Tatar (1987), Knoepflmacher and Auerbach (1992); Warner (1994); and Knoepflmacher (1998).

41. The story of 'Hansel and Gretel' provides an interesting example, for while it does not contain any dryadic transformations, the forest space is particularly threatening for the young boy; it is Hansel whom the witch at the centre of the forest wants to 'make fat' — a clear allusion to sexual tumescence. Her repeated testing of his phallic finger makes the sexual threat even more apparent. His 'little bone' (*The Complete Fairy Tales of the Brothers Grimm*, trans. by Padraic Colum (London: Wordsworth, 1997), p. 88) keeps him in a state of arrested development (and safe) until the witch's frustration makes her impatient. The threat of her 'oven' again becomes a sexual one, as a kind of *vagina dentata* that no undeveloped boy should enter. That Gretel saves Hansel from his fate points to a more age-appropriate sexual union (and, importantly, Hansel and Gretel are lovers in other tales recorded by the Grimms). For these children, sexual threat does not require physical transformation, but rather a more normative escape from the transgressive forest space. Their ability to find their way home immediately coincides with the ending of the sexual threat of the witch, and of course 'the woman' at home, who herself had led the children into the threatening forest, also turns out to be dead. The forest has offered a sexual threat, only to be overcome by resistant innocence. Although this story, like the adaptations of many fairy tales, comes to a happy ending, it highlights a sense that male children can also be sexually vulnerable in the forest. Bettelheim (1975) has famously explored the 'destructive aspects of orality' in this story. See esp. p. 162.

42. Jacob and Wilhelm Grimm, *The Complete Fairy Tales*, p. 584.

43. See Thomas Bulfinch on the tale of Rhœcus: *Bulfinch's Mythology* (London: Spring Hill, 1967), p. 160.

44. Perhaps the most famous encounter between a young man and a sexually threatening plant occurs in Antoine Saint-Exupéry's *The Little Prince* (1943), trans. by Irene Testot-Ferry (London: Wordsworth, 1995), where the flower becomes a type of siren that the prince needs to avoid as part of his development. During his first experience of her, the Little Prince determines that '[t]his flower is indeed a very complex creature' (p. 37). While exquisitely beautiful, the flower is a vain and demanding female: 'The Little Prince, watching the growth of an enormous bud, sensed that this could well lead to a miraculous apparition, but the flower continued her preparations for her beauty in the shelter of her green chamber. She chose her colours with great care. She dressed slowly, carefully arranging her petals one by one. She didn't wish to appear crumpled, like a poppy. She only wished to appear in the full glory of her beauty. Oh yes! She was Vain!' (p. 35) The Prince's voyeurism becomes heightened by what he cannot see. Through her alluring beauty she enslaves the Prince into fulfilling her continual whims and fancies — 'Thus it was that she began from the outset to torment him with her demanding vanity' (p. 36). The implication that any beautiful woman is a kind of siren, even if the male is willing to serve that beauty, becomes apparent. The Prince swiftly learns that while the flower is truly a 'complex creature', she is also one he should never listen to or trust: 'I shouldn't have listened to her,' he confided to me one day, 'one should never listen to flowers. One must admire them and breathe their fragrance. Mine perfumed all my planet, but I did not know how to enjoy her' (p. 36).

45. Dollimore (2003), p. xii.

46. William Shakespeare, 'Sonnet 130', *The Complete Works*, ed. by Stanley Wells et al. (Oxford: Oxford University Press, 1986). Italics mine.

47. Andersen, *The Complete Fairy Tales*, p. 297.

48. Ovid, *Metamorphoses*, VIII. 720.

49. Andersen, *The Complete Fairy Tales*, p. 302.

50. Frank Stockton, *Old Pipes and the Dryad* [1885] (London: Franklin Watts, 1969), p. 7.

51. Ibid., pp. 16–17.

52. Ibid., p. 42.

53. Ibid., p. 24.

54. J. R. R. Tolkien, *The Letters of J. R. R. Tolkien*, ed. by Humphrey Carpenter (London: HarperCollins, 2006), p. 43.

55. See, for example, Smol (2004). For a more conservative take on Tolkien's views of sex, see Rosenthal (2004).

56. J. R. R. Tolkien, *The Lord of the Rings: The Two Towers* [1954] (London: HarperCollins, 1999), p. 86.

57. J. R. R. Tolkien, *The Lord of the Rings: The Return of the King* [1955] (London: HarperCollins, 1999), p. 312.

58. Ibid., p. 313.

59. J. R. R. Tolkien, *The Two Towers*, p. 87.

60. Ibid., p. 88.

61. Philip Pullman, *The Amber Spyglass* [2000] (London: Scholastic, 2001), p. 537.

62. Shohet (2005), p. 33.

PART II

Christianity and Classicizing

Introduction to Part II

Ingo Gildenhard & Andrew Zissos

When Pausanias (*c.* 110/115–*c.* 180), in his *Description of Greece*, reaches Arcadia, his narrative takes a turn into the domain of the metamorphic.[1] If in earlier portions of his travelogue he dismissed tales of transformation as incredible on principle or obliquely rationalized traditional stories of transformative change, here he shows himself willing to entertain, indeed to argue for, the historicity of certain instances of metamorphosis that took place in the distant past.[2] His entry into the topic is by way of contrasting the religious practices of the 'historical contemporaries' Lycaon, Arcadia's most famous legendary figure, and the equally legendary Athenian king Cecrops. While the latter receives credit for being the first to name Zeus the Supreme god (ὁ μὲν γὰρ Δία τε ὠνόμασεν Ὕπατον πρῶτος) and refusing to sacrifice anything that was alive (he opted to burn sacrificial cakes instead), the former comes under heavy criticism for having sacrificed a human baby at the altar of Lycaean Zeus, which entailed (people say) his instant transformation from a man into a wolf (καὶ αὐτὸν αὐτίκα ἐπὶ τῇ θυσίᾳ γενέσθαι λύκον φασὶν ἀντὶ ἀνθρώπου).[3]

Surprisingly (in the light of his earlier scepticism), Pausanias is quite willing to believe that this actually happened: apart from the authority of age, the story, he submits, has the additional merit of probability (VIII. 2. 4: καὶ ἐμέ γε ὁ λόγος οὗτος πείθει, λέγεται δὲ ὑπὸ Ἀρκάδων ἐκ παλαιοῦ, καὶ τὸ εἰκὸς αὐτῷ πρόσεστιν).[4] He glosses this claim by invoking a contemporary variant of Hesiod's notion of successive ages, each featuring its own distinct interface between the natural and the supernatural spheres. In the old days, Pausanias recalls, human beings, because of their righteousness and piety, consorted and feasted with the gods, and the gods in turn took an active and immediate interest in human conduct: they openly honoured the good, and visited sinners with their wrath. In that bygone age, he notes, gods came into being from the ranks of humans (θεοὶ τότε ἐγίνοντο ἐξ ἀνθρώπων; he mentions Aristaeus, Britomartis of Crete, Heracles, Amphiaraus, Polydeuces and Castor, all of whom continue to receive cultic honours); so one might as well also believe, he goes on to suggest, that Lycaon was turned into a beast and Tantalus' daughter Niobe into stone (VIII. 2. 5: οὕτω πείθοιτο ἄν τις καὶ Λυκάονα θηρίον καὶ τὴν Ταντάλου Νιόβην γενέσθαι λίθον).

Pausanias' careful use of moods indicates that he is rather conscious of the fact that some of his readers may not be quite as willing to accept the veracity of the tale as he is. If in VIII. 2. 4 he stated in the present indicative that *he* finds the story of Lycaon's sacrifice and transformation plausible (καὶ ἐμέ γε ὁ λόγος οὗτος πείθει), he now employs the optative mood and a generalizing 'one' (πείθοιτο ἄν τις) in encouraging belief that such transformative changes occurred 'way back when'. Pausanias knows that argument is needed to render his view plausible and goes on to discuss why people might find such tales — mistakenly — *in*credible. Returning to the contrast between past and present or, rather, the Greek past and the Graeco-Roman present, he makes two related points.[5] First, the current state of humanity's sinful degeneracy has put an end to both apotheosis and punitive transformation: the former is now observable only as a discursive phenomenon of flattery at court; and as for the latter, the gods nowadays wait to unleash their wrath until the sinners have departed for the afterlife.[6] And secondly, he criticizes the habit of embedding actual events within artifices of falsehood, a discursive practice that has the unfortunate consequence of rendering historical facts seemingly unworthy of belief as well; he specifically singles out those who enjoy listening to marvellous reports, insofar as they have the tendency to embellish and exaggerate what they have heard, thereby ruining truth by mixing it with lies.[7] Apart from some natural marvels, he uses the fabulous elaborations that the stories to do with the transformation of Lycaon and Niobe accrued over time as examples of fiction contaminating fact: people now say that ever since the time of Lycaon a man has changed into a wolf at the novennial sacrifice to Lycaean Zeus, with the possibility of re-transformation after nine years if he abstained from devouring human flesh during this period; and they say that Niobe on Mount Sipylus sheds tears during the summer season (VIII. 2. 6–7). Pausanias dismisses all this as bogus, but insists that such nonsense ought not to affect our acceptance of the original transformations undergone by Lycaon and Niobe as genuine parts of the historical record. In short, he presents a three-pronged argument, designed to (a) confirm the truthfulness of certain tales of metamorphosis that record such incidents of transformative change as having occurred in the distant past; (b) deny the truth value of reports of contemporary instances of marvellous transformations; and (c) explain both why people doubt the truth of the old and invent new falsehoods.

Whatever the idiosyncrasies of the present passage, the key figures of thought that Pausanias brings into play resonate in a traditional key. He reasons according to a watershed moment à la Hesiod that allows him to separate the present from a past age, which not only featured social interactions and easy-going familiarity that crossed the mortal–immortal divide, but actual transformative change across this and other ontological boundaries. In this former age human beings could be turned into gods or, as the case may be, animals, through divine intervention (though Pausanias remains reticent about agency: he uses the Greek word 'to become' throughout, without specifying who actually caused the transformation to occur). He operates in a critical Euhemeristic spirit by mocking the discursive elevation of 'post-lapsarian' mortals in positions of power to the status of gods. And he approaches mythology and the marvellous like Palaephatus by clinging to a core of historical truth that, in time, has become overgrown and embellished by much fanciful falsehood — though of course without endorsing the Palaephatean principle of ontological continuity throughout history, which would have been irreconcilable with the Hesiodic idea of a succession of ages and his insistence on a past era in which divinely induced transformative change of human beings was a distinct possibility. The selective activation of views and positions makes a strategic contribution to Pausanias' own agenda, which includes the validation of the old over the new, the sacred over the profane.[8] As such, he employs the theme of metamorphosis and the discourse of truth that evolved around it to provide a critique of present circumstances he finds unpalatable (rampant sin and obsequious flattery in a world dominated by Roman power) and to endorse a specific outlook on religion: Pausanias invokes the existence of a supreme divinity, disapproves of blood-sacrifice, maintains belief in the existence of an afterlife, and, most importantly, upholds the gods as arbiters of justice who reward the good and punish the wicked. To illustrate the last point, metamorphosis is his motif of choice. The passage, then, shows very well the evolution and sedimentation of ideas within a cultural tradition, as well as the emergence of new vistas and viewpoints triggered by developments in such cultural spheres as politics and religion — all contributing to a complex and ongoing meditation on (historical) truth and falsehood to do with the limits and possibilities of metamorphic change.

The density of reflection on religious phenomena and their credibility at the beginning of Book VIII is unusual for Pausanias; soon after, he revisits the issue of (metamorphic) truth in legendary lore in a slightly more sceptical vein.[9] Paul Veyne has even suggested that the experience of Arcadia brought about this momentary change in outlook.[10] But we have spent some time on Pausanias not primarily because of the vagaries of his own belief system or his authorial strategies (interesting though these are in their own right), but because his reflections on the historicity of metamorphosis belong to a distinct cultural configuration that can be traced back in our literary record to archaic Greece and beyond, but was about to come to an end: at the time Pausanias wrote his *Description of Greece*, Christianity was spreading rapidly throughout the Roman Empire and, within another century and a half, would become its official religion. The triumph of Christianity irrevocably altered the cultural standing of classical metamorphoses (from then on stigmatized as 'pagan'): for the next millennium and a half, the transformative tales of Greece and Rome had to find a place and mode of existence within a profoundly hostile environment, dominated as it was by a Judeo-Christian view of the universe that was grounded in divinely revealed truth and sacred scripture and that dismissed pagan religion as, at best, fiction and, at worst, blasphemy. Judaism and Christianity cultivated their own notions of transformative change, but, with some scattered exceptions recounted in the Old Testament, did not endorse the classic 'pagan' metamorphosis of human beings into flora, fauna, or inanimate objects. Pausanias thus provides a *summa*, as it were, of traditional Graeco-Roman thinking on transformative change (in part critical, in part credulous) shortly after the emergence of the religion that would soon come to dominate the discourse on metamorphosis and to shape conceptions of (supernatural) reality in the Western world for more than a thousand years, until modern science began to displace sacred scripture as the dominant source of truth in Western society.

If in the Introduction to Part I we covered roughly a millennium (800 BC–AD 200), we now take our story forward by a further millennium and a half, up to what tends to be referred to as 'the eighteenth-century Enlightenment' and the onset of modernity. Here, even more than in the Introduction to Part I, a detailed survey (let alone exhaustive coverage) of all pertinent material is impossible to achieve:

in telling our story, we will have to content ourselves with a sketch of the most significant historical trends and the analysis of selected texts and artefacts. Given the vast expanse of time that we are about to traverse, it might be useful to outline a roadmap here, to avoid disorientation during our march down the centuries.

To begin with, we consider the presence and significance of transformative change in New Testament and Christian theology. This forms the requisite back-drop for an exploration of how dominant Christianity handled the classical heritage of metamorphic thought (in particular as codified in Ovid's *Metamorphoses*) in late antiquity and the Middle Ages: myth as an alternative discourse on religion and supernatural truth constituted toxic material in general that required techniques of accommodation, but could also be co-opted to advance the plausibility of marvellous and miraculous aspects of the Christian faith and the *historia sacra* recorded in the Bible. A closer look at two figures in equal measure unique and foundational then serves as a Janus-faced pivot between the Middle Ages and early-modern times: the way in which Dante (1265–1321) conceptualizes (the truth of) metamorphosis in his *Divine Comedy* serves as our epitome for medieval thinking on the theme, whereas Petrarch's (1304–1374) brand of Ovidian humanism and metamorphic experience, especially in his *Canzoniere*, betokens (apparent) affinity with modern forms of subjectivity and modes of truth. In the concluding section, we outline the phenomena and developments in the half millennium between these towering intellects of the Italian *Trecento* and the eighteenth century, in which transformative change and the notion of metamorphosis played a significant role, not least practices of magic, witchcraft, and alchemy. Our end point is the (gradual) rise of a scientific worldview that operates with a 'demystified' concept of nature and disowns the possibility of miraculous transformations (or, more generally, supernatural interventions in human affairs). Like Christianity before it, modern science has had a profound impact on the cultural standing of metamorphosis in its diverse classical, classicizing, and biblical variants.

The Transforming Passion of Christianity

Christian dogma, as we had occasion to note in the Introduction to Part I, sub-sumes a range of metamorphic moments focused on Jesus Christ, in particular his incarnation (which coincides with a change in ontological status from purely divine to partly divine, partly human), his transfiguration — or, to use the Greek term Matthew and Mark employ to describe the event, 'metamorphosis' — shortly before his crucifixion (which announces his return from humanity to divinity), and his resurrection after suffering death on the cross, followed by his eventual ascent to heaven.[11] In addition to these metamorphic events in his biography, Jesus during his Last Supper instituted the celebration of the Eucharist by taking the bread he broke and the wine he served at table and proclaiming them to be — turning them into? — his body and his blood. The ritual gesture has been re-enacted ever since during the celebration of the Holy Communion, even though the precise meaning of Jesus' pronouncement, not least in terms of transformative change, has remained a hotly contested issue in Christian theology. (Positions range from a strictly symbolic interpretation to the notion of the 'real presence' of Christ in the bread and wine to the (medieval) doctrine of transubstantiation.) Whatever the truth may be, the sacrament of the Eucharist holds out the promise that all of us, or at least those of us who — in the idiolect of Paul — 'metamorphose themselves' and their lives in the process of imitating Christ, will, at the day of Judgement, undergo a change similar to His resurrection and ascent. What follows is a more detailed look at each of these transformative moments in Christian creed and scripture, along with examination of their epistemic status.

The incarnation

In the General Introduction, we drew attention to the presence of metamorphic moments in the Old Testament; the phenomenon of marvellous transformation tends to occur in contexts concerned with the assertion of divine power. What is largely absent from the Old Testament is traffic from the human to the divine sphere; it bears stressing, however, that, just like Greek and Roman literature and culture, ancient Judaism at times recognized the possibility of deification. The elevation of Enoch at Genesis 5. 22–24 is a notable case in point: 'And Enoch walked with God after he begat Methuselah three hundred years, and begat sons and daughters: And all the days of Enoch were three hundred sixty and five years: And Enoch walked with God: and he *was* not; for God took him' ([...] καὶ εὐηρέστησεν Ενωχ τῷ θεῷ καὶ οὐχ ηὑρίσκετο, ὅτι μετέθηκεν αὐτὸν ὁ θεός).[12] The text leaves it unclear whether or to what extent Enoch underwent a genuine transformation from mortal to immortal; but his removal from the world of humans through an act of God at least leaves open the possibility that he has since enjoyed continued existence in the supernatural realm. The episode has apparent affinities with similar phenomena in Graeco-Roman culture, such as the apotheosis Hercules was commonly held to have undergone upon his death, the offer of immortality made by Calypso to Odysseus in Homer's *Odyssey*, the transformation of Romulus into the god Quirinus that Ennius recounts in his *Annals*, or the posthumous deification of Roman emperors. Outside the core biblical canon, the figure of Enoch became the protagonist of a tradition that explored two-way traffic across the boundary between divine and human, as in 1 Enoch, which begins with the fall of the angels in the Book of Watchers and concludes with an account of Enoch's (visionary) ascent to heaven and his encounter with the divine.[13] Enoch describes this experience as transformative of both body and soul: 'I fell on my face; my whole body melted, and my spirit was transformed. Then I cried out with a loud voice, in a spirit of power, blessing, glorifying, and exalting' (1 Enoch 71. 11).[14]

In all examples from ancient Judaism and the classical cultures of Greece and Rome transformative change that consists in a movement across the mortal–immortal divide happens in one direction only, that is, from human to divine. No supernatural being ever turns into a mortal creature; even the angels, in their fallen state, retain their divine nature. Christianity, by contrast, is grounded in a crossing in the opposite direction: from divine to human (and then back again). At the core of Christian religion stands the paradox that, as Walter of Châtillon (twelfth century) put it, 'the Creator became creature' (*factor factus est factura*): Jesus Christ is both the immortal second person of the Trinity and the mortal Son of God, conceived and born by the Virgin Mary. He thus occupies a special ontological niche, corresponding to his function as an intermediary between the human and the divine. Accordingly, his career on earth is shaped by two moments of transformative change: the transformation of word into flesh (Καὶ ὁ λόγος σὰρξ ἐγένετο/*et Verbum caro factum est*, in the pregnant formulation of the Gospel of John, I. 14); and the resurrection and ascension.

The *duplex natura* of Jesus Christ enables and underwrites the incarnation, but defies conventional thinking. Christ's duality as both God and human breaks with all known ontological protocols. The trope of paradox accordingly dominates endeavours to capture the nature of Christ — or, to use Augustine's pithy formulation (and a case in point), the *humana divinitas et divina humanitas Christi*.[15] The uniqueness of Christ has given rise to a special branch of theological thought, that is, Christology. The incarnation in particular has exercised the theological imagination, from patristic authors such as Tertullian (*de Carne Christi*)[16] or Athanasius (*De Incarnatione Verbi*) to post-Reformation thinkers, notably Martin Chemnitz (*De duabus naturis in Christo*, Leipzig 1578), to contemporary theologians.[17] In the period AD 300–600, the nature of Christ became a matter of divisive controversies within the Christian church and resulted in church councils and official pronouncement in the form of creeds — from the Nicean (formulated in response to the heresy of Arius) to the Chaldean, which proclaimed Christ to possess two natures in one person, forming a 'hypostatic union', and the creed of Athanasius (*Quicumque vult*).[18] Still, the incarnation remains the *mysterium* par excellence, a unique event in the history of the world.[19]

The transfiguration

In between the incarnation and the resurrection the so-called 'transfiguration' (from the Latin *transfiguratio*) occurred: it took place shortly before Jesus' death and prefigures his return to a divine existence. The Greek term behind the Latin *transfiguratio* is *metamorphosis*. In their accounts of the events on Mount Tabor, Matthew and Mark both use the verb μεταμορφόω ('to transform'), the only two occurrences of the term in the gospels. Here is Mark's version (9. 1–7):[20]

> And after six days Jesus taketh *with him* Peter, and James, and John, and leadeth them up into an high mountain apart by themselves: and he was transfigured before them (καὶ μετεμορφώθη ἔμπροσθεν αὐτῶν | *transfiguratus est coram ipsis*). And his raiment became shining, exceeding white as snow; so as no fuller on earth can white them. And there appeared unto them Elias with Moses: and they were talking with Jesus. [...] And there was a cloud that overshadowed them: and a voice came out of the cloud, saying, This is my beloved Son: hear him.

Theologians still debate how this episode ought to be situated within contemporary traditions of religious thought, such as Greek mystery religion, epiphany, the Jewish belief in the eschatological transformation of the righteous (Daniel 12. 3;

1 Enoch 38. 4, 39. 7; IV Ezra 7. 97), or Christology.[21] In terms of reception, the transfiguration has played a more prominent role in Eastern Christianity than in the West, where 'the liturgical feast of the Transfiguration was not officially recognized [...] until 1475' — even though 'discussions of the Transfiguration play a significant role in Medieval debates concerned with the metaphysics of light, and in mystical-contemplative texts.'[22] For our purposes, it is significant that the tradition of exegesis that has accrued around the Gospel reports of this event features interesting parallels to critical reactions to myths of metamorphosis in Graeco-Roman culture. In the face of a miraculous event that is unaccountable in terms of everyday experience, impulses to rationalize may kick in that challenge the literal meaning of the text. The Venerable Bede, for instance, in his commentary on Mark 9. 3, reassures his readers:

> transfiguratus salvator non substantiam verae carnis amisit sed gloriam futurae vel suae vel nostrae resurrectionis ostendit qui qualis tunc apostolis apparuit talis post iudicium cunctis apparebit electis.

> [The transfigured saviour did not lose the substance of his actual body but showed forth the glory of his own or our future resurrection by appearing to the apostles then how he shall appear to all the elect after the Judgement.]

In other words, Bede turns the metamorphosis into an allophany or epiphany (cf. *apparuit*) that does not involve a material change in substance. Those of a more pragmatic bent have mooted the possibility of an optical illusion caused either by Jesus himself or some opportune lightning; others have mused that the evangelists here recount a subjective experience of Jesus. One of the reasons why the passage causes discomfort in theological circles is the lexical coincidence between the metamorphosis of Jesus and the metamorphoses of Greek and Roman literature. Up comes the *cordon sanitaire*: 'The transformation of Jesus is to be kept apart from the Greek idea of metamorphosis — despite the same word.'[23]

Crucifixion, resurrection, and ascension

The death of Jesus of Nazareth on the cross during the reign of Tiberius, around AD 29, is an incident that can be accepted as historical on the basis of the available evidence, without the need to resort to the supernatural registers of magic, marvel, or miracle. The same is not the case with the subsequent events, that is, his resurrection from the dead on the third day after his entombment and his ascension to heaven soon afterwards. As Geza Vermes puts it, 'unlike the crucifixion, it is an unparalleled phenomenon in history. Two types of extreme reactions are possible: faith and disbelief.'[24] The notion of a crucified saviour is as paradoxical as, and closely related to, the divine becoming human in the incarnation and has required hermeneutic efforts from the outset, not least since it breaks with conceptions of the Messiah in the Jewish tradition and therefore had to overcome steep barriers of plausibility within the milieu in which Christianity first spread.[25] The theology of the cross requires the imagination to cope with paradoxa, insofar as it simultaneously signifies death and life, humiliation and elevation, defeat and triumph. Tertullian, for one, explicitly turned the apparent absurdity of incarnation and resurrection into the reason and foundation of his faith (*de Carne Christi* 5.4):[26]

> Crucifixus est dei filius: non pudet quia pudendum est. Et mortuus est dei filius: credibile est quia ineptum est. Et sepultus resurrexit: certum est quia impossibile.
>
> [The Son of God was crucified: it is not shameful because one has to be ashamed. The Son of God died: it is believable because it is absurd. Buried, he has risen: it is certain because it is impossible.]

Markus Bockmuehl draws attention to the spectrum of options available to classify the claim that Christ has risen from the dead by means of the alliterative sequence 'miracle, myth, metaphor'. Each term points to a different conception of the reality of the resurrection: miracle recognizes the possibility of an event that defies conventional protocols of experience; myth, itself a protean concept, suggests that the story lacks a referential basis in reality and is a figment of the imagination; metaphor strikes a compromise: it indicates a way of speaking that points to something else, which could be profound or, indeed, real, even though it defies a literal articulation in human language.[27] The accounts of the ascension — which, according to Acts 2. 33, constitutes the culmination of Christ's mission, resulting in the outpouring of the spirit — equally confront readers with the choice between faith and fiction. As Dunn puts it, 'for anyone with a historical turn of mind, it is one of the most troublesome of all episodes recorded in the first five books of the NT'.[28] He notes that those who are uncomfortable with the notion of a material ascent to Heaven prefer the non-spatial term 'exaltation'.

The Eucharist and transubstantiation

During the last supper that Jesus shared with his apostles before his betrayal and execution, he identified the bread and the wine that he served to his followers with his body and his blood. Here is Matthew's account of the episode (26. 26–28):[29]

> 26   Ἐσθιόντων δὲ αὐτῶν λαβὼν ὁ Ἰησοῦς ἄρτον καὶ εὐλογήσας ἔκλασεν καὶ δοὺς τοῖς μαθηταῖς εἶπεν, Λάβετε φάγετε, τοῦτό ἐστιν τὸ σῶμά μου.
>
> > cenantibus autem eis accepit Iesus panem et benedixit ac fregit deditque discipulis suis et ait accipite et comedite hoc est corpus meum
> >
> > And as they were eating, Jesus took bread, and blessed *it*, and brake *it*, and gave *it* to the disciples, and said, Take, eat; this is my body.
>
> 27   καὶ λαβὼν ποτήριον καὶ εὐχαριστήσας ἔδωκεν αὐτοῖς λέγων, Πίετε ἐξ αὐτοῦ πάντες,
>
> > et accipiens calicem gratias egit et dedit illis dicens bibite ex hoc omnes.
> >
> > And he took the cup, and gave thanks, and gave *it* to them, saying, Drink ye all of it;
>
> 28   τοῦτο γάρ ἐστιν τὸ αἷμά μου τῆς διαθήκης τὸ περὶ πολλῶν ἐκχυννόμενον εἰς ἄφεσιν ἁμαρτιῶν.
>
> > hic est enim sanguis meus novi testamenti qui pro multis effunditur in remissionem peccatorum.
> >
> > For this is my blood of the new testament, which is shed for many for the remission of sins.

The episode is of vital importance for the Christian faith: the Eucharist epitomizes the very notion of the New Testament, insofar as it constitutes the ritual enactment of Christ's salvific mission of personal sacrifice for the ultimate salvation of all of humanity, the undoing of the history of sin that began with Adam. Yet what exactly did Jesus mean when he used the deictic pronoun 'this' and the copula 'is' in seemingly *identifying* the bread and the wine with his body and his blood? Was he speaking literally or metaphorically? Are the bread and the wine he served to be understood as a symbol or do these substances actually begin *to be* His divine flesh and blood? And if Jesus affected a real transformation at the time, does such a transformation continue to occur whenever Christian communities celebrate the Eucharist? And, if so, in whom is the power of transformation vested: the celebrant priest or God?

From medieval times until today, these questions have given rise to considerable controversy. An early endorsement of a literal reading of the Gospel passages and the continual re-enactment of a change in substance during the celebration of the Holy Mass was Paschasius Radbertus' *De Corpore et Sanguine Domini* (written between 831 and 833), a treatise on the nature of the Eucharist that insists on the physical presence of Christ during the sacrament of the Mass and the actual transformation of bread and wine into his body and blood. One of the arguments that Paschasius advanced to render this apparently counterintuitive claim plausible was that God, the Creator, retains unlimited rights of transformative intervention in his creation. In other words He can do with or in the physical universe whatever He pleases, including the repeated transformation of bread and wine into the flesh and blood of His son, without violating any apparent law of nature since nature itself is the outgrowth of His will.[30] Paschasius' case rested entirely on theological speculation, rather than empirical evidence, since the sacred flesh and blood of Christ that is being consumed must have looked, felt, and tasted exactly like ordinary bread and wine: in other words, despite the assertion that the substances in question before and after the miraculous transformation are utterly different, this difference does not manifest itself in any qualities open to normal sense perception. Dissenting voices arose almost instantaneously, resulting in the Carolingian Eucharist Controversy, but Paschasius' view ultimately prevailed and became a mainstream article of faith in the Catholic Church.[31]

The elevation of his interpretation into dogma was a decision of momentous consequences that has continued to exercise the theological imagination till today, but resonated with particular force during the High Middle Ages and, again, in early-modern times.[32] Thus about two hundred years after Paschasius, Berengar of Tours challenged the doctrine on the grounds of logic and common sense: he argued that the demonstrative pronoun *hoc* in the consecrating phrase *hoc est corpus meum* initially refers to the bread and cannot logically change its referent without invalidating the utterance; and he raised the interesting problem of what happens to crumbs of what others take to be Christ's body nibbled at by mice.[33] This latter question soon gave rise to a variety of opinions, including those of Stephen Langton (*c.* 1150–1228), Archbishop of Canterbury, who asserted that contact with the teeth of a mouse re-transubstantiated the consecrated host into ordinary bread

([...] *dicendum esset, quod corpus Christi transsubstantiatur in panem in comestione muris*) and Gerald of Novara (writing *c.* 1200–09), who consigned the answer to the knowledge of God, while dismissing Berengar's objection (and the contempt for mice it implies) as irrational, given that the host is also consumed by the most evil of humans.[34] Berengar of Tours, at any rate, was forced to abjure his heretical views in 1079, pronouncing the following oath in front of a Roman Church Council presided over by Pope Gregory VII:[35]

> I, Berengar, believe with my heart and confess with my mouth that the bread and the wine that are put upon the altar are substantially changed into the true, proper, and vivifying flesh and blood of our Lord Jesus Christ through the mystery of holy prayer and the words of our Redeemer and, after the consecration, are the true body of Christ, which was born of the Virgin and which hung on the cross, offered for the salvation of the world, and which sits at the right of the Father, and the true blood of Christ, which poured forth from his side, not only through the sign and the power of the sacrament, but in the propriety of its nature and in the truth of its substance [...].

Yet silencing the troublemaker did not solve the philosophical problem of how to explain the phenomenon of transubstantiation. Different schools of thought emerged as to what precisely happens to the elements or substances of bread and wine during the Eucharist, such as (a) coexistence, (b) substitution, or (c) transformation.[36] In a letter, in which he addressed the theme *De forma sacramenti Eucharistiae eiusque elementis*, Pope Innocent III (1198–1216), for instance, argued that in the sacrament of the Eucharist three discrete aspects must be carefully distinguished: the visible appearance, the true nature of the substance, and the spiritual quality; thus what is bread and wine in terms of its form is in truth the body and blood of Christ, signifying divine love and the unity of the church.[37] And Aquinas tried to reconcile theology with Aristotelian physics and sensual experience by arguing that the bread and the flesh of Christ into which it is transformed are two qualitatively different substances that happen to have the same accidental properties open to our sense perception — in other words, Christ's flesh and blood feels, looks, and tastes like bread and wine, even if it is something entirely different.[38]

The basic principle of substantial transformation remained in force, even when Enlightenment thinkers such as Descartes started to challenge medieval conceptions of the natural world. While reformation thinkers developed a range of positions that accommodated doubts and scepticism, and resolutely objected to the idea that the 'real presence' of Christ (however conceived) in the Eucharist had anything to do with the transformative power of the celebrant, the Catholic Church has continued to affirm the actual transformation of substances in the moment of the Eucharistic consecration of bread and wine. In the twentieth century, some theologians tried to solve the problem through the invention of neologisms, designed to move away from the Paschasian tradition of a literal understanding of the Gospel passages. But Pope Paul VI, in his encyclical *Mysterium fidei* (1965), rejects as 'false and disturbing opinions' conceptions of what happens during the Eucharist as 'transignification' and 'transfinalization', reaffirming 'the marvellous conversion of the whole substance of the bread into the Body and the whole substance of the wine into the

Blood of Christ' (10–12) and devoting several paragraphs to 'The Various Ways in Which Christ Is Present' (34–39). Even after the Second Vatican Council, then, the Eucharist has remained 'a paschal banquet in which Christ is eaten' (4).[39]

The transubstantiation is one the most remarkable phenomena of transformative change in Western culture. It grounds the Christian message in a divinely enabled metamorphosis, a moment of ontological flux, continually re-enacted in memory of Jesus' sacrifice for humankind and in anticipation of ultimate salvation. It is the institutionalization and continual reiteration of a miracle and arguably the one instance of miraculous, transformative change originating in antiquity (both in its original moment in history and its ritual re-enactment) that continues to command belief within a significant institution in modern society. But whereas in medieval and early-modern times, theologians and philosophers tried to reconcile the phenomenon with contemporary knowledge about the natural world, such endeavours at a 'rational scientific' explanation have ceased to dominate Catholic discourse. In the encyclicals of Paul VI and John Paul II the dominant mode is dogmatic assertion, rather than natural-philosophical argument.[40]

Imitatio Christi

To conclude this section, it is worth casting a glance at the two instances of the verb μεταμορφόω in the Letters of Paul, who applies the term to describe the 'upward transformations' that human beings undergo if they devote their lives to belief in, and the imitation of, Christ:

> καὶ μὴ συσχηματίζεσθε τῷ αἰῶνι τούτῳ, ἀλλὰ μεταμορφοῦσθε τῇ ἀνακαινώσει τοῦ νοός, εἰς τὸ δοκιμάζειν ὑμᾶς τί τὸ θέλημα τοῦ θεοῦ, τὸ ἀγαθὸν καὶ εὐάρεστον καὶ τέλειον.

> [And be not conformed to this world: but be ye transformed by the renewing of your mind,[41] that ye may prove what is that good, and acceptable, and perfect, will of God.] (Romans 12. 2)

> ἡμεῖς δὲ πάντες ἀνακεκαλυμμένῳ προσώπῳ τὴν δόξαν κυρίου κατοπτριζόμενοι τὴν αὐτὴν εἰκόνα μεταμορφούμεθα ἀπὸ δόξης εἰς δόξαν, καθάπερ ἀπὸ κυρίου πνεύματος.

> [But we all, with open face beholding as in a glass the glory of the Lord, are changed into the same image (*in eandem imaginem transformamur*) from glory to glory, even as by the Spirit of the Lord.] (II Corinthians 3. 18)

These passages have apparent affinities with Hellenistic mystery religions and specific texts that thematize ecstatic religious experience, proximity to the divine, or salvation in terms of metamorphosis, such as Apuleius' *Golden Ass* or the *Corpus Hermeticum*.[42] This does not mean that Paul here draws on the idiom of pagan mystery cults as some scholars have suspected; rather, he seems to stand in the tradition of apocalyptic Judaism.[43] Paul's use of μεταμορφοῦσθαι captures the 'before' and 'after' of experiencing divine revelation, coinciding with an assimilation of the believer to Christ. Like Mark and Matthew with reference to the transfiguration, Paul uses the notion of metamorphosis as a dynamic principle at work in the universal and personal history of salvation.[44] There exists, indeed, a structural analogy between transformation and conversion: both involve a decisive rupture in the continuity of selfhood, an event that generates a before and an after, and two states of existence that are related but distinct. From this point of view, conversion emerges as the Christian equivalent to pagan metamorphosis.[45]

Meaning, doubt, and dogmatism: In all, Christianity introduced something qualitatively new into ancient Mediterranean thought on transformative change, not least in asserting that the most decisive sequence of metamorphic moments in the history of humankind (incarnation, transfiguration, death and resurrection, ascension) had just happened in the here and now. Yet even for those who purported to be eyewitnesses to these events, the full significance of Jesus' life often remained obscure. Indeed, the Gospels themselves deliberately stage interpretative aporias around the figure of Jesus and the meaning of his words, deeds, and experiences. Thus his followers, after he announced that they should keep silent about what they had seen during the transfiguration until the son of man had risen from the dead, were not at all sure what 'rising from the dead' was supposed to mean and quizzed each other about it.[46] If the challenge before the passion was one of hermeneutics, afterwards it became one of authentication. Somehow, the apostles managed to render the claim plausible that they had indeed seen the risen Jesus with their eyes (rather than in a vision).[47] And ultimately even 'doubting Thomas', whom later ages imagined as being in need of putting his finger into the physical body of Christ as a means of grasping metaphysical Truth, was convinced that Jesus had undergone resurrection.[48] Objections to this claim have accompanied its dissemination ever since it was first asserted: the physical reality of resurrection did not command widespread plausibility (if any) in first-century Palestine;[49] and the status of Jesus as Christ is, naturally, Christianity-specific, the main dividing line between Christianity and Judaism or, indeed, any other religious faith.[50] But against all gainsayers, within a mere three centuries, the apostles, their successors, missionaries, and church officials managed to establish their faith as the dominant religion of the Roman Empire. While controversies over the orthodox understanding of Christ and the Christian conception of the supernatural continued to rage, the transformative events surrounding Jesus became binding articles of faith for communities of believers, within an evolving theological paradigm that included a proto-scientific discourse about the nature of the universe and retained a powerful influence on, if not hegemonic sway over, Western conceptions of (supernatural) reality until the rise of modern science.

Policing (and Exploiting) the Pagan

With Constantine enthroned, for the first time in world history a religion grounded in the Mosaic distinction between one true God and many idols (or demons) acquired imperial sway.[51] God's claim to exclusivity has of course a commanding presence in Jewish Scripture, as the second statement in his ground rules for his chosen people, reinforced by the pronouncement of jealous, cross-generational, and inexpiable wrath in the case of violation; it comes immediately after his self-identification as the agent of historical salvation and right before the prohibition of idolatry and the vain use of his name.[52] And the elevation of Christianity to the official religion of the Roman Empire meant that the Christian version of the Mosaic distinction could rely on the resources of imperial power to enforce religious orthodoxy. From the start, Christian writings had engaged rival versions of religious thought found in the pagan classics; and if previously Christians had been the victims of persecution for not recognizing the divinity of the emperor, after Constantine's reforms they began to launch their own acts of aggression against what they construed as the world of false belief. Polytheistic cult practices, not least various forms of blood sacrifice, were discontinued; temples were burned down or rededicated; statues of Olympian divinities and deified emperors were smashed to smithereens.[53]

Myth, too, continued to be attacked as a rival system of theology.[54] But the pagan classics, including Ovid's *Metamorphoses*, with their tales of gallivanting gods, whose sexual exploits, often achieved via metamorphic strategems, would be the envy of any perverse polymorph, and their broad conceptualization of the world as a domain of supernaturally induced transformative change, proved more durable than the practices, buildings, artworks, or institutions of pagan cult. While we no longer sacrifice oxen and burn the bones and the fat as offerings to the gods, we still read Ovid's poetry and other works of classical literature radically at variance with Christian doctrine. The reasons why no all-consuming bonfire of pagan vanities occurred are complex and have to do, not least, with education: the classical texts remained at the core of a curriculum grounded in the study of grammar and rhetoric, designed to enable its elite beneficiaries to speak eloquently in public as a key dimension of their social and cultural identity and self-promotion.[55] The remarkable resilience of classical modes of education ensured the continuing presence of pagan figures and concepts, including classical notions of transformative change, in a Christian universe. As Momigliano put it: 'The new history could not suppress the old. Adam and Eve and what follows had in some way to be presented in a world populated by Deucalion, Cadmus, Romulus, and Alexander the Great.'[56]

In Seznec's arresting phrase, the pagan gods and heroes of classical antiquity, as well as the tales of their exploits, 'survived' in a world profoundly hostile to much of what they represented, not least in terms of reproductive morality and religious experience.[57] Yet from the outset the resulting frictions solicited diverse strategies of coping, to subordinate, but also to utilize, pagan falsehood within Christian truth.[58] In what follows, we pick out some of the figures of thought that influenced the epistemic repositioning of Graeco-Roman mythology (especially its metamorphic elements) undertaken by Christian thinkers from late antiquity to the Middle Ages and beyond.[59]

Fabula: from fiction to falsehood

The most basic stratagem consisted in refusing to grant the tales about gods, heroes, and ordinary mortals undergoing miraculous transformations not only any claim to historical veracity, but also the status of imaginary entertainment — what we (and Aristotle) would classify as (historical) fiction.[60] By collapsing the distinction between literary invention and lying, Christian writers condemned the *muthoi* or *fabulae* recounted by classical authors as outright falsehood, designed to deceive.[61]

To pick just one illustrative and influential example: a 'classic' confrontation between the rival systems occurs in the so-called *Ecloga Theoduli*, which was part of the anthology known as the *Auctores Octo*, the 'Eight Authors', who occupied a central position in the schoolrooms of medieval Europe.[62] It stages a musical contest in the Virgilian tradition of agonistic bucolic poetry between the maiden Alithia ('Truth') of Davidian lineage and the shepherd Pseustis ('Falsehood'), who, envious of the sweetness of Alithia's music, challenges her to a competition in song, with their mutual friend Phronesis ('Wisdom') sitting in judgement. In reply to mythic tales by Pseustis (often clearly drawn from Ovid's *Metamorphoses* but also drawing upon other classical sources), Alithia counters with stories from the Old Testament: thus Lycaon's habit of slaughtering guests and his transformation into a wolf gets juxtaposed to the deification of Enoch on account of his justice (61–68), Noah trumps Deucalion and Pyrrha (69–76), and the myth of Daedalus and Icarus finds its match in the story of Abraham and Isaac (101–08). The *Ecloga Theoduli* thus epitomizes an episteme in which the classical tales of metamorphosis, as well as Greek and Roman myth more generally, are turned into deceitful lies that mimic and rival scriptural truth.[63]

Demonic demotions

An alternative to turning the pagan figures into figments of the imagination lay in reducing them to the status of demons. Drawing their inspiration from Psalm 95. 3–5, some Christian authors (notably Augustine) kept the pagan divinities very much alive, but located them on a lower ontological register.[64] Demons were thought to be active in the service of the devil, not least in fostering belief in pagan divinities, plagiarizing and then distorting the religious truths of Christianity, and — according to Augustine in particular — causing (belief in) the occurrence of miraculous transformative change.[65]

Christian nuggets in pagan horseshit

A more charitable approach to pagan lore was to recognize that, while most of it was nonsense, it nonetheless contained some truthful information about the workings of the divine from which a Christian might benefit. And thus the *magister* in Conrad of Hirsau's *Dialogus super auctores* (c. 1130) counters his student's protest that by reading Ovid's *Metamorphoses* he besmears himself with the 'manure' of pagan blasphemies by explaining that even Ovid's poem of marvellous transformation contains 'nuggets' of genuine insight, not least in the creation narrative.[66] Already Lactantius gave voice to this conviction: *Ovidius quoque in principio praeclari operis sine ulla nominis dissimulatione a deo, quem 'fabricatorem mundi', quem 'rerum opificem' vocat, mundum fatetur instructum.*[67] The question naturally arises: how did the nuggets (i.e. partial insight into absolute Christian truth without the benefit of revelation) find their way *into* the manure? Christian authors suggested various possibilities, such as plagiarism of the Bible, the nature of the human soul (knowledge of God as inborn, rather than learned through experience), or the conception of pagan culture as *praeparatio evangelica*, in parallel to Judaism and the Old Testament.[68]

Degrees of credibility

Yet another ploy demands some attention, even if its overall significance in Christian apologetics is not particularly pronounced: the use of *pagan* implausibilities to render *Christian* implausibilities more plausible. A striking instance of this rhetorical strategy occurs at Tertullian, *de Carne Christi*, 4.6, within an attack on Marcion, who had questioned the true humanity of Jesus:

> et tamen apud illam [*sc.* sapientiam] facilius creditur Iuppiter taurus factus aut cycnus quam uere homo Christus penes Marcionem.

> [And yet, on the basis of this wisdom, as far as Marcion is concerned, it is more easily believed that Jupiter became a bull or a swan than that Christ truly became a man.]

The reference is of course to the animal-allophanies in which Jupiter abducted or impregnated Europa and Leda.[69] The same rhetorical strategy also helps Jerome to address the problem of credibility in his *Commentary on The Book of Jonah*. Conceding that some pagans may not consider Jonah's three-day stay in the bowels of a whale particularly believable, he surprisingly recommends perusal of Ovid's *Metamorphoses* as a reminder of divine omnipotence:[70]

> But if they will be pagans, let them read the fifteen books of Ovid's *Metamorphoses* and all of Greek and Latin history. There they will perceive Daphne turned into a laurel tree or the sisters of Phaethon into poplars; how Jupiter, their highest divinity, changed himself into a swan, flowed in the form of gold, abducted in the form of a bull and all the rest of it, in which the very shamelessness of the fables belittles the sanctity of divinity. They believe in those and say that everything is possible for God. And although they believe in shameful matters and defend the universal power of God, they refuse to ascribe the same quality also to matters that are honourable.

Pagan myths — though Jerome here classifies the *Metamorphoses* obliquely as *historia* — are thus cited in order to increase the plausibility of elements of Christian doctrine that defy norms of rationality and empiricism. In effect, Jerome argues that one should believe in incredible biblical tales because they are less absurd records of divine activity than classical myths of transformative change, which too find credulous, yet mistaken, believers. (Ironically, Jerome thereby ascribes greater credibility to Ovid's tales than Ovid and his original readership would have.) It is a stratagem that the church fathers passed down to theologians of the Middle Ages and early-modern times. The *Defensorium inviolatae virginitatis beatae Mariae* by Franz von Retz (*c.* 1420), for instance, is a grandiose attempt to render the inexplicable (the virgin birth) plausible with the help of what Ohly calls a '"wenn-warum dann nicht?"-Gefüge': a two-step argument grounded in the principle 'if "x" is the case, why not "y" as well?', even though that of course implies granting the pagan stories, at least notionally, referential value and some measures of historical truth. Retz repeatedly juxtaposes biblical, legendary, and classical material, and one of his sources for the latter is, again, Ovid's *Metamorphoses*: Danae, Circe's transformation of Odysseus' companions, the transformation of the companions of Diomedes into birds, Europa kissing Jupiter in the guise of a bull.[71]

Christian truths encoded in pagan lies

Closely related to the 'nugget-in-manure' approach, but shifting the emphasis from 'discovery' to 'decoding', from identification to interpretation, is the notion that classical texts *conceal* (allegorical) Christian truths behind the (literal) veneer of pagan falsehoods.[72] The resort to allegorical reading was a widespread hermeneutic practice in antiquity, across a range of cultural traditions.[73] Allegoresis offered a convenient means of endowing a text that, taken literally, was thought to signify something unpalatable but was nevertheless judged to be of sufficient cultural value to call for engagement and transmission (rather than outright dismissal as rubbish), with a more acceptable meaning.[74] Examples include Jewish (and later Christian) allegorical readings of the apparent celebration of sex and eroticism in the Song of Songs, allegorical readings of anthropomorphic divinities in Homer as standing in for forces of nature, and Neoplatonic allegorical readings of ancient myths in late antiquity.[75] In general terms, allegoresis is ideally suited to the integration of aspects of a cultural heritage that seem problematic or alien, and it can be applied on a large scale — as seen with the Christian allegorical co-option of Jewish Scriptures (codified and integrated into the Christian Bible under the label 'Old Testament', which, in Christian usage, is taken to prefigure allegorically the 'new covenant'). But it was also a technique employed to endow holy writ with meaning and significance beyond the literal sense of the text. The poly-semantics of Scripture found its classic articulation in the doctrine of the 'four senses': the literal, the allegorical, the moral, and the anagogical.[76] The medieval recuperation of pagan mythology as a discourse of hidden truths could thus build on and merge with well-established traditions of allegorical exegesis, Christian and otherwise.

One of our earliest testimonies for Christian allegoresis of Ovid comes from the ninth century. Theodulf of Orléans, in a poem with the rather prolix title *About the Books I was in the Habit of Reading and How the Myths of the Poets are Interpreted by Learned Men in an Allegorical Sense* (17–20), writes: 'Now I was reading Pompeius, now you, Donatus, now Virgil, and now you, garrulous Ovid. Although their writings contain many absurdities, a great many truths lie hidden under the false trappings.'[77] More systematic endeavours followed, notably by Arnulf of Orléans (active in the 1170s), who followed up a series of glosses on Ovid's *Metamorphoses* with a highly influential *Allegoriae*, and John of Garland's *Integumenta Ovidii* (c. 1234). The approach ultimately culminated in the French vernacular rewriting and expansion of the *Metamorphoses* in a Christian key known as the *Ovide moralisé* (around 1300) and Pierre Bersuire's *Ovidius moralizatus* (c. 1348). The tradition petered out in early-modern times, when thinkers and theologians started to consider Christian allegorical readings of Ovid's *Metamorphoses* even more unsavoury than its literal meaning. Luther famously declared that he 'hated allegory' and portrayed Bersuire's allegoresis of Ovid as a 'beautiful whore' (*formosa meretrix*) that seduced leisured minds with her apparent innocence and moral verve; in his view there was little value and less virtue in seeing Maria behind Daphne or Christ behind Apollo.[78] And Rabelais, in his *prologue de l'auteur* to *Gargantua*, refuses to believe in the allegorical readings of classical authors such as Homer or Ovid: 'Homer dreamt as little of those allegories as Ovid in his *Metamorphoses* dreamt of the mysteries of the

Christian Gospel, which a certain Brother Lubin [*sc.* Bersuire] has tried to prove are in there.'[79]

But before Christian allegoresis began to lose its plausibility, the practice had become embedded within a tradition of systematic commentary on the *Metamorphoses*, which devoted significant space to the discussion of transformative change.[80] Thus, the *accessus* to the 'vulgate commentary' (*c.* 1250) distinguishes four different types of transformation that can be found in Ovid's poem: natural, moral, magical, and spiritual. Natural transformations include the combination and recombination of natural elements or biological processes of change, including the phenomena mentioned by Pythagoras in his discourse; moral transformations refer to a change in ethics, from (say) benign to cruel, which has given rise to such stories — to be understood allegorically — as Lycaon's mutation into a wolf; magical transformation occur through the practice of witchcraft (*ars magica*), as when the sorceress Circe turns Odysseus' companions into swine; and spiritual transformations refer to diseases that affect both the body and the mind, such as the fit of insanity that caused Agave to tear her son Pentheus to pieces.[81] What is remarkable is the panoramic approach to the phenomenon of transformative change that identifies a range of types, each with its specific 'referential' status, depending on whether the instance under consideration is to be understood literally or figuratively. Most of Ovid's tales are taken to belong to the metaphorical variety, where a fictional metamorphosis illustrates an issue in ethics (*moralis*), but his epic is also seen as recording actual transformations, such as natural processes, changes in form caused by magic, or altered states of consciousness. This tradition of allegoresis and commentary on the *Metamorphoses* forms the backdrop for Dante and Petrarch, who both operate within and against these modes of engaging with Ovid and thinking about transformative change. Both succeed in making Ovidian metamorphosis resonate in a novel key.

Dante and Petrarch: Ovid's *Metamorphoses* as Fiction and Experience

As recent scholarship — and especially a series of studies by Brownlee — has shown, Ovid is a subliminal presence throughout the *Divine Comedy*, including Paradiso.[82] Still, the only place where Dante mentions Ovid by name outside 'la bella scola' of Inferno IV (88–90: *Quegli è il Omero poeta sovrano;* | *L' altro è Orazio satiro che viene;* | *Ovidio è terzo, e l'ultimo Lucano*) is in Inferno XXV, the canto of the thieves, where he is ordered, together with Lucan, to be silent, on the grounds that the accounts of metamorphosis contained within the *oeuvres* of these two classical poets vanish into insignificance when juxtaposed to the kind of transformative changes Dante himself has witnessed in Hell (Inferno XXV, 94–99):[83]

> Taccia Lucano omai là dov' e' tocca
> del misero Sabello e di Nasidio,
> e attenda a udir quel ch'or si scocca.
> Taccia di Cadmo e d' Aretusa Ovidio,
> ché se quello in serpente e quella in fonte
> converte poetando, io non lo 'nvidio.

> [Let Lucan now fall silent where he tells
> of poor Sabellus and Nasidius,
> and let him wait to hear what comes forth now!
> Let Ovid not speak of Cadmus or Arethusa,
> for if his poem turns him into a serpent
> and her into a fountain, I grudge it not.]

Dante implicitly accepts the historicity of Lucan's account in *Bellum Civile* IX of what happened to Sabellus and Nasidius, two soldiers in Cato's army, after they were bitten by snakes during a march through the African desert: one melted like snow, the other swelled up before bursting. In contrast, he obliquely asserts his superiority over Ovid by dismissing his epic of transformative change as fiction. The key term that does the polemic work is 'poetando', which contains a double thrust. First, in a passage of highly Latinate Italian (*serpente, fonte, converte, 'nvidio*) it actually *is* (also) Latin — as Guido da Pisa's translation from the Italian to the Latin in his *Deductio textus de vulgari in latinum* evinces: *taceat etiam de Cadmo et Arethusa Ovidius; quia si illum in serpentem <u>poetando</u> convertit, nullam invidiam illi porto*.[84] And secondly, 'poetando' implies that the transformations one finds in Ovid's *Metamorphoses* are figments of the poet's imagination. Benvenuto da Imola glosses the term with 'poetice fingendo', that is, 'by inventing in his poetry'.[85] Dante thus distinguishes between the metamorphoses recorded by Lucan in his *Bellum Civile* (as well as, as we shall see, those he himself has witnessed in Hell) and those that Ovid recounts in his *Metamorphoses*. The former are real; the latter mere figments of the imagination. Ovid (unlike Lucan, who wrote historical epic) is a creative artist whose tales have no grounding in empirical reality. By turning (two of) Ovid's metamorphoses into fictions by means of the simple term *poetando*, Dante in part follows the tradition of allegorical exegesis, which also argued that most of the instances of transformative change recounted by Ovid (including those of Cadmus and Arethusa) ought not to be taken literally; but unlike practitioners of allegoresis, he does not probe the myths for a non-literal 'moral truth'. Rather, Dante here outs Ovid's Latin as a medium of falsehood and, to use the terms of *de vulgari eloquentia*, artifice, implicitly endorsing his native (and hence natural) Italian as the language of verisimilitude and truth, the perfect medium to recount *actual* metamorphoses — including those he has himself witnessed in Inferno.[86]

The lines thus put Ovid in his place, and in more ways than one. But, regardless of Dante's pronouncement, Ovid cannot simply be silenced. And as it turns out, in outdoing Ovid, Dante (unwittingly?) outs himself as Ovidian through and through, not least in the play with basic categories of scholastic ontology that occurs within this particular canto. The ontological confusion (man merging with snake) in lines 48–78 and its final outcome are based in no small part on the imagery and idiom of Ovid's Salmacis and Hermaphroditus episode in *Metamorphoses* IV, where the nymph Salmacis merges with the boy Hermaphroditus to produce the sexually ambiguous Hermaphrodite that is both and neither of the two sexes, just as Dante's sinner is both snake and human as well as neither — a being, in other words, that appears not to find a rung on the divine ladder of nature. Dante's debt to Ovid is less obvious, but arguably even more intriguing, in the passage on transformative exchange, which begins as follows (Inferno XXV, 100–03):

> ché due nature mai a fronte a fronte
> non trasmutò sì ch'amendue le forme
> a cambiar lor matera fosser pronte.
> Insieme si rispuosero a tai norme [...]

> [for never did he change two natures, face to face,
> in such a way that both their forms
> were quite so ready to exchange their substance.
> Their corresponding changes went like this:]

Ovid's *Metamorphoses*, one recalls, opens with *In nova fert animus mutatas dicere formas | corpora* ['My mind carries me to sing of forms changed into new bodies']. The Ovidian formulation implies a basic synonymity of *forma* and *corpus*, not least since one would expect the inverse: bodies changed into new forms, rather than forms changed into new bodies. But for Dante and medieval intellectuals more generally — and Dante commentators up to the present day — *forma* and *corpus* (or, in the vernacular: *forma* and *matera/materia*) had a distinct meaning in scholastic philosophy. Very succinctly put, in the Aristotelian-Thomic tradition, *forma* represents the active principle, the soul, whereas *materia* refers to (inert) matter. Put differently, what Dante does in this *terzina* is to gloss Ovid's key categories of *forma* and *corpus*, soul and substance, from an Aristotelian-scholastic point of view, to set up a kind of transformation unheard of in, and difficult to reconcile with, orthodox Christianity and its conception of human nature and the union of body and soul: the human soul becomes one with the body of a beast, and the soul of the beast becomes one with a human body. Given his breach of ontological decorum, it comes as no surprise that Dante concludes his account with an apologetic comment (Inferno XXV, 142–44):

> Così vid' io la settima zavorra
> mutare e trasmutare; e qui mi scusi
> la novità se fior la penna abborra.

> [Thus I saw the seventh rabble change
> and change again, and let the newness of it
> be my excuse if my pen has gone astray.]

His apologetic faltering in the face of the new strikes an apposite contrast with the bold declaration of Ovid that his mind carries him into the telling of novelties, in particular novel transformations.[87] Dante thus presents himself not as a bragging artist, but as God's archivist, who records not the wilful rampages of pagan divinities, but the enactment of divine justice. After an address to the reader saying that he wouldn't be surprised if what he is about to describe was not believed — since he could scarcely believe it himself (46–48) — and the injunction addressed to Lucan and Ovid to fall silent (94–99), the apologetic exclamation in lines 143–44 is the third instance of meta-commentary in the canto that resonates in an Ovidian key: both the practice of sprinkling his narrative with poetological interventions and the issues raised therein — the credible mimesis of the marvellous, the emulation and silencing of literary predecessors, and the apologetic faltering in the face of the new — recall the meta-poetic discourse that programmatically traverses Ovid's *Metamorphoses*.

Overall, then, we capture in Dante a new way of engaging with Ovid, coming out of the medieval tradition of allegorical reading, but going beyond the confines of allegoresis in employing Ovid as a resource for reflecting upon (supernatural) reality and its representation in poetry. He uses Ovid both as foil and as inspiration in his efforts to bear witness to divine Truth — or, to put it differently, Ovid helps him to articulate in words and images the (ineffable) autopsy of Christian Inferno (and later also Purgatorio and Paradiso). At the same time, Dante keeps Ovid firmly subordinate to his Christian project and thereby epitomizes the prevailing medieval approach towards classical thinking about transformative change. The first major author who explicitly plays off Ovid against Christ is Petrarch, an epoch-making individual par excellence, who also marks a significant watershed in the history of metamorphosis.

While literary scholars nowadays like to downplay historical caesuras in favour of emphasizing continuities, in terms of theme and overall outlook the contrast between Dante and Petrarch remains stark, not least in how the two authors configure love, glory, and the Ovidian world of transformative changes. Thus Dante frames his account of the Christian Heavens with two programmatic periphrases of God: the first and the last lines of Paradiso are 'La gloria di colui che tutto muove' and 'l'Amor che muove il sole e l'altre stelle'. The pair of *Gloria* and *Amor*, Love and Glory, reappears in Petrarch's *Secretum*; but rather than being attributes or qualities of God, the terms here signify sinful desires. According to St Augustine, Francesco's critical interlocutor in the dialogue, the pursuit of secular love and literary glory keeps Petrarch from attaining what, according to Christian doctrine, ought to be the alpha and omega of our worldly endeavours: a life in Christ and hence salvation. Petrarch agrees that his love for Laura and the laurel, a woman and fame as a poet, has made him oblivious to the world of the Eternal Maker. The *Canzionere* can be, and has been, read as his version of Augustine's *Confessions* or, for that matter, Dante's *Divine Comedy* — a Petrarchan counterpart to the autobiographies of his patristic and medieval predecessor, in which he looks back and takes stock of a life in sin that contained within itself a movement towards God. But while the overall plot and basic figures of thought evoke Christian models, the spirit of the undertaking and the artistic outlook of the autobiographical record of his love for Laura signal a new departure, not least in how Petrarch handles the themes of love, glory, and transformation. His main source of inspiration is Ovid.[88]

This emerges most famously in *Canzone* 23, 'Nel dolce tempo de la prima etade', Petrarch's 'exemplary *Canzone*', as his self-citation of the opening line in *Canzone* 70 demonstrates, and the founding manifesto of what one could call 'Ovidian Humanism'.[89] In this *Canzone*, Petrarch recalls undergoing a sequence of seven transformations caused by Cupid, the God of Love, and his beloved Laura, all of them prefigured in Ovid's *Metamorphoses*: he successively turns into a laurel tree (like Daphne in *Met.* I), a swan (like Cygnus in *Met.* II), a stone (like Battus in *Met.* II or Niobe in *Met.* VI), a fountain (like Byblis in *Met.* IX), a stone once more, an echo (re-enacting the experience of the eponymous nymph in *Met.* III), and, finally, a stag (like Actaeon in *Met.* III). Thus, instead of striving for the 'upward' metamorphosis delineated by Paul, that is, the transformation of our selves through exclusive focus on our divine Creator and *imitatio Christi*, he here confesses to have thrown himself into the world of erotic passion and its sublimation in art, experiencing as a consequence the 'downward' metamorphosis into flora, fauna, and inanimate matter. Put differently, he gives up God in the (Ovidian) quest to find, or rather explore, himself.[90] Petrarch thereby fashioned himself as a Renaissance man *avant la lettre* or perhaps even as the first 'modern' individual.[91]

Indeed, the ultimate, self-reflective stanza strikes a note of existential triumph at his literary achievement — as well as his sexual ethics — as Petrarch implicitly demotes both God *and* Ovid in promoting himself and his poetry:

> Canzon, i' non fu' mai quell nuvol d'oro
> che poi discese in preziosa pioggia
> sì che 'l foco di Giove in parte spense;
> ma fui ben fiamma ch' un bel guardo accense,
> et fui l'uccel che più per l'aere poggia
> alzando lei che ne' miei detti onoro;
> né per nova figura il primo alloro
> seppi lassar, ché pur la sua dolce ombra
> ogni men bel piacer del cor mi sgombra.

[Song, I was never the cloud of gold that once descended in a precious rain so that it partly quenched the fire of Jove; but I have certainly been a flame lit by a lovely glance and I have been the bird that rises highest in the air raising her whom in my words I honour; nor for any new shape could I leave the first laurel, for still its sweet shade turns away from my heart any less beautiful pleasure.]

At the end of his poem, then, Petrarch alters, indeed inverts, his perspective on transformative change: instead of the metamorphoses of human beings into lower categories of nature, he here recalls divine allophanies. The 'shower of gold' that Jupiter turned into in order to impregnate Danae was among the most allegory-prone myths, but Petrarch prefers to read the incident historically (*poi discese*) to gain a negative foil for his own passion for Laura:[92] unlike Jupiter he never consummated his love in sex, but if Jupiter descended from the sky in the form of golden rain or carried off skyward the objects of his desire in the form of an eagle, Petrarch's elevation of his beloved is achieved through the medium of poetry: he remains committed to an existence devoted to love and poetry, which he turns into a secular medium of immortality both for himself and his Laura.[93]

Petrarch, in his metamorphic pursuit of Daphne/Laura and worldly laurel, is the first representative of what has been called 'Ovidian humanism', which explores secular subjectivities (if always within a wider Christian horizon) rooted in erotics and the arts (including the quest for immortality through literary fame). This movement finds its centre in the celebration (and exploration) of the human being, not least as a creature of desire. In the wake of Petrarch, classical myth, as mediated, primarily, by Ovid's *Metamorphoses*, increasingly re-emerges as a medium in which members of the cultural elite (artists, authors, princes, politicians, even church officials) promoted and negotiated their self, their experiences, and their surrounding world, in particular when it came to sex and power, destiny and death. Myth in general, and myths of transformation in particular, despite continued criticisms of their literal meaning from rationalizing or Christian perspectives, thus became an alternative preserve of (imaginary and subjective) truths. As Bynum puts it: 'For my self is my story, known only in my shape [...] I am my skin and scars [...] The power of myth demands that "this really happened": the horror and pain come because the wolf was (is?) Lycaon, the tree was (is?) Daphne.'[94] The use of myth as a medium for self-promotion, self-exploration, and socio-political commentary underwrites the innumerable instances of creative reception of specific mythic tales, in particular those canonized in Ovid's *Metamorphoses*, in the Western classical tradition from the Renaissance onwards.[95]

Metamorphosis in Renaissance Europe and the Rise of Modern Science

From the Middle Ages until well into the early-modern period, thinkers tried to reconcile an empirical view of the world around them with the theologically grounded belief in the existence of supernatural figures and forces, such as an omnipotent deity, the devil, or demons. In his *De mirabilibus sacrae scripturae*, for instance, the so-called 'Irish Augustine', writing in the middle of the seventh century, tackles the problem of how to reconcile the implications of divine omnipotence (meaning that everything is possible for God at all times, including the causation of miracles of transformation) with a rational approach towards the world founded on the recognition that nature operates according to fixed principles and with a certain regularity that can be studied and utilized. Keen to downplay the marvellous nature of the miracles recorded in the Bible, he tries to render them explicable (and hence believable) with reference to shared human knowledge about, and experience of, natural phenomena. His discussion of the transformation of the wife of Lot into a pillar of salt, for instance, starts with the observation that the human body contains this substance (suffice it, he notes, to taste tears to ascertain this empirically), from which he concludes that God simply enacted the rhetorical figure of *pars pro toto* in a transformative procedure.[96] The same rationalizing impulse to enhance the plausibility of supernatural events through recourse to natural science animates his discussion of the virgin birth of Christ, insofar as he notes that various animals, such as bees, different types of birds and fish, as well as worms (a Psalm reference is provided to render this *comparandum* acceptable), are born without prior sexual intercourse having taken place.[97] The distinction that the Venerable Bede drew a generation or so later between nature during the six days of creation *ex nihilo* and the subsequent period in which natural laws or regularities apply betokens a similar attempt to accommodate theological dogma with the desire to understand the surrounding world according to empirical and proto-scientific principles.[98]

Similar endeavours to correlate natural laws and divine omnipotence informed early-modern alchemy, that science of transformative change, not least in those of its branches influenced by the Humanist revival of classical learning. This resulted in various syncretistic efforts to reconcile different bodies of knowledge from various cultural traditions (Judaism, Christianity, Neoplatonism, natural and occult sciences, hermeticism).[99] Basic premises of this proto-science included a sympathetic conception of the universe as open to rational understanding, as well as manipulation. Nature thereby became a source of insight into the workings of God, an alternative mode of unveiling supernatural truth to revelation through Scripture, though the aim was to decode the secret interface between supernatural causation and physio-chemical processes. The declared objective was to discover the forces that animate the universe, which would empower humanity to effect seemingly supernatural changes on matter — most notoriously, of course, the transformation of base substances (such as lead) into gold by means of the philosopher's stone.[100] Renaissance practitioners of alchemy tried to endow their undertaking with the authority of tradition and the patina of age; and one way of doing so was the large-scale co-option of ancient mythography as a body of alchemical writing *avant la lettre*.[101] On the subject of transformative change no author had, naturally, more to offer than Ovid and his *Metamorphoses*, with Virgil coming a close second.[102] Mytho-alchemists read the text as a pragmatic piece of work on transformative change, from chaos to the preparation of the elixir needed to turn base material into precious metal: for obvious reasons, the Medea episode attracted the alchemists' special attention, as a treasured piece of writing in which there were thought to be encoded the secret laws of nature.[103] Overall, the mytho-alchemists initiated a different way of reading classical mythology allegorically, focused not on pagan demons, moral messages, or Christian truths, but the reconciliation of poetry and physics, ancient wisdom and contemporary science, in the quest to articulate a *physica poetica harmonica*.[104]

Alongside alchemy, belief in the efficacy of magical practices remained widespread from antiquity to early-modern times, within the context of both Christian belief and the classical tradition.[105] The divine shape-shifter par excellence is the devil, a creature of transformation both in the popular imagination and high literature (from Milton's *Paradise Lost* to Goethe's *Faust*), often appearing in the shape of a goat or (as in *Faust*) a black dog.[106] Throughout early-modern times, the master deceiver, who also came to preside over the domain of 'experimental knowledge', operated at the interface between science and the supernatural, though generally speaking God himself tended to remain firmly in charge of (un)natural events as the first and final cause.[107]

And yet, the proto-scientific qualities of magic, alchemy, and demonology not-withstanding, the key development for our concerns in the period 1300–1800 is a gradual, if significant parting of the ways of theology and science.[108] Nowadays scholars routinely, and rightly, emphasize that this development was not uni-directional and continue to argue over the main factors and forces that brought the modern age into being — in reaction to such classic accounts as that of Max Weber, who, in his *The Protestant Ethic and the Spirit of Capitalism*, sought to identify the Reformation as the decisive influence in the gradual rise of a secular and materialist conception of nature, to be exploited for capital ventures.[109] Yet while one would be wise to abstain from incorporating the numerous transformative processes that took place in early-modern Europe into a coherent, let alone linear, plot, it remains beyond dispute that radical changes occurred, especially if one fast-forwards to the end of the eighteenth century. By then, the repercussions of the Reformation, the impact of rationalist philosophy in the tradition of Descartes, the empiricism and scepticism of such British and Scottish Enlightenment figures as John Locke, George Berkeley, and David Hume, the 'scientific revolution' more generally, the emergence of capitalist modes of production and the industrial revolution, fuelled by the exploitation of natural resources on an unprecedented scale, as well as a host of other phenomena that we associate with the onset of the modern age, had resulted in a novel conception of nature as the basis for much societal autopoiesis. This entailed, not least, a restrictive reconfiguration of the domains of discourse and practice, in which assertions about the occurrence or possibility of supernaturally induced, and scientifically inexplicable, instances of transformative change could still command respect.

Overall, a shift took place from a view of the natural world as liable to unpredictable supernatural interventions to a universe that follows reliable, mechanical patterns (and hence rules out instances of inexplicable transformative change).[110] Divine omnipotence got curtailed; the devil lost his hold over nature, if not over the imagination. There was a 'growing tendency to regard God less as a busy and unpredictable meddler, than as a distant and passive spectator, a clockmaker deity who did not normally need to tinker with the machine he had created'.[111] In 1788, Friedrich Schiller captured the realities of this brave new world — a universe disenchanted, nature reduced to mechanics — in a wistful evocation of classical Greece via a digest version of Ovid's *Metamorphoses* ('Die Götter Griechenlands', Stanzas 3–5):[112]

> 3
> Wo jetzt nur, wie unsre Weisen sagen,
> Seelenlos ein Feuerball sich dreht,
> Lenkte damals seinen goldnen Wagen
> Helios in stiller Majestät.
> Diese Höhen füllten Oreaden,
> Eine Dryas starb mit jenem Baum,
> Aus den Urnen lieblicher Najaden
> Sprang der Ströme Silberschaum.

> 4
> Jener Lorbeer wand sich einst um Hilfe,
> Tantals Tochter schweigt in diesem Stein,
> Syrinx Klage tönt' aus jenem Schilfe,
> Philomelens Schmerz in diesem Hain.
> Jener Bach empfing Demeters Zähre,
> Die sie um Persephone geweint,
> Und von diesem Hügel rief Cythere,
> Ach, vergebens! ihrem schönen Freund.

> 5
> Zu Deukalions Geschlechte stiegen
> Damals noch die Himmlischen herab;
> Pyrrhas schöne Töchter zu besiegen,
> Nahm Hyperion den Hirtenstab.
> Zwischen Menschen, Göttern und Heroen
> Knüpfte Amor einen schönen Bund,
> Sterbliche mit Göttern und Heroen,
> Huldigten in Amathunt.

> [There, where now, as we're by sages told,
>   Whirls on high a soulless fiery ball,
> Helios guided then his car of gold,
>   In his silent majesty, o'er all.   20
> Oreads then these heights around us filled,
>   Then a dryad died in yonder tree,
> From the urn of loving naiads rilled
>   Silver streamlets foamingly.
>
> Yonder Laurel once imploring wound,   25
>   Tantal's daughter slumbers in this stone;
> From yon rush rose Syrinx' mournful sound,
>   From this thicket Philomela's moan.
> Yonder brook Demeter's tears received,
>   That she wept for her Persephone,   30
> From this hill, of her loved friend bereaved,
>   Cried Cythera, fruitlessly!
>
> To Deucalion's race from realms of air
>   Then the great Immortals still came down;
> And to vanquish Pyrrha's daughter fair,   35
>   Then a shepherd's staff took Hyperion.
> Then 'tween heroes, deities, and men
>   Was a beauteous bond by Eros twined,
> And with deities and heroes then
>   Knelt in Cyprus' Isle mankind.][113]

After deploring the destruction of natural beauty, which, for Schiller, coincided with the extinction of the pagan divinities that animated the classical world (and nature more generally), he singles out two historical forces as the principal culprits: first, Christianity: '*Einen* zu bereichern unter Allen | Mußte diese Götterwelt vergehn' ['To enrich One among all | this world of divinities had to vanish']; then, science:

> Unbewußt der Freuden, die sie schenket,
> Nie entzückt von ihrer Trefflichkeit,
> Nie gewahr des Armes, der sie lenket,
> Reicher nie durch meine Dankbarkeit,
> Fühllos selbst für ihres Künstlers Ehre,
> Gleich dem todten Schlag der Pendeluhr,
> Dient sie knechtisch dem Gesetz der Schwere,
> Die entgötterte Natur.

[Unconscious of the joys she bestows, never enraptured by her own excellence, never aware of the arm that guides her, never richer through my gratitude, insensitive even to the honour of her artist, like the dead beat of the pendulum clock, she slavishly serves the law of gravity, disenchanted Nature.]

Because of its apparent heathen sensibilities, the elegy got a frosty reception in Christian circles.[114] And this reception in itself betokens that Schiller pessimistically overstated the case; miracles and the marvellous, and belief in the existence of supernatural forces that intervene in human affairs, have continued to maintain a presence even after the Enlightenment, and not just in religious institutions (such as the Catholic Church) but in society at large; there are interesting continuities from medieval to modern times in how religious institutions construe perceived interferences of supernatural beings (such as saints) in human affairs.[115] But it is also the case that in a post-Enlightened world certain conceptions of the universe that allowed for various types of transformative change caused by supernatural agents no longer command *scientific* plausibility.

Yet metamorphosis did not simply disappear from the cultural record. Once more the notion proved sufficiently protean to adapt to altered circumstances and new regimes of truth and retain its hold over the imagination. To begin with, during the early-modern period, metamorphosis helped European thinkers, at a time when their geographical horizons were expanding, in negotiating new data and novel experiences. The intermingling of science and fiction in the Age of Discovery in many ways resembles the paradoxography of the Hellenistic age and imperial Rome, not least in the obsession with wonders and marvels.[116] Classical texts contributed their share to efforts to make sense of the new.[117] These included Ovid's *Metamorphoses*: as Marina Warner has shown, in the early-modern period metamorphosis, especially as conceptualized by Ovid, functioned at the interface of the old and the new, the mythic and the scientific, Europe and the newly discovered Americas, as a dynamic principle of creation and as a creative idiom to explore novel insights and experiences.[118] And with the onset of modernity around 1800, metamorphosis had already become established as a key concept in two spheres of endeavour: science and conceptions of the human self.

When the symbolic-theological view of nature as a book of divine creation began to give way to scientific study of natural phenomena, aided, among other things, by the invention of the microscope by the painter Johannes Goedaert (1620–1668), the term 'metamorphosis' was employed to denote transformative biological processes, especially in insects, plants, and amphibian creatures such as frogs. Works from this period, which feature metamorphosis in their title, include Goedaert's own *Metamorphosis et historia naturalis insectorum*, Maria Sibylla Merian's (1647–1717) *Metamorphosis insectorum Surinamensium* (as well as her posthumously published collection *Erucarum ortus alimentum et paradoxa metamorphosis*), and Johann Wolfgang von Goethe's (1749–1832) *Metamorphose der Pflanzen*.[119] The scientific career of metamorphosis in early-modern Europe seems to have had its origins in the renaissance of Ovid.[120] But it is crucial to stress the semantic differentiation of metamorphosis in this period into a scientific and a theological meaning of the term. This differentiation does not come without paradoxical effect: by applying a concept that, in its classical usage, implies a supernatural agent to entirely natural processes of transformative change, early-modern authors used metamorphosis metaphorically (i.e. stripped of its implication of divine involvement) to describe real (in the sense of empirically verifiable) change, while scientists meanwhile stripped the old meaning of metamorphosis of validity, asserting that any supposedly historical record of this phenomenon ought to be either dismissed as fiction or understood metaphorically. Put differently, the old, literal use of metamorphosis came to be perceived, even more strictly than before, as a metaphor, whereas in scientific discourse the new, metaphorical use of the term has come to designate something quite real, shedding its (by now metaphorical) supernatural past.[121] In the medium of poetry, the scientific and the theological meaning of metamorphosis could, of course, still find reconciliation where the latter was allegorical. This can be seen in the song *Raupenleben* by Luise Hensel (1798–1876), in which the transformation of the caterpillar into a butterfly stands allegorically for the ascent of the human soul to heaven. A metamorphosis in nature thus functions here as allegory for the metamorphosis of the soul that Paul mentions in II Corinthians.

The second domain in which metamorphosis has continued to resonate in what could be labelled the modern 'post-metamorphic' age of disenchanted nature is 'the self'. Petrarch's use of Ovid to explore a proto-modern subjectivity in the pursuit of worldly fame — in conscious departure from Christian scripts and expectations — heralded a shift from the divine to the human as the (self-)transformer par excellence. Humanity (as it were) began to make good the power vacuum left by the supernatural beings that science increasingly relegated to the margins. The most striking articulation of the human being as a protean creature arguably occurs in Pico della Mirandola's treatise *De hominis dignitate*, which we already had occasion to cite in the General Introduction. Here are some further sentences:[122]

> Quis hunc nostrum chamaeleonta non admiretur? aut omnino quis aliud quicquam admiretur magis? Quem non immerito Asclepius Atheniensis versipellis huius et se ipsam transformantis naturae argumento per Proteum in mysteriis significari dixit. Hinc illae apud Hebraeos et Pythagoricos metamorphoses celebratae.

> [Who does not admire this our chameleon, or who, at least, feels greater admiration for anything else? Asclepius the Athenian quite rightly said that, on account of his mutability and his self-changing nature, the human being is symbolically represented by Proteus in the mysteries. This is the source of those metamorphoses recorded among the Hebrews and Pythagoreans.]

In his syncretistic citing of evidence, Pico still operates very much within religious traditions of thought: apart from his reference to natural history (the chameleon), he alludes to pagan myth and its divinities (Asclepius, Proteus), occult sciences and hermeticism (*in mysteriis significari*), the Hebrew Scriptures (*apud Hebraeos*) and Greek philosophy (the Pythagoreans). In what follows, he further adduces the transformation of Enoch into an angel and various other humans into other divine beings and makes reference to the New Testament and the Chaldeans. Yet the point of his theological witnesses is a novel emphasis on the power of human beings to transform themselves (and, one might add, each other). In his version of Genesis, the emphasis is on human freedom and emancipation from divine prescriptions and this prefigures both the metamorphic self-fashioning that informs the posthumanist striving of a Nietzsche and the desire of the creature to turn into creator, in what one may call the Frankenstein impulse.

The frontispiece of John Bulwer's *Anthropometamorphosis* nicely epitomizes most of the main issues of the preceding discussion.[123] To begin with, the book has as its central theme various practices of human self-transformation, that is, human beings modifying their bodies in one way or another.[124] Bulwer's use of the term 'metamorphosis' is metaphorical insofar as the changes under discussion

Fig. 4. Frontispiece of John Bulwer, *Anthropometamorphosis*, 1654
Credit: © The British Library

are not genuine instances of transformations in form or substance, but 'cosmetic' interventions and alterations. Crucially, however, the agent of change has become humanity — even though Bulwer situates the practices (of which he disapproves) within a wider supernatural context. His benchmarks are the Judeo-Christian Bible and Nature, while the devil is featured as applauding the deformations. Yet he appears relegated to the margins, as he cackles at God's supreme creature making a mockery of its divine likeness by lowering itself to the level of the beasts: his is the secondary role of cheerleader at the transformative outrages that an emancipated humanity performs upon itself, in violation of divine and natural laws.[125] Furthermore, Bulwer develops his argument within an ethnographic context: his evidence for blasphemous body art comes from across the globe, and he uses the English gentleman as his norm and standard to appraise tribal practices from other geographic regions, achieving a sublime and oblique coincidence of nature and civilization in English Christendom, while portraying other nations as degenerate apostates. In short, the main protagonists and points of reference of transformative change in early-modern Europe — God and his Creation, the Judeo-Christian Bible, natural laws, the devil, the movement of humanity up and down the Ladder of Nature, the tension between divine norms and human agency, Europe (or England) and the wider world — here all come together around the notion of man-made metamorphosis, capturing as in a snapshot the gradual transition from the medieval and early-modern emphasis on supernaturally induced transformative change to the modes of human self-transformations that come to dominate the discourse of metamorphosis in the modern period. But this is the story of Part III, which brings our history of transformative change from the eighteenth century to the present.

The Chapters

The first chapter, by Robert Carver, entitled 'Of Donkeys and D(a)emons: Metamorphosis and the Literary Imagination from Apuleius to Augustine', offers a case study of the crucial transition from a classical-pagan to a biblical-Christian episteme that took shape in late antiquity. His discussion of Apuleius rounds off our coverage of ancient Greece and Rome by bringing into focus the author whose influence on Western conceptions of transformative change has been second to only one, i.e. Ovid and his *Metamorphoses*. But in terms of overall sense and sensibility his novel about Lucius as a protean ass, with its climactic evocation of Eastern mystery religion, comes closer in spirit to Christian experience than the tales from Ovid, not least in its affinity with Platonism — even though he arguably outdoes his Augustan predecessor in ribaldry. Carver then takes his detailed analysis of the types of transformative change present in Apuleius as his point of departure for exploring pagan and patristic views on metamorphosis, culminating in a discussion of the church father Augustine, whose views proved highly influential in defining the place and cultural value of metamorphic possibilities during the medieval period and beyond.

Carlo Caruso's chapter 'Adonis as Citrus Tree: Humanist Transformations of an Ancient Myth' explores the creative engagement of one of the foremost Humanist poets, Giovanni Pontano (1426–1503), with one of the best-known myths from antiquity, the tragic love story of Venus & Adonis. In the unfolding story of this volume, his learned analysis offers a case study from the Italian Renaissance, in which the classical heritage of thought and literature on transformative change itself underwent a radical transformation in terms of cultural value and significance. Caruso uses Pontano's polemic engagement with Ovid and other classical authors for a more general discussion of the various modes in which Renaissance poets and scholars positioned themselves vis-à-vis their classical models, whom they frequently accepted as authorities only to go beyond them. Thus Pontano used the fact that certain pieces of botanical knowledge were not available in antiquity to outdo ancient authors by presenting them as outdated, entailing the need to revisit and update the classical heritage in a contemporary key. The chapter's emphasis on the interface between myth and astrology is particularly welcome, given the crucial importance that astrological implications assumed in the transmission (and the Renaissance revival) of pagan mythology.

Robert Carver's second contribution to the volume, 'Defacing God's Work: Metamorphosis and the "Mimicall Asse" in the Age of Shakespeare', offers a counterpart to Caruso's focus on Italy with a discussion of metamorphosis in the English Renaissance. This chapter also continues the story of the reception of Apuleius within the context of Christian daemonology, considering the playwrights John Lyly (1553/54–1606), Christopher Marlowe (1564–1593), and, above all, William Shakespeare (1564–1616), with a coda on Milton's *Paradise Lost*. Among other things, Carver's discussion brings out the complex interlacing of various ways of thinking transformative change in the early-modern period.

In the final chapter of Part II, '*Phantastica Mutatio*: Johann Weyer's Critique of the Imagination as a Principle of Natural Metamorphosis', Guido Giglioni uses the Dutch physician Johann Weyer (1515–1588), to whom Carver gestures briefly, to trace a gradual shift in how early-modern thinkers conceived of the transformative powers of the human imagination. If figures such as Pietro Pomponazzi (1462–1525) and Paracelsus (1493–1541) supposed that our imagination, especially when under the influence of demonic forces and the devil, could alter reality in its most physical aspects, Weyer rejected this view. He confined the impact of the imagination on reality to the domain of appearances, wishful thinking and storytelling. While Weyer remained convinced of the ability of demons and the devil to modify *perceptions* of reality and desires in the human mind, he was one of the pre-Enlightenment thinkers who helped to move Western cultural history into its 'post-metamorphic' phase.

Appendix: The Verso to the Frontispiece of Bulwer's *Anthropometamorphosis*

The Intent of the Frontispiece Unfolded

The high *commission* from Heaven granted for the triall of the *Artificiall changling* upon the matter of *Fact*, touching *Man's Transformation*, is exhibited by the *Letters Pattents*, or *Great Charter of Nature*, ingrossed with a *Sun beame*, and signed with the *Broad-Seale of Heaven*, presented by a *Hand*, extended out of a *Cloud*: The *crowned Scepter* in the other *out-stretched Hand*, shews the *Government of the World* is by the *Laws of Nature* established from the Creation, and that the forme of proceedings is according to that *un-repealed Statute*. The *perpendicular Ray* intimates that formidable sentence which (as it is to be feared) shall be pronounced at the generall day of Judgement against all *abusers of their Bodies*, who have new-made and deformed themselves. *I know you not, neither are you the workes of my Hands*. The *Angell*, by motto, expresseth, *That God made man righteous, but he hath found out many inventions*. The *Devill* is figured rejoycing at the practicall and abusive *Metamorphosis of Man*, with a *ha, ha, he; In the image of God created he them! but I have new-moulded them to my own likenesse*. The *Creatures*, the *Asse*, the *Leopard*, the *Hound*, and the *Ape*, admiring at the degenerate *Apostasie of Man*, from the originall perfections of his true Shape, cry out, *Behold Man is become as one of us!* A *Tent* being pitched *sub Dio*, over the *Valence*, whereof, the title is inscribed *Anthropometamorphosis*, or the *Transformation of Man*, *Nature*, with all the *Hieroglyphicall Equipage of her Power*, being seated upon the *Tribunall*, our *Prototypes Adam* and *Eve* Assessors, the *two Books* being laid open, one of the *use of parts*, the other of the *abuse of parts*, is read, at which the Ghost of *Galen* appears, as raised up at the report of the prodigious *abuse of parts*: Which being urged and prosecuted by *Natures Solicitor* against the *Nations at the Bar*, who plead *Guilty*, and submit themselves to be try'd by *God* and *Nature*, thereupon the *Ocular witnesses* are brought into Court, and sworne upon a *Book* to testifie and give in evidence of the whole truth, and nothing but the truth. A *Jury* being Empannelled, the *Foreman*, after consultation, brings in a *Bill*, signed *Billa Vera*, which implies the Inditement is sound; whereby these Nations are judged guilty of *high Treason* against *Nature*, *Judgement* is passed on them to suffer according to their demerits, the *Court* rose up, and adjourn'd untill the last *Great Assizes* and *Session*.

Notes to the Introduction

1. For context see e.g. Bowie (2001).
2. See e.g. I. 30. 3, where Pausanias mentions Cycnus' transformation into a swan as defying belief (γενέσθαι δέ μοι ἄπιστον ὄρνιθα ἀπ᾽ ἀνδρός) or I. 41. 9, where he touches upon the story of Tereus, Procne, and Philomela. In his version, Tereus committed suicide, whereas Procne and Philomela both died of grief, after which people invented their metamorphosis into nightingale and swallow on account of the plaintive song of the birds. See further Buxton (2009), p. 136.
3. VIII. 2. 3. For the archaeological evidence of Arcadian cult practice and the mythic discourse of Arcadia see the studies by Jost (1994) (1998).

4. Contrast the view of Pausanias' near-contemporary Pliny the Elder, who dismisses the Arcadian tales of human-wolf transformations (and vice versa) as an example of the extent to which Greek credulity will go, disapprovingly generalizing, from the imperial superiority of Roman common sense, that in Greece one can find a (false) witness for any nonsense imaginable (*Natural History*, viii. 80–82; *mirum est quo procedat Graeca credulitas! nullum tam impudens mendacium est, ut teste careat*). Despite Pliny, werewolves have, of course, persisted to haunt the Western imagination, from Petronius' *Satyricon* to those of medieval Ulster (recorded by Gerald of Wales in 1187: Bynum (2001), pp. 15–18 and 195 n. 1) to the American werewolves of modern cinema in London (1981) and Paris (1997). The literature is vast: see e.g. Copper (1977), Wooward (1979), Otten (1986), Douglas (1994), and Veenstra (2002). For more on werewolves, see Chapter 8 (Guido Giglioni), which includes a discussion of Johann Weyer's (1515–1588) rationalization of lycanthropy as a mental illness induced or strengthened by the devil.

5. For the wider significance of the cross-cultural dimension of this chronological distinction, see e.g. Elsner (1992) and Bowie (1996).

6. viii. 2. 5: οὔτε θεὸς ἐγίνετο οὐδεὶς ἔτι ἐξ ἀνθρώπου, πλὴν ὅσον λόγῳ καὶ κολακείᾳ πρὸς τὸ ὑπερέχον, καὶ ἀδίκοις τὸ μήνιμα τὸ ἐκ τῶν θεῶν ὀψέ τε καὶ ἀπελθοῦσιν ἐνθένδε ἀπόκειται. His attack on apotheosis by flattery prefigures his sarcastic comments on the deification (entailing an empire-wide cult) of Hadrian's darling Antinoos at viii. 9. 7. See Hutton (2005), pp. 318–21 and, more generally, Lafond (2001).

7. viii. 2. 6–7: [...] καὶ οὕτω τοῖς ἀληθέσιν ἐλυμήναντο, συγκεραννύντες αὐτὰ ἐψευσμένοις.

8. See Habicht (1985), p. 220.

9. See esp. viii. 3. 6–7, where he recounts the story of Callisto (Lycaon's daughter), including her transformation into a bear and ultimate catasterism. Pausanias here stresses that he is (merely) repeating the story as told by the Greeks and concludes by suggesting that the constellation may simply have been *named* in Callisto's honour given that the Arcadians showcase her grave.

10. Veyne (1988), pp. 99–100, 151 n. 194. Pausanias himself seems to suggest that the experience of Arcadia constituted something of a caesura in his thinking about old religious lore, acknowledging the possibility that some of the ancient tales are riddles (*ainigmata*) full of wisdom that require decoding: viii. 8. 2; see further Hutton (2005), pp. 303–11. This approach has strong affinities with practices of allegoresis, on which see further below.

11. We limit our discussion to the metamorphic aspects of the Christian faith as set out in the New Testament, where they are confined to bare essentials — in contrast to apocryphal texts, some of which configure Christ as inherently polymorph: see Klauck (2008), ch. 7 ('Christus in vielen Gestalten: Die Polymorphie des Erlösers in apokryphen Texten'), who begins his discussion with the programmatic quotation of the proem to Ovid's *Metamorphoses*.

12. We give the Greek of the Septuagint. See further Bachmann (2009) and Reed (2005).

13. Cf. Genesis 6. 4, which is rather reminiscent of Hesiod's *Catalogue of Women*: 'There were giants in the earth in those days; and also after that, when the sons of God came in unto the daughters of men, and they bare *children* to them, the same *became* mighty men which *were* of old, men of renown.' The King James Version appears to flatten out the Greek of the Septuagint, where the offspring of the sons of God and the daughters of men clearly *are* the giants: οἱ δὲ γίγαντες ἦσαν ἐπὶ τῆς γῆς ἐν ταῖς ἡμέραις ἐκείναις καὶ μετ' ἐκεῖνο, ὡς ἂν εἰσεπορεύοντο οἱ υἱοὶ τοῦ θεοῦ πρὸς τὰς θυγατέρας τῶν ἀνθρώπων καὶ ἐγεννῶσαν ἑαυτοῖς· ἐκεῖνοι ἦσαν οἱ γίγαντες οἱ ἀπ' αἰῶνος, οἱ ἄνθρωποι οἱ ὀνομαστοί. In Genesis, of course, divine displeasure at human sinfulness and the Flood follows right after the quoted passage, wiping this hybrid generation of heroic (or gigantic) individuals from the face of the earth and enacting a watershed that divides human history into two ages, each with its own peculiar interface between the human and the supernatural spheres. Giants, let alone sex between divine offspring and mortal women, disappear from the narrative world of the Bible. Genesis thus operates with a periodization not unlike that of Hesiod and Pausanias.

14. We cite the translation of D. C. Olson, *Enoch: A New Translation. The Ethiopic Book of Enoch, or 1 Enoch, Translated with Annotations and Cross-References* (North Richland Hills, TX: BIBAL Press, 2004).

15. *Sermo*, xlvii. 12. 21; see e.g. Dunn (1989).

16. See also his *Adversus Praxeam*, 27. 10–11, a treatise in which Tertullian tries to refute the heretical

opinion that God the Father was incarnate. He rejects this on the grounds that this would imply God to have undergone a metamorphosis — a clear impossibility.

17. See e.g. Kuschel (1990) with O'Leary (1992) or Swinburne (1994), Chapter 9: 'The Possibility of Incarnation', who argues that the human nature that God assumed in the incarnation 'must be regarded not as a substance, but as the contingent properties [...] that make someone human.'

18. For a detailed account see Clauss (2011).

19. For its influence in Western literature and thought from the point of view of cultural history (rather than theology) see Kablitz (2003).

20. Compare Matthew 17. 1–8, esp. 2: καὶ μετεμορφώθη ἔμπροσθεν αὐτῶν, καὶ ἔλαμψεν τὸ πρόσωπον αὐτοῦ ὡς ὁ ἥλιος, τὰ δὲ ἱμάτια αὐτοῦ ἐγένετο λευκὰ ὡς τὸ φῶς ['And he was transfigured before them: and his face did shine as the sun, and his raiment was white as the light']. With its insistent focus on light (and his choice of the sun, rather than the bleaching capabilities of a fuller, as a point of comparison) Matthew's account puts much greater emphasis on the transcendent qualities of the event. Even the cloud that appears to throw its shadow over the proceedings, which in Mark has no attribute, Matthew calls 'shining' (17. 5: νεφέλη φωτεινὴ ἐπεσκίασεν αὐτούς), establishing a lexical nexus between the shining of Jesus and the sphere of the divine: the shining cloud is the site of the voice of God, claiming Jesus as his son (ἰδοὺ φωνὴ ἐκ τῆς νεφέλης λέγουσα, Οὗτός ἐστιν ὁ υἱός μου ὁ ἀγαπητός). Classical rhetoricians would have drawn attention to the alliteration, or indeed faux *figura etymologica*, that links the different aspects of the multi-media spectacle λευκὰ ὡς τὸ φῶς, νεφέλη φωτεινὴ and φωνὴ ἐκ τῆς νεφέλης. Luke (9. 28–36) avoids the verb μεταμορφόω in noting that the appearance of Jesus' face changed and his clothes became shining white: καὶ ἐγένετο ἐν τῷ προσεύχεσθαι αὐτὸν τὸ εἶδος τοῦ προσώπου αὐτοῦ ἕτερον καὶ ὁ ἱματισμὸς αὐτοῦ λευκὸς ἐξαστράπτων; in his account, the cloud has no attribute, but envelops Jesus' followers (9. 34).

21. Mystery religion: Reitzenstein (1927); epiphany: Heil (2000); Jewish eschatology and Christology: Kee (1972), pp. 137–52, Mach (1992), Fossum (1995), Fletcher-Louis (1997), pp. 38–50 and 223–24, and (2001).

22. Schnapp (1986), p. 91 n. 25. For the Eastern tradition see Andreopoulos (2005); for the notion in patristic literature, Chamberas (1970).

23. Gnilka (1988), p. 94.

24. Vermes (2008), p. 2.

25. Mark 8. 32, 9. 32; Luke 9. 45, 18. 34. See also e.g. 1 Corinthians 1. 23–24 and, more generally, Cousar (1990). In classical literature and culture, the resurrection of the dead belongs into the domain of necromancy: see Ogden (2001) and, for Greek beliefs in the resurrection of the body as a key enabling factor in the spread of Christianity, Øistein Endsjø (2009).

26. For discussion, see e.g. Götz (2002), pp. 25–27 (including references to earlier literature) and, for the history of reception (notably in Kierkegaard), Bühler (2008).

27. Bockmuehl (2001), p. 103.

28. Dunn (2001), p. 301.

29. See also Luke 22. 19–20; 1 Corinthians 11. 17–34. The literature is of course vast. See e.g. Klauck (1982) and Klawans (2002).

30. *De corpore et sanguine Domini* I.

31. Chazelle (1992), Zirkel (1994).

32. For medieval times, see e.g. Jorissen (1965), Macy (1984) and (1994), Goering (1991), Rubin (1991), Laarmann (1999); for early-modern times, the collection of primary sources edited by Scheib (2008); and for contemporary views, Ratzinger (1967) and Wohlmuth (2002).

33. Scheib (2008), p. 15 n. 11; Macy (1991).

34. *queritur si mus sumit corpus christi. Respondet magister, non. Sed quod sumat? Deus novit. Potest tamen dici quod mus sumat cum enim pessimus homo ipsum sumat. Quare non mus? Non est ratio (Summa, c. 7); see Macy (1991), p. 160 (Langton) and p. 159 (Gerald).*

35. *Ego Berengarius corde credo et ore confiteor, panem et vinum, quae ponuntur in altari, per mysterium sacrae orationis et verba nostri Redemptoris substantialiter converti in veram et propriam ac vivificatricem carnem et sanguinem Iesu Christi Domini nostri et post consecrationem esse verum Christi corpus, quod natum est de Virgine et quod pro salute mundi oblatum in cruce pependit, et quod sedet ad dexteram Patris, et verum sanguinem Christi, qui de latere eius effusus est, non tantum per signum et virtutem sacramenti, sed*

in proprietate naturae et veritate substantiae [...]: H. Denzinger, *Enchiridion symbolorum, definitionum et declarationum de rebus fidei et morum (Kompendium der Glaubensbekenntnisse und kirchlichen Lehrentscheidungen)*, revised by P. Hünermann, 37th edition (Freiburg: Herder, 1991).

36. (b) and (c) imply a departure from the principles of Aristotelian metaphysics, 'which set the parameters concerning how the structure and characteristics of material beings had to be understood', or, put differently, involve a miracle — an anomaly that could not be accounted for on the basis of the prevailing knowledge about nature: Colish (2004), pp. 381–82.

37. *Distinguendum est tamen subtiliter inter tria, quae sunt in hoc sacramento discreta, videlicet formam visibilem, veritatem corporis et virtutem spiritualem. Forma est panis et vini, veritas carnis et sanguinis, virtus unitatis et caritatis.* He presided over the Fourth (ecumenical) Lateran Council of 1215, which uses the formulation *transsubstantiatis pane in corpus et vino in sanguinem potestate divina*: H. Denzinger, *Enchiridion symbolorum, definitionum et declarationum de rebus fidei et morum (Kompendium der Glaubensbekenntnisse und kirchlichen Lehrentscheidungen)*, revised by P. Hünermann, 37th edition (Freiburg: Herder, 1991), p. 802; Scheib (2008), p. 11.

38. *Summa contra gentiles*, IV. 61 and 63–65; Scheib (2008), pp. 39–53.

39. A further reiteration of the Church's commitment to the reality of the event occurs in the encyclical *Ecclesia de Eucharistia*, published on 17 April 2003, by Pope John Paul II: '*The Eucharist is a true banquet*, in which Christ offers himself as our nourishment' (Chapter 1. 16). See Pitchers (2004).

40. See further the papers in Burnham and Giaccherini (eds) (2005).

41. The pair of conform ~ transform reproduces the etymological play of the Latin: *et nolite conformari huic saeculo sed reformamini in novitate sensus vestri.*

42. Furnish (1984), pp. 240–41.

43. Back (2002) offers an exhaustive discussion of the cited passages and parallel texts.

44. According to Paul, Christ's death on the cross has opened the path to heaven for humanity at large. As discussed in the General Introduction, 1 Corinthians 15. 51–53 explores the eschatological significance of the event in terms of a transformative change from mortality to immortality. For discussion of the historical background and history of reception, see e.g. Day (1995), Perkins (2009), Bynum (1995); Nicklas, Reiterer, and Verheyden (2009).

45. See e.g. Freccero (1975) p. 36: 'Conversion demands that there be both a continuity and a discontinuity between the self that is and the self that was.'

46. Mark 9. 9–10; see Harvey (1994).

47. Davis (1997).

48. For the figure and his reception, see Most (2005), who gives special attention to Caravaggio's iconic painting. For a recent response, see Chris Gollon's painting 'Doubting Thomas (After Caravaggio)': illustration and discussion in Pickeral (2010), pp. 168–69.

49. Stanton (1994). For the historical context see e.g. Mettinger (2001) and Vermes (2008).

50. See Lapide (1983), further: Avery-Peck and Neusner (2000).

51. For the 'Mosaic distinction', see Assmann (2003).

52. Exodus 20. 2–17; Deuteronomy 5. 6–21.

53. We simplify, of course. For a more complex version of the story see Dowden (2000).

54. Horstmann (1979), p. 7: 'Das *frühe Christentum* sieht in den antiken Mythen durchweg das konkurrierende System heidnischer Theologie, deren Gehalt an Lehre es folglich auszuschalten sucht'. For recent work, including on the shift from apologetics to aggression in the wake of the Constantinian turn, see the papers in Ulrich, Jacobsen, and Kahlos (2009).

55. See Kaster (1988) and now also Cameron (2011).

56. Momigliano (1963) p. 81.

57. Seznec (1953).

58. A much-investigated phenomenon: see e.g. the studies by Gnilka (1984) (1993), Fuhrmann (1990), Fiedrowicz (2000), and the papers in Haehling (2005).

59. Different texts presented different challenges: in the case of Cicero, for instance, it was not primarily the contents of his writings that caused Christians problems (though that, too) as the aesthetic allure of his Latinity, which is stylistically far superior (and hence pleasurable) than the — from a classical point of view substandard — Latin in which the Scriptures were written, a fact that caused many an educated Christian considerable nightmares, most notably Jerome.

60. Christians were of course preceded by classical thinkers in using this ploy (notably Plato); and the concept of fiction (and its historical variations) is, as goes without saying, itself a fraught and problematic concept. See above Introduction to Part I.

61. For a medieval perspective on the phenomenon see Dronke (1974), pp. 13–78 ('Chapter 1: *Fabula*: Critical Theories').

62. Recent secondary literature includes: Green (1982), Meyers (2004), Herren (2007). For the history of reception of this highly popular work, which has survived in more than two hundred manuscripts, see Quinn (1971).

63. Given the lack of reliable information about author and date, the poem has proven notoriously difficult to contextualize. Herren (2007) argues that the poem reflects an age in which the 'hidden truth' of pagan fables began to exert a renewed fascination as a source of insight into morality, happiness, truth and hope of salvation that could rival Scripture. If Phronesis in the end decides in favour of Alithia (how could she not?), the contest over Pseustis is hard-won: the *Ecloga* 'appears to represent a growing realization that pagan literature was not as harmless as it purported to be' (pp. 216–17).

64. ὅτι μέγας κύριος καὶ αἰνετὸς σφόδρα, | φοβερός ἐστιν ἐπὶ πάντας τοὺς θεούς· | ὅτι πάντες οἱ θεοὶ τῶν ἐθνῶν δαιμόνια, | ὁ δὲ κύριος τοὺς οὐρανοὺς ἐποίησεν· ['For the Lord *is* great, and greatly to be praised: he *is* to be feared above all gods. For all the gods of the nations *are* idols: but the Lord made the heavens']. The King James Version turns what are literally 'demons' in the Septuagint into objects. See Horstmann (1979), pp. 8–9 with references to demons in patristic sources in n. 25.

65. Augustine, *de Civitate Dei*, XVIII. 18. For further elaboration of this tradition of thought see Chapter 5 (Robert Carver).

66. See Whitbread (1972), Tunberg (1987), and Rädle (1997), pp. 156–62, who discusses passages in which the teacher argues that even the producers of falsehoods are creatures of the Divine Creator and have thereby some connection to the realm of truth.

67. *Divine Institutes*, I. 5. 13: 'Ovid, too, at the beginning of his work, acknowledges without any verbal subterfuge that the world was made by God, whom he calls "craftsman of the world" and "artisan of all"'; cf. *Met.* I. 57 and 79; See also II. 8. 63–64: *sanctae litterae docent hominem fuisse ultimum dei opus; [...] idem [...] poetae fatentur. Ovidius perfecto iam mundo et universis animalibus figuratis hoc addidit: 'sanctius his animal [...] natus homo est'* (= *Met.* 1.76/8) ['Holy Scripture teaches that the human being was the work of God. [...] even the poets acknowledged it. Ovid, after recounting the creation of the universe and the formation of all the animals, added the following: "an animal more sacred than these [...] the human was made".'] Lactantius subtly reinforces his point by oblique lexical parallels: *sanctae litterae ~ sanctius his animal*.

68. Fiedrowicz (2000), pp. 152–54.

69. Cf. *Apologeticum*, XXI.8.

70. *Sin autem infideles erunt, legant quindecim libros Nasonis Metamorphoseos, et omnem Graecam, Latinamque historiam, ibique cernent vel Daphnen in laurum, vel Phaetontis sorores in populos arbores fuisse conversas: quomodo Jupiter eorum sublimissimus deus, sit mutatus in cygnum, in auro fluxerit, in tauro rapuerit, et caetera, in quibus ipsa turpitudo fabularum, divinitatis denegat sanctitatem. Illis credunt, et dicunt Deo cuncta possibilia: et cum turpibus credant, potentiaque Dei universa defendant, eamdem virtutem non tribuunt et honestis.* See Hagendahl (1958), pp. 210–11.

71. See Ohly (1979), p. 149 n. 35. He notes: 'Die Herkunft dieser Typen aus Ovid hat Franz von Retz kaschiert, indem er jeweils Augustin als Quelle nennt.'

72. An early proponent of this approach is Lactantius, *Divine Institutes*, I. 11. 30: *nihil igitur a poëtis in totum fictum est: aliquid fortasse traductum et oblique figuratione obscuratum, quo veritas involuta tegeretur* ('No poetical work is a total fiction. There is some element perhaps of adaptation and concealment by metaphor so that the truth can be hidden in wraps', trans. by Bowen and Garnsey).

73. Some recent bibliography includes Allen (1970), Pépin (1976), Haug (1979), Whitman (1987) (2003), Copeland and Melville (1991), Horn and Walter (1997), Boys-Stones (2003), Pérez-Jean and Eichel-Lojkine (2004); Dahan and Goulet (2005), Copeland and Struck (2010).

74. See the papers in Copeland and Struck (2010) for a cutting-edge discussion of allegory from antiquity to the present and up-to-date bibliography.

75. See e.g. Hagedorn (2005).

76. *Littera gesta docet, quid credes allegoria,* | *Moralis quid agas, quo tendas anagogia* ['The letter teaches what happened, the allegorical what to believe, the moral what to do, the anagogical toward what to aspire']. Two classic studies are De Lubac (1959–64) and Auerbach (1959).

77. Theodulf, *Carmen* 45 (*De libris quos legere solebam et qualiter fabulae poetarum a philosophis mystice pertractentur*), 17–20: *Et modo Pompeium, modo te, Donate, legebam,* | *et modo Virgilium, te modo, Naso loquax.* | *In quorum dictis quamquam sint frivola multa,* | *plurima sub falso tegmine vera latent.*

78. Luther, *Commentary on Genesis*, ch. 30, quoted in J. Engels, 'Berchoriana I: Notice bibliographique sur Pierre Bersuire, Supplement au Repertorium Biblicum Medii Aevi', *Vivarium*, II (1964), p. 69; see Allen (1971) p. 12 n. 20.

79. For discussion of the quotation and the broader spirit of Humanism that animates it see Moss (1997). She observes that with the rise of humanism and in the aftermath of the Reformation the paradigm of reading that applied techniques of allegoresis both to Scripture and pagan fables broke down (p. 397).

80. Good accounts of the basic trends are available in Coulson (1987) (2007).

81. For the Latin text, see Coulson (1991): *Notandum autem est quod quadruplex est mutacio: naturalis, moralis, magica, et spiritualis. Naturalis est que fit per contexionem elementorum et retexionem uel mediante semine uel sine semine. Per contexionem enim conueniunt elementa et de spermate nascitur puer, et de ouo pullus, et de semine herba siue* | *arbor, et sic de consimilibus et hoc mediante semine; per retexionem uero sicut fit dissolucio in quolibet corpore, et hoc sine semine, et quantum ad elementa <et> quantum ad yle. Elementa, sicut fit quando terra rarescit in aquam, aqua leuigatur in aera, aer tenuatur in aquam, aqua conglobatur in terram. Et hec mutacio naturalis est de qua facit mencionem in ultimo Pitagoras dicens 'quatuor eternus genitalia corpora mundus continet' etc. Moralis est que attenditur circa mores, uidelicet cum mores inmutantur, vt de Licaone dicitur quod de homine mutatus est in lupum, quod est dicere de benigno in raptorem, et sic de consimilibus que in moribus attenduntur. Est autem magica mutacio que circa artem magicam attenditur et fit tantum in corpore quando uidelicet magi aliquid alterius essencie quam sit per artem magicam faciunt apparere, vt ostendit de Circe que per artem magicam legitur socios Vlixis in porcos mutauisse. Hec autem ars, scilicet magica, fuit antiquitus in ualore, in dampnacionem cuius lex dedit preceptum tale: 'alienam segetem ne pellexeris' id est ne transtuleris. Segetes enim de agro in agrum per artem magicam transferebant. Spiritualis mutacio est que attenditur in corpore et in spiritu, quando scilicet corpus sanum efficitur morbidum, et inde uexatur spiritus et sic spiritus cum corpore pariter inmutatur, ut apparet in freneticis et in aliis morbidis; in spiritu quidem tantum ut de sano fit insanus, sicut legitur de Horeste et de Agaue que proprium filium, scilicet Pentheum, membratim dilacerauit et <sic> de consimilibus. In presenti opere de omnibus agit actor.*

82. Brownlee (1978) (1984a) (1985) (1986) (1993); see also Barolini (1987/1989), Levenstein (1996), Wetherbee (2008).

83. We cite the translation of Inferno by R. and J. Hollander (New York: Doubleday/Anchor, 2000). For Dante's use of metamorphosis in this canto, see e.g. Gross (1985), and for his engagement with Ovid (including the metapoetic theme of theft), Ginsberg (1991) and Cioffi (1994).

84. The text is available via the Dartmouth Dante Project at <http://dante.dartmouth.edu/>.

85. Benvenuto da Imola's commentary can be accessed on the Dartmouth Dante Project (see preceding note).

86. On Dante's championship of his native Italian over Latin see further Brownlee (1984b).

87. The first four words of the *Metamorphoses* (*in nova fert animus*) form a self-contained unit of meaning; the reader only realizes when reaching the first word of line 2 (*corpora*) that *nova* is an attribute, rather than an adjective functioning as a noun ('novel things').

88. Bibliography comes in bulk. But see e.g. Sturm-Maddox (1985), Marcozzi (2001) and Cipollone (2009).

89. Bibliography includes: Brenkmann (1974), Freccero (1975), Rivero (1979), Stierle (1991), Cipollone (1998).

90. Stierle (1991), p. 27: 'Erst Petrarca gelingt es, die Tiefe des poetischen Ich wirklich zur Anschauung zu bringen. "Nel dolce tempo" ist das Gedicht einer bis zu den Grenzen der Ich-Gefährdung und Ich-Zerstörung reichenden psychischen Spannung des durch die unerfüllt bleibende Liebe in Grenzsituationen der Erfahrung getriebenen Ich.' But his (conventional) contrast between Ovid and Petrarch (p. 33: 'Der Schauplatz der Ovidschen Metamorphosen

ist die Welt. Der Schauplatz von Petrarcas Metamorphosen ist das Ich') is too sharp: Ovid was interested in both. See Frécaut (1985).

91. Barkan (1975), p. 6: 'It is a truism that in the Renaissance men turned from pure contemplation of God to contemplation of themselves'; Stierle (2003).

92. The choice of the golden shower as iconic image of the sex Petrarch did not have may contain an implicit dig at Augustine, who, in his *Confessions*, indexed the myth as an instance of pagan blasphemy (I. 16. 26), but admitted to being unable to abstain from the pleasures of the flesh.

93. Unsurprisingly, the final stanza also engages Dante: see Cipollone (1998).

94. Bynum (2001), p. 177, cited by Fowler (2006), p. 389, whose own study illustrates the enduring power of myth as a medium to articulate personal experience and fashion an 'I' in contemporary writing. See further Introduction to Part III.

95. Literature on the reception of Ovid's *Metamorphoses* is legion, both in terms of general surveys and studies of particular Ovidian myths and their resonance and re-appropriation through the ages. A selective bibliography includes Barkan (1986), Wall (1988), Barnard (1987), Mayer and Neumann (1997), Stoichita (2008), Martindale (1988), Lyne (2001), the chapters on reception in Hardie (2002b) and the papers in Dente, Ferzoco, Gill, and Spunta (2005), Keith and Rupp (2007), and Coelsch-Foisner and Görtschacher (2009).

96. Book I, Chapter 11: *De uxore Loth in statuam salis mutata*; PL 35, 2161–62: *[...] Et non solum in lacrymis, sed etiam in phlegmate, et tussi expresso sputo pectoris sapitur, quod salis natura per humanum corpus inseratur. Potens ergo rerum gubernator, cum totum in partem vertere cupit, quod in modica parte latebat, per totum infundit. Atque hac ex causa, cum uxorem Loth in statuam salis vertere voluit, pars illa tenuissima salis quae carni inerat, totum corpus infecit. [...]*

97. Book III, Chapter 2: *De Incarnatione Domini nostri Jesu Christi, et nativitate ex Maria Virgine: Quam rem ne sine exemplo naturae alicujus, velut novam in Dei creaturis dimittamus, multa animantia absque parentum coitu progigni comprobamus. Qualiter apes sine patribus fotu materni corporis tantummodo crescunt, et omnia illius modi volatilia fetus suos taliter concipiunt. Sed et multae aves absque maribus ova gignere possunt. Et talem conceptum in multis piscium generibus esse physiologi aiunt. In sola quoque carne sine patre vermis nascitur, cui se Dominus hac de causa similem dicere per prophetam non dedignatur* (Psal. XXI, 7). *Quod ergo in multis rebus consueto more Dominus operatur, quid, naturae contrarium dicendum est, si quando ipse voluit, ut in virginali utero Spiritus sancti dispensatione filius sine viri coitu nasceretur.*

98. *De Natura Rerum* 1–2.

99. Telle (1980), p. 154: 'Ausgelöst durch Impulse des Renaissancehumanismus und durch die Wirkkraft italienischen Platonismus zusätzlich bestärkt, nahmen Alchemisten in einem gegenwärtig nur unzureichend bekannten Ausmaß antike Dichtungen in die Reihe ihrer Informationsquellen auf.' The most famous representative of this tendency is Pico della Mirandola who features prominently in our story: Telle (1980), p. 139 n. 14. For the evolution of early-modern alchemy into modern chemistry, see e.g. Read (1957). Critical voices — notably Francis Bacon — emerged early: Rossi (1974).

100. Borchardt (1990). (The article begins with a good survey of the development of this field of scholarship from the beginnings in the late nineteenth century (pp. 57–59) and stresses that 'among the *magi* around the year 1500, magic was an act of piety, even of intense piety', based on the premise that God existed and had created an orderly universe that operated according to a secret code that could be cracked and then put to use (p. 72).)

101. Telle (1980), esp. 143–44. He notes that the identification of medieval precedents proves difficult: 'Verläßliche Aussagen über das Fortleben mythologischer Überlieferungen in der Alchemieliteratur des lateinischen Mittelalters sind uns beim gegenwärtigen Stand der Texterschließung verwehrt' (p. 138).

102. Rice (1976), DeVun (2008), Kuntze (1912), Zika (2002). Virgil became a 'magician' in the Middle Ages: see Comparetti (1966). Alchemists were particularly intrigued by his story of the golden bow.

103. See e.g. [Anon.], *Medea spagyrica, seu Metamorphoseos Ovidiane pars ea quae artis physiochem. arcana continet* (seventeenth/eighteenth century): Telle (1980), p. 141.

104. Telle (1980), p. 148. He refers to J. H. Alsted, 'Physica poetica harmonica: hoc est, Consensus poëtarum et physicorum', in *Physica harmonica* (Herborn 1616), pp. 271–81.

105. Studies include Thorndike (1923–58), Walker (1958), Thomas (1971), Bremmer and Veenstra (2002), Burnett and Ryan (2006), Zambelli (2007), Saunders (2010).

106. See e.g. Brunner Ungricht (1988), pp. 103–04 for the role of the devil in German fairy tales.

107. Walsham (2008), p. 524, with reference to Schmidt (1998); Clark (1991) (1997).

108. For the big picture, see e.g. Luhmann (1997). More fine-grained historical accounts of modern science include the papers in Daston and Lunbeck (2011) and Livingstone and Withers (2011) with Jardine (2011).

109. The work first appeared as two essays in 1904 and 1905 in *Archiv für Sozialwissenschaft und Sozialpolitik* XX and XXI, which Weber republished in the form of a revised monograph in 1920 (*Die Protestantische Ethik und der Geist des Kapitalismus*); for critique and discussion of the Weberian paradigm and the foregrounding of the Reformation, see e.g. Walsham (2008), Borutta (2010), Steinert (2010), and Weltecke (2010), pp. 96–99.

110. In a sense, this constitutes a return to a Lucretian-Epicurean conception of the world, and recent scholarship has emphasized the importance of the rediscovery of a manuscript of the *De Rerum Natura*, which had fallen out of circulation, in 1417 by Poggio Bracciolini for the development of scientific thinking in the West. See Brown (2010), Greenblatt (2011), and Passannante (2011).

111. Walsham (2008), p. 524.

112. Edition: Friedrich Schiller, *Werke und Briefe*, vol. 1, ed. by G. Kurscheidt (Frankfurt a. M.: Deutscher Klassiker Verlag, 1992), first version: pp. 285–91; second version: pp. 162–65. We are citing from the first version. The translation is by E. A. Bowring (slightly adjusted), in *Poems of Places: An Anthology in 31 Volumes*, ed. by Henry Wadsworth Longfellow. Boston: James R. Osgood & Co., 1876–79. Bibliography includes Berghahn (1985), Koopmann (1996), Frick (1998), Zimmermann (2008).

113. The references are to *Met.* I. 451–567 (laurel, i.e. Apollo and Daphne), VI. 146–312 (Tantalus' daughter, i.e. Niobe), I. 689–712 (Pan and Syrinx), VI. 412–674 (Philomela), V. 332–571 (Demeter and Persephone), X. 503–739 (Cythera, i.e. Venus, and Adonis), I. 313–415 (Deucalion and Pyrrha), and II. 676–85 (Apollo as shepherd). Amathus is a city on the southern coast of Cypris, famous for its rich ore and sacred to Aphrodite. Ovid mentions the place at *Met.* X. 220, 227, and 531.

114. On the reception, see Gerhard (1942), Fambach (1957), Frühwald (1969), Dahnke (1989), Oellers (2002); on Schiller and religion more generally: Oellers (2006).

115. For medieval times, see the recent study by Koopmans (2011); for today, the procedure that led to the elevation of the former Pope John Paul II to the status of a saint on 1 May 2011 after Vatican officials had ascertained that he miraculously cured a French nun of Parkinson's disease from the beyond.

116. This phenomenon has received much attention in recent years: see Ryan (1981), Kenseth (1991), Greenblatt (1991), Biow (1996), Platt (1999), Daston and Park (1998), Campbell (1999), Warner (2002), Evans and Marr (2006), Stagl (2008).

117. Grafton and Siraisi (1992).

118. Warner (2002).

119. See further Introduction to Part III.

120. See Heselhaus (1953), pp. 144–45.

121. See General Introduction.

122. For recent scholarship see Dougherty (2008).

123. The first edition appeared in 1650; the frontispiece reproduced here comes from the 1654 edition. The substantial subtitle runs as follows: *A view of the people of the whole world, or, A short survey of their policies, dispositions, naturall deportments, complexions, ancient and moderne customes, manners, habits & fashions: a worke every where adorned with philosophicall, morall, and historicall observations on the occasions of their mutations & changes throughout all ages: for the readers greater delight figures are annexed to most of the relations.*

124. Body-modification has been a widespread practice in many cultures, from antiquity to the present day. See Lee (2009) and Schildkrout (2004), who surveys recent, mainly anthropological literature on body art and the cultural construction of the inscribed body.

125. Importantly, the devil is not entirely disempowered: in the body of the text Bulwer discusses the devil's power to transform normal men into midgets and giants. Still, restrictions apply: Bulwer maintains that it is beyond the devil's ability to change a midget into a giant or *vice versa*.

CHAPTER 5

Of Donkeys and D(a)emons: Metamorphosis and the Literary Imagination from Apuleius to Augustine

Robert H. F. Carver

Introduction

Ovid and Apuleius

The grip of Ovid's *Metamorphoses* on the Western imagination during the last two millennia has been so strong that it is easy to underestimate the significance of Apuleius' (almost) identically titled work about a man who is transformed into a donkey following his affair with a witch's slave-girl.[1] There are interesting points of contact — as well as contrast — between Apuleius' prose *Metamorphoses* (also known as the *De asino aureo*, or *Golden Ass*) and its Ovidian precursor.[2] Ovid — notorious for the erotic content and often cynical tone of his elegiac poetry — chooses to write, at epic length and in the heroic metre, a metamorphic history from the world's beginnings in chaos to the age of Augustus, concluding the work with a philosophical justification of his choice of theme that is celebrated more for its rhetorical virtuosity than its argumentative cogency. Apuleius, in contrast, enjoyed a reputation as a *philosophus platonicus*, and his choice of subject perplexed admirers such as Macrobius who wondered why a serious philosopher would indulge (*Apuleium nonnumquam lusisse miramur*) in fictions fit only for the nursery (*in nutricum cunas*).[3]

While Ovid aspires from the outset to fuse his poetic narratives into something lofty and sublime, invoking the gods (*di*) to 'draw down' (*deducite*) a *perpetuum [...] carmen* (I. 4), Apuleius' opening words call attention to the disreputable genre in which (ostensibly, at least) he will be working: *at ego tibi sermone isto Milesio uarias fabulas conseram* ['But I shall weave together various tales for you in that Milesian discourse'] (*A.A.* I. I).[4] Like Ovid, however, he supplies an ending (a vision of Isis, followed by a return to human form and service as the goddess' disciple) that has seemed, to many readers, to be out of keeping with the tone and content of the earlier books.

In the *Tristia* (II. 64), Ovid refers to the *Metamorphoses* as a poem about 'bodies changed in an unbelievable manner' (*in non credendos corpora uersa modos*). Apuleius' reference to 'Milesian discourse' seems to be an invitation to readers to distance themselves from the fictions presented; but, as a first-person prose narrative, *The Golden Ass* makes very different claims from Ovid's *Metamorphoses* on our belief and disbelief. Apuleius' prologue invites us to wonder at 'the figures and fortunes of men transformed into other shapes and restored again to themselves in a reciprocal binding' (*figuras fortunasque hominum in alias imagines conuersas et in se rursus mutuo nexu refectas*, I. I).[5] The phrase *in alias imagines conuersas* maps readily onto Ovid's *in noua ... mutatas ... formas | corpora* (I. I–2), but Apuleius simultaneously broadens the Ovidian brief (by including the 'fortunes' as well as the 'figures' of men) and narrows it (by introducing the limiting term of reverse metamorphoses that provide a *restitutio in integrum*). By concentrating his attentions on the adventures of a single man — transformed into an ass and forced to wander for a full year before being returned to his human skin — Apuleius may seem to have reneged on his original promise of plurality, but he offers, by way of compensation, a whole series of mini- and para-metamorphoses. In so doing, he significantly expands the remit of metamorphosis and opens up new rhetorical, mimetic, and hermeneutic possibilities.

The parodic 'paideia' and the metamorphic book

Notions of metamorphosis are, of course, embedded in the very building blocks of Western fiction. *The Golden Ass* (like Petronius' *Satyrica*) is an ironic (at times, parodic) counterpart to Homer's *Odyssey*. In Book IV of the *Odyssey*, Menelaus famously has to pin down the Old Man of the Sea as Proteus changes shape in his attempts to avoid giving an answer. But Odysseus is himself a protean figure — the epithet πολύτροπος ('much turned', but also 'much turning') suggests that the 'versatility' of the hero depends on a co-dependent, self-reinforcing relationship between *gnosis* and *praxis*, ingenuity and experience. The *Odyssey* is not merely a domestication of Iliadic epic, providing (as Longinus saw it) a 'comedy of character';[6] it also serves as a prototype (in its relation of action, journey, time, and place) for romance and picaresque, and (in its emphasis on the development of character, e.g. in the so-called 'Telemachia') for the novel (particularly the *Bildungsroman*). Apuleius plays constantly with both Homeric epics, but while engaging the reader's sympathy for Lucius, he also exposes his protagonist to critical scrutiny; and Lucius himself admits, even as late as Book IX, that his acquisition of asinine ears has produced an imperfect imitation of Odysseus, rendering him 'much-knowing, albeit less wise' (*etsi minus prudentem, multiscium reddidit, A.A.* IX. 14).[7]

Moreover, the very act of reading is presented, from the outset, as a metamorphic process: the reader who obeys the injunction to pay attention (*lector intende*) will be transformed (*laetaberis*: 'you will be delighted', I. I), but s/he will also be engaged — as a *lector scrupulosus* (IX. 30) and *lector studiosus* (XI. 23) — in the transformation of the text. The bogus seer, Diophanes, displays a rare example of prescience when he foretells that Lucius will become 'a mighty history, an unbelievable fable, and a multi-volume book' (*historiam magnam et incredundam fabulam et libros me futurum*, II. 12) — a prophecy fulfilled, figuratively (and meta-fictionally), in the novel as a whole, but more particularly (and metamorphically) in the Prologue, where the speaker's question *Quis ille?* ['Who is this?'] (I. 1) elicits an account of origins that seems to refer as much to the literary and philosophical antecedents of the novel (e.g. Plutarch's *Moralia*) as to the narrator's ancestry.[8] The relationship between text, protagonist, and author is further complicated by the fact that Apuleius seems to insert himself (as the 'poor man from Madauros') in the final book of the novel (*mitti sibi Madaurensem sed admodum pauperem*, XI. 27), despite the fact that Lucius (the character being referred to — or displaced — at this point) has previously been described as coming from Corinth (e.g. II. 12). [9]

Origins and (ex-)Changes: The Second Sophistic

This fluid approach to origins is partly a reflection of the intellectual milieu within which Apuleius is operating at the end of the second century AD — the so-called 'Second Sophistic'. Some of the phenomena that we associate most readily with this philosophically inflected rhetorical and literary movement may appear to be inherently anti-metamorphic — the tendency to 'Atticize', for example (to speak and write the 'pure' Greek of classical Athens), or the studied avoidance (amongst many Greek writers, at least) of any explicit acknowledgement of the reality of Roman *imperium*. But such 'conservative' (or 'reactionary') tendencies can also be read dynamically, as strategies of cultural resistance; and while the Atticizers may have drawn their validation from, and fixed their system of signification in, the classical Athens of half a millennium earlier, orators, teachers, and writers of the period (whether working in Greek, or Latin, or both) proved adept at negotiating (and exploiting) the complex political, economic, and intellectual matrices of Roman hegemony.[10] And the linguistic hyper-sensitivity and rhetorical self-consciousness required of (and displayed by) professional orators, philosophers, and *littérateurs* produced some very interesting effects, including certain congruences with the self-referential preoccupations of postmodernist discourse.

Apuleius embeds (indeed, embodies) in his work the notion of the *translatio studii et imperii* ['the transfer of learning and of power']. The choice of adjective in the narrator's announcement, *Fabulam graecanicam incipimus* ['We begin a Greekish story'] (I. 1) calls attention to the fact that the narrative at hand involves not only borrowing from, but transformation of, a Greek source (the lost *Metamorphoses* attributed by Photius, in the ninth century, to one 'Lucius of Patras').[11] The prologue's apology for being the 'rude speaker of an exotic language of the forum' (*exotici ac forensis sermonis rudis locutor*, I. 1), constructs both self and text as a site of cultural, linguistic, and economic exchange: the rhetorician's strategies of self-presentation are deployed in a market-place of words and affect.

It is surely not accidental that Lucius' host, Milo (husband of Pamphile, the metamorphic witch), is a money-lender. Almost the first words that Photis speaks to Lucius (when he arrives, unannounced, outside the house) are: *sub qua specie mutuari cupis?* (I. 22).[12] Hanson's translation is appropriate to the immediate context: 'What kind of security [gold or silver?] do you offer for the loan you want?' But an alert (second-time) reader cannot help making a connection between *mutuor* ('I borrow'), *muto* ('I change'), and the phrase *mutuo nexu* ('in a reciprocal binding' or 'interwoven knot') used to describe the metamorphic programme of the novel (1. 1). And this points to a crucial difference between Apuleian and Ovidian metamorphoses: while Pythagoras' speech in *Metamorphoses* XV stresses the general condition of flux in the universe, the individual transformations in Ovid (particularly those of an aetiological nature) tend to have a stabilizing effect (whether serving as punishment, reward, or mitigation). Reverse metamorphoses do occur (e.g. Tiresias and the companions of Ulysses), but they are the exceptions that prove the rule. In Apuleius, on the other hand, one can never be certain whether a metamorphosis is going to be reversed, or lead to a further change; and internal states are at least as important as physical forms.

The Road to Hypata

Lucius' first experience of Hypata is emblematic of the all-pervasive nature of metamorphosis within the novel.[13]

> nec fuit in illa ciuitate quod aspiciens id esse crederem quod esset, sed omnia prorsus ferali murmure in aliam effigiem translata, ut et lapides quos offenderem de homine duratos et aues quas audirem indidem plumatas et arbores quae pomerium ambirent similiter foliatas et fontanos latices de corporibus humanis fluxos crederem; iam statuas et imagines incessuras, parietes locuturos, boues et id genus pecua dicturas praesagium, de ipso uero caelo et iubaris orbe subito uenturum oraculum. (*A.A.* II. 1)

> [Nothing I looked at in that city seemed to me to be what it was; but I believed that absolutely everything had been transformed by some deadly mumbo-jumbo: the rocks I hit upon were feathered human beings, the trees that surrounded the city walls were humans with leaves, and the liquid in the fountains had flowed from human bodies. Soon the statues and pictures would begin to walk, the walls to speak, the oxen and other animals of that sort to prophesy; and from the sky itself and the sun's orb there would suddenly come an oracle.]

Everything that subsequently happens to Lucius (good as well as bad) stems from this initial fascination with transformative magic. It is important to observe, however, that Lucius' perception of the city has been shaped by a pre-existing narrative that he heard (from the lips of a purported eye-witness, Aristomenes) in the course of his journey to Hypata — the story of Socrates' fatal entanglement with an 'elderly but still quite attractive' inn-keeper (*caupona*) named Meroe (*anum sed admodum scitulam*, *A.A.* 1. 7).[14] Like Cervantes' Don Quixote (slaughtering wine-skins, tilting at windmills), or like many a prosecutor in the witchcraft trials of the early-modern period, Lucius 'sees' what he expects (or desires) to see.[15]

Figure 5 reproduces a woodcut from the first printed edition (1538) of Johann Sieder's German translation of *The Golden Ass*, showing Meroe's transformations of fellow citizens who have offended her (*A.A.* 1. 9–10).[16] To the right, Meroe is placing a spell on the trussed-up figure of a rival innkeeper who can also be seen (to her left) in the process of being transformed into a frog (note the hypertrophied thighs and webbed feet). In the centre — thanks to a single word from the witch (*unico uerbo mutauit*) — an unfaithful lover has assumed the features of a beaver (a

FIG. 5. *Meroe and her Metamorphosed Victims*, Sieder (1538),
fol. 2ʳ (= sig. A2ʳ) (cf. Apuleius, *A.A.* 1. 9–10)

precursor to cutting off his own genitals to evade capture), and is seated on a beer barrel. On the far left, Meroe transforms (*deformauit*) an opulently gowned lawyer who continues to practise law 'as a ram' (*nunc aries ille causas agit*); while, at the top of the picture, a naked Meroe (mounted not on a broomstick but — in deference to her occupation — on what I suspect is a brewer's 'mash oar'[17] or a maltman's shovel) is transporting the entire house of her chief accuser to a waterless town which lies 100 miles away atop a jagged mountain.

The German woodcut foregrounds these physical metamorphoses, but they only reach us, in Apuleius' text, through Socrates' *recordatio* of the deeds (*eius ... facta*, 1. 8) committed by Meroe 'in full view of multiple witnesses' (*quod in conspectu plurimum perpetrauit*, 1. 9). The account serves as a parodic *aristeia*, designed to impress upon Aristomenes the dangers posed by the innkeeper. But Apuleius seems to be far more interested in Socrates' own experience of transformation, which is rather subtler. Having been stripped by robbers of everything he possessed (*omnibus priuatus*, 1. 7), he is hospitably received by Meroe. She begins by treating him 'with more than human kindness' (*nimis quam humane*, 1. 7), but then takes him into her bed. By this 'single act of intercourse' (*ab unico congressu*), Socrates binds himself to 'a destructive relationship lasting many years' (*annosam ac pestilentem coniunctionem contraho*, 1. 7). Having been a 'reasonably wealthy' businessman (*nummatior*), he becomes a 'sack-carrier' (*saccariam faciens*, 1. 7), giving everything he earns to Meroe (figuratively anticipating Lucius' asinine role as a beast of burden), and is finally reduced, by 'his good wife and evil Fortune' (*bona uxor et mala Fortuna*), to the appearance (*ad istam faciem*, 1. 7) of a ghost (*laruale simulacrum*, 1. 6).

When Aristomenes stumbles across his old friend by chance, he finds Socrates 'deformed' (*deformatus*) and 'almost someone else on account of his sallowness' (*paene alius lurore*, 1. 6), resembling a beggar on a street-corner. There are obvious structural parallels with the Parable of the Good Samaritan (Luke 10. 29–37), but Apuleius concentrates more on the psychological than the moral ramifications of encountering someone transformed by circumstances. Even though Socrates is a 'close friend and extremely well known' (*quamquam necessarium et summe cognitum*), Aristomenes approaches him 'with a doubtful mind' (*tamen dubia mente propius acessi*). He does, however, take him to the baths, where he applies oil (*quod unctui ... praeministro*) and, 'with great labour', scrapes 'the thick crust of scurf' (*sordium enormem eluuiem operose effrico*) from his body.

Aristomenes complements this physical transformation with rest, food, wine, and story-telling (*fabulis permulceo*, 1. 7), but, just after he has fallen asleep that night, the doors of the room in the inn are burst open, and Meroe enters with her sister, Panthia. Hiding beneath his upturned cot, as though 'turned into a tortoise' (*de Aristomene testudo factus*, 1. 12), Aristomenes watches as Meroe plunges a sword into Socrates' neck and pulls out his heart, while Panthia blocks the wound with a sponge. The sisters contemplate dismembering Aristomenes 'in a Bacchic frenzy' (*bacchatim discerpimus*, 1. 13 — a fitting transformation for an inn-keeper to make) or castrating him (reprising the beaver motif), but content themselves with squatting over his face and discharging their bladders (*super faciem meam residentes uesicam exonerant*, 1. 13). As they leave, the doors and bars and bolts are restored to their original condition in a miraculous reverse transformation, while Aristomenes is left (in one of the novel's many metamorphic anointings) 'covered in urine, as though newly issued from [his] mother's womb' (*lotio perlitus, quasi recens utero matris editus*, I. 14). By a curious hypallage, he has become, in structural terms, the child born to an earlier victim of Meroe's malevolent magic, the woman condemned to perpetual pregnancy when her womb was stopped up at I. 9.

More terrors ensue, as Aristomenes (anticipating being charged with his companion's murder) attempts first to flee, and then to hang himself. But Apuleius now supplies the first of those transformative 'twists in the tail' that can be considered a defining characteristic of Milesian story-telling: the rope breaks, causing Aristomenes to fall upon the supposed corpse; Socrates wakes up and chides his room-mate for smelling like a latrine as Aristomenes hugs and kisses him in relief (I. 16–17). They depart, laughing and joking, but still rather uneasy after their supposed 'nightmares'. Stopping for breakfast (*ientaculum*, I. 18), Socrates eats greedily, but when he bends over the river to assuage his thirst, the wound in his neck reopens, 'the sponge suddenly rolls out' (*illa spongia de eo repente deuoluitur*, I. 19), and he dies instantly. There is an obvious epic precedent, in the accounts of the Wooden Horse, for introducing a concentrated, but catastrophic narrative 'charge' into a context of relief and relaxation. Indeed, Aristomenes adapts Virgil's description of the Greeks emerging from the belly of the Horse and invading a city that is 'buried in sleep and wine' (*inuadunt urbem, somno uinoque sepultam, Aeneid*, II. 265) when he tries to persuade himself that he merely 'dreamed the worst things, being buried in cups and wine' (*poculis et uino sepultus extrema somniasti*, I. 18).[18] But the precise sequence in Apuleius (apparent climax, illusory relief, real climax) anticipates the cinematic technique of 'double-take' that has become a staple of horror movies.[19]

Diana and Pamphile

As we see from Meroe, the depiction of witches in Apuleius tends to follow the Thessalian and (sub-)Homeric Circean traditions, in which metamorphic punishments are erotically charged and usually deeply (or pettily) personal; but the novel also incorporates more exclusively Ovidian transformations at certain points: as he enters the *atrium* of his kinswoman, Byrrhena (II. 4–5), Lucius marvels at the verisimilitude of a statue group depicting Diana and Actaeon (Figure 6).[20] He admires the 'sheen' (*nitor*) of the marble, and the 'skilfully polished grapes' (*uuae faberrime politae*), and takes extraordinary delight in exploring every curve and fold of the carving with his eyes (*haec identidem rimabundus eximie delector*), but despite the dramatic irony of his hostess' welcome — 'All that you see is yours' (*tua sunt ... cuncta quae uides*, II. 5) — he fails to connect Actaeon's fate to his own predicament as a handsome (and inquisitive) young man living in the household of a powerful and amorous witch.[21]

His hostess, Pamphile, is (as her name — 'Love all' — might suggest) an anti-Diana: while Ovid's goddess displays an elegant economy in response to an unwitting violation of her modesty (condemning Actaeon to be torn apart by his

FIG. 6. Byrrhena's Statuary of Diana and Actaeon
(cf. Apuleius, *A.A.* II. 4), Sieder (1538), fol. 7ʳ (= sig. B3ʳ)

own hounds with a mere aspersion of bath-water), Pamphile deforms any man who dares to resist her advances, turning them 'on the spot, into stones or sheep, or any other kind of animal', or simply 'annihilating them completely' (*in saxa et in pecua et quoduis animal puncto reformat; alios uero prorsus exstinguit*, II. 5).

At the same time, Apuleius quietly undercuts these reports of cosmic power by emphasizing how easily merely physical transformations can be achieved. Desirous of imitating Pamphile's metamorphosis into an owl, Lucius asks what would be required to reverse the process (*quo dicto factoue exutis pinnulis illis ad meum redibo Lucium?*). Photis replies:

> specta denique quam paruis quamque futilibus tanta res procuretur herbulis: anethi modicum cum lauri foliis immissum rore fontano datur lauacrum et poculum.

> [Look, then, with what small and trifling little herbs so great a thing is obtained: a small amount of dill mixed in spring-water with bay leaves is given as a bath and a drink.] (*A.A.* III. 23)

One of the many ironies of Apuleius' narrative is that Lucius is left unmolested by Pamphile, both erotically and magically. There is no (apparent) supernatural involvement in Lucius' change of shape: he actively pursues metamorphosis, and only acquires the form of a donkey rather than an owl because of Photis' confusion of ointments. Of course, such a transformation readily invites a moralizing reading. Mithras, the priest of Isis, sees it as the 'perverse reward of [Lucius'] unfortunate curiosity, having slipped into slavish pleasures' (*ad seruiles delapsus uoluptates, curiositatis improsperae sinistrum praemium reportasti*, XI. 15). In the illustration to Sieder's translation (Figure 7), Photis stands in front of a richly draped bed (a reminder of voluptuary indulgence), holding a jar (*pyxis*) of transforming ointment, while Lucius is in the process of changing into an ass (one arm still human, the other a hemi-ithyphallic leg and hoof, pointing to the trouble-inducing contents of his jock-strap).[22]

In order to assume the form of an owl, Pamphile, the (supposedly) all-powerful witch, has to have a 'long and secret conversation with her lamp' (*multumque cum lucerna secreto collocuta*, III. 21) before the ointment begins to take effect. But Lucius shows how very easy it is for a philosophically trained *alumnus* of Athens to make an ass of himself: he embraces and kisses the *pyxis*, prays for a 'prosperous flight', strips off his clothes, and covers himself with ointment (III. 24). The unlooked-for transformation begins immediately: hair thickens, skin hardens, ears lengthen, and a 'great tail' (*grandis cauda*) appears. The only 'consolation' that he can see in this 'wretched transformation' is the fact that his 'generative organ was growing', just at (or to) the point where he 'could no longer embrace Photis' (*nec ullum miserae reformationis uideo solacium, nisi quod mihi iam nequeunti tenere Photidem natura crescebat*, III. 24). One of the most dramatic transformations of the novel is the way that Lucius' attitude towards Photis changes, almost in the instant of assification, from ardent affection (often expressed in elegiac terms) to murderous hatred (III. 26). But Lucius has already been subjected to significant metamorphoses even before he anoints himself, most obviously when he watches Pamphile:

FIG. 7. Lucius becomes an Ass (cf. Apuleius, *A.A.* III. 24);
Sieder (1538), fol. 17ᵛ (= sig. E1ᵛ)

> et illa quidem magnis suis artibus uolens reformatur. at ego nullo decantatus carmine, praesentis tantum facti stupore defixus, quiduis aliud magis uidebar quam Lucius. sic exterminatus animi, attonitus in amentiam uigilans somniabar.

> [Whereas hers was a willing metamorphosis brought about by her powerful arts, I, who had not been enchanted by any spell, yet was so transfixed with awe at the occurrence that I seemed to be something other than Lucius. I was outside the limits of my own mind, amazed to the point of madness, dreaming while awake.] (*A.A.* III. 22)

It is in passages such as these that Apuleius' real originality (and significance for the development of the 'Western imaginary') can be found. We might compare the transformation induced by the spectacle of Photis wiggling her buttocks in the kitchen — *isto aspectu defixus obstipui et mirabundus steti; steterunt et membra quae iacebant ante* ['I was transfixed by the sight, utterly stunned. I stood in amazement, as did a part of me which had been lying limp before'] (II. 7) — while noting similar figurative transformations in the novel as a whole.

The Festival of Laughter

One of the most entertaining (but also disturbing) episodes in the novel occurs shortly before the protagonist's physical transformation, when Lucius figuratively 'makes an ass of himself' through the very eloquence of his own defence at his trial for homicide (in reality, utricide) during the Festival of *Risus* (*A.A.* III. 1–11; III. 18). The God of Laughter's festival not only celebrates (cf. II. 31), but enacts, the transformative power of humour. On the way home from Byrrhena's tale-enriched party,[23] Lucius (well tippled, and in the dark) suffers another failure in perception and cognition, running his sword through three magically animated wine-skins that he mistakes for robbers attacking Milo's house (II. 32). He enters the house 'panting and bathed in sweat' (*anhelans et sudore perlutus*) and falls asleep comparing himself to Hercules, the slayer of three-bodied Geryon (II. 32); but he wakes in the morning filled with anguish, and feeling 'besmeared with the gore of a triple slaughter' (*trinae caedis cruore perlitum*, III. 1). That transition — from (genuine) 'sweat' to (imagined) 'gore' — constitutes a mini-metamorphosis (we should note the transformative associations of several other viscous liquids in the course of the work: urine, amniotic fluid, unguents, honey, and perfume), but it is also an example of psychological realism that we would recognize as 'novelistic' (an aspect enhanced by the fact of taking place between the end of one 'book' — effectively, a long 'chapter' — and the beginning of the next).

Lucius is arrested and dragged to the forum to stand trial, but the crowd is so large that — in the alleged interest of public safety — the setting is changed ('with amazing speed', *mira celeritate*, III. 2; cf. *repente* and *nec mora* — all terms appropriate to the abrupt shifts in a dream or nightmare) to a theatre (*theatrum*). The 'public ministers' (*publica ministeria*) lead him 'like some victim' (*uelut quondam uictimam* — already, figuratively, a quadruped in a sacrificial religious setting) 'across the middle of the stage' (*per proscaenium medium*) and stand him in the middle of the *orchestra*.

The speeches for the prosecution and defence parody both historiographical and forensic reconstructions of events. The nightwatchman's 'wakeful diligence' (III. 3) is the ironic counterpart of Thelyphron's vain boast at II. 23, and his account of himself 'considering individual details with scrupulous care' (*scrupulosa diligentia ... singula considerans*) while creating a false picture of the whole, provides us with a paradigm of how (and how not) to read the narrative, as well as anticipating much of the forensic practice of Renaissance witch-hunters (see Chapter 7, *infra*).

While protesting his innocence and veracity, Lucius concocts an eloquent but wholly fictitious account of his epicized battle with the animated wine-skins, complete with verbatim reports of the speeches made by the supposed 'robbers'. The performance simultaneously parades and parodies the sophist's oratorical art. At the micro-level, rhetorical tropes or 'figures of speech' (from τρέπειν, 'to turn, to direct, to alter, to change') typically involve linguistic plays or deformations that allow the listener or reader to keep the original form or meaning in mind while also relishing the successive instars in that metamorphic process. And within the Ciceronian tradition, at least, the role of oratory or rhetoric at the macro-level is not merely to 'delight' (*delectare*), but to 'teach' (*docere*), and by means of that 'delightful teaching' (as Sidney calls it in the *Defence of Poesie*), to 'move' (*mouere*) the audience to (virtuous) action.[24] Lucius, despite his youth and the obvious strain of being on a capital charge (*reus capitis inducor*, III. 7), has been well taught: he is able to marshal not only his words, but also his gestures in the appropriate order, deferring his clinching appeal to 'the eye of the Sun and of Justice' (III. 7) until the spectators have been, he believes, sufficiently 'moved' (*commotos*) by 'humanity', and 'affected' (*affectos*) by 'pity'. But, as he raises his gaze to meet theirs, he finds that the transformation wrought by his rhetoric differs completely from what he expected: he sees 'the entire population dissolved in raucous laughter' (*risu cachinnabili diffluebant*, III. 7).

Confined to a stage, Lucius becomes the unwitting actor in his own play. Instruments of torture are brought on (*ignis et rota*, 'fire and the wheel', III. 9), and he fears the loss, not only of life, but of corporeal integrity (*integro saltim mori non licuerit*, III. 9). The comic peripeteia occurs before he can be fastened to the 'cross', however, when he is forced to draw back the sheet covering the bodies of his 'victims': *Quod monstrum! Quae fortunarum mearum repentina mutatio!* (III. 9). His exclamation, *Quod monstrum!* ('What a marvel!' or 'What a monster!'), does not so much describe the perforated wine-skins that he sees (in place of corpses) on the bier, as concretize the 'swift' *mutatio* — a 'change' not only in his 'fortunes' (that is the result), but also (immediately prior to that product of cognitive processing) in his expectation-shaped perception. The sudden reversal of appearances leaves Lucius 'dumbfounded' and stuck to the spot (*subito in contrariam faciem obstupefactus haesi*, III. 9). The audience is still in its state of liquefaction — they depart 'drenched with happiness' (*laetitia delibuti*, III. 10) — while Lucius remains 'frozen into stone just like one of the other statues or columns of the theatre' (*fixus in lapidem steti gelidus nihil secus quam una de ceteris theatri statuis uel columnis*, III. 10), *transformed* into part of the very material structure in which his humiliation has been *performed*. When he is finally induced to return to Milo's house, the magistrates appear again, to inform him of the city's decree that his 'likeness should be preserved in bronze' (*ut in aere staret imago tua decreuit*, III. 21) — a metamorphic honour that Lucius politely, but firmly declines.

Cupid and Psyche

The heroine of the tale of 'Cupid and Psyche' (which forms the centre-piece of the novel, occupying most of Books IV to VI) mimics Lucius' predicaments, adventures, and (apparent) redemption in multiple respects, including the unwelcome experience of resembling a statue (IV. 32). Psyche shares a name not only with 'soul' in Greek, but also with that most metamorphic of natural creatures, the butterfly.[25] The whole story is fraught with figurative transformations and reversals, many of them seemingly in response to the demands of the plot: Psyche's sisters change character, switching from grief-stricken mourners (following her exposure on the rock) to jealous precursors of Shakespeare's Goneril and Regan (when they witness the opulence of her invisible husband's palace). Psyche momentarily changes sex (*sexum audacia mutatur*) as she approaches the conjugal bed (decapitating razor in hand), but the light of the lamp transforms the monstrous serpent of her expectations into that 'mildest and sweetest beast of all wild creatures', Cupid himself (*uidet omnium ferarum mitissimam dulcissimamque bestiam*, A.A. V. 22).[26] She briefly changes character again after Cupid's desertion as she exacts revenge upon her sisters (V. 26–27), but soon reverts to a state of passivity and despair. She is almost destroyed by an ill-advised attempt at metamorphosis — appropriating some of the infernal 'beauty' that Proserpina supplies to Venus in a *pyxis* (VI. 20; the same word describes the container of Lucius' ointment at III. 24) — but is revived by Cupid and taken to heaven, where the previous impediment of *nuptiae impares* (marriage between social unequals) is removed by the conferring of immortality (VI. 23). Jupiter proposes to marry Cupid to Psyche as a way of grounding him, of containing his disruptive and destructive energies; and all seems to be resolved in the time-honoured way, with a wedding-feast, Venus' dance, and the birth of a child, *Voluptas* (VI. 24).

Charite and Aftermath

The fate of Charite and Tlepolemus (hero and heroine of the narrative that frames 'Cupid and Psyche') reveals, however, the failure of Jupiter's attempted trans-formation of Cupid. Tlepolemus is killed by a lust-maddened rival (VIII. 5), and Charite commits suicide after blinding her husband's murderer with a pin (VIII. 14). The dissolution of their household leads us into some of the most harrowing stories in the novel. The feeble old man who solicits help for his 'nephew' transforms himself into a man-devouring snake (VIII. 21), giving physical expression to the fears voiced earlier by Psyche's sisters about the true nature of her unknown husband (V. 17–18). The servant who violated social hierarchies by 'burn[ing] with love for a freewoman' (VIII. 22) is stripped naked, smeared with honey (*nudum ac totum melle perlitum*), and tied to a tree. Misdirected desire leads (once again) to an anointing, followed by a metamorphosis, as his body is reduced by ants to a pile of gleaming white bones (VIII. 22).[27]

Book VIII ends with Lucius being sold to a band of debauched eunuch priests of the Syrian goddess, who not only 'beautify themselves hideously' (*deformiter quisque formati*, VIII. 27), with garish clothes and cosmetics, but transform their appearance by cutting and flagellating themselves, until the ground is wet with their blood (VIII. 27–28). Books IX and X are dominated by tales of adultery, unnatural passions, and acts of egregious violence, a highlight being Lucius' asinine congress (X. 19–22) with a beautiful *matrona* at Corinth (see Figure 8, p. 294).

There is an extraordinary moment in Book X when, in the midst of a description of the pantomime depicting the Judgement of Paris (a prelude to Lucius' scheduled coupling with a condemned murderess), the speaker suddenly launches into a tirade against judicial corruption, addressing the 'cattle of the courts, nay, rather, vultures in togas' (*forensia pecora, immo uero togati uulturii*, X. 33).[28] The epanorthosis (*immo uero ...*) has the effect of extending the critique from those who merely collude (or acquiesce passively) in Injustice (the dumb beasts for sale in the *forum* that had evolved into a court and has now become a market-place again) to the judges and jurors who feed actively on the flesh of Injustice's victims. But the rhetorical trope (also known as *correctio*) is itself metamorphic, reconfiguring the *iudices* to reveal their true(r) bestial selves.[29]

As *lectores scrupulosi*, however, we ought to ask, 'Who is the speaker of this apostrophe?' Is it (to employ Winkler's terminology) Lucius *actor* (the assified protagonist), or Lucius *auctor* (the reflective first-person narrator)?[30] The speaker ends on a note of rhetorical self-depreciation, imagining his audience objecting to a 'philosophizing ass' (*ecce nunc patiemur philosophantem nobis asinum?*, X. 33), but we are left again with the sense that, in the case of Apuleian metamorphoses, notions of 'before' and 'after' rarely indicate rigid divisions between states: there is an enduring potential for slippage and reversal.

Book XI: The Final Twist?

Apuleius makes meta-discursive references at several points in the work, signalling the change, for example, from comedy to tragedy: *iam ergo, lector optime, scito te tragoediam, non fabulam, legere et a socco ad cothurnum ascendere* ['So now, excellent reader, know that you are reading a tragedy, and no light tale, and that you are rising from the lowly slipper to the lofty buskin'] (X. 2). But he saves the most remarkable transformation of all until the end. In Book X, facing the degradation (and potential danger) of being publicly mated with a woman condemned to be devoured by beasts, Lucius takes comfort in the prospect of a double metamorphosis induced by Spring 'painting everything' (*cuncta depingeret*, X. 29). As the emerging roses cast off their thorny covering (*dirrupto spineo tegmine*), they offer Lucius the possibility of escaping from his own thick hide and returning to human form.

But in the final book (XI), credit for the reverse metamorphosis is given to the goddess who appears to Lucius in a vision, and instructs him to receive the roses from the hands of her own priest, Mithras: Lucius complies, is duly restored, undergoes a religious conversion, and dedicates himself to a new life in the service of Isis (and Osiris).

The orthodox response to the Isiac intervention is that, 'For Apuleius, metamorphosis is essentially a paradigm of conversion.'[31] While the terrestrial lover (Photis) fails to supply the remedy of roses required at III. 25, and Lucius' attempts at self-help at IV. 2 almost prove fatal when he mistakes toxic 'laurel-roses' (oleander) for the genuine article, the theophany in Book XI ensures that Lucius' tribulations result in a return, not merely to his original human form, but to a higher state as an initiate of the goddess.

As Winkler and others have shown, however, this final (religious) metamorphosis is deeply problematic.[32] Milesian tales rely (as we have seen) on a 'twist' or 'sting in the tail' — an anticipated, but nevertheless surprising ending. Apuleius, I suggest, is not merely stringing together a collection of short *Milesiae*, but is imagining the work as a whole as a demonstration of *sermo Milesius* ('Milesian discourse', I. 1). We should therefore hold onto the possibility that the religious transformation in Book XI is functioning, at some level, as a comic device.

It may be significant that Lucius' first prayer is addressed to that embodiment of mutability, the Moon (XI. 1–2). The combination of Mithras and the Festival of Isis has a structural (as well as onomastic) parallel in the appearance of Zatchlas (a linen-clad Egyptian priest, II. 28) in a tale told during the Festival of *Risus* (God of Laughter). And Lucius' final role as a 'shrine-bearer' (*pastophorus*) may prompt (in the *lector studiosus*, at least) an unsettling memory of Socrates' time as a 'sack-carrier' (I. 7) in the service of another powerful (and jealous) female, the witch with an Egyptian name (Meroe).

As I have argued elsewhere, the 'ass with glued-on wings' (*asinus pinnis adglutinatis*, XI. 8) at the end of the *anteludia* (the pageants preceding Isis' *peculiaris pompa*, XI. 9) encapsulates many of the tensions of the novel:

> at one level, it carnivalizes (in a hermeneutically reconcilable blend of *iocum* and *serium*) the imminent translation of Lucius from the plane of sluggish quadruped to that of winged soul; at another level, it merely underscores (by its emphasis on gluing) our doubts both about the *integritas* ('wholeness') of Lucius' transformation and about the nature of the junction between the creature's wings (Book 11) and body (Books 1–10). It is difficult to avoid the conclusion that, at the end of the work, Lucius, despite all his earnest flappings towards the divine, is still (in many respects, at least) an ass — earth-bound and somewhat risible (*tamen rideres*, XI. 8).[33]

Our reading of Book XI is further complicated by the fact that Lucius' physical re-transformation and religious conversion occur within an Egyptian context that is fundamentally therianthropic. The procession of Isis features theriocephalous gods such as Anubis (the dog- or jackal-headed son of Osiris and Nephthys) who embodied much that was inimical to Roman tradition. In Virgil's depiction of the Battle of Actium on the Shield of Aeneas (*Aeneid* VIII), Cleopatra is a frenzied version of Isis, 'inciting her forces with the native *sistrum*' (*patrio uocat agmina sistro*), while 'Anubis the Barker' (*latrator Anubis*) and 'monstrous gods of every kind' (*omnigenumque deum monstra*) 'brandish weapons against Neptune and Venus, and against Minerva' (*contra Neptunum et Venerem contraque Mineruam | tela tenent*, 696–700).[34] The separate itemization of the Goddess of Wisdom may suggest that the multi-form Egyptian deities (and the faith placed in them) offend against Reason itself.[35] According to Plutarch (*Moralia* 379e), '[t]he notion that the gods, in fear of Typhon, changed themselves [μεταβαλεῖν] into these animals [...] is a play of fancy surpassing all the wealth of monstrous fable' (πᾶσαν ὑπερπέπαικε τερατείαν καὶ μυθολογίαν).

Apuleius seems to be negotiating with Rome's anti-Egyptian prejudices when he promises to 'soothe' the 'benevolent ears' of his listeners 'with a charming whisper' (*auresque tuas beniuolas lepido susurro permulceam*), provided that they do not 'disdain to look upon an Egyptian papyrus inscribed with the sharpness of a reed from the Nile' (*modo si papyrum Aegyptiam argutia Nilotici calami inscriptam non spreueris inspicere*, I. I).[36] There is an implicit reference to the physical transformation of (exotic) plant matter into writing materials,[37] and (for the 'initiated' second-time reader) a coded allusion to the Isiac finale; but I would argue that in the prologue (I. I) and in the appropriation — in the following sentence — of 'the renowned Plutarch' as an ancestor (I. 2), Apuleius is subtly drawing attention both to the challenges and the originality of his programme: he builds upon Plutarch's attempt in the *De Iside et Osiride* to interrogate the Egyptian mystery religions and accommodate them to the demands of Middle Platonism, but he gives bodily shape to such ideas in the form of Milesian story-telling (*sermone isto Milesio*, I. I), creating, in the process, a novel form of philosophical entertainment.[38]

From Apuleius to Augustine: Pagan and Patristic Views of Metamorphosis

Pagan and Christian attitudes towards metamorphosis do not form a neat dichotomy. In the *Odyssey*, Poseidon's lapidification of the Phaeacians' preternaturally swift ship (XIII. 153–83) marks a significant transition — from the fabulous (Scheria, and the tales told on it) to the realistic ('rocky' Ithaca) — and the closure of one of the portals linking the two. But Virgil's decision to transform ships into nymphs (*Aeneid* IX) has struck critics (from Servius right up until the modern day) as incongruous, or even indecent.[39] And while epic abounds in similes and metaphors that 'figure' heroes in animal terms (as a means of conveying, say, speed, or strength, or ferocity), it tends to protect its central characters from physical metamorphoses.[40]

We find similar restraint in pagan science. The *Historia naturalis* contains many strange phenomena, but Pliny the Elder 'confidently' rejects the notion of lycanthropy, confining werewolves to the realm of the fabulous:

> homines in lupos verti rursusque restitui sibi falsum esse confidenter existimare debemus aut credere omnia quae fabulosa tot saeculis conperimus.
>
> [But we ought confidently to consider as false [the notion of] men being turned into wolves and restored again to themselves, or else give credence to all those matters which we have known, for so many ages, to be fabulous.][41]

Indeed, he seems to think that there is something rather un-Roman about the whole business:

> mirum est quo procedat Graeca credulitas! nullum tam inpudens mendacium est, ut teste careat.[42]
>
> [It is a marvel how far Greek credulity extends! There is no lie so impudent that it lacks an eye-witness.]

Works of pagan mythography like Ovid's *Metamorphoses* also offered abundant ammunition to Christian polemicists. In his commentary on the Book of Jonah, St. Jerome declares:

> sin autem infideles erunt, legant quindecim libros Nasonis Metamorphoseos, et omnem Graecam, Latinamque historiam, ibique cernent uel Daphnen in laurum, uel Phaetontis sorores populos arbores conuersas fuisse; quomodo Jupiter eorum sublimissimus deus, sit mutatus in cygnum, in auro fluxerit, in tauro rapuerit, et cetera, in quibus ipsa turpitudo fabularum, diuinitatis denegat sanctitatem.

> [But if they will be pagans, let them read the fifteen books of Ovid's *Metamorphoses* and every Greek and Latin (hi)story, and there discern either Daphne turned into a laurel, or the sisters of Phaethon changed into poplar trees, or how Jupiter — the most elevated god of theirs — was changed into a swan, flowed in gold, abducted in the form of a bull, and those other cases, in which the very shamefulness of the fables denies the holiness of divinity].[43]

In classical mythology, the Olympian deities usually transform themselves in order to satisfy particular appetites. As Marlowe puts it, in his exuberant description of the crystal pavement in the Temple of Venus: 'There might you see the gods in sundry shapes, | Committing heady riots, incest, rapes' (*Hero and Leander*, 46–47). The Christian experience of divine auto-metamorphosis is rather different.[44] Because God created man 'in His own image' (*ad imaginem Dei*/κατ' εἰκόνα θεοῦ, Genesis I. 27: KJV, Vulgate, Septuagint), there is a general reluctance to contaminate divine substance with animal form. John the Baptist's exclamation, at his first (adult) meeting with Jesus, 'Behold the Lamb of God who takes away the sin of the world' (John I. 29), has always been understood symbolically rather than metamorphically.[45] Similarly, the dove has proved useful in giving visible expression to the Holy Spirit.

Despite humankind's participation in the *imago Dei*, the Incarnation of God the Son required a transformation — *Et homo factus est*/καὶ ἐνανθρωπήσαντα, as the Niceno-Constantinopolitan Creed (AD 325 and 381) puts it — but of a disenabling and (ultimately) self-sacrificial kind. Christ is theanthropic — fully God and fully Man — but his assumption of humanity involved a temporary 'self-emptying' (κένωσις), a voluntary giving up of certain divine attributes.[46] The Transfiguration serves as a quasi-metamorphosis that reveals the glorified Christ to His disciples; and while the Gospels stress the physical reality of the Resurrection (the risen Christ eats grilled fish at Luke 24. 43, and places Thomas' hand in the hole in His side at John 20. 27), it is also clear that His resurrected body is somehow different: Mark states (16. 12) that 'He appeared in another form' to two of the disciples (*in alia effigie*/ἐν ἑτέρᾳ μορφῇ), while the disciples on the road to Emmaus only recognized Him 'in the breaking of the bread' (*cognoverunt eum in fractione panis*: Luke 24. 35; cf. 24. 13–32).[47]

The (prefigurative) echo of the Last Supper may remind us that the Eucharist depends — within the Roman Catholic tradition, at least — on a double metamorphosis: the scholastic formulation of the theory of transubstantiation describes how the substance of the bread and wine (things made by 'work of human hands') is changed into the Body and the Blood of Christ, while the accidents (or *species* — 'outward appearance') remain the same.[48] But, for the faithful, reception of the Eucharist is also transformational:

> Domine non sum dignus ut intres sub tectum meum, sed tantum dic verbo et sanabitur anima mea
>
> [Lord, I am not worthy that you should enter under my roof, but only say the word, and my soul shall be healed][49]

In the *Confessions*, Augustine describes how he heard a divine voice:

> cibus sum grandium: cresce et manducabis me. nec tu me in te mutabis sicut cibum carnis tuae, sed tu mutaberis in me.
>
> [I am the food of grown men; grow and you shall feed upon me; nor shall you change me, like the food of your flesh, into yourself, but you shall be changed into me.][50]

The metamorphic effects of Divine Grace receive different emphases in the various parts of the Christian tradition, but the notion of *theosis* or 'divinization' of human beings (particularly prominent in Eastern Orthodox thought) has scriptural authority. As St Paul puts it II Corinthians 3. 18):

> But we all, with open face beholding as in a glass the glory of the Lord, are changed into the same image [τὴν αὐτὴν εἰκόνα μεταμορφούμεθα/*in eandem imaginem transformamur*] from glory to glory, *even* as by the Spirit of the Lord.

The possibility of mortals experiencing an ascending metamorphosis stands in chiastic relation to the descending metamorphosis of God the Son becoming Incarnate. In the words of Augustine (echoing St Athanasius):

> Deos facturus qui homines erant, homo factus est qui Deus erat.[51]
>
> [To make gods of those who were men, He was made man who was God.]

It is also clear, however, that the Church recognized, very early on, the disruptive and transgressive potential of metamorphosis.[52] St Paul speaks of 'false apostles [ψευδαπόστολοι], deceitful workers, transforming themselves [μετασχηματιζόμενοι/ *transfigurantes*] into apostles of Christ.' He links such tendencies to the Arch-Deceiver:

> [And no wonder! For Satan himself transforms [μετασχηματίζεται/*transfigurat*] himself into an angel of light [*in angelum lucis*]. Therefore it is no great thing if his ministers also transform themselves into ministers of righteousness, whose end will be according to their works] (II Corinthians 11. 13–15)

Augustine and Apuleius

In the Western tradition, one of the foundation texts of d(a)emonology is Augustine's engagement with Apuleius' *De deo Socratis* in Books VIII and IX of the *De ciuitate dei* (begun in AD 413).[53] Augustine is very clear that, of all the pagan philosophies, Platonism approximates most closely to Christianity (he even toys with the idea that Plato acquired an inkling of the Truth through contact with Jewish Scriptures during his visit to Egypt, VIII. 11), and he accords Apuleius a high place among Platonists; but he refutes Apuleius' notion that *daemones* (like Socrates' supposed supernatural *amicus*, VIII. 14) can mediate positively between men and the gods, arguing instead that they are merely 'demons' in our modern (wholly pejorative) sense of the term.[54] And he establishes an intimate connection between demons, theatre, pagan worship, and Plato's decision to expel poets from his ideal state (*Republic* III, 398a). Once one has read Apuleius' *De deo Socratis*, Augustine tells us,

> one can no longer be astonished that these demons wish the obscenities of the stage [*scaenicam turpitudinem*] to have a place among divine ceremonies, and that while eager to be accounted gods, they could find pleasure in the scandals of the deities [*deorum criminibus*], and that everything in the sacred rites which arouses laughter or disgust [*uel ridetur uel horretur*] by reason of its celebration of obscenity or its degraded barbarity is very much to their taste.[55]

Egypt has a special place in Augustine's account. He relates the story that 'Io was the daughter of Inachus, and she was afterwards called Isis, and was worshipped in Egypt as a great goddess'; but he also notes an alternative (Euhemeristic) tradition that she was accorded divine honours after her death because she had 'established many useful practices, especially the art of reading and writing'. Indeed, 'so great was the honour in which she was held that anyone who asserted that she was a mere human being was liable to a capital charge' (XVIII. 3).[56] Augustine suppresses the detail of Io's bovine metamorphosis, but he does dwell on the way in which 'Egypt, infatuated by a strange delusion' (*mirabili uanitate decepta Aegyptus*, XVIII. 5) worships a living bull (*bos*) named Apis which manages to maintain an identical set of white patches through multiple generations. Invoking the precedent of Jacob's rods (Genesis 30. 37–43), Augustine explains how demons, intent on deceiving the Egyptians into perpetuating animal worship, 'display unreal shapes' to pregnant cows, causing their offspring to give physical expression (in their hides) to the visual impressions received by their mothers (*hoc daemones figuris fictis facillime possunt animalibus concipientibus exhibere*, XVIII. 8).

The introduction of the pagan pantheon into Greece (and the proliferation of classical mythology) follows directly, in Augustine's account, from the Hebrews' Exodus from Egypt (XVIII. 12–13). But it is surely not coincidental that, amongst the plethora of attacks upon the (generally unspecified) 'enormities' of the stage, Augustine should mention the contention of goddesses 'for a golden apple' (*pro malo aureo*) in an 'all-singing, all-dancing' performance of the Judgement of Paris (*inter theatricos plausus cantantur atque saltantur*, XVIII. 10). The spectacle readily matches the (highly titillating) pantomime described by Apuleius at the end of Book x — a performance which serves as a prelude to the (projected) 'theatrical' climax (Lucius copulating in public — and for real — with a condemned murderess who is then to be devoured by a wild beast), and which is closely followed by the Isiac theophany, return to human form, and conversion in Book XI.[57]

These engagements with the daemonic theory of the *De deo Socratis* provide an essential context for Augustine's hugely influential discussion of 'transformations which seem to happen to men by the craft of demons' (XVIII. 16–18). Augustine begins with supposedly 'historical' accounts of survivors of the Trojan War such as Diomedes, who was 'made' a god (*et Diomeden fecerunt deum*) despite the fact that he had been prohibited from returning home by a divine punishment. The transformation of his companions into birds is presented by pagan authors (like Varro) not 'as a baseless poetic fantasy', but 'as historical fact' (*eiusque socios in uolucres fuisse conuersos non fabuloso poeticoque mendacio, sed historica adtestatione confirmant*, XVIII. 16). In order to 'bolster up' (*ut astruat*) this story, Varro tells 'other, no less incredible' tales (*alia non minus incredibilia*): of Circe changing Ulysses' companions into animals (*socios ... mutauit in bestias*); of the Arcadians, who were metamorphosed into wolves, but could regain their original form if they had not eaten human flesh for nine years; and (finally) of Demaenetus, who was transformed into a wolf (after eating the flesh of a boy sacrificed by the Arcadians to the god Lycaeus), but was then 'restored to his proper shape' in the tenth year (*in lupum fuisse mutatum et anno decimo in figuram propriam restitutum*). Having trained as a boxer, he won a prize at the Olympic games (*pugilatum sese exercuisse et Olympiaco uicisse certamine*, XVIII. 17).

It is easy to hear the mockery behind Augustine's use of the word *historicus* ('historian') in relation to Varro; but there is more to his relation of the (otherwise unknown) story of Demaenetus's lycanthropy than meets the eye. The ten-year sojourn has an obvious Homeric dimension, but the language of 'restitution' recalls Lucius' desire to be restored to his former self' (e.g. *quae me priori meo Lucio redderent*, X. 29) and the detail of post-restoration Olympian victories has a structural resonance with Lucius' successes as a lawyer in Rome (*A.A.* XI. 28). We should also note (as, I am sure, Augustine did), that Demaenetus is a character in Plautus' *Asinaria*, a play about asinine folly which contains the famous line, *Lupus est homo homini, non homo, quom qualis sit non nouit* ['One man to another is a wolf, not a man, when he doesn't know what sort he is'] (495).

The reference to *The Golden Ass* comes only a few sentences later, when Augustine decides to tell a few stories of his own. In a meta-discursive (and characteristically Apuleian) opening, he imagines his readers waiting for him to say what he thinks of 'such an egregious piece of play-making by the demons' (*sed de ista tanta ludificatione daemonum nos quid dicamus, qui haec legent, fortassis expectent*, XVIII. 18). His instinctive response is spiritual and scriptural: we should 'escape from the midst of Babylon' (*de medio Babylonis esse fugiendum*; cf. Isaiah 48. 20), and the greater the power that we detect in demons, 'the more tenaciously we should cling to the Mediator through whom we climb from the depths to the heights' (*tanto tenacius Mediatori est inhaerendum per quem de imis ad summa conscendimus*). He balances the impulse to say that such things are simply 'not to be believed' (*ea non esse credenda*) with the observation that 'there are some men, even now' (*non desunt etiam nunc*) who will assert 'that they have heard well-attested cases of this sort, or even that they have had first-hand experiences of them' (*qui eius modi quaedam uel certissima audisse uel etiam expertos se esse adseuerent*). This hedging-about with veridical qualifications and asseverations establishes a discursive space within which Augustine can indulge in his own fabulations (XVIII. 18):

> Nam et nos cum essemus in Italia audiebamus talia de quadam regione illarum partium, ubi stabularias mulieres imbutas his malis artibus in caseo dare solere dicebant quibus vellent seu possent viatoribus, unde in iumenta

illico verterentur et necessaria quaeque portarent postque perfuncta opera
iterum ad se redirent; nec tamen in eis mentem fieri bestialem, sed rationalem
humanamque servari, sicut Apuleius in libris, quos Asini aurei titulo inscripsit,
sibi ipsi accidisse, ut accepto veneno humano animo permanente asinus fieret,
aut indicavit aut finxit.

[For even when we ourselves were in Italy, we heard such things of a certain
region in those parts where, they said, lady innkeepers, steeped in these wicked
arts, used to give [substances] in cheese to any travellers they wished to (or were
able to), whereby they were changed on the spot into pack-animals and carried
whatever was required and, upon completion of the task, returned to their true
selves. Their mind, however, did not become bestial, but remained rational and
human, just as Apuleius, in those books which he inscribed with the title, *The
Golden Ass*, either believed or feigned to have happened to himself — that, on
taking a potion, he became an ass while his mind remained human.]

The Golden Ass is introduced as a way of glossing reports to which Augustine claims
to be an 'ear-witness' (*audiebamus talia*), but there is surely some artful (and even
mischievous) manipulation at work here: the account of Italian innkeepers seems
to involve a conflation of Socrates' figurative transformation at the hands of the
innkeeper, Meroe (cheese and the bearing of burdens featuring significantly in
both authors), with the explicitly asinine transformation of Lucius in the house of
Pamphile (*A.A.* I. 5–7; I. 19; III. 24–25).

Augustine's stated attitude towards such apparent wonders is ambivalent: *Haec
vel falsa sunt vel tam inusitata, ut merito non credantur* ['These things are either false or
so unusual that they might deservedly not be believed']. He is willing to concede,
however, that demons might be able to change the *appearance* of things created by
the true God, so that they seem to be what they are not (*specie tenus, quae a vero Deo
sunt creata, commutant, ut videantur quod non sunt*). Neither the soul nor even the body
can truly be changed by the power of demons, but a man's phantom (*phantasticum
hominis*) may appear to others in the form of some animal and the man himself may
imagine that he is such a creature. Augustine cites the case of a certain Praestantius
(one of those people 'whom we could never consider to have lied to us', *quos nobis
non existimaremus fuisse mentitos*) whose father took the potion in some cheese and fell
into a deep, unbreakable sleep. Upon waking, some days later, he described how he
had seemingly been 'transformed into a horse and, along with other pack-animals,
carried grain to soldiers' (*caballum se ... factum annonam inter alia iumenta baiulasse
militibus*). It was then discovered that this had happened just as he had said.

Augustine uses the term *uenenum* ('potion' or 'drug') — usually a liquid taken
into the body — rather than Apuleius' own term, *unguentum* (something applied
to the surface). *Venenum* offers at least the potential for viewing the apparent
transformation as a product of hallucinogenesis; but it is worth considering other
ways in which Augustine may have transformed his source material. The final story
that Augustine tells us in this group of metamorphic narratives concerns a man,
at home (but not yet in bed), who sees a philosopher coming towards him. The
philosopher explains to him 'a number of Platonic matters' which he had previously
been unwilling to explain in his own house (*exposuisse nonnulla Platonica quae antea
rogatus exponere noluisset*, XVIII. 18). When asked later to clarify his contradictory

behaviour, the philosopher replies: 'I did not do it; I merely dreamed that I did' (*Non feci, inquit, sed me fecisse somniaui*). Augustine articulates an important element of (subsequent) dream theory when he observes that 'what one man saw in his sleep was displayed to the other, while awake, by means of a phantom appearance' (*Ac per hoc alteri per imaginem phantasticam exhibitum est uigilanti, quod alter uidit in somnis*, XVIII. 18), but the tale itself remains very strange, and his choice of subject is highly suggestive.

Could we not read this account as a joco-serious dramatization of Augustine's own engagement(s) with Platonism? The philosopher who is 'extremely well known' to the enquiring man (*philosophum quendam sibi notissimum*) would stand, on this reading, for his fellow country-man, Apuleius, that famed (and familiar) mediator of Platonic doctrine (cf. Augustine, *Epistulae*, 138. 19: *Apuleius, qui nobis afris afer est notior* ['Apuleius, who, as an African, is better known to us Africans']; and *De ciuitate dei*, VIII. 12: *Apuleius Afer Platonicus nobilis*).[58] And the moral would seem to be that the (partial) truths contained within the (often contradictory) Platonic tradition only become explicable when translocated to Christianized home ground (*domi*, XVIII. 18).

Augustine's reference to Apuleius' novel may well have been crucial to its survival during the Middle Ages, and his use of the title *De asino aureo* (the earliest known instance) has significant implications for our understanding of the wider textual tradition (the oldest manuscript, F, preserves only the title *Metamorphoses*, yet it was based on the recension produced by Sallustius who was working in Rome under Endelechius in 395).[59] Augustine had connections with the same rhetorical circle (Symmachus had recommended him to Ambrose) and he probably knew the title *Metamorphoses*, but he is insistent that Apuleius 'inscribed' the books 'with the title of *Golden Ass*' (*quos Asini aurei titulo inscripsit*).[60] And it is that very particularity of phrasing that makes me (increasingly) suspicious. It is possible that Augustine is claiming superior local knowledge of the work's 'proper' title, and (perhaps) showing evidence of the continuing circulation in north Africa of a manuscript tradition independent of Sallustius. I should like, however, to float the possibility that *Asinus aureus* is Augustine's own (derogatory) title, and that — responding to the word *inscriptam* in the opening sentence of the novel (and to the identification of the character, Lucius, with the author, Apuleius, at *A.A.* XI. 27: the 'poor man from Madauros') — Augustine is transforming Apuleius' 'Egyptian papyrus' (*A.A.* I. 1) into a palimpsest, which he (re-)'inscribes' (*inscripsit*, appropriating Apuleius' authorial rights), with the 'sharpness' (*argutia*, *A.A.* I. 1), not of a 'Nilotic' but of a Judaeo-Christian 'reed'.[61] By means of this transformation, he reveals the Egyptian mystery cults (which Apuleius was supposedly promoting) to be not simply a 'load of Old Bull' (Apis) but profoundly asinine (the ass being — in an added irony — an animal antipathetical to Isis because of its associations with Seth-Typhon, the murderer of Osiris).[62] The devotion shown by the asinine Lucius/Apuleius to a bovine Egyptian goddess (the procession of Isis includes a cow, 'the fertile symbol of the divine mother of all', *bos, omniparentis deae fecundum simulacrum*, *A.A.* XI. 11) may recall, for Augustine, an earlier seduction of a people (who should have known better) by Egyptian idols, more specifically, the Golden Calf.[63]

At the midpoint of his *Confessions* (VII. 9. 13), Augustine describes a crucial moment in his intellectual and spiritual development, when God 'procure[d] for me, through one inflated with the most monstrous pride, certain books of the Platonists, translated from Greek into Latin' (*procurasti mihi per quendam hominem immanissimo typho turgidum quosdam platonicorum libros ex graeca lingua in latinam versos*).[64] Within these pagan works, Augustine found the truths of Christian revelation, 'not indeed in the same words, but to the selfsame effect' (*non quidem his verbis sed hoc idem omnino*). In *De ciuitate dei*, VIII. 12, Augustine observes that among 'modern philosophers the most highly esteemed of the Greeks are Plotinus, Iamblichus, and Porphyry; while Apuleius of Africa stands out as a notable Platonist, writing in both Greek and Latin'.[65] The contents of the work discussed in the *Confessions* do not match any specific text of these Platonizing philosophers (Porphyry has been the most touted candidate), but it may be significant that while the period of Augustine's life alluded to here is around AD 386, the actual writing of the *Confessions* immediately follows the editing of Apuleius' *Metamorphoses*, *Apologia*, and *Florida* at Rome and Constantinople (AD 395–97). The attitude displayed by Augustine to Middle- or Neoplatonic discourse in this chapter of the *Confessions* is fundamentally transformative. While claiming to find common content, he rewrites the pagan texts in explicitly Christian terms, using verbatim quotations from the New Testament. And in the following passage, he balances appreciation of Egypt (acknowledging it as the source of 'Egyptian gold', i.e. Platonism) with an awareness of its potential to abuse both spirit and intellect, through the worship of 'four-footed beasts' and 'idols [...] fashioned of gold':

> et ideo legebam ibi etiam immutatam gloriam incorruptionis tuae in idola et varia simulacra, in similitudinem imaginis corruptibilis hominis et volucrum et quadrupedum et serpentium [...]. quoniam caput quadrupedis pro te honoravit populus primogenitus, conversus corde in Aegyptum et curvans imaginem tuam, animam suam, ante imaginem vituli manducantis faenum [...]. et ego ad te veneram ex gentibus et intendi in aurum quod ab Aegypto voluisti ut auferret populus tuus, quoniam tuum erat, ubicumque erat [...]. et non attendi in idola Aegyptiorum, quibus de auro tuo ministrabant qui transmutaverunt veritatem dei in mendacium, et coluerunt et servierunt creaturae potius quam creatori.

> [I also read there how 'they changed the glory of thy incorruptible nature into idols and various images — into an image made like corruptible man and to birds and four-footed beasts, and creeping things' [Romans 1. 25]: [...]. so that thy first-born people worshiped the head of a four-footed beast instead of thee, turning back in their hearts toward Egypt and prostrating thy image (their own soul) before the image of an ox that eats grass. [...]. I had sought strenuously after that gold which thou didst allow thy people to take from Egypt, since wherever it was it was thine.[66] [...] But I did not set my mind on the idols of Egypt which they fashioned of gold, 'changing the truth of God into a lie and worshipping and serving the creature more than the Creator.' [Romans 1. 25]] (*Confessions*, VII. 9. 15)

All literary critics are necromancers to an extent. It is possible, of course, that the image we have conjured up in our interpretation is less a *simulacrum* of authorial intentions than a *corpus phantasticum*, assembled from the *disiecta membra* of Augustine's writings. But a collocation of two other passages displays the tension between unity and plurality in the authors. In Apuleius' description of the debauched woman who believes in a single god 'whom she would call "one and only"' (*quem praedicaret unicum*, IX. 14), we are almost made to feel that the repressive force of her monotheism creates a disequilibrium in Nature, which is counter-balanced — in rhetorical as well as moral terms — by her polymorphous perversity, as represented in a succession of verbal deformations: she is *saeua scaeua, uirosa ebriosa, peruicax pertinax* ['cruel and perverse, crazy for men and wine, headstrong and obstinate'].[67] Augustine, in contrast, concludes his chapter on pagan transformations with the observation that demons aim 'to deceive humans into worshipping many false gods, at the expense of the one true God' (*ad decipiendos homines, ut falsos deos cum ueri Dei iniuria multos colant*, XVIII. 18).

Patristic Legacies: Early-Medieval Views of Metamorphosis

Most of the subtleties (suggested above) of Augustine's engagement with Apuleius seem to have been lost on his successors, but his theory of demonic agency (together with his objections to theatrical shows) had a profound influence on medieval attitudes. In a sermon entitled *De kalendis ianuariis*, Saint Caesarius of Arles (AD 468/470–542) excoriates those who engage in transvestite revels to mark the New Year: it is bad enough that heathens (*pagani homines*) cover their human selves with 'obscene deformities' (*obscenis deformitatibus teguntur*), so that worshippers make themselves resemble the animal-god which is being worshipped (*utique ut tales se faciant qui colunt, qualis fuit ille qui colitur*); but, at this time of year, 'even some Christians take on adulterous forms [belonging to something other than human] and monstrous appearances' (*etiam aliqui baptizati sumunt formas adulteras, species monstruosas*):

> Alii vestiuntur pellibus pecudum; alii adsumunt capita bestiarum, gaudentes et exultantes, si taliter se in ferinas species transformaverint, ut homines non esse videantur. Ex quo indicant ac probant, non tam se habitum beluinum habere quam sensum: nam quamvis diversorum similitudinem animalium exprimere in se velint, certum est tamen, in his magis cor pecudum esse quam formam.[68]

> [Some dress themselves in the skins of cattle; others put on the heads of beasts, rejoicing and exulting, as though, by so doing, they have transformed themselves into the appearances of wild animals, so that they do not seem to be men. By so doing, they indicate and prove that they have, not so much the appearance of beasts, as the understanding; for although they wish to express, in themselves, the likeness of different animals, it is certain that they have the heart, rather than the form, of cattle.]

Masquerades and carnival of this kind are prohibited by various ecclesiastical edicts (e.g. the Council of Auxerre in AD 578 [or 585]), and penitential handbooks prescribe the penalties for abuses, as in the *Liber poenitentialis* formerly attributed to Theodore of Tarsus, Archbishop of Canterbury (AD 668–90):

> §19. Si quis in Kalendas Januarii in cervulo aut vetaula vadit, id est, in ferarum habitus se [commutant?] communicant, et vestiuntur pellibus pecudum, et

assumunt capita bestiarum, qui vero taliter in ferinas species se transformant, III annos poeniteat, quia hoc daemoniacum est.

[(19. If anyone at the calends of January goes about as a stag or a bull; that is, making himself into a wild animal, and dressing in the skin of a herd animal, and putting on the heads of beasts; those who in such wise transform themselves into the appearance of a wild animal, penance for three years; because this is devilish.][69]

In pseudo-Theodore's case, the putting on of animal costume is construed as 'demoniacal', but in the codifications of Canon Law that occur from the Carolingian period onwards, the proscriptive emphasis seems to shift to *belief* in the efficacy of bestial transformations. The most important medieval formulation of the Church's teaching on metamorphosis is the so-called Canon *Episcopi* (named after its opening noun). The provenance of the canon is obscure: some recensions suggest that it resulted from the Council held in Ancyra (Galatia) in AD 314 (hence, *Concilium anquirense*), but its contents do not match any of the extant decrees of that event.[70] The earliest version may be found in the *Libri duo de synodalibus causis et disciplinis ecclesiasticis* (no. 364), a collection of canons compiled by Regino of Prüm (d. 915). It passed into section 10 (*De incantatoribus et auguribus*) of Burchard of Worms' *Decretum* (c. 1012), and gained authoritative status from its inclusion in the great *Concordia* of Canon Law compiled (c. 1141) by Master Gratian (*Decretum Gratiani, causa 26, quaestio 5, canon 12*). The crucial feature of the Canon is its condemnation of the belief 'that any creature can be made, or transmuted for better or worse, or transformed into some other species or into any other likeness, except by the Creator Himself'.[71]

This Canon (and the weight of tradition behind it) may account for the caution with which authors approach the subject of metamorphosis during the Middle Ages; but (as we shall see in Chapter 7, below), it also posed significant challenges during the early-modern period, both for prosecutors of witchcraft, and for dramatists wishing to represent physical transformations on stage.

Notes to Chapter 5

1. On the reception of Apuleius' novel, see Carver (2007); Gaisser (2008); and Carver (2010).
2. See, generally, Scotti (1982); Krabbe (1989), pp. 37–81; Graverini (2004–05).
3. Macrobius, *Commentarii in Somnium Scipionis*, I. 2; Carver (2007), pp. 30–33.
4. The *Milesiaka* of Aristides of Miletus have not survived, but on the basis of tiny fragments of Cornelius Sisenna's Latin translation, brief (and invariably critical) ancient references, and some of the intercalated tales found in Petronius and Apuleius, it is possible to identify sexual and/ or supernatural content, cynical or realistic attitudes to human motivation and behaviour, tight structure, and an element of surprise in the conclusion, as characteristic features of Milesian tales. See Harrison (1998) and Carver (2007), pp. 15–17.
5. Latin text (with 'u' substituted for 'v') from Loeb edition of Apuleius, *Metamorphoses*, ed. and trans. by J. Arthur Hanson. In the quotations that follow, I move freely between Hanson's translations and my own.
6. οἱονεὶ κωμῳδία τίς ἐστιν ἠθολογουμένη, *On the Sublime*, 9 (Penguin trans., pp. 112–13).
7. On epic intertextuality, see Harrison (2000), pp. 222–23.
8. See Carver (2001), p. 163.
9. This has been variously explained as a *lapsus calami* or as an example of *sphragis* (the author placing his 'seal' on his work). Neither solution disposes of the hermeneutic problem. Cf. Griffiths (1975), p. 5; and van der Paardt (1981). In *The Golden Ass*, while Lucius is transformed

into a donkey, the first-person narrator seems to be simultaneously Greek (*A.A.* I. 1–2) and Roman (*A.A.* III. 29 and IV. 32). In the *Apologia* (24), Apuleius jestingly describes himself as 'half-Numidian' (*seminumida*) and 'half-Gaetulian' (*semigaetulus*).

10. See, generally, Gleason (1995); Goldhill (2001); and Whitmarsh (2005).

11. Photius, *Bibliotheca*, Cod. 129. Cf. S. J. Harrison and M. Winterbottom's observation that *Graecanicus* is a technical term used by Varro (*De lingua latina*, X. 70) for words which are 'Greek in origin but adapted for Latin use' (2001), p. 15. On Renaissance receptions of the passage, see Carver (2007), pp. 251 and 255; and (on Photius) pp. 55 and 275, n. 151.

12. Note, in a different context, Anderson (2005), p. 133: 'Here the Ciceronian word for borrowing, *mutuatio*, derives from *mutuor*, ... *mutuus*, "given in exchange," and whose root is *muto*, "to change, exchange, barter."'

13. See Carver (2013a). The passage is singled out by Godwin (1834), pp. 164–65. Godwin notes the 'misapprehension' of writers like Augustine and Lactantius 'respecting his principal work, the *Golden Ass*, which is a romance detailing certain wonderful transformations, and which they appear to have thought was intended as an actual history of the life of the author'; but he includes the work in his study as 'a curious representation of the ideas which were then prevalent on the subjects of magic and witchcraft.'

14. See Carver (2013a).

15. On Cervantes' debts to Apuleius, see Carver (2007), pp. 375–77.

16. *Ain schön lieblich auch kurtzweylig Gedichte Lutij Apuleij von ainem gulden Esel* (Augsburg: Alexander Weissenhorn, 1538), fol. 2ʳ (= sig. A2ʳ). Forty-one of the seventy-eight woodcuts are attributed to Hans Schäufelein.

17. A wooden implement used 'to stir the malt in the mash-tub'. See *The Complete Farmer: or, A General Dictionary of Husbandry*, 3rd edn (London: J. F. and C. Rivington et al., 1777), sig. L2ᵛ, s. v. 'Brew-House'.

18. On Apuleius' transformations of source material, see Finkelpearl (1998).

19. The parallels with Ridley Scott's genre-(re-)defining 'sci-fi horror movie', *Alien* (1979), are striking. The parasitized Executive Officer Kane (John Hurt) is used as an unconscious Wooden Horse (cf. Virgil, *Aeneid*, II. 237–38: *fatalis machina [...] feta armis*, 'the fateful engine [...] pregnant with weapons') to gain admittance to the space-ship, *Nostromo* (Science Officer Ash serving as an androidal Sinon), but the infamous 'Chestburster' scene, in which the xenomorph that has been incubating in his thoracic cavity suddenly emerges in the middle of a communal meal, resembles the Socrates-Aristomenes episode in its combination (and sequence) of details: terror, relief, allusion to nightmare ('Just some horrible dream about smothering'), thirst, hunger, eating, joking, sudden death by eruption or ejection (xenomorph/sponge), and perfunctory corpse disposal.

20. Sieder (1538), fol. 7ʳ (= sig. B3ʳ). Note how the mimetic limitations of the medium of woodcut actually enhance the impression of the verisimilitude of the original statue-group encountered by Lucius: for the consumer of Sieder's text, there is nothing (apart, perhaps, from the goddess' height) to differentiate the onlookers (Lucius and Byrrhena) from the sculpted dogs and mythological figures in the atrium.

21. Apuleius subtly transmutes his Ovidian source, taking pains to present Actaeon as an emblem of misdirected erotic curiosity, rather than a hapless victim: the statue depicts him 'stretched out towards the goddess with an inquisitive gaze' (*curiosu optutu in deam uersum proiectus*, II. 4). On the further implications of *rimabundus*, see Carver (2007), pp. 200–02. Lucius' inability to 'read' the statuary matches his failure to absorb the lesson contained in Aristomenes' story in Book I.

22. On alternative interpretations of *seruiles uoluptates*, and the Platonic implications of Photis' failed attempt to transform Lucius into a 'winged creature', rather than a sluggish quadruped, see Carver (2013b).

23. The initiating narrative is the tale told at Byrrhena's house by Thelyphron about his experience of guarding a corpse. He is warned that witches are willing to transmute themselves (*reformatae*, II. 30) into all manner of animals (birds, dogs, mice, and even flies) in order to gain access to corpses and bite pieces from their faces. At the end of the night, the corpse is pronounced intact but the watchman subsequently discovers (when the prosthetics fall off) that his own nose and ears have been removed and replaced with wax ones.

24. On the Ciceronian triad, *docere, mouere, delectare*, see Vickers (1988), p. 77; Calboli Montefusco (1994).

25. On the interplay of etymology and entomology, see Warner (2002), pp. 84–93. We might add an example from modern cinema: in David Cronenberg's *The Fly* (1986), the 'telepods' resemble giant cocoons, and the film concentrates on metamorphic process rather than product (in the early stages, the protagonist — like Lucius — enjoys certain advantages derived from his transformation, e.g. more acute perception and enhanced sexual powers; cf. Lucius' tale-collecting ears at *A.A.* ix. 15, and his enlarged 'natural endowment' at *A.A.* iii. 24). The naming of 'Seth Brundle' (Jeff Goldblum's character) may also be Cratylic: if 'Brundle' suggests the 'bundling' together or fusion (*mutuo nexu*) of human and muscine elements to form that (still protean) hybrid, 'Brundlefly', there may also be an Egyptian resonance in 'Seth' that conveys his fissive function. The scientist's 'world-changing' discovery, teleportation (involving disintegration followed by reintegration), structurally mimics Plutarch's account of Osiris being dismembered by Seth-Typhon and reconstituted by Isis (*Moralia* 358a–b). The (post-transformation) relationship between the Geena Davis and Jeff Goldblum characters also participates in the 'Beauty and the Beast' complex (which is linked, in turn, to 'Cupid and Psyche'). The deleted 'Butterfly baby' dream scene adds to the entomological dimension, while also strengthening the Isiac parallels: the endangered (because, potentially, mutant) unborn child resembles Horus, the threatened fruit of the union between Isis and the re-assembled Osiris (a prosthetic — in some versions, made of gold — having supplied the missing phallus, *Moralia* 365c). If the foregoing analysis seems entirely fanciful, we might note that Cronenberg was a top-ranking student of literature at the University of Toronto during the reign of Northrop Frye, and admits to a long-standing interest in *Lepidoptera* and the works of Nabokov. His co-writer, Charles Edward Pogue, was also responsible for the TV mini-series, *Hercules* (2005).

26. We might note Isis' role in changing Iphis into a boy in order to enable her marriage to Ianthe (Ovid, *Met.* ix. 773–97).

27. Cf. Socrates (i. 7), Pamphile (iii. 21), Psyche (vi. 20), and (of course) Lucius (anointing and assification at iii. 24; the anointing by the Corinthian *matrona* at x. 21, followed by the reverse metamorphosis in xi. 13).

28. On the 'similarity of this tirade to Cynic diatribes', see Zimmerman (2000), p. 393.

29. The scene takes us back to i. 9, where Meroe's transformation of 'someone from the court/ market-place' (*alium de foro*) does not prevent him from pleading cases 'as a ram' (*nunc aries ille causas agit*).

30. See Winkler (1985), pp. 135–79.

31. Krabbe (1989), p. 38.

32. Winkler (1985), pp. 204–47; Harrison (2000), pp. 235–59; Carver (2013b).

33. Carver (2013b).

34. Cf. *OCD3* (s.v. 'Anubis', p. 117): in 'the Principate, [Anubis] stands for the absurdity or wickedness of Egyptian religion (Ver. *Aen.* 8. 696–700 ...).' Tacitus observes (*Histories*, v. 5) that 'The Egyptians worship many animals and monstrous images; the Jews conceive of one god only, and that with the mind alone' (Loeb translation).

35. In 'The Statues', W. B. Yeats invokes a similarly critical encounter between Eastern multiplicity and Western *integritas*, though he claims that it was 'not the banks of oars that swam upon | The many-headed foam at Salamis' (the Greek victory over the Persians in 480 bc), but classical sculptors like Phidias who 'put down | All Asiatic vague immensities' by 'modell[ing]' the 'Calculations' of Pythagoras in such a way that they 'look but casual flesh'.

36. Hanson's decision to take *beniuolas* proleptically ('caress your ears into approval') emphasizes the transformative nature of Apuleian discourse.

37. Platonically minded readers may also connect the passage with Thamus' warning to Thoth-Theuth (*Phaedrus* 274c–275b) that his invention of writing is a bane rather than a boon. See Trapp (2001), pp. 40–41.

38. On Apuleius' engagement with Plutarch, see Carver (2013b).

39. Servius on *Aeneid*, iii. 46 and ix. 77–122. See Fantham (1990). In Peter Carey's Lucianically titled (cf. the *Vera historia*) and Booker Prize-winning novel, *True History of the Kelly Gang* (St Lucia, Qld: University of Queensland Press, 2000), one of Australia's most iconic (indeed, epicized)

figures, the bushranger, Ned Kelly, represents himself as a ship at the climax of the Siege of the Inn at Glenrowan, when he emerges from the early-morning mist (and into the firing range of befuddled police), clad in armour forged from plough-iron, beating the butt of his revolver against the side of his helmet, and shouting, 'I am the bl----y Monitor, my boys' (cf. the USS Monitor, one of the first of the ironclads — equipped with a rotating turret — built during the American Civil War). Kelly is, figuratively at this moment (p. 1), both a ship and a *monstrum* of hybridity (a minatory 'Minotaur' of sorts), but he is also giving (transposed) fulfilment to his childhood ambition to be the 'ink monitor' (p. 29) at school (a role long denied him as an Irish Catholic).

40. In the Epistle Dedicatory to *The. xv. bookes of P. Ouidius Naso, entytuled Metamorphosis, translated oute of Latin into English meeter* (London: William Seres, 1567), Arthur Golding refers to the prophylactic given by Hermes to Odysseus before his encounter with Circe: 'And what is else herbe Moly than the gift of stayednesse | And temperance?' (sig. aiv^v).

41. *Natural History*, VIII. 80.

42. *Natural History*, VIII. 82. In Petronius' *Satyrica* (62), it is a freedman with a Greek name who tells what looks very much like a Milesian tale about his companion (a soldier) changing into a wolf. Trimalchio remarks (63) that he knows Niceros to be someone who 'does not narrate trifles; nay, he is steady and not loquacious' (*scio Niceronem nihil nugarum narrare: immo certus est et minime linguosus*).

43. *Commentarii in prophetas minores*, Cl. 0589, SL 76, *In Jonam*, cap. (s.s.): 2, linea: 57.

44. Yeats, meditating on the seminal significance of the rape of Leda for Western civilization (Helen, Clytemnestra, the Trojan War, etc.) gave the title 'Annunciation' to an early draft of 'Leda and the Swan', but the contrast between the 'indifferent beak' of the theriomorphic Zeus and the self-sacrificial love of the theanthropic Christ could not be more marked.

45. We have become used, in the West at least, to (highly stylized) depictions of the *Agnus Dei* (whether in church windows or on the signs of public houses such as 'The Lamb and Flag'). But that familiarity with the symbolism does not lessen the impact of Jan Van Eyck's brilliant yet unsettling 'Ghent Altarpiece' or 'Adoration of the Mystic Lamb' (*c.* 1432), where the divine substance is represented (in the lower-centre panel) in an uncompromisingly ovine form: a bleeding sheep standing (with all four feet) on an altar. Medieval representations (drawing on Revelation 5) will often show the hybrid form of the Lamb/Lion of Judah, a figure which is anything but 'realistic' or 'naturalistic'. The Eastern Orthodox tradition of representing God pictorially is resolutely anthropomorphic. Canon 82 of the Quinisext Synod (AD 692) declared that Christ should be depicted 'in human form, instead of the ancient lamb'. See Louth (2007), p. 35.

46. On *kenosis*, see Philippians 2. 5–8 and associated commentary. Cf. Hebrews 2. 9: 'But we see Jesus, who was made a little lower than the angels for the suffering of death, crowned with glory and honour; that he by the grace of God should taste death for every man' (KJV).

47. Luke's Christ declares emphatically (at 24. 39) that he is not a 'ghost' (πνεῦμα/*spiritus*). Mark's reference to Christ appearing 'in another form' may have given ammunition to the Gnostics who denied the physical reality of the Crucifixion. Cf. the heresy of docetism — the belief that the human form of Jesus was merely semblance (from δοκεῖν, 'to seem') rather than reality — and the apocryphal Acts of John (94–102 and 109).

48. The attempts of theologians such as Edward Schillebeeckx and Karl Rahner at the time of the Second Vatican Council to move away from the Aristotelian/Thomist 'theory of substance' towards a notion of 'transignification' or 'transfinalization' were met by Paul VI's papal encyclical *Mysterium Fidei* (3 September 1965) which reaffirmed traditional Catholic teaching on transubstantiation.

49. e.g. *Prymer of Salisbury vse* (Paris: Per Fra[n]ciscu[m] Regnault, 1533), fol. 89^v; and current *Missale Romanum*. Cf. the Roman centurion's words in Matthew 8. 8 and Luke 7. 6–7. In an anonymous late medieval drama, *The Croxton Play of the Sacrament* (which purports to depict a 'miracle' that occurred in Aragon and was then presented in Rome in 1461), a group of 'Jews' (who swear, oddly, by 'Mahommed so mighty', and seem to stand for 'heretics' or unbelievers more generally) subject a consecrated Host (purchased from a merchant for 100 ducats) to a new Passion by nailing it to a pillar, boiling it, and burning it in an oven, but the Christ present in the *species* of the 'cake' overcomes their attempts (bursting the bounds of the oven, for example,

just as He broke the bonds of Death and emerged from the tomb) and the Jews are so impressed that they convert. See *The Non-Cycle Mystery Plays, together with the Croxton Play of the Sacrament and the Pride of Life*, ed. by Osborn Waterhouse, EETS, extra series, no. 104 (London: Early English Text Society, 1909). I am grateful to Dr Barbara Ravelhofer for bringing this play to my attention, as well as for helpful criticisms.

50. Augustine, *Confessions*, VII. 10. 16; *Patrologia Latina*, ed. by J. P. Migne, XXXII. 742.

51. *Sermo* CXCII. 1. 1; cf. Athanasius, *De incarnatione* 54. 3. The Church Fathers make it clear that 'Only the Word is the Son of God by nature; the redeemed are children of God by participation'. See Bonner (1999), p. 265.

52. This sense of pluripotentiality is embodied in the motto '*Nothing is one*' (81; 231; cf. Plato, *Theaetetus*, 152d) in Murray Bail's *Eucalyptus* (Melbourne: Text Publishing, 1998), which provides postmodern variations on several Ovidian themes: a latter-day Actaeon (Molloy) is blinded and has most of his nose (a nod to Publius Ovidius *Naso*?) torn off by a barbed-wire fence after spying on the heroine (Ellen) as she bathes (and 'pisses') in a 'sandy pool' between River Red Gums which 'appeared as an entourage of sturdy older women' (pp. 47–48); an English Tiresias visiting Bathurst strikes a brown snake and is 'turned into a woman' (p. 98); and a voyeuristic travelling salesman is transformed into a telegraph pole hewn from *Eucalyptus diversicolor* (p. 195).

53. See, generally, Hunink (2003); Carver (2007), pp. 23–29. Cf. Hagendahl (1967), II, 680–81: 'No post-classical Latin author has such a place in Augustine's writings [681] as Apuleius.'

54. Socrates refers to his invisible companion as a *daimonion* (a 'divine something') rather than a *daemon* (e.g. *Apology* 31c–d; 40a). Love is described as a 'great daemon' in the *Symposium* (202d) and *Amor* is counted among the *daemones* in the *De deo Socratis* (ch. 16).

55. *De ciuitate dei*, VIII. 14, trans. by Henry Bettenson (Harmondsworth: Penguin, 1972), p. 319.

56. Citing Varro, he refers to the image (*simulacrum*) 'found in nearly all the temples where Isis and Serapis were worshipped [*ubi colebantur Isis et Serapis*], which had a finger pressed to its lips, apparently enjoining silence, thus indicating that not a word should be said of their having been human [*ut homines eos fuisse taceretur*]' (XVIII. 5; Penguin edn, p. 767).

57. Cf. Zimmerman (2000), p. 366, on *A.A.* x. 30.

58. There may be a playful echo of the moment in *A.A.* XI. 27 when the newly reformed Lucius has a vision of a man with a twisted left heel which is answered the following day when he encounters (the appropriately named) Asinius Marcellus. Asinius informs him that he, in turn, had dreamed the previous night that a certain 'poor man from Madauros' was being sent to him (*audisse mitti sibi Madaurensem sed admodum pauperum*).

59. Carver (2007), pp. 12–23.

60. Cf. Winkler (1985), pp. 293–98.

61. In Book x, the word *argutiae* is used to describe the 'clever tricks' which Lucius is taught to display as a performing ass (*A.A.* x. 17).

62. Cf. Isis' description of the ass at *A.A.* XI. 6.

63. Tacitus (*Histories*, v. 4) conflates the 'golden calf' with an ass when he describes how the Hebrews 'dedicated, in a shrine, a statue of that creature [the ass] whose guidance enabled them to put an end to their wandering and thirst [...]. They likewise offer the ox, because the Egyptians worship Apis.' Plutarch brings together (in highly suggestive ways) gold, asses, Apis, Typhon, the Jews, and 'wicked men transformed into animals' at *Moralia* 362e–363d.

64. *Confessions*, ed. by James J. O'Donnell (Oxford: Oxford University Press, 1992). Glossing *immanissimo typho turgidum* ['inflated with the most monstrous pride'], O'Donnell comments that '*Typhus* is a non-biblical Grecism already Christianized' and 'becomes a favorite expression' which Augustine applies even to himself. We should, however, note Plutarch's observation that Isis and Osiris' enemy, Typhon, 'is conceited, as his name implies, because of his ignorance and self-deception' (*Moralia*, 351f). See Carver (2013b).

65. *recentiores tamen philosophi nobilissimi quibus Plato sectandus placuit noluerint se dici peripateticos aut academicos, sed platonicos. ex quibus sunt valde nobilitati graeci Plotinus, Iamblichus, Porphyrius; in utraque autem lingua, id est et graeca et latina, Apuleius Afer extitit platonicus nobilis.*

66. 'The Egyptian gold is Platonism' (O'Donnell).

67. Thus Hanson. In an earlier translation of *The Golden Ass* (New York: The Limited Editions

Club, 1932), p. 277, Jack Lindsay tries to replicate the original's verbal tricks: 'She was lewd and crude, a toper and a groper, a nagging hag of a fool of a mule'.

68. *Caesarii Arelatensis Opera, pars I, 2* (Turnhout: Brepols, 1953), pp. 779–83 (p. 780).

69. Summers (1926), p. 134, calls it 'a distinct prohibition of this foul mummery'. Cf. William Prynne, *Histrio-mastix* (London: E[dward] A[llde] et al. for Michael Sparke, 1633), pp. 197–98: 'Our learned Country-man, *Alcbuvinus* [*sc. Alchuvinus* = Alcuin], writing, *of the practices of the Pagan Romanes on the Kalends of Ianuary*, now our New-yeeres day; informes us; *that divers of them did transforme themselves into monstrous* [198] *shapes, and into the habit of wilde beasts. Others* (saith hee) *changed in a feminine gesture, did effeminate their manly countenance: neither unworthily haue not they a manly fortitude, who have changed themselves into a womans habit, or have put on a womans attire.*'

70. The decrees do, however, include sliding scales for offences involving bestiality, depending upon the age and marital status of the offender.

71. For the Latin text, see the discussion of *A Midsummer Night's Dream* in Chapter 7 of this volume. The Third Council of the Lateran (AD 1179) provides a *terminus ad quem* for Gratian.

CHAPTER 6

Adonis as Citrus Tree: Humanist Transformations of an Ancient Myth

Carlo Caruso

The revival of classical antiquity that took place in Italy at the end of the Middle Ages brought about a keen new interest in classical mythology. While this is a well-known phenomenon whose importance hardly needs to be stressed, its progressively changing nature has not always received adequate acknowledgment.[1] In the heyday of Italian Humanism, which one identifies *grosso modo* with the period between the second half of the fourteenth century and the early sixteenth century, fascination with pagan myths was not necessarily or primarily engendered by mere antiquarian curiosity, or by pride in the strict imitation of the classics. In fact, one of its most striking features was a fresh, uninhibited and emulation-driven approach to the ancient models — something which later authors, increasingly preoccupied with issues of classicizing decorum to the point of fastidiousness, would rather be inclined to ban as inappropriate. Ancient myths of transformation proved particularly inspirational in this respect, and the myth of Adonis provides a good case in point.

The offspring of incestuous passion between King Theias of Assyria and his daughter Smyrna (or rather, according to alternative sources, between King Cinyras and his daughter Myrrha), Adonis was extracted from the womb of his mother after she had been turned by the gods into a myrrh tree. When he had reached youth, the extraordinarily handsome ephebe attracted the attention of Venus, surrendered rather passively to her seductive arts, and indulged with her in an idle life of sensual pleasures until he decided to go off hunting a wild boar. The hunt resulted in the inexperienced Adonis getting killed by the beast. After lamenting his untimely departure, Venus turned him, or rather his blood, into an anemone.[2]

This simple story won perpetual literary fame mainly thanks to Ovid's popular adaptation (*Met.* x. 532–739). However Sappho, Plato, Aristophanes and the Greek bucolic poets had already alerted their readers to the existence of female cults of the young hero in Attica, Egypt and Asia Minor.[3] Later authors — Plutarch, Pausanias, Lucian, Ammianus Marcellinus, Macrobius, and Martianus Capella amongst others — stressed the similarities between the cult of Adonis and those of comparable Babylonian, Egyptian and Anatolian gods or demi-gods like Tammuz, Osiris and Attis, with further emphasis on the myth's association with sacrificial rites of fertility and the cult of the Sun.[4] This brought Adonis dangerously close to the figure of Christ, and led the anxious Church Fathers to denounce any proximity of such kind as fallacious and misleading.[5] After the end of antiquity, interest in Adonis seems to have declined. Except for the exegetic tradition to Martianus Capella II. 191–92 and to Book X of Ovid's *Metamorphoses*, nothing particularly significant appears to have emerged for a period of over eight centuries — although research in this field has admittedly been far from exhaustive.[6] Adonis' lack of status during this long period is conveniently summarized in Jerome's periphrastic designation of him as a mere lover of Venus, *Veneris amasius*.[7]

A noticeable change occurred when the ancient mythological lore was revived in new works of antiquarian erudition, among which Giovanni Boccaccio's *Genealogie deorum Gentilium* (*The Genealogies of the Ancient Gods, c.* 1355–70) stands out as most authoritative. Arranged like a long gallery of portraits distributed in obeisance to genealogical patterns, Boccaccio's encyclopaedic repertoire was to establish itself as the standard work on classical mythology for almost two centuries.[8] It was Boccaccio's minute attention to antiquarian detail, complemented with a euhemeristic approach of both pagan (mainly Ciceronian) and Christian inspiration, which secured for his work unprecedented prestige, even despite its patent faults and extravagant misunderstandings.[9] The very design of the *Genealogie* came to exercise a tangible influence over the production of early Renaissance poets and writers. By assigning each character a section, however small, of their own, Boccaccio ensured they could all be granted, at least potentially, equal or near-to-equal dignity. Minor mythical personages were thus offered a degree of autonomy they had never enjoyed in ancient literature. An immediate consequence of this was a flourishing production of 'new' myths in both neo-Latin and vernacular poetry, where characters from secondary episodes of Ovid's *Metamorphoses* or from such other works as Statius' *Silvae*, the pseudo-Ovidian *Nux*, the *Appendix Virgiliana*, the poems of Ausonius etc., were deliberately placed at the centre of new narrations. In the second half of the fifteenth century reputed scholars like Domizio Calderini and Angelo Poliziano went so far as to declare that such smaller formats well became modern poets, for they, unlike the ancients, would not be capable of sustaining their inspiration successfully over the span of longer and more ambitious poems.[10]

Broad convictions of this kind, and the fact that Boccaccio had placed renewed emphasis on Macrobius' interpretation of the Adonis myth as an allegory for the sun's seasonal cycle,[11] provided the handsome ephebe with the essential requisites for attracting the attention of the literary world again. Not until the end of the fifteenth century did his story catch the eye of a truly gifted poet in the person of Giovanni Pontano. From that moment onwards, however, the somewhat colourless *Veneris amasius* went through an extraordinary transformation that was to culminate with James G. Frazer's interpretation of Adonis as one of the archetypal 'dying gods'.[12]

Pontano and the Myth of Adonis

Not unlike many other fifteenth-century humanists, Giovanni Pontano (1426–1503) pursued a political career in the service of an Italian potentate. A native of Cerreto di Spoleto, a charming hilltop village in the Umbrian valley of the river

Nera, Pontano moved to Naples in 1454, where he progressed through the ranks to the eminent position of secretary and minister of the Aragonese kings (1486). His political career came to an end in the aftermath of the French conquest (and subsequent loss) of Naples in 1494–95. Thus unburdened of the heavy duties of a busy court, Pontano was free to channel all his energies into literary activity. He would survive the demise of his office for only eight years. Yet the quantity and quality of the work he produced during this period outclassed his previous and by no means irrelevant production, and remained unequalled among the humanists of his time.[13] Long after Pontano's death his sometime pupil and friend Iacopo Sannazaro still remembered the old man bustling with daimonic energy while showing indignation at his younger colleagues' apathy. 'When dear old Pontano wanted to challenge us while he was putting forth verse after verse, he was wont to say: "You men of straw, and what are *you* doing?"'.[14]

Pontano's prodigious activity as witnessed by his contemporaries receives further confirmation from the available manuscript evidence. Many works he had drafted in the 1460s were brought to maturity and saw the public light no earlier than the following century after undergoing substantial changes and frequent restyling. The chronology of such revisional work is not always known or clear; it is therefore difficult to ascertain the dating of any specific attention Pontano may have devoted to classical myths in general and to the myth of Adonis in particular.[15] Allusions to Adonis detectable in the 'earlier' sections of such works as *De amore coniugali* (*On Marital Love*, 1467–84, rev. 1490s) and *Eridanus* (1482–84, rev. 1490s), appear to be rather conventional, as Adonis tends there to conform to his usual background role of Venus' lover.[16] Conversely, some of the shorter poems collected under the titles of *Tumuli* (*Tombs*, viz. 'Epitaphs') and *Iambici* (*Iambic poems*), datable with good approximation to the last decade of the fifteenth century, suggest that by this time Pontano had come to explore a different aspect of the same myth. The imagery dominating the *Tumuli* is one of pathetic contrast between the graves as symbols of the soulless coldness of death and the plants beside them as tokens of perpetually renewable life.[17] In the *Iambici* the ephemeral life of flowers and herbs is compared with the longer and only apparently happier life of human beings, who are nevertheless denied the privilege of a new birth.[18] Such moving variations on the ancient theme of death affecting the whole of the human race, yet sparing plants (no matter how humble) which are bound to revive at every spring, show Pontano a keen reader of Hellenistic bucolic poetry, where such a theme is closely associated with the Adonis myth. They also denote an attention to what the ancients called 'the gardens of Adonis' — pots where fragile herbs were grown, only to wither rapidly under the unrelenting summer sunbeams in resemblance of the young hero's premature fate.[19]

When put in relation to these ancient sources, a chronology of Pontano's readings can perhaps be established on relatively firmer ground. Eighteen idylls by Theocritus, including Idyll 15 on the *Adoniazusae*, had been published for the first time in Milan in 1480. Shortly afterwards Pontano spent a period of two years in Ferrara (1482–84), where, in the circle of Battista Guarino, Theocritean poetry had been fashionable for over twenty years.[20] A further crucial moment for the growing popularity of the Greek Bucolics came in 1495, when the first printed edition of the *Corpus Theocriteum* appeared in Venice from the workshop of Aldo Manuzio with a dedication to Guarino, Manuzio's old teacher. It included amongst others Theocritus 15, the Anacreontic poem *The Dead Adonis* on the guilty boar put under trial by Venus (often ascribed, though not by Manuzio, to Theocritus), Bion's *Lament for Adonis*, and ps.-Moschus' thematically related *Lament for Bion* (as of anonymous in the Aldine print).[21] The following passage from the *Lament for Bion* in particular must have proved inspirational for Pontano:

> Alas, when in the garden wither the mallows, the green celery, and the luxuriant curled anise, they live again thereafter and spring up another year; but we men, we that are tall and strong, we that are wise, when once we die, unhearing sleep in the hollow earth, a long sleep without end or wakening. Lapped in silence therefore will thou lie beneath the ground [...]. (98–105, trans. by Gow).[22]

Clearly reminiscent of this old song is Pontano's dirge for the death of his son Lucius in 1498:

> Foliis quid heu, amarace, heu quid floribus
> Nudata squales maestula? Heu quid languida
> Arentibus comis et horrido sinu,
> lugubri amictu fles, misella amarace?
> [...]
> Deest enim, te qui rigabat [...]
> His tu viresces et novam indues comam,
> beata amarace, foliis novis, novo
> amictu; at ego senex subarescam miser
> umore vacuus [...].[23] (*Iambici*, 5.1–21)

> [Alas, why, amaracus, why, alas, are you languishing, sad and barren of your leaves and flowers? Why, alas, are you crying, your foliage withered, your bosom barren, in such mournful fashion, sad little amaracus? [...] He who used to water you is now gone [...] You will live again with a new crown, happy amaracus, with new leaves and a new attire; but I, poor old man, emptied of my vital sap, I shall wither [...].]

The fragile and now untended plant of marjoram (*amaracus*), dried up by the heat after the death of the poet's son had interrupted its watering, bears a revealing likeness to the herbs of the gardens of Adonis.[24]

The Solar Myth of Adonis in Pontano's *Urania*

At the turn of the new century it became clear that Pontano's curiosity for the Adonis myth had increased over the years, as Adonis features in two of the three poems posthumously published by Aldo Manuzio in 1505, *Urania* and *De hortis Hesperidum libri duo* [*Two Books on the Garden of the Hesperides*].[25]

Conceived shortly after 1469 and progressively expanded, *Urania* was declared ready for the press more than thirty years later, when Pontano gave his friend Suardino Suardo permission to supervise its printing in Venice.[26] The poem represents the culmination of an illustrious tradition started off by Poggio's rediscovery of

Manilius' *Astronomica* in 1417 and continued by one of Pontano's mentors, Lorenzo Bonincontri, who exercised a lasting influence upon his pupil. Bonincontri's poem *Rerum naturalium et divinarum sive de rebus coelestibus libri tres* [*Three Books on Natural and Divine, that is, Celestial Matters*] provided a much-admired model for the future author of *Urania*,[27] and the editorial work done by Bonincontri for the 1484 Roman edition of Manilius proved of such quality as to win the praise of no less demanding a critic than A. E. Housman.[28] Pontano on his part considered *Urania* his most challenging poetic enterprise, so much so that he came to be regularly associated with it in the mind of his admirers.[29] Manuzio, while soliciting the privilege of being Pontano's publisher, hailed the poem as 'a divine piece'.[30] Pontano's long-time friend and posthumous editor, Pietro Summonte, writing to Manuzio about his own editorial plans in Naples, promised to leave *Urania* for Manuzio to publish 'as a work of paramount importance',[31] and in dedicating to Sannazaro his edition of Pontano's lyrics openly declared *Urania* to stand at the summit of his late friend's production.[32]

Both Manilius' *Astronomica* and Pontano's *Urania* share an equal number of books as well as a broadly similar subject matter, even though the latter never gets quite as technical as the former.[33] *Urania* deals with three main topics: the planets (Book 1), the fixed stars (Books 2–4), and the stars as patrons of the various regions and peoples of the Earth (Book 5). In Book 1 the author proceeds to describe the celestial bodies according to the traditional Ptolemaic sequence: the Moon, Mercury, Venus, the Sun. After a series of myths connected with the sun-god Apollo two short digressions follow, designed to highlight the relations of both Mercury and Venus with the Sun.[34] The transition between the two episodes is secured by one of those thematic links that readers of Ovid's *Metamorphoses* are able to recognize at once.[35] Following Macrobius, and indeed Ovid,[36] Pontano claims that Argos is the sky and that its hundred eyes are the stars, which are bound to die out when the rising sun-god Apollo vanquishes them with his radiant light (*Phoebo exoriente [...] candenti lampade victa | emoriuntur*, 1. 471–73). The hint to an image of death evoked by the catch-word *emoriuntur* ['they die out'], combined with the subsequent echoing of a line from Ovid's *Ars amatoria* (*Nec te praetereat Veneri ploratus Adonis*, 1. 75: 'You won't omit to remember Adonis, bewailed by Venus'), offers the prompting for the mournful story of the young hero.

> Nec deploratum Veneri linquamus Adonim,
> Venantem quem durus aper sub dente peredit.
> Non illum fontes nec amici flumina Nili
> infletum voluere. (*Urania*, 1. 474–77)

[Let us not forget Adonis, bewailed by Venus, devoured by the cruel boar's tusk while hunting. Neither did the springs nor the waters of the friendly Nile wish to leave him unlamented.]

The lines that follow present a female figure that looks like an artful combination of Venus, Nature and Mother Earth, shedding tears on the untimely death of her paramour. For seven full days, urged by their irrepressible grief, the swollen river joins her in mourning by flooding the neighbouring countryside and laying waste of plants, animals and human beings alike. Trees and shrubs, too, lament Adonis' lot, and the myrtle sacred to Venus strives in vain to follow the funeral procession by repeatedly and pathetically stretching its branches.

> Ter myrtus conata sequi miserabile funus,
> Ter radice retenta sua est, ter brachia flexit,
> Ter frustra lentos conata est flectere ramos. (*Urania*, I. 485–87)

> [Thrice did the myrtle attempt to follow the sad funeral, thrice was it held back by its roots; thrice did it stretch its arms, and thrice it attempted to flex its pliant branches in vain.]

This image, too, stems from Ovid — it harks back to the plants drawn from their roots by Orpheus' song in *Met*. X. 86–105.[37] But the threefold iteration recalls further Ovidian and Virgilian passages, and the resulting effect is one of sophisticated mosaic-like design. The myrtle stretching its branches is an imitation of Medea stretching her arms to the stars (*Met*. VII. 188–89: 'sidera sola micant: ad quae *sua bracchia tendens*, | *ter* se convertit, *ter* [...]'). Also Ovidian is the construction *ter conata* followed by the bisyllable infinitive of a deponent verb, *sequi* in Pontano, *loqui* in Ovid (*Met*. XI. 419: '*ter conata loqui, ter* fletibus ora rigavit'; *Her*. 4. 7–8: '*Ter* tecum *conata loqui ter* inutilis haesit | lingua [...]'). Virgilian, as well as Ovidian, is the triple vain attempt, made especially memorable by two famous lines occurring twice in the *Aeneid*: '*ter conatus* ibi collo dare *bracchia* circum; | *ter frustra* comprensa manus effugit imago' (*Aen*. II. 792–93 and VI. 700–01) — both referring to the shades of deceased persons (Creusa and Dido), and therefore thematically appropriate in a funeral context.

Yet the main novelty deriving from Pontano's combinatory technique resides in those stretched branches which, as is successively made clear, are but the shrub's longer shadows cast by the gradually receding autumn sunlight. The death of Adonis is presented here as the progressive disappearance of the sun from the autumn and winter horizon; so that Pontano's narrative is in this respect an elegant re-phrasing in smooth hexameters of the allegory expounded at length and with characteristic slow pace by Macrobius in his *Saturnalia*. There Adonis stands allegorically for the sun, the killing boar for winter, and Venus for the earth's boreal hemisphere, 'going into mourning [in Macrobius' own words] when the sun, in the course of its yearly progress through the series of the twelve signs, proceeds to enter the sector of the lower hemisphere'.[38]

Macrobius had interpreted the Adonis myth as an allegory for vegetal regeneration in harmony with the changing of the seasons, while suggesting a comparison between Adonis and the Egyptian god Osiris (as well as Attis): which is essentially what Pontano also does.[39] Yet Macrobius was not a source Pontano would be comfortably ready to acknowledge. Macrobian prose offended his finely tuned humanist ear, for it combined a lack of linguistic and stylistic refinement with inappropriate sententious tones in Virgilian matters. How dared that barbarian, born under distant skies and unable to express himself in acceptable Latin, pass judgment *tanquam praetor*, like a magistrate, on the greatest of all Roman poets?[40] Moreover, because of his frequent use of Greek, Macrobius was likely to be implicitly ascribed by Pontano — as he would later by Erasmus — to the unflattering category of *graeculi*.[41] Pontano was therefore willing to improve on his source, and no one was better qualified than he to perform the job. The old Senecan ideal of allusive as well as elusive imitation, according to which references to one's sources were to be made palatable yet not immediately recognizable even for a highly perceptive reader, had already and very effectively been adopted and promoted by Petrarch, and was now being further refined by Pontano, who was genuinely believed by his contemporaries to embody the humanistic ideal of the 'Poet as Proteus', *Poëta Proteus alter*, graced by an uncanny ability to re-adapt metamorphically, and even excel, his own models.[42]

The effectiveness of Pontano's technique may be appreciated from the way in which he transformed Macrobius' account of Venus recovering from the sad winter months.

> Sed cum sol emersit ab inferioribus partibus terrae, vernalisque aequinoctii transgreditur fines augendo diem: tunc est Venus laeta, et pulchra virent arva segetibus, prata herbis, arbores foliis. (*Saturnalia*, I. 21. 6)

> [But when the sun has come up from the lower parts of the earth and has crossed the boundary of the spring equinox, giving length to the day, then Venus is glad and fair to see, the fields are green with growing crops, the meadows with grass and the trees with leaves.] (trans. by P. V. Davies)

> Ac ueluti uirgo, absenti cum sola marito
> Suspirat sterilem lecto traducere uitam
> Illius expectans complexus anxia caros,
> Ergo, ubi sol imo uictor conuertit ab Austro,
> Tum grauidos aperitque sinus et caeca relaxat
> Spiramenta, nouas ueniat qua succus in haerbas,
> Et tandem complexa suum laetatur Adonim. (*Urania*, I. 500–06)

> [But like a maiden that has been waiting anxiously for the affectionate embrace of her absent man, while sighing and leading a lonely and sterile life on her bridal bed, then, as soon as the victorious sun rises above the southern horizon, she opens up her florid bosom, and unlocks her inner pores, and lets the life juice flow into the tender blades, rejoicing at last in the arms of her Adonis.]

The stock of Macrobius' dreary prose is revived by Pontano's grafting onto it the striking Virgilian image *et caeca relaxat | Spiramenta, nouas ueniat qua succus in haerbas* ['[the Earth] unlocks her inner pores, whereby the sap flows into the tender blades'], which is lifted verbatim from *Georgics* I. 89–90, but not without a twist. In Virgil the picture is one of rustic vividness, referring as it does to the soil releasing its secluded humidity when stubble is burnt in the fields. In *Urania* those very words are dexterously made to convey a description of the Great Mother in Cytherean attire, with her sensuous body being gradually resuscitated by the warmth of spring for a glorious celebration of Nature's regenerative powers.

The Garden of the Hesperides: Adonis as Citrus Tree

In one of his last great works written at the cusp of the new century, *De hortis Hesperidum sive de cultu citriorum libri duo* [*The Garden of the Hesperides, or The Cultivation of Orange Trees, in Two Books*], Pontano came up with yet another re-interpretation of the Adonis myth. The subtitle of the work is misleading, as the poem in fact deals with the cultivation of three different varieties of citrus trees — oranges (the 'sour' variety, bot. *Citrus aurantium*), citrons (bot. *Citrus medica*) and lemons (bot. *Citrus limonum*).[43] The title contains an allusion to the mythical garden situated in the African Atlas, where golden apples were grown under the surveillance of a dragon and three nymphs, the Hesperides. The raiding of the Garden of the Hesperides had constituted the eleventh labour of Hercules, who after killing the dragon had carried the precious fruits off with him to Greece.[44] With characteristic boldness, Pontano disallowed the classical myth and turned it into an *aition* intended to explain the presence of citrus trees on the Neapolitan shore. He declared their extraordinary fruits to be the genuine issue of the mythical golden apples of the Hesperides, and their noblest variety, the orange, the plant in which Adonis had been transformed after succumbing to the fury of the boar. This matter Pontano poured into the mould of a didactic poem on husbandry in emulation of Virgil's *Georgics*.

Competition with the ancients was once again the main driving force behind Pontano's accomplishment.[45] More specifically, two passages from Virgil's *Georgics* must have played a decisive role in motivating his emulative approach. Virgil had famously declared that he was leaving orchards for others to sing (*Georg.* IV. 144–48). In fulfilment of such auspices, Columella had already responded by producing the tenth book of his *De re rustica* in hexameters — where, however, citrus trees are not mentioned; nor are they recorded in the anonymous treatise *De arboribus liber*, traditionally ascribed to Columella and transmitted by manuscripts and early editions together with his *De re rustica*.[46] Furthermore, Virgil's invitation was presumably read by Pontano in the light of another passage from the *Georgics*, where the citron or Median tree — the only known variety of citrus in antiquity — is mentioned (II. 126–35). In it, Virgil claims that the tree producing the 'Median apples' is worth being compared with the bay tree, for which it could easily be mistaken were it not for its scent.

This was an enticing, but also problematic passage, as ancient readers already knew. Servius thought the tree to which Virgil was referring was not a citron tree.[47] Virgil's comparison is in fact inaccurate, as it is based on a misunderstanding (presumably generated by a corrupt reading) of a passage from Theophrastus' *Historia plantarum* (IV. 4. 2), the work on which the Roman poet depended for most of his botanical information. Virgil may have never seen a citron tree after all — and Renaissance readers were quick to realize that.[48] Whether Pontano also identified Virgil's blunder remains a matter open to debate. He certainly was aware of what the Elder Pliny had stated, viz., that even citron trees had only been familiar to the Romans as pot plants imported from Media (*Hist. nat.* XII. 7. 14–16). Another source with which he was undoubtedly familiar, namely Macrobius, had reported from Oppius' lost work *De silvestribus arboribus* [*On Woodland Trees*] the distinction between a variety of citron trees (*citrea malus*) that grew in Italy and another, called 'Persian [tree]' (*Persica [malus]*), which grew in Media (*Sat.* III. 19. 3–5) — unless the latter was recognized as a mere peach tree. At all events, the ancient sources confirmed the ancients' ignorance of the most valuable varieties of citrus trees, that is to say oranges and lemons, introduced in the West by the Arabs during the Middle Ages.[49] But on top of everything stood the intriguing suggestion, made by no lesser author than Virgil, that citrus trees could be compared with, and therefore be a match for, bay trees. There was enough scope for Pontano to add an original chapter to the Virgilian topic of orchards — also considering the renewed preoccupation with the aesthetic qualities of country life that characterized the second half of the Italian Quattrocento, and inspired in literature a vigorous revival of the georgic and bucolic genres.[50]

Not unlike other georgic poets like Hesiod, Virgil, Columella, Walahfrid Strabo and Petrarch, Pontano was himself a passionate gardener and an accomplished agronomist, who enjoyed busying himself with his orchard on the hill of Antignano overlooking the bay of Naples. It is therefore legitimate to ask of him the same question that R. A. B. Mynors once asked of Virgil: 'How much about husbandry did he already know?'[51] The answer is easily provided. The *Horti Hesperidum* delivers not just first-rate Latin poetry but also detailed accounts of specific cultivation techniques, and even some little jewels like, for instance, what looks like one of the first allusions to 'sweet oranges' or *portogalli*, thus named after the Portuguese crew of Vasco de Gama that first came upon them (*Hort. Hesp.* 1. 343–63).[52] The 'sweet orange' (bot. *Citrus sinensis*) is the tree, then still unknown to the Western world, from which all the currently commercialized varieties of orange derive.[53] News of its discovery was propagated in private letters by members of Vasco de Gama's crew on their return home in 1499.[54] When one year later Pontano announced in a letter to the future dedicatee that the poem was finished and only in need of some polish, the passage on the sweet oranges may have been already there.[55] At any rate it must have been inserted before Pontano's death, which occurred in 1503. The *Horti Hesperidum* is among the earliest texts, almost certainly the first published text in verse, to report on the existence of the newly discovered variety of oranges.[56]

Had Pontano any direct predecessor for this unusual reformulation of the Adonis myth? A revealing source may emerge one day showing him in significant debt to previous authors. In the current state of affairs, however, a comparable equivalent is still to be identified. Given Pontano's fondness for literary cross-contamination, one is tempted to surmise that he devised his topic independently through his usual blend of ancient and modern sources.

One thing is certain — Pontano did take pride in the originality of his own approach to the matter. In a passage of his dialogue *Aegidius* (last revised 1501 or later), the then still unpublished *Horti Hesperidum* is introduced as an object of admiration on the part of contemporary scholars.[57] One of the characters in the dialogue, Hieronymus Carbo (Girolamo Carbone), asks for the opinion of another interlocutor, Puccius (Francesco Pucci), about the topic of didactic poetry. Puccius obliges by citing Virgil, Columella, and Lucretius, as well as expanding on the Virgilian and Lucretian masterful 'art of beginning'.[58] At this point Hieronymus incidentally voices his expectation on Pontano's forthcoming poem 'on the nature of oranges, on the rarity of such trees and cultivation thereof, which nobody has [yet] put on record' (*a nemine tradito*). The absolute novelty of the subject matter is further confirmed by another interlocutor, Thamyras (Piero Tamira), as well as Puccius.[59] The interesting element here is that both Thamyras and Puccius are purposely called upon in their role as pupils of two great humanistic schools, Pomponio Leto's in Rome and Poliziano's in Florence respectively. Both of them attest to their teachers' omission in dealing with oranges while commenting on the crucial passage of *Georgics*, II. 126–35:[60] a statement that can be easily confirmed through direct scrutiny of the texts in question. Neither Leto's commentary on the *Georgics*, elaborated in the years 1469–71 and published for the first time in an unauthorized edition at Brescia in 1490, nor Poliziano's unpublished lecture notes for the course on the *Georgics*, which the humanist had delivered in the Florentine Studio in 1483–84, contain any reference to orange trees.[61]

Pontano's self-reference in *Aegidius* betrays the highly erudite nature of his endeavour, performed in competition with not just poets but also scholars. That of amalgamating citrus trees, the Hesperides and the Adonis myth into one single narrative was undoubtedly a brilliant idea; its originality and complexity, however, suggests that it must have dawned on him only gradually. Even the association of citrus fruits with the fabulous golden apples of the Garden of the Hesperides was far from being straightforward. In his *De re rustica* (II. 1. 6–7), Varro had offered an allegorical interpretation of the 'golden apples' (*aurea mala*) of the Hesperides as 'sheep' — by proposing the etymological reading of Lat. *mala* < Gr. μῆλα ('sheep'). In the works of Lucretius, Virgil, and Ovid, the *aurea mala* or *aurea poma* of the Hesperides were (and are) commonly understood to be not citrons but rather quinces.[62] Pontano seems to have shared the same belief at first, for in *De amore coniugali* II. 4. 14, *aurea mala* does not stand for citrus fruits but for small apples called *azariole*.[63] In that very same poem Venus and Adonis are exposed as the cause of moral corruption among mankind after all the other gods had abandoned the Earth dominated by vice (II. 4. 63–70 — a transparent imitation of the Astraea episode in Ovid, *Met*. I. 149–50). It thus appears that this piece is likely to represent a phase prior to Pontano's interest in the Macrobian interpretation of Adonis, as well as the myth of the Hesperides.[64]

Citrus trees and the Garden of the Hesperides could be correlated on the assumed authority of several later Latin and Greek authors, like the Elder Pliny (*Hist. nat.* V. 1. 12; XIII. 29. 91), Martial (XIV. 89), and Athenaeus (*Deipn*. III. 83 a–d)[65] — an authority, however, riddled with uncertainties. There existed a terminological confusion between Lat. *citrus* ('citron' and/or '[Atlas] cedar') and *cedrus* ('cedar', 'juniper'), and among Gr. κίτριον/κίτρεον ('citron'), κέδριον ('juniper-berry') and κέδρος ('cedar tree').[66] Although denounced by Athenaeus at *Deipn*. III. 84c–d, such confusion perpetuated itself throughout the Middle Ages: the alternation of variant readings like *cetrus/cedrus/citrus* in medieval manuscripts of ancient Latin works is revealing enough, and doubly confusing when occurring in works to which people confidently turned to obtain reliable factual information, like e.g. the Elder Pliny's *Natural History*.[67] Moreover, ever since the Middle Ages one single term (*cedro*) has been used in the Italian vernacular to designate the citron tree and its fruit, as well as the cedar tree. The location of the wonderful trees and fruits, too, was uncertain. In Athenaeus' dialogue the character maintaining that the Africans call 'the apples of Hesperia [...] citrons' is immediately silenced by his opponent who points to Theophrastus (*Hist. plant.* IV. 4. 2) as proof that citrons originated from the East, namely from Media and Persia, and not from the West.[68] A further reference to the western regions of northern Africa may have reached Pontano via the Greek–Latin Glossaries and *Hermeneumata*, which in different versions circulated widely in fifteenth-century classrooms and provided young pupils with the earliest rudiments of Greek.[69] Terms like *citrium*, *citrum* are there consistently translated as εσπερις, εσπεριον or suchlike (< Gr. ἕσπερος, Lat. *vesper* 'evening', 'West').[70] This would have easily authorized etymological word-play on Hesperides as well as Hesperia, one of Italy's traditional names in antiquity, and of course on *Hesperus* as 'the evening star', viz., the planet Venus. Finally, in yet another source — Antonio Mancinelli's commentary on Virgil's *Bucolics*, read in the Roman Studio in 1486–87 and first published in 1490 — etymological word-play seems to have been silently stretched to produce *citereum*, an apparent conflation of *citreum* ('of the citron') and *cythereum* ('Cytherean').[71]

For a humanist such scattered elements were in themselves valuable pieces of rare and remote information, but a poet like Pontano must have cast his eye beyond their informative value, looking forward towards their potential re-use in a literary context. Moving on from the lexical to the narrative level, one realizes that a first hint might have come to him from a mere statement of fact — that a relationship between the Adonis myth and that of the Hesperides, at least by contiguity, already existed in ancient literature. As a keen admirer of Ovid's *Metamorphoses*, Pontano could not have failed to notice that the Adonis episode includes as an inset digression the story of Atalanta and Hippomenes (*Met.* X. 560–707), where the deployment of the apples of the Hesperides constitutes Hippomenes' decisive stratagem for defeating Atalanta in the field race. A further association between the Hesperides and Adonis also existed insofar as their names had been mentioned together by Pliny in connection with the fabulous gardens of old — 'the garden of the Hesperides and of the kings Alcinous and Adonis, and also [the] hanging gardens' of Semiramis (XIX. 19. 49: *Hesperidum hortos ac regum Adonidis et Alcinoi, itemque pensiles*). It was a very well-known statement for anybody fostering an interest in garden cultivation: Pomponio Leto used it to introduce his commentary on Columella's Book X.[72]

But it was one particular detail that made Pontano's association of the Adonis myth with citrus trees not just persuasive but also compelling. The metamorphosis of Adonis as a symbol of life's perpetual renewal was deemed by him to be uniquely enshrined in a distinctive feature of such trees — that of being, in Pontano's own words, 'always graced with new fruits, blossoms and leaves' across the whole year (*Hort. Hesp.* I. 571: *Et fructu felix et flore et fronde recenti*). It was a feature that Theophrastus, Pliny, Solinus, Servius, Palladius, Macrobius and Isidore of Seville had already noticed and recorded when illustrating citron trees.[73] In the medieval and early-modern age similar observations occur — as one would expect — in the work of a famous medieval agronomist like Pietro de' Crescenzi,[74] but also in Boccaccio's *Decameron*, where a garden is described as 'surrounded by most green and luxuriant orange- (*aranci*) and citron-trees (*cedri*), which showed not only flowers but fruits both old and new'.[75] Even more remarkable is the imagery conveyed by a text chronologically close to the *Horti Hesperidum*, the *Hypnerotomachia Poliphili* (1499). There a cloister is said to be adorned 'with admirable citron-, orange- and lemon trees' (*di spectatissimi citri, di naranci et di limoni*), with oranges in particular sporting their 'candid flower' and their 'fruits both ripe and unripened', while in a further passage the same tree varieties border a garden sacred to Venus, notably comprising the sepulchre of Adonis.[76]

The awe-inspired tone of these descriptions shows wonder for a natural phenomenon that seemed to make dreams of a fantasy world concrete. Indeed citrus trees offered a natural equivalent of the fantastic plants in Alcinous' garden that Homer had described at *Odyssey* VII. 113–32:

> But without the courtyard [...] is a great orchard of four acres [...]. Therein grow trees, tall and luxuriant, pears and pomegranates and apple-trees with their bright fruit, and sweet figs, and luxuriant olives. Of these the fruit perishes not nor fails in winter or in summer, but lasts throughout the year; and ever does the west wind, as it blows, quicken to life some fruits, and ripen others; pear upon pear waxes ripe, apple upon apple, cluster upon cluster, and fig upon fig. There, too, is his fruitful vineyard planted, one part of which, a warm spot on level ground, is being dried in the sun, while other grapes men are gathering, and others, too, they are treading; but in front are unripe grapes that are shedding the blossom, and others that are turning purple. [...] Such were the glorious gifts of the gods in the palace of Alcinous. (trans. by A. T. Murray)

The Orange and the Bay Tree

As in *Urania*, transformation of the ancient sources occurs in the *Horti Hesperidum* through 'crossing' at several levels. This is already evident from the organisation of the poem's proemial lines. According to the hierarchy of styles, the *Horti Hesperidum* was supposed to rank well below *Urania*: hence the initial invocation of lesser local deities, such as the water-nymphs (Naiads) and the nymphs of forests (Napaeae) dwelling in the river Sebethus and on the slopes of Mount Vesuvius. But this apparently humbler approach is rapidly subverted by what follows. The name of Virgil, whose tomb tradition has located in nearby Posillipo, is evoked first (*Hort. Hesp.* I. 9); then Urania is introduced as gracefully granting her benevolent patronage to the modern poet (I. 26). At this point a sudden change of tone occurs, and the poet's voice rises to a passionate prayer in characteristic Lucretian style and energy, asking his beloved Muse to assist his enterprise — the celebration of the orange as the noblest among all citrus trees (*citrigenum decus*) and the glory of the Sebethian groves, just like the Phoebian bay tree is the pride of Tempe (I. 30–45).

This declaration is the prelude to an even greater surprise. Orange trees are sacred to Venus, Pontano explains, for this is the plant into which the dead Adonis was converted by the will of the goddess, its ever-present blossoms and fruits being 'a perpetual and sad memento to Venus' grief' (I. 67, *Perpetuum Veneris monumentum at triste dolorum*). No reference is given to any previous mythological tradition. With a single stroke Pontano obliterated the Ovidian version of the myth and replaced it with a brand new *aition* — which he characteristically obtained by borrowing from Ovid himself, for he saw no impediment in drawing on the death of Adonis as narrated in *Met.* x. 708–39 and 'improving' upon his model. If Ovid's Venus had just sprinkled nectar over Adonis' blood, then Pontano's Venus would indulge in a much longer rite, pouring ambrosia over the youth's hair, washing his body, and murmuring unintelligible spells. And while Ovid had had Adonis' blood turned into an anemone, Pontano would rather have the whole body of Adonis turned into a tree, so that the story of the child born of a myrrh tree could come full circle.

> Ambrosio mox rore comam diffundit et unda
> Idalia corpus lauit incompertaque uerba
> Murmurat ore super supremaque et oscula iungit.
> Ambrosium sensit rorem coma, sensit et undam
> Idaliam corpus diuinaque uerba loquentis;
> Haeserunt terrae crines riguitque capillus
> Protenta in radice et recto in stipite corpus,
> Lanugo in teneras abiit mollissima frondes,
> In florem candor, in ramos brachia et ille,
> Ille decor tota diffusus in arbore risit;
> Vulnificos spinae referunt in cortice dentes,
> Crescit et in patulas aphrodisia citrius umbras. (*Hort. Hesp.* I. 77–88)

[She then showers his hair with ambrosia and washes his body with her Idalian wave while murmuring incomprehensible words, and gives him a final kiss. The hair sensed the ambrosian shower, the body sensed the Idalian wave and the words uttered by the goddess; the hair clinged to the soil stretching rigidly into a root, and his body into an upright trunk; his soft body-hair dissolved into tender leaves, his white skin into blossoms, his arms into boughs, and that old grace pervaded the whole tree like a radiant smile. The thorns on the bark reproduce the wound-making teeth, and Venus' orange tree grows casting around its broad shadow.]

The long quotation makes it apparent that for the actual description of Adonis' metamorphosis Pontano did not hesitate to bring in Ovid's most spectacular showpiece, the metamorphosis of Daphne (*Met.* I. 548–56), conveniently and antagonistically rearranged by reversing the original descriptive sequence.[77] Further textual resemblances suggest that the Ovidian transformation of the Heliades (*Met.* II. 343–66) was also drawn upon — no doubt to offer the knowledgeable reader another ably disguised but eventually recognizable source. As for the language, Pontano hardly left a single Ovidian expression untouched, brilliantly and perilously bordering on parody yet never actually crossing over to it. At the sight of such 'wonderful dexterity' (*prodigiosa maestria*), an expert judge like Vladimiro Zabughin was encouraged to declare Pontano's consummate art only comparable to that of Dante's.[78] But Pontano's dexterity was not confined to the language of the ancients. While writing his poems in Latin, he could not resist drawing upon the parallel vernacular tradition — as indeed most neo-Latin poets of the Italian Quattrocento would be wont to do. Once the metamorphosis of Adonis has reached its conclusion, the newly born tree gratefully shakes its top in response to Venus' woeful attentions, and lets its blossoms shower into the goddess's lap:

> Illa uelut dominae luctum solata recentes
> Excussit frondes, resupinaque uertice canos
> Diffudit florum nimbos, quis pectora diuae
> Impleuitque sinum et lacrimas sedauit euntes;
> Exin hesperiis arbor nitet aurea siluis. (*Hort. Hesp.* 1. 97–101)

[As if to comfort its lady in mourning, [the tree] shook its new leaves, and bending its top poured white showers of blossoms into the goddess's bosom and lap, and calmed her flowing tears. Thereafter the golden tree shines amidst the Hesperian groves.]

Readers of Petrarch will not fail to recognize in this passage an allusion to a celebrated scene from his *Rerum vulgarium fragmenta*, where Laura is depicted under a shower of blossoms:

> Da' be' rami scendea
> (dolce ne la memoria)
> una pioggia di fior sovra 'l suo grembo [...]
> (*Rer. vulg. frag.* 126. 40–42)

[A rain of flowers descended (sweet in the memory) from the beautiful branches into her lap [...]]]

Scanty as they may seem, the examples offered in this chapter should help explain why Pontano was felt to be the only modern poet who had genuinely challenged the otherwise undisputed supremacy of the ancients. It comes as no surprise that many of his contemporaries and followers saw in his orange trees, fruits and blossoms the token of a new radiant age for Latin poetry, one that could stand up to classical poetry and to its noblest symbol, the Phoebian bay tree — as indeed Pontano had himself wished (*Hort. Hesp.* 1. 39–42). It is an episode of Renaissance literary history that has strangely gone unnoticed, or perhaps simply misinterpreted as mere ornamental stock-verse, and dismissed accordingly. Yet at a time when the prestige of Latin could still mark an advantage upon the vernacular closing up, it was only natural that some of the foremost Italian poets should decide to produce their ultimate effort for a poem written in the ancient language. Works like Sannazaro's *De partu Virginis* (1526), Girolamo Fracastoro's *Syphilis* (1530), and Marco Girolamo Vida's *Christias* (1530) clearly show that confidence in the power of Latin was still unshaken in the third decade of the sixteenth century. That confidence had in no small part been inspired by Pontano.[79]

The testimony of the Neapolitan Sannazaro deserves to be mentioned first. When in 1501 Sannazaro decided to follow in exile king Frederick of Aragon, he was said to have bid goodbye to Naples and 'its gardens and Hesperides' in elegant Latin distichs while the boat was leaving the harbour, and the moving scene was recorded in Pontano's *Aegidius*.[80] Sannazaro's was no passing fantasy. As late as 1526, when he finally published his eagerly expected poem *De partu Virginis*, readers apprehended from the final lines that the poet's coveted prize for his most ambitious poetic enterprise was nothing but a wreath of Neapolitan — and one could as well say, Pontanian — orange leaves:

> Mergillina, novos fundunt ubi citria flores,
> citria Medorum sacros referentia lucos:
> et mihi non solita nectit de fronde coronam.
> (*De part. Virg.* III. 511–13)

[Mergillina — where orange orchards put forth ever new blossoms, orange orchards that evoke the sacred groves of the Medians — weaves me a crown from unusual leaves.][81]

It was not just Naples that honoured its old *vates* in such guise. While describing Agostino Chigi's Roman residence (now Villa Farnesina) in 1512, Blosius Palladius sang the praises of Pontano's Hesperides as soon as he came across an orange tree in the villa's garden (*Suburbanum Augustini Chisii*, 196–207).[82] Another acknowledged master of Latin verse and one of the beacons of the Roman court, Francesco Maria Molza, devoted one of his elegies (3.2) to Pontano's Hesperides and his new Adonis myth.[83] The Florentine Ludovico Alamanni, on putting out the first georgic poem in any European vernacular (*Della coltivazione libri sei*, first published in 1546 but written over a period of twenty years), referred to the orange as the 'tree [...] descended from Heaven' (*pianta* [...] *che fu trovata in ciel*, v. 674–75), and commiserated the 'uncouth ancient world' for 'having been deprived of so noble a tree' (*O rozza antica età, che fusti priva | Di questo arbor gentil* [...], v. 694–95).[84] More prominent than anyone else in his support of Pontano's new poetry, however, was the Veronese physician and poet Girolamo Fracastoro. In the proemial lines of his aetiological poem and masterpiece, *Syphilis sive De morbo gallico* [*Syphilis, or The French Disease*, 1530], Fracastoro invoked the protection of Pontano's Muse Urania (I. 24–52), and went on honouring Pontano himself (II. 38–49) and his 'Cytherean tree' (*arbor cithereïa*, II. 220), cultivated by Venus in remembrance of her Adonis.[85] Sannazaro's fantasy about a garland weaved with orange leaves had in the very same years grown to be the ambition of many a fellow poet.

Nevertheless, as anticipated at the beginning of this paper, the days of radical innovations and transformations in the realm of ancient lore, of which Pontano had been the most inspiring representative, were to be over soon. Among Pontano's fiercest critics was the humanist and poet Pietro Bembo, who advocated a strict imitation of selected authors both in Latin and the vernacular, and could not therefore share his contemporaries' enthusiasm for Pontano's bold contaminations of sources and re-formulations of ancient myths.[86] When in 1526 Fracastoro asked Bembo to revise a draft version of his *Syphilis*, the latter did praise the former's enterprise, but sharply stigmatized his excessive mythographical inventiveness blaming it on the deleterious examples provided by Pontano:

> I won't say a word about Pontano — for if I were to imitate anything [from his works], I would rather imitate his virtues, not his faults. That habit of his of inventing new myths is so despicable that one can hardly stomach the reading of any of his poems.[87]

Classicizing decorum had by the 1520s begun to hamper the self-assured, uninhibited approach to ancient mythology that had characterized the neo-Latin poetry of the previous century; and Bembo in particular had come to feel more and more uneasy with imitative practices which, by boldly elaborating on the works of both ancient and modern 'classical' authors, produced in his view nothing but an unwelcome sense of stylistic distortion. Moreover, as the champion of that Petrarchism that had by then become the dominating trend of Italian lyric poetry and was about to spread all over Europe, Bembo would have hardly tolerated that the laurel of his beloved Petrarch, as well as of the ancient poets, should give way to Pontano's orange tree.

Notes to Chapter 6

1. For an overview see Alessio (2005).
2. For a thorough survey of the sources and their mutual relations see Roscher (1884–86); Frazer (1919), I, 1–159; Atallah (1966); Ribichini (1981); Tuzet (1987); Reed (1995). For a revision of the traditional approaches to the myth see Detienne (2001).
3. Sappho, *Fragments* 140, 168 and 211; Plato, *Phaedrus*, 276b–277a; Aristophanes, *Pax*, 416–20; *Lysistrata*, 393; Theocritus, 15.
4. Plutarch, *De Iside et Osiride*, 15–17; Pausanias, II. 20. 6; III. 17. 5; Lucian, *De dea Syria*, 6–7; Ammianus Marcellinus, XIX. I. 11, XXII. 9. 15; Macrobius, *Saturnalia*, I. 21; Martianus Capella, II. 191–92. For further significant sources on the cult of Adonis see Roscher (1884–86), cols 73–75.
5. Origen, *Selecta in Ezechielem*, 8 (= *Patrologia Graeca* 13, 797–99); Jerome, *Commentariorum in Ezechielem Prophetam libri quatuordecim*, III. 13–16 (= *Patrologia Latina* 25, 82–84); Cyril of Alexandria, *Commentarius in Isaiam Prophetam*, 18. 1–2 (= *Patrologia Graeca* 70, 440–41).
6. Cf. e.g. Alain de Lille's *Anticlaudianus*, VI. 226, VII. 42–44; John of Garland's *Integumenta Ovidii*, 419–20; Giovanni del Virgilio's commentary on Ovid's *Metamorphoses* (Ghisalberti (1933), pp. 91–92). On the medieval exegesis of Ovid's *Metamorphoses* see Coulson (1991).
7. Jerome, *Epistulae*, 58. 3 (= *Patrologia Latina* 22, 281); *Commentariorum in Ezechielem Prophetam libri quatuordecim*, III. 13 (= *Patrologia Latina* 25, 82: *amasius Veneris*).
8. On Boccaccio's predecessors see Seznec (1953), pp. 167–79; Hankey (1998), pp. 81–94, with bibliography.
9. See Gruppe (1921), pp. 22–26; Seznec (1953), pp. 220–24; Pfeiffer (1976), pp. 20–22; G. Boccaccio, *Genealogie deorum Gentilium*, ed. by V. Zaccaria, 2 vols (Milan: Mondadori, 1998–99), II, 1613; Zaccaria (2001), pp. 112–26.
10. On Statius in the fifteenth century see Reeve (1977). On Statius and fifteenth-century Italian poetry see Tissoni Benvenuti (2000), pp. 5–10; Caruso (1997); on the *Nux* see Jensen (1968).
11. Boccaccio, *Genealogie*, II. 51. Cf. Macrobius, *Sat.* I. 21. Macrobius is listed in the catalogue of the library of Santo Spirito in Florence, which absorbed Boccaccio's *parva libraria*: see Mazza (1966), p. 19.
12. Frazer (1914) and (1919).
13. For Pontano's biography see Pèrcopo (1936–37); Kidwell (1991).
14. Naples, 15(?) April 1521 to Antonio Seripando: 'Il povero Pontano, quando facea versi assai e volea increpitare a noi, dicea: "Uomini di paglia, e voi che fate?"' (I. Sannazaro, *Opere*, ed. by A. Mauro (Bari: Laterza, 1961), p. 387). The anecdote is recalled by Sannazaro in regard with the use of Lat. *increpito* ('I challenge') in his *De partu Virginis* (III. 463), like Virgil (*Aen.* I. 738, X. 900; *Georg.* IV. 138), and unlike the Gospels (Luke 8. 24).
15. On the textual tradition of Pontano's poems see the Introduction to G. Pontano, *Carmina*, ed. by B. Soldati, 2 vols (Florence: Barbèra, 1902–05), I; Dionisotti (2009b); De Nichilo (1975) (1977).
16. Pontano, *Am. Coniug.* II. 4. 63–70 (see also *infra*, p. 256); II. 7. 25–34; *Erid.* I. 28. 1–6; I. 36; I. 39; II. 3; II. 21. 9–12. Cf. also Monti Sabia (1996), discussing and solving the doubts expressed by Parenti (1985), pp. 92–99.
17. On ancient precedents see Forbes Irving (1990), p. 129.
18. Pontano, *Iambici*, 1.17–19, 2.17–20.
19. Plato, *Phaedrus*, 276b. A recent revision of this traditional interpretation has been offered by Dillon (2006).
20. Tissoni Benvenuti (1979).

21. Gow (1952), p. xii.

22. *Theocritus*, edited with a translation and commentary by A. S. F. Gow, 2 vols (Cambridge: Cambridge University Press, 1950), I, 190.

23. For the marjoram (*amaracus*) as a plant sacred to Venus, cf. *Eridanus*, I. 39. 67–68.

24. The wide-ranging surveys of the Greek Bucolics' popularity among modern authors by Mustard (1909) (1918) strangely ignored Pontano. A double variation on Bion's theme of the anemone born of Venus' tears and the rose of Adonis' blood (*Lament for Adonis*, 64–68) occurs in Pontano's *Eridanus*, I. 36 and I. 39, both of uncertain dating. At Ps.-Moschus' *Lament for Bion*, 80–84, Venus is said to long more for Bion than for the kiss she 'printed on Adonis' dying lips'. On the revival of pastoral poetry in the early Italian Renaissance see Carrara (1936), chapters III and IV; Grant (1965); Carrai (1998).

25. The Manutian edition includes the *Meteororum libri* as well, and constitutes the first neo-Latin collection of didactic poetry to appear in print: cf. Ludwig (1982), pp. 151–52.

26. Naples, 31 December 1502, to Suardino Suardo, in Pontano (1948), p. 461: 'Possete attendere ad la stampa de la *Urania* liberamente' ['You may start the printing of *Urania*']. Cf. Pontano, *Carmina*, pp. xxv–xxxv; Soldati (1986), p. 260; De Nichilo (1975), pp. 11–12.

27. Soldati (1986), chapters I–IV. Manilius' *Astronomica* features in the short and presumably incomplete list of Pontano's books (Pèrcopo (1936–37), pp. 246–47). On Bonincontri, who lived in Naples from 1450 to 1475, see Soldati (1986), chapters II–III; Grayson (1970).

28. On Bonincontri's edition of Manilius (Rome 1484) see Sabbadini (1899), pp. 110–14; Reeve (1986), pp. 236 and 238. Housman had no direct access to it, but saw a selection of Bonincontri's valuable emendations in the apparatus of a late sixteenth-century edition and had words of commendation for them, while lamenting that 'Scaliger and Bentley and the modern editors [had] unduly neglected [them]' (1937), I, p. xii. On another contemporary and highly influential astrological poet, Basinio Basini of Parma, see Soldati (1986), chapter I; Campana (1962) (1965).

29. A medal by Adriano Fiorentino, struck not long after 1500, shows Pontano on the obverse, and Urania on the reverse holding a globe and a lyre (reproduced in Nicolini (1925), p. 167, and in Kidwell (1991), p. 313). In the fresco portrait painted in 1536 in the town hall of Cerreto, the poet's birthplace, Pontano is sitting at his desk drafting his verses while Urania crowns him with laurel (reproduced in Kidwell (1991), p. 299).

30. Manuzio in the dedication of his Statius (August–November 1502) to Pontano. Cf. Giovanni Pontano, *Carmina*, ed. by J. Oeschger (Bari: Laterza, 1948), p. 459; *Aldo Manuzio editore. Dediche, prefazioni, note ai testi*, ed. by G. Orlandi, intro. by C. Dionisotti, 2 vols (Milan: Il Polifilo, 1975), I, 62: 'diuinum illud opus tuum' ['that divine poem of yours'].

31. Naples, 29 August 1505: 'riseruando pur ad uoi la *Urania* come cosa maiore' (Pontano, *Carmina*, ed. Oeschger, p. 464). On the transactions between Summonte and Manuzio see Monti Sabia (1969); on Summonte as editor, see Monti Sabia (1985).

32. Pontano, *Carmina*, ed. by Oeschger, p. 469: 'Quis hunc putet a *Naeniolis* illis depressisque versiculis ad *Uraniae* gradatim sublimitatem ascendisse?' ['Who would have thought that he could gradually ascend from those pretty *Lullabies* and humble little pieces to the sublime heights of *Urania*?'].

33. *Urania*'s books were originally four, until the structure of the poem was revised again in 1496 (De Nichilo (1975), pp. 25–26). Firmicus Maternus' *Stromata* also played an inspiring role: see Soldati (1986), p. 244; Rinaldi (2002) (2003).

34. The rubrics read 'De Mercurio et Argo' (*Ur.* I. 464–73) and 'De Adonide et Venere' (*Ur.* 1.474–506).

35. See e.g. the theme of blood linking the successive episodes of the Iron Age, Astraea, the Giants, Lycaon and Caesar, in *Met.* I. 149, 157, 162, 201, 235. On Ovid's presence in *Urania* see Tateo (1995).

36. Macrobius, *Sat.* I. 19. 12, 14, based on Ovid, *Met.* I. 720–21.

37. The myrtle (*bicolor myrtus*, *Met.* x. 98) is among the plants mentioned by Ovid as moving towards Orpheus; Pontano's motionless myrtle seems to emphasize by contrast the finality of death. It is worth remembering that the Adonis episode is also located in *Met.* x.

38. Macrobius, *Sat.* I. 21. 1: 'lugens [...] dea, quod sol annuo gressu per duodecim signorum ordinem pergens partem quoque hemisphaerii inferioris ingreditur, quia de duodecim signis zodiaci sex superiora sex inferiora censentur'.

39. Macrobius, *Sat.* I. 21. 11: 'For it is no secret that Osiris is none other than the sun and Isis, as we have said, none other than the earth or world of nature, and the explanation which applies to the rites of Adonis and Attis is applicable also to the Egyptian rites, to account for the alternation of sorrow and joy which accompany in turn the phases of the year' ('Nec in occulto est neque aliud esse Osirin quam solem, nec Isin aliud esse quam terram, ut diximus, naturamve rerum: eademque ratio, quae circa Adonin et Attinem vertitur, in Aegyptia quoque religione luctum et laetitiam vicibus annuae administrationis alternat').

40. Pontano, *Antonius*, in G. Pontano, *Dialoghi*, ed. by C. Privitera. Edizione critica (Florence: Sansoni, 1943), pp. 75–76. Foreign origin and linguistic inability had been admitted by Macrobius himself in *Sat.* Praef. I. 11.

41. Cf. Erasmus, *Ciceronianus*, in *Opera omnia*, 10 vols (Leyden: Petrus van der Aa, 1703–1706), I, col. 1007A (Philoponus speaking): '[Macrobius] sua lingua non loquitur, & si quando loquitur, Graeculum Latine balbutire credas' ['He doesn't speak with his own voice; and if ever he does, you may well believe it's some poor Greek stammering in Latin'] (trans. by B. I. Knott).

42. Parenti (1985), pp. 8–11. On Seneca's much-quoted passage on 'honey-making' as a metaphor for eclectic imitation (*ad Luc.* 84) see Petrarch, *Fam.* 23.19, and also the less frequently cited Macrobius, *Sat.* VI. 1. 6 and v. 16. 12 (as suggested by Cadili (2001), p. 10). On the art of literary allusion see Pasquali (1994), II, 275–82; Conte (1996).

43. Many critics have reported confusedly on this matter. In the dedicatory epistle of Pontano's *Opera* (May–August 1505) to Johannes Collauer, Aldo Manuzio omits lemons: 'Delectabunt [te] *horti Hesperidum* citriorum et citrorum cultu peruario' ['With its description of the varied cultivation of oranges and citrons, the *Horti Hesperidum* will delight you'], in Pontano, *Carmina*, ed. by Oeschger, p. 467; *Aldo Manuzio*, 1975, I, 90. Grant (1965), p. 59, omits citrons, while Zabughin (2000), II, 76–77, only mentions *cedri* ('citrons'), and so do Rossi (1938), p. 486; Pèrcopo (1936–1937), II, 117–22; Monti Sabia in Arnaldi, Monti Sabia, Gualdo Rosa (1964), p. 780; De Nichilo (1977), pp. 225, 245. Kidwell (1991), p. 295, vaguely refers to 'a citrus tree'. All varieties are correctly identified by Roscoe (1805), IV, 91; Soldati (1986), p. 271; Lanza (1930), p. 8; Floridia (1936), pp. 26–27, 71–72; Ludwig (1982), p. 151; Calabrese (2004), p. 24. The distinction between *citrius* ('orange') and *citrus* ('citron') is explicitly made by Pontano at *Hort. Hesp.* II. 180–95, and emphasized by the marginal rubric 'Quo differat citrius a citro' ['In what respect the orange differs from the citron']. Contemporary authors may occasionally use a different terminology: cf. e.g. Celio Calcagnini's *De citrio, cedro et citro commentatio*, dedicated to the famous physician and botanist Antonio Musa Brasavola, where *citrius* stands for the orange tree, and *cedrus* and *citrus* for two different varieties of cedar tree (C. Calcagnini, *Opera aliquot* (Basel: Froben, 1544), pp. 479–83). In the popular Byzantine collection of treatises on agriculture known as *Geoponica*, Gr. κίτριον is used for 'citron' (*Geop.* x. 7. 8): cf. Rodgers (2002), p. 167. See in general Olck (1899) and the chapter on 'Agrumi' in Hehn (1911), pp. 442–56; (1885), pp. 329–39.

44. For the variants of the myth see Seeliger (1886–90).

45. See *Hort. Hesp.* 1.9, where Virgil's shade is evoked, and *Aegidius*, in Pontano, *Dialoghi*, pp. 260–61, for Pontano's comparison between his own *Horti Hesperidum* and Virgil's *Georgics*. On the revival of didactic poetry in humanistic circles see Ludwig (1982). On the composition and textual tradition of the *Horti Hesperidum* see Soldati's Introduction to Pontano, *Carmina*, I; De Nichilo (1977).

46. On the popularity of the *Georgics* and of Columella's Tenth Book in fifteenth-century Italy see below, footnote n. 50. See also the Introduction to L. Iuni Moderati Columellae *Res Rustica*. Incerti auctoris *Liber de arboribus*, ed. by R. H. Rodgers (Oxford: Clarendon Press, 2010).

47. Servius, *In Georg.* II. 131.

48. Thomas (1988), I, 179; Mynors (1994), pp. 117–18; Olck (1899), col. 2613. The problem was e.g. identified and discussed in the commentary on Dioscorides by the sixteenth-century botanist Pietro Andrea Mattioli, *I discorsi [...] nelli sei libri di Pedacio Dioscoride Anazarbeo della materia Medicinale*, 5 vols (Venice: Vincenzo Valgrisi, 1568), I, 268.

49. Cf. Poliziano's commentary on Virgil, *Georg.* II. 126–27 (in Angelo Poliziano, *Commento inedito alle Georgiche di Virgilio*, ed. by L. Castano Musicò (Florence: Olschki, 1990), pp. 106–09) for a significant overview of what humanist scholarship could achieve when reading and interpreting the Virgilian passage in question. Oranges and lemons were brought to Western Europe from

China and India via Persia by the Arabs (Hehn (1911), pp. 444–45; (1885), pp. 331–32; Olck (1899), col. 2612; Floridia (1936), pp. 15–19, 22, 56–62). It has been suggested that the ancient Romans simply lacked the terminology to distinguish among different types of citrus trees and fruits, and that archaeological evidence from Pompeii, Carthage and the basilica of Santa Costanza in Rome should authorize the view that the ancients cultivated not only citrons but also lemons and oranges (Tolkowsky (1938), pp. 90–100). See however the more prudent opinion of Olck (1899), col. 2612; and of Calabrese (2004), p. 16.

50. See Zabughin (2000), I, 234, 254, on the relevance in this respect of the fifteenth-century Virgilian commentaries by Cristoforo Landino (1424–1492) and Antonio Mancinelli (1452–*c.* 1505). Of Columella's Book X four fifteenth-century commentaries survive today — by Giulio Pomponio Leto, Curio Lancillotto Pasio, Giovanni Battista Cantalicio and Giovan Battista Pio (cf. Brown (1976)). On the effects of this new trend on neo-Latin and vernacular poetry see Caruso (1997); and the collective volumes Carrai (1998); *Letteratura di villa* (2004).

51. Reported by R. G. M. Nisbet in his Preface to Mynors (1994), p. vi.

52. *Portogalli* was the common Italian name for 'oranges' until the early twentieth century (cf. Pasquali (1985), p. 318). Etymologically related forms survive in several southern Italian dialects and in various other languages (notably Greek and Arabic) along the coasts of the eastern Mediterranean.

53. Floridia (1936), pp. 25–26; Calabrese (2004), p. 32. Cf. also Calcagnini, *Opera aliquot*, p. 481. For later testimonies see Floridia (1936), pp. 74–75.

54. A selection of letters by the crew members can be read in Radulet (1994).

55. On the chronology of the composition see De Nichilo (1977), pp. 218–28. Gallesio (1811); Floridia (1936); Tolkowski (1938); and Calabrese (2004): all seem to have by-passed Pontano's reference.

56. Pontano does however refer to both 'sweet' and 'sour' local *citria*, apparently obtained through crossing (*Hort. Hesp.* II. 432–75); see also Floridia (1936), pp. 22, 23, 26–29. Gallesio (1811), pp. 297–322, maintained that the sweet oranges cultivated in Southern Europe during the late Middle Ages had been imported from the East by the Genoese. Tolkowski (1938), p. 238, thought them to be the progeny of those cultivated in the early Christian era, of which however no written record survives (for a discussion of the archaeological evidence see *supra*, footnote n. 49).

57. In *Aegidius* reference is made to the recent death (1501) of Gabriele Altilio, bishop of Policastro: cf. Pontano, *Dialoghi*, p. 255.

58. Pontano, *Dialoghi*, pp. 261–63. The proem of the *Horti Hesperidum* does indeed present a combination of Virgilian and Lucretian elements very skilfully intertwined: see *infra*, p. 263.

59. Pontano, *Dialoghi*, p. 261. On Piero Tamira see Gualdo Rosa and Osmond (2009).

60. Pontano, *Dialoghi*, p. 261.

61. On Leto's commentary on Virgil see Lunelli (1983) (1997); Abbamonte (2004) (2008). Poliziano's commentary remained unpublished until 1990 (cf. Poliziano, *Commento inedito alle Georgiche*).

62. Lucretius, *De rer. nat.* V. 32 (*aureaque Hesperidum [...] fulgentia mala*); Virgil, *Ecl.* 3.71 (*aurea mala*), 6.61 (*Hesperidum [...] mala*); Ovid, *Met.* X. 650 (*aurea poma*). See in general Sargeaunt (1920), p. 75.

63. Text in Pontano, *Carmina*, ed. by Soldati, II, 144; Pontano, *Carmina*, ed. by Oeschger, pp. 156–57; *Poeti latini del Quattrocento*, pp. 478–79.

64. *Poeti latini del Quattrocento*, pp. 478 and 475.

65. Cf. also the three epigrams 'De citro' from the *Codex Salmasianus* (*Anthologia latina*, ed. by A. Riese, 2 vols (Leipzig: Teubner, 1894–1895; 1st edn 1868), I.1, pp. 150–51). For earlier Greek sources not available to Pontano see Olck (1899), col. 2614.

66. Fully discussed by Olck (1899), cols. 2616–17.

67. Cf. e.g. Pliny, *Hist. nat.* V. I. 12 and XIII. 29. 91. Note the repeated attempts made by Ermolao Barbaro in his *Castigationes Plinianae* (1493) to explain the presence of such confusing variant readings in the tradition of Pliny, *Hist. nat.* V. I. 12, XIII. 29. 91, XVI. 26. 66 (E. Barbaro, *Castigationes Plinianae et in Pomponium Melam*, ed. by G. Pozzi, 4 vols (Padua: Antenore, 1973–1979), II, 322, 712; III, 1251).

68. Cf. also Calcagnini, *Opera aliquot*, p. 479. On the reception of Athenaeus in the fifteenth century see Di Lello-Finuoli (2000).

69. On the *Hermeneumata* as a didactic tool for learning Greek in the fifteenth century see Dionisotti

(1982). In his youth Pontano took Greek classes under Gregory Tifernas and George of Trebizond (Pèrcopo (1936–37), p. 125).

70. *Corpus Glossariorum Latinorum*. II. *Glossae Latinograecae et Graecolatinae*, ed. by G. Goetz and G. Gundermann (Leipzig: Teubner, 1888), p. 315 (24); *Corpus Glossariorum Latinorum*. III. *Hermeneumata Pseudodositheana. Accedunt Hermeneumata medicobotanica vetustoria*, ed. by Gustav Goetz (Leipzig: Teubner, 1892), pp. 26 (22), 358 (75), 442 (9), 477 (41), 545 (71).

71. As cited in Zabughin (2000), I, 228. Mancinelli's phrase 'to some of my "citerean" trees' (*meis quibusdam citereis arboribus*) occurs in his note to Virg. *Ecl*. 7.6 (*a frigido vento*). It refers to the damage done by the March and April winds to his own citrus (?) trees, and sounds like a personal response to the line where Meliboeus says that he is constructing a repair to defend myrtles from the cold wintery wind. On Mancinelli see Sabbadini (1877); Zabughin (2000), *ad indicem*; Mellidi (2007).

72. See Brown (1976), pp. 181–84. Note that while the text in the surviving MSS of Leto's commentary reads *Adonis vero regis*, in at least three fifteenth-century printed editions (Venice 1480, Bologna 1494, Reggio Emilia 1499) the text reads *Ante omnes* (or *omnis*) *vero regis*, where the name of Adonis disappears altogether.

73. Theophrastus, *De causis plantarum*, I. 11, I. 18. 5; Pliny, *Hist. nat*. XII. 7. 15; Solinus, *Epit*. 46. 4; Servius, *In Georg*. II.127; Palladius, *Opus agriculturae*, IV. 10. 16; Macrobius, *Sat*. III. 19. 4; Isidore of Seville, *Etym*. XVII. 7. See Hehn (1911), pp. 444–45; (1885), p. 335; Pasquali (1985), p. 317.

74. P. de' Crescenzi, *Ruralia commoda*, ed. by W. Richter and R. Richter-Bergmeier, 2 vols (Heidelberg: Universitätsverlag C. Winter, 1995–98), II, 112.

75. Introduction to Day 3.8, in G. Boccaccio, *Decameron*, ed. by V. Branca (Turin: Einaudi, 1985), p. 325.

76. Cf. Francesco Colonna, *Hypnerotomachia Poliphili*, ed. by L. A. Ciapponi and G. Pozzi, 2 vols (Padua: Antenore, 1980), I, 80 and 365.

77. As Zabughin had observed as early as 1923: Zabughin (2000), II, 176.

78. Zabughin (2000), I, 242–43, providing an excellent analysis of Pontano's treatment of Virgilian and Ovidian sources.

79. Cf. Dionisotti (2009a), pp. 21–29 for a masterly analysis of the relationship between Latin and the Italian vernacular in the early decades of the sixteenth century.

80. Sannazaro, *Epigrams*, 3. 9, in I. Sannazaro, *Latin Poetry*, trans. by M. C. J. Putnam (Cambridge, MA, and London: Harvard University Press, 2009), p. 360. For the scene in *Aegidius* see Pontano, *Dialoghi*, p. 267. Cf. also the ominous dream of 'a magnificent orange tree' (*un albero bellissimo di arangio*) felled to the ground at the end of Sannazaro's pastoral romance *Arcadia* (1504), 12.7 (in Sannazaro, *Arcadia*, ed. by F. Erspamer (Milan: Mursia, 1990), p. 213), which scholars have interpreted as an allegory for the end of the Aragonese rule in Naples.

81. Nash (I. Sannazaro, *The Major Latin Poems*, trans. by R. Nash (Detroit, MI: Wayne State University Press, 1996), p. 63) translates *citria* with 'orange trees', whereas Putnam (Sannazaro, *Latin Poetry*, p. 93) offers 'orchards'. As is well known, the fruit is ordinarily designated by the neuter, the tree by the feminine gender. *Citria* may have been given in this context the meaning of *citreta* ('citrus groves').

82. Text edited in M. Quinlan-McGrath, 'Blosius Palladius. *Suburbanum Agustini Chisii*. Introduction, Latin Text and English Translation', in *Humanistica Lovaniensia*, 39 (1990), 93–157 (p. 127).

83. F. M. Molza, *Elegiae et alia*, ed. by M. Scorsone and R. Sodano (Turin: RES, 1999), pp. 63–66. The elegy is entitled *Ad Octavium Farnesium iuventutis principem* ['To Ottavio Farnese [1523–1586] prince of youth']. It must have been written before 1538, when Ottavio married Margherita of Austria, and certainly before 1540, when he became Duke of Camerino — a dignity not mentioned in the poem's title.

84. L. Alamanni and G. Rucellai, *La coltivazione e Le api* (Padua: Comino, 1718), pp. 181–82.

85. He also addressed Matteo Giberti, *Datarius* to Pope Clement VII and Bishop of Verona, eulogizing in one epistle and two epigrams the citrus groves on the shores of Lake Garda, 2 vols (G. Fracastoro et al., *Carminum editio II* (Padua: Comino, 1739), I, 117, 154, 155; cf. also the Appendix, I, 22, 24, 29, for autograph fragments of poems to Giberti where the same topic is introduced).

86. On the debate on imitation see McLaughlin (1995); *Ciceronian Controversies*, ed. by J. DellaNeva, trans. by B. Duvick (Cambridge, MA: Harvard University Press, 2007).

87. Fracastoro, *Carminum editio II*, 1, Appendix, p. 61: *Del Pontano non parlo. Del quale se io avessi ad imitar cosa alcuna, vorrei imitar di lui le virtù, e non i vitii. Questo finger le favole in esso è così vizioso, che per questo non si può leggere alcun de' suoi poemi senza stomaco.*

CHAPTER 7

Defacing God's Work: Metamorphosis and the 'Mimicall Asse' in the Age of Shakespeare

Robert H. F. Carver

Introduction

If the English Middle Ages can be characterized by their general reticence in metamorphic matters (a tendency to avoid the subject altogether, or to concentrate on allegoresis, while passing up opportunities to describe physical processes, or to explore — and exploit — transitional states), we might instinctively expect more liberal attitudes and expressions in the early-modern period.[1] After all, our very conception of 'the Renaissance' has been shaped by the metamorphic (and especially the auto-metamorphic) discourses of Humanism, most famously, God's description (*teste* Pico) of Adam as 'the free and extraordinary shaper of yourself, [able to] fashion yourself into whatever form you prefer'.[2] John Donne's declaration, 'Change is the nursery | Of music, joy, life and eternity' ('Elegy III') reflects the age's abiding concern with the related phenomenon of mutability.

In the last decade and a half alone of Elizabeth's reign, explicit advertisements of metamorphic content can be found in the titles of Thomas Lodge's *Scylla's Metamorphosis* (1589); John Marston's *The Metamorphosis of Pigmalions Image* (1598); and an anonymous play (based on Ovid's story of Iphis), *The Maydes Metamorphosis* (1600). Nor should we overlook Sir John Harington's attempt to transform the plumbing arrangements of England's upper classes with his design for a flushing water-closet ('a jakes') in *A New Discourse of a Stale Subject, called the Metamorphosis of Ajax* (1596); or Sir John Beaumont's *The Metamorphosis of Tabacco* (1602).

The theme of metamorphosis features extensively in the two most 'epical' achievements of the Elizabethan age, Sidney's *Arcadia* and Spenser's *Faerie Queene* — unexpectedly, perhaps, given the Protestant framework (with its ideological concerns about verbal as well as visual images) within which they were operating.[3] Their experiments with transformation had significant benefits for the development of characterization in general, but they were employing a very different mimetic medium from the Elizabethan play-maker. As E. Henry has observed (in a classical context), 'Metamorphosis is hardly a tractable theme for drama, except by the device of a messenger, or by prophecy.'[4] More fundamentally, the reservations voiced in Chapter 5 (*supra*) about metamorphosis are still very much present in the Renaissance. Nevertheless, even given the physical limitations of the early-modern stage, and continuing anxieties about the adulteration of the divine image, Renaissance dramatists were able to use metamorphosis in interesting ways.

John Lyly

John Lyly (*c.* 1553–1606) is hardly the first name that comes to mind today in a litany of English Renaissance dramatists.[5] Grandson of the Latin grammarian, William Lyly, he is best known as the inventor of Euphuism, that self-consciously mannered rhetorical style which (replicating many of the effects of an overblown Asiaticism) enabled a generation of aspirant courtiers and would-be wits to re-fashion (and re-present) themselves in words:

> It is virtue, yea virtue, gentlemen, that maketh gentlemen; that maketh the poor rich, the base-born noble, the subject a sovereign, the deformed beautiful, the sick whole, the weak strong, the most miserable most happy. There are two principal and peculiar gifts in the nature of man, knowledge and reason; the one commandeth, and the other obeyeth: these things neither the whirling wheel of fortune can change, neither the deceitful cavillings of worldlings separate, neither sickness abate, neither age abolish.[6]

But Lyly is also the most metamorphically minded of Shakespeare's immediate precursors in the drama.[7] In *Love's Metamorphosis* (perf. *c.* 1589; pr. 1601), a tree speaks in response to the blows of Erisichthon's axe, revealing an inner (pre-play) identity as Fidelia, a nymph of Ceres who (like Daphne) invoked metamorphosis to elude 'a Satyre' in pursuit:

> [...] whose body now is growne ouer with a rough barke, and whose golden lockes are couered with greene leaues; yet whose mind nothing can alter, neither the feare of death, nor the torments. (I. 2, sig. B2^v)[8]

In the course of the play, three other nymphs are metamorphosed (off stage: into a stone, a rose, and a bird) because (like Ovid's Anaxarete) they have rejected the entreaties of 'worthy' suitors (Cupid tells the spurned lovers, 'Your reuenges are reasonable, and shall bee graunted', IV. 1, sig. D4^v).[9]

Meanwhile, Erisichthon tries to reverse the economic effects of the famine Ceres has inflicted upon him by selling his daughter, Protea, to a wealthy merchant. Protea reluctantly complies ('I yeeld father, chop and chaunge me, I am readie', III. 2, sig. D1^v), but not before entreating her former lover:

> Sacred *Neptune*, whose godhead conquered my maiden-head, bee as ready to heare my passions, as I was to beleeue thine, and performe that now I intreate, which thou didst promise when thy selfe didst loue. Let not me bee a pray to this *Marchaunt*, who knowes no other god then Gold, vnlesse it be falsely swearing by a god to get gold; let me, as often as I be bought for money, or pawnd for meate, be turned into a Bird, Hare, or Lambe, or any shape, wherin I may be safe, so shall I preserue mine owne honour, my fathers life, and neuer repent me of thy loue [...] (III. 2, sig. D2^r)

Neptune obliges her (as we learn in a *recordatio*) by turning her 'to a Fisherman on the shore, with an Angle in my hand, and on my shoulder a net' (IV. 2), but the metamorphosis is merely a temporary expedient (as befits her name) and she gives dramatic expression to the economic/linguistic nexus of 'change' and 'exchange' that we also noted (ch. 5, *supra*) in Apuleius (*muto* and *mutuor*) with her claim that 'My father cannot be miserable, if *Protea* be happie, for by selling me euerie day, hee shall neuer want meate, nor I shiftes to escape' (IV. 1, sig. E1^v).[10]

Lyly seldom employs metamorphosis without making some play (often in the context of gender relations) between the physical and the metaphorical. The Siren who tempts Petulius attributes her own hybrid state to the 'subtleties' of males:

> Of all creatures most vnkind, most cunning, by whose subtilties I am halfe fish, halfe flesh, themselues being neither fish nor flesh, in loue luke warme, in crueltie red hot, if they praise, they flatter; if flatter, deceiue; if deceiue, destroy. (IV. 1, sig. E2^r)

The Siren may make some telling points in her critique of masculine nature, but her pernicious hybridity prompts Protea to shift shape for amatory rather than mercantile purposes. In the only on-stage metamorphosis of the play, she asks Neptune to let her 'take suddenly the shape of an olde man' in order 'to preuent this mischiefe' and 'marre what shee makes' (IV. 1, sig. E2^v). Telling Petulius that 'I am the Ghost of *Vlisses*', she exhorts him to 'curse this hag, who onely hath the voice and face of a Virgine, the rest all fish and feathers, and filth' (IV. 1, sig. E3^r).[11]

As she walks, still disguised, with Petulius, she points out 'what miraculous punishments here are for deserts in loue; this Rocke was a Nymph to *Ceres*, so was this Rose, so that Bird'. The transformed nymphs are re-configured as admonitory emblems:

> *Pet.* All chaung'd from their shapes?
> *Prot.* All chaung'd by *Cupid*, because they disdain'd loue, or dissembl'd in it.
> *Pet.* A faire warning to *Protea*; I hope shee will loue without dissembling. (v. [2], sig. F1^r)

In the final scene, the three nymphs enter in their normal shapes, having been restored (again, off stage) by Cupid in the expectation that they will now 'yield' to their suitors. In a proto-feminist permutation on the Plutarchan theme of Gryllus (the companion of Odysseus who did not wish to be retransformed, from a swine back into a man), all three reject the deal:

> *Nisa.* Not I, *Cupid*, neither doe I thanke thee that I am restored to life, nor feare againe to be chaunged to stone: for rather had I beene worne with the continuall beating of waues, then dulled with the importunities of men [...] (v. 5, sig. F3^r)[12]

Cupid threatens them with far worse transformations:

> [...] if they yeeld not, I will turne them againe, not to [F4^r] flowers, or stones, or birds, but to monsters, no lesse filthie to be seene, then to bee named hatefull: they shall creepe that now stand, and be to all men odious, and bee to themselues (for the mind they shall retaine) loathsome. (v. 5, sig. F3^v–F4^r)

At the very end of the play, following Ceres' entreaty, the nymphs agree to marry, but Cupid's victory does not involve a complete subjugation of female will or nature:

> *Nisa.* I am content, so as *Ramis*, when hee finds me cold in loue, or hard in beliefe, hee attribute it to his owne folly, in that I retaine some nature of the Rocke, he chaunged me into. (v. 5, sig. F4^r)

In the reverse metamorphoses and in the (metaphorical) exchanges of natures that have occurred (*mutuo nexu*, as Apuleius puts it, *A.A.* i. 1), we see dramatic expression being given to some of the central themes outlined in the prologue to *The Golden Ass.*

Apuleian themes are more explicitly present in Lyly's *Midas* (1592), where the protagonist undergoes two (ultimately reversed) metamorphoses. His courtier, Mellacrites, guides his choice of gift from Bacchus:

> Wish Gold *Mydas*, or wish not to be *Midas*. In the counsell of the Gods, was not *Anubis* with his long nose of Gold, preferred before *Neptunes*, whose stature was but brasse? And *Æsculapius* more honoured for his golden beard, than *Apollo* for his sweet harmonie?[13]

Midas finds a physical solution to his aurifying touch by bathing in the river Pactolus (cf. Ovid, *Met.* xi. 142–45), but his innate foolishness leads to an auricular transformation when (fulfilling Mellacrites's unwitting prophecy) he judges a music competition in Pan's favour:

> *Myd.* What hast thou done *Apollo?* the eares of an Asse vpon the head of a King?
> *Ap.* And well worthy, when the dulnes of an asse is in the eares of a King. (iv. 1, sig. E1^v)

Midas laments:

> If I returne to *Phrygia*, I shall bee pointed at; if liue in these woods, sauage beasts must be my companions: and what other companions should *Mydas* hope for than beasts, being of all beasts himselfe the dullest? Had it not bin better for thee to haue perished by a golden death, than now to lead a beastly life? Vnfortunat in thy wish, vnwise in thy iudgment; first a golden foole, now a leaden asse. (iv. 1, sig. E2^r)

There is a latent allusion here to a 'golden ass', but it is only rendered visible to rhetorically *in*formed readers who can appreciate the *trans*formative effects of chiasmus.[14]

Lyly teases us with the prospect of a complete metamorphosis ('Ah *Mydas*, why was not thy whole body metamorphosed, that there might haue been no parte left of *Mydas*?', iv. 1, sig. E2^r), but he indicates, again and again, that he is far less interested in the theatrical impact of physical transformation than in its tropological significance, its potential to establish (in audiences and readers) a pattern for moral change:

> *Amint.* Well, then this I say, when a Lyon doeth so much degenerat from Princely kind, that he will borow of the beasts, I say he is no Lion, but a monster; peec'd with the craftines of the fox, the crueltie of the tyger, the rauening of the woolfe, the dissembling of Hyena, he is worthy also to haue the eares of an Asse. (iv. 2, sig. E3^r)[15]

By the end of the play, Midas has regained his human ears, but only through Lyly's addition of a daughter, Sophronia ('sensible', 'prudent', 'of sound mind'), who is able to guide her father to better judgment (v. 3).

Lyly's exploration of the rhetorical potential of metamorphosis (particularly the elements of exchange, reciprocation, and resistance) opened up opportunities that his successors (especially Shakespeare in his early comedies) were able to exploit and develop. In terms, however, of dramatic technique or willingness to challenge conventional structures of belief, Lyly seems a very static figure when compared to Shakespeare's exact contemporary, Christopher Marlowe (1564–93).

Christopher Marlowe

Marlowe appropriates the homiletic structures of medieval Morality Play and *De casibus* tragedy, but he populates his works with hyperbolic versions of Pico's auto-metamorphic Man: the lowly shepherd (or 'sturdy Scythian thief', *1 Tamburlaine*, I. I. 36) who conquers half the world while spouting the rhetoric of Humanism ('Nature [...] Doth teach us all to have aspiring minds', II. 7. 18–20); Barabas, the Machiavellian merchant (heaping up 'Infinite riches in a little room', *Jew of Malta*, I. I. 37), whose willingness to poison his own daughter (together with a whole convent of nuns) in response to a spiritual transformation (her conversion to Christianity) may be an extension of a deeper difficulty in differentiating between animate and inanimate substances ('O my girl, | My gold', II. I. 47–48);[16] and Dr Faustus, the poor boy from Wittenberg who fashions himself into a myriad-minded scholar but then sells his soul to the Devil in exchange for twenty-four years of being served by a demon.[17] Marlowe's protagonists are defiers of limits, embodiments of excess, and the ends that they meet satisfy at least the formal expectations of orthodoxy ('Faustus is gone. Regard his hellish fall [...]' as the Epilogue puts it in line 4); but Marlowe forces us to engage imaginatively with his high-fliers, and his use of myth is almost always creative, or even subversive. Faustus may be an Icarian figure ('His waxen wings did mount above his reach [...]' in the words of the Prologue, line 21), but the Chorus' next line mischievously suggests that the divine economy of double pre-destination (as articulated by Calvin and incorporated within the Elizabethan Settlement) may be responsible for his downfall ('And melting heavens conspired his overthrow').

Faustus' opening words to Mephistopheles are metamorphic:

> I charge thee to return and change thy shape.
> Thou art too ugly to attend on me.
> Go, and return an old Franciscan friar;
> That holy shape becomes a devil best (I. 3. 23–26)

Mephistopheles' re-entry, *fratris imagine* ('in the image of a friar', I. 3. 34), continues the tradition of anti-clerical satire that we find, for example, in Chaucer's Wife of Bath's Tale,[18] but he makes it clear (with a flourish of scholastic terminology) that Faustus' 'conjuring speeches' were only the apparent 'cause' of his arrival ('but yet *per accidens*', I. 3. 45–46): he is 'a servant to great Lucifer' and he 'came now hither of mine own accord' after hearing Faustus 'Abjure the Scriptures and his Saviour Christ' (I. 3. 48).

At the end of the first act, Faustus' servant, Wagner, promises to teach Robin 'to turn thyself to anything, to a dog, or a cat, or a mouse, or a rat, or anything' (I. 4. 58–59). Robin provides what looks like an orthodox objection to debasing the *imago dei* ('How? A Christian fellow to a dog or a cat, a mouse or a rat!', I. 4. 60), but immediately undercuts it with a declaration of his willingness (in the cause of venereal pleasure) to be degraded to the form of an insect:

> No, no, sir. If you turn me into anything, let it be in the likeness of a little, pretty, frisking flea, that I may be here and there and everywhere.[19] O, I'll tickle the pretty wenches' plackets! I'll be amongst them, i' faith. (I. 4. 61–64)

The scene comically foreshadows the end of Act II, where Lucifer gives Faustus a book: 'Peruse it throughly, and thou shalt turn thyself into what shape thou wilt' (II. 3. 162–63). Faustus promises to keep the book 'as chary as my life' (II. 3. 165) — a hollow promise, perhaps, given the ease with which he has signed himself over, body and soul, to the Prince of Darkness), but it is clear that, by the end of the following act, this book (or one like it) has fallen into the wrong hands.

An abortive attempt at asinine transformation on stage occurs in III. 2 in the first edition (the so-called 'A-text') of *Doctor Faustus* (1604), where the compositor (probably working from improperly edited copy) appears to have set two versions of the same episode in which Robin, trying to avoid returning a goblet that he and Rafe have stolen from a vintner, conjures up Mephistopheles using one of Faustus' books. Enraged at being summoned from Constantinople, 'Mephostopholis' (as the A-text names him) 'sets squibs at their backs' and punishes the three parties indiscriminately as 'They run about': 'Vanish vilaines, th'one like an Ape, an other like a Beare, the third an Asse, for doing this enterprise'.[20] The combination of sizzling fireworks and rapid (perhaps criss-crossing) movement may have provided cover for the pulling on of a mask, or the substitution of characters on stage required to effect the metamorphosis.[21]

In most modern editions, this punishment is excised, leaving only the second version, in which the innocent vintner is spared the form of an ass, and Rafe is turned, not into a bear, but into a dog which (like the simified Robin) retains the power of speech:

> MEPHISTOPHELES Well, villains, for your presumption I transform thee [*to Robin*] into an ape, and thee [*to Rafe*] into a dog. And so, be gone!
> [*They are transformed in shape.*] Exit [*Mephistopheles*].
> ROBIN How, into an ape? That's brave. I'll have fine sport with the boys; I'll get nuts and apples enough.
> RAFE And I must be a dog.
> ROBIN I'faith, thy head will never be out of the pottage pot.
>   *Exeunt.*
>
>   (III. 2. 37–43)

A similarly punitive transformation occurs in IV. 1, when a knight doubts Faustus' ability to 'bring Alexander and his paramour before the emperor', observing: 'I'faith, that's as true as Diana turned me to a stag' (53–54; 56). Faustus quips, 'No sir, but when Actaeon died, he left the horns for you' (57), and he ensures (through Mephistopheles' agency) that when the Knight returns to the stage, he does so '*with a pair of horns on his head*'. The Knight berates Faustus for his violation of social hierarchy ('How dar'st thou thus abuse a gentleman? | Villain, I say, undo what thou hast done', 75–76), but his opening sally, 'Thou damnèd wretch and execrable dog' (73), is doubly ironic, unwittingly confirming his tormentor's spiritual destiny, but also his own vulnerability (as Actaeon) to canine attack. The reverse metamorphosis (theatrically, the easier direction) occurs on stage ('Mephistopheles, transform him straight',) and Faustus assures the Emperor that the transformation had been motivated by the desire 'to delight you with some mirth' (IV. 1. 83).

For most of the play, the protagonist makes little or no use of his supposed power to shift his own shape, although there are some para-metamorphic moments (he asks Mephistopheles to 'charm me that I may be invisible' while playing tricks on the Pope and friars in Rome at III. 1. 56; and he appears to allow a disgruntled horse-courser to pull off his leg while he is sleeping at IV. 1. 160–63). In the climactic final scene, however, Faustus seeks, by invoking metamorphosis (and metempsychosis), to escape the full effects of eternal damnation:

> Why wert thou not a creature wanting soul?
> Or why is this immortal that thou hast?
> Ah, Pythagoras' *metempsychosis*, were that true,
> This soul should fly from me, and I be changed
> Unto some brutish beast.
> All beasts are happy, for, when they die,
> Their souls are soon dissolved in elements. (v. 2. 97–103)

As the clock strikes twelve, he attempts both a corporeal transformation ('Now, body, turn to air, | Or Lucifer will bear thee quick to hell', v. 2. 108–09) and a spiritual dissolution ('O soul, be changed into little water drops, | And fall into the ocean, n'ere be found', v. 2. 110–11).[22] The fact that the Devils '*exeunt with him*' suggests one (or more) of three possibilities: a) he has attempted these metamorphoses too late (immediately after the expiry of the twenty-four year term granted to him by Lucifer); b) such attempts violate the conditions of the diabolical contract; or c) (most orthodoxly) transformations of this kind were never possible as they exceeded the divinely circumscribed powers retained by (fallen) angels. But the imagined change of the soul into 'little water drops' also resonates with the earlier image that appeared to Faustus in the night sky (at some point between 11 o'clock and midnight):

> O, I'll leap up to my God! Who pulls me down?
> See, see where Christ's blood streams in the firmament!
> One drop would save my soul, half a drop. [...] (v. 2. 69–71)

From an orthodox Elizabethan perspective, Faustus acknowledges here the redemptive potential of Christ's sacrifice even as he demonstrates the hubris of an over-reaching Renaissance Humanist by imagining that he can initiate his own salvation — 'leaping up', rather than waiting for Divine Grace to (con)descend. But it can also be argued that Marlowe is playing a subtly subversive game, using Christ's metaphorical (or — as in the rejected Catholic understanding of the Eucharist — metamorphosed) 'blood' to expose the constraints of Calvinist double pre-destination: on this reading, God is taunting Faustus not merely as a grave (though, momentarily repentant) sinner, but as one pre-destined to damnation.[23]

For our present purposes, however, the most interesting example of transformation in the play is an inexplicit one. At the beginning of Act V, 'two or three Scholars' ask Faustus to confirm the results of their 'conference about fair ladies' by allowing them to see 'that peerless dame of Greece, whom all the world admires for majesty' (V. 1. 9–10; 13–14). Faustus complies, and Helen '*passeth over the stage*'; but she is almost immediately followed by an Old Man who counsels Faustus to repent for the 'flagitious crimes of heinous sins' (43). Faustus comes close to repentance ('I do repent, and yet I do despair', 63), but is persuaded by Mephistopheles to 'confirm | My former vow I made to Lucifer' (71–72). As a reward (or consolation), however, he asks:

> That I might have unto my paramour
> That heavenly Helen which I saw of late,
> Whose sweet embracings may extinguish clean
> These thoughts that do dissuade me from my vow,
> And keep mine oath I made to Lucifer. (V. 1. 83–87)

Mephistopheles had previously rejected Faustus' request to supply him with 'a wife, the fairest maid in Germany' (II. 1. 140), bringing on stage instead '*a Devil dressed like a woman, with fireworks*'. His sardonic 'Tut, Faustus, marriage is but a ceremonial toy. If thou lovest me, think no more of it' (II. 1. 150), conceals the fact that the union of man and wife involves a transformation (becoming 'one flesh') that is beyond the powers of the Devil. He does not hesitate, however, to grant Faustus a 'paramour' in order to secure his soul: 'this [...] Shall be *performed* in twinkling of an eye' (V. 1. 88–89; emphasis added).

The re-appearance of Helen inspires the most famous lines in the play:

> Was this the face that launched a thousand ships
> And burnt the topless towers of Ilium?
> Sweet Helen, make me immortal with a kiss.
> Her lips suck forth my soul. See where it flies! (V. 1. 90–93)

Faustus' cry, 'Was this the face [...]?', serves, in immediate theatrical terms, as a rhetorical question, a way of drawing attention to the wonder that has been wrought (indeed, 'performed'), in study, and on stage, before Faustus' eyes, as well as our own. The enhancing rhetoric does, however, conceal a real question, the answer(s) to which can only be negative: in meta-theatrical terms, of course, the vision of 'heavenly' beauty standing before the enraptured 'Faustus' is a bewigged, cross-dressed, and unguented boy actor, the subject of a metamorphosis (from male to female) which so many critics (especially patristic and Puritan writers) found repugnant, as being contrary to the teachings of Exodus and Leviticus.[24] But even within the fictional world generated and sustained by the play, Faustus — with all his theological and philosophical learning — ought to know that the vision is not of Helen herself, but of a demon who has assumed her form, either by animating a whole corpse or by piecing together spare body parts.[25] Rather than initiating some kind of Platonic *ekstasis* (the separation from the body, and super-corporeal union of souls experienced by true lovers, as celebrated in Donne's 'The Ecstasie'), Helen's kiss poses significant spiritual perils ('Her lips suck forth my soul: see where it flies!'). Indeed, according to some critics, this is the point at which Faustus seals his damnation by committing the sin of demoniality.[26] Nevertheless, this remains one of the most memorable moments in the entire Western dramatic tradition. However well catechized we may have been — however fortified against the false shows and empty pomps of Satan — the power of theatrical illusion is so great that it is difficult for us *not* to suspend our disbelief. We collude with Faustus in our enjoyment of something that we all know (or ought to know) to be spurious. The cooperation of demonic agency and human imagination in a theatrical context has helped to fulfil Faustus' request: 'Sweet Helen, make me immortal with a kiss'.[27]

William Shakespeare

Shakespeare borrowed a good deal from Marlowe as well as from Lyly, and he played with metamorphosis throughout his career. Proteus is the name given to the embodiment of erotic 'inconstancy' in what appears to be Shakespeare's earliest attempt at comedy, *The Two Gentlemen of Verona*. But the god also figures explicitly in *3 Henry VI*, where Richard laments how Love 'forswore me in my mother's womb':

> And, for I should not deal in her soft laws,
> She did corrupt frail nature with some bribe
> To shrink mine arm up like a withered shrub,
> To make an envious mountain on my back —
> Where sits deformity to mock my body — (III. 2. 153–58)[28]

He considers his arm and back to have been *trans*formed ('shrub' and 'mountain'), but he also compares himself to something *un*formed, 'to a chaos, or an unlicked bear-whelp | That carries no impression like the dam' (III. 2. 161–62); and he sees the trappings of power as a way of correcting his natural defects:

> I'll make my heaven to dream upon the crown,
> And whiles I live, t'account this world but hell,
> Until my misshaped trunk that bears this head
> Be round impalèd with a glorious crown. (III. 2. 168–71)

By the end of the soliloquy, he has changed from dejection (at his physical limitations) to Machiavellian (indeed, Marlovian) ebullience (at his manipulative potential):

> I can add colours to the chameleon,
> Change shapes with Proteus for advantages,
> And set the murderous Machiavel to school.
> Can I do this, and cannot get a crown?
> Tut, were it farther off, I'll pluck it down. (III. 2. 191–95)

The opposite metamorphic trajectory is described in *2 Henry IV* where the heir to the throne asks Poins how they might 'see Falstaff bestow himself tonight in his true colours, and not ourselves be seen?' He is told that they should 'Put on two leathern jerkins and aprons, and wait upon him at his table like drawers' (II. 2.

161–64). Prince Harry comments:

> From a god to a bull — a heavy decension — it was Jove's case. From a prince
> to a prentice — a low transformation — that shall be mine; for in everything
> the purpose must weigh with the folly. (II. 2. 165–68)[29]

The Prince's 'low transformations' (this is merely one of many) will prove (in the
language of *1 Henry IV*, I. 3. 210–12) to be a 'foil', giving an added lustre to his
'reformation, glitt'ring o'er my fault', and ultimate transfiguration as Henry V,
victor of Agincourt.

In *Hamlet*, Claudius' dissection of another prince's 'transformation' may also draw
attention to the gap between the 'exterior' and the 'inward man' in the (new) king
himself (as judicious regicide and avuncular fratricide):

> Something have you heard
> Of Hamlet's transformation — so I call it,
> Since not th'exterior nor the inward man
> Resembles that it was. What it should be,
> More than his father's death, that thus hath put him
> So much from th'understanding of himself,
> I cannot dream[30] of. (II. 2. 4–10)

The rhetorical reference to the unfathomability of Hamlet's melancholy ('I cannot
dream of [...]') may also convey Claudius' inability to surrender his mind to
Morpheus, that fashioner of forms which might give expression to his guilt.[31]

The revelation of guilt in *Titus Andronicus* involves a meta-dramatic exposure
of source, when the mutilated Lavinia pursues her nephew, young Lucius, as he
'*flies from her with his books under his arm*' (IV. 1). Lavinia turns the leaves of 'Ouid's
Metamorphosis'[32] until she finds the appropriate tale, allowing Titus to declare:

> This is the tragic tale of Philomel,
> And treats of Tereus' treason and his rape,
> And rape, I fear, was root of thy annoy. (IV. 1. 47–49)

Shakespeare suppresses the metamorphic conclusion of Ovid's story, forcing us to
preserve the impact of her earlier entrance at II. 4:

> Enter the Empress' sons [...] with Lavinia, her hands cut off and her tongue cut
> out, and ravished

There is nothing to distract us from the transformation wrought by 'a craftier
Tereus' who has removed from Lavinia the means, not only of speech, but of sewing
her 'mind' (as Philomel did) in 'a tedious sampler' (II. 4. 39–41).

Shakespeare's engagement with Ovid culminates in the remarkable (and possibly
'miraculous') transformation at the end of *The Winter's Tale*, where a 'statue' of
Hermione (allegedly fashioned, not by Pygmalion, but by an historical Renaissance
artist, 'that rare Italian master Giulio Romano', V. 2. 96) appears to come to
life, restoring to Leontes (albeit somewhat 'wrinkled', V. 3. 28) his 'dead' wife,
Hermione, after the passage of sixteen years.[33]

Comedy is, almost by definition, transformational.[34] In what has sometimes (if
over-romantically) been taken as Shakespeare's 'Farewell to the Stage', Prospero

plays the part of an internal dramaturge. But amongst all the metamorphoses that feature in *The Tempest* (and in Shakespearian comedy generally), we might single out one that does *not* take place. At the end of the play, having undertaken to break his staff and drown his magic book (v. 1. 54–57) and after reconciling (through transformative charms)[35] almost all the disjointed parties, Prospero (a 'whiter' version of that earlier Humanist-turned-Magician, Faustus) directs our attention to Caliban, the misshapen product of a union between an Algerian witch (Sycorax) and (if we are to believe Prospero) 'the devil himself' (1. 2. 321) — a semi-piscine creature ('not honoured with | A human shape', 1. 2. 284–85) who has repaid Prospero's efforts to transform him through education, by trying to rape Miranda. Prospero's laconic utterance, 'This thing of darkness I | Acknowledge mine' (v. 1. 278–79), conveys the limits, not only of magic, but of comedy itself, in effecting *substantial* change.[36]

Shakespeare also indulges in more obviously satirical metamorphoses, drawing on the Lucianic and Apuleian traditions. In *The Merry Wives of Windsor*, Falstaff reflects on his figurative 'transformation' at the hands of the very women he was intending to dupe:

> I would all the world might be cozened, for I have been cozened, and beaten too. If it should come to the ear of the court how I have been transformed, and how my transformation hath been washed and cudgelled, they would melt me out of my fat, drop by drop, and liquor fishermen's boots with me. I warrant they would whip me with their fine wits till I were as crestfallen as a dried pear. I never prospered since I forswore myself at primero. Well, if my wind were but long enough, I would repent. (IV. 5. 87–96)

In *Troilus and Cressida*, Thersites describes Menelaus (next to Agamemnon) as:

> the goodly transformation of Jupiter there, his brother the bull, the primitive statue and oblique memorial of cuckolds, a thrifty shoeing-horn in a chain, hanging at his brother's leg: to what form but that he is should wit larded with malice and malice farced with wit turn him to? To an ass were nothing: he is both ass and ox. To an ox were nothing: he is both ox and ass. To be a dog, a mule, a cat, a fitchew, a toad, a lizard, an owl, a puttock, or a herring without a roe, I would not care; but to be Menelaus! — I would conspire against destiny. Ask me not what I would be if I were not Thersites, for I care not to be the louse of a lazar, so I were not Menelaus. — Hey-day, sprites and fires. (v. 1. 50–63)

And in *Timon of Athens*, we revisit the Gryllus theme, but in a more obviously Cynical setting:

> TIMON [...] What wouldst thou do with the world, Apemantus, if it lay in thy power?
> APEMANTUS Give it the beasts, to be rid of the men.
> TIMON Wouldst thou have thyself fall in the confusion of men, and remain a beast with the beasts?
> APEMANTUS Ay, Timon.
> TIMON A beastly ambition, which the gods grant thee t'attain to. If thou wert the lion, the fox would beguile thee. If thou wert the lamb, the fox would eat thee. If thou wert the fox, the lion would suspect thee when peradventure thou

wert accused by the ass. If thou wert the ass, thy dullness would torment thee, and still thou lived'st but as a breakfast to the wolf [...]. What beast couldst thou be that were not subject to a beast? And what a beast art thou already, that seest not thy loss in transformation!
APEMANTUS If thou couldst please me with speaking to me, thou mightst have hit upon it here. The commonwealth of Athens is become a forest of beasts.[37]
TIMON How, has the ass broke the wall, that thou art out of the city? (IV. 3. 323–52)

Case Study: *A Midsummer Night's Dream*

Asinine imagery features elsewhere in Shakespeare's plays, but there is nothing in his other works (or, indeed, in English Renaissance literature as a whole) that quite prepares us for the uncompromising physicality of the metamorphosis at the heart of *A Midsummer Night's Dream*, where a character appears, for an extended period on stage, sporting the head of a donkey. Shakespeare's debt to Apuleius in the play is now firmly established,[38] though for a long period critics preferred to locate the immediate source of Bottom's transformation in the 'receipt for making a man resemble an ass' given by Reginald Scot in *The Discoverie of Witchcraft* (1584),[39] or his quip about '*Bodins* asseheaded man' who 'must either eat haie or nothing'.[40]

Yet while Scot is regularly acknowledged as the source of specific details in the characterization of Bottom (and of Puck or 'Robin Goodfellow'), the wider thematic considerations of the *Discoverie of Witchcraft* (and their implications for Shakespeare) are often overlooked.[41] Scot's task is to expose ('discover') the illusory nature of witchcraft and, in so doing, protect English women from the hysterical attacks on alleged witches being made on the Continent. Thousands of supposed witches were hanged, burned, or otherwise punished in the sixteenth century, some of them for the crime of turning themselves (or others) into (the semblance of) animals (including asses).[42]

Before the reappearance of *The Golden Ass* (*c.* 1300), a number of accounts of asinine, equine, or lupine transformation were in circulation: whatever their ultimate relation to Apuleius, they all seem to derive from the cluster of stories surrounding Augustine's discussion (*De ciuitate dei* XVIII. 18) of d(a)emonic agency and the *De asino aureo* (see ch. 5, *supra*). In the *Gesta regum anglorum* (completed by 1125), William of Malmesbury relates how two innkeepers on the highway leading to Rome receive as a guest 'a certain young man who made his living by histrionic movements' (*quendam ephoebum, qui motibus histrionicis victum exigeret*, II. 171). They transform him (to all intents and appearances) into an ass and then exhibit him for money.[43] His fame as a performing ass spreads far and wide; a rich man buys him for a pretty sum but is warned not to lead him over water.[44] The ass escapes from a negligent custodian, leaps into a pond, and (after a decent wallow) is re-humanized. The account ends with a tantalizing reference to Peter Damian (*literaturae peritus*, 'a man of great literary learning').[45] Damian, William tells us, assured a sceptical Pope Leo that such things were possible, adducing the example of Simon Magus who caused his own visage to appear in the face of Clement's father, Faustianus.[46]

Roger of Wendover (fl. 1215) repeats the story in his *Chronica* under the entry for 1048.[47] In one manuscript of the chronicle attributed to (the probably fictitious)

'Matthew of Westminster', the story is followed by Augustine's account of assification (*De ciuitate dei*, XVIII. 18) and an anecdote (from the *Life of Saint Macarius*) of
a girl who appears (in the eyes of everyone except the Egyptian saint) to have been
turned into a horse.[48] 'Matthew' concludes:

> unde apparet demones humanas formas immutare in bestias non posse, sed
> oculos hominum suis machinationibus falsitare, ita ut aliud sit corpus et aliud
> videatur

> [Hence it is obvious that demons are not able to change human shapes into
> bestial ones; though by their stratagems they can deceive men's eyes so that a
> body remains one thing while seeming to be another.]

In *Lo specchio della vera penitenzia* (wr. *c*. 1350; pr. 1495), the Florentine Dominican
theologian, Jacopo Passavanti (d. 1357), repeats the story of the apparent
equinification of a girl, observing:

> [...] in the books of the poets there are accounts of plenty of these transformations,
> as is shown in the *Metamorphoses* of Ovid and *The Golden Ass* of the Platonist
> Apuleius. And all of these things, as St. Augustine shows in his book called *The
> City of God* do not happen truly, but only appear to happen, since the devil plays
> and fascinates both by his intelligence and by his ability to control the eyes of
> those who see his wonders.[49]

A further comment (which may derive from Augustine's account of the dreaming
philosopher at the end of *De ciuitate dei* XVIII. 18) conveys powerfully the belief that
the imagination can extend or project into the external world, taking on (as it were)
corporeal forms:

> And it also follows from this that the devil knows what men fantasize and
> imagine, and what they dream, insofar as the actions of imagination are not
> closed within the human intellect or will, but are corporeal sentiments, and can
> be perceived by external signs.[50]

We might also note the story told by Gerald of Wales ('Giraldus Cambrensis',
1147–1223) at the head of a catalogue of recent marvels in Ireland, of a priest's
encounter, datable to 1183 or 1184, with a man and woman who had been turned
into wolves, while retaining human minds and speech. Gerald validates the story
by claiming to have met the priest personally, and provides patristic authority
for such transformations by quoting Augustine's comments on Apuleius' asinine
metamorphosis in *De ciuitate dei*, XVIII. 18.[51]

The three main traditions of asinine (or equine) metamorphosis (those of Apuleius,
Augustine, and William of Malmesbury) become incorporated into early-modern
debates over the existence and extent of demonic powers. But in grappling with
this deadly question, 'Can the Devil and his agents (demons and witches) transform
men into beasts?', the Renaissance treatises on witchcraft also address issues that are
fundamental to all verbal art: the relationship between reality and illusion, essence
and appearance, reason and imagination.

One problem for Renaissance witch-hunters was the existence of the canon
Episcopi (referred to in ch. 5, *supra*). For the early and medieval Church, still
competing with pagan cults and deeply ingrained superstitions, it was important

to *limit* the powers to be attributed to demons, powers that might detract from the primacy, the unique potency, of the one Creator. Hence the Canon:

> Quisquis ergo credit posse fieri aliquam creatura̲m, aut in melius, aut in deterius immutari, aut transformari in aliam speciem vel aliam similitudinem, nisi ab ipso creatore qui omnia fecit, & per quem omnia facta sunt: procul dubiò infidelis est, & pagano deterior.[52]

> [Anyone who believes that any creature can be made, or transmuted for better or worse, or transformed into some other species or into any other likeness, except by the Creator Himself who made all things and through whom all things were made, is undoubtedly an unbeliever and worse than a pagan.]

In the early-modern period, the argument becomes curiously invaginated: the persecutors of witchcraft are obliged to construct arguments that lend credence to the potency of the demonic powers that they are striving to combat. Heinrich Kramer and Jacob Sprenger, Dominican Inquisitors and co-authors of the *Malleus maleficarum* ('Hammer for Witches', first published in 1486–87), try to reconcile their own evidence for the occurrence of bestial transformations (and the apparent support to be found in Augustine) with the ecclesiastical text.[53] The Canon, Kramer and Sprenger tell us, though much quoted, is greatly misunderstood. Those preachers who proclaim in public that such 'illusory transformations' (*transmutationes præstigiosæ*) cannot be made by demons, apply themselves only to the outer husk (*cortex*) of the Canon's words and not to the marrow (*medulla*). The verb *fieri* can be taken in two ways: as a synonym for *creari* (the creation of *aliquid ex nihilo*, a function proper to God alone), and in the sense of the 'natural production of something' (*pro naturali productione alicuius rei*). Here intrudes the old theory of spontaneous generation. When the Canon speaks of creatures 'being made', it refers to 'complete creatures' (*creaturæ perfectæ*) such as men, asses, etc. (note the choice of examples), which clearly can only be created by God. But 'imperfect creatures' (such as snakes, frogs, and mice), which can be generated *ex putrefactione*, can also be made by the power of demons, although, as Albertus shows in *De animalibus* (citing the authority of Exodus 7), demons cannot do this instantaneously (as can God) but over some period of time, however brief. The concession is significant since it gives demons (and their agents, witches) control over a range of lower-order animals ('vermin', as we might term them) that feature in narratives involving magic or witchcraft from the earliest to the latest periods.[54]

On the second issue, that of *transmutatio*, the authors distinguish, in the traditional scholastic manner, between substantial (*substantialis*) and accidental (*accidentalis*) transformation. The first (transformation of a creature's substance) can be effected only by God. The second (*accidentalis*) is also two-fold (*duplex*): transformation of a) the shape (*forma*) natural to, and inherent in, the thing seen; or, b) the shape inherent, not in the thing seen, but in the organs and faculties of the person seeing.[55] The Canon, Kramer and Sprenger say, precludes substantial transformations. It also refers to the second sort (2[a]), although the devil can, with God's permission (one thinks of the case of Job), cause certain changes to the accidental body (such as making a face appear leprous). But this leaves an enormous scope for apparent transformations under 2(b).

Much of the argument (if one allows the basic premises) seems (comparatively speaking!) reasonable (one does not, after all, have to believe in ghosts to accept that people 'see things'); and the philosophical hair-splitting actually leads to some interesting discussions of the ways in which the faculties of perception and imagination interact with the real world.[56] Scot's attack (as Montague Summers — a hostile reader — noted) misrepresents his Continental adversaries at many points (in the case of Kramer and Sprenger's remodelling of the Canon, he simply ignores the subtle philosophical distinctions being proffered in their attempt to reconcile Augustine, Aquinas, and Saint Antoninus, Bishop of Florence). And he derides the credence given by scholars such as Bodin to the *Malleus'* account of the young merchant (visiting Salamis in Cyprus) who spends three years labouring, in the (apparent) form of an ass, for a local woman from whom he had purchased eggs. In the fourth year, a remedy for the collective (and demonically induced) delusion finally presents itself:

> [...] he passed by a church where Holy Mass was being celebrated, and heard the sacred-bell ring at the elevation of the Host (for in that kingdom the Mass is celebrated according to the Latin, and not according to the Greek rite). And he turned towards the church, and, not daring to enter for fear of being driven off with blows, knelt down outside by bending the knees of his hind legs, and lifted his forelegs, that is, his hands, joined together over his ass's head, as it was thought to be, and looked upon the elevation of the Sacrament.

The pious response of an 'ass' to the Eucharistic miracle of transubstantiation attracts the attention of passing Genoese merchants (note the interconnection, once again, of 'change' and 'exchange'). They take the witch before a judge, 'where, being questioned and tortured, she confessed her crime and promised to restore the young man to his true shape'.[57]

Johann Weyer (Johannes Wier), who anticipated Scot in his sceptical view of witchcraft, is dismissive of all these accounts of quadripedic transformation:

> *hæ & similes nugæ eandem sortiantur fidem, quam Apuleij & Luciani metamorphosis meretur.*[58]
>
> [These trifles — and ones like them — ought to be given the same credence that the metamorphosis of Apuleius and Lucian deserves.]

Lambert Daneau's *A Dialogue of Witches*, which appeared in English translation in 1575, takes a middle course. In his prefatory note to the Reader, Daneau warns that his treatise 'containeth no olde wyues tales' but 'only such matter as most credible hystories doe reporte'.[59] Scot classes Daneau with the likes of Jacob Sprenger ('a special mainteiner of their follies'),[60] but crows over the fact that Daneau, nonetheless, rejects the veracity of accounts of bestial transformation:

> *Theophilus.* What if I should also ad that which will seeme much more meruelous, which notwithstanding S. *Augustine* and *Apuleus* [*sic*] doe credibly wryte, yet am I of opinion that it can not be so.
> *Anthony.* What is that?
> *Theophil.* Forsooth, that Sorcerers can chaunge men into other formes & shapes, that is to wit, into wolues, Beares, & Asses.[61]

On the other hand, the jurist, Jean Bodin (1530–90) — acclaimed by Montaigne as 'the highest literary genius of his time'[62] — was quite ready to give credence to William of Malmesbury's account:

> *il fut conclud, que cela estoit possible: qui seroit bien pour confirmer, ce qui est escript en Lucian & Apulee atheistes changez en asnes*[63]

> [it was concluded that this was possible; this was sufficient to confirm what was written in Lucian and Apuleius — atheists [pagans] changed into asses]

Scot ridicules Bodin's credulity:

> Nevertheles, Bodin saith it as a cleare case: for the matter was disputed upon before pope Leo the seventh, and by him all these matters [73] were judged possible: and at that time (saith he) were the transformations of *Lucian* and *Apuleius* made canonicall.

Scot's account is inaccurate in many respects. The important point for our immediate purposes, however, is the 'canonicall' status that he attributes (ironically) to the transformations of Lucian and Apuleius. Writers from Augustine to Bodin return again and again to the same questions: did the transformations described in the accounts of Nebuchadnezzar, in Homer's Circe episode, in Ovid, Apuleius, St Macarius of Egypt, and so on, actually happen? One of the things that separate the likes of Augustine, Sprenger, and Bodin from most modern audiences is their failure (often a wilful one) to discriminate between veridical (and/or mimetic) categories: fiction, biblical allegory, and (allegedly) empirical accounts are mixed up together. Bodin's apparent belief in 'poets fables' invites Scot's derision:

> Item, he mainteineth, as sacred and true, all *Homers* fables of *Circes* and *Ulysses* his companions: inveieng against *Chrysostome*, who rightlie interpreteth *Homers* meaning to be, that *Ulysses* his people were by the harlot *Circes* made in their brutish maners to resemble swine.
>
> But least some poets fables might be thought lies (whereby the witchmongers arguments should quaile) he mainteineth for true the most part of *Ovids Metamorphôsis*, and the greatest absurdities and impossibilities in all that booke: marie he thinketh some one tale therein may be fained. Finallie, he confirmeth all these toies by the storie of Nabuchadnez-zar. And beicause (saith he) Nabuchadnez-zar continued seven yeres in the shape of a beast, therefore may witches remaine so long in the forme of a beast;[64]

Even Scot, however, wants to apply to Homer — a pagan author (albeit a revered one) — the same exegetical techniques that had been used on a biblical narrative to make the transformation of Nebuchadnezzar figurative rather than literal (the king, Scot tells us, was 'for his beastlie gouernement and conditions, thrown out of his kingdom [...] there in exile to lead his life in beastlie sort').[65]

Nicholas Remy (Remigius)

One of the most disturbing examples of the interpenetration of fact and fiction, reality and fable, is Nicholas Remy's *Demonolatry*, a text which (to my knowledge) has not previously featured in discussions of *A Midsummer Night's Dream*.[66] The *Demonolatry* was published in Lyons in 1595, coinciding precisely with the likely period of composition of Shakespeare's play.[67] It advertises itself on its title page as being based on the trials of around 900 individuals convicted on capital charges of witchcraft over the span of fifteen years in the Duchy of Lorraine (*Daemonolatreiae Libri Tres Ex Iudicijs capitalibus nongentorum plus minus hominum; qui sortilegij crimen intra annos quindecim in Lotharingia capite luerunt*).[68]

Remy is evidently a man of enormous erudition and pronounced literary appetites and ambitions. In his prefatory address 'To the Courteous Reader', he plays both sides of the metamorphosis debate: he talks of his head being almost completely filled with the 'frequent transmutations into other shapes and forms (for so it seemed)' of the witches (*oppleui quasi totum caput mihi sagarum [...] crebris, vt videtur, in alienas formas mutationibus*, sig. B1^r); but he also points out 'how easily simulated or feigned things can deceive [literally, 'creep into' the eyes and minds of] wretched mortals [and be taken] for true things' (*vti facilè miseris mortalibus simulata fictàue pro veris obrepere solent*). It is not simply the harm that witches do through their *maleficium*. More significant still is the idolatrous devotion to the Devil into which they fall through their relations with demons: for 'Who indeed would not worship as a god a being who can at will change the shape and appearance of things [...] ?' (*Quis enim pro numine non colat; qui rerum formas, ac species ad nutum vertere, atque immutare [... possit]*; Summers, p. xi; Remy, sig. β2^r).

Remy anticipates the accusation 'of being nothing but a retailer of marvellous stories' (p. xii), but claims that 'it was from no scattered rumours, but from the independent and concordant testimony of so many witnesses' that he has 'reported these things as certain facts' (p. xii). He condemns as 'utterly ridiculous' reports 'that witches can by their spells change men from being men and turn them into beasts' (*sagas suis pharmacis homines ex hominibus exuere, atque in feras vertere*, Summers, p. xiii; Remy, sig. β3^v). At the same time, he stresses the protean powers of the demons themselves:

> Qua verò forma, ac specie id præstant tam infinitum sit dicere, quàm Protheum in omnes suas figures distinguere. [p. 75 (sig. K2^r, −Summers 27, I. vii)]
>
> [their different shapes and appearances may be said to be as limitless as those adopted by Proteus in his various forms]

They 'will roar like lions, or leap like panthers, or bark like dogs; and at times will transform themselves into the shape of a wine-skin or some other vessel' (*Leonis more frementes; saltantes, vt pardalis; latrantes, vt canis, atque in vtris, vasisque figuram sese aliquando transformantes*).[69]

Remy presents his shift away from scepticism to 'knowledge' as a positive transformation which he hopes to replicate in his readers:

> Before I became a Public officer of Justice I had often heard stories of this impudent behaviour of the Demon: but I took no more notice of them than if they had been tales of hobgoblins and bugaboos told by nurses to frighten naughty children [*nihilque magis me afficiebant, quam quos nutrices vagientibus infantibus de lemurum, laruarumque occursationibus terrores affere solent*]. Now that I have given personal attention to the matter and have been convinced by unassailable proofs [*Nunc postquam praesens attentius obseruaui omnia, exque manifestissimis argumentis rem totius cognoui [...]*], I do not hesitate to hand on

my knowledge to others, who, however, must not, if they refuse to believe me, deem me more biased than I once thought they were who told me these things when I was inexperienced. Therefore of many examples I shall give you one, reader, as to the truth of which I stake my honour; for I witnessed it with my own eyes in the exercise of my judicial office. (Remy, p. 368; Summers, p. 174)

Remy goes on to recount the story of 'a witch, commonly called Lasnier [*Asinaria*] because her husband was a donkey-man, whom I pressed so hard in respect of the evidence against her that she was left with no loophole for evasion or escape'. She resolves to confess, but is checked by the sight of 'her Little Master' (*Magistellus*), 'fiercely threatening her with hands forked and clawed like a crab'. Remy tries to stiffen her confessional resolve:

> But again she saw him monstrously threatening in another corner and, like a play-actor, in another shape [*vti qui scenae alicui seruiunt [...] mutata iam persona*]; for he had horns growing straight out from his forehead and seemed as if he would gore her with them. (Remy, III. ix, p. 369; Summers, p. 174)

Remy congratulates himself on the fact that his grappling with the demon has been effective: 'after he had been ridiculed and utterly reviled he departed and was seen no more by [Lasnier], as she declared when she was just about to be led to the fire' (Summers, p. 174). But, within only a few pages, Remy is endorsing Lucius' absurdly credulous reaction to Aristomenes' tale, as an appropriate response to occurrences that seem to go beyond 'what is credible according to nature':

> 'Ego vero' inquam 'nihil impossibile arbitror, sed utcumque fata decreuerint ita cuncta mortalibus prouenire: nam et mihi et tibi et cunctis hominibus multa usu venire mira et pæne infecta, quae tamen ignaro relata fidem perdant [...].'

> ['I think nothing impossible; but as the fates have decreed, so do all things happen for mortals. For to all men there happen many marvellous and almost impossible experiences which, when told to the ignorant, cannot be believed'] (Remy, III. xii, pp. 382–83; Summers, p. 182; cf. *A.A.* I. 20)

One is occasionally tempted to suspect that the entire work is some kind of elaborate joke; but Remy proves, again and again, to be (like Lucius with his asinine ears) *multiscius* ('knowing many things') but *minus prudens* ('not particularly wise').[70]

Remy decides at one point to quote *verbatim* a long passage from Apuleius (describing the self-flagellating priests of the Syrian goddess, *A.A.* VIII. 28), 'because of its old-time elegance and the rare splendour of its ornate and flowery style' (*propter eius antiquam elegantiam, ac bracteati, floridíque styli rarum nitorem*).[71] Note how Remy is seduced by the 'sheen' (*nitor*) of Apuleius' style, just as Lucius was seduced by the 'sheen' of the statue at II. 4–5 (see Figure 6, *supra*). Both are examples of highly eloquent misreaders of the 'texts' presented to them.[72]

We also notice how Remy uses a fictional narrative to bolster his 'factual' or 'eyewitness' account, but suppresses the detail of Pamphile's avine metamorphosis:

> Tum visae, quæ statim ac se eis illinendi ac perfricandi potestatem à Iudice accepissent, momento sursum efferrentur, ac disparerent: vti de Pamphile sua recitat Lucius 7 [7. Apud Apuleum [*sic*] lib. III. De As. Aue[*sic*].] quæ inquit,

indidem in se ingesto tali vnguine, iam sui periclitabunda paulatim terra resultauit, ac mox in altum sublimata forinsecus totis alis euolauit.

[Again, there have been cases of witches who as soon as the Judge has given them permission to rub or anoint themselves with the unguent, have at once been carried aloft and have disappeared. Lucius Apuleius (Bk. III, *The Golden Ass*) tells of Pamphile that she in the same way applied such an unguent to herself and, after a few tentative leaps from the ground, flew up and away in full flight.] (Remy, I. iv, p. 44, sig. F2^v; Summers, pp. 6–7)

There are various small details in Remy that are paralleled in Shakespeare. The love-juice which Oberon orders Puck to pour on the sleeping Demetrius' eyes so that he will redirect his attentions from Hermia back to their former object, Helena, may owe a debt to Remy's account of the 'the porter of the Fortress of Bassompierre' who 'had married a young wife, but continued to maintain connubial relations with a woman who had been his mistress before his marriage.' Her neighbour (Lahire) 'gave her a herb plucked from her garden and said that if she put the juice of it in her husband's food, he would immediately forget his other love' (though the effect is to make his manhood disappear).[73]

But I would like to float the possibility that the transformation of Bottom in *A Midsummer Night's Dream* may be a deliberate answer to the challenges implied in Remy's statement:

Hic non est animus Apuleij asinum denuò in scenam producere: aut qua poëtæ comminiscuntur, Metamorphoses nouis exemplis tueri, ac defendere: sed hoc quod multorum assertione contestatum, ac ipsa experientia comprobatum habeo, in medium proferre. (III. v, sig. Ff1^v, p. 226)

[It is not my intention here to bring the Ass of Apuleius again on to the stage, or to adduce fresh examples to support the old tales of the poets of men being changed into beasts; but only to bring forward such instances as are attested by the evidence of many witnesses and are proved by actual experience.] (Summers, p. 108)

The beginning of Act III of *A Midsummer Night's Dream* finds the mechanicals rehearsing their production of 'Pyramus and Thisbe' in the woods. Their writer-cum-director, Peter Quince, calls attention to a theatrical structure that is of particular significance for Shakespeare's own play: 'This hawthorn-brake [shall be] our tiring-house' (the room in which actors are 'attired' in their costumes, III. 1. 4). Ned Bottom's Pyramus exits with the line, 'And by and by I will to thee appear' (l. 82), but he is intercepted by Puck, and fails to enter after Thisbe's compliment, 'As true as truest horse that yet would never tire' (l. 91). It is only after Flute has repeated Thisbe's line that Bottom bursts onto stage wearing the head of a donkey. The imaginative space allocated to a metaphorical 'tireless' horse is suddenly usurped by a physical creature 'tired' in a different sense: '*Enter BOTTOM with the ass-head*' (l. 97).[74] An equine metaphor is displaced by an asinine metamorphosis. We have encountered enough discussions by now to know that human-to-animal transformations are always controversial; but Quince's exasperated direction to Bottom immediately before his entry ('Your cue is past; it is "never tire" ', l. 96) may remind us of theatre's more fundamental transgressions. Shorn from its context,

Pyramus' cue can easily be (ironically) redeployed as a Puritan imperative: 'Never tire!'

William Prynne's *Histrio-mastix* (1633) was published nearly forty years after the first performance of *A Midsummer Night's Dream*, and is particularly associated with theatrical entertainments in the Caroline court; but Prynne draws on two thousand years of anti-theatrical diatribe, and many sections of *Histrio-mastix* read as though they could be a Puritan's response to Shakespeare's play:

> For the strange disguisednesse of theatricall attires, it is most apparant: For doe not all Actors, Mummers, Masquers usually put on [...] *the persons, the representations of Devils, Satyrs, Nymphes, Sylvanes, Fayries, Fates, Furies, Hobgoblins, Muses, Syrens, Centaures, and such other Pagan Fictions? yea, the portraitures and formes of Lyons, Beares, Apes, Asses, Horses, Fishes, Foules, which in outward appearance metamorphose them into Idols, Devils Monsters, Beasts*, whose parts they represent? [891]

Attacking 'Stage-disguises', he notes that Scripture

> *condemnes mens disguising of themselves like women, and womens metamorphosing themselves into men either in haire, apparell, offices, or conditions:* how much more then mens transfiguring of themselves into the shapes of Idols, Devils, Monsters, Beasts, &c. betweene which and man there is no Analogie or proportion, as is betweene men and women [...] . [893] [...] so I may likewise condemne these Play-house Vizards, vestments, images and disguises, which during their usage in outward appearance offer a kinde of violence to Gods owne Image and mens humane shapes, metamorphosing them into those idolatrous, those bruitish formes, in which God never made them.[75]

One of the many original aspects of Shakespeare's play is the lack of any obvious justification or explanation for Bottom's assification (beyond Oberon's desire to punish Titania for her refusal to hand over the 'changeling boy' by making her fall in love with a 'monster'). Metamorphosis usually serves as punishment, reward, escape-mechanism, or mitigation, but *Histrio-mastix* may provide some light. When Prynne comes to retell the story of assification given by William of Malmesbury ('a grave English Historian'), the 'young man who made his living by histrionic movements' (*quendam ephoebum, qui motibus histrionicis victum exigeret*) is figured unambiguously as 'a certaine Stage-player who got his living by acting', rather than a 'juggler' or 'acrobat' (which might be more appropriate to the period).[76] People flock 'to behold the rare feates of this Mimicall Asse, who strucke the Spectators with great admiration of his strange gestures'. Prynne concludes:

> If this bee but an *Ovids Metamorphosis*, or an *Apuleius his Golden Asse*; we may laugh at the conceit, and so passe it by: but if it bee a truth, as the Historian confidently affirmes it, wee may deeme it a just judgement of God upon this Actor, who for his acting of other mens parts in jest, was thus enforced to play the Asses part in earnest. (554)

There is also a natural affinity between demons and dramaturgy: as Remy points out repeatedly, 'Satan is before all the imitator of God'.[77] Puck's initial reaction to Peter Quince and his troupe ('What hempen homespuns have we swaggering here | So near the cradle of the Fairy Queen?', III. 1. 73–74) and his cry, 'I'll be an auditor;

| An actor too perhaps, if I see cause' (III. I. 74–75), may suggest that Bottom's 'crime' is presumption, a mere 'mechanical' encroaching upon the preserve of the daemonic by engaging in histrionics (when Puck, at III. 2. 13, calls Bottom 'The shallowest thick-skin of that barren sort', he is referring to his pre-asinine state).

But, as elsewhere in Shakespeare, the apparent punishment is also a source of greatness. The part of Bottom seems to have been taken by that most celebrated of Elizabethan clowns, William Kemp. As other critics have noticed: 'Bottom is far too richly characterized to be merely an embodiment of asininity. During his period of change (about which he understands little) he is gloriously himself, ridiculous, vain, cocksure, ebullient, kindly, an inspirer of affection in others, a source of life and delight.'[78]

Placed in a similar position to (the fully asinine) Lucius (*A.A.* x. 19–22) when he finds himself, suddenly, the recipient of a powerful and beautiful woman's affections, Bottom displays bestial appetites, but only with regard to food ('Sweet hay hath no fellow') — inverting the traditional trope of the mind remaining human within the animal body.

Puck's epilogue ('If we shadows have offended', v. I. 409) serves the conventional purposes of seeking indulgence for 'this weak and idle theme' and inviting the audience's applause.[79] The imaginative liberation afforded by the notion of the play as a 'dream' carries with it a freedom from responsibility that equally affects author, characters, and audience. Yet it is worthwhile asking in what other ways the play might have 'offended'. Critics are generally agreed that Oberon's promontory-with-dolphin speech contains *some* political allusion, although there is no consensus as to its particular referent.[80] Nevertheless, it must have been difficult for an educated Elizabethan audience to see Titania ('the Fairy Queen', III. I. 74) represented on stage without recalling Spenser's figuring of the reigning monarch in his *Faerie Queene* of 1590 and 1596. And we need not make so precise an identification as to link Titania and Bottom with the (already long-stale) issue of Elizabeth's proposed match with Alençon, to see potential cause for offence in the depiction of the regal in the embrace of the bestial, particularly given the Apuleian sub-text of Lucius' congress with the *matrona* of Corinth (see Figure 8).[81]

There may also be cause for offence at an even more fundamental level. Having ridiculed the accounts of asinine metamorphosis given by Sprenger and Bodin, Scot asks:

> What a beastlie assertion is it, that a man, whom GOD hath made according to his owne similitude and likenes, should be by a witch turned into a beast? What an inpietie is it to affirme, that an asses bodie is the temple of the Holy-ghost? Or an asse to be the child of God, and God to be his father; as it is said of man? Which *Paule* to the *Corinthians* so divinelie confuteth, who saith that Our bodies are the members of Christ. In the which we are to glorifie God: for the bodie is for the Lord, and the Lord is for the bodie. Surelie he meaneth not for an asses bodie [...]. Now, if a witch or a divell can so alter the shape of a man, as contrarilie to make him looke downe to hell, like a beast; Gods worke should not onelie be defaced and disgraced, but his ordinance should be wonderfullie altered, and thereby confounded.[82]

After discussing examples of bestialization, Kramer and Sprenger distinguish

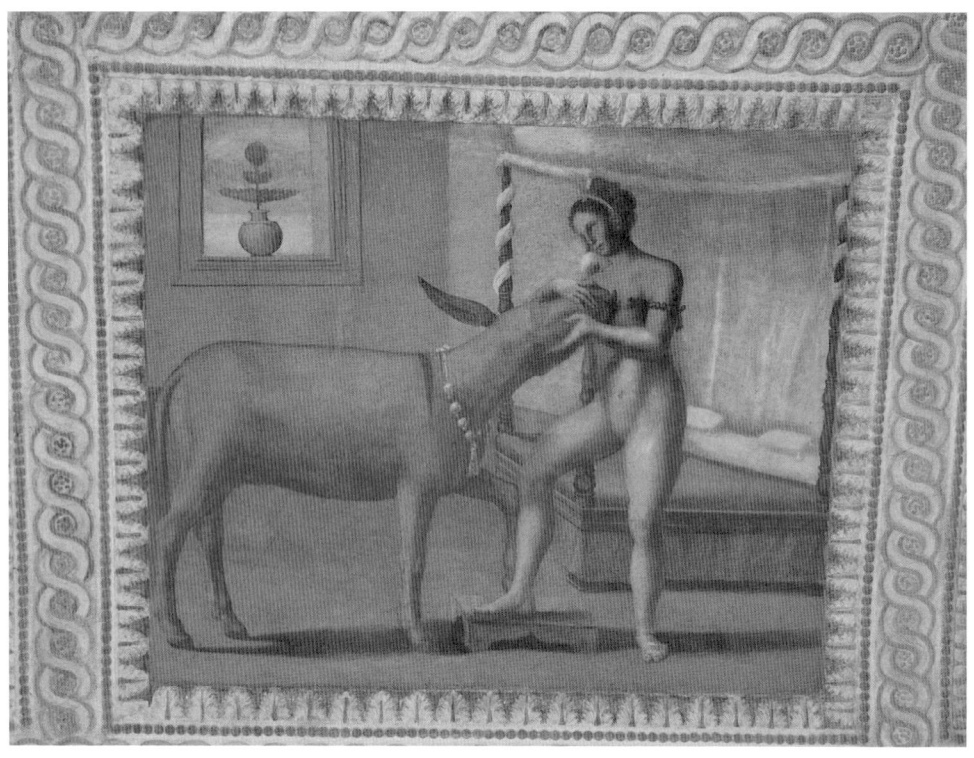

FIG. 8. Lucius and the *matrona* of Corinth (*A.A.* x. 19–23),
Sala dell'Asino d'Oro, La Rocca dei Rossi at San Secondo (*c.* 1525–32)

between a wonder (*mirum*) and a miracle (*miraculum*). A miracle must be i) performed by God; ii) beyond the existing order of nature (*præter existentiam naturæ, contra cuius ordinem fit;* iii) manifest (*euidens*); and iv) for the strengthening of the Faith (*ad fidei corroborationem*).[83] Bottom's transformation satisfies points ii) and iii), but fails on count i) (the metamorphosis occurs through the agency, not of God but of a *daemon*, Puck) and on count iv) (it asserts the potency of a natural and supernatural world that is oblivious to the workings of a higher Christian deity). Bottom's unknowing burlesque of 1 Corinthians 2. 9 has a triple significance in this context: it directs us to the same text discussed by Scot, a text which condemns the Jewish emphasis on the importance of miracles (1 Cor. 1: 22) while developing the notion of 'Pauline folly' (1 Cor. 1. 20–27) which was to feature so importantly in Erasmus' *Encomium moriae*. The version in *A Midsummer Night's Dream* has the theologically subversive effect of elevating a daemonic *mirum* to the status of a divine *miraculum*: 'The eye of man hath not heard, the ear of man hath not seen, man's hand is not able to taste, his tongue to conceive, nor his heart to report, what my dream was' (IV. 1. 209-12).

All this material, arcane and convoluted as it is, supplies a web of sub-texts, both to the metamorphosis itself and to Theseus' famous speech on Reason, Poets, Madmen, and Imagination. At the beginning of Act V, Hippolyta and Theseus reflect on the wonders that they have seen wrought upon the affections of the four young lovers in the wood:

> *Hip.* 'Tis strange, my Theseus, that these lovers speak of.
> *The.* More strange than true: I never may believe
>   These antique fables, nor these fairy toys.
>   Lovers and madmen have such seething brains,
>   Such shaping fantasies, that apprehend
>   More than cool reason ever comprehends.
>   The lunatic, the lover, and the poet
>   Are of imagination all compact:
>   One sees more devils than vast hell can hold;[84]
>   That is the madman:[85] the lover, all as frantic,
>   Sees Helen's beauty in a brow of Egypt:[86]
>   The poet's eye, in a fine frenzy rolling,
>   Doth glance from heaven to earth, from earth to heaven;
>   And as imagination bodies forth
>   The forms of things unknown, the poet's pen
>   Turns them to shapes, and gives to airy nothing
>   A local habitation and a name.
>   Such tricks hath strong imagination,
>   That if it would but apprehend some joy,
>   It comprehends some bringer of that joy:
>   Or, in the night, imagining some fear,
>   How easy is a bush suppos'd a bear! (V. 1. 1–23)

Theseus, of course, is unaware that he himself is one of these 'antique fables', given 'shape' by the metamorphic 'pens' of a succession of 'poets', the last of whom has provided 'A local habitation' both on the page of the text, and in the theatre in which the play is being performed. But, as ruler of Athens, Theseus is also a dispenser of justice, and his threat of capital punishment (or, in comedic terms, something even worse: perpetual virginity) hangs over Hermia's head for most of the play ('Either to die the death, or to abjure | For ever the society of men', I. I. 65–66). That threat has just been removed by Theseus' *fiat* ('Egeus, I will overbear thy will', IV. I. 178), but this scene serves instead, I suggest, as a kind of 'trial' of the imagination. Hippolyta's brief response points, at one level, to the power of comedy to harness the protean forces of metamorphosis and direct them to stability (marriage) rather than entropy:[87]

> But all the story of the night told over,
> And all their minds transfigured so together,
> More witnesseth than fancy's images
> And grows to something of great constancy;
> But, howsoever, strange and admirable. (V. I. 24–28)

But if we have been spending too much time in the company of jurists and demonographers (locked — or looped — inside their self-reinforcing hermeneutic of guilt), we may also be reminded (unsettlingly) of the ways in which justice can function in the real world: 'witness' statements being gathered, and forensic 'evidence' being weighed, within communities whose 'minds' have been 'transfigured so together' by the 'fancy' of witchcraft that conviction is almost inevitable.[88] We noted, earlier, the passage in which Remy cites Apuleius' Pamphile as an illustration of the use of ointments in flight. He concludes with a demonstration of judicial 'proof' and the difference between 'dream' and reality:

> Et omnino de vnguinis istius Magici vsu, facultate, ac viribus conueniunt quotquot hactenus etiam diuersi, super ea re sunt interrogati sortilegi. Immo & colorem etiam studiosè designant, quo fides magis sit no̲n̲ esse somnium, sed rem oculis ipsis visam, ac perceptam.

> [And however much witches may differ concerning other matters, they are all, when questioned, agreed about the magic use, properties and powers of this ointment. They are even particular in describing its colour; and this provides further proof that the matter is no dream, but visible and perceptible to the eyes.] (Remy, I. iv, p. 44, sig. F2ᵛ; Summers, p. 7)

Shakespeare, in contrast, invites us to revel in the wonder (whether *mirum* or *miraculum*) of dramatic mimesis. He has transmuted scholastic philosophizing and judicial deliberations into rich theatrical substance, in the process simply dissolving the distinctions between the real and the illusory. Bottom — as man, ass-man, and ass — is uncompromisingly present, unequivocally real; and, while reflecting on the 'most rare vision' that he has had (an experience which seems to combine the sublimity of Lucius' Isiac theophany with at least the voluptuary potential of his encounter with the Corinthian *matrona*), Bottom manages once again to deflect (or transfer) the charge of asininity, by suggesting that the very process of interpretation is assifying: 'I have had a dream, past the wit of man to say what dream it was. Man is but an ass if he go about to expound this dream' (IV. I. 203–07).[89]

Bottom's Legacy

The issue of bestial transformations remained topical long after *A Midsummer Night's Dream*. The Ambrosian friar, Francesco Maria Guazzo, devotes one chapter of his *Compendium maleficarum* (1608) to the question *An possint Magi transformare corpora ex una specie in alium*, concluding with the orthodox statement that man and beast cannot truly be interchanged but that, through 'feats of legerdemain' (*præstigiæ*), one may have the appearance (*species*) though not the real nature (*veritas*) of the other.[90]

We see, even as late as the year of Shakespeare's death, a process of confusion and contamination between Apuleius' summary of Platonic daemonology (*De deo Socratis*), his self-defence against the charge of magic (*Apologia*, or *De magia*), and his fictional narrative about encounters with magic (*De asino aureo*). In *The Triall of Witch-craft* (1616), having 'produced diuers sorts of noted Practisers' of the 'inhibited contract' with the Devil, John Cotta chooses to

> conclude as a corallary [*sic*] vnto all that went before, with the testimonie and confirmation of *Lucius Apuleius*, that famous, expert, & learned *Magician*, in his booke *de Aureo Asino*, from his long proofe and acquaintance with the Diuel: *Dæmones* (saith he) *præsident Augurijs, Aruspicijs, oraculis, Magorum miraculis*, that is, the Diuels are chiefe presidents, haue chiefe power or authoritie are chiefe Maisters, Guides, or Rulers ouer Diuination, or reuelation by the signes taken in flying of fowles, of diuination by inspection of the entralls of beasts, of Oracles, and of all the miracles or miraculous workes of *Magicians*.[91] They that will not beleeue the holy Scripture, nor the testimony of so many men and ages, that the Diuell is the sole Author of vaine miraculous reuelations, diuinations and workes, let them credit the *Magician* his owne mouth.

From this farrago of category errors, Cotta proceeds (in the very next sentence) to the practicalities of prosecuting and convicting witches:

> As we haue hitherto viewed, how Witch-craft and Witches may be, first, by sense manifestly detected: secondly, by reason euidently conuicted: so let vs now consider, how they may be both produced vnto the barre of Iustice, and bee arraigned and condemned of manifest high treason against Almighty God, and of combination with his open & professed enemy the Diuell.[92]

A continental scholar like Gabriel Naudé (1600–53) shows a serious regard for Apuleius as the author of philosophical works and as the undeserving target of witchcraft accusations, but in *The History of Magick* (1625; trans. 1657), he derides the failure of modern writers on the subject to distinguish between fact and fiction:

> [...] they have so outvied one another in the allegations of these fabulous stories, that the impertinences of old Romances, the fooleries of I know not what books, the tales of old wives, and such fictions, as those of *Lucian*'s Dialogues, and *Apuleius*'s Metamorphoses, have these Authours taken for irrefragable Demonstrations [...][93]

Naudé later speaks of 'our Daemonographers' who 'quote upon all occasions' 'the Metamorphosis of Apuleius' as

> a manifest history to prove *Lycanthropie*. Out of some such jealousie it was, that

the Authour thought himself oblig'd to give us all the precautions possible, to shew that his transmutation was a meer Fable and Romance, when he sayes in the first page of his Book, *At ego tibi sermone isto Milesio varias fabellas conseram*, and a little after, *Fabulam Graecam* [*sic*] *incipimus, lector intende, laetaberis.* [...] those are deservedly laugh'd at, who would establish and confirm a proposition of such consequence by a relation acknowledged to be fabulous, even by the Authour of it [...].[94]

Epilogue

However much we may regret the lines of popular and judicial thinking that led to the prosecution, conviction, and execution of so many alleged witches in the early-modern period, we should acknowledge the role played by the witchcraft debates in developing and articulating an understanding of the metamorphic processes involved in perception, cognition, and the imagination. Moreover, many of the same themes and issues presented in literary works like *The Golden Ass* and *A Midsummer Night's Dream* continue to manifest themselves, even in what we fondly call 'real life'. *The Daily Telegraph* for 26 October 2011 carried a report of a man in Africa arrested for bestiality:

> A Zimbabwean man has told a court that he hired a prostitute who during the night transformed into a donkey, and that he is now 'seriously in love' with the animal, according to state media. 'I think I am also a donkey. I do not know what happened when I left the bar, but I am seriously in love with (the) donkey,' Sunday Moyo told the court, according to *The Herald* newspaper.

The story has been widely syndicated, doubtless for its comic and novelty value, but, in certain respects, an educated Elizabethan reader was better equipped to engage with such a narrative than a modern Western one (whose reaction is likely to be simple incredulity).[95] In George Gifford's *A Dialogue concerning Witches and Witchcrafts* (1593), Samuel relates his experience as a juror in the (non-capital) trial of 'a woman indicted for a witch, but not for killing any man or child':

> A third man came in, and he sayd she was once angry with him, he had a dun cow which was tyed vp in a house, for it was in winter, he feared that some euill would follow, and for his life he could not come in where she was, but he must néedes take vp her tayle and kisse vnder it. (sig. L4^r)

Samuel asks his more cautious and rationally inclined interlocutor what he makes of 'the man which could not chuse but kisse vnder his cowes tayle'.[96] Daniel replies:

> I say he was farre in loue with his cow. Let such men learne to know God, & to expell fantasies out of their mindes that the deuill may not haue such power ouer them, for he worketh in the fantasies of mans mind, and the more strongly where they feare him, as it appeareth this man did. Satan did worke in this mans minde many foolish imaginations, and to make him beleéue he was bewitched he maketh him fall out with one that may be suspected. And thus you Iurie men take your oath & condemne many innocent persons, because you beleéue the deuill, & imagine that witches do that which they can not do.

But even if the Devil has the best tunes, he should not, perhaps, be left with the last laugh. Towards the end of Book x of *Paradise Lost* (1667), Milton depicts Satan's triumphant return to Hell, having unseated his rivals from the Garden of Eden by deceiving Eve in the form of a serpent.[97] He describes his deeds in detail and ends with an exhortation to his comrades:

> Ye have the account
> Of my performance: what remains, ye Gods,
> But up and enter now into full bliss. (*Paradise Lost*, x. 501–03)

Satan's rhetorical promotion of his fellow fallen angels to the ranks of 'Gods' is in keeping with his role as the 'Father of all Lies' (and of a piece with his claim at v. 860 that they were 'self-begot, self-raised'). But there is more truth than Satan realizes in his description of his achievements as a 'performance'. As the following lines make clear, he has (rather like Lucius during the Festival of Laughter in *A.A.* iii) been playing a part in a covert drama, the production of the divine dramaturgist which is destined to be subjected (along with Satan's immediate audience as well as the principal players) to unexpected transformations:

> So having said, a while he stood, expecting
> Their universal shout and high applause   505
> To fill his ear, when contrary he hears
> On all sides, from innumerable tongues
> A dismal universal hiss, the sound
> Of public scorn; he wondered, but not long
> Had leisure, wondring at himself now more;   510
> His visage drawn he felt to sharp and spare,
> His arms clung to his ribs, his legs entwining
> Each other, till supplanted down he fell
> A monstrous serpent on his belly prone,
> Reluctant, but in vain: a greater power   515
> Now ruled him, punished in the shape he sinned,
> According to his doom: he would have spoke,
> But hiss for hiss returnd with forked tongue
> To forked tongue, for now were all transformed
> Alike, to serpents all as accessories   520
> To his bold riot: [...] (*Paradise Lost*, x. 504–21)

Satan's involuntary metamorphosis into a serpent is a visible demonstration of a higher authority and power. It may take our minds back to other responses to transgression (such as the fusion of body parts and civic structures following the execution of political rebels;[98] or the public reduction to ashes of the witches convicted, in Cotta's words, 'of manifest high treason against Almighty God'), although it sits uneasily with Milton's previous support for the deposing and execution of England's anointed king, Charles I, in 1649. But the moment when, 'contrary' to Satan's expectation of 'high applause', he hears 'A dismal universal hiss, the sound | Of public scorn', closely matches Lucius' experience of a failed (or unexpected) rhetorical transformation at *A.A.* iii. 7, when his eloquent self-defence elicits universal laughter rather than sympathy (see ch. 5, *supra*).[99]

Many critics, especially those hostile to Christianity, have been disturbed by the 'derision' (xii. 52) shown by God in response to a related act of 'rebellion', the attempt (on 'The plain, wherein a black bituminous gurge | Boils out from under ground, the mouth of hell', XII. 41–42) to build the Tower of Babel.[100] God thwarts the construction by a simple transformation of language:

> Forthwith a hideous gabble rises loud
> Among the builders; each to other calls,
> Not understood, till hoarse, and all in rage,
> As mocked they storm; great laughter was in heaven
> And looking down, to see the hubbub strange
> And hear the din; thus was the building left
> Ridiculous [...]. (*Paradise Lost*, XII. 56–62)

There is no simple or absolute way of resolving these conflicting vectors (like all great works of literature — not least, *The Golden Ass* — Milton's epic remains dialogical), but God's metamorphic intervention at the supposed climax of the Satanic 'account' serves as a confirmation that the demonic ability to deceive and harm is merely a licensed or delegated power, carefully circumscribed. And the celestial laughter might also be heard as a reminder (closing the circle with Dante's *Divina Commedia*) that, from a soteriological perspective, the human drama is ultimately comedic, not tragic. Satan's mischief seems to engender confusion and woe for humankind, but the 'Fall' is transmuted into something 'fortunate' (a *felix lapsus*) since it precipitates that grandest of all metamorphoses, the Incarnation, bringing with it, Redemption and (for the spiritually transformed, at least), the promise of a final escape from Mutability into life everlasting.[101]

Notes to Chapter 7

1. See Cooper (1988), esp. pp. 75–76.
2. Pico della Mirandola, *Oratio de hominis dignitate* (wr. 1486, pr. Bologna, 1496), fol. 132[r–v]: *ut tui ipsius quasi arbitrarius honorariusque plastes et fictor, in quam* [132[v]] *malueris tute formam effingas.* On the need for restraint in reading Pico in terms of 'Protean Man', see Craven (1981), pp. 35–36. Cf. Greenblatt (1980).
3. See Carver (1998a) and (1998b); Burrow (1988); Chaudhuri (1990). On Sidney and Spenser's use of Apuleius, see Carver (2007), pp. 365–83, and 384–428.
4. (1988), p. 44.
5. Times and tastes, however, have changed. In his *Palladis Tamia. Wits treasury* (London: P. Short for Cuthbert Burbie, 1598), Francis Meres includes 'eloquent and wittie Iohn Lilly' in his list of 'the best Poets for Comedy' (sig. 283[v]).
6. *Euphues, the Anatomy of Wit* (London: T. East for Gabriel Cawood, 1578), fol. 54[r] (spelling modernized).
7. On Lyly and Apuleius, see Carver (2007), pp. 331–32.
8. *Loues metamorphosis. A vvittie and courtly pastorall. [...] First playd by the Children of Paules, and now by the Children of the Chappel* (London: [S. Stafford] for William Wood, 1601). The felling of the 'tree' is mitigated by a further metamorphosis: we learn from Cupid that '*Diana* hath chaunged her bloud to freshe flowers, which are to be seene on the ground' (v. 1, sig. E4[r]).
9. Ceres takes a different view of 'reasonableness': '*Cupid*, thou hast transformed my Nymphes and incensed me, them to shapes vnreasonable, me to anger immortall [...]' (v. 1, sig. E3[v]).
10. Cf. Thomas Cooper's *Thesaurus linguae Romanae & Britannicae* (London: Henry Denham, 1578), sig. Lllll3[v]: '*Muto, mutas, mutâre. Var. To change: to translate: to batter* [*sc.* barter] *or exchange one thing for another: to change from one nature or colour to another.*' Protea's strategic response to her own commodification echoes that of Tarsia in *Apollonius of Tyre* (and anticipates that of Marina in Shakespeare's *Pericles*) — sold into a brothel, but managing to earn money (while maintaining her virginity) by telling her pitiful story (or giving music lessons).

11. The episode acts, figuratively, as a kind of reverse metamorphosis, forcing the erotically deluded Petulius to see the ugly reality beneath the beautiful surface. Cf. the forced disrobing of Duessa in Spenser's *Faerie Queene*, i. viii. 45–49; Carver (2007), pp. 404–05.

12. See Plutarch, *Bruta animalia ratione uti, siue Gryllus* (*Moralia*, 985d). Cf. Spenser, *Faerie Queene*, ii. xii. 86: 'But one aboue the rest, in speciall, | That had an hog beene late, hight *Grille* by name, | Repined greatly, and did him miscall, | That had from hoggish forme him brought to naturall'. Sir Guyon observes (ii. xii. 87): 'See the mind of beastly man, | That hath so soone forgot the excellence | Of his creation, when he life began, | That now he chooseth, with vile difference, | To be a beast, and lacke intelligence.'

13. *Midas Plaied before the Queenes Maiestie vpon Tvvelfe day at night, by the Children of Paules* (London: Thomas Scarlet for I[ohn] B[roome], 1592), i. 1, sig. A2^r.

14. Cf. Erato's comment, 'Hee hath the aduantage of all eares, except the mouse; for else theres none so sharpe of hearing, as the Asse' (iv. 1, sig. E2^r), and Lucius' auditory enhancement at *A.A.* ix. 15 (discussed in connection with David Cronenberg's *The Fly*, ch. 5, *supra*).

15. In the same year as the play, a translation appeared of Jean de L'Espine's *A very excellent and learned discourse, touching the tranquilitie and contentation of the minde* ([Cambridge]: John Legate, 1592). In reference to 'choler', he asks: 'What shall we then say of that which maketh such a Metamorphosis of the whole bodie?' (fol. 48^r).

16. Cf. Solanio's mimicry of Shylock: 'My daughter! O my ducats! O my daughter!' in Shakespeare's *Merchant of Venice* (ii. 8. 15). The Christian prohibition of usury was based on the Augustinian notion that money was inanimate and therefore could not 'grow' through the accumulation of interest. The transformation of Western society from feudalism to capitalism depended on the services of money-lenders like Shylock (as well as the ultimate relaxation of the prohibition).

17. Christopher Marlowe, *Tamburlaine, Parts I and II*; *Doctor Faustus, A- and B-Texts*; *The Jew of Malta*; *Edward II*, ed. by David Bevington and Eric Rasmussen (Oxford: Oxford University Press, 1995). All quotations from *Doctor Faustus* derive from the A-Text (1604).

18. In the introduction to her tale, the Wife declares that 'fayeryes' are no more to be seen (872). The place of the 'elf' (873) has been taken by the 'lymytour' (mendicant friar) who haunts the countryside in which he is licensed to beg: 'Ther is noon oother incubus but he' (880).

19. This display of entomological salaciousness draws on the pseudo-Ovidian poem, *De pulice* ('Concerning the Flea').

20. *The tragicall history of D. Faustus* (London: V. S[immes] for Thomas Bushell, 1604), sig. D[4]^r.

21. We need not assume that such metamorphoses were intended to be permanent. In ch. 43 of *The historie of the damnable life, and deserued death of Doctor Iohn Faustus*, trans. by P. F., gent. (London: Thomas Orwin for Edward White, 1592), the 'merry pranks' with which Faustus entertains his 'scholars' include (amongst much eating and drinking and the appearance at table of a 'monstrous greate Ape') taking them into neighbours' houses as 'maskers' and playing metamorphic tricks upon them: 'Doctor *Faustus* made that euery one had an Asses head on, with great and long eares, so they fell to dansing and to driue away the time, vntill it was midnight, and then euery man departed home, and assoone as they were out of the house each one was in his naturall shape againe' (pp. 62–63).

22. A nineteenth-century theologian might relate Faustus' wishes to the (speculative) theories of Conditionalism (that the human soul is naturally mortal and only rendered immortal by divine gift) and Annihilationism (that the souls of those who are not saved are totally destroyed after death, rather than having to endure everlasting torment). I have enjoyed discussing this topic with Dr Sheridan Gilley.

23. On the notion of 'Subversion through Transgression' in *Doctor Faustus*, see Dollimore (2004), ch 6.

24. Thus Stephen Gosson, *Plays Confuted in Fiue Actions* (London: Thomas Gosson, [1582]), sig. E3^v: 'Whatsoeuer he be that looketh narrowly into our Stage Playes, or considereth how, and which ways they are represented, shall finde more filthines in them, then Players dreame off. The Law of God very straightly forbids men to put on womens garments, garments are set downe for signes distinctiue betwene sexe & sexe, to take vnto vs those garments that are manifest signes of another sexe, is to falsifie, forge, and adulterate, contrarie to the expresse rule of the word of God. Which forbiddeth it by threatning a curse vnto the same. All that do so are abhomination

v<nto> the Lord, which way I bsch you shall they bée excused, that put on, not the apparrell onely, but the gate, the gestures, the voyce, the passions of a woman?' Cf. the attacks by William Prynne (*infra*).

25. In the earlier scene (IV. 1), where Faustus agrees to 'bring Alexander and his paramour before the Emperor' (53–54), he acknowledges that 'it is not in my ability to present before your eyes the true substantial bodies of those two deceased princes, which long since are consumed to dust' (43–45), but merely 'such spirits as can lively resemble' them (48). The Emperor, however, remarks: 'Sure these are no spirits, but the true substantial bodies of these two deceased princes' (IV. 1. 65–66). In *The Devil is an Ass* (which blends together themes from *Doctor Faustus* and *A Midsummer Night's Dream*), Ben Jonson's Satan is scrupulously orthodox in describing the limits of his power: 'But you must take a body ready made, Pug | I can create you none: nor shall you form | Yourself an airy one' (I. 1. 135–36).

26. Greg (1946). Cf. Kiessling (1975). Kiessling makes some telling points about the soteriological implications of having congress with an incubus or succubus, but fails to address the question of who (or what) 'Helen' might be if she is not a demon. In *The historie of the damnable life*, we have a report of progeny, but the disappearance immediately after Faustus' death of 'both mother and sonne' suggests their illusory quality: 'And you haue heard that he held by him in his life the Spirit of fayre *Helena*, the which had by him one sonne, the which he named *Iustus Faustus*, euen the same day of his death they vanished away, both mother and sonne' (ch. 63, sig. L2^v).

27. The moment, in the 1967 OUDS production (directed by Neville Coghill), when Elizabeth Taylor (as Helen) glided across the stage in front of Richard Burton's Faustus lives on in Oxford's folk-memory. Proceeds from the production (for which the principals took no fee) were used to build the Burton-Taylor Rooms.

28. Except where indicated to the contrary, all quotations are from William Shakespeare, *The Complete Works*, 2nd edn, ed. by Stanley Wells, Gary Taylor, John Jowett and William Montgomery (Oxford: Clarendon Press, 2005).

29. Harry has already observed the negative transformation wrought on the page-boy given to Falstaff, who 'had him from me Christian, and look if the fat villain have not transformed him ape' (II. 2. 63–65). In *1 Henry IV*, the 'misuse' (*sc.* emasculation) of the thousand 'butchered' 'men of Herefordshire' is described as a 'beastly shameless transformation' effected upon a collective 'corpse' by 'Welshwomen' who are, effectively, configured as metamorphosing witches in the service of 'the irregular and wild' Glendower (I. 1. 38–46).

30. I restore here the reading of the 1604 quarto ('dreame', sig. E2^v) in preference to Wells and Taylor's 'deem'.

31. See Ovid's description of Somnus (god of Sleep), rousing his son, Morpheus, 'the creator and imitator of form': *At pater [...] | excitat artificem simulatoremque figurae | Morphea [...].* (*Metamorphoses*, XI. 633–35). Cf. John Gower: 'Morphe[u]s [...] whos nature | Is forto take the figure | Of what persone that him liketh' (*Confessio amantis*, IV. 3039–41).

32. 1594 quarto (sig. F4^r; = IV. 1. 42). This is the only occurrence of the word 'metamorphosis' in the accepted Shakespearian canon. In *A pleasant conceited historie, called The taming of a shrew* (London: Peter Short for Cutbert Burbie, 1594) — usually taken as an adaptation (or a 'bad quarto' version) of Shakespeare's *The Taming of the Shrew*) — upon seeing the change wrought in the Shrew's behaviour, Polidor exclaims: 'Oh wonderfull metamorphosis' (sig. G1^r). In an apocryphal play, *The London prodigall*, Flowerdale Senior declares, 'Looke on me better, now my scarre is off. | Nere muse man at this metamorphosie', as he doffs the disguise adopted to uncover his son's errancy. But he forgives 'the follyes that are past', and takes 'ioy' in the 'change' wrought in his son by Luce, 'this vertuous maide, | Whom heauen hath sent to thee to saue thy soule'. See *The London prodigall As it was plaide by the Kings Maiesties seruants. By VVilliam Shakespeare* (London: T[homas] C[reede] for Nathaniel Butter, 1605), sig. G4^r.

33. See, generally, Bate (1994).

34. See Nevo (1980). In an early comedy like *The Taming of the Shrew*, Katherine's apparent transformation is marked by the moment when she accepts Petruchio's wilfully arbitrary identification of 'sun' and 'moon': 'Then, God be blessed, it is the blessèd sun, | But sun it is not when you say it is not, | And the moon changes even as your mind. | What you will have it named, even that it is, | And so it shall be still for Katherine' (IV. 6. 19–23). The passage may seem to anticipate the capitulatory moment in Orwell's *1984* where Winston Smith's perception

and cognition begin to be shaped by O'Brien's insistence that the four fingers he is holding up are actually five. It can also be argued, however, that the changes in Katherine's language are an adaptive strategy, and that she has succeeded in figuring her husband in lunar terms, transferring to the male the image of the moon which has traditionally been an emblem of feminine mutability.

35. Cf. v. 1. 30–32: 'Go release them, Ariel. | My charms I'll break, their senses I'll restore, | And they shall be themselves.'

36. It is difficult to tell how sincerely we should read Caliban's parting comment, 'I'll be wise hereafter, | And seek for grace' (v. 1. 298–99). More interesting, from an Apuleian point of view, is Caliban's description of his mis-directed religious devotion as a form of asinine transformation: 'What a thrice-double ass | Was I to take this drunkard for a god, | And worship this dull fool!' (v. 1. 299–300).

37. Cf. the characterization of Rome as 'a wilderness of tigers' in *Titus Andronicus* (III. 1. 53).

38. Carver (2007), pp. 433–45 (with reference to earlier secondary literature).

39. Francis Douce, *Illustrations of Shakspeare and of Ancient Manners*, 2 vols (London: Longman, Hurst, Rees, and Orme, 1807), I, 193. The passage occurs in Bk XIII, ch. 19 of Reginald Scot, *The Discoverie of Witchcraft*, ed. by Bradley Nicholson (London: Elliot Stock, 1886), p. 258. Scot derived the recipe from the *Magiae Naturalis* (1558) of Johannes Baptista Neapolitanus (Giambattista Della Porta, 1535–1613).

40. See Scot, Book v, ch. 5, p. 79. For two near-by references to Apuleius, see Book v, ch. 1, pp. 72–73, and Book v, ch. 4, p. 78.

41. Charles and Michelle Martindale (1990), p. 201, n. 40, express the general view when they note: 'Shakespeare also extracted some amusing material about asses' heads from Reginald Scot's *Discovery of Witchcraft* (1584).'

42. See Henri Boguet, jurist and judge of Saint-Claude in Burgundy, *Discours des Sorciers* (Lyon, 1590); Hirsch (2005). The discussion of the *Malleus Maleficarum*, Scot, Bodin, and Daneau given below, draws on unpublished material in Carver (1991), pp. 279–87.

43. Lib. II. s. 171. The most striking resemblance is to the account of Lucius earning money as a performing ass in *A.A.* 10.

44. Scot, p. 76; cf. Marlowe, *Doctor Faustus*, 4.5.

45. William of Malmesbury, *Gesta regum anglorum*, ed. and trans. R. A. B. Mynors, R. M. Thompson, and M. Winterbottom, 2 vols (Oxford: Clarendon, 1998-99), I, 292-93. Cf. Carver (2007), pp. 88-89.

46. For the marvel itself, see *The Clementine Recognitions*, ed. by Alexander Roberts and James Donaldson, trans. by Thomas Smith, in *Ante-Nicene Christian Library*, vol. III (Edinburgh: T. & T. Clark, 1867), pp. 459–60.

47. *Rogeri de Wendover Chronica sive Flores Historiarum*, ed. by H. O. Coxe (London: English Historical Society, 1841), I, 485–86. The authorship of the early English chronicles is extremely problematic. The same work is variously attributed to Roger of Wendover and Matthew of Paris. See *Matthæi Parisiensis, monachi sancti Albani Chronica majora*, ed. by Henry Richard Luard (London: Rolls Series, 57a, 1872), I, 519, for an almost identical version of the story assigned to the year 1049.

48. *Flores historiarum*, ed. by Henry Richards Luard (London: Rolls Series 95a, 1890), p. 567. On the complex question of the interrelationship of the various traditions of ass-story, see Scobie (1983), pp. 258 ff. On Macarius, see Frankfurter (2001).

49. See Charles and Peters (2001), p. 109.

50. Charles and Peters (2001), p. 107.

51. *Topographia Hibernica* (II. 19), in *Giraldi Cambrensis opera*, 8 vols (London: Longmans, 1861–91), vol. V, ed. J. F. Dimmock, pp. 105–06. See, also, Bynum (1998), p. 1011; (2001), p. 107; and Carver (2007), p. 89.

52. *Decretorum Canonicorum collectanea* (Antwerp: Christopherus Plantinus, 1570), II, 919. For a more modern text, see *Corpus Iuris Canonici: Pars prior decretum Magistri Gratiani*, ed. by Aemilius Friedberg (Leipzig: Bernhardus Tauchnitz, 1879), *Decreti secunda pars causa xxvi. Quest. v. c. xii*, cols. 1030–31.

53. *Malleus maleficarum in tres divisus partes. Auctore Iacobe Sprengero Ordinis Prædicatorum, olim Inquisitore* (Frankfurt on Meine: Nicolaus Bassaeus, 1580). Sprenger gives his text (and interpretation) of the canon at pp. 276–77. In the introduction to his English translation, *Malleus Maleficarum*

(London: Pushkin Press, 1948), p. xiv, Montague Summers — an interested party — ranks Sprenger's work 'among the most important, wisest, and weightiest books of the world.' Cf. Henricus Institoris, O. P. and Jacobus Sprenger, O. P., *Malleus Maleficarum*, ed. and trans. by C. S. Mackay, 2 vols (Cambridge: Cambridge University Press, 2006), I, pp. 321-28; II, pp. 153-60 (Part I, quest. 10).

54. In George Gifford's *A dialogue concerning witches and witchcraftes In which is laide open how craftely the Diuell deceiueth not onely the witches but many other and so leadeth them awrie into many great errours* (London: John Windet for Tobie Cooke and Mihil Hart, 1593), Daniel claims that the choice of 'paltrie vermine' on the Devil's part is strategic: 'now, when they take vpon them the shapes of such paltrie vermine, as Cats, Mise, Toads, and Weasils, it is euen of subtiltie to couer and hide his mightie tyrannie, and power which he exerciseth ouer the heartes of the wicked' (sig. C2^r). Cf. Remy, I. xxi; Summers, p. 67.

55. *Malleus* (1580), p. 276.

56. *Malleus*, Part II, ch. 4.

57. *Malleus*, Part II, quest. ii, ch. 4; trans. Summers, p. 173; cf. Mackay I, pp. 519–21, II, pp. 385–88. The authors (Heinrich Kramer and Jacob Sprenger) state that they 'have learned much of this matter from the Knights of the Order of S. John of Jerusalem in Rhodes'. We should note how the setting in Cyprus (where the Roman rite was in use) obviates any awkward questions that might arise in a Greek Orthodox context as to whether the 'mystery' of the Eucharist should be understood loosely as a 'change' (*metabole*) undergone by the bread and wine, or (accommodating western Scholastic notions of Transubstantiation) as a 'change in essence' (*metousiosis*). Cf. Bodin, Book II, ch. 6, fol. 100^r; Scot, Book V, chs. 4, 5. Scot also classes as 'the starkest lie that ever was invented' Augustine's story (*De ciuitate dei*, xviii. 18; see ch. 5, *supra*) 'of the two alewiues that used to transforme all their ghests into horses' (Book V, ch. 3). He finds such stories 'too common in his books' and says, 'I judge them rather to be foisted in by some fond Papist or Witchmonger, then so learned a mans doings', though he notes that Augustine 'concludeth against *Bodin;* for he affirmeth these Transubstantiations to be but fantastical, and that they are not according to the verity, but according to the appearance'.

58. *Ioannis VVieri de praestigiis daemonum, & incantationibus ac ueneficiis libri sex, postrema editione quinta aucti & recogniti* (Basil: Ex officina Oporiniana, 1577), col. 268 (IV. x). Leo IX died in 1054. See in more detail Chapter 8 (Guido Giglioni).

59. Lambertus Danæus, *A Dialogue of Witches, in foretime named Lot-tellers, and novv commonly called Sorcerers. VVherein is declared breefely and effectually, vvhat soeuer may be required, touching that argument. A treatise very profitable, by reason of the diuerse and sundry opinions of men in their question, and right necessary for Judges to vnderstand, which sit vpon lyfe and death*, [trans. by Tho: Twyne] ([London]: [T. East? for] R. W[atkins], 1575), sig. A.iii^r.

60. Scot, p. 78.

61. Daneau, sig. F1^r.

62. Summers, p. xiii.

63. Jean Bodin, *De la Démonomanie des sorciers* (Paris: Iacques du Puys, 1582), fol. 100^v.

64. Scot, Book V, ch. 1, p. 72.

65. Scot, Book V, ch. 6. In the case of biblical narrative, there is actually no need in the first place to use a figurative interpretation to explain away something which contradicts the established order of nature since, as Scot observes (in a codicil which reflects the confusions in the whole debate), God is able 'to bring to passe such workes at his pleasure'.

66. On Remy, see Monter (2007). On the verso of the fly-leaf of his copy of Remy (Oxford, Bodleian Library, Douce RR 146), Francis Douce (1757–1834) has written: *Liber rarissimus omnium qui de Magia scripti sunt, et vere singularis* ['The rarest of all the books that have been written about Magic, and truly singular'].

67. Note the Arden editor's conclusion that it was composed 'in the winter of 1595–96'. See *A Midsummer Night's Dream*, ed. by Harold F. Brooks (London: Methuen, 1983), p. lvii (all quotations are taken from this edn). Ben Jonson cites Remy (Remigius) — along with Apuleius — several times in the notes to his *Masque of Queenes* (1608; pr. 1609): e.g. sigs. A4^v; A[*sc.* B]3^v. Cf. William Perkins, *A discourse of the damned art of witchcraft so farre forth as it is reuealed in the Scriptures, and manifest by true experience* ([Cambridge]: Cantrel Legge, printer to the Vniuersitie

of Cambridge, 1610). In answer to the question, 'Whether the Witches of our times, be the same with those that are here condemned by Moses Law?', Perkins states: 'The confessions of Witches recorded in the Chronicles of countries through all Europe, doe with common consent declare and manifest this point.' The marginal note (Chap. 7, Sect. 1, p. 187) points us to: 'Nicol. Remigius, Dæmonolatr. c. 1. c. 5.' Biblical authority for executing witches is found in Exodus 22. 18: 'Thou shalt not suffer a witch to live.'

68. For translation, see Nicolas Remy, *Demonolatry: An Account of the Historical Practice of Witchcraft*, trans. by E. A. Ashwin, ed. by Montague Summers (London: John Rodker, 1930; repr. Mineola, NY: Dover Books, 2008).

69. Summers, p. 27; Remy, p. 76. Cf. Puck's delight in shape-shifting as he persecutes the mechanical actors: 'Sometimes a horse I'll be, sometime a hound, | A hog, a headless bear, sometime a fire; | And neigh, and bark, and grunt, and roar, and burn, | Like horse, hound, hog, bear, fire, at every turn' (III. 1. 103–06).

70. *A.A.* IX. 14. See Chapter 5 in this volume.

71. I. ix, p. 91; Summers, p. 36. The word *bracteatus* ('gilt, covered in gold leaf') is obviously appropriate to *The Golden Ass*: in the pantomime, Mercury carries an 'apple gilded with gold leaf' (*malum [...] bracteis inauratum*, *A.A.* X. 30); the stern of the ship in the *nauigium Isidis* ceremony is 'clothed in gold leaf' (*bracteis aureis uestita*, XI. 16).

72. Details from the description of Socrates 'baring the rest of his body from his navel to his loins' (*ab umbilico pube tenus cetera corporis renudaret*, *A.A.* I. 6) seem to have dripped into Remy's (immediately following) account of a flagellant in Mirecourt who 'would sit down [...] naked to the navel' (*procumbebat nudus vmbilico tenus*, p. 92; Summers, p. 36).

73. Remy, p. 234; Summers, p. 112.

74. As the Arden editor notes (Brooks, p. 52), this is '*OED*'s earliest instance' of the term.

75. pp. 892–93. There is much more in the same vein. We might note his citing of 'Saint Chrysostome' in support of his argument that '*Players and Play-haunters by acting and seeing Playes became more barbarous then the most savage beasts*'. Those 'who were reasonable men before, are metamorphosed into beasts or monsters now' (p. 280).

76. *Histrio-mastix* (1633), p. 553.

77. I. ix; Summers, p. 36. Cf. ch. 6 ('The Devil, God's Ape') of Clark (1997), pp. 80–93. Cf. Summers, p. 29: Demon imitating voice = 1595, p. 79. Cf. Gifford, *A Dialogue* (1593), sig. E1ᵛ, on Satan as 'iugler'.

78. Martindale, C. and M. (1990), p. 65.

79. Compare the epilogues of such ancient dramatists as Plautus.

80. II. 1. 148–54.

81. Carver (2007), pp. 438–43; Carver (2013b).

82. Scot, Book V, ch. 5, p. 80.

83. *Malleus*, Part II, quest. i, ch. 9, p. 285.

84. William Prynne relates the story of 'the visible apparition of the Devill on the Stage at the Belsavage Play-house, in Queene *Elizabeths* dayes, (to the great amazement both of the Actors and Spectators) whiles they were there prophanely playing the History of *Faustus* (the truth of which I have heard from many now alive, who well remember it,) there being some distracted with that fearefull sight' (*Histrio-mastix* [1633], fol. 556ʳ). For another version of the story (featuring 'certaine Players at Exeter, acting upon the stage the tragical storie of Dr. Faustus the Conjurer'), see Chambers (1923), vol. III, p. 424.

85. Cf. Pierre de La Primaudaye (b. *c.* 1545), *The second part of the French academie*, trans. by T. B. (London: G. B[ishop] R[alph] N[ewbery] R. B[arker], 1594), ch. 27 ('Of the internall senses, and of men possessed with devilles'), p. 166: 'Example heereof is daily seene in many that are frensie and madde, hauing all their senses troubled, which sometimes they had sound and perfect. Yea there are some that behaue themselues like dogges and wolues as Physicions report, because they thinke they are transformed into those kinde of beasts, by reason of the violence of Melancholy, and of that malady, which is thereupon named by the Graecians *Cynanthropie* and *Lycanthropie*. It pleased God to punish *Nebuchadnezzar* with this kinde of chastisement, to beate downe his glorie and pride, when his wittes were taken from him, in so much that hee did not thinke himselfe to be a man any more but a beast, and so indeede liued in the fieldes like a wilde beast.'

86. Cf. the response of Marlowe's Faustus (and his audience) to (the boy actor playing the part of) the phantom Helen (*supra*).

87. Cf. Oberon's earlier rebuke to Puck after mixing up suitors when applying the love-herb: 'Of thy misprision must perforce ensue | Some true love turn'd, and not a false turn'd true' (III. 2. 90–91).

88. Cf. Remy, p. 44, sig. F2^v.

89. Cf. Lucius' response to Aristomenes' tale at *A.A.* I. 20 (discussed, *supra*, in context of Remy, III. xii, pp. 382–83; Summers, p. 182) and his teasing allusion to the need not to divulge details following his initiation into the Egyptian mysteries at XI. 23. Note also how Bottom suggests that those engaged in perceiving him are creating the image of an ass: 'What do you see? You see an ass-head of your own, do you?' (III. i. 111–12).

90. See *Compendium maleficarum [...] per Fratrem Franciscum Mariam Guaccium [...] compilatum*, 2nd edn (Milan: Ex collegii Ambrosiani Typographia, 1626), pp. 96–97.

91. The Latin is not from *The Golden Ass* (or any of Apuleius' works), but looks like a paraphrase (doubtless from a further intermediate source) of Augustine's summary of Apuleian daemonology in *De ciuitate dei*, VIII. 16: *Inter cetera etiam dicit ad eos [sc. daemones] pertinere diuinationes augurum, aruspicum, uatum atque somniorum; ab his quoque esse miracula magorum.* Cf. Apuleius, *De deo Socratis*, 6: *Per hos eosdem, ut Plato in Symposio autumat, cuncta denuntiata et magorum uaria miracula omnesque praesagiorum species reguntur.*

92. *The triall of vvitch-craft shewing the true and right methode of the discouery: with a confutation of erroneous wayes. By Iohn Cotta, Doctor in Physicke* (London: George Purslowe for Samuel Rand, 1616), p. 80. The passage is repeated in *The Infallible True and Assured Witch; or, The Second Edition of the Tryall of Witch-Craft Shewing the Right and True Methode of the Discouerie* (London: I. L. for Richard Higginbotham, 1624), pp. 102–03.

93. *The history of magick by way of apology, for all the wise men who have unjustly been reputed magicians, from the Creation, to the present age. / Written in French, by G. Naudaeus late library-keeper to Cardinal Mazarin. Englished by J. Davies* (London: John Streater, 1657), p. 60. This is a translation of *Apologie pour tous les grands personnages qui ont esté faussement soupçonnez de magie* (1625).

94. *The History of Magick,* ch. XI, p. 115.

95. The corresponding headline in *The Sun* read, 'Man claims prostitute turned into a donkey'.

96. sig. M2^v. Gifford expects his own dialogue to have a transformative effect upon his readers. M. B. (a former believer in the power of 'the cunning folk') remarks to wife, 'I was of your minde, but I am not nowe, for I seé how foolish I was'. The wife of Samuel observes: 'I thinke my husband is turned also: here hath bene one reasoning with them threé or foure howers' (sig. M4^r).

97. On other aspects of Milton's use of Ovid, see Green (2009), and (*non vidi*) Kilgour (2012); on his use of Apuleius, see Carver (2007), pp. 356–57.

98. Edward Hall provides one of the earliest applications of the word 'metamorphosis' in English when he comments on Jack Cade's attempts to evade capture in the course of the popular revolt of 1450 by 'depart[ing] secretly in habite disguysed, into Sussex: but all his metamorphosis or transfiguracion, litle preuailed.' The 'caitiff' is cornered and killed, and his transgressive tendencies are redirected by an exemplary corporeal transformation ('This is the successe of all rebelles, and this fortune chaunceth euer to traytors') as his head is 'set on Londo[n] bridge' and the four quarters of his body are 'sent to be displayed at Blackheath, Norwich, Salisbury, and Gloucester'. See *The vnion of the two noble and illustre famelies of Lancastre [and] Yorke* (London: Richard Grafton, 1548), fol. Clxi^r [28 Henry VI]; and *ODNB*, 'Cade, John'.

99. Cf. X. 545–47: 'Thus was th' applause they meant, | Turn'd to exploding hiss, triumph to shame | Cast on themselves from thir own mouths'. The metamorphosis is eventually reversed ('Thus were they plagu'd | And worn with Famin, long and ceasless hiss, | Till thir lost shape, permitted, they resum'd', X. 572–74), though some authorities maintain that the devils were required to undergo an 'annual humbling' in this serpentine form, 'To dash thir pride, and joy for Man seduc't' (X. 575–77).

100. See C. S. Lewis (1960), p. 131; W. Empson (1981), pp. 119–21; Bate (1997), 1–26. Cf. critical reactions to God's alleged mocking of Faustus in Marlowe's final scene: 'See, see where Christ's blood streams in the firmament' (*supra*).

101. Cf. Remy, II. v; Summers, p. 113.

CHAPTER 8

Phantastica Mutatio: Johann Weyer's Critique of the Imagination as a Principle of Natural Metamorphosis

Guido Giglioni

A large number of pre-modern and early-modern philosophers, theologians, physicians and rhetoricians agreed that the imagination had the power to represent — more or less faithfully — reality. Their opinions, however, varied significantly when they had to assess the extent to which the imagination could change reality or even produce new reality. Some agreed with the rhetoricians that 'visualization' (*enargeia*) had the power to move the affects and provoke bodily reactions. Others shared the characteristically medical view that confidence in the physician's skills could boost the energy of the patient's imagination and lead him or her to a full recovery or that, conversely, mistrusting the doctor's abilities might impair his or her level of self-confidence to such a degree that the ailing body might release all sorts of pathological symptoms. Not many could deny the fact that maternal imaginations had the power to impress marks on the supple flesh of the foetus or even to shape it in monstrous fashions every time the mother's senses and imagination underwent strong emotions of fear and hatred. Very few went so far as to embrace the radical opinion (held among others by Avicenna during the Middle Ages and Paracelsus in the Renaissance) that the imagination could alter not just one's own body, but other people's bodies and even their surrounding environment. Theories of enchantment, from Al-Kindi to Pietro d'Abano to Tommaso Campanella, shared the ancient belief that images (and words in their mimetic and representative functions) could convey properties and powers from the objects they represented.[1]

This, in a nutshell, may be considered the spectrum of the various positions concerning the relationship between the imagination and reality in the Renaissance. It should not therefore come as too much of a surprise to discover that the imagination — often characterized as the most protean of the human faculties — became the subject of a heated debate over the scope and the limits of the human ability to represent or even change reality. In addition, starting from the end of the fifteenth century, as a result of the widespread belief that the world was bewitched and under attack by the forces of Satan, the question concerning the limits of changeability with respect to both souls and bodies had become increasingly more urgent. This belief had often been taken as an indication that human beings were unable to distinguish between the imaginary and the real in an unequivocal manner, or as evidence of the diabolical conspiracy's progress.[2]

Consequently, from both a philosophical and a theological point of view, the imagination was at the centre of ongoing discussions about the ontological conditions of metamorphosis, especially every time unnatural transformations of human bodies or their fabled transformations into animals called into question the stability and constancy of natural species. The role that philosophers, physicians and theologians assigned to the imagination in the explanation of such transformations could vary from that of a physical force of nature to that of narrative plausibility. If we want to trace a trend in such an intricate matter, we might say that, with the demise of Renaissance cosmologies, the imagination was deemed to have gradually lost its power to cause physical change and instead it became a literary force moving from physical transformations to transformations in words and images. This does not mean that the metamorphic power of the imagination lost its hold on human souls and bodies, for the narrative imagination continued to affect the identities of the persons involved in stories of bodily transformations. By becoming a narrative force, the imagination was increasingly associated with fictional accounts of reality, involving aspects of theatrical illusion, suspension of disbelief and preternatural bewitchment. In the debate over the nature of diabolical interventions, possessions by the devil were often described as the state of being possessed by the imagination, a state in which there was no actual physical change. As a narrative force capable of feeding on the credulous anxiety of human beings, the imagination was seen as the main culprit behind distorted representations of reality. Within this context of imaginary (though extremely powerful) transformations, the Augustinian concept of human 'phantom' (*phantasticum hominis*), understood as the surrogate of a ceaselessly changeable body, came in handy. The power and scope of the imagination could thus be defined in an acceptable and plausible way, for, in the neo-Augustinian reading, both the imagination and the devil were indeed still 'Protei, but 'Protei' without an impact on physical reality.[3]

This is precisely the position embraced by a sixteenth-century inquirer into the world of the imagination and unnatural transformations of human bodies: Johann Weyer. Court physician to Duke Wilhelm V of Jülich-Cleves, Weyer (1515? — 1588) was the typical humanist doctor of the Renaissance, who in his work combined medical expertise with an impressive level of historical and literary erudition, knowledge of legal thought and natural philosophy.[4] With his *De praestigiis daemonum et incantationibus ac veneficiis* ('On the illusions of demons and on spells and sorcery', published originally in 1563 and then, in several enlarged editions, in 1564, 1566, 1568, 1577, 1583), Weyer penned what we might call an exhaustive critique of the imagination, assessing the prerogatives and powers of the faculty under examination. In keeping with Augustine's account of the structure and function of images, Weyer stressed the special relationship that images entertained with the objects they represent: 'images of objects are usually called by the names of the objects which they represent. Who would hesitate to call a man in a picture a man?'[5] This, though, was not the only property that could be attributed to images. While retaining something of the original thing, images and names could trigger tropological shifts and perpetuate the characteristic condition of suspension and ambivalence conveyed by appearances, that is to say, a reality that is not really a reality, an appearance that is not only an appearance. In Weyer's opinion, the belief that the appearances of things could induce physical changes and symbolic associations represented a threat for a number of intellectuals, divines and rulers, especially when the flickering and changeable world of natural appearances was interpreted as the very kingdom of Satan. To this diffident and largely negative characterization of appearances and imaginations, Weyer added his own distinctively phenomenological attitude towards the figments of the imagination. He took appearances for what they are in the first place, i.e., pure semblances of things, and yet he saw them as ontologically relevant in making human beings aware of being irredeemably prisoners of a deceitful world. In Weyer's universe, reality meant, first and foremost, God, and, secondarily, the world he had created according to natural laws and logical principles mirroring the foundations of His eternal wisdom. All the rest he deemed to be made up of varying degrees of appearances. This world of appearances was for him the world of the imagination.

In all his works, Weyer describes the imagination as the faculty of false impressions, long-held beliefs, misleading opinions and fixed ideas. The imagination constitutes a universe of knowledge in which mental representations are not corroborated by an unambiguous reference to reality or validated by ethical principles. Its representative power is marred both by the distorting mirror of lustful anticipations and by the constitutively faulty mechanism of human perception. Only the innermost part of the soul can escape this process of representative adulteration of reality. Indeed, the *sanctum sanctorum* of men's inner thoughts is for Weyer such a genuine manifestation of being that the devil has no access to it.[6] This has important consequences on a legal level. One should not invoke the law to punish the imagination. If the witches are actual 'poisoners' (*veneficae*), then the law of the Empire (*lex Caesarea*) must be enforced. But if they are deluded witches (*lamiae*), then they are seriously disturbed but inoffensive women 'whose imagination or imaginative power has been so injured by that crafty spirit of deviation and dizziness (*veteratorius ille vertiginis spiritus*) that they think they have done what in fact they did not or what does not even exist in nature'.[7] Only God knows the mind of the guilty and He is the only one who can punish a crime of the mind (*Flagitium mente conceptum Deus punit, qui mentem novit*).[8] Because of his faith in the ultimate reality and autonomy of the intelligible world, Weyer finds support even among Neoplatonic philosophers. It may sound unusual at first, but Iamblichus is quite an important authority for Weyer. Significantly, he quotes his words more than once throughout his *De praestigiis daemonum*:

> The things that we imagine when bewitched have no reality of action and being, except as imaginings.[9]

One might object to Weyer's position that the bewitched condition of the imagination postulated by Iamblichus cannot be taken to represent a paradigm of perception. However, as I will argue in the course of this essay, it was precisely because Weyer resolved almost all phenomena of bewitchment and possession into neuro-physiological states of altered perception that possession and bewitchment could be assimilated to ordinary forms of imagination. In *De praestigiis daemonum*, Weyer set out to show that, in order to free human knowledge from the enchantments of the imagination, the first thing to do was to demonstrate that the oddest and most extraordinary phenomena of nature were in fact the product of ordinary operations pertaining to the representative faculties of the human mind.

In Weyer's opinion, one of the most ordinary among these operations was the tendency to surrender to the power of the imagination, seen as a natural desire to escape into a reassuring world of self-serving figments. That people tend to give up reason, base their lives on unfounded imaginations, and accept a condition of self-delusion is one of the basic assumptions underlying Weyer's theory of witchcraft. The rationale behind this otherwise irrational behaviour is that reality is simply too painful to bear. No doubt, by reality Weyer means such hardships as disease, famine and poverty, but he is also convinced that reality in its truest sense is God in all His formidable power. Here one may understand why Sigmund Freud was so fascinated by *De praestigiis daemonum*: for Weyer the imagination represents a dangerous substitute of reality, especially when the 'reality principle' is too harsh a principle to come to terms with. For instance, Weyer ends the description of a case involving the use of witchcraft by saying that all the characters in the 'drama' 'have much preferred to believe that this was an instance of witchcraft'.[10] Furthermore, Weyer is convinced that *credulousness* as a result of fear leads to *unbelief*. It is easier and safer to believe in the evil intentions of a witch than in the just but inscrutable will of God. One of Weyer's principal arguments is that the mocking illusions of the devil are allowed by God because of the lack of faith displayed by human beings. The 'children of unbelief' (*filii diffidentiae*), says Weyer borrowing Paul's expression (Eph. 2. 3), prefer to attribute their misfortunes to the activity of some poor old woman rather than to 'a flaw of nature' or 'the will of God'.[11] Instead of being responsible and honest believers, they accuse other people of crimes they did not commit. Belief in the power of the devil is no superstition for Weyer, for he maintains that the devil and his actions are real. Superstition is to mistake human feats for the actions of the devil. While cases of possession may be real attacks of the devil, episodes of witchcraft are always delusions. No real action of natural magic is permitted in Weyer's universe. All magic is diabolical because all preternatural phenomena purported to result from acts of human sorcery are in fact caused by the devil. In the final analysis, the misfortunes that afflict people are a divine punishment for their lack of faith: 'unbelief is strengthened when we abandon God in adversity, and lose faith in the means graciously granted to us by Him who can truly heal our languors'.[12] Weyer is as scrupulous as a doctor as he is pious as a Christian. Indeed, he often puts his medical expertise to the test to decide what belongs to nature and what to the devil.

Since it is God that sends tribulations to men to try their faith, the ultimate cause of all natural events remains therefore God's will.[13] Weather catastrophes, like the hail storm which in the summer of 1562 destroyed crops and vines, are not caused by the devil or witches, but by God.[14] However, the fact that Weyer acknowledges the extent of God's power in nature does not mean that he is a supporter of theological voluntarism. His view of divine causality privileges the aspects of God's *potentia ordinata* rather than His *potentia absoluta*.[15] This means that natural phenomena follow the laws established by God at the moment of creation. Such laws impose regularities and a number of conditions that cannot be violated, not even by God's will. There cannot be such things as interruptions of regular relationships of causality, actions at a distance, unnatural stretching of bodily parts and anomalous dilations of the pores of the skin so that all sorts of objects can be introduced in someone's body. If human beings happen to be present at such phenomena in nature, then the only plausible explanation is that these marvels are appearances caused by demonic theatrics. And it is a theatre — 'a theatre of ignorance' (*inscitiae theatrum*)[16] — with a precise didactic purpose: to edify or punish the 'children of unbelief'. In this sense, natural and demonic metamorphoses are in fact illusions staged by God, both director and impresario of the great theatre of nature.

Weyer's Demonology

We can sum up the argument developed so far by saying that, while limiting the power of the imagination within carefully circumscribed boundaries, Weyer expanded the domain of representations and appearances by making the devil, under the providential regime of God, the great illusionist. And yet, ironically, it is the devil who, in the final analysis, is called to certify the veridical nature of some of the most implausible stories. In a way, he is the witness par excellence. Even a most unlikely story like the legend of the lost children of Hamelin has him as its main character, for Weyer identifies the piper with the devil: 'here we have a case of the devil appearing as a piper who thirsts for blood'.[17]

A telling case is the story set in Bruges, reported by Weyer in book 3, chapter 32 ('An extraordinary account of childbearing on the part of a possessed woman, caused by a witch (*lamia*)'). All the typical circumstances and characters are in place: a woman tormented by a demon, a maid suspected of witchcraft and acting as Satan's accomplice, episodes of demonic rape and, as a result, a demonic pregnancy with a final act of infant snatching. The source of the story meets all the requirements one would expect for a witness to be reliable: 'These facts were reported to me by my brother-in-law, a man renowned for his nobility, learning, and piety, and most deserving of belief', who has family ties with 'Antonius Sucquetus, a Knight of the Golden Order, well known through all of Flanders and an honoured member of the Privy Council of the Court of Brabant'. More importantly, Weyer's brother-in-law had heard the event directly from the mouth of the possessed woman's husband and from other people 'who had been present on many occasions'.[18] We are therefore given standards of objective report: the direct witnessing of the event, the careful scrutiny and comparison of various accounts and different sources, the moral and social reliability of the witnesses. From a literary point of view, Weyer's report reads like a detective story. Or rather (to avoid careless anachronisms), I should say that Weyer is, in fact, writing a tragicomedy. After all, he likes to call episodes of witchcraft and demonic possession silly plays that end in tragic finales.[19] In this particular case, when everything seems to have found a perfectly 'reasonable' explanation and all the circumstances seem to point to the only possible culprit, that is, the maid suspected of witchcraft (her motive being her jealous infatuation with her mistress' husband), Weyer interrupts the telling of the story and takes on the role of the critical examiner by revealing the real culprit and the real motive. Rather than relying on the usual *dea ex machina* (the witch), and embarking instead on a rational inquiry substantiated by correct theological views, Weyer discloses the real engine behind such an intricate plot:

> Lest I seem to be stunned into speechlessness — a silent character (κωφὸν πρόσωπον) in this artfully constructed drama — I should like to add briefly what I think about the matter.[20]

In Weyer's opinion, the whole story can be described as a well-arranged display of illusory effects performed by the devil following the strict rules enforced by the providential supervision of God. The devil inflated the woman's womb with air, assumed the semblance of a midwife and induced the image of a newborn in the imagination of all those who were present at the event (or maybe the child had been stolen somewhere for a short while). The motive behind the diabolical farce is also grander than the petty vendetta of a jealous woman: while the devil's purpose is to spread the seeds of unbelief, God's purpose — if it is legitimate to glance at the unfathomable abysses of His will — is to test man's faith.[21]

Undoubtedly, there is an element of self-fashioning involved in Weyer's disparaging inquiry: it is precisely when the evidence of the devil's power seems to be particularly compelling that Weyer is eager to show his ability in dismantling even the most elaborate plot orchestrated by the subtle cunning of the devil. Weyer is able to demonstrate his expertise every time he is faced with intricate and perplexing cases which everyone fails to solve by relying on natural and rational explanations. As a result, he can strengthen his point that witches are in the end only deluded women. The real danger lurking behind the spread of witchcraft is the increase in human unbelief and the advance of the diabolical conspiracy. In Weyer's opinion, the farcical nature of demonic theatrics should alert human beings to the most tragic implications of such a farce, namely, that the diabolical conspiracy grows in inverse ratio to the decrease of faith.

An important part in Weyer's strategy to unmask the devil's plotting activities is the ability to recognize the real power of appearances. As already observed, it is to Weyer's credit that he never assumes moralistic or patronizing poses to downplay the influence that *phantasmata* exercise on human imagination. The world inhabited by the witches is a world of dreams and images, and yet such dreams and images represent a powerful reality for them:

> it is not to be denied that these poor silly women 'know' these things just as if they were true, because they have been so maddened by the demon through forms impressed upon their powers of imagination. Therefore, when they are subjected to questioning and brought near to the flames, they openly acknowledge as their own crimes which are known to them only by dreams and images.[22]

When one considers that the only world they have is a world of images, it is fair to say that they tell the truth. Not only are their imaginations more than simple imaginations; they are also irrefutable evidence that the devil is the real actor and that he has the power to mislead human minds. 'It thus becomes obvious', says Weyer, 'that virtually all of the actions hitherto attributed to the Lamia — actions to which the crazed woman even confesses, because her powers of imagination have been corrupted by the Deceiver — proceed not from the Lamia but from Satan himself'.[23] One can say that the transformations are real — or that they at least have a certain degree of reality — when they are seen from the point of view of the devil (in that the devil and its influence are real); from the point of view of the witch, though, they are purely imaginary (in that the world of witchcraft is a world of appearances).

For Weyer, to imagine is the same as to be deluded, and the devil is simply taking advantage of this natural tendency among human beings by adding tricks and special effects. By staging the theatre of the imagination — 'a spectacle of empty images' — he has easy access to the world of human credulousness, passions and mental weakness.[24] It should not come as too much of a surprise, says Weyer, that the imagination can be manipulated so easily by the devil if we think that even the imagination of people of a sound mind has the ability to produce and shape all the forms it likes and to store and recall them any time it wishes.[25] If the tendency to be deceived is imbedded in the very faculty of the imagination, then the devil may be said to be the great enabler of human gullibility:

> He tries to 'enrich' the desperate, the credulous, and the infirm with promises of glory, and to destroy them after they have been lured into the hope of happy prospects, or torture them by instilling in them the fear of an unhappy future.[26]

Once the devil has corrupted the opinions and passions of his victims, their bodies, too, become docile prey of his machinations. Bodies are twisted with spasms and convulsions, forced to mimic real movements, but in fact they move like puppets in the hands of the devil.

A result of Weyer's approach to the study of witchcraft is that the range of demonic interventions in nature is strikingly widened. It is as if everyone, in Weyer's world, were more or less possessed, in the sense that his or her eyes and imagination are prone to all sorts of perspectival accidents put into effect by the devil. Accordingly, possessions become events that are quite ordinary and prosaic in a world dominated by the wiles of the devil. They are the result of external, make-believe strategies rather than of an internal, visceral turmoil caused by the devil pervading the bodies of his victims in a direct way. Being possessed means to be part of an intellectual game, in which the limits of believability are constantly challenged by tricks and illusions, rather than to undergo a corporeal transformation induced by the actual physical presence of the devil in one's own body. This is the ever-recurrent plot and the following are the typical characters of all demonic tragicomedies: a victim who is unaware of the impending threat is used by the devil as an opportunity for exploiting his or her inability to come to terms with reality. Human intentions and passions are pretexts and occasions through which the devil creates erroneous beliefs among people of weak faith and inclined to scepticism. Weyer does not deny the existence of real cases of demonic possession or the possibility that demons can take advantage of people suffering from melancholy. However, he is more interested in finding ways to distinguish the active intervention of the devil from the natural process of falling ill. What is more, he thinks that there is nothing demonic in the actions of demons. The little they accomplish — Weyer never tires of repeating — is the result of following the rules of natural reason and exploiting the natural properties of matter. Weyer reports an anecdote involving Philipp Melanchthon, in which, once again, it is difficult to dispel a certain impression of tragicomic incongruity. Melanchthon is reported to have deceived a demon using ordinary instead of holy water, an episode that has a double debunking effect: it reveals the theatrical nature of the devil's performance and the purely symbolical power of the *sacramentals*, that is, the material objects and rites considered indispensable for the proper administration of the sacraments.[27] In the hands of Weyer, demonic possessions, being the same as being possessed by false beliefs, turn into sophisticated processes of deception. Make people believe is all the devil can really do — which is not an easy task, if we think how hard it is for human beings to pass from the state of imagining things to that of believing them.[28]

Weyer's Theory of the Imagination

Because of the negative connotations which Weyer attributed to the imagination, *De praestigiis daemonum* can be seen as a thorough account — a phenomenology as it were — of the human tendency to be deluded rather than a treatise on the actual powers of the imagination. Such a tendency depends on a condition of vulnerability affecting human beings in three particular areas of experience: a delicate mental health (always exposed to the bodily ravages of intense fear and melancholy), a liability to succumb to the lure of egotistical passions (such as anger, vanity, envy and distrust) and a disposition to believe and to be carried away by distorted, fictional accounts of reality. In other words, in Weyer's account, the imagination has a special relationship with melancholy, vanity and fiction. As a result, all metamorphic changes instigated by the imagination affect the virtual reality of human passions and dreams. They are real to the extent that they are *imagined* metamorphoses.

Physiology of the imagination

Weyer's medical expertise comes to the fore every time he needs to explain the way in which the imagination affects man's sense perceptions, emotions and understanding and the way in which demons interfere in the processes of sensation, emotional response and mental elaboration of sense data. By shaping atmospheric air, stirring bodily humours or scattering vapours of black bile into the vessels of their victims, demons can imbue the optic spirit with all the images they like.[29] They can alter the functioning of visual nerves and make fake images correspond to acoustic hallucinations.[30] They have the power to induce all sorts of sensations in the bodies of their victims,[31] or, by contrast, they can impair their senses to the point that they become unable to feel anything.[32]

In all these cases, the pain suffered by the devil's victim is both real and imaginary: real, in that the devil recreates the experience of pain and suffering by manipulating actual physiological factors such as humoural motions and flatulencies; imaginary, in that the connection between the injuring object and the subjective feeling in the patient is arbitrary and established by demonic conventions.[33] Weyer relies on previous medical literature to provide explanations in line with the characteristic tenets of medical environmentalism. Among others, he quotes from Giambattista Della Porta:

> So great is the power of their imagination and the character of their impressions that the part of the brain called 'memorative' is virtually filled with this sort of images; since they are quite ready to believe things because of the inclination of their nature, they take on these impressions in such a way that their spirits are changed and they think of nothing else night and day, and they are assisted in this by the fact that they eat nothing but beets, radishes, chestnuts and legumes.[34]

On this matter, he also reports Girolamo Cardano's opinion: this behaviour 'is caused by the black bile which comes partly from food and drink, from the air, from grief, from the fear of poverty, partly from the constitution of the sky and climate, and partly from associations with other delirious persons'.[35] It may sound trivial, but it is correct to say that we imagine according to what we eat. The imagination affects nutrition and digestion, and conversely nutrition and digestion affect the representative abilities of our mind. As is proved by dreams, sensory impressions can linger in the organs of sense for a long time and still affect human thinking.[36] By intensifying the very physiological processes that underlie the normal activity of dreaming, the devil clogs men's sense organs with empty images even when they are awake.[37]

Of all the temperaments, the melancholic one is undoubtedly the most prone to demonic illusions.[38] Weyer uses the condition that is characteristic of the imagination poisoned by melancholic effluvia as an explanatory model to understand the rationale behind the actions and statements of witches.[39] The devil uses the atrabilious humour as his favourite prop every time he stages his attacks on the imagination of his victims:

> the devil loves to insinuate himself into the melancholic humour, as being a material well suited for his mocking deceptions; St. Jerome has therefore most appropriately termed melancholia 'the devil's bath'.[40]

Finally, there is the way in which the imagination affects the physiological condition of one's body, that is, through feelings of trust and distrust. As a physician, Weyer is well aware that 'confident belief' restores and maintains one's health (*plurimum valet confidentia*), but he is also keen to distinguish the vital confidence that is inextricably intertwined with the affects of hope and anxiety concerning one's own health from the 'living faith produced from a true awareness of God and the inspiration of the Holy Spirit'.[41] Religious belief has to be the expression of sincere faith, which 'takes root in our hearts' and does not get lost in mechanical practices and formal rituals:

It is clear from this what sort of faith I speak of here: a faith that one should embrace, a faith upon which he should firmly take a stand. I do not propose a mere recitation of a prescribed formula of faith (which the devil too might readily utter), nor again the faith loudly vaunted by those whose hearts are far from Christ — a hidden, sluggish, dead, and barren faith. I urge the faith that renews the whole man, manifesting itself with lively virtue among the members of Christ — a fruitful faith which by God's power brings safety to its possessor — the hallowed anchor, stem, and stern of our salvation — a rock set immovably against all Satan's storms and onsets.[42]

Passions and imagination

Due to the special relationship, which connects the force of the imagination to passions and appetites, the devil takes great advantage of superstitions, fears and feelings of anger and desperation. Emotional instability is often behind human proneness to demonic illusions. Weyer's list of individuals who are more likely to become victims of diabolical manipulations includes 'the people without faith in God, the impious, the illicitly curious, the people wrongly trained in the Christian religion, the envious, those who cannot restrain their hatred, the malicious, old women not in possession of their faculties, and similarly foolish women of noted malice or slippery and wavering faith'.[43] It is no wonder that Weyer puts women (together with children and madmen) in the category of people leading a life based on delusions.[44]

By bodily and emotional constitution, witches are women who are less in control of their affects and more exposed to the lures of the imagination. Weyer describes them as worn-out old women 'given to imagining things'.[45] 'Persons who stray from common sense', explains Weyer, 'are sometimes popularly said to be "imagining things" (*phantastici*), and their distortion of understanding or reasoning or thought is termed their "imagination" (*phantasia*)'.[46] The difference between witches and 'ordinary' people is that witches have a more corrupted imagination.[47] A witch is a gullible or mentally ill woman whose imagination has been perverted by the temptations of the devil, and witchcraft is 'a most severe illness'.[48] The much-vaunted pact that the witch allegedly established with the devil is simply the result of 'the deceptive appearance of a phantasm, or a fancy of the mind or the phantastical body of a blinding spirit'.[49] Witches and sorcerers do not acquire a specific expertise through knowledge, study and work. The contrast between the boundless scope of their ambition and the narrow compass of their mind leads them to resort to quick fixes: 'They revere and cherish one teacher only, their imagination, which is corrupted by the various imaginings introduced by an unclean spirit'.[50] Unlike many contemporary authors, Weyer is convinced that the faculty of the imagination is barren of knowledge and works. It is a shortcut leading nowhere apart from self-delusion and sin.

A particularly dangerous emotion in combination with the imagination is anger. Weyer believed that Europe was in the grip of an anger epidemic and that some sort of anger management was urgently needed. Unsurprisingly, he was of the opinion that one of the causes of anger was to be looked for in the malfunctioning of the sense organs. Nature has provided human beings with the use of the senses, so that they may take care of their physical wellbeing (*corporis commoditas*) and strive for the improvement of their souls (*animae perfectio*). Through the senses and the representations of the imagination (*phantasmata*), and through mental apprehension (*antilepsis*), the intellect judges the perceptions of reality as good or bad. We get angry, says Weyer 'when something that we should have avoided happens to us and when we are deprived of what we were entitled to have, for then is when the belief that we are wronged by other people (*injuriae ab aliis illatae opinio*) insinuates itself'. The fact that we have a perception of reality that is inevitably filtered through the representations of various cognitive faculties increases the chances that we get angry with other people and frustrated at how things happen to us: 'when we cannot rely on the services of the sense organs, we can be deceived more quickly'.[51] Proneness to anger is a sign of our tendency to be deceived by the imagination's *phantasmata*, a trait that human beings share with other animals.[52] When we yield to anger it means that we surrender to the imagination: 'We proceed with the imagination (*pergamus ad phantasiam*). And the imagination finds no safety anywhere, nor does it allow any to itself, and it is convinced that everything is suspicious and hostile'.[53]

Metamorphoses of narrative imagination

Weyer attributes the spiralling self-referential and self-fuelling tendency of the imagination to the power that fiction and mimesis exercise on human minds. At the end of one of the numerous stories reported in his work, Weyer concludes with a bit of Platonic acrimony:

> for me these stories will stand as fables, upon which many persons in that benighted age wasted their good time, handing products of the imagination down to posterity in their writings as though they were real.[54]

Elsewhere, he uses the colourful expression of 'archives of foolish and deluded men' to refer to the supposed wisdom of folklore.[55]

However, it must be said that, treacherous as they may be, narrative and fictional mechanisms are crucial aspects of Weyer's inquiry. The range of genres to which he refers or which sometimes he himself applies is indeed impressive: medical reports, biblical stories, ethnographic accounts, folk tales, legal documents, textual amulets, *facetiae*, jokes, magical formulas and moral exempla. Readers of *De praestigiis daemonum* cannot help but notice the extent to which Weyer interweaves his debunking arguments with tales (more or less tall, more or less believable). However, this elaborate pastiche of literary genres has a very specific aim: to show the natural but dangerous collusion between the human urge to recount and listen to stories and the related activities of imagining and suspending one's disbelief. Stories are precisely the stuff on which the faculty of the imagination feeds. We could sum up this important point by saying that for Weyer fiction is the very soul of the imagination, for in satisfying mimetic and empathetic tendencies the imagination provides fictional accounts of reality.

Weyer's notion of metamorphic imagination requires an active role from the readers of his stories. He often limits his analysis of the fictionalized products of the imagination to the mere reporting, without inquiring about the truthfulness or likelihood of unlikely stories. He seems to leave to the reader the task of assessing their plausibility. In this sense, Weyer's writing technique presupposes a faith in the reader's ability to discern the truth from falsehood, the real from the apparent. A supercilious censor might object that letting laymen know magical formulas, ritual procedures and incantatory orations might lead them to their perdition. On the contrary, Weyer is confident that man's good sense and sense of humour will inevitably expose the ridiculous and ineffectual character of all magical procedures. Readers will finally realize that the only persons to be offended by the activities of a sorcerer are the sorcerers themselves and God. Referring to a magical curse used to recover stolen objects, Weyer explains his reasons behind his candid reports:

> I do this so that everyone may see more clearly the hidden impiety of actions of this sort practised by many churchmen.[56]

In this, his approach is strikingly similar to that of his former mentor, Heinrich Cornelius Agrippa von Nettesheim, who wrote an up-to-date summa of occultism (*De occulta philosophia libri tres*, 'Three books on hidden philosophy', 1510) and then a key to question everything that he had written in that summa (*De incertitudine et vanitate scientiarum et artium*, 'On the uncertainty and vanity of the arts and sciences', 1526). As in Agrippa's case, the reader needs to apply a certain level of irony not to misinterpret the meaning of the literary operation. Take, for instance, the chapter dealing with various magical methods for tracking down thieves. In it Weyer expands on long quotations from Cardano, who, while examining a set of procedures on how to evoke and read images from a bottle, had wondered whether all the stories he was hearing were truthful accounts of events that really happened or mere old wives' tales.[57] But this is precisely the point: Weyer is not sure that he can always distinguish between a fact and a tale, and maybe such a distinction is not even relevant for his inquiry.

Weyer is well aware that literature exercises a fictive and mimetic force on human minds. It is in this context that he devotes particular attention to the question of the incantatory power of words and its real efficacy.[58] Examining the transformative energy of words, he rules out the possibility that inanimate nature or irrational beings can be moved or changed by words, for they are unable to understand their meanings. He also criticizes Al-Kindi's influential theory of enchanting words by following the procedure of atomising words down to their syllable and physical sounds and thus demonstrating that there is no active energy of any kind in such sounds.[59] And yet Weyer is fully aware that words are something more than physical sounds, all the more so because the success of his investigation as a literary enterprise rests on precisely the very disposition to suspend disbelief that is at work in the ceremonies he has been reviewing so carefully. Stories of demonic metamorphoses are elaborate constructions of words and appearances, and yet they suggest that human desire and imagination have some power, limited as it may be, to modify the physical reality of bodies. Because of their sentient and appetitive nature, animal bodies respond to all sorts of representations and phantoms. Within the world of the imagination, as we will see in the next section, the scope of imaginary change (*phantastica mutatio*) spans across various level of being. However, it never crosses the boundaries of species and natures originally established by God.

Becoming Animal

As already said, Weyer's rational inquisitiveness and expertise in medical knowledge, combined with a sceptical tendency, allow him to explain or debunk the oddest phenomena occurring in one's body. The belief in prodigious bodily changes represents a characteristic example of the kind of delusions that may affect man's imagination. More often than not, such transformations are nothing but sports (*ludificationes*), whirls of deceitful appearances that demons stage when they want to take advantage of human credulousness. The reason why they resort to illusions is that, despite their inventive mind and nimble spirit, demons cannot produce or alter reality. In the great majority of cases, the alleged transformations caused by their intervention are the result of a cunningly well-ordered sequence of transient appearances.

Consequently, Weyer is of the opinion that unnatural transformations, including animal metamorphoses, are not actual events occurring in nature. Laws of physics, theological dogmas and principles of human legislation rule out the possibility that a created being, however powerful, may ever be able to cross the boundaries that delimit natural species and genders. For all his cunning, swiftness and strength, the devil cannot contravene the basic laws of nature established by God, such as the production of matter out of nothingness or its annihilation into nothingness, the transformation of natural species through unnatural copulation, the alteration of regular causal relationships, the penetrability of material substances, the transmission of energy without the use of material media, the rarefaction or condensation of material substances against their natural limits, the production of special powers out of the mixture of the natural qualities of the elements, the superimposition of miraculous powers on human artefacts made up of elemental matter.[60] As Weyer points out, the fact that the imagination can easily picture such anomalous events does not mean that they can really happen.[61] It is a testament to the imagination's power that in the world of fiction it can break laws of the strictest causality and logical cogency. In the field of knowledge, though, the same ability is seen as a sign of unreliability. To make sense of the bodily alterations purported to be real transformations one should presuppose a sort of 'demonic' physics, in which natural changes can be affected by the direct intervention of the devil, that is, a hybridization of ordinary physics and diabolical manipulations. In fact, the devil himself cannot do more than follow the laws of nature. He simply stretches the limits of believability by building imaginary worlds that feed upon man's anxiety and gullibility.

Weyer does not deny the reality of change in nature and the possibility that natural bodies may undergo all sorts of anomalous changes. Post-mortem dissections and a whole range of anatomical findings demonstrate that the human body is capable of producing its own excrescences, protuberances, pebbles, stones, hair and filaments, all material concretions resulting from the coagulation of phlegm and melancholic humours.[62] He also reminds the medically untrained reader that worms 'of prodigious size' can be generated inside the cavities of the human body.[63] In keeping with Aristotle and Galen, Weyer acknowledges that the natural faculties of the body are endowed with plastic virtues of their own. However, even in this case, their artistic potential is limited by the same laws that apply to all processes of nature.

In the case of the remarkable transformations of human bodies, Weyer explains these physical alterations by resorting to the devil's ability to modify perceptions of reality and desires in the human mind. Episodes of altered metabolism, for instance, are less dramatic and invasive than direct acts of possession, and certainly they are more real than any condition of bewitched delusion, and yet their effects on the vital economy of human bodies are strikingly powerful. By poisoning the mind of their victims and taking advantage of their need for food, demons stealthily transform the physical appearances of human bodies. By instilling illicit desires, they prompt processes of bodily decay through ingested food and unbridled lusts.[64]

However, fully-fledged metamorphoses in which bodies lose their very identity belong to a different category. Here the natural power underlying the action of nutritive and plastic faculties is too feeble to account for such dramatic forms of shape-shifting as men turned into animals. Admittedly, demons can assume the semblance of living beings; they can look like cats, dogs and other animals.[65] But even in these cases, argues Weyer, demons are not undergoing real transformations; they are simply using natural effects in a shrewd way. In doing so, they create a carefully crafted world of appearances, and as demonic doubles are creatures made up of appearances, they do not interact with reality. For instance, even assuming that demons can take on the semblance of a human body by condensing atmospheric air, Weyer rules out that 'an airy body can unite sexually with a body composed of a tempered mixture of the four elements in an act of normal intercourse'.[66] Demons cannot introduce into women's womb the semen they are purported to be collecting through the elaborate practice of succubus and incubus. Weyer concludes the discussion on semen-snatching with an ironic remark: 'if this could happen, how fertile a mother of monsters the human race would have become in so long a period of time, with seed being borrowed from wild animals or beasts and carried by a demon incubus to be instilled in the lap of a woman!'[67]

In the case of alleged metamorphic transformations of human beings, the level of deluded belief is even higher, all the more so because the imaginative processes that affect the mind of people who believe they have been transformed into animals are not spontaneous, but imposed by demons. Demons cause their victim to imagine things that are not happening.[68] Ultimately, Weyer redefines — perhaps it would be more correct to say 'dilutes' — the notion of possession from being a physical turmoil happening inside one's body to a condition of imaginary oppression induced by demons. In Weyer's universe, unnatural transformations of bodies are thus conflations and rearrangements of semblances resulting from the devil's ability to manipulate the appearances of things. Such transformations are instances of 'imaginary change' (*phantastica mutatio*).[69] The devil

> knows how to display various forms, fashion empty idols with wondrous skill,

confound the organs of sight, blind the eyes, substitute false things for true with remarkable dexterity (lest they be detected), cover over things which really exist, so that they are not apparent, and show forth things which in reality do not exist, in such a way that they seem to do so. He knows how to transform itself into a thousand appearances and play the part of Proteus.[70]

As already pointed out, Weyer's inquiry draws on the world of literature, on stories, myths and folktales. Classical writers are widely represented as authoritative repositories of pertinent source material. For example, Weyer compares the exploits of the devil to the mythical feats of Proteus and he quotes from Virgil's *Georgics* to corroborate his point:

> Then do various bestial shapes and countenances mock and deceive. For he [Proteus] will become at once a bristling boar, a tigress fell, a scaly serpent, and a lioness with tawny neck; or he will shoot flames with a piercing sound, transforming himself into all sorts of wondrous things: fire, a fearsome beast, a flowing stream.[71]

Some of the most famous stories of animal metamorphoses of the classical world are retold by Weyer through the mediation of Augustine. Ancient myths of transformation are brought back to life by means of important pages in *De civitate Dei*: Ulysses' companions turned into pigs, Lycaon and the Arcadians changed into wolves and Diomedes' fellow soldiers mutated into birds. Weyer considers these stories as a typical product of superstitious credulity.[72] His scepticism is even stronger in his later *Liber apologeticus*, where he defends his position from a certain Paul Skalić de Lika, author of an *Encyclopediae epistemon* (1559), in which, against Weyer, he had strongly advocated the reality of human metamorphoses. Apparently, Skalić had argued that, 'if souls are like angels in their essence', they are 'able to take on the body of a weasel, or a dove, or a man'. Weyer's answer is unequivocally negative:

> I am amazed that a most acute philosopher and most learned theologian may have come up with and defended such a thesis, unless you have been granted the special privilege to determine what you like. Human souls always long for the bodily structure (*corporaturam*) to which they have been destined by God, and not the body of a weasel. Otherwise, the consequence would be that, first, there is one soul common to men and animals, and that that soul informs two bodies'.[73]

An intriguing aspect of Weyer's discussion concerns the political consequences that may derive from assuming that the soul has the ability to take on any kind of body it likes. 'That the prince uses both his own vehicle and that of a cobbler', Weyer argues, 'does not become a well-ruled state'.[74] In Skalić's bizarre account, the principle of metamorphosis justifies the fact that angels can mutate into weasels, that is, that ontological differences in the hierarchical layering of the universe have no place any longer and that everything can become everything else.

On this matter, Weyer confirms that it is much safer to follow Augustine. More specifically, with respect to the question of *ludificatio daemonum*, Augustine had acknowledged that demons could in fact transform (*commutare*) the appearances of things (*specie tenus*), but he ruled out the possibility that they could create actual beings (*naturae*). What demons are able to do is to induce in the mind of human beings the impression that other human beings are being transformed into animals. Augustine's explanation, adopted by Weyer, hinged upon the intriguing notion of 'phantom' (*phantasticum*). He argued that

> a man's phantom (*phantasticum hominis*) — which also in his thoughts and dreams is changed by the countless variety of objects it receives, and though it is not a body, still with astonishing swiftness receives shapes that are like material bodies (*cum corpus non sit, corporum tamen similes mira celeritate formas capit*) — this phantom, I hold, can in some inexplicable way present itself to the senses of others in bodily form, when their physical senses are dulled or blocked out.[75]

Although, properly speaking, the 'phantom' is not a body, nevertheless, it can assume a bodily shape and can be perceived by the human senses. Bodies (and minds) cannot take on all the forms the devil wishes to impose on them, but the imagination can undergo countless forms and the devil uses this virtually infinite reservoir of deceptive forms for his vicious ends. Furthermore, he can direct the *phantasticum* to other people's imagination as a sort of dreaming activity controlled at a distance. Weyer reports another important passage from the Pseudo-Augustinian *De spiritu et anima*, where it is stated that 'demons cannot create natures'; what they can do is to 'somehow bring it about that things seem to be what they are not'.[76] Here it is worth remembering that for Augustine, even at the level of sense apprehension, perception is always apprehension of images. He held a view of sensation as an active process controlled by the soul's power of attention (*attentio*) and concentration (*intentio*).[77] For Augustine, sense perception is always perception of images, not bodies, and images are not corporeal. This means that the world conveyed by our sense perceptions is already, irredeemably, a world of images.

A particular case of *phantastica mutatio* examined by Weyer is that of werewolves. Weyer argues that these creatures may be either ordinary men who are made to believe they are wolves through demonic impairment of the organs of their imagination, or they are real wolves affected by demons and made to behave as if they were humans possessed by some demonic entity, or, finally, they are the very same demons who have assumed the form of wolves by exploiting the natural properties of the material elements or the principles of human vision.[78] In all three cases, the alleged metamorphic entities are theatrical werewolves, with men, wolves or demons alternatively playing the role of the main actor. Weyer the pious doctor sees lycanthropy as a mental illness induced or strengthened by the devil. He reports the case of a peasant living around Padua, who believed that he was a wolf whose pelt was turned inside out, and who had on occasion attacked and killed people in the fields. When he was captured,

> certain persons stripped themselves of all humanity, and (as truly savage and ravenous wolves) hacked at his arms and legs with a sword and cut them off, to find the truth of the matter. And when they realised that the man was innocent, they handed him over to the surgeons to cure him, but he expired after a few days.[79]

One should ask who the real wolf is in this story, the person who is convinced he is a wolf because of a disorder of the imagination, perhaps reinforced by a diabolical illusion, or the people who believe they see a wolf where in fact they have a fellow human being in front of them. In a way, the metamorphosis of human nature that takes place in both the alleged werewolf and his captors results from distorted perceptions, precipitous judgement and reported stories. Weyer maintains that the supposed transmogrification of the Paduan peasant into a wolf does not affect the core of his humanity, whereas the men chasing the wolf-man are the real wolves of the episode. However, it seems most correct to say that all characters involved in the story are inescapably entangled within a web of delusions. Be that as it may, it cannot be denied that, from a rhetorical point of view, the way Weyer describes the event accentuates the elusive and destabilizing power of appearances. Imagination does not alter reality; it simply distorts our perception of it. This point is even clearer in Weyer's response to another of his critics, this time the French Paracelsian Jacques Gohory (1520–1576), also known as Leo Suavius. Relying on Pietro Pomponazzi and Paracelsus, Gohory had accepted the story of the transformation of the Arcadians into wolves reported by Pliny in his *Natural History* (VIII. 80–82) (*veram transmutationem fuisse Pomponatium dicere, uti et Paracelsum*).[80] Gohory's reference to Pomponazzi and Paracelsus is particularly significant in this context: they were the authors who perhaps more than any other during the Renaissance had emphasized the extent to which the imagination could alter reality in its most physical aspects. For them the imagination was a force of nature affecting both the human mind and the life of the universe — a real Proteus. Weyer rejected this radical assumption and confined the imagination to the domain of appearances, wishful thinking and story-telling. His was an imaginary Proteus of diabolical origin.

Conclusions

When one considers the early-modern debate concerning the nature of meta-morphosis, it is almost impossible to keep the idea of metamorphic change separate from that of the imagination. To be sure, if by imagination we mean simply a faculty of representation — a sense that, as we have seen, Weyer defends throughout his critical inquiry — then the cultural and symbolic reality of metamorphosis and change vanishes together with that of the imagination. Instead, if we consider the broad scope covered by the early-modern notion of imagination (which is not only a faculty of re-presentation, but also of original presentations and material productions), then the imagination becomes a key component in early-modern accounts of metamorphosis. Weyer's position is particularly important here because he reacted decisively against all attempts to credit the imagination with a natural and material productivity. In so doing, he made the difference between the imagination (*phantasmata*) and reality (*res gestae*) irrevocable.[81]

It would not be stretching the point too far to say that Weyer has a distinctive Platonic-Augustinian view of the imagination, seen as a faculty prone to self-deception and capitulation to the lures of unbridled desire. This is the background against which he advocates a characteristically medical understanding of melancholic imagination, which in turn provides a physiological basis to his carefully crafted phenomenology of deceptive appearances. In addition to this philosophical and medical framework, Weyer proves to be clearly aware of the power that literature and tale-telling exercise on human minds through the shaping of symbolic universes and belief systems, for narrative imagination creates real expectations and strong beliefs out of imaginary worlds. He looks at the imagination as an inexhaustible repository of fictive entities, i.e., of dreams, visions and hallucinations, of myths, legends and tales, opinions, rumours, gossip, delusions and self-delusions. As already pointed out, he accuses witches, sorcerers, and unlearned people in general of taking the imagination as their only 'teacher' and source of knowledge. The problem is that, far from teaching anything real or ethically valuable to them, the imagination perpetuates their state of ignorance by making them even more eager to escape reality. For all these reasons, Weyer's largely negative attitude towards the imagination is rather ambivalent, being both a severe criticism of the superstitious fabrications produced by the imagination and an unstinting acknowledgement of its inexhaustible creativity.

On the one hand, *De praestigiis daemonum* can be seen as an extraordinary collection of beliefs, legends and customs. On the other — and this is particularly clear when Weyer pauses to give meticulous descriptions of magical rituals — such a collection is not meant to provide knowledge as such. Rather, it has a preventive function, ensuring that the 'pious reader' will be dissuaded from indulging in superstitions and vain ceremonies. This applies in particular to stories of metamorphosis. Once the imagination has been deprived of the ontological, cosmological and physiological rationales that account for its power to alter reality, what remains is the fictional aspect of mimesis, understood in a narrowly edifying and didactic sense. In Weyer's work, animal metamorphoses become fictionalized, be they the theriomorphic myths of antiquity or the unnatural changes involving the intervention of the devil. While Weyer tolerates forms of suspension of disbelief when they are used to convey a cautionary tale to the reader, he undermines all claims of reality and truth made by the imagination, and, in doing so, he demystifies and rationalizes a whole universe of meaningful symbols and rites, bodily changes and narrative strategies. His approach is both radically destructive and patronizingly pious.

Weyer makes up for his demise of the world of the imagination by presenting the battle of humankind against the devil in heroic and tragic terms. It is a battle that gives structure and purpose to a world otherwise devoid of hope and in the clutches of fear. At the end of his critique of the imagination, the everyday world of common people is left with the menacing presence of the devil, a situation that is a characteristically Lutheran predicament. Weyer's disenchanting view of the world lays bare the reality of the devil in all its obscene glory, a reality that is tolerated by a God whose motives for doing so remain frustratingly opaque to men. As a result, the imagination is emptied of its meanings and we are left with the husk of what was once a rich and complex life. No wonder, then, that Weyer's critique of the imagination develops along the lines of ironic (sometimes even tragicomic) forms of anthropology and ethnography. Once the contriving and smoothing effect of the imagination is removed, the contrast between beliefs and knowledge becomes too sharp, and irony is the only means that is left to mediate between the two. And when, later in the eighteenth century, the devil, too, is removed from the picture, the crisis of human beliefs concerning the relationship of natural and supernatural will reach a new level of intensity. Weyer's contrast between reckless credulity (*temeraria credulitas*) and living faith (*viva fides*) disappears to be replaced by the irreconcilable opposition between superstition and reason.

Notes to Chapter 8

1. On the subject of early-modern imagination see Harvey (1975); Zambelli (1991); Yates (1992); Fattori and Bianchi (1998); Mack (2004), pp. 59–76; Roling (2006); Clark (2007); Giglioni (2012).
2. See Maxwell-Stuart (2007).
3. On Proteus, the mythical sea-demon who could change his outward appearance at will, interpreted by a number of early-modern philosophers (from Giordano Bruno to Francis Bacon) as a symbol of material changeability, see Zatta (1997); Pesic (1999); Pesic (2008); Pesic (2010).
4. On Weyer see Anglo (1976); Clark (1997); Midelfort (1999), pp. 168–81, 196–217; Valente (2003); Cameron (2010); Hoorens (2011).
5. Johann Weyer, *De praestigiis daemonum, et incantationibus ac veneficiis libri sex. Ab auctore sexies aucti et recogniti, juxta exemplar Basiliense 1583* (II, x), in *Opera omnia* (Amsterdam: Peter van den Berge, 1660, henceforth abbreviated as *OO*), pp. 129–30: 'solent imagines rerum earum nominibus, quarum imagines sunt, appellari. Quis enim, qui hominem pictum dubitet vocare hominem?'; English translation by John Shea, in *Witches, Devils, and Doctors in the Renaissance: Johann Weyer, De praestigiis daemonum*, ed. by George Mora and Benjamin Kohl (Binghamton, NY: Center for Medieval and Early Renaissance Studies, 1991, henceforth abbreviated as *WDD*), p. 132.
6. Weyer, *De praestigiis daemonum* (I, xxv), *OO*, p. 87 ('non [potest] introspicere ac integre pernoscere sensus et cogitata hominum'), *WDD*, p. 87; (I, xxvi), *OO*, p. 88, *WDD*, p. 89; (IV, xvii), *OO*, p. 321 ('Nec hominum cogitationes novisse daemonem, tradit quoque Augustinus'), *WDD*, pp. 326–27. See Augustine, *De ecclesiasticis dogmatibus*, in *Patrologia Latina*, LXXII, col. 1221 ('Internas animae cogitationes diabolum non videre, certi sumus: sed motibus eas corporis ab illo et affectionum indiciis colligi, experimento didicimus'), cit. in *WDD*, p. 639.
7. Weyer to Johann Brenz, 10 October 1565, in *Liber apologeticus*, *OO*, p. 584: 'ad nostrarum lamiarum punitionis modum vel statuendum vel confirmandum, nullo modo debet torqueri lex Imperatoria, cujus ne ullum quidem verbum illas concernit, quarum phantasiam aut vim imaginativam, ut se fecisse opinentur quae revera non fecere, aut quae etiam saepenumero in rerum natura non sunt, tantopere laesit veteratorius ille vertiginis spiritus'.
8. Weyer to Johann Brenz, 10 October 1565, in *Liber apologeticus*, *OO*, p. 585. And if one thinks that will and assent, too, should be punished, then we should distinguish between sound and ill will: 'Si insuper voluntatem et consensum puniri debere, quis contentiosius urgeat, hunc certe distinguere ad minimum oportet inter voluntatem sanae mentis, qui facinus in politiam publicam animo decreverit, idque exequi potuerit, atque in actum perducere coeperit tentaritque: et inter eum qui non itidem mentis confirmatae, imaginetur se velle facere, imo fecisse, quae nec fecit, nec in rerum natura etiam plerunque consistere queunt: alioqui tale voluntatis et consensus flagitium quoque impingi possit melancholicis, fatuis et pueris, qui saepenumero falsa persuasione inducuntur, ut se haec vel illa scelera commisisse credant fateanturque' (ibid.).
9. Weyer, *De praestigiis daemonum* (II, viii), *OO*, p. 121: 'Quae fascinati imaginamur, praeter imaginamenta, nullam habent actionis et essentiae veritatem'; *WDD*, p. 123. Weyer uses Marsilio Ficino's paraphrasis of Iamblichus' *De mysteriis Aegyptiorum*. See Ficino, *Opera omnia*, 2 vols (Basel: Heinrich Petri, 1576; repr. Turin: Bottega d'Erasmo, 1962), II, 1890. See also *De praestigiis daemonum* (III, xxviii), *OO*, p. 251; *WDD*, p. 254. On Iamblichus's view of the imagination as the principle that accommodates external to internal reality, the senses to the intellect, see ibid. (III, viii), *OO*, p. 183: 'De phantasia sic scribit Jamblichus: Phantasia omnibus animae viribus est adnata, omnesque figurat atque effingit similitudines specierum, et apparitiones, visaque seu impressiones virium aliarum transmittit in alias: quae quidem a sensu micant, in opinionem excitat: quae vero ab intellectu, secundo loco offert opinioni, sed in seipsa ab omnibus imagines suscipit. Haec utique omnes actiones animae fingit et exprimit, atque externas accommodat

intimis'; *WDD*, p. 186. In the same page, Weyer also refers to Marsilio Ficino's commentary on Priscianus Lydus' *Metaphrasis in Theophrastum*: 'Hic Marsilius Ficinus Platonicus, in explicatione Prisciani Philosophi Lydi, interpretantis librum Theophrasti de phantasia et intellectu, cap. 2. ait: Imaginatio actiones rationis effingit sub rerum sensibilium conditione, ac potest ultra sensuum actus latius phantasmata promere. Superat sensum: quia enim nullo movente, imagines edit, imaginatio est tanquam Proteus vel chamaeleon'. *WDD*, pp. 186–87.

10. Weyer, *De praestigiis daemonum* (IV, xvi), *OO*, p. 315: 'omnes siquidem maleficium esse arbitrari penitus maluissent'; *WDD*, p. 320.

11. Ibid. (IV, vii), *OO*, p 295; *WDD*, pp. 299–300; (V, xvii), p. 401; *WDD*, p. 414. Augustine had often characterized demonic mockery as a form of divine punishment for men's evil will. See, for instance, *De doctrina Christiana*, II. 23. 35; *De civitate Dei*, XI. 17.

12. Weyer, *De praestigiis daemonum* (IV, ix), *OO*, p. 298 ('quo id, in cujus finem hanc instituerat tragoediam, nempe incredulitatem, stabiliret. Ubi scilicet in rebus adversis, Deo relicto, eiusque medijs ex gratia donatis ab eo, qui languoribus nostris vere mederi potest'), *WDD*, p. 303. See also (IV, xxx), *OO*, pp. 349–50; *WDD*, p. 357; (V, i), *OO*, p. 352, *WDD*, p. 362.

13. Ibid. (V, xvii), *OO*, p. 402, *WDD*, p. 414.

14. Weyer to Johann Brenz, 10 October 1565, in *Liber apologeticus*, *OO*, p. 582: 'sed Deum omnipotentem solum esse grandinis et authorem et creatorem, eoque nomine ab illo effici et produci, ut ejusdem potentia impios puniat, iique ad peccatorum agnitionem compellantur resipiscantque'.

15. On the theological notions of *potentia Dei ordinata* and *absoluta*, with special attention to the early-modern context, see Funkenstein (1986); Scribano (1988).

16. Weyer, *De praestigiis daemonum* (V, iii), *OO*, p. 360, *WDD*, p. 370.

17. Ibid. (I, xvi), *OO*, p. 47 ('En diabolum tibicinem sanguinarium'), *WDD*, p. 51.

18. Ibid. (III, xxxii), *OO*, p. 258, *WDD*, p. 261.

19. Ibid. (V, xi), *OO*, p. 385 ('nugatorii actus scena'), *WDD*, p. 396; (V, xv), *OO*, p. 397 ('secundus fabulae actus'), *WDD*, p. 409.

20. Ibid. (III, xxxii), *OO*, p. 258 ('ne in hoc actu tam artificiose instructo velut attonitus, κωφὸν πρόσωπον agere videar, succincte quid hic sentiam, adjicere volui'), *WDD*, p. 262.

21. Ibid. (III, xxxii), *OO*, p. 258, *WDD*, p. 262. See ibid. (III, xxxiii), p. 261 ('Id [i.e., poisoning through action at a distance] porro nihil eatenus posse, jam demonstravi. Si tamen nocumentum hinc subsequi videatur, certum est ab ipso Satana, ex Dei assensu, ob hominis laedendi incredulitatem, vel etiam, ut hic probetur cum Jobo, idipsum excitari'), *WDD*, p. 264.

22. Ibid. (III, iv), *OO*, p. 173 ('negandum non est, miseras has mulierculas ita formis virtuti phantasticae impressis, a daemonio dementatas, non aliter ac si haec ita vere fierent, scire: uti fere omnes illarum praeter naturam actiones, imaginariae saltem videntur: et propterea quaestionibus adactae, flammisque propinquae, sua aperte confitentur flagitia, per somnum vel simulachrum illis solummodo cognita'), *WDD*, p. 176.

23. Ibid. (III, iii), *OO*, p. 169 ('Sic plerasque omnes actiones Lamiae hactenus attributas, quas suas esse, malesana quoque fatetur, ex corrupta a praestigiatore virtute imaginativa, non Lamiae, sed ipsius Satanae existere, palam fit'), *WDD*, p. 173.

24. Ibid. (I, xxv), *OO*, p. 87 ('Sed visu tandem quaedam inania suis cultoribus afferunt, varia prorsus et instabilia, quae tamen impii divina esse spectacula putant'), *WDD*, p. 88. On demons' love for theatrical deceptions in Augustine's demonology, see Evans (1990), p. 105.

25. Ibid. (III, viii), *OO*, p. 186 ('Nec mirum videri debet, daemonem potentia sua naturali id valere, cum etiam homo insomnis et sanae mentis pro suo arbitrio, quas velit in suis organis proponere producereque formas, atque in iis imaginationes conquiescere, possit facile: quemadmodum ii omnes qui rerum expetitarum et absentium desiderio languent, experiuntur'), *WDD*, p. 189.

26. Ibid. (I, xii), *OO*, p. 31 ('desperantes, credulos, maleque sanos pollicitationibus et gloria ditare, in spem felicium successuum illectos perimere, aut tristium eventuum metu injecto cruciare'), *WDD*, p. 34.

27. Ibid. (IV, xvii), *OO*, p. 321, *WDD*, p. 327. On the evolution of the meaning of *sacramentalia* after the Reformation, see Scribner (1993).

28. The *locus classicus* of the discussion concerning the relationship between imagination and belief is Aristotle's *De anima*, III. 3. On a historical contextualization of this question, see Giglioni (2010).

29. Weyer, *De praestigiis daemonum* (II, viii), *OO*, p. 122, *WDD*, p. 124; (III, vii), *OO*, p. 183, *WDD*, p. 186; (III, viii), *OO*, p. 185, *WDD*, p. 188; (III, x), *OO*, p. 190, *WDD*, p. 193; (IV, i), *OO*, p. 278, *WDD*, p. 283.

30. Ibid. (III, iii), *OO*, p. 169, *WDD*, p. 173.

31. Ibid. (IV, xiv), *OO*, pp. 309–13, *WDD*, pp. 314–18.

32. Ibid. (V, xii), *OO*, pp. 387, 389, *WDD*, pp. 398, 401.

33. Ibid. (IV, ix), *OO*, p. 298, *WDD*, p. 303.

34. Giambattista Della Porta, *Magiae naturalis libri viginti* (Frankfurt: Wechel, 1591): 'tanta est imaginationis vis, impressionum habitus, ut fere cerebri pars ea quae memorativa dicitur, huiusmodi sit plena: cumque valde sint ipsae ad credendum naturae pronitate faciles, sic impressiones capessunt, ut spiritus immutentur, nil noctu diuque aliud cogitantes: et ad hoc adiuvantur, cum non vescantur nisi betis, radicibus, castaneis et leguminibus' (Shea's translation). See Weyer, *De praestigiis daemonum* (III, xvii) *OO*, pp. 222–23, *WDD*, p. 226.

35. Girolamo Cardano, *De varietate rerum*, in *Opera omnia*, ed. by C. Spon, 10 vols (Lyon: Jean Antoine Huguetan and Marc Antoine Ravaud, 1663; repr.: Stuttgart and Bad Cannstatt, Frommann, 1966), III, 292a: 'causam horum in atram bilem (ut dixi) reiicere oportet, quae partim cibis ac potibus et aere et moerore timoreque paupertatis, partim a coeli constitutionibus, partim ex consuetudine aliorum delirantium contingit'. Weyer, *De praestigiis daemonum* (III, xiv), *OO*, p. 203, *WDD*, p. 206. On Cardano and witchcraft, see Ernst (2006).

36. Weyer, *De praestigiis daemonum* (II, v), *OO*, p. 110, *WDD*, p. 112.

37. Ibid. (III, v), *OO*, p. 177, *WDD*, p. 181.

38. Ibid. (III, v), *OO*, p. 177, *WDD*, p. 180; (IV, xiv), *OO*, p. 309 ('quanto affectu in hunc succum *analogikos* sibi suisque actionibus peculiarem se immergere solet, ejusque adminiculo admirabilia inducere phantasmata et imaginationes raras'), *WDD*, p. 315.

39. Ibid. (III, vii), *OO*, p. 180, *WDD*, p. 183.

40. Ibid. (IV, xxv), *OO*, p. 339 ('Humori etenim melancholico, uti materiae suis ludibriis consentaneae, diabolus se, ut antea memini, insinuat libentissime: propterea et perquam apposite, melancholiam esse diaboli balneum, dixit D. Hieronymus'), *WDD*, p. 346. On melancholy as the devil's bath, see Schmidt (2007), pp. 64–77.

41. Weyer, *De praestigiis daemonum* (V, viii), *OO*, p. 378, *WDD*, p. 389; (V, xiii), *OO*, p. 393 ('viva fide, ex vera Dei agnitione et Spiritus sancti inspiratione prognata'), *WDD*, pp. 405–06. For some examples of what *temeraria credulitas* (rather than *viva fides*) can accomplish, see also ibid. (V, xviii), *OO*, pp. 403–06, *WDD*, pp. 416–18.

42. Ibid. (V, i), *OO*, p. 354 ('Unde satis liquet, de qua hic fide loquar: quam amplecti, cuique firmiter insistere oporteat. Non simplicem formulae fidei praescriptae enarrationem propono, quam et facile pronunciaret diabolus: non etiam ore iactatam ab iis, quorum cor a Christo procul est, quae consopita, mortua, sterilisque delitescit, nusquam se prodens, velut infoecunda arbor exscindenda, ignique mandanda: sed hanc urgeo, quae totum innovat hominem, virtute viva se in Christi membris exerens, fructificans, efficax potentia Dei ad salutem habenti, sacra salvationis nostrae ancora, prora et puppis, petra contra quamcunque Satanae tempestatem impetumque immobilis'), *WDD*, p. 364.

43. Weyer, *De praestigiis daemonum* (III, v), *OO*, p. 177: 'Sunt item Deo diffidentes, impii, illicite curiosi, perverse in religione Christiana instituti, invidi, impotentis odii, maliciosi, vetulae vix mentis compotes, similesque lubricae fidei (qui enim facile credit, facile et recedit) vel insignis maliciae mulierculae'), *WDD*, p. 181.

44. Ibid. (III, viii), *OO*, p. 184 ('Ejusmodi autem simulachra frequentius obvia sunt pueris, mulieribus, vaecordibus, mollibus, atque aegrotis, qui propter imbecillitatem animi et corporis, assidua formidine vanisque insomniis quatiuntur'), *WDD*, p. 187. See also Weyer to Johann Brenz, 10 October 1565, in *Liber apologeticus*, *OO*, p. 585.

45. Witches are just deluded old women, 'cum sint indoctae, ineptae et stupidae, tum ob sexum, tum ob aetatem' (Weyer to Johann Brenz, 10 October 1565, in *Liber apologeticus*, *OO*, p. 583).

46. Weyer, *De praestigiis daemonum* (III, xv), *OO*, p. 209 ('Phantasticos enim quandoque a communi sensu devios appellat vulgus: et phantasiam, intellectus vel rationis, vel cogitationis depravationem'), *WDD*, p. 213.

47. Ibid. (II, i), *OO*, p. 94 ('Nostris adhaec Germanis uno eodemque nomine Zauberer nuncupatur

magus, ex professo illusor, et frequenter eruditus, Saga vel Lamia ob mentis imbecillitatem et corruptam phantasiam a diabolo delusa, et venenum studio usurpans veneficus'), *WDD*, p. 97; (III, xvi), *OO*, p. 213, *WDD*, p. 217; (IV, i), *OO*, pp. 280–81, *WDD*, p. 285.

48. Weyer to Johann Brenz, 10 October 1565, in *Liber apologeticus*, *OO*, p. 585: 'gravissimus animi morbus'.

49. Weyer, *De praestigiis daemonum* (III, iii), *OO*, p. 169 ('Foedus autem esse praestigiosum, phantasmate aut imaginatione, vel phantastico praestringentis spiritus corpore fallaciter apparente: vel nervis opticis seu visoriis indita subdole, quam Satan vult, specie, commotis huc humoribus et spiritibus idoneis: vel sibilo, susurro aut murmure in organis auditus, vitiatae formis imagini respondente, spiritus maligni arte excito conflatum stabilitumque, ac inde nullius esse ponderis, haud obscure cognoscitur'), *WDD*, p. 173.

50. Ibid. (III, xxxiii), *OO*, p. 260 ('corruptam variis imaginibus ab immundo spiritu ingestis, phantasiam solummodo doctorem venerantur et colunt: cui utplurimum propensius confisae, misere decipiuntur, ac in perniciem ruunt'), *WDD*, p. 263.

51. J. Weyer, *De ira morbo, eiusdem curatione philosophica, medica et theologica liber*, in *OO*, p. 784: 'Tertiam ponimus caussam irae internam, vitium instrumentorum quae sensui inserviunt. Nam quum natura et ad animae perfectionem et corporis commoditatem, sensus in nobis crearit, quibus obiecta phantasmata aut bona aut mala per *antilepsin* ad intellectum deducuntur: indignamur, quando nobis aliquid accidit quod erat fugiendum, et eo privamur quod fuerat percipiendum: quoniam tunc obrepit injuriae ab aliis illatae opinio, propterea quod destituti sensoriorum ministerio, citius falli queamus'.

52. Ibid., pp. 792–93: 'Huic etiam partitioni vicina sunt illa signa, quae ab interioribus sensibus desumuntur. Vigilia siquidem homines iratos torquet maxime, ut tum sedeant in lecto, tum surgant, tum ambulent, situ in momenta mutato propter inquietudinem: ac si aliquando succedat somnus, ille est mirifice interruptus occursu terribilium insomniorum, quae repraesentant aut hominem praesentem, aut nos jugulari a latronibus, aut daemonibus circumdari, aut enormibus periculis obiici, aut in duelli lucta ancipitem exspectare eventum. Et illud sane nobis cum brutis propter sensus communis participationem est commune. Canes siquidem ex repraesentatione inanium simulachrorum in somno, in latratus erumpunt'.

53. Ibid.: 'Pergamus ad phantasiam. Ea nullibi securitatem invenit, nullam sibi promittere audet, omnia sibi suspecta et invia opinatur'.

54. Weyer, *De praestigiis daemonum* (III, xxx), *OO*, p. 254 ('At mihi fabulae erunt, quibus bonas horas male nimis seculo illo caeco impenderunt plerique, chartulisque phantasmata pro rebus gestis ad posteritatem transtulere'), *WDD*, p. 257.

55. Weyer, *De praestigiis daemonum* (v, x), *OO*, p. 382 ('ex ineptorum delusorumque hominum archivis'), *WDD*, p. 393.

56. Ibid. (v, vi), *OO*, p. 370 ('Anathema hoc S. Adalberti magicum potius ob divini nominis et sacrae Scripturae abusum, quam Christianum, hic ea adijcio ratione, ut occulta ejusmodi actionum plerisque religiosis hominibus usitatarum impietas oculis omnium magis eluceat'), *WDD*, p. 381.

57. Ibid. (v, v), *OO*, p. 369, *WDD*, p. 378. See Cardano, *De varietate rerum*, in *Opera omnia*, III, p. 326.

58. Ibid. (v, viii), *OO*, pp. 376–79, *WDD*, pp. 387–91.

59. Ibid. (v, viii), *OO*, p. 379 ('O delirium incomparabile! Quaenam vis haec quaeso, unde derivata, ubi recepta? Si etenim pendet ab harmonia coelesti tota verborum virtus, ut Alchindus contendit: cur non ipsa per sese operari id potest, cum sit causa superior? Dicet fortasse, coelum media et proxima causa, hoc est verbis agere. At hoc doceat, in sonone, aut in voce, an in verbis exterioribus operandi vis recipiatur. Prior enim natura sonus quam vox, et vox quam verba: haec enim ex illa, illa vero ex alio conficiuntur, cum verba vocem et sonum includant, et in definitione vocis contineatur sonus. Sine voce sonus esse potest, quia natura prior: pari ratione sine verbis vox: sine voce autem et sono verba non sunt. Si igitur vis in sono recipitur, et qua sonus movet elementa, omni sono etiam inanimatorum corporum poterit ea virtus communicari: quare nec voce, nec verbis opus erit. Si autem in voce, cum ea plerisque etiam animantibus praeter quam homini, competat, idipsum poterit a brutis etiam fieri. Si vero in humanis verbis tantum recipi dixeris, rogo, unde accipiatur vis, in primane syllaba, aut medijs, an ultima? Si in syllaba, iam

non in verbis, ea vero mox perit. Eadem in aliis erit ratio. Quare colligitur, nullo modo verbis inesse hanc posse virtutem coelitus operantem'), *WDD*, pp. 390–91.

60. Ibid. (v, ix), *OO*, p. 381, *WDD*, p. 393; (v, xiii), *OO*, pp. 391–93, *WDD*, pp. 403–05.

61. Ibid. (iv, xv), *OO*, p. 314 ('Talia quidem phantasia facile imaginatur; at in actum non item deducuntur'), *WDD*, p. 319.

62. Ibid. (iv, xvi), *OO*, pp. 315–16, *WDD*, p. 321.

63. Ibid. (iv, xvi), *OO*, p. 319, *WDD*, p. 325.

64. Ibid. (i, xx), *OO*, pp. 59–60, *WDD*, pp. 62–63.

65. Ibid. (iii, x), *OO*, p. 301, *WDD*, pp. 306–07; (iv, xiii), *OO*, p. 308, *WDD*, p. 313.

66. Ibid. (iii, xxvii), *OO*, p. 248 ('Et si demus, spiritus aliquos elemento aëreo corporatos esse: minime tamen hinc sequetur, ab aëreo corpore, cum eo, quod contemperata quatuor elementorum permixtione consistit, naturalem, vel similem ei, qui inter paria, terrena magis contemperatione imbuta contingit corpora, exerceri congressum'), *WDD*, p. 251. See Augustine, *De civitate Dei*, xv. 23; *Quaestiones super Genesim*, i, q. 3: 'non hic temere aliquid audeo definire, utrum aliqui spiritus, elemento aëreo corporati (nam hoc elementum etiam cum agitatur flabello, sensu corporis tactuque sentitur) possint etiam pati hanc libidinem, ut quo modo possunt, sentientibus foeminis misceantur'.

67. Weyer, *De praestigiis daemonum* (iii, xxvi), *OO*, p. 247 ('Si enim hoc fieri posset, quam foecunda monstrorum mater tam longo tempore extitisset humanum genus, semine ex feris vel bestiis permutato, translatoque ab incubo daemone, et mulieris sinui infuso? En horribilem consequentiam'), *WDD*, p. 250.

68. Ibid. (iii, xi), *OO*, p. 191 ('In hujusmodi vero cogitationes se ingerens daemon, earum seriem texit, hancque variat mira arte et scite, repetitis praeteritis, annexis praesentibus, et aspersis etiam quibusdam admonitionibus de futuris, ne in suspicionem anilium fabularum, aut temere cogitatarum ineptiarum veniant: inducta etiam persuasione, ut coram spectasse, quae diabolus offudit, imaginentur, ita dementat eos, quos ad talia usurpat ministeria, ut sui prorsus non sint compotes'), *WDD*, p. 194.

69. Ibid. (iii, x), *OO*, p. 189: 'De phantasticae porro mutationis hominum in bestias opinione'. *WDD*, p. 192.

70. Ibid. (i, xii), *OO*, p. 31 ('Novit adhaec varias ostentare formas, inania idola arte mira conformare, visus organum turbare, oculos perstringere, falsa pro veris singulari dexteritate ne agnoscantur, proponere: quae vere sunt, ut non appareant, velare: et quae revera non existunt, ut esse appareant exhibere: se in mille species transformare, Proteumque agere'), *WDD*, p. 34.

71. Virgil, *Georgics*, iv, 406–09; 441–42 (Shea's translation). Weyer's text is slightly different from Virgil's original. See Weyer, *De praestigiis daemonum* (i, xii), *OO*, p. 31; *WDD*, p. 34.

72. Weyer, *De praestigiis daemonum* (iv, xxii), *OO*, pp. 331–35, *WDD*, pp. 337–42.

73. Weyer, 'Apologia adversus quendam Paulum Schalichium, qui se Principem de la Scala vocitat', in *Liber apologeticus*, *OO*, pp. 602–03: 'Quomodo praeterea cohaereant illae particulae, transformationis diabolicae causam esse, subjectorum variorum assumptionem, et diabolum non indigere medio, item in momento subjectum suae actioni et proposito conveniens facere, non video'. Paul Skalić de Lika (1534–1573), born in Zagreb, a humanist and encyclopaedist who wrote the *Encyclopediae seu orbis disciplinarum tam sacrarum quam prophanarum epistemon*, published in Basel in 1559. In this work, at the end of the third book, Skalić had launched an attack on Weyer.

74. Weyer, 'Apologia adversus quendam Paulum Schalichium', in *Liber apologeticus*, *OO*, p. 603: 'Subjungit deinde paulo post: "Et si quidem animae essentia angelis pares sunt, anne subjectum sive mustelae, sive columbae, sive hominis, sive alterius cujuspiam rei assumere possunt?". Nequaquam, respondeo: et miror ab acutissimo philosopho, et doctissimo scilicet Theologo talia excogitari, proponi et defendi, nisi peculiari privilegio indultum tibi sit decernere quod voles. Animae siquidem humanae hanc corporaturam semper expetunt, cui a Deo destinatae, et non corpus mustelae. Sequeretur alioqui primum unam animam esse et hominis et bruti communem, et informare duo corpora. Non convenit bene institutae civitati, ut princeps tum proprio, tum cerdonis vehiculo utatur.'

75. Augustine, *The City of God*, xviii. 18. See Weyer, *De praestigiis daemonum* (iv, xxii), *OO*, pp. 332–33, *WDD*, p. 339; 'Apologia adversus quendam Paulum Schalichium' in *Liber apologeticus*, *OO*, pp. 605–06.

76. Pseudo-Augustine, *De spiritu et anima*, in *Patrologia Latina*, xl, col. 798: 'phantasticum hominis (quod etiam cogitando sive somniando per rerum innumerabilium genera variatur, et cum corpus non sit, corporum similes formas mira celeritate capit), sopitis aut oppressis corporeis hominis sensibus, ad aliorum sensuum figuras corporeas perduci potest: ita tamen quod corpora ipsa hominum alicubi jaceant, viventia quidem, sed multo gravius atque oppressius quam somno suis sensibus obseratis; phantasticum autem illud veluti formatum in alicujus animalis imaginem, alienis sensibus appareat, talisque homo sibi videatur, qualis sibi videri posset in somnis'; Weyer, *De praestigiis* (iv, xxii), *OO*, p. 332; *WDD*, p. 339.

77. Augustine, *De musica*, in *Patrologia Latina*, xxxii, cols 1167–71.

78. Weyer, *De praestigiis daemonum* (iii, x), *OO*, p. 190, *WDD*, p. 193.

79. Ibid. (iv, xxxiii), *OO*, pp. 335–36 ('Adhaec Patavii lupus sibi videbatur agricola, anno millesimo quingentesimo quadragesimo primo: multosque in agris insiliit, trucidavitque. Tandem non sine multa difficultate captus, confidenter asseveravit se verum esse lupum, discrimen solum existere in pelle cum pilis inversa. Quapropter quidam omnem exuti humanitatem, vereque lupi truces voracesque, tibias et ejus brachia gladio feriunt amputantque, veritatem rei exploraturi: cognita vero hominis innocentia, eum chirurgis tradunt curandum, sed post dies non multos expiravit'), *WDD*, p. 342.

80. Weyer, 'Adversus Leonis Suavii calumnias', in *Liber apologeticus*, *OO*, p. 637. On Pliny dismissing the tales concerning the Arcadian wolves as a lying fantasy of the Greek imagination, see 'Introduction to Part II' in this volume.

81. Weyer, *De praestigiis daemonum* (iii, xxx), *OO*, p. 254.

PART III

Science

From the 'Post-Metamorphic'
to the Posthuman

Introduction to Part III

Ingo Gildenhard & Andrew Zissos

> Il n'est point de peuple dans le monde, chez qui la croyance aux métamorphoses ne soit encore vivante aujourd'hui même; [...] dans les pays civilisés elle se cache au fond des compagnes, où elle inspire de naïfs récits, que les savants se hâtent d'enregistrer, de comparer et de classer.

> [There are hardly any peoples in the world among whom the belief in metamorphosis persists in the present day; [...] in civilized countries this belief hides deep in the countryside, where it inspires naïve tales that scholars hasten to record, to compare and to classify.]

So opens Georges Lafaye's landmark study on Ovid's *Metamorphoses*, published at the very beginning of the twentieth century. This scholarly incipit attests to the prevalence of what we might call a 'post-metamorphic' sensibility, to the marginalization of the idea of transformative change within the collective imaginary of the West ('les pays civilisés', no doubt). The notion of metamorphosis belonged to the world-view of what anthropologist Lucien Lévy-Bruhl (1857–1939) termed a 'pre-logical mentality', to the imaginary of non-modern peoples. It had, it seemed, run its course, and now stood irrevocably banished by scientific rationality to the cultural and geographical fringes of the modern world.

But if Lafaye, scrupulous classical scholar that he was, was right to diagnose the demise of tales of metamorphosis as we have considered them so far, he failed to recognize that new narratives of metamorphosis were already rising in their wake. These were, ironically, born of the scientific revolution to which Lafaye implicitly claims affiliation, and would become fully entrenched in a world in which science had assumed a virtual monopoly on the production of accredited conceptions of reality. These new narratives have restored the legitimacy of transformative change in the discourses of mainstream society — indeed, they have raised metamorphosis to the status of a modern cultural icon.[1] And by addressing, in an increasingly systematic and plausible way, the prospect of the posthuman, they have made metamorphosis a singularly compelling and urgent topic in contemporary culture.

Anthropocentrism, whether implicitly assumed or explicitly stated, has, in one form or another, dominated virtually all phases of Western thought. The human being has almost invariably been assigned a privileged status in the world, as the animal closest to the gods, or indeed the one fashioned in God's image. But advances in science and technology in the modern age have posed two colossal challenges to such convictions, both of which are fundamental to the re-emergence of metamorphosis in modern thought. The first challenge arose in the late eighteenth century with Darwin's theory of evolution, which compelled a reconsideration of the privileged status of the human species in the natural world, in no small part through examination of its evolutionary past. In one fell swoop *Homo sapiens* lost its status as Creation's culminating achievement, and was unceremoniously cast back into Nature's experimental laboratory, with all the other species.[2] Implicit in Darwinian evolutionary principles is the prospect — almost, from a deep-time perspective, the inevitability — of a fitter species arising to displace *Homo sapiens* from its dominant position in the animal world.

The second challenge, already anticipated in nineteenth-century science fiction literature, is upon us in the present day, as advances in cybernetics, robotics and artificial intelligence progressively erode the once firm ontological divide between human and machine.[3] Like Darwinism, these advances have reintroduced notions of metamorphosis into human thought and experience, now in a technological key. And, again like Darwinism, they raise the spectre of a posthuman world — either a world in which humankind asserts technological control over biological evolution through a cybernetic merger of its own organic life form with mechanical systems or, more diabolically, a world in which humankind is superseded by sentient machines of its own creation.

In this final introductory essay we propose to chart out the curious narrative, driven almost entirely by scientific developments, of the demise and resurrection of transformative change in the modern age.

I. The 'Post-Metamorphic'

In the West science gradually emerged, and was eventually institutionalized, as a privileged venture for the production of knowledge about the world. Science proposed a new way to apprehend reality, a way that was empirical, objective and rational, a way that was not conditioned by religious or other supernatural pre-suppositions.

With the progress of empirical science a realm of transformative possibilities was effectively abandoned. The new parameters of plausibility were governed by a materialist rationality that reduced all phenomena to the consequences or manifestations of matter, denying the existence of anything that could not be investigated via the methods of science.

As we saw in the Introduction to Part II, in his poem 'Die Götter Griechenlands' (1788), Friedrich Schiller famously bemoaned the desacralization ('Entgötterung', literally the 'de-godding') of Nature, the diminishing of its magical and spiritual dimensions that had resulted from the triumph of monotheistic Christianity over the polytheistic religious systems of the ancient world. Schiller's celebrated lament was self-consciously reworked in the early twentieth century by the sociologist Max Weber, who mused that it was the fate of the modern age to be subject to rationalization, intellectualization, and above all 'the disenchantment of the world' ('Entzauberung der Welt'). If Christianity had imposed certain restrictions on the magical and the metamorphic, it was the rise of science and rationality, as Weber implies, that had dispensed with them altogether.

With modern science's redefinition of the parameters of the possible, conceptions of the universe that allowed for supernatural forces to effect miraculous transformations, which had captivated the western imagination from the dawn of our literary record, lost their consensual plausibility. This is not to say that traditional forms of transformative change (or belief therein) such as transubstantiation or various modes of metamorphoses that earlier ages ascribed to the interference of demons or the devil entirely ceased to find their communities of believers. But in a modern, functionally differentiated society, religious discourse and dogma as well as religious practices and institutions of whatever creed no longer possess the same central cultural standing that they had in pre-modern times.

Against this backdrop, metamorphosis as such became marginalized in 'mainstream' literature. Of course we do not mean to suggest that narratives of transformation were no longer written. It is more the case that such narratives were banished to the literary margins, above all to children's literature. Here, at least, transformative change continued to thrive: among the best-known and most exuberantly metamorphic of all children's tales is Carlo Collodi's *Le avventure di Pinocchio: storia di un burattino* (1881), in which a mysteriously animated piece of wood, given human shape by the poor carpenter Geppetto, undergoes various metamorphoses, en route to a culminating transformation into fully human form.[4]

Tales of transformative change thus continued to be written, but often in circumscribed imaginative spaces and restricted generic domains. In this sense, early modernity could be called a 'post-metamorphic' age — an age, in other words, in which modes of transformative change that previous centuries considered distinct possibilities lost their credibility or at least (as in the case of Christian dogma) their hegemonic status.

In the sceptical climate of modernity, there is also a broad reprocessing of ancient myths of transformation. These myths, like other traditional resources of our cultural memory, continue to be employed to make sense of collective and individual experience.[5] But in the 'post-metamorphic' age they reappear most prominently as vehicles of metaphor.[6] Such usage is essentially abstract and self-conscious, typically manifesting an awareness of its own fictive status. Metamorphosis in this transposed and diluted sense is repeatedly pressed into service by thinkers, authors and artists as a privileged trope to reflect upon contemporary issues. Despite the fact that these transformations are figural, the persistence of the motif as a means of commentary on ourselves, as well as our position in the world, is striking.

It will be illuminating to chart out the 'troping' of one of ancient myth's most notorious metamorphic agents, the Homeric enchantress figure of Circe, who famously transformed Odysseus' men into swine.[7] In the modern period Circe becomes a popular and mobile metaphor across a range of discourses and cultural domains, and with multiple opprobrious connotations. A striking instance of metamorphosis turned into metaphor occurs in a passage from Gautier's *Le Capitaine Fracasse* (1863), where the Circean tenor is drunkenness, with the character Malartic rousing his comrades with the following exhortation:

> 'Holà! vous autres, aimables brutes, tâchez de vous dresser sur vos pattes de derrière, et allez dans la cour vous répandre un seau d'eau froide sur la tête. La Circé de l'ivresse a fait de vous des pourceaux, redevenez hommes par ce baptême [...].' (*Le Capitaine Fracasse*, ch. 16)

['Here, you fellows! You lovely brutes! Try to get up on your hind legs and trot into the yard, where you can souse your heads with cold water. The Circe of drunkenness has turned you into swine; let that baptism make men of you again [...].']

In Victorian Britain, the Circean tenor shifts to the sexual, and speaks to an attendant metaphorical debasement of those falling under the enchantress' spell. Circe becomes a widespread figure for carnality, particularly in excess or perverse form, as well as prostitution. This was, as Goldhill well observes, 'an easy metaphor' for the culture.[8] And it was not by chance, the same scholar notes, that James Joyce, in *Ulysses* (1922), made his Circe the Madam of a brothel.

Joyce's 'Circe' episode (*Ulysses*, pp. 561–704) merits further examination as a particularly elaborate and ruthlessly degraded metaphoric recasting of the Homeric tale. This episode differs strikingly from other episodes in the novel in that it is composed as a play complete with stage directions, and that it partially forsakes the realistic portrayal of action in favour of a more dreamlike atmosphere in which distinctions between reality and illusion are not easily made. As Bloom and Stephen enter 'Nighttown', Dublin's red-light district, the Joycean equivalent of Circe's island, the narrative shifts to a surreal mode, a veritable dreamscape in which objects talk and characters seem to morph into one another. This oddly metamorphic atmosphere notwithstanding, the 'Circe' episode follows Joyce's procedure elsewhere in the novel by ironically and self-consciously enacting a systematic translation of the mythical content of Homer's *Odyssey* into the mundane and sordid realities of contemporary Dublin. Bella Cohen, the 'massive whoremistress' (p. 641) of the brothel in which the action unfolds, plays Circe to Leopold Bloom's Odysseus. The transformation of Odysseus' men into pigs is metaphorically reprised as various male figures act out their carnal desires under the degrading influence of the brothel and its madam. Peculiar details reinforce this metaphoric recasting: Bloom's purchase of a pig's foot subtly signals the Homeric metamorphosis, while Bella Cohen's sexual intercourse with a veterinarian (which takes place off stage) neatly recapitulates the Homeric Circe's connection to the animal world.

Still in the 'roaring twenties', another modern and 'post-metamorphic' Circe appears in George Grosz' eponymous watercolour (Figure 9).[9] This ironic image, completed in 1927, involves a ruthless attack on the perceived decadence of contemporary German society during the Weimar Republic. As such, it amounts to a visual rendering of contemporary allegorical readings of the Homeric Circe episode.[10] As one critic puts it, with his 'Circe' Grosz suggests that 'Homer's premise is not so remote after all. Grosz' cutting irony, his lambasting of the bourgeois morals and social vices of the difficult period between the two world wars, presents us with a modern, paid Circe who turns her clients into pigs.'[11] We might add that this modern Circe not only metaphorically bestializes men, but, unlike her Homeric archetype, lusts after them in their debased condition.

The metaphoric apprehension of myth that characterizes the 'post-metamorphic' sensibility is well illustrated by Walter Crane's painting 'Neptune's Horses' (Fig. 15), completed in 1892.[12] In it the sea god Neptune (Greek Poseidon) drives forward a cresting wave that is presented as so many galloping white horses. Here is what Crane himself had to say on the genesis of the painting in his literary reminiscences:[13]

> Watching the sea breaking all day along the long line of shore — the wind often catching the crests of the waves just as they curled over to break, and blowing the spray out like the mane of prancing steeds — the motive suggested itself which I afterwards carried out in my picture 'Neptune's Horses', the first sketch for which was made at Wauwinet. As a child in the early days at Torquay I had been accustomed to hear the waves spoken of as 'white horses', and the idea seemed to be a perfectly natural and familiar one — though it was only now that I attempted to give it form.

So the origins of 'Neptune's Horses' reach back to a local metaphor that Crane has in a sense 'remythologized', but which remains in the realm of metaphor. Indeed, the painting is almost a visual theorization of the mythological more generally, for Neptune is the god of horses as well as god of the sea, and Crane's image ingeniously brings these two spheres of divine competence into contact. The approach is, at the same time, highly abstract and self-conscious: a figure of speech brought to life in a way that sheds light on the interface between human imagination and the natural world. 'Neptune's Horses' thus amounts to something like an artistic 'reverse engineering' of the mythological imagination.

As in earlier periods, so in the modern age metamorphosis is frequently pressed into service as a metaphor for the poetic imagination.[14] Speaking more broadly, it might be observed that the ancient and medieval notion of metamorphosis as a physical event ceded ground to the use of the theme to explore the vagaries of the human mind. Indeed, it is a peculiarly modern insight that the metamorphic and the monstrous may be intrinsic products of the human psyche. From a psychological perspective then, fantastical metamorphosis is not an external event, but an inner one, part of a psychological drama played out in the human mind. In this sense transformative change might be regarded the embodiment of the morphism of the human psyche, the instrumentalization of its metaphoric production.

A famous etching by Francisco Goya, completed between 1797 and 1799, shows the artist, perhaps asleep, with his head buried in his arms, which are resting on a table. In the background monstrous bats and owls swoop in, while a big-eyed cat looks on. The caption reads: 'El sueño de la razón produce monstruos' ['The Sleep of Reason Produces Monsters']. This suggests, as Freudian psychological theory would later confirm, the inner reality of an ongoing struggle within the human psyche itself. Goya's message is polyvalent, not least since image and caption keep in unresolved balance a fundamental tension between three vital aspects: first, reason 'polices' the production of imaginary monsters, that is, it keeps them at bay; second, the vigilance of reason has its limits: it is susceptible to nodding off; and thirdly, while the loosening of rational inhibitions and control enables monsters to appear, the nightmarish creatures brought into being by inattentive reason are exactly the monstrous creations that appear in Goya's art — which is populated by monsters, classical and otherwise. In short, the sleep of reason not only induces nightmares, but also unleashes human creativity.[15]

Goya's visual reflections on the apparent powerlessness of reason to maintain a

FIG. 9. Grosz, George (1893–1959): *Circe*, 1927. New York, Museum of Modern Art (MoMA). Watercolour, pen and ink, and pencil on paper, 26 x 191/4" (66 x 48.6 cm). Gift of Mr and Mrs Walter Bareiss and an anonymous donor (by exchange) 73.1981 © 2011. Digital image, The Museum of Modern Art, New York/Scala, Florence © Photo SCALA, Florence, and DACS 2012

FIG. 10. Füssli, Johann Heinrich, 'Nachtmahr', 1790
Credit: © akg-images

world without monsters speaks to a broad phenomenon of particular interest to our history of metamorphosis: recognition that even in an age of materialist rationality, the monstrous and the metamorphic will not be banished altogether. They continue to subsist, even if under comparatively restricted conditions, because they conform to the human imagination.

Just a few years before Goya's 'El sueño de la razón', the Anglo-Swiss artist Johann Heinrich Füssli had produced in multiple versions a painting entitled simply 'Nachtmahr' ['Nightmare'], the first of which was completed in 1781. The essential image seems to present both the woman and her nightmare, and seems to reflect German folkloric beliefs about dream visitations by monstrous supernatural beings. All versions are highly eroticized, showing a woman asleep, lying on her back with a small monstrous creature (an incubus) perched on or above her, and a horse appearing in the background. Particularly striking is a version completed in 1790–91 (Figure 10), in which the woman lies with her head to the right, and the monstrous creature gazes directly at her.

It would appear that monstrous amalgams — whether from dreams, ancient mythology or modern literature — are inevitable products of human fantasy, displaced symbols of the intrinsic hybridity of human identity.[16] Monsters are 'metamorphic' creatures that fulfil a 'kaleidoscopic mirror function'.[17] This is a powerful insight of modern thought, but one that restricts monstrous creatures to the 'inner space' of the human psyche, denying them material reality.

For many modern readers, the apparent inability of vigilant reason to hold off the monstrous and the metamorphic will call to mind the psychological theories of Sigmund Freud, and in particular his notion of the human unconscious as a repository of suppressed irrational and monstrous aspects of the human psyche. A play between the rational and the irrational aspects of the mind ensues, with the former in tenuous control, the latter forcing its way into consciousness, though the actual contents are disguised or transmuted, to render them unrecognizable (as well as less objectionable) to conscious thought. Thus the human psyche is discovered to be a kind of oneiric producer of metamorphosis. The set of operations by which representation takes place in dreams and fantasy — condensation, displacement, symbolization — is obviously in some relationship to the metaphoric.[18]

Freud's psychological theory represents a moment of rupture in Western thought, and one with profound consequences for humanity's sense of itself. The discovery of the human unconscious proved devastating for the notion of *Homo sapiens* as a creature of *logos*: human rationality was debunked, and indeed forsaken as a plausible aspiration or transcendent force in the newly complex economy of the warring psyche.

A suggestive cinematic articulation of such ideas is the science fiction film *Forbidden Planet* (1956), now widely recognized as a masterpiece of the genre.[19] Drawing a measure of inspiration from Shakespeare's *The Tempest*, this film opens with a spaceship landing on a recently colonized planet, to investigate the fate of the human colonists, of whom only two survive, the scientist Dr Morbius and his daughter Altaira. The crew is threatened by the same invisible power that exterminated the colonists, which is finally discovered to be a 'monster from the

Id' of Morbius himself. The monster is actualized by the advanced technology of a now extinct race, the Krell, which, as its crowning achievement, acquired the capacity to 'instrumentalize' thought, i.e. achieve its concrete realization. Like the Krell before him, Morbius is unwittingly destroyed by the monstrous contents of his own psyche, the 'mindless beasts of the unconscious', which the Krell, for all their advanced science and technical genius, had failed to take into account.

With *Forbidden Planet* our analysis of the 'post-metamorphic' has in a certain sense come full circle. Outer space has become a platform for the expression of, even the concrete realization of, the 'inner space' of the human psyche.[20] We are back to Goya's 'sleep of reason', to the conviction, that is, that the monstrous and the metamorphic are ineradicable components of the human psyche.[21] Indeed, *Forbidden Planet* is striking for its insistent location of the monstrous and metamorphic in the human mind. It is only the technology of a species unimaginably more advanced than *Homo sapiens* that can achieve a physical realization of these monstrous shifting figments. The machine of the Krell instrumentalizes thought, and by so doing it translates the 'morphism' of the human psyche into embodied metamorphosis. This is metaphor made flesh — but in a 'scientific' domain rather than a mythic one. As such it signals a kind of usurpation that is both conceptual and generic.

But with this venture into modern cinema — and into science fiction as well — we are getting ahead of ourselves. It is time to shift back 200 years or so, to the emergence of the 'fantastic' and related literary genres.

II. Literary Equivocations

The triumph of materialist rationality in the West was, of course, never total. For one thing, there were periodic 'great awakenings' of religious (which is to say Christian) faith in the nineteenth and twentieth centuries. The rise of modern science also coincided with the emergence (or re-emergence or reconfiguration) of domains of experience that defy explication by means of scientific protocols. In such domains, transformative change of one kind or another continues to feature — even if only in a vestigial or hesitant manner.

The modern period saw the rapid development and articulation of the sciences (biology emerges as a distinct field in the nineteenth century, for example, as does psychiatry); but it also saw a striking counter-thrust in the emergence (or re-emergence) of the so-called 'occult sciences' — illuminism championed by Swedenborg, magnetism championed by Messmer, and many others besides — that often attracted large followings. Such occult sciences both influenced, and found a literary outlet in so-called 'fantastic' literature, a new genre (according to Todorov) that emerged towards the end of the eighteenth century. The literary antecedent (or perhaps better, older sibling) of the 'fantastic' was Gothic literature, its successor was magical realism. In terms of our overall critical narrative, such literary movements might be thought of as metamorphic 'holdouts'.

Gothic Literature

The Enlightenment of the eighteenth century famously championed contemplation of a real world stripped of all supernatural explanation. But the same century also saw the beginnings of Gothic literature, a mode of writing in which strange events and figures point to the existence of alternate realities of a mysterious and unsettling kind.[22] If its menacing forces are generally otherworldly, a primary function of Gothic literature is to explore the condition of being human through the generation of horror.[23]

Gothic literature is defined by certain characteristic elements — most obviously the presence of the supernatural, the charged, sensationalist atmosphere, and the antiquated setting. The Gothic novel is responsible for establishing, inter alia, the clichéd setting of the 'haunted house' and for making prominent use of ghosts and diabolical apparitions.

Early Gothic literature sees a profusion of stories of ghosts and vampires.[24] The latter is of particular interest, as a protean creature with the power to dissolve ontological boundaries — above all by transmuting its chosen human victims into vampires in their own right. 'The vampire is a liminal creature, neither fully alive nor dead. At this monster's core lies an affinity for rupture, change, and mutation.'[25] Popular belief in the existence of vampires can be traced back to antiquity, but becomes particularly widespread in eastern Europe in the eighteenth century. The theme inspired many writers, including Théophile Gautier, whose *La Morte amoureuse*, the story of a young priest who falls in love with a vampire, appeared in 1836. But it was, of course, Bram Stoker who in the novel *Dracula* (1897) afforded the vampire its most memorable and fully developed literary articulation, as well as bequeathing its emblematic figure.

Stoker famously endorsed the popular belief that vampires required the blood of the living to maintain the vigour of their own life force. Another interesting trait ascribed to Dracula is a developed para-psychological capacity: the Count is not merely a shape-shifter and metamorphic agent, but also influences the disposition of animals, and has a degree of control and influence over the minds of his victims. The transformation of Mina Harker is thus psychological as well as physical: as her human nature is progressively eroded, she becomes a kind of medium for the Count. In certain respects, Stoker's treatment of vampirism constitutes a reaction to the Romantic ideal of love, 'a nightmarish version of the ideal of two individuals who willingly dissolve the boundaries of the Self, losing themselves in an all-encompassing bond of love. Stoker's vampire is a perversion of the lover, who must drink the latter's blood in order to continue its own existence'.[26]

Gothic underwent a resurgence in the nineteenth century, with new characteristic elements updating the conventions, including modern settings and the airing of scientific theories. A pre-eminent work of the nineteenth-century Gothic Revival is Wilde's *The Picture of Dorian Gray* (1890).[27] This, Wilde's only novel, draws inspiration from Balzac's *La Peau de Chagrin* and Stevenson's *The Strange Case of Dr Jekyll and Mr Hyde*, which had been published with spectacular success a mere four years earlier.[28] Like Stevenson, Wilde splits the psyche of his titular protagonist, but in a very different way. Dorian Gray, a fashionable inhabitant of contemporary

London, lamenting the fact that his physical resplendence will fade with advancing age, expresses the whimsical desire to sell his soul to ensure the portrait that his friend has painted would age rather than he. Dorian's wish is mysteriously granted, thereby introducing a Faustian theme into the plot. Through this supernatural 'pact', a ubiquitous metamorphic process inherent in organic nature is arrested in the protagonist's physical body, and transferred to a non-organic object that bears its likeness.[29] Dorian then proceeds to pursue a life of decadence and vice. But in addition to registering the displaced process of ageing, the portrait is mysteriously transformed with each of Dorian's depraved acts, thereby signalling through disfigurement of form the effect that each act of depravity has upon his soul. As the novel progresses, the focus increasingly shifts from the striking physical beauty of Dorian to the horrific metamorphosis that his portrait undergoes. The latter becomes for the protagonist a kind of supernatural mirror that reflects his own spiritual condition. It becomes so loathsome to Dorian that he finally attempts to destroy it with a knife, an action that leads to his own destruction, through a final metamorphic transposition that is discovered by Dorian's servants:

> When they entered, they found, hanging on the wall, a splendid portrait of their master as they had last seen him, in all the wonder of his exquisite youth and beauty. Lying on the floor was a dead man, in evening dress, with a knife in his heart. He was withered, wrinkled, and loathsome of visage. It was not until they had examined the rings that they recognized who it was. (*Picture of Dorian Gray*, ch. 20)

The Picture of Dorian Gray employs the supernatural to articulate a widespread conviction of the period. As Mighall observes, the novel 'operates within a frame-work of expectations about the visibility of vice'.[30] Basil Hallward, the artist friend who creates the portrait, is made to express the Victorian conviction that

> Sin is a thing that writes itself across a man's face. It cannot be concealed. People talk sometimes about secret vices. There are no such things. If a wretched man has a vice, it shows itself in the lines of the mouth, the droop of his eyelids, the moulding of his hands even. (*Picture of Dorian Gray*, ch. 12)

A momentary point of contact with contemporary science is established in a suggestive passage in which Dorian contemplates not his own portrait, but that of an ancestor, Herbert Gray, in whom he recognizes his own physical traits. This leads him to muse upon the extent of his genetic inheritance:

> Was it young Herbert's life that he sometimes led? Had some poisonous germ passed from body to body till it had reached his own? Was it some dim sense of that ruined grace that had made him so suddenly, and almost without cause, give utterance, in Basil Hallward's studio, to that mad prayer that so changed his life? (*Picture of Dorian Gray*, ch. 11)

Here the novel engages the theory of atavism, but 'takes up the scientific discourse and adds a supernatural touch to it.'[31]

As already observed, one of the strongest influences upon Wilde's *Picture of Dorian Gray* was Balzac's *La Peau de Chagrin* (1831). This is a work inflected with its author's characteristic realism, establishing a backdrop of everyday Parisian life into which the supernatural irrupts.[32] The novel begins with its protagonist Raphael accepting from an elderly Jewish shopkeeper the *peau de chagrin*. This magical object fulfils its owner's every wish, but each time at the expense of his vital force: with the fulfilment of each desire it miraculously shrinks, assuming a size in proportion to the remaining life force of its owner. Unable to heed to the shopkeeper's warning, Raphael proceeds to satisfy his various desires; the skin shrinks progressively until it becomes naught, at which point he dies. An essential theme of *La Peau de Chagrin* is thus the struggle between desire and life, which is played out in a supernatural key.

The informing scheme of Balzac's 'Comédie Humaine', to which *La Peau de Chagrin* belongs, is a classificatory analysis of human beings along parallel lines to zoology. At the same time his broader purpose was to identify driving forces and principles at work in contemporary human society. *La Peau de Chagrin* is particularly concerned with the latter purpose. Balzac himself characterized it as a middle or connecting term between *Les Études de Mœurs* and *Les Études Philosophique*, the two divisions of his great literary enterprise. The fact that it is but one component of 'Comédie Humaine' makes clear that we are dealing here with almost explicit allegory. Balzac's point is to demonstrate that desire is a natural force that can act constructively or destructively according to moral inclination.

The other major influence on Wilde's novel was, as noted, Robert Louis Stevenson's *The Strange Case of Dr Jekyll and Mr Hyde* (1886). This is a work that defies easy categorization: it has unmistakable Gothic elements, but also ventures into the realm of scientific transformation — though the science is decidedly 'fuzzy'. The civilized and well-mannered Dr Jekyll in the course of his scientific experimentation undergoes an initial, chemically induced transformation (affecting both form and psyche) to the monstrous Mr Hyde. This lasts for a number of hours, after which the protagonist oscillates between the two conditions, with Hyde gradually 'taking over'.

In generic terms, Stevenson's tale constitutes an interesting fusion of the form of the modern medical case history with the Gothic novel. Its unfolding psychomachia invites reading as a moral allegory, with the negative psychological impulses of Victorian man given bodily form in the person of Mr Hyde. But there is obviously another, more direct reading available, thanks to the trappings of the medical case history: this has Mr Hyde arising from a metamorphosis caused by 'science'. For Suvin, who locates the novel in the sub-genre of horror–science fiction, this vague and unresolved ambivalence suggests that Stevenson is 'cheating' in terms of his basic narrative logic:

> On the one hand his moral allegory of good and evil takes bodily form with the help of a chemical concoction. On the other, the transmogrification Jekyll-Hyde becomes not only unrepeatable because the concoction had unknown impurities, but Hyde also begins 'returning' without any chemical stimulus, by force of desire and habit. This unclear oscillation between science and fantasy, where science is used for a partial justification or added alibi for those readers who would no longer be disposed to swallow a straightforward fantasy or moral allegory, is to my mind the reason for the elaborate, clever, but ultimately not satisfying exercise in detection from various points of view — which in naturalistic fashion masks but does not explain the fuzziness at the narrative nucleus.[33]

That the disparate generic elements coexist in the same narrative is a testament to the brilliance of Stevenson's storytelling. But the very existence of these contrary elements, the need for an 'alibi' for readers 'no longer [...] disposed to swallow a straightforward fantasy' attests to a certain ambivalence towards the metamorphic that emerges more strongly in fantastic literature.

Fantastic Literature

The pioneering work of Todorov in the 1960s was crucial for identifying the 'fantastic' as a category of literature and focussing critical attention on it. His monograph *Introduction à la littérature fantastique* (1970) remains foundational to the field. Todorov proposed a well-delineated set of criteria for fantastic literature that has inevitably encountered resistance.[34] As often in literary studies, definitions remain elusive and critical consensus hard to achieve.

For Todorov, the fantastic derives its generic distinctness from its underlying ambiguity. It applies the narrative techniques of realism to describe supernatural events for which no explanation is provided, and ends on a note of indeterminacy — with a culminating ellipse of meaning, a hesitation. It compels the reader to question whether the events described are natural or supernatural, reality or dream, without providing a definitive answer.[35] This indeterminacy or uncertainty is the crucial feature: as Todorov explains, 'once we choose one answer or another, we leave the fantastic for a neighbouring genre'.[36]

Much like Gothic, then, fantastic literature proposes, against the dictates of empirical science, the existence of alternate realities that maintain interfaces with our own. But, unlike Gothic, which freely admits supernatural and metamorphic phenomena, fantastic literature represents a more delicate compromise, a strategic ceding of terrain to scientific rationality and empiricism. It characteristically concedes the possibility that the supernatural phenomenon reported may be just an oneiric phenomenon, or even the product of delirium.[37] Moreover, fantastic literature is premised on the quasi-rationalist conviction that the magical and supernatural cannot occur in normal empirical experience; it posits alternate realms in which supernatural events do occur, but these realms are connected to normal experience by a somewhat vague and unpredictable interface.[38] The fantastic thus belongs to the irrational; it stands opposed to the materialist rationality of modern scientific thought, and yet attempts more than other genres to accommodate it. The genre's tentative appeals to supra-mundane powers are not religious in any conventional sense. The supernatural is not represented according to Christian teaching or other religious dogma, but remains unexplained, shrouded in mystery.

Fantastic literature emerges in the Age of Reason, a period in which belief in the supernatural, as already noted, is being subjected to enormous pressure by the advance of science. The genre's confrontation with this broader societal trend typically finds its textual embodiment in the stock figure of the sceptical academic, scientist, or doctor. This materialist sceptic marks the intrusion of scientific cognition into the literary imaginary, standing as an internal 'representative' of science whose role is to impose protocols of plausibility and to police (at least initially) the credulous acceptance of supernatural causation.

Two great early exponents of the genre are E. T. A. Hoffmann and Théophile Gautier. In the latter, who was very much a disciple of Hoffmann, the genre perhaps reaches its fullest stage of development. Gautier makes particularly full use of occult sciences. In terms of the potentialities of human experience, he freely admits soul migration but is more wary of bodily transformation as such.[39] But the metamorphic occurs in such themes as the murderous action of the gaze and of thought, the animation of objects of art, and the much-favoured theme of the dead woman resurrected through the action of desire.

A characteristic fantastic tale of the latter type is Gautier's *Arria Marcella* (1852). This novella is an ingenious variation on the tale of demonic seduction, in which the seductress is not a malignant being but rather the form of the titular character, an attractive young woman who perished by the volcanic eruption that buried the city of Pompeii in 79 AD. Her enticing physical form has been reconstructed by archaeological technique in quasi-sculptural form from the impress of the hardened ash and is on display in a museum in Naples. This eerie aesthetic object captivates the story's protagonist, the young French tourist Octavien, when he visits the museum. Thereafter he proceeds with his companions to Pompeii itself, where they examine, inter alia, the home of Arria's father, Arrius Diomedes. After dinner, Octavien returns alone, and finds that the ancient city has somehow come to life: the roads are full of people, the markets abuzz with transactions. The detailed elaboration of daily life in ancient Pompeii endows the experience with a characteristic aura of realism. Octavien presently meets his beloved, and they proceed to consummate their union. But their passionate embrace is ultimately put to an end by the intervention of Arria's father, a disciple of Christ and his new religion, who admonishes her perceived immorality. Arria protests; but even as Octavien clasps her in his arms, she disintegrates into a handful of ashes. The following day Octavien's friends find him unconscious, and they revive him only with great difficulty. He does not tell them of his remarkable experience, but instead vaguely explains that he experienced a harmless lapse of consciousness, a fit of some kind.

In Gautier's fantastic account, then, the beautiful young Pompeian woman who died nearly two thousand years ago appears momentarily to be reanimated, even reconstituted by Octavien's passion. As Arria herself tells him, 'Ton désir m'a rendu la vie' ['Your desire brought me to life'] (p. 242). The story embodies a familiar theme in Gautier's *oeuvre*, namely, the power of love to transcend the limits of temporality and reconstitute the beloved. A belief in alternate domains of reality is also expressed: 'En effet, rien ne meurt, tout existe toujours; nulle force ne peut anéantir ce qui fut une fois' ['Nothing dies; everything exists for all time: no force can annihilate what once was'] (p. 242). Gautier also expresses the conviction that the phenomena of these domains are not reducible or subject to the materialist logic of quotidian reality: Octavien's experiences are characterized as 'circonstances inquiétants et fantastiques que la raison ne peut expliquer' ['troubling and fantastic circumstances that reason cannot account for'] (p. 255).

Arria Marcella manifests the characteristic hesitation of fantastic literature: both author and protagonist acknowledge the possibility that Arria Marcella's animation is merely a delusional product of Octavien's profound passion.[40] The protagonist is evidently a person easily given to fantasy, and it is undoubtedly significant that he tries unsuccessfully to repeat his encounter. But though he can neither replicate nor understand his experience, he regards it as a lived reality. To be sure, the encounter with Arria Marcella profoundly affects Octavien's 'real life': even after he marries, his love for Arria Marcella never abates, and his wife searches in vain for the mistress who has, so she intuitively senses, captured her spouse's heart.

Magical Realism

Gothic fiction and fantastic literature have interesting affinities with a later mode of writing called magical realism, which deliberately breaks down the distinction between the real and the supernatural. Magical realism constellates literary universes that resemble the one we live in, while also deviating from it in crucial respects — such as admitting the possibility of metamorphosis. Instead of a tenuous or intermittent interface between quotidian reality and a supernatural realm, the genre opts for a radical merging of the two, with no attempt to justify the plausibility of the result. Magical realism rises to prominence in Latin America in the second half of the twentieth century, as a self-conscious, post-colonial literary movement. The term itself emerges in the 1960s among scholars of Latin American literature and has a particularly strong association with Gabriel García Márquez's *Cien años de soledad* (1967, published in translation as *One Hundred Years of Solitude* in 1970).[41]

Its identification with Latin American literature notwithstanding, the earliest example of magical realism is arguably Franz Kafka's *Die Verwandlung* (1915), entitled *Metamorphosis* in English translations.[42] To be sure Kafka's well-known novella defies attempts at categorization. Though sometimes classified as a work of fantastic literature, it is perhaps better regarded as either a direct precursor to, or even a straightforward instance of magical realism.[43]

Kafka's novella breaks with classical versions of human-animal transformations in important ways.[44] It opens with an abrupt and startling sentence: 'Als Gregor Samsa eines Morgens aus unruhigen Träumen erwachte, fand er sich in seinem Bett zu einem ungeheueren Ungeziefer verwandelt' ['When Gregor Samsa woke up one morning from uneasy dreams, he found himself transformed in his bed into a monstrous vermin'] (ch. 1). Kafka proceeds to relate Gregor's various experiences, including the discovery of the possibilities and limitations of his insectile body, and his increasingly difficult interactions with members of his family, who gradually cease to believe that the oversized cockroach in the bedroom is indeed Gregor. In the course of the novella, the circumstances of the family as a whole improve in inverse proportion to the worsening of Gregor's condition. And yet Gregor becomes more humane as the narrative progresses. His abiding human spirit achieves a partial transcendence of his bestial physiology and instincts. Despite the increasingly evident loathing of his father and sister, Gregor's thoughts show him ever more concerned with his family and its welfare.[45] This disjunction manifests itself decisively in a final moment of rupture, when his sister Grete's violin playing entices Gregor out of his room, the door of which had accidently been left open. 'War er ein Tier, da ihn Musik so ergriff?' ['Was he an animal that music could move him so?'] (ch. 26). He is drawn out by fraternal love, but is promptly rebuffed by his sister's disgusted reaction — including her denial of his human identity, and her stated wish to be rid of him. Not long thereafter Gregor is found dead. The novella ends with his family celebrating his death with a trip to the countryside, full of joy and planning optimistically for the future.

Scholars have debated the degree to which Kafka's novella stands in dialogue with Ovid's *Metamorphoses*, and some have even denied any direct connection whatsoever.[46] Ultimately, though, the degree of direct engagement with his Roman predecessor is of less importance than the fact that Kafka's handling of metamorphosis radically deviates from classical and classicizing conventions, and in various ways.[47]

To begin with, Kafka's story begins where Ovid's stories tend to end. Whereas in Ovid the transformation tends to conclude a tale, in Kafka the metamorphosis has already befallen Gregor before the narrative even begins. In this sense the novella is not about the physical metamorphosis as such, but rather about its psychological consequences.

With this idiosyncratic starting point, Kafka deprives his readers, at least initially, of a wider context that might explain what caused the transformation to occur. Indeed, the factors responsible for Gregor's unfortunate plight remain obscure throughout, though Kafka clearly implies that social forces are at work, in particular his protagonist's dysfunctional relationships with other members of the family. But there is no explanation of how these social forces could have resulted in this miraculous biological outcome.

Secondly, there is Gregor's transformation into a species of insect — or rather of vermin (the term *Ungeziefer* carries a more unpleasant implication than 'insect', denoting something particularly objectionable — something that might crawl out of a sewer, or that one would tend to squash under the heel of one's shoe). Kafka's choice underscores retrospectively the point that classical tales of transformation tend to explore a relatively circumscribed — one might go so far as to say sanitized — selection of possibilities offered by the animal kingdom. Very few transformations in Ovid, for instance, deal with insects and none with vermin; the few admitted cases of the former — such as Arachne's metamorphosis into a spider — are specific and well motivated, and often emphasize 'elevated' animal traits (such as weaving) as residual traces of an original human nature.

Die Verwandlung therefore shocks not just in terms of contents, but also in its violation of an unspoken principle of decorum in traditional metamorphic art and literature; the modernity of the tale manifests itself not least in this break with convention. But if Kafka's treatment lacks precedent, it is responsible for setting a trend: in the cultural industry of the twentieth century (and beyond), insects, and transformation into insects, figure prominently in thinking about what it is to be human.[48]

Finally, Kafka explores far more persistently than any classical predecessor the experience of a human consciousness trapped in an animal body. Ovid and Apuleius, of course, explore this constellation. But in the overwhelming majority of Ovidian tales, the flora and fauna arising from the reported metamorphoses retain only vestigial traces of the human mind of the metamorph. More importantly, in those cases where human consciousness continues to reside within the animal frame (such as Io, Callisto, or Actaeon in Ovid, or Lucius' asinine existence in Apuleius) it remains by and large intact.[49] One of the most haunting aspects of Kafka's tale, by contrast, is his exploration of a middle way between the two extremes of retention and obliteration: the partial assimilation of the human mind to the animal body.[50]

So, for example, consciousness and insectile body are initially at odds. Gregor discovers that he has 'numerous little legs, which were in every different kind of perpetual motion and which, besides, he could not control' (ch. 1). He promptly exhibits involuntary insect behaviour when he cannot resist snapping his jaws several times at the sight of his distraught mother's spilling coffee ('dagegen konnte er sich nicht versagen, im Anblick des fliessenden Kaffees mehrmals mit den Kiefern ins Leere zu schnappen', ch. 1). Here Gregor acts purely (and irrepressibly) out of animal instinct, signalling 'the invasion of his private self by a new motivating agency'.[51] Further indications of an insect nature soon appear. Gregor discovers a sense of wellbeing when he behaves in the manner of a cockroach. His diet changes; his eyesight grows progressively weaker; insectile cycles of wakefulness and sleeping emerge; he discovers with some delight that he can crawl up the walls and on to the ceiling, and derives comfort from doing so.

A particularly important physiological transformation involves Gregor's voice, which devolves into a chirping sound that humans cannot understand. He makes several attempts to talk on the first morning, over the course of which his voice becomes increasingly unintelligible. After this Gregor makes no more attempts at human communication — a development that leads his family to the false conclusion he has likewise lost understanding of their speech.

By having Gregor's consciousness affected by his radical physiological metamorphosis, Kafka arguably puts more critical pressure on the nexus between transformation and identity (Heidegger's 'Jemeinigkeit') than any of his predecessors, not least since he explores the phenomenon of transformed identity both from the inside, that is, Gregor's own perspective, and the outside, as betokened by the observations of his family and other members of the household, thereby establishing a tight interface between biological processes and social commentary.

The entire narrative of *Die Verwandlung* is premised upon Gregor's initial metamorphosis. But no agency is attributed, and no attempt is made to account for the process of transformation. Indeed, Kafka seems to invite disbelief in literal truth from the outset. The transformation is associated with dreaming ('unruhigen Träumen', ch. 1), and, even if it is punctually affirmed as real ('"Was ist mit mir geschehen?" dachte er. Es war kein Traum', ch. 1), doubts quickly re-emerge.[52] As he lies in bed, Gregor thinks to himself that he has often in the past had mildly traumatic experiences of this order that turned out to be purely imaginary, and 'he was eager to see how today's fantasy would gradually fade away' ('er war gespannt, wie sich seine heutigen Vorstellungen allmählich auflösen würden', ch. 1). In the event, of course, Gregor's own observations are confirmed by other characters, but the reader cannot entirely banish the doubts that were raised at the outset. Kafka's treatment thus encourages a somewhat fluid apprehension of reality.[53]

Gregor's metamorphosis finds a suggestive precedent in the fragments of an unfinished novel, *Hochzeitvorbereitungen auf dem Lande* ['Wedding Preparations in the Country'], which Kafka began in 1906–07, and reworked in 1909. The novel begins on the day its protagonist, Eduard Raban, who is engaged to an older woman, is to meet his future parents-in-law and make wedding arrangements. Lying in bed that morning, Eduard fantasizes about a fantastical splitting of his being that would resolve his feelings of ambivalence:

> Ich brauche nicht einmal selbst aufs Land fahren, das ist nicht nötig. Ich schicke meinen angekleideten Körper. [...] Ich habe, wie ich im Bett liege, die Gestalt eines großen Käfers, eines Hirschkäfers oder eines Maikäfers, glaube ich. [...] Ich stellte es dann so an, als handle es sich um einen Winterschlaf, und ich preßte meine Beinchen an meinen gebauchten Leib. Und ich lisple eine kleine Zahl Worte, das sind Anordnungen an meinen traurigen Körper [...]. (*Hochzeitvorbereitungen auf dem Lande*, ch. 1)

> ['I don't even need to go to the country myself. It isn't necessary. I'll send my clothed [*sc.* human] body. [...] As I lie in bed I assume the form of a big beetle, a stag beetle or a june beetle, I think. [...] Then I pretend it is a matter of hibernating, and I press my little legs against my bulging body and I whisper a few words of instruction to my sad [*sc.* human] body [...].']

The striking similarities to *Die Verwandlung* leave no doubt that this fragment represents the genesis of the later novella's metamorphic premise. Eduard Raban fantasizes a split into two distinct selves, a giant beetle who remains at home, and a human body that goes to meet his obligations in the world of human intercourse. Gregor's metamorphosis, in other words, was originally an act of the imagination belonging to a kind of fantasy world in which a person can evidently split apart and then merge again.[54]

Kafka's novella has, of course, spawned a huge body of critical commentary.[55] Problems of interpretation and categorization abound, and they have proven to be largely intractable. We have opted to classify it as a work of magical realism, but are well aware that this is a controversial choice. Whatever formal category one assigns it to, *Die Verwandlung* is clearly a foundational text of modern and post-modern thought on transformative change, with its emphasis on insects and identity, dehumanization and alienation, exploitation and dysfunctionality, as well as the complex interlocking of the social and the biological.

A more straightforward case of magical realism is Salman Rushdie's controversial fourth novel, *The Satanic Verses* (1988), which looks at the experience of Indian expatriates in contemporary England, while drawing partial inspiration from the life of Muhammad. This novel features transformative change quite prominently, though in a highly self-conscious fashion. Metamorphosis, such as the transformations from human to animal that affect members of the immigrant population in Britain, is a characteristic magical-realist element that even the characters themselves identify and discuss. Thus a fellow immigrant, now a manticore (man-tiger) explains to Saladin Chamcha, who has been metamorphosed into a goat-like devil figure, that such transformations are the result of racist perceptions of the indigenous population: '"We're going to bust out of here, before they turn us into anything worse…" "But how do they do it?" Chamcha wanted to know. "They describe us", the other whispered solemnly. "That's all. They have the power of description, and we succumb to the pictures they construct"' (p. 168). Here, then, metamorphosis is little more than a symbolic code, and one that is dissolved back into tenor and vehicle by the characters themselves. It points to an issue already raised in reference to Kafka, namely, our power to dehumanize and hence transform fellow human beings. As with Kafka, so Rushdie's magical-realist fiction suggests that the continuing ability of the marvellous, the monstrous, and the metamorphic to engage our attention arises from the fact that they are ideally suited to comment on, and cope with, key aspects of the modern condition, in particular such phenomena as racism, imperialism, and social 'othering'.

In a similar spirit, the metamorphic art of the contemporary South African artist Jane Alexander uses often grotesque visual metaphors to articulate Kafka-esque preoccupations with dehumanization and alienation, exploitation and dysfunctionality, as well as the complex interlocking of the social and the biological. Her work presents a world in flux, where boundaries between self and other, human and animal, are inherently unstable. Ontological categories dissolve and leave the spectator puzzled: we not only wonder *who* her *Bom Boys* are (or the *Custodian*, the *Hobbled Ruminant*, the *Beast*, or the *Scavenger*), but also *what* they are: her anthropomorphic animals and zoomorphic humans defy easy classification. In her universe of mutants, 'common sense' undergoes surreal permutations with at times grotesque results. Alexander's very style is paradoxical, combining as it does the classical with the grotesque: exposed bodies with a ripped physique and smooth elegant surfaces are used for apocalyptic monsters, such as *Butcher Boys* and divine creatures, such as the *West Coast African Angel* (both sculptures date from 1985–86).

Butcher Boys (Fig. 11), in particular, has strong thematic affinities with Kafka, insofar as here too socio-political and ethical failures entail biological consequences. The three life-size figures, virtually naked, are deprived of sense perception, but their bodies have been split open for inspection. They are missing mouths, ears, genitals, and spine, but are still endowed with a powerful physique and a muscular torso — spineless creatures, in other words, who look quite capable of perpetrating violence, but seem disinclined to prevent it: their active or passive participation in oppression, their perpetration or toleration of violence, is slowly transforming these fraying figures into subhuman monsters. Disintegration and metamorphosis here negotiate between the spheres of ethics and aesthetics: the loss of standards, the inability or unwillingness to stand up for what is just and right, deforms identity, and the subjects mutate into a subhuman condition. The Butcher Boys are apocalyptic creatures, yet both here and in Alexander's *oeuvre* more generally, the metaphysical, so insistently alluded to, is ultimately cancelled out. Her apocalyptic visions do not point us to a beyond, but to hell on earth. Her 'forsaken people' are the products of a human-made inferno — as well as agents within it, even though their free will and dignity are severely compromised through injustice and violence. Alexander employs metamorphosis to represent and condemn the human capacity to inflict suffering on others, to torture and oppress, as well as to show the deforming consequences of these practices for the perpetrator.

Fig. 11. Jane Alexander, 'Butcher Boys' (1985–86)
Reinforced plaster, oil paint, animal bones, horns, wood; 128.5 × 213.5 × 88.5 cm
Collection of the South African National Gallery, Cape Town
Photograph: Mark Lewis
© Jane Alexander, reproduced by kind permission of the artist

In artistic movements, the figure of metamorphosis becomes the visual icon for the paradox of 'irrational knowledge', a knowledge that resides in the subconscious and is surreal, an alternative vision to the protocols of reality that shape our everyday life. Salvador Dalí (1904–1989), for instance, in his fluid dreamscapes depathologizes paranoia and ascribes to it a status as a normal dimension of human existence, a complementary status to rationality, and asserts irrational flux as an ineluctable dimension of being human.[56] More generally, the surrealists drew on creatures of Greek myth and figures from classical literature, in particular Attic tragedy, Ovid's *Metamorphoses*, and Apuleius' *The Golden Ass*, to evoke the mysterious, the erotic and the ecstatic, transgression, speed and mobility, and virtual existence.[57]

III. The Transformations of Science

With Genesis losing its cultural standing as the first and the last word on creation, new notions and narratives of metamorphic change came into vogue in the eighteenth and nineteenth centuries. These were the product of advances in science, and underwritten by science's displacement of religion as western civilization's preeminent venture for producing knowledge about the world.

The scientific paradigm is characterized by the systematic acquisition of knowledge of the physical world gained through empirical observation and the relentless testing of hypotheses through experimentation. It is premised on the transparency and communicability of knowledge, and embraces a 'mathematicalization' of physical events. As already observed, its underlying materialist ontology endows it with a scepticism that had eliminated a number of metamorphic and other supernatural possibilities. At the same time it is, in many respects, a more all-embracing and pervasive paradigm than it might at first appear to be. There is, for example, a scientific aesthetic — an idea popularized by Robert Hunt's *The Poetry of Science* (1848). And science would quickly acquire (or, perhaps better, inspire) its own mode of fantasy, in the form of the literary genre of science fiction. This is a genre of speculative ideas and 'thought experiments', with anti-anthropocentric tendencies, that places a premium on the plausibility of its scientific and technological extrapolations.[58] It was through science fiction, above all, that transformative change would stage its triumphant return from literary exile.[59]

Like science itself, science fiction is premised on 'the necessity and possibility of explicit, coherent, and immanent or non-supernatural explanation of realities'.[60] For Suvin what differentiates science fiction from supernatural genres (mythical tales, fairy tales, fantastic literature) is 'the presence of scientific cognition as the sign or correlative of a method (way, approach, atmosphere, sensibility) identical to that of a modern philosophy of science'.[61] He takes a purist's hard line (perhaps too hard a line) in asserting that it is 'intrinsically or by definition impossible for science fiction to acknowledge any metaphysical agency, in the literal sense of an agency going beyond *physis* (nature)'.[62] Whenever it does so, in Suvin's view, it should not be classified as science fiction, but rather as a metaphysical or supernatural fantasy tale.

In 1771 the Italian scientist Luigi Galvani discovered, by investigating the effect of electricity on dissected animals, the electrical activity of the nervous system, thereby establishing the crucial relationship between electricity and life.[63] Galvani's research led to a radical reconception of electricity: it was no longer merely a phenomenon of the external world, but was now implicated in the physical constitution and vitality of organic life forms, human beings included. This breakthrough led to widespread speculation about what came to be known as *galvanism*, or animation through electricity. Many scientists believed until well into the Victorian Age that the suitable application of electricity to the brain of a corpse would revive it for a short period. Galvanism thereby became, for a time, a key 'scientific' descendant of a crucial demiurgic metamorphic capacity ascribed to gods in ancient myth and Christianity.

The fictional application of this idea to the generation of a new life form appears a few decades later in Mary Shelley's masterpiece *Frankenstein or the Modern Prometheus* (1818). Shelley's novel, often identified as the earliest work of science fiction, is very much a meditation upon recent scientific advances, with galvanism holding pride of place.[64] Galvani's discovery is signalled when Dr Frankenstein reminisces about 'a man of great research in natural philosophy [... who] entered on the explanation of a theory which he had formed on the subject of electricity and galvanism, which was at once new and astonishing to me' (vol. I, ch. 2). Although the precise means by which Frankenstein creates new life is necessarily somewhat vague, the reference to the 'spark of being' (vol. II, ch. 5) that animates the assemblage of body parts clearly signals galvanism.

A suggestive feature of the novel is Shelley's choice of Prometheus as her classical archetype for generating a human being,).[65] Prometheus' activity as creator was a challenge to Jovian authority, for which he endured (in some versions) everlasting torture. Victor Frankenstein, Shelley's modern Prometheus, likewise strives after divine prerogatives. In his Faustian quest for knowledge and power he seeks to originate a new life form:

> Life and death appeared to me ideal bounds, which I should first break through, and pour a torrent of light into our dark world. A new species would bless me as its creator and source; many happy and excellent natures would owe their being to me. No father could claim the gratitude of his child so completely as I should deserve theirs. (*Frankenstein*, vol. II, ch. 4)

As Bloom has well observed, Frankenstein embodies a concept of scientific practice that Mary Shelley deplored, namely 'the notion that science should manipulate and control rather than describe, understand and revere nature.'[66] Here we have the scientist as metamorphic agent — and the genesis of the literary figure of the 'mad scientist'. It is precisely the reckless impulse to manipulate and transform (rather than merely observe) nature that defines this stock character, of which Dr Frankenstein is the archetype. Shelley writes of 'unhallowed arts' (vol. II, ch. 8), and *Frankenstein* is in no small part an ethical exploration of the limits of human knowledge and power. It is also a cautionary tale, inasmuch as Victor Frankenstein's initial objectives are largely benevolent: 'to banish disease from the human frame, and render man invulnerable to any but a violent death' (vol. I, ch. 2).

Frankenstein touches on both scientific hubris and a failure of Promethean paternity. Here it is important to recall that the creature of Shelley's novel is not, as in its later Hollywood incarnations, bestial and inarticulate. The new being constructed from assorted human body parts is essentially humanoid: it shows its humanity in desiring to participate in human society and culture. It acquires a human sensitivity and dignity, and develops a prodigious intelligence. It learns to speak and acquires literacy, reading various literary classics — including Plutarch's *Lives*, Milton's *Paradise Lost*, and Goethe's *The Sorrows of Young Werther* — which it uses as a spur to its own intellectual and moral development. The terrible vengeance it exacts on its creator results from the latter's rejection and abandonment. In short, Dr Frankenstein's creature is not created a monster, but becomes one. Bloom well observes that 'The greatest paradox and most astonishing achievement of Mary Shelley's novel is that the monster is *more human* than his creator.'[67]

Its unattractive appearance notwithstanding, Frankenstein's creature is in nearly all respects endowed with abilities and capacities that exceed the human norm. In this Shelley inaugurates the science fiction idea of the 'superman', a characteristically tragic figure, whom science has equipped with superior abilities that threaten to eclipse the human race, or achieve its subjection. This prospect is explicitly aired by Frankenstein, and supplies a fundamental motivation for not providing the monster with a mate and enabling procreation:

> Even if they were to leave Europe, and inhabit the deserts of the new world, yet one of the first results of those sympathies for which the daemon thirsted would be children, and a race of devils would be propagated upon the earth, who might make the very existence of the species of man a condition precarious and full of terror. (*Frankenstein*, vol. III, ch. 3)

In post-Darwinian science fiction this idea would crystallize as the threat of evolutionary replacement.

Evolution

In the course of the Enlightenment, the Christian view of Creation as a singular metamorphic act came under the ever-increasing pressure of scientific observation. An exemplary figure in this paradigm shift is the Swedish botanist and zoologist Carl Linnaeus (1707–1778). Linnaeus initially held the firm conviction that God had created all the species by divine *fiat* in a single moment in time — the standard Christian view — and that no more could come into existence, whether by a new act of divine intervention, natural processes, hybridization, or any other means.[68] In his *Systema Naturae*, he famously declared *nullae species novae* ('no new species').[69] But this view of a zoomorphically static universe was gradually overturned in the eighteenth century by discoveries in fields like palaeontology and botany; and Linnaeus removed that declaration from the twelfth edition (1766). He came to accept that hybrids could be generated from the species that the Almighty had created.[70]

Several decades later, partly in response to Linnaeus, Johann Wolfgang von Goethe (1742–1832), a self-proclaimed polyhistor (*Universalgelehrter*), though today famous principally for his literary *oeuvre*, formulated a theory of metamorphosis as a natural principle of generation. He developed his understanding of nature through research in, above all, the field of botany. In 1790, he published the treatise *Versuch die Metamorphose der Pflanzen zu erklären*, and several years later composed a corresponding didactic elegy entitled *Die Metamorphose der Pflanzen* (1798), soon followed by *Die Metamorphose der Tiere* (1799), written in the same genre.[71] For Goethe, metamorphosis was the basic principle at work throughout the cosmos, underwriting and informing the development of both natural and cultural entities and formations.[72] Insight into the principle of metamorphosis was held to explicate the laws of nature that manifest themselves in the transformative change that all flora and fauna undergo, from conception to maturity and death. His theory of metamorphosis, so Goethe thought, enabled a hermeneutics of depth that penetrated to the principle of life informing the infinite variety of living forms. And Goethe extended the principle to human nature and human consciousness, culture, and civilization.[73] The history of the reception of his theory, especially in the arts, is phenomenal.[74] Later ages, particularly in the German-speaking world, would regard Goethe's works on metamorphosis as important Romantic precursors to Darwin.[75]

Another important precursor to Darwin is the Chevalier de Lamarck (1744–1829), whose *Philosophie Zoologique* (1809), a treatise on evolutionary philosophy, anticipates some elements of *The Origin of Species* (1859), and is emblematic for the Christianity–Science watershed. Lamarck was the first to advance a fully coherent evolutionary theory. He proposed that the environment gives rise to changes in animals, and noted the tendency of organisms to become more complex over time, ascending, as it were, a ladder of progress. He referred to this phenomenon as 'le pouvoir de la vie' or 'la force qui tend sans cesse à composer l'organisation' ['the power of life' or 'the force that perpetually tends to produce order'] (*Philosophie Zoologique*, p. 127).

Such precursors notwithstanding, the decisive watershed in scientific conceptions of change occurred midway through the nineteenth century with Charles Darwin's theory of evolution. There are, to be sure, continuities with earlier thought.[76] But this should not obscure the fact that Darwin's ideas represent something qualitatively new. *The Origin of Species* (1859) is a landmark work of science that dramatically redefined for the modern world the terms of discussion for transformative change.

Darwin is *the* crucial figure in the modern reconception of metamorphosis. He is responsible for decisively overturning the Christian tenet of zoomorphic stability by demonstrating that species evolve over time, and that they do so according to the principle of 'natural selection'. That is to say, mutations occur randomly in individual creatures, but only those that are advantageous, that improve 'viability', will influence, over time, the form of the species in question. *The Origin of Species* thus authenticates the notion of transmutation of the form of all animals, albeit on a very different time-scale than that of a typical tale of transformative change. If one takes the long view, then, bodily transformation is natural rather than supernatural: 'biological evolution is natural metamorphosis'.[77]

The Darwinian notion of evolution forced a fundamental paradigm shift. Natural science no longer called for the study of Nature's animate elements as so many fixed species or biological objects. Nature was now reconceived as process — that is, as a ceaseless and eternal experiment in zoomorphic transformation. All planetary life forms were henceforth seen as united in a single chain of being, with *Homo sapiens* merely the current apex of an ongoing procedure that began with the emergence of single-celled plasma many millions of years ago.

As already noted, one of the consequences of Darwin's scientific breakthrough was to reposition humanity itself, to reconceptualize *Homo sapiens* not as the transcendent term of a fixed and divinely imposed zoomorphic scheme, but rather as one more, probably transient, stage in nature's ongoing evolutionary story. Being human was by implication stripped of its sanctity — and its teleological finality. This anti-anthropocentrism is expressed with particular eloquence by Margulis and Sagan in the preface to the second edition of *Microcosmos: Four Billion Years of Evolution from Our Microbial Ancestors*. The authors make it their primary objective to strip away the aggrandizing self-image of the human race, to overturn the dictum of Protagoras that 'Man is the measure of all things'.[78] *Homo sapiens* is characterized more humbly as a 'latter-day permutation in the ancient and on-going evolution of the smallest, most ancient, and most chemically versatile inhabitants of the Earth, namely, bacteria.'[79] The principles of evolutionary theory thus make it possible to conceive of the posthuman as an essentially natural process: the human race could — and in all probability will — go the way of the dinosaur.[80]

The cultural impact of Darwinism would prove to be profound and enduring. Popular scientific works brought to public consciousness the multiplicity of bizarre and exotic life forms in the natural world that had been a particular focus of Darwin's research. The German naturalist Ernst Haeckel, whose *Natürliche Schöpfungsgeschichte* (1868; translated into English as *The History of Creation* in 1876) did much to popularize Darwin's theories, subsequently published *Kunstformen der Natur* (1899–1903), which included 100 colour illustrations of species from protozoa to exotic tropical birds. This served as a veritable handbook for the *Jugendstil* art movement, with its rich proliferations of swirling mineral, plant, and animal forms.[81] The movement is nothing less than a visual celebration of Nature's limitless capacity for zoomorphic variation — that is, for metamorphosis in the *longue durée*.

Darwin's theory also drives the development of science fiction, not only shaping the imagery deployed in representing the past and future of humankind, but also providing guidelines for the estimation of the nature of alien life. In the post-Darwinian literary imagination, moreover, metamorphosis becomes almost inextricably intertwined with Darwinian theory; the metamorphic imaginary henceforth has a distinctly evolutionary valence.[82] As already noted, evolution came to be treated as a kind of massively decelerated process of metamorphosis.[83] In literature (and in film as well) this gives rise to an important subgenre of science fiction, so-called 'evolutionary fantasy'.[84]

The fiction of H. G. Wells remains among the most brilliant and striking literary responses to Darwinism.[85] Two works in particular call for our attention: *The Time Machine* (1895), and *The Island of Dr Moreau* (1896). The former is a science fiction novella that features as its hero a British gentleman-scientist who is never named, but is referred to simply as the Time Traveller. The story initially unfolds over consecutive weekly dinner parties, hosted by the unnamed protagonist. In the first he reveals to his guests a newly invented device that permits time travel; in the second he reports on his use of it. His initial journey takes him to 802,701 AD. There he encounters two species, the Eloi and the Morlocks, evidently the complex product of a socially conditioned bifurcation in human evolution.[86] The delicate and effete Eloi have evolved from the upper classes; the bestial, subterranean Morlocks from the proletariat. The two species are the product of a 'natural' evolution from the protagonist's own time. Thus, the device of time travel permits the hero and the reader to experience the evolution of the human race over 800 millennia as an essentially instantaneous metamorphosis, rather than a lengthy process unfolding in deep time. In a striking effect, rarely matched by Wells' many imitators, the transformations of the Earth's surface and environment wrought by natural processes and its human inhabitants are visually apprehended by the Time Traveller:

> The landscape was misty and vague. I was still on the hill-side upon which this house now stands, and the shoulder rose above me grey and dim. I saw trees growing and changing like puffs of vapour, now brown, now green; they grew, spread, shivered and passed away. I saw huge buildings rise up faint and fair, and pass like dreams. The whole surface of the earth seemed changed — melting and flowing under my eyes. (*Time Machine*, ch. 3)

In his second voyage, the Time Traveller proceeds millions of years into the future, and witnesses the expiration of the earth's ecosystem and complex life forms:

> So I travelled, stopping ever and again, in great strides of a thousand years or more, drawn on by the mystery of the earth's fate, watching with a strange fascination the sun grow larger and duller in the westward sky, and the life of the old earth ebb away. At last, more than thirty million years hence, the huge red-hot dome of the sun had come to obscure nearly a tenth part of the darkling heavens. Then I stopped once more, for the crawling multitude of crabs had disappeared, and the red beach, save for its livid green liverworts and lichens, seemed lifeless. (*Time Machine*, ch. 9)

Wells' choice not to name the protagonist is a device that has an important over-arching effect, as Suvin observes:

> The Time Traveller is a generic representative of *Homo sapiens*, an Everyman defined in terms of biological rather than theological classification, as a species-creature and not as a temporarily embodied soul. The medieval Everyman was an immortal soul in a mortal body; the principle of individuation was saved. Symmetrically but inversely, the Darwinist Everyman is a quasi-immortal species (germ-plasm) in a mortal body. The principle of individuation is lost. But quasi-immortal is not immortal: even the generic principle could get lost, and biology is full of cautionary tales about dominant species or whole orders (such as the giant reptiles, significantly absent in *The Time Machine* though a staple of much science fiction since Jules Verne's *Journey to the Centre of the Earth*) that disappeared in the depths of geological time.[87]

The Time Machine is Wells' most fully articulated, and most seminal, response to Darwinism. It offers the vision of a chronologically distant future in which the human race has given way to other life forms. In this it is also an important, almost inaugural, foray into the posthuman. In retrospect it can be seen to have set the agenda for much subsequent science fiction.[88]

Scarcely less important in Wells' oeuvre is *The Island of Dr Moreau* (1896), in which the titular character uses his highly developed surgical abilities to effect excruciating, and excruciatingly modern, metamorphoses, creating new hybrid and quasi-human species by vivisection. The novella, which appeared one year after *The Time Machine*, has been well characterized as 'a seminal narrative of technoscientific modernity and its discontents'.[89] It describes a stark, even brutal, instance of a technologically and scientifically empowered humanity arrogating to itself the power of creator.[90] Like Shelley's Dr Frankenstein, Moreau is a developed instance of the 'mad scientist', a diabolical metamorphic agent given to transforming, rather than merely observing the natural world. This contrast is subtly brought out in Moreau's disdainful words to the narrating character Prendick:

> 'It may be, I fancy, that I have seen more of the ways of this world's Maker than you; for I have sought his laws, in my own way, all my life, while you, I understand, have been collecting butterflies.' (*Island of Dr Moreau*, ch. 14)

There is a Promethean undercurrent to Moreau's activity: he describes his creatures as having been 'moulded' (ch. 14). He proceeds on the assumption that scientific advances, and Darwinian theory in particular, have rendered God's creativity redundant.[91] This is a comprehensive position: in addition to the outward form of an animal, he has acquired the ability to transform physiology and 'chemical rhythm'. Wells thus imaginatively anticipates the kinds of experimentation with and applications of recombinant DNA (i.e. genetically engineered DNA, usually involving combinations from multiple species) that have flourished since the 1970s. No less striking is Moreau's challenge to the essentialist view of 'being human'. The motley collection of 'Beast People' that arise from Moreau's surgical experimentation are subsequently made capable of rudimentary speech and demonstrate other human capacities, including collective ritual. He explains that

> '[...] the possibility of vivisection does not stop at a mere physical metamorphosis. A pig may be educated. The mental structure is even less determinate than the bodily. In our growing science of hypnotism we find the promise of a possibility of superseding old inherent instincts by new suggestions, grafting upon or replacing the inherited fixed ideas. Very much indeed of what we call moral education', he said, 'is such an artificial modification and perversion of instinct.' (*Island of Dr Moreau*, ch. 14)

This is a subtly anti-anthropocentric position, a non-essentialist view of 'being human', an undermining of the long-standing Western philosophical and religious view of humanity as radically different from all other planetary species. As noted earlier, one consequence of Darwinism was to diminish the once seemingly unbridgeable chasm between *Homo sapiens* and all other members of the animal kingdom.

In *The Island of Dr Moreau*, then, Wells offers a chilling account of a scientifically imposed upwards 'evolution': Moreau 'stamped the human form' on various species of animal (ch. 15). But this is followed by a seemingly ineluctable devolution. Moreau himself laments that 'As soon as my hand is taken from them the beast begins to creep back, begins to assert itself again' (ch. 14). Here Suvin well observes:

> Dr Moreau's fashioning of humans out of beasts is clearly analogous to the pitiless procedures of Nature and its evolutionary creation. He is not only a latter-day Dr Frankenstein but also a demonically inverted God of Genesis, and his surgically humanized Beast Folk are a counterpart of ourselves, semibestial humans.[92]

As with the creature of *Frankenstein*, Wells' Beast People are inserted into a space they share with a human collective (albeit a minimal one) and a good deal of pathos arises from their unsuccessful efforts to achieve social inclusion, to gain acceptance from their human creator. Moreau characterizes them to Prendick as 'a travesty of humanity' and declares 'I take no interest in them' (ch. 14). As an alienated and non-uniform collective, these creatures form their own social hierarchy according to physical proximity to the human form — those few with five digits regarded as superior to those with less. And they collectively 'perform' their humanity through the ritual chanting of articles of 'The Law', a series of prohibitions against instinctual animal behaviour (walking on all fours, hunting and eating the flesh of their prey, etc.) that Moreau embeds in their psyche via hypnosis before letting them loose on the island. As Clarke observes,[93]

> The most prescient stroke of the narrative is the way the Beast people suffer en masse their promotion to and relapse from a marginal humanity. [...] [T]he cruelest twist of the narrative lies in the way that Dr Moreau ultimately forecloses the Beast Peoples' desires — posed in the rhetorical question of their pitiful chant 'Are we not men?' — by his persuasion to the contrary. Had he held faith with his own creations, as it were — had he lived up to his own Promethean aspirations — that alternative persuasion might have tipped the scales in the other direction.

Instead, the novella ends in 'an apocalyptic cascade of reverse metamorphoses'.[94]

With *The Island of Dr Moreau*, Wells gives us transformative change in a modern, scientific key. Its topical verisimilitude resides in its 'knowledgeable depiction and intermingling of vivisection and devolution, those hot-button, scientific-ethical issues of the Victorian fin-de-siècle.'[95]

Up to this point we have considered the impact of Darwin's theory of evolution in creating a new conception of nature as process, as intrinsically metamorphic. But the scientific picture was as yet unfinished. Although Darwinian thought continued to hold a preeminent position in both science and culture, the theoretical model remained tantalizingly incomplete for the better part of a century. What was lacking was a grasp of the mechanism of transformation, that is, the precise means by which nature generated variations or mutations. The missing piece of the puzzle was supplied in 1927 by Wilhelm Müller, who showed that exposure to radiation promoted mutation in fruit flies. This was a momentous discovery that has continued to resonate in popular culture. In fantasy as much as in fact, radiation has become a primary agent of mutation and change, a crucial and defining element in the modern reconception of metamorphosis. In *Starship Troopers* (1959), for example, Robert Heinlein ingeniously acknowledges its fundamental importance by considering the consequences of its absence, describing a popular resort-planet called Sanctuary, which is 'like Earth, but retarded' thanks to low radiation levels:

> With its evolutionary progress held down almost to zero by lack of radiation
> and a consequent most unhealthily low mutation rate, native life forms on
> Sanctuary just haven't had a decent chance to evolve and aren't fit to compete.
> Their gene patterns remained fixed for a relatively long time; they aren't
> adaptable — like being forced to play the same bridge hand over and over again
> for eons, with no hope of getting a better one. (*Starship Troopers*, p. 155)

But fictional extrapolations of the effects of radiation are rarely so sanguine. Here
we touch on a remarkable imaginative conjunction. Since the identification of
radiation as nature's mechanism for producing mutations, the emergence of nuclear
technologies, in both the military and civic spheres, has significantly increased the
risks of radiation exposure at all levels. This unsettling reality — made even more
fearful by the invisibility of radiation — drives the 'teratological imagination' of
much of twentieth-century science fiction.

Accidental Mutation

A troubling metamorphic possibility, then, arising above all from human experimentation with or exploitation of nuclear fission, is inadvertent or accidental
transformation. In literature this is frequently framed as the product of a kind of
'technological hubris'; such cautionary themes have become increasingly popular,
and poignant, in a post-Hiroshima world. The later twentieth- and early twenty-
first-century fascination with the monstrous, and the new plausibility afforded its
physical instrumentalization may be linked to the historical emergence of a 'post-
nuclear sensibility'.[96]

The possibility of consequential alterations to an organism's genetic code through
non-fatal exposure to radioactivity became a stock guiding premise for many
post-World War II films. *The Incredible Shrinking Man* (1957) and *The Attack of the
Fifty-Foot Woman* (1958) are two well-known Hollywood entries in the field, with
each titular character undergoing the indicated transformation of scale as a result
of radiation exposure. Here we see sinister modern metamorphic reinscriptions
of fantasy motifs familiar from Jonathan Swift's *Gulliver's Travels*. Modulations
of scale, then, dominate the comparatively muted teratological approach of post-
Hiroshima American cinema.[97] But more extravagant notions quickly prevail in
other spheres.

In the 1960s the mutation fantasy develops in an oddly positive (or mostly
positive) direction among American comic book writers, who developed a number
of superheroes whose extraordinary powers are the result of (usually accidental)
radiation exposure.[98] Here we have a veritable mutant chic, a privileging of terato-
logically deviant forms over the conventional version of the human being. Perhaps
the most pertinent for a study of metamorphosis is the Hulk, created by comic book
writer Stan Lee and illustrator Jack Kirby. The Hulk comes into being when the
scientist Bruce Banner suffers accidentally radiation exposure, and is consequently
transformed into a huge green raging beast with immense physical strength. The
Hulk is a humanoid monster — although greatly enlarged and chromatically altered,
it retains a recognizable human form. A striking detail, quite unusual among comic

book superheroes, is that the metamorphosis is not permanent: the monster emerges whenever Banner is aroused in some fashion, but only for a time: the human features and character eventually reassert themselves. As Packer observes,[99]

> The Hulk is a Jekyll and Hyde-type of character who retains a painful memory of his past, his pre-exposed, pre-metamorphosed self. But he has no control over his transformation, other than to take measures to prevent the adrenergic overload that triggers his transformation. He cannot get angry. He cannot get sexually aroused. He cannot have a full love affair. The Hulk is a sad monster.

An important difference, though, resides in the respective shifts in scale. Stevenson's Hyde is physically smaller than Jekyll, and this has prompted critics to see the monstrous figure as representing something 'inside' the man himself — some manner of negative psychological content. The Hulk, by contrast, is a physically enhanced version of his human form. It is also significant that *The Hulk* involves a kind of pseudo-scientific 'update' of *Jekyll and Hyde*. Whereas Stevenson, as noted earlier, was obliged to remain vague about the impure chemicals that constituted the metamorphic agent, the storyline of *The Hulk* offers a full (albeit implausible) explanation: the reversible mutation is caused in the first instance by radiation exposure and specific instances are triggered by the onset of an excited physiological condition.

A non-radioactive instance of catastrophic accidental transformation of the human genetic code is supplied by *The Fly*, a 1958 film, now better known through David Cronenberg's superb 1986 remake.[100] The basic premise of both films is that a scientist becomes accidentally hybridized with a fly in the course of teleportation experiments. This results from the insect's unnoticed presence in the teleporting chamber with the scientist. Cronenberg himself has characterized his version of *The Fly* as an updating of the 1958 original in the light of intervening scientific advances — a 'DNA re-think'.[101] Technically speaking, this entails reframing the accident as an unintended transgenosis — that is, the introduction of exogenous genes into an organism and their subsequent 'expression' in that organism. In one of the film's most devastating scenes, the computer system that manages the teleportation reveals to the protagonist that he and the fly have been 'fused at the molecular-genetic level'.[102]

Croneberg's attempt to capture and represent a physiological dynamic of transformation — the 'expression' of the exogenous genes — is a striking improvement over the earlier film, which does not treat this in any depth, simply having the scientist emerge from the teleportation mishap with a fly head and claw (Fig. 12). Cronenberg's remake, by contrast, has the metamorphic consequences emerge over several weeks, in an increasingly grotesque fashion. Another consequence of the 'DNA rethink' is that the metamorphic mishap does not result in a 'clean' mixture of well delineated insectile and human body parts, but rather involves a molecular fusion that manifests itself in systemic changes (Fig. 13). The two films thus display very different approaches to the notion of hybridity metamorphosis.

In Cronenberg's version, the initial effects of the teleporting disaster seem largely positive: Seth Brundle, the scientist, discovers that he has gained enhanced physical strength and athletic ability (which he promptly puts to use in Herculean feats of arm-wrestling and sexual intercourse). In his ignorance of the metamorphic calamity

Fig. 12 and 13. Above: *The Fly*, 1958, dir. Kurt Neumann
Below: *The Fly*, 1986, dir. David Cronenberg

that has already befallen him, Brundle deems his increased physical capacity to arise from a purifying effect inherent in the teleporting experience.[103] But things begin to unravel soon thereafter, as the initially invisible genetic fusion manifests itself and the disturbing transgenic hybridity of 'Brundlefly' (the scientist's wry term for the blended creature he has become) becomes manifest. Indeed, Brundlefly does not reach a point of equilibrium, but progressively becomes more fly and less Brundle, shedding human attributes and body parts over time. The metamorphosis is not merely physical: Brundle is tragically aware of the gradual overpowering of his human nature. This is made clear by his ingenious exposition on the nonexistence of 'insect politics', used to warn Veronica, his erstwhile female companion, of the threat he will pose for her as his insect nature becomes dominant.[104] This plays out as a tragic, drawn-out case of 'devolution'.[105]

As the scientist Seth Brundle becomes more fly-like in physical terms, he gradually takes on fly-like behavioural traits. Perhaps most notoriously, he starts involuntarily vomiting an acidic liquid on food before ingesting it (Fig. 13) — an authentic physiological detail.[106] But if this is a sign of the protagonist's devolutionary progress, his 'becoming-insect', it also becomes a sign of human adaptivity. Near the end of Cronenberg's film, 'Brundlefly' uses this liquid as a weapon, projectile-vomiting onto a human adversary to devastating, limb-dissolving effect. This attests to a residual intelligence in 'Brundlefly', who is able to exploit a reflexive digestive mechanism as a combat weapon. It is a brilliant, if grotesque, embodiment of the hybridity metamorphosis, showing human ingenuity allied with insectile physiology.

The fascinating complexity of Cronenberg's film derives from more than a mere scientific updating of the original film — one senses other influences as well, Kafka prominent among them. On the broad thematic level, both Kafka's *Die Verwandlung* and Cronenberg's *Fly* involve metamorphoses of their respective protagonists into oversized insects — and not insects with positive associations, but 'unwholesome' species that elicit involuntary human revulsion. The metamorphosis of Brundle into 'Brundlefly' is Kafka-esque in other fundamental respects, most significantly in its gradual psychological unfolding, the progressive encroachment of insectile instincts and emotions upon the subject's human psyche.[107] Cronenberg's film also shares with Kafka's novella an attention to physiological and environmental changes, such as the modifications in diet and the progressively deteriorating habitats, including odours offensive to humans, to which the metamorph is oblivious.

Clarke draws attention to a powerful moment in Cronenberg's film. Brundle has been using his computer system in a vain attempt to arrest or correct his devolutionary descent into bestiality. Because of the secretive nature of his research he had used voice recognition software as a means of data security. Some weeks after his metamorphic misadventure when Brundle attempts to access his computer system the security program replies with the devastating message: 'Voice not recognized'. As Clarke well observes, this is 'a cybernetic twist' on a key transformational moment of realization in classical metamorphic tales, 'that aphasic moment when the metamorph first tries to speak but can only, like Apuleius' Lucius, bray like an ass, or Kafka's Gregor, chirp like an insect ('Piepsen', ch. 1)'.[108]

For all its similarities to Kafka's *Die Verwandlung*, Cronenberg's film is at pains to establish a plausible scientific and technological basis for the metamorphic event. The mysterious and unelaborated physical metamorphosis that is the premise of Kafka's tale is now carefully embedded in a rationalized, scientific frame. Put another way, if Smith is right to insist that 'absurdist, existentialist literature, the type in which human beings are inexplicably transformed into cockroaches, does not qualify as science fiction', then *The Fly* is remarkable for achieving just such a generic transposition in its elaboration of Kafka's premise.[109]

Genetic Engineering

Advances in science (long since anticipated by science fiction) mark our entry into a new age of metamorphosis, in which the dominant agents of transformative change are not the supernatural forces of pre-modern times, nor even natural evolution, but a technologically empowered humanity that has gained control over the building blocks of life. The scientific decoding of these building blocks has resulted in an ever-increasing capacity to intervene and manipulate creation and reproduction through genetic engineering, putting 'real' transformative change on the agenda of modern civilization.

This situation was partially anticipated by H. G. Wells in his novel *The Food of the Gods* (1904). This is a cautionary tale that raises the spectre of *Homo sapiens* being supplanted by a fitter race of its own creation. The story features two British scientists, Redwood and Bensington, who collaborate in the discovery of a food that magnifies dramatically the growth patterns of infants. The result is a new race of human giants (and, by way of accident, rats and various insects including wasps, which in their magnified dimensions constitute a mortal threat to unaltered human beings). The scientists dub the metamorphic substance Herakleophorbia ('the food of Hercules'). The novel touches on the unintended results of science's blind pursuit of knowledge. This aggressive exploration is encapsulated in Bensington's secret testing of Herakleophorbia on his own infant son, who as a consequence grows up to be a giant. At length outbreaks of 'giganticism' become a global phenomenon, raising the prospect of the human race (along with other species of fauna and flora) being replaced by an over-sized version of itself, a species of 'supermen' (the allusion in the food's name to the greatest hero of antiquity, emphasizing strength more than size is not accidental). This idea is linked to Darwinian thought, with the colossi representing a scientifically induced mutation, a seemingly fitter species than the current version of the human race. Some two decades later, Bensington's son, now an adult giant, confides to his lover: 'We are at the beginning of the beginning [...]. My father believes, and I believe, that there will come a time when littleness will have passed altogether out of the world of man' (*Food of the Gods*, book III, ch. 2). Anxieties over the prospect of evolutionary displacement prompt the 'little people' to wage war on the giants; when the campaign comes to a standstill and negotiations are attempted the humans make two demands: that the giants live apart from regular humanity, and that they do not procreate. The giants, whom Wells consistently treats with sympathy, reject the latter demand, and the novel ends on an indeterminate note, with the giants preparing for further confrontation. *Food of the*

Gods reprises from Shelley's *Frankenstein* the science fiction idea of the 'superman', usually a tragic figure, whom science has equipped with superior abilities. In a Darwinian universe the threat such figures represent is nothing less than the eclipse of the human race — that is, its evolutionary replacement by a fitter version (or mutation) of itself.[110]

For all its imaginative brilliance, Wells' speculations about scientific advances in *Food of the Gods* pale before the techno-scientific reality of the present day. Simply put, the human race has put itself in a position to assert technological control over biological evolution. A pivotal scientific breakthrough came in 1953 when two scientists in Britain, Francis Crick and James Watson, deciphered the structure of DNA. Since then science has increasingly usurped supposed divine prerogatives in transforming existing life forms and generating entirely new ones.[111]

With the discovery that DNA sequencing variation constituted the essential mechanism for evolution, modern science has raised not so much the spectre as the promise of a new age of profound biological transformation. The close of the twentieth century saw the inception of the 'Genome Era', an evident supplanting of the 'Space Age' that marks a significant realignment of the priorities of the scientific community and the various agencies, both public and private, that fund its projects and research. The first major milestone of the new era was the publication, in 2001, of a 'working draft' of the human genome, that is, a genetic blueprint accounting for well over 99% of its roughly three billion base pairs. The sheer scale of the project, undertaken by an international consortium of scientists (with a biotechnology firm promptly setting itself up as a corporate rival) makes it one of the most successful collaborative research endeavours in human history. The symbolic, if fortuitous, timing of the working draft's publication underscores that the twenty-first century promises to be, at least initially, an 'era of biological transformation'.[112] According to one popular writer, biotechnology 'promises the greatest revolution in human history, [outdistancing even] atomic power and computers in its effects on our everyday lives'.[113]

Genetic engineering and cloning are already in our power. Human beings now possess the capacity to intervene in natural process and generate new species by reassembling the building blocks of life — by breeding fluorescent mice that feature a jellyfish gene, for example, which makes them glow in the dark; or by splicing human genes into pig genes in order to make the latter grow at a faster rate and to a larger size. Many hundreds of transgenic plants and animals have already been created through biotechnology. Much of this scientific activity is driven by economic imperatives.[114]

The newly acquired human capacity for transformation of animal species and the creation of new life forms comes with significant potential, as well as great attendant risk. Science fiction considers both. In *Starship Troopers* (1959), for example, Robert Heinlein imagines a genetically engineered improvement on 'man's best friend' in the 'neodog', an artificial creature endowed with rudimentary speech that is, as the narrating character explains, much more than just a dog that talks:

> A neodog is not a talking dog; he is not a dog at all, he is an artificially mutated
> symbiote derived from dog stock. A neo, a trained Caleb, is about six times as

> bright as a dog, say about as intelligent as a human moron — except that the
> comparison is not fair to the neo; a moron is a defective, whereas a neo is a
> stable genius in his own line of work. (*Starship Troopers*, p. 37)

As with canine units in contemporary police forces, the neodog is paired with a particular member of its military unit, and develops a very close bond:

> The emotional relationship between the dog-man and the man-dog in the K-9
> team is a great deal closer and much more important than is the emotional
> relationship in most marriages. If the master is killed, we kill the neodog — at
> once! It is all we can do for the poor thing. A mercy killing. (*Starship Troopers*,
> p. 37)

It is, however, more characteristic of science fiction tales to speculate about the generation of new life forms in a cautionary framework. Writers typically depict scientists playing with the building blocks of life without fully considering the potential consequences of their experimentation. Michael Crichton's novel *Jurassic Park* (1990) and its film version (1993) are among the most prominent recent warnings of the attendant perils of genetic engineering.[115] With *The Island of Dr Moreau* and *Food of the Gods*, H. G. Wells explored the theme of disaster brought about by scientists tampering with forms of organic life. Themes from both are reworked in *Jurassic Park*, with contemporary advances in genetics and biotechnology providing a concrete basis for Wells' unavoidable scientific vagueness. As in *Island of Dr Moreau*, Crichton places his protagonists on a remote island where a 'mad' scientific project develops over some years unknown to the rest of humanity.[116] On both islands, scientists develop new transgenic species — Moreau's assorted Beast People, Crichton's various species of dinosaurs — with no serious thought as to the potential consequences.[117] Both Moreau and Hammond demonstrate a casual hubris in their willingness to tamper with nature.[118] The results follow the paradigm of Shelley's *Frankenstein*, with the creatures going on the rampage, and killing their human creators. But the global threat to humankind posed by the proliferating dinosaur population in *Jurassic Park* differs from the more limited consequences in *Island of Dr Moreau*, and in this more resembles *Food of the Gods*.

IV. The Technological Posthuman

As discussed so far, the posthuman is a prospect and a category of thought that involves evolutionary replacement. The human race could be supplanted through the normal workings of nature, or, more diabolically, from a new species of its own creation that has been inserted into the natural order. But there is another, more radical version of the posthuman that involves technological advances and maintains a more tenuous contact with Darwinian principles. If the first prospect puts pressure on anthropocentric ideologies by casting doubt on the human–animal binary opposition, the latter tends to do so by calling into question the human–machine dichotomy.

Directly pertinent to the notion of the technological posthuman is the rise (or re-emergence) of materialist philosophy.[119] A central document belonging to this movement is *L'Homme Machine* (1748), by Julien Offray de La Mettrie, one of the earliest French Materialists of the Enlightenment. In *L'Homme Machine*, La Mettrie extends Descartes's argument that animals were automatons or machines to human beings, denying the existence of the soul as a substance separate from matter: 'the soul is merely a vain term of which we have no idea [that should be used] only to refer to that part of us that thinks' (*L'Homme Machine*, p. 26). La Mettrie has frequent recourse to the term 'mécanique' ('mechanical') in describing the functioning of the human organism, brain included. The human body is thus reconceived as an abstract machine. Implicit in this view is the impossibility of metamorphosis in the Ovidian sense of an alienated mind, of the substitution of bodies experienced by a stable psyche. The body–soul dyad does not pertain.

La Mettrie uses the notion of *ressorts* or 'springs' (in the mechanical sense: 'ressorts de la Machine humaine') to describe the microscopic internal mechanics of the human body that produce the various impulses of the human organism: 'l'Homme n'est qu' un [...] Assemblage de ressorts' ['Man is nothing but an assemblage of springs'] (*L'Homme Machine*, p. 128). The human body is likened to a clock (*horloge*), that remarkable achievement of mechanical miniaturization that was among the finest technological feats of the day.

The spectre of the technological posthuman is the flip-side, as it were, of the materialist physiology that denied the existence of the soul as a substance separate from matter. If, as La Mettrie argues, human beings, like animals, are automatons or machines, then there is, a priori, no reason why machines cannot become 'human'. Man as machine clearly raised the possibility of machine as man.

The twentieth-century French philosopher Georges Canguilhem has argued that a kind of primitive anthropomorphism underwrites all human technology. On this view every technological device, every machine, can be seen on some level as an imitation of the human organism. Canguilhem thereby affirms the priority of the organic over the technological in all respects, and sees the history of machines as a series of progressive approximations at reproducing the functions of the human organism. As Braidotti observes,

> All technologies become biotechnologies. Especially since the nineteenth century, Western culture has been faced with the promise or threat, of meta(l)morphoses, that is to say, a generic becoming machine. The great advantage of Canguilhem's technophilic bio-philosophy is that it paves the road for rethinking the symbiotic relationship between the human and the technological.[120]

To be sure, the evolving relationship between the human being and technology makes for a complex story, and one replete with ironies. Even if, as Canguilhem asserts, technology is fundamentally anthropomorphic in its impulses and structures, the inevitability of feedback loops means that influence is bidirectional. Simply put, humans are by no means exempt from the influence of the machines they create.

A crucial document in this history of mutual convergence, and one that has resonated with particular power for the better part of a century, is Charlie Chaplin's *Modern Times* (1936). This film uses the setting of the Fordist factory assembly line to show human beings suddenly made slaves to their own machines — or, perhaps better, reduced to a small element in the overall manufacturing mechanism. The

FIG. 14. *Modern Times*, 1936, dir. Charles Chaplin

objective is of course to maximize profit through maximizing productivity —
a goal that is achieved through a 'rationalization' of procedures that results in
dehumanizing 'mechanization' of the workers. A fundamental insight of *Modern
Times* is the convergence of human being and machine.[121] The factory workers are
assimilated to the mechanical by the necessity of repetitive physical actions. The
film's protagonist is even, in a celebrated scene that has become iconic, 'ingested' by
one of the machines (Fig. 14), thereby achieving a striking visual fusion of the human
body and its mechanized counterpart. As critics have frequently noted, Chaplin's
factory worker becomes, in metaphor as in reality, just one more machine part.

Modern science and technology hold out three principal prospects for a posthuman
organism, all long since anticipated in science fiction literature: the robot, the
android, and the cyborg. Since terminological slippage within these categories
is rampant, it will be as well to start with definitions.[122] A robot is an artificial
humanoid, made from inorganic (usually mechanical) components; an android is an
artificial humanoid constructed from synthetic biological components; a cyborg is a
merger of a normal human being with one or more mechanical systems.

Cyborgs

The term 'cyborg', first coined in 1960, is a contraction of 'cybernetic organism'.
It designates a life form with both organic and artificial — usually electronic and
mechanical — components. The broad project of cybernetics is the implementation

of such mergers with the aim of improving the functionality of the original organic life form. Though the latter may come from any species, in practice cybernetics has focused overwhelmingly on the technological enhancement of the human being. Cybernetics thus touches on the improvement, even the 'perfectibility', of the human body through transplants, implants and prosthetics. The resulting compound form is a collage, a mixture of organic and replaceable mechanical components, with the latter offering greater control over life and death, even raising the spectre of quasi-immortality.

The transformation of the human organism through human–machine hybridization is already well underway.[123] The advent of machine intelligence coupled with micro-circuitry and progress in biotechnology has made the cyborg a partial reality in the early twenty-first century.[124] Seismic shifts in the modern media environment anticipate those changes most characteristic of the cybernetic. Braidotti already speaks of the posthuman body, which is 'shot through with technologically mediated social relations. It has undergone a meta(l)morphosis and is now positioned in the spaces in between the traditional dichotomies, including the body–machine binary opposition'.[125] But this is just the beginning; in the view of many the future of the human species lies in a progressive movement away from organic embodiment, a transformative migration with uncertain, but no doubt far-reaching, consequences for the anthropocentric humanistic subject.

Cybernetic engineering, aiming at the construction of organisms that possess characteristics of both machines and living beings has thus emerged as a disciplinary domain focusing on postmodern metamorphosis.[126] It stands in a kind of complementary opposition to genetic engineering, as a rival technological strategy for positively transforming the human species (or subsets thereof), whether to make good functional deficiencies in the present environment, or, more speculatively, to prepare it for future environments.[127] Both disciplines demonstrate the Promethean imagination of humankind, its interest in altering the form and capacity of life forms, above all its own. Together they have brought humanity to the point where a posthuman condition has become an almost inevitable prospect, and one that continues to provoke a great deal of speculative discussion.[128] David Rorvik's *As Man Becomes Machine* (1971) represents an early milestone in such discussion, importantly heralding a new era of 'participant evolution'.

From its outset, science fiction has obsessively generated fantasies, many now on the verge of realization, of the manipulation and transformation of the human body by science and technology. The idea of the cyborg (though not the term itself) was developed with astonishing precocity in literature. Already Edward Page Mitchell's ingenious science-fiction fantasy *The Ablest Man in the World*, published in 1879, features a cyborg with a computer for a brain.[129] The titular character, Baron Savitch, born mute and retarded, and raised in a mental asylum, has been surgically transformed by Rapperschwyll, a Swiss doctor. The latter, relying on his knowledge of human physiology and psychology, along with a prodigious skill in watch making (an ingenious pre-digital anticipation of the miniaturization achieved by modern micro-circuitry), fashions and surgically implants in Savitch's cranium a mechanical brain.[130] This enhancement renders

Savitch vastly superior to normal human beings and sets him on a course for world dominion, until his brain is removed and destroyed by Fischer, the American hero of the story.

In television and film the cyborg is typically humanoid and barely distinguishable from ordinary human beings. Such cyborgs are almost invariably supermen, whether acting for good (as in the 1970s television *The Six Million Dollar Man*) or for evil (as in the *Terminator* film franchise).

Androids

The term 'android' originates in alchemical literature, where it was used in reference to the creation of artificial humans.[131] Its first literary use, in Villiers de l'Isle-Adam's *L'Ève future* (discussed below), is inconsistent with its now established usage as a designation for artificial humanoids made from organic rather than inorganic components.

Even more than other forms of artificial life, the android poses fundamental and searching questions about the essence of 'being human'. In works of science fiction, these questions are often driven by the difficulty, in some cases the impossibility, of distinguishing between individual human beings and androids, along with the often superior physical and mental capacities of the latter. Behind these questions lurk broader ethical concerns arising from the human exploitation of androids, which are typically produced as a servile species intended to enhance the material conditions of human existence.

Karel Čapek's play *R. U. R.* (1926) treats with astonishing precocity and comprehensiveness themes related to the android, and to biotechnology more broadly, themes that would eventually become central concerns of science fiction literature.[132] The elder Rossum, a scientist, discovers a process for organizing living matter that is faster and more versatile than that used by nature. After experimenting with simpler life forms, he sets his sights on constructing a fully complex humanoid species.[133] The younger Rossum, however, has other ideas and, driven by the lure of measureless profit, simplifies his father's design, removing 'unnecessary' human qualities such as creativity, emotions, even the experience of pain. As the character Domin explains:

> 'When [Young Rossum] took a look at human anatomy he saw immediately that it was too complex and that a good engineer could simplify it. So he undertook to redesign anatomy, experimenting with what would lend itself to omission or simplification [...]. He chucked everything not directly related to work, and in so doing pretty much discarded the human being and created the Robot. My dear Miss Glory, Robots are not people. They are mechanically more perfect than we are, they have an astounding intellectual capacity, but they have no soul. Oh, Miss Glory, the creation of an engineer is technically more refined than the product of nature.' (*R. U. R.* prologue, pp. 7–8)

This proves to be a successful capitalist venture (*R. U. R.* stands for the corporation *Rossum's Universal Robots*), with these androids — called 'robots' by Čapek (from Czech *robota*, meaning 'forced labour'); but this coinage has become inconsistent with subsequent usage — gradually taking over the burden of all human work, including military service. The play poignantly points to the degrading effects such a development, an industrialist's dream, would have on humanity.[134] The subservient 'Robots' in due course develop feelings of some kind — some apparently spontaneously, some through the surreptitious design alterations of Dr Gall — and rebel against their human masters.[135]

The android rebellion results in the extermination of the human race. The 'Robots' too face extinction since their lifespan is a mere twenty years, they are not capable of organic reproduction, and knowledge of Rossum's biotechnological procedure, a closely guarded industrial secret, has perished with the human race. This doubly apocalyptic conclusion is mitigated by the revelation that two of the 'Robots' have fallen in love, and may have become a kind of android Adam and Eve — that is to say, they hold out the prospect of a new, properly biological, moment of origin for their species, an insertion of the android into the natural order.

A complex cinematic vision of the biotechnological posthuman is offered by *Blade Runner* (1982), a 'neo-noire' film loosely based on Philip K. Dick's science-fiction novel *Do Androids Dream of Electric Sheep?* (1968).[136] The film is set in 2019, in a technologically advanced but dystopian Los Angeles whose urban landscape blends magnificent pyramidal corporate complexes, abuzz with aerial vehicles landing and departing, and slum-like districts with chaotic, garbage-strewn streets and decaying apartment buildings.[137] In this grim world of 'industrial imperialism', genetically engineered androids called 'replicants' are manufactured by the powerful Tyrell Corporation and one or two rivals. The latest version of Tyrell's android species, Nexus-6, is visually indistinguishable from human beings — the advertising slogan is 'more human than human' — and in many respects exhibits superior functionality. The androids, all physically individuated, are not only stronger and generally more attractive than human beings, but are also in many respects more intelligent.[138] At the same time, despite being made of biological materials, replicants are regarded as machines by their human owners and creators, and are employed for menial or dangerous work on off-world colonies.[139] Their presence on Earth is banned. Replicants who defy the ban and return to Earth are hunted down and eliminated by special operatives known as Blade Runners. The plot follows the actions of one such Blade Runner, Rick Deckard, as he tracks down a group of renegade replicants hiding in Los Angeles.

Both novel and film explore the ever-narrowing ontological divide between humans and androids, in a world in which exemplars of the latest replicant version, Nexus-6, are securely distinguishable from human beings only via a complex psycho-physiological examination, the Voigt-Kampff test.[140] That this is commonly referred to as an 'empathy test' makes for lingering irony, in that replicants consistently exhibit more sympathy and loyalty to one another than do the film's human characters. A central figure in *Blade Runner's* elaboration of this category confusion is Rachael, an experimental android who initially believes she is human, a delusion fed by the provision of extensive memory 'implants' that equip her with the memories of an actual human being. Revelation of the truth is emotionally wrenching for her.[141] In *Do Androids Dream of Electric Sheep?* the possibility is briefly raised that Deckard himself is an android. The film makes this a more persistent question — and one that has remained controversial thanks to the discrepant views of those most closely connected with the film. The actor playing Deckard (Harrison Ford) insisted that he was human; the director (Ridley Scott) thought of him as an android; the original screenwriter (Hampton Fancher) regarded the matter as ambiguous.

The film is not only more invested than Dick's novel in the exploration of human–android category confusion, but also more willing to entertain the possibility of the superiority of the non-organic creatures over their organic creatures. The implications of *Blade Runner*'s treatment of androids are far-reaching, and the implicit contrast with a degraded humanity significant. As Solomon observes, one message of the film appears to be that 'having created a dehumanized and dehumanizing civilization, modern humanity is losing faith in itself and beginning to dream of a new, unfallen, synthetic "humanity" that might takes its place. Perhaps humanoid machines will succeed where we have failed, *Blade Runner* intimates.'[142]

In the film Deckard accomplishes his mission through the assistance of Rachael who eventually falls in love with him, and the film ends with the human–android couple departing hand in hand to share a life together.[143] This revisits themes from Villiers de l'Isle-Adam's *L'Ève future*, discussed in more detail below, but with important differences. The French novel is interested primarily in the pheno-menological experience of a machine as 'human' — the robotic machine built by Edison is a mechanical reproduction of an existing human being, Lord Ewald's unworthy love object Alicia, with a full range of pre-programmed behaviours and responses. *Blade Runner* is more interested in the fundamentally ontological question of whether an android — and here it is no doubt important that these artificial beings are genetically engineered and 'organic' — can acquire a 'human nature', at what point it becomes intrinsically 'human'. The French novel and the Hollywood film are thus in the end asking different questions.

As Solomon observes, *Blade Runner* 'suggests that that there is something fascinating for postmodern culture in the prospect of designing creatures who are superior to their creators: robots whose intelligence dwarfs our own, and whose robotic bodies are stronger, and sexier, than anything nature can produce.'[144]

Robots

A crucial development in the late twentieth and early twenty-first centuries is the gradual migration of intelligence and sensory apprehension from human beings to machines.[145] This is a transformative trend with profound and far-reaching impli-cations.

In the twentieth century, of course, the intelligent robot emerged as a practical reality, with robotics emerging as a distinct and increasingly important techno-scientific discipline. The emphasis of robotics has largely shifted from mechanics to electronics. Arguably the first properly modern, digitally driven robot, was the 'Unimate', invented by George Devol in 1954, and put to work in a General Motors factory in 1961.

There has already been a great deal of speculation on how robots might act in society, to what degree they might be capable of moral apprehension, and what they should or should not be empowered to do. From the earliest imaginings, the intelligent robot has been a source of considerable human anxiety, as a potentially super-human, non-organic species created by human beings that might eventually supplant or destroy its creators. The source of that anxiety is the robot's perceived (or real) autonomy, their apparent agency. Here we touch once again on the existentialist fantasy, and the so-called 'Frankenstein complex'. An early alarmist warning was sounded by David H. Keller in his short story *The Threat of the Robot* (1929).[146]

Isaac Asimov is a central figure in this discussion, and an important counterweight to alarmist voices. His more sanguine views are found throughout his corpus, but particularly in various short stories that were eventually gathered in the collections *I, Robot* (1950) and *The Rest of the Robots* (1964). Asimov famously imagined that all robots would have encoded in their programming fundamental behavioural imperatives and restrictions, the so-called 'Three Laws of Robotics'. The most fundamental of these was an injunction against doing harm to human beings.[147]

One important vision of the technological posthuman carries an explicit evolutionary valence. The Austro-American scientist Hans Moravec, an expert in robotics and artificial intelligence, has suggested that the age of carbon-based life forms is coming to its end.[148] According to this view, scientific and technological advances are quickly propelling the planet to a point at which the human race will be supplanted by intelligent machines as the dominant terrestrial 'life-form'.[149]

Moravec is not the only one to see this possibility in essentially positive terms. Edith Milton, in her essay 'The Track of the Mutant', has piercingly observed that machines 'are now the icons of all our best qualities. Freed from human needs and greeds [...] our logical computer-selves [...] can develop epic amounts of decency.'[150] The possibility that machine nature could prove to be an improvement on human nature is already raised in Asimov's short-story collection.

The virtually intelligent robot first appears in literature in E. T. A. Hoffmann's short story *Der Sandmann* (1816, translated into English as *The Sandman*).[151] In this tale the protagonist Nathaniel, a university student, falls in love with Olympia, a robot passed off as the daughter of his physics professor Spalanzani. The latter presents Olympia to society at a lavish party, during which she plays the harpsichord, and dazzles all with her beauty, but otherwise disconcerts the guests by her stiff and strangely mechanical motions and the coldness of her touch. Whereas Olympia's limited speech — she repeatedly answers with the versatile ejaculation 'ah, ah!' — convinces the other guests of her limited mental capacity, Nathaniel reads it as a sign of her understanding. Some time later he resolves to propose to her, but discovers the truth when he comes upon Spalanzani arguing with his associate Coppola over who deserves credit for the construction of the robot's various components — including Olympia's eyes, which Nathaniel sees lying on the ground. This discovery drives Nathaniel mad: he is committed to an asylum for a time and, some time after his release, takes his own life.

A mere handful of years after Mitchell's *Ablest Man*, Villiers de l'Isle-Adam published *L'Ève future* (1886), a novel that features a much more capable robot than Hoffmann's Olympia, designed and constructed by a fictionalized Thomas Edison.

Edison's friend Lord Ewald, despairing of the shortcomings of his flesh-and-blood fiancée Alicia, takes up the inventor's offer to build him a perfect bride — of the mechanical variety — matching Alicia in all physical respects, but much 'improved' in disposition.[152] A striking feature of the tale, and one that complicates generic classification, is that the robot comes to house the spirit of the inventor's female assistant Sowana by a process of metempsychosis.[153] This touch of supernatural fantasy notwithstanding, *L'Ève future* is a decidedly precocious treatment of a popular science fiction motif in the later twentieth century, as well as the first literary work to use the term android (French *andréide*) — though it is used in reference to what would now properly be termed a 'robot'. In any event, this remarkable text is an important anticipation of the twentieth-century literary fascination with androids and robots. This interest finds its earliest cinematic expression in the demonic robot fashioned in the likeness of the heroine Maria in *Metropolis* (1927), Fritz Lang's masterpiece of silent film.[154]

Villiers blends two ancient myths of transformation here, those of Pygmalion and Prometheus. The figure of Lord Ewald, like Pygmalion, despairs of real women and happily accepts an artificial substitute. Edison, on the other hand, takes on the role of Prometheus. The inventor has already delivered a kind of Promethean fire to the human race in the form of electricity, and now sets about the business of fashioning pseudo-human beings.

Stanislaw Lem's ingenious satire *Cyberiad* (1967) offers a vision of the posthuman in which intelligent machines have transcended their human creators and displaced humanity from evolutionary pre-eminence. In this post-Darwinian narrative universe, evolution is no longer the product of random natural processes, no longer a matter of biology: it is now the product of technology. The new species of robots, arising from *Automatus Sapiens*, has its own version of Creation that expunges the messy biology of its organic antecedents:

> 'There are legends, as you know, that speak of a race of paleface, who concocted robotkind out of a test tube, though anyone with a grain of sense knows this to be a foul lie [...]. For in the Beginning there was naught but Formless Darkness, and in the Darkness Magneticity, which moved the atoms, and whirling atom struck atom, and Current was thus created, and the First Light [...] from which the stars were kindled, and then the planets cooled, and in their cores the breath of Sacred Statisticality gave rise to microscopic Protomechanoans, which begat Proteromechanoids, which begat the Primitive Mechanisms. These could not yet calculate, nor scarcely put two and two together, but thanks to Evolution and Natural Subtraction they soon multiplied and produced Omnistats, which gave birth to the Servostat, the missing Clink, and from it came our progenitor, Automatus Sapiens.' (*Cyberiad*, p. 200)

The spectre of the technological posthuman has penetrated into children's literature and cinema, as with the animated film *WALL-E* (Pixar Films, dir. Andrew Stanton, 2008). This computer-animated post-apocalyptic science fiction film, set in 2805, features as its protagonist a garbage-processing robot (of the type Waste-Allocation Load Lifter — Earth: whence WALL-E, pronounced 'Wally') that has acquired sentience at some point in his 700-year-career of cleaning up the heavily polluted planet Earth, almost totally devoid of complex life forms, and long since abandoned by the human race. Wall-e pursues a love interest with another robot, the suggestively named EVE (Extraterrestrial Vegetation Evaluator), whose assigned task it is to seek out surviving plant specimens. This mechanical couple help to re-establish plant and animal life on earth, while saving an indolent and conspicuously obese humanity stripped of agency and subjected to (essentially benign) domination by intelligent machines led by Auto (pronounced 'Otto') that have taken over all decision-making, along with industrial, regulatory, and service functions. In this film, as in *Blade Runner*, there is a sense that the robot protagonists are somehow more 'human' (in a conspicuously twentieth-century sense) than the examples of decadent humanity that the film initially presents. Wall-e and Eve, indeed, represent a residual and 'unfallen' humanity — a condition illustrated by the former's fondness for 1950s-era Hollywood musicals, the latter's none too subtle name, and their shared concern for and preservation of the few organic life forms they come across in their adventures. These humanized machines succeed where an indolent humanity has clearly failed. The radical implications of this dichotomy are, however, 'contained' by their pivotal role in assisting the human race to regain its autonomy and dignity through a return to Earth and the resumption of a wholesome, agricultural way of life.

Along with such visions of a more-or-less benign supplanting of the human race from global dominance, science fiction writers have frequently invoked the idea of a more revolutionary supersession, that is, a violent and abrupt 'takeover' by sentient machines.

This theme is developed in full in the *Terminator* film franchise, with computer systems gaining autonomy and rising against their human creators.[155] Prominent in the series is the Frankenstein's monster motif, which develops after the computer systems created by humankind acquire sentience and turn against their human creators, endeavouring to gain global mastery. The acquisition of autonomous consciousness is a metamorphosis belonging to the broad repertoire of 'existentialist fantasy' that is never adequately explained — attesting to an accepted convention, fuelled by anticipation of advances in artificial intelligence, as much as to the necessarily 'fuzzy' science underwriting such a transformation. Likewise the *Battlestar Galactica* television series, first aired in 1978, with four seasons of episodes over the period 2003–09 made this idea its founding premise. It begins with the destruction via nuclear weapons of a human civilization (distributed over a dozen planets known as The Twelve Colonies) by the Cylons, a robotic race created by human beings as mechanical servants.[156] As in the *Terminator* film franchise, the Cylons develop autonomous consciousness and then turn against their creators. Here, as in Lem's *Cyberiad*, there is a political idea adapted from Čapek's play *R. U. R.* (discussed above) — the rebellion of machines against the conditions of servitude under their human masters.

For completeness we should mention the extra-terrestrial posthuman: the idea that beings from other planets will attempt to destroy or supplant the human race. The idea of discovering other forms of life in the cosmos — and in particular 'intelligent' species, possibly more advanced than *Homo sapiens* — amount to one more challenge (albeit still a theoretical one) to the privileged status of humanity in the universe. The space invader theme receives its first literary articulation with H. G. Wells' *The War of the Worlds*, in which an advanced race of aliens from Mars, driven by the depleted biosphere of its own planet, attempts to conquer and colonize Earth.[157] This premise has been reworked countless times since. One variation on this idea is the 2007 science fiction film *Transformers*, based on the popular children's toy line of the same name. This Hollywood blockbuster, which spawned three sequels within six years of its theatrical release, narrates a war between the benevolent Autobots and the sinister Decepticons, two factions of an alien robot species, whose members, like so many post-industrial Proteuses, have the capacity endlessly to transmute themselves into different mechanical forms. The Decepticons seek control of AllSpark, the demiurgic entity that created their species, with which they intend to engineer a second robotic genesis by giving life to the machines on Earth, thereby mustering an unconquerable intergalactic army with which to dominate the universe.

But perhaps the most striking feature of *Transformers* is the easy assumption that machine-like entities can be sentient, living beings. The mechanical has become a plausible life form, attesting incidentally to the erosion of the machine–human distinction in the technological imaginary of the early twenty-first century.

The Chapters

In the foregoing pages, we have traced the impact of the scientific revolution in first applying pressure to, and then reconfiguring and raising to prominence notions of transformative change in the Western cultural imaginary. Though the onset of modernity seemed initially to herald the dawn of a 'post-metamorphic' age, subsequent increases in the metamorphic powers of humanity have ensured that transformative change has remained on the agenda — has, indeed, re-emerged as an urgent concern of contemporary culture. The four chapters that follow all broaden and deepen our understanding of this complex story — across a wide range of distinctly modern media and genres, including the novel, horror stories, war fiction, and Hollywood film. In Chapter 9 '"Our Mind Is the Ancient Proteus": Proust, the Poets, and the Sea', Francesca Spiegel considers in detail a passage from Proust's *A la recherche du temps perdu*, which offers an elaborate illustration of how a modern author of the first rank both acknowledges conventional metamorphosis as one of the 'things past' and revalidates the concept as a heuristic device to explore key aspects of his culture. Spiegel shows how Proust plays with the dubious ontological status of (imaginary) metamorphosis to capture and negotiate his world and its problems (such as differences in class and social status), while at the same time entering into a dialogue with the classicizing predecessors of the Parnassian literary movement. In Chapter 10, '"Horror in a Covered Platter": H. P. Lovecraft and the Transformation of Petronius', Luke Pitcher serves up a reminder that Ovid and Apuleius are by no means the only Latin authors who explore the possibilities of transformative change. In his obsession with various modes of food processing in his *Satyrica* more generally and the stomach-churning glory of the *cena Trimalchionis* ('the Dinner of Trimalchio') in particular, Petronius has clearly offered several modern authors much food for thought. But while his intertextual presence in

T. S. Eliot and F. Scott Fitzgerald has received attention from literary scholars, the revolting use that the horror-writer H. P. Lovecraft makes of Petronius still awaits critical recognition: it is a particularly lurid instantiation of the anxiety of influence — i.e. the phenomenon that authors try to displace, kill, or, indeed, cannibalise their predecessors. Thematically, Lovecraft's deliberate blurring of the interface between (degenerate) humans and swine in the context of food processing and meat consumption has interesting affinities with the hyperrealist sculptures of the contemporary Australian artist Patricia Piccinini: both author and artist draw attention to the potential monstrosities that ensue once the distinction between human and animal collapses — either because humans degenerate into animals (as in Lovecraft) or animals are recognized as quasi- human (as in Piccinini). In Chapter 11, 'Transforming the Experience of War in the Fiction of Marcel Aymé, René Barjavel and Michel Tournier', Christopher Lloyd demonstrates how modes of transformative change retain their power of illumination in the strongly realist aesthetic of twentieth-century French novelists. His main theme is the horror of industrialised warfare and its transformative impact on humanity. Specifically, he identifies and discusses the presence of 'fantastic' elements in the oeuvres of his chosen authors, not least as a (futile) means of escape from the brutal realities of war. Lloyd's theoretically sophisticated analysis further illuminates key texts and categories of transformative change in a 'post-metamorphic' age, such as the fantastic, science fiction, and Kafka's *Die Verwandlung*. In the concluding Chapter 12, 'The Parabola Paradox: Transformation and Science Fiction', Sarah Annes Brown explores how science fiction reflects upon and critiques various forms of trans-humanist, indeed trans-human, striving. She shows that the human desire to be transformed 'upwards' — into semi-divine, or at least posthuman creatures — continues to attract ambivalent, if not outright negative appraisals in the contemporary cultural industry: the prospect of a collective improvement of the human species is often presented as a story of ultimate loss, in which humanity comes to resemble insects, in particular ants.

Notes to the Introduction

1. Braidotti (2002), pp. 178–79.
2. The subversive implications of Darwinism for the contemporary world-view are perhaps less evident in the predictable resistance of some members of the scientific community than in the virulent negativity of the initial literary reaction. It is striking that in the immediate aftermath of the publication of Darwin's theories, there appeared a number of metamorphic novels seeking to ridicule evolutionary thinking: see Asker (2001), p. 34 with further bibliography.
3. A challenge explored with astonishing sensitivity and imagination in Asimov's justly renowned short-story collection *I, Robot*.
4. Most famously, Pinocchio's nose magically grows in length as a result of his telling of lies (ch. 17). Rather more strikingly, and in a narrative sequence clearly inspired by Apuleius' *Metamorphoses*, Pinocchio is, in the 'Paese dei Balocchi' ['Land of Toys'], transformed into an ass and in this form lives for some time in the company of clowns (chs. 32–33). Like Apuleius' Lucius, Pinocchio undergoes both physical and psychological metamorphosis, with a triumphant finale in which he emerges as an enlightened human being.
5. Cf. Fowler (2006), p. 382: 'Myth, as both theme and method, was at the heart of Modernism; its central trope, metamorphosis, shaped and defined Modernist texts from *The Waste Land* and *Ulysses* to *The Tower* and *Mrs Dalloway*.'

6. The close connection between metamorphosis and metaphor has long been recognized. In an influential study, Barkan (1986), p. 23 observes that to relate a tale of metamorphosis is 'to make flesh of metaphors'. Cf. Perry (1990), pp. 13–14: 'metamorphosis is associated by some critics with the more poetical figures of rhetoric, those figures that can somehow distort logic or render the incredible credible: metaphor and metonymy.' Critics have often regarded metamorphosis as a destroyed metaphor; but from the viewpoint of our diachronic survey it might not be altogether inappropriate to invert the terms of this formulation and regard metaphor in the post-metamorphic phase as an eclipsed or sublimated metamorphosis.

7. For earlier discussion of the Circe myth, see pp. 40–42, 48–49, 58 above.

8. Goldhill (2011), p. 56, with a valuable following discussion.

9. For Victorian images of Circe, see Goldhill (2011), pp. 58–62.

10. In reference to 'Circe', Dantini (2008), p. 94 observes that 'Grosz was an assiduous collector of pornographic photographs and drawings: he used them as ideas for his images of seduction and prostitution, almost as though to provide allegorical portrayals of the dark, contemptible, greedy side of society.'

11. Zuffi (2008), p. 280.

12. The image is discussed in a Proustian context by Spiegel, p. 390.

13. *An Artist's Reminiscences* (1907), p. 408.

14. Cf. Perry (1990), p. 7: 'Metamorphosis becomes the operative image for a theory of the poetic imagination [...] figures of metamorphosis often represent the imagination at work'. The same scholar points to J. W. L. Mellmann's treatise *Commentatio de causis et auctoribus narrationum de mutatis formis* (Leipzig, 1786), which lists ambiguities of speech, metaphors, poetic elaborations of actions and philosophical allegory as types of metamorphoses; this slippage belongs to the post-metamorphic. For metamorphosis as a trope for artistic creativity in earlier periods see Baumbach, Chapter 3 in this volume.

15. Further complexities ensue if one ponders the meaning of the genitive: are the monsters the product of the human imagination when reason has fallen asleep or of *reason* sleeping?

16. Here it may be poignant to anticipate our discussion of H. G. Wells' *The Island of Dr Moreau*, a work of 'hard' science fiction that characteristically insists on rigorous verisimilitude and scientific plausibility. The titular character creates various hybrid creatures through advanced techniques of vivisection. Its scientific pretensions notwithstanding, the narrator calls attention, in the course of a group encounter with the hybrids, to their monstrous, dream-like quality: 'Imagine the scene if you can! We three blue-clad men [...] surrounded by this circle of crouching and gesticulating monstrosities — some almost human save in their subtle expression and gestures, some like cripples, some so strangely distorted as to resemble nothing but the denizens of our wildest dreams' (ch. 16). It is worth noting as well an overt connection to ancient mythology in the creature called 'the Satyr', which the narrating character Pendrick assesses as 'a gleam of classical memory on the part of Moreau' (ch. 16).

17. Braidotti (2002), p. 200.

18. One thinks here of the emphasis throughout Freudian theory on the significance of metaphor as an essential mechanism of psychic life. Orthodox Lacanian thought posits metaphor and metonymy, along with condensation and replacement, as the fundamental operations of the human unconscious.

19. *Forbidden Planet* (1956), directed by Fred Wilcox; screenplay by Cyril Hume, based on a story by Irving Block and Allen Adler.

20. As Strick (1982), p. 34 nicely puts it, *Forbidden Planet* represents a fresh direction in science fiction film: it is the genre's first 'inner space' story. The film is not about technology per se, but rather about 'the equivocations of scientific power'.

21. Cf. the observation of Williams (2007), p. 166 that *Forbidden Planet's* 'central topos is a kind of "sleep of reason", in which the latent consequences of the dreams of the Renaissance magus Prospero are transformed into futuristic inventor Morbius' nightmare'.

22. The genre is generally thought to begin with Horace Walpole's *Castle of Otranto* (1764). On the Gothic generally, see Spooner and McEvoy (2007); for discussion of particular elements, such as sexuality and gender or Gothic notions of self, Anolik (2007), pp. 1–24 (esp. p. 5: 'there is usually slippage between sexual danger and supernatural danger') and Cameron (2010). As critics

have often noted, it is significant that the Gothic novel emerges in the context of the Industrial Revolution, in which European societies were transformed from an essentially agricultural structure to an urban organization based on factory production and the emergence of a new industrial working class.

23. As Botting (1995), p. 131 observes, 'horror constitutes the limit of reason, sense, consciousness and speech, the very emotion in which the human reaches its limit. Horror is thus ambivalently human.'

24. See Smith (2010).

25. Butler (2010), p. 1. Clarke (2008), p. 166 qualifies this picture, pointing out that not all vampires are equally protean: 'The elite among them, such as Stoker's count, may be metamorphic, but most are only marginally so, as their bodily differences are largely concealed and held away from the sunlight. As metamorphs go, they remain liminal, hovering at the boundary between day and night, mortality and immortality.'

26. Clarke (2008), p. 166, opining further that the figure of the vampire has subsequently come to represent 'a kind of Gothic, anachronistic posthumanity'.

27. It was initially published, in thirteen chapters, in the July 1890 issue of *Lippincott's Monthly Magazine*; it was released the following year, in twenty chapters but otherwise little changed, in a single volume. Quotations are from the latter.

28. Wilde's indebtedness to Balzac extends beyond *La Peau de Chagrin* to *Splendeurs et Misères*; other influences include Gautier's *Mademoiselle de Maupin*.

29. Cf. Paglia (1992), pp. 528–29: 'What is odd about the picture of Dorian Gray is that it is in Dionysian metamorphosis. The changing painting insults beauty and form: Dorian calls it "the misshapen shadow", "the hideous painted thing", "this monstrous soul-life". [...] Painting is invaded by a daemonic, form-altering power, because [Dorian] has tried to make nature surrender her authority.'

30. Mighall (2003), p. 195.

31. Gerken (2007), p. 11.

32. See Suvin (1979), p. 69.

33. Suvin (1979), p. 69.

34. Some have found his distinction between 'fantastic' and 'strange' or 'weird' literature too rigid. So, for instance, Edgar Allan Poe is excluded from fantastic literature. For Todorov the crucial point is Poe's tendency to locate supernatural phenomena unambiguously in the protagonist's mind.

35. Modern cinema has demonstrated a peculiar fondness for this kind of uncertainty or hesitation. A well-known example is the figure of Freddy Krueger in Wes Craven's classic horror film *A Nightmare on Elm Street* (1984). Krueger is a lynched serial killer who returns from the dead to attack his victims while they dream. He gains in power the more the community he haunts believes in his existence, and vanishes as soon as his chosen victims stop considering him 'real'. But Craven thwarts any easy resolution by leaving uncertain the status of key frames — a dream or reality? As a result, the story hovers between the properly metamorphic realm of the fantastic, in which the dead may come back to life and haunt the living, and the merely 'strange', or what Freud called the *Unheimlich*.

36. Todorov (1970), p. 25.

37. Fantastic narratives are often recounted in the first person. The narrating protagonist reports his experiences and his understanding of those experiences as supernatural phenomena; but this is a non-omniscient mode, a subjective account, that leaves open the possibility of another interpretation.

38. Another interesting attempt at distinction is by Caillois (1966). He distinguishes between fairy tales and fantastic literature. In fairy tales the fantastic, the metamorphic, is integral to the narrative world. One common element of children's literature is the sense of crossing a threshold, of entering into a realm in which the normal rules of reality, the conventional parameters of the possible, no longer hold. The most explicit examples of this are found in children's literature — as, for example, when in Lewis Carroll's *Through the Looking Glass* Alice passes through the mirror and thereby enters a metamorphic world in which conventional principles of logic and causation are suspended.

39. Gautier's hesitation in the face of overt supernatural metamorphosis is well illustrated in *Le*

Roman de la momie (1858), set in the Egypt of the pharaohs, and touching on events from the biblical story of *Exodus*. This novel features various biblical episodes, including Moses and Aaron's confrontations with pharaoh, in which they petition for the freedom of the Jewish people. In a series of metamorphic competitions between Aaron and the Pharaoh's own magicians, the former gradually establishes the supremacy of his transformative powers. This begins with the miraculous scene, reprised from *Exodus* 7. 10, in which Aaron magically transmutes his staff into a serpent: 'Aharon jeta son bâton devant le roi, et le bois commença à se tordre, à onduler, à se couvrir de écailles, à remuer la tête et la queue, à se dresser, et à pousser des sifflements terribles. Le bâton s'était changé en serpent' (ch. 15). But all this is carefully hedged by the author's use of a distancing narrative structure. The events are reported in an ancient Egyptian novel, written in hieroglyphics, that the protagonists discover during an excavation in Egypt, along with the extraordinary find of a female mummy, the authoress. Gautier's own account is the scholar's translation of this text — so a story within a story written in a mysterious 'dead' language deriving from a mysterious, impossibly remote, and fantastic civilization, long since expired — a civilization whose landscape was dotted with rows of crouching sphinxes, curious obelisks, and monstrous hybrid idols with animal heads. On the one hand the magical metamorphic sequence is given a full airing; on the other it is hard to imagine how Gautier, one of the nineteenth century's most daring writers, could have distanced himself more fully from the supernatural events described.

40. E.g. 'Octavien [...] se demandait s'il dormait tout debout et marchait dans un rêve. Il s'interrogea sérieusement pour savoir si la folie ne faisait pas danser devant lui ses hallucinations; mais il fut obligé de reconnaître qu'il n'était pas ni endormi ni fou' (p. 254).

41. Hegerfeldt (2005), p. 42 well observes that, precursors notwithstanding, García Márquez may be regarded as playing a foundational role, popularizing and institutionalizing what was, in effect, a new kind of literature.

42. As Koelb (2010), p. 117 points out a more accurate translation would be *The Transformation*. 'The allusions the English title makes to both Ovid's *Metamorphoses* and the process of maturation in certain insects are appropriate but they were not foremost in Kafka's imagination. The original title suggests something miraculous and radical, as when a magician turns a white scarf into a white rabbit. It can also suggest a religious conversion, a chemical transmutation, a theatrical change of scenery, and a theological transubstantiation.'

43. Hegerfeldt (2005), pp. 41–42.

44. For background, genesis, and impact of the story see Corngold (1996); Binder (2004). Discussions include Rudloff (1988); Matz (1994), pp. 73–85; Michel (1992).

45. Koelb (2010), p. 118.

46. For the opposite view, and some general reflections on the debate, see Neumann (2006).

47. For Kafka's place in Jewish traditions of thought, see Bruce (1987).

48. Indeed, insects take on an important cultural coding in the twentieth century. They become, particularly in the post-nuclear historical context, phobic objects: see Braidotti (2002), p. 148. Insects also offer models for the extra-terrestrial posthuman (H. G. Wells' spider-machines in *War of the Worlds*; Robert Heinlin's 'Bugs' in *Starship Troopers*). They are also, in scenarios of nuclear holocaust, the inheritors of the Earth after the self-inflicted demise of the human race.

49. For a recent discussion see Tornau (2008).

50. Cf. Sweeney (1990), p. 28: 'insect-character and human-character are unfused; no unified personality integrates both insect and human traits. Aside from a few acknowledgements of their existence, Gregor's new insectile attitudes and dispositions remain outside his consciousness [...]. Although at times Gregor ponders their presence, he does not consciously claim them as his own. Thus, instead of a unified self, Gregor is fissured into two characters, clashing yet jointly existing in the same body.'

51. Sweeney (1990), p. 28.

52. See further Holland (1958).

53. Cf. Sweeney (1990), p. 26: 'The possibility that Gregor's predicament might be imaginary, even though the experience be vivid, challenges the reliability of his narrative point of view. By raising questions about the veracity of Gregor's self-conscious narration, the text makes room for an alternative conceptual explanation of Gregor's identity.'

54. A number of critics have insisted on its metaphoric status, interpreting *Die Verwandlung* as a narrative of psychotic breakdown: see, e.g., Michel (1992); cf. Skulsky (1981), pp. 171–73. But through sheer persistence in developing the initial premise this metaphor becomes unmoored from its genesis in psychological fantasy, and the narrative fact of Gregor's status as an oversized insect is difficult to deny. Again, one does better to think of the fluid reality of magical realism.

55. On the question of how to interpret the novella, see Corngold (1973).

56. Dalí's art also seems to exhibit correspondences with the instabilities mapped out by contemporary science; cf. Raquejo (2004), p. 112: 'his painting offers an alternative to the fixed perception of the real, to open another where images, and hence thoughts, flow to the sound of a constant metamorphosis. In that flow in constant change Dalí gives us a version of the real that is close to that raised by science nowadays, thus being ahead of his time.'

57. Roloff (2006), p. 17: 'Die Surrealisten konzentrieren sich auf die mythischen Figuren der Rätselhaftigkeit und Mehrdeutigkeit (das Labyrinth, Orakel, Sphinx und Chimäre), Figuren des Rauschs, der Erotik und Ekstase (Dionysos, die Bacchantinen, Sirenen), der Doppel-geschlechtigkeit (Hermaphrodit), der Transgression und der verbotenen, tödlichen Blicke (Orpheus, Medusa, Amor und Psyche, Melusine) aber auch der Geschwindigkeit und Mobilität (Hermes) und der Virtualisierung (Pygmalion).'

58. Cf. Braidotti (2002), p. 183: 'Science fiction is a genre that accepts full responsibility for its attempt to imagine things differently and thus enacts a sort of cognitive responsibility for its own imaginative flights. As such it is beneficial not only to society but also to science, which needs to be imaginative and speculative in order to progress.'

59. Cf. the observation of Asker (2001), p. 14 that there is a sense in which 'contemporary science [...] is moving to meet metamorphosis in some confused and ethically awkward middle ground'.

60. Suvin (1979), p. 66.

61. Suvin (1979), p. 65, adding that 'this does not mean that novelty is primarily a matter of scientific facts or even hypotheses'; and finally stating that 'Science in this wider sense of methodologically systemic cognition cannot be disjoined from the SF innovation.' Suvin draws a useful distinction between 'naturalistic' fiction, fantasy, and science fiction: 'naturalistic fiction does not require scientific explanation; fantasy does not allow it; science fiction both requires it and allows it'.

62. Suvin (1979), p. 66.

63. It was, to be sure, a very tentative first step: Galvani initially referred to 'animal electricity', assuming that it was a distinct form of electricity from that found in the external environment.

64. It is certainly important to acknowledge the presence of alchemical texts in the tale. But, as Reichart (1994), pp. 136–37 has observed, Frankenstein 'is not a story about alchemy and magic, but about science, [...] natural philosophy, chemistry and galvanism.' In other words, Shelley's novel documents the fault-line, the transition from the alchemical to the scientific.

65. Rather than, say, Pygmalion (who would re-emerge as a paradigm in much later literature), whose demiurgic activity is more ambiguously situated vis-à-vis the divine. Reminiscences of both Pygmalion and *Frankenstein* seem to coexist in the film *La piel que habito* (2011; directed by Pedro Almodóvar), in which a skilled surgeon captures and imprisons his daughter's rapist, and progressively transforms him, both surgically and chemically, into a physical doppelganger of his dead wife. The ability surgically to alter an individual's gender (a possibility for which ancient myth showed a certain fascination) is a crucial new capacity of modern medicine, which exploits advances in surgical technique and biochemistry. This is combined brilliantly with the mad-scientist motif and, ultimately, the revenge of his creation.

66. Mellor, *Mary Shelley*, p. 100.

67. Bloom (2004), p. 4.

68. He shares this belief in utter ontological stability across time with Palaephatus. See Introduction to Part I.

69. A related theological problem for the next century arose from evidence for the apparent existence of old, or extinct species. When the bones of dinosaurs were discovered in the early nineteenth century, many scientists identified them as extraordinarily large specimens of known species, since it was for them inconceivable that God would permit any part of Creation to expire. The solution of the British anatomist Richard Owen, famous for coining the term

'dinosaur', but also a devout Christian, was to link such extinct species to the global flood of Noah's day.

70. Cf. Asker (2001), pp. 5–6: 'Whatever Linnaeus' role in the history of evolutionary theory, it is quite clear that he was deeply involved in thinking around the topic of change of form among species and evolution: the notion of metamorphosis/evolution was current as he looks over his shoulder at the hybrid beasts described by early natural historians and in his crystal ball at what would become evolutionary science. Of course, Linnaeus was neither a metamorphosist (in the pejorative pseudo-scientific sense) nor an evolutionist (in the Darwinian). He was a Creationist-Scientist, itself a curious but far from uncommon hybrid being, blended if not confused.'

71. Lichtenstern (1990), pp. 1–10 (p. 2). For background, see Boyle (1999), pp. 824–49.

72. See Breidbach (2006) and, most recently, (2011), esp. pp. 67–74 and pp. 186–93 ('Die Idee der Metamorphose').

73. Jaeger (2007).

74. See Lichtenstern (1990).

75. Goethe's works contributed to a more general contemporary debate, which produced a range of scientifically informed 'poetics of procreation' that correlated biological phenomena of growth and reproduction with literary creation and processes in culture. Controversies raged (in such diverse fields of human endeavour as literature, philosophy, and science) as to whether procreation should be conceived in terms of epigenesis or pre-formation. Put differently, does procreation occur by means of the growth of cells into a differentiated whole (epigenesis); or does the outcome already exists *in nuce* in the seed, pre-formed as it were? See further Müller-Sievers (1997); Richards (2002); Holland (2009). For us, these debates are primarily of historical interest.

76. Some have even found Darwin prefigured in Ovid: Warner (2002), p. 75 observes that the tension between 'due organic change on the one hand and incongruous and disruptive mutation' on the other are already embodied in the *Metamorphoses*.

77. Following Clarke (2008), p. 1: 'Charles Darwin's *Origin of Species* told an old story in a new way: bodily metamorphosis is not supernatural but natural. Given deep time, biological evolution is natural metamorphosis.'

78. Margulis and Sagan (1997), p. 13.

79. Ibid.

80. Science fiction often considers the possibility that such evolutionary replacement might be catalysed by human folly, as with H. G. Wells' *The Food of the Gods* (discussed below). Likewise the conclusion to the film *Planet of the Apes* (1968; dir. Franklin J. Schaffner) suggests that the supplanting of *Homo sapiens* by a different branch of the primate family is the consequence of some man-made global apocalypse. This is a noteworthy departure from Pierre Boulle's *La Planète des singes* (1963), the science fiction novel from which the film was adapted, which follows the scenario of Karel Čapek's play *R. U. R.* (discussed below): human beings enslave apes to provide a servile species of manual labourers, eventually becoming totally dependent on them. The apes then overthrow their masters, and become the dominant global species, while the defeated humans lapse into a primitive, pre-technological condition. There is, of course, a more radical posthuman scenario in which the human race destroys itself via nuclear holocaust or like catastrophe of such magnitude as to eradicate all mammals and most other complex life forms as well. As scientists have often pointed out, though, this would not be a total apocalypse: the bacteria that are the backbone of planetary life would doubtless survive, as perhaps would some of the hardier species of insects, leaving a new and vastly simplified terrain, a clean slate as it were, for the process of evolution to once again churn out new species.

81. Anderson (1992), p. 50.

82. Clarke (2008), p. 2.

83. The evolutionary process, of course, occurs at a speed that is in inverse proportion to the lifespan of the species in question, so that scientists can observe changes over generations of very short-lived organisms.

84. Stableford (2004), p. 106. The evolutionary fantasy has also found its way into comic books, most notably Stan Lee's *X-Men* series. It features 'mutants', gifted with a bewildering assortment of special powers, and thereby superior to ordinary humans, who have, in effect, been left on a lower rung of the evolutionary ladder. The special powers were initially vaguely attributed to

mutations in DNA; more recently a more specific explanation has been supplied, both in comic books and film: the special powers of the mutants are attributed to a single gene, the X-gene. Though *X-men's* titular characters themselves are sworn protectors of humanity, much of the action, in both comic book and film series, is driven by the anxiety of the unaltered masses of humanity, for whom the various extraordinary capacities of the mutants are a source of envy and fear. Here the archetype is H. G. Wells' *The Food of the Gods*, which, in a sharp parody of contemporary politics, has unaltered humanity rise up against the new race of giants in their midst, ultimately resulting in all-out warfare.

85. Wells began his literary career as an author of non-fiction, much of which featured speculation over the evolutionary destiny of the human race. Of this early literary output, which was published in popular magazines, the essay 'The Man of the Year Million' (1893) is generally regarded as the finest specimen. Like many others, Wells was deeply influenced by the writing of Thomas Henry Huxley, a populariser of Darwin's theory of evolution.

86. An altogether different evolutionary destiny for humankind, based on the perceived advantages of the (more advanced) Martian species that invades Earth is implicitly aired by the internal narrator in *The War of the Worlds* (Book II, chapter II): 'To me it is quite credible that the Martians may be descended from beings not unlike ourselves, by a gradual development of the brain and the hands [...] at the expense of the rest of the body.'

87. Suvin (1979), pp. 238–39.

88. Cf. Stableford (2004), p. 106: 'American science fiction accepted from the beginning that one of its central tasks was to figure out where future human evolutionary progress might lead — a prospect dominated by psi powers [*sc.* paranormal psychic abilities] until a mature appreciation of the transformative potential of biotechnology emerged in the 1970s. Some far-futuristic fantasy looks forward to a time when humankind's descendants will have given way to other life forms, but designing the posthuman superman [...] has always been the subgenre's core enterprise.'

89. Clarke (2008), p. 8.

90. Suggestive in this respect is Prendick's suspicion that Moreau, after fashioning his monstrous creatures, 'had infected their dwarfed brains with a kind of deification of himself' (ch. 12).

91. Here, as Stableford (2004), p. 106 observes, Wells set the trend for British and American writers of science fiction; French evolutionary fantasy, by contrast, pioneered by Camille Flammarion's *Lumen* (1872) retained a framework of religious fantasy well into the twentieth century.

92. Suvin (1979), p. 214.

93. Clarke (2008), p. 159.

94. Ibid.

95. Ibid.

96. Braidotti (2002), p. 186.

97. This can be seen in the film *Them!* (1954; dir. Gordon Douglas, based on an original story by George W. Yates), which features giant post-nuclear ants. *Them!* is the first of the 'big bug films' and one of the earliest nuclear monster films. The 'big bug films', and in particular the human–insect combat scenario, hark back to the vivid accounts of such in H. G. Wells' *The Food of the Gods* (discussed below), which likewise features a careless and inadvertent, albeit non-nuclear, transformation of the natural world by the pursuits of science. In contrast to their American counterparts, Japanese post-war science fiction films, particularly those produced by Toho Studios, have tended to feature post-nuclear monsters modelled after large prehistoric reptile species, now extinct, such as Ishirō Honda's *Godzilla* (1954), and his less well-known *Rodan* (1956), which has a mutant pterosaur in the starring role. There is thus a suggestive reverse-evolutionary thrust to the post-nuclear scenario, a devolution or 'relapse' brought about by humankind's reckless treatment of the planetary ecosphere.

98. The superheroes of this so-called 'Silver Age' of comic book superheroes differ from their counterparts from the 'Golden Age' (from the late 1930s to the late 1940s) in the greater use of science-fiction premises, above all the widespread attribution of their extraordinary powers to the transformational effect of radiation exposure.

99. Packer (2010), p. 124. Lee himself acknowledged the literary debt not just to Stevenson, but also to Shelley, observing that 'I combined *Jekyll and Hyde* with *Frankenstein* and got the monster I wanted, who was really good, but nobody knew it' (*Washington Times*, May 12, 2012).

100. *The Fly* (1958, directed by Kurt Neumann; screenplay by James Clavell), with sequels in 1959 and 1965; remade in 1986 (dir. David Cronenberg; screenplay by Charles E. Pogue and David Cronenberg), with a sequel, *The Fly II*, in 1989. In its earliest incarnation *The Fly* was a short story by George Langelaan, published in *Playboy* magazine in June 1957. Pogue and Cronenberg substantially rewrote the screenplay from the first film, which had already significantly re-elaborated Langelaan's original story.

101. Cronenberg's act of updating is also signalled metatheatrically in various ways. So for instance, the protagonist is constantly recording his experiments, so the act of filming is present in some scenes; this detail is reinforced by the fact that his girlfriend Veronica is a reporter — and so constantly looking for 'the story'.

102. *The Fly* (1986), dir. Cronenberg; screenplay by C. E. Pogue and D. Cronenberg.

103. 'It's somehow a purifying process [...]. Human teleportation, molecular decimation, breakdown and reformation is inherently purging' (*The Fly* (1986), dir. Cronenberg; screenplay by C. E. Pogue and D. Cronenberg).

104. Seth: 'Insects don't have politics [and so] we can't trust the insect. I'd like to become the first insect politician.' Veronica: 'I don't know what you are trying to say.' Seth: 'I'm saying that I am an insect who dreamt he was a man and loved it. But now the dream is over and the insect is awake.' (*The Fly* [1986], dir. Cronenberg; screenplay by C. E. Pogue and D. Cronenberg).

105. Another striking difference in the two filmic versions involves the final demise. In the first the scientist–fly hybrid asks his wife to kill him as he feels the insect nature growing stronger; she mercifully does so, crushing his fly-head under an industrial press. In the later film, by contrast, 'Brundlefly' tries to dilute the effects of the metamorphosis by attempting a second genetic fusion with a human, thereby lowering the insect genetic component as against the human (while at the same time creating a hybrid female counterpart to himself, in a reprise of the desire of the Frankenstein monster). It is only when this goes awry and 'Brundlefly' is fused with an inanimate object to excruciating effect that he reprises the culminating gesture of the initial film, asking his erstwhile girlfriend Veronica to put him out of his misery.

106. Prior to ingestion flies regurgitate an acid that dissolves solid food into a fluid that they can then suck up through their proboscis. Flies have no teeth: the audience is not spared the spectacle of the protagonist losing these, as part of his progressive insectile metamorphosis.

107. In both cases the initial reaction includes a certain exhilaration arising from new physical capabilities: both Gregor and 'Brundlefly' take some delight in their new-found ability to defy gravity, to crawl up walls, across ceilings, and so on.

108. Clarke (2008), p. 152. To these examples should be added the Ovidian archetype: the transformed Io mooing like a cow when attempting to speak (Met. 1. 637–38, discussed in the Introduction to Part I, above, p. 45).

109. Smith (1982), p. 9.

110. Similar evolutionary thematics are explored in J. D. Beresford's *The Hampdenshire Wonder* (1911) and Olaf Stapledon's *Odd John* (1931). Broadly speaking, such works are the literary antecedents of the comic book superhero. Even closer in conception to the comic book superhero is the protagonist of H. G. Well's *The Invisible Man* (1897), a scientist who discovers the means to render animate life-forms invisible, and hastily applies this metamorphic procedure to himself, without having developed the means to reverse the transformation, and giving insufficient thought to the consequences of invisibility. After early experiences he settles on a plan of tyrannizing the human race, which is forestalled in the event by prompt recognition of the threat by a friend in whom he confides, and his hunting down and extermination by local authorities. The novel ends with an almost Ovidian account of the metamorphic reversion of his corpse to visibility.

111. <http://news.nationalgeographic.com/news/2002/01/0111_020111genmice.html>. Unsurprisingly, artists have turned to hybridity to represent and think through the new porosity of ontological distinctions. Already Ovid's *Metamorphoses* contains an extensive meditation on, and has inspired countless engagements with, hybridity, though his choice here is selective: his epic features centaurs, Glaucus, and Scylla, but steers clear of werewolves and vampires. See Cole (2008), p. 60 for the restraint; for the presence and exploration of theme in the poem and how Ovid's treatment of hybridity inspired later ages see Casanova-Robin (2009).

112. Stableford (2004), p. xxvii.
113. Crichton (1990), p. vi.
114. Biotechnology companies have not only created thousands of transgeneric species, but also patented them. A 1987 United States Supreme Court ruling crucially determined that genetically engineered species are legitimate inventions that may be patented and 'owned'. This has given rise to what Crichton (1990), p. vi characterizes as 'a scientific gold rush of astonishing proportions' in the late twentieth century. The commercialization of molecular biology is, still according to Crichton, 'the most stunning ethical event in the history of science'.
115. *Jurassic Park* (1993), directed by Steven Spielberg; screenplay by David Koepp and Michael Crichton. In the preface to the novel, Crichton (1990), p. xi inveighs against the greed and irresponsibility of the biotechnology industry, whose research is carried out 'in secret, and in haste, and for profit'. The novel was a bestseller; the film's worldwide box office revenue exceeded 900 million dollars, making it fourth all-time in that category.
116. Though both figures work in secrecy and seclusion in order to evade the scrutiny and interference of public authorities, Hammond has an additional motivation, namely to beat his competitors in the biotech industry (and patent the 'new' species produced). His secrecy is thus tactical rather than ingrained: his ultimate objective is the world's first dinosaur theme park featuring genetically reconstructed dinosaurs, and all the profit and fame that would accrue from it. As he explains, 'we set out to make biological attractions. *Living* attractions. Attractions so astonishing they would capture the imagination of the entire world' (p. 61). Hammond is not a scientist himself, but a capitalist who habitually uses money to persuade scientists to realize his reckless but visionary project.
117. In *Jurassic Park* the problem of retrieving dinosaur DNA from species extinct millions of years ago is ingeniously solved by a massive search for mosquitoes that were trapped in amber, and so preserved, in the Jurassic Age. Those that had recently bitten dinosaurs would have ingested retrievable dinosaur DNA in the drawn blood. The extracted DNA is supplemented, where damaged, with gene strands from other species, and further modified for various practical reasons, as well as 'to make them patentable' (p. 122). The on-going practice of transgenic modifications of DNA in successive generations of dinosaur species causes the scientists to assign them 'release versions' (4.1, 4.3, and 4.4 are mentioned), like so many editions of computer software. As one character explains, 'as we discover glitches in the DNA, Dr Wu's labs have to make a new version' (p. 128). Later Crichton acknowledges the artistic element of the fashioning of these life forms via a Pygmalion-esque simile: 'In making his dinosaurs, Wu had manipulated the DNA as a sculptor might clay or marble. He had created freely' (p. 209).
118. In *Jurassic Park* the critique is delivered by one of the characters, the mathematician Malcolm, with a suggestive inversion of the 'Sleep of Reason' motif: 'You decide you'll control nature, and from that moment on you're in deep trouble, because you can't do it. Yet you have made systems that require you to do it [...] Your powers are much less than your dreams of reason would have you believe' (p. 351).
119. A movement whose impetus owed much to the rediscovery and circulation of Lucretius' masterpiece *De Rerum Natura*; see now Greenblatt (2011).
120. Braidotti (2002), p. 215.
121. *Modern Times* presents this as a devastating experience for the human being. Chaplin's character, a reincarnation of the 'Little Tramp' of earlier films, has a breakdown and spends a good deal of time recovering in a mental institution.
122. One should perhaps not insist on terminological rigour, given that the term 'android' was first used by Villiers de l'Isle-Adam in *L'Ève future* (1886), in reference to what is properly a robot. Likewise the term 'robot' was coined by Karel Čapek in his science fiction drama *R. U. R.* (1926) in reference to what would now be thought of as an android. The titular abbreviation stands for 'Rossum's Universal Robots', but Rossum's artificial humanoids are the products of biotechnology, not mechanics.
123. Cf. Clarke (2008), p. 195: 'Human technologies have produced a hyper complex environment for which humanist distinctions between the natural, the human, and the technological are increasingly nonfunctional. Cybernetics has allowed us to embed mechanisms within our bodies and to insert vast mechanical and computational systems into the world around us.'

124. With respect to biotechnology, we are well into the early stages of machine hybridization, with devices such as pacemakers in widespread use, and more dramatic innovations (e.g. artificial forms of sensory perception for the deaf and blind) on the cusp of realization.

125. Braidotti (2002), p. 228.

126. What happens in the natural sciences has a counterpart in the social sciences and attempts at social engineering. See W. S. Gilbert, *Pygmalion and Galatea*, and, most famously, George Bernhard Shaw, *Pygmalion: A Romance in Five Acts*, as well as the musical film adaptation *My Fair Lady*.

127. Stableford (2004), p. 83.

128. Haraway (1991); Hayles (1999); Graham (2002); Fukuyama (2002); Liveley (2006); Clarke (2008); Wolfe (2010).

129. It might be argued that the brain is the one part of the body that cannot be swapped out in the construction of a cyborg, but we take the term in its broadest sense of any integrated system composed of organic and artificial components.

130. The reference to the miniaturizing technology of the clock calls to mind La Mettrie, and demonstrates that, in effect, the flip side of the man-machine is the machine-man. It is worth noting in passing that mention is made of Babbage's calculating machine, which Rapperschwyll's mechanical brain is said vastly to surpass.

131. Stableford (2004), pp. 9–10.

132. Some of the broader themes in *R. U. R.*, particularly those relating to industrialization, are elaborated from a short story entitled *The System*, which Čapek co-authored with his brother Josef, and published in 1908.

133. As the character Domin explains: 'Old Rossum [...] wanted to somehow scientifically dethrone God. He was a frightful materialist and did everything on that account. For him the question was just to prove that God is unnecessary. So he resolved to create a human being just like us, down to the last hair' (*R. U. R.* prologue, p. 7).

134. Among other problems, the human fertility rate plummets to near zero: Dr Gall explains this collective psycho-physiological symptom as arising from the reality that 'man is virtually an anachronism' (*R. U. R.* Act I, p. 39).

135. As Radius, the eventual 'Robot' leader, explains to his human interlocutor, 'You are not like Robots. You are not as capable as Robots are. Robots do everything. You only give orders — utter empty words [...]. I do not want a master. I know everything' (*R. U. R.* Act I, p. 37).

136. *Blade Runner* (1982), dir. Ridley Scott; screenplay by Hampton Fancher and David Peoples.

137. The film thereby changes or mutes many of the premises of Dick's novel, which is set in 2021 San Francisco, in an explicitly post-nuclear world suffering the lingering effects of radioactive fallout from World War Terminus (WWT). This has caused a massive depopulation, both through the war itself and subsequent waves of extra-terrestrial emigration.

138. A legend (text scroll) at the beginning of the film announces that 'The Nexus 6 Replicants were superior in strength and agility, and at least equal in intelligence to the genetic engineers who created them' (*Blade Runner* (1982), dir. R. Scott; screenplay by H. Fancher and D. Peoples). Again, this represents a significant departure from Dick's novel, in which the Nexus 6 androids have evolved beyond those humans whose mental capacity, along with their genes, has been significantly eroded by radiation fallout (a group collectively referred to as 'specials'). This means that the androids have merely 'evolved beyond a major — but inferior — segment of mankind' (p. 30).

139. 'The big religious boys said that replicants, no matter how human, were objects; only God could make people' (*Blade Runner* (1982), dir. R. Scott; screenplay by H. Fancher and D. Peoples).

140. In the film it is stated that even the difference detected by the Voigt-Kampff test vanishes after a Nexus-6 android has four to five years of life experience. As a 'fail-safe', therefore, in order to ensure preservation of this difference, these androids are limited to a built-in four-year life span.

141. *Blade Runner* thus clarifies a deliberate ambiguity in Dick's novel, which hints at various moments that Rachael may have known all along that she was an android.

142. Solomon (1998), p. 45.

143. The love story between replicant and replicant hunter is a marked departure from Dick's novel, in which Deckard is married and Rachael has sex with him only as a ploy, successful with other

Blade Runners but not with Deckard, to persuade him to give up android hunting. At the close of the novel Deckard discovers that Rachael has exacted revenge for Deckard's slaying of her android friends by killing his pet goat. The film was made with two romantic endings, the first with Deckard and Rachael leaving his apartment to share an unspecified future together, the second with them enjoying a romantic car ride in an alluring rural landscape. It is hard to resist the observation that one seemingly immutable element in our modern age of cultural flux is the Hollywood happy ending.

144. Solomon (1998), p. 45.

145. Clarke (2008), p. 4.

146. Originally published in the June 1929 edition of *Science Wonder Stories*.

147. Asimov (1950), p. 37: 'A robot may not injure a human being or, through inaction, allow a human being to come to harm'. The second and third laws were 'A robot must obey the orders given to it by human beings, except where such orders would conflict with the First Law', and 'A robot must protect its own existence as long as such protection does not conflict with the First or Second Laws'.

148. Moravec (1988).

149. Well discussed in Hayles (1999), pp. 235–39. The subfield of artificial intelligence known as 'evolutionary computation' might offer a glimpse into how machines themselves could 'evolve' quite independently of direct human intervention. Evolutionary computation uses the same Darwinian principles of natural selection (e.g. by privileging the 'fittest' members of successive, randomly generated groups of solutions to particular problems) to achieve autonomous problem solving in a variety of areas, including engineering.

150. Milton (1987), p. 12.

151. The simpler idea of the unintelligent robot is considerably older. In the West it can be traced at least back to Leonardo da Vinci, in whose notebooks, rediscovered in the 1950s, is a sketch for an automaton able to sit up and move various body parts, including its arms and head.

152. For Braidotti (2002), p. 219 *L'Ève future* expresses 'the desire to perfect the female sex as fetishized, commodified, mechanical body-other, a topos that is dominant in the social imaginary of modernity.' Be that as it may, the basic premise of Villiers de l'Isle-Adam's novel is reprised, with gender inversion, in the science fiction/comedy film *Making Mr. Right* (1987; dir. Susan Seidelman).

153. The novel thus climaxes with a decidedly metaphysical flourish, abandoning the insistent aura of scientific plausibility (incarnated in the character of Thomas Edison himself) that characterized the narrative up to that point. In the end, the scientific yields pride of place to a transcendent 'occult' logic, and the novel takes on elements of supernatural fantasy.

154. Metropolis (1927), dir. Fritz Lang; screenplay by Thea von Harbou and Fritz Lang, adapted from Thea von Harbou's novel of the same name.

155. *Terminator* (1984; directed by James Cameron; screenplay by James Cameron, Gale Anne Hurd, William Wisher Jr.); *Terminator II: Judgment Day* (1991); *Terminator III: The Rise of the Machines* (2003). Though they provide the focus of much of the films' action, the production of 'Terminators', a class of cyborg assassins (replaced in *Terminator II* by the more advanced T-1000, a Protean robot constructed from a 'mimetic poly-alloy' metal that enables it to assume the form of anything it touches) to hunt down human beings is a secondary development vis-à-vis the initial rebellion of the artificially intelligent, self-aware Skynet computer system, which triggers a nuclear holocaust and then relentlessly wages war against the human survivors.

156. The Cylons are in fact variously conceived in different stages of the television franchise — sometimes as robotic, sometimes as an organic alien race.

157. That the invasion is ultimately unsuccessful is not attributed to effective resistance on the part of humankind, but rather to that of planetary microorganisms. That is to say, the Martian's lack of immunity to the various bacteria that populate the ecosphere causes them to perish in short order. The nod to Darwinian theory is here explicit: '[...] by virtue of this natural selection of our kind we have developed resisting power [*sc.* to bacteria]; to no germs do we succumb without a struggle, and to many [...] our living frames are altogether immune. But there are no bacteria in Mars, and directly these invaders arrived, directly they drank and fed, our microscopic allies began to work their overthrow' (*War of the Worlds*, ix).

CHAPTER 9

'Our Mind Is the Ancient Proteus': Proust, the Poets, and the Sea

Francesca Spiegel

This chapter began as a brief series of observations on a particular passage in Proust's 1922 novel *A la recherche du temps perdu*, describing what seemed to be a visual transformation of women into sea-goddesses, in the eye of the beholding narrator ('Marcel') as he attends the opera in Paris, admiring the fine ladies above in the boxes, from below, where he is seated in the orchestra. My comments were concerned with Proust's literary heritage and his reception of Graeco-Roman myth in this narrated metamorphosis, and my suggestion that much of Proust's understanding of classical antiquity seemed to have come through his reading of French nineteenth-century poetry by various movements or authors, such as Parnassianism, Symbolism, and of course Baudelaire. Starting from this short note about Parnassian influences in Proust's text — an influence which has perhaps not received sufficient attention in Proust studies so far — the paper has since turned into a more ample discussion of the history of ideas in continental mid-nineteenth and early twentieth centuries, more particularly a review of just how such supernatural or surreal events as metamorphoses have been received and described by modern poets and novelists. I thought it advisable to provide some socio-cultural background to help the reader understand the historical context of what seems to be a post-enlightenment aversion to all things miraculous in literature, whilst examining those authors who did essay the inclusion and vivid representation of supernatural events in their writing, frequently, but not always, by adopting themes, whether directly or through intermediaries, from classical authors.

The topics I have alluded to just now roughly provide the structure and subject matter of this essay. After a detailed reading of, and commentary on, the above-mentioned passage from Proust, I will explore his connection with Parnassianism through discussion of a number of short poems. Lastly, I will briefly offer some thoughts on metamorphosis as a theme in modern (French) literature and its place in the history of ideas.

Noble Nymphs: A Look at the Text

D'abord il n'y eut que de vagues ténèbres où on rencontrait tout d'un coup, comme le rayon d'une pierre précieuse qu'on ne voit pas, la phosphorescence de deux yeux célèbres, ou, comme un médaillon d'Henri IV détaché sur un fond noir, le profil incliné du duc d'Aumale, à qui une dame invisible criait: 'Que Monseigneur me permette de lui ôter son pardessus', cependant que le prince répondait: 'Mais voyons, comment donc, Madame d'Ambresac.' Elle le faisait malgré cette vague défense et était enviée par tous à cause d'un pareil honneur.[1]

[At first there were only vague shadows, in which one suddenly encountered, as rays from an unseen precious gem, the phosphorescence of two illustrious eyes or, as a medallion of Henry IV on a pitch black background, the inclined profile of the Duke of Aumale, to whom an invisible lady cried out 'my dear sir must allow me to take his cloak', to which the prince answered 'Oh come, come, my dear Lady Ambresac', but she did so, despite his vague demurral, and was envied by all for such an honour.]

Marcel is at the Opéra in Paris, awaiting the beginning of Act I of Racine's *Phèdre*, and looking around the theatre. He notices, in the boxes, the members of high society, and imagines the women as Nereids and the men as Tritons. The eyes of members of the aristocracy, gleaming like precious gems, promise an imaginary voyage; the description entirely leaves aside the potential character and psychological interest of these persons, instead endowing them with an inanimate charm.[2] Then follows a brief mannerist vignette of aristocratic life with its almost comic code of behaviour.

Immediately thereafter, introduced by 'mais' [but] (a strong coordinating conjunction in French, almost always suggesting a break in the line of thought), follows the first long set of paragraphs in which the ladies of the aristocracy are described as if they were Nereids, nymphs of the sea:

Mais, dans les autres baignoires, presque partout, les blanches déités qui habitaient ces sombres séjours s'étaient réfugiées contre les parois obscures et restaient invisibles. Cependant, au fur et à mesure que le spectacle s'avançait, leurs formes vaguement humaines se détachaient mollement l'une après l'autre des profondeurs de la nuit qu'elles tapissaient et, s'élevant vers le jour, laissaient émerger leurs corps demi-nus, et venaient s'arrêter à la limite verticale et à la surface clair-obscur où leurs brillants visages apparaissaient derrière le déferlement rieur, écumeux et léger de leurs éventails de plumes, sous leurs chevelures de pourpre emmêlées de perles que semblait avoir courbées l'ondulation du flux;[3]

[Yet in the remaining boxes,[4] almost everywhere, the white deities that dwelt in those dim abodes had taken refuge between dark walls, and remained invisible. But gradually, as the show went on, their vaguely human forms gently detached themselves, one by one, from the depths of the night that they inhabited, and as they rose to daylight, letting their half-naked figures emerge, they came to halt by that vertical frontier, that chiaroscuro surface on which their radiant faces appeared behind the cheerful surge, foamy and light, of their feathered fans, under their crimson hair interspersed with pearls that appeared to curve with the motion of the flow;]

There is no transitional phase to the metamorphosis that seems to have occurred here. In the mind of the narrator, the individuals in question have evidently taken on the form of sea-creatures before he begins his description. Indeed, one of the most striking aspects of this passage is the oscillation between the narrator's (presumably accurately captured) sensory perception and his imagination, rich in mythical imagery, which is grafted onto his vision, and the fact that he is clearly aware of this oscillation, going so far as to supply reasons why he is reminded of nymphs when he looks at these women.

In an earlier sketch, Proust had imagined the aristocratic ladies as flowers — bunches or bouquets — as they flocked towards the front of their boxes.[5] In the finalized passage as transmitted by the editors, Proust paints the picture of these ladies as 'white deities' in dark–light visual interplay with the 'dim abodes' where they have sought 'refuge', as helpless Nereids, a group of minor goddesses in the shade of their governing, principal goddess. They remain 'invisible' at first and then, slowly, as the show progresses, their 'vaguely human forms' begin to detach themselves one by one from the 'depths of the night', both a visual contrast and, by synaesthesia, an illustration of Proust's internal perception of feelings associated with recognition, doubt, understanding and human existence.

Raising themselves towards the 'daylight' (which is, of course, not daylight at all but the brighter lighting inside the Palais Garnier), they let emerge their 'half-naked bodies'. Clearly, they are not in reality half-dressed, so again, the description must be understood as highly imaginative. Indeed, Proust's use of marine idiom and imagery calls to mind Walter Crane's painting 'The Horses of Neptune' (Fig. 15), which the editors, in the Introduction to Part III, aptly characterise as 'an artistic reverse-engineering of the mythological imagination'.

After this description, Proust turns his attention to the orchestra stalls:

> [...] après commençaient les fauteuils d'orchestre, le séjour des mortels à jamais séparé du sombre et transparent royaume auquel çà et là servaient de frontière, dans leur surface liquide et pleine, les yeux limpides et réfléchissant des déesses des eaux. Car les strapontins du rivage, les formes des monstres de l'orchestre se peignaient dans ces yeux suivant les seules lois de l'optique et selon leur angle d'incidence, comme il arrive pour ces deux parties de la réalité extérieure auxquelles, sachant qu'elles ne possèdent pas, si rudimentaire soit-elle, d'âme analogue à la nôtre, nous nous jugerions insensés d'adresser un sourire ou un regard: les minéraux et les personnes avec qui nous ne sommes pas en relations.[6]

> [[...] here began the orchestra stalls, dwelling of mortals forever separate from the shadowed and transparent kingdom to which, here and there, in their liquid and even surfaces the clear and reflecting eyes of the aquatic goddesses served as a boundary. For the folding seats on the shore and the figures of monsters in the orchestra were mirrored in these eyes, according to the sole laws of optics and according to their angle of incidence, as happens with those two parts of external reality which, knowing that they do not, even in the most rudimentary way, possess a soul analogous to ours, we would deem ourselves lunatic to address with a look or a smile: minerals, and persons with whom we are not acquainted.]

Fig. 15. Crane, Walter, 'Neptune's Horses', 1893
Credit: © akg-images

The author contrasts the noble and enticing 'kingdom' of the water goddesses to the 'monstrous' human beings. The separation of the two worlds is already implied by the word 'royaume' ('realm' or 'kingdom'), which is resonant of fairy tale, of the oriental tales of the *One Thousand and One Nights* so dear to Proust, or the Old Testament[7] or of Flaubert's novelistic depiction of the princess Salammbô, who lives in a secluded sphere inaccessible to most and visible only on her balcony. It designates the abode of the nymph-like aristocrats as very distant from that of common mortals; and going even further, Proust states that these creatures do not have a 'soul analogous to ours', adding that persons with whom one is not acquainted are as minerals to one's perception, i.e. like inanimate objects.

There are many elements here — the cave-like obscurity, the limits of understanding, the separation of soul and body, the uncertain nature of appearance, the vulgar situation of those seated in the orchestra — which bring to mind Plato's allegory of the cave and the broader philosophical metaphor equating clear understanding with unimpeded vision. All of this Proust most likely had learnt in school; he is, at any rate, known to have been impressed by Henri Bergson's contemporary teachings on this philosophical tradition as well as his theories on memory.[8] It is worth bearing this conceptual background in mind as we continue our reading of this passage. The philosophical image of looking glasses, and, perhaps more specifically, the philosopher Baruch Spinoza's memorable professional training in the making and maintenance of optical instruments such as telescope lenses,[9] which became a symbol of rationalist philosophy itself in traditional French philosophical teaching,[10] seems to have found its way into Proust's thinking when he writes that the composition of the *Recherche* was to him as the process of polishing a looking glass to provide clearer introspection.[11]

The motif of minerals, already touched upon in the opening of Proust's passage, is given fuller development through the detail of light reflection in the description of 'the clear and reflecting eyes of the aquatic goddesses' with their polished-stone-like quality mirroring light 'according to the laws of optical science'. More 'lapidary' still are the aquatic demigods:

> En deçà, au contraire, de la limite de leur domaine, les radieuses filles de la
> mer se retournaient à tout moment en souriant vers des tritons barbus pendus
> aux anfractuosités de l'abîme, ou vers quelque demi-dieu aquatique ayant pour
> crâne un galet poli sur lequel le flot avait ramené une algue lisse et pour regard
> un disque en cristal de roche.[12]

> [To the other side, however, of the boundary of their domain, the sea's
> luminous daughters were frequently turning to smile upon bearded tritons
> suspended from the crevices of the abyss, or upon some aquatic demigod with
> a polished stone for skull, onto which the waves had brought sleek seaweed,
> and for gaze, a crystal rock.]

Taken together with Proust's earlier remark 'if only they had had minds'[13] and
the idea that they 'do not possess a soul analogous to ours', this description of the
aquatic demigods' anatomy as inanimate objects does not leave these aristocratic
characters with much humanity in their nature and gives the impression that
Marcel, while not acquainted, is fairly deferent to them.

Proust then changes the point of view from what the 'monsters' can see from the
orchestra seats to describe what happens within the secluded sphere of the 'radieuses
filles de la mer' ['luminous daughters of the sea'], with the close-up detail of an
ekphrasis,[14] almost as if he were present in the box:

> Elles se penchaient vers eux, elles leur offraient des bonbons; parfois le flot
> s'entr'ouvrait devant une nouvelle néréide qui, tardive, souriante et confuse,
> venait de s'épanouir du fond de l'ombre; puis l'acte fini, n'espérant plus
> entendre les rumeurs mélodieuses de la terre qui les avaient attirées à la surface,
> plongeant toutes à la fois, les diverses sœurs disparaissaient dans la nuit.[15]

> [They were leaning towards them, offering sweets; on occasion the wave parted
> in front of a new Nereid, who, arriving belatedly smiling and apologetic,
> blossomed from the depth of the shade; then, when the act was over, no longer
> hoping to hear the melodious rumours of the earth that had drawn them to the
> surface, plunging all at once, the several sisters vanished into the night.]

Their turning and bowing to 'bearded tritons' or 'aquatic demigods' are narrated in
the imperfect tense, imparting an almost mechanical, puppet-like repetitiveness to
their actions. The offering of sweets jars ironically with the marine setting; and yet,
the candied fruit is a recurring image in the passage, externalizing the vanity and
artificiality of their activity, perhaps even affording a note of ridicule. It is perhaps
possible to see implied in the symbolism of candied fruits (as opposed to fresh ones)
a state of artificial preservation and latent decay in the life that Proust describes.
A core concern of the entire *Recherche* is of course the novelistic recreation of an
era that has ended, as discussed below. In the immediate context, the symbolism
of candied fruits, though jarring with the marine setting, works in harmony with
the ancient mythological symbolism, in as far as both entail 'preservation' set agains
the ravages of time.

After the Nereids disappear into the night, Proust brings another key figure into
focus:

> Mais de toutes ces retraites au seuil desquelles le souci léger d'apercevoir
> les œuvres des hommes amenait les déesses curieuses, qui ne se laissent pas

approcher, la plus célèbre était le bloc de demi-obscurité connu sous le nom de baignoire de la princesse de Guermantes.[16]

[Yet, of all these retreats, to the threshold of which their frivolous desire to see in the works of mankind was leading these curious goddesses, who do not let anyone approach them, the most illustrious was the cube of half-obscurity, known as the box of the Guermantes princess.]

At this point, Proust's narration begins to merge back from what seemed a description of inanimate objects, to a description of a human being, when he opens the new paragraph with a simile: 'Like a great goddess'. This is in contrast to the treatment of the other aristocratic figures, whom he referred to directly in terms of divinity, without indicating that he was making a comparison, or mobilizing any other mediating trope:

Comme une grande déesse qui préside de loin aux jeux des divinités inférieures, la princesse était restée volontairement un peu au fond sur un canapé latéral, rouge comme un rocher de corail, à côté d'une large réverbération vitreuse qui était probablement une glace et faisait penser à quelque section qu'un rayon aurait pratiquée, perpendiculaire, obscure et liquide, dans le cristal ébloui des eaux. A la fois plume et corolle, ainsi que certaines floraisons marines, une grande fleur blanche, duvetée comme une aile, descendait du front de la princesse le long d'une de ses joues dont elle suivait l'inflexion avec une souplesse coquette, amoureuse et vivante, et semblait l'enfermer à demi comme un œuf rose dans la douceur d'un nid d'alcyon. Sur la chevelure de la princesse, et s'abaissant jusqu'à ses sourcils, puis reprise plus bas à la hauteur de sa gorge, s'étendait une résille faite de ces coquillages blancs qu'on pêche dans certaines mers australes et qui étaient mêlés à des perles, mosaïque marine à peine sortie des vagues qui par moment se trouvait plongée dans l'ombre au fond de laquelle, même alors, une présence humaine était révélée par la motilité éclatante des yeux de la princesse.[17]

[Like a great goddess presiding from afar over the games of inferior divinities, the princess had deliberately remained somewhat in the background on a sofa which was red as a coral reef, adjacent to a large glassy reverberation, a mirror no doubt, that called to mind a section, perpendicular, dark and liquid, cut by a ray of light, in the dazzling crystal of the waters. Both plume and petrol, like certain marine flora, a large white flower, downy as a wing, hung down from the princess's head along one cheek of which it followed the curve with coy suppleness, fond and vivacious, half-enclosing it, as it seemed, as a rose egg in the comfort of a halcyon's nest. On the princess's hair, descending down to her eyebrows and attached lower down at the level of her throat, was spread a fine net made of those white shells retrieved from certain southern seas, and mingled with pearls, marine mosaic just barely emerged from the waves, which at times found itself drowned in a darkness, at the bottom of which, even then, a human presence was revealed by the flashing mobility of the princess's eyes.]

It is worth pointing out some of the comparative formulations used by Proust here: notice that the couch on which the princess reclines is 'red as' a coral reef, the mirror behind her 'recalled' the section of a ray through water; the flower in the princess's hair is 'just as some marine flora', 'downy as a wing', and encloses the face of the princess 'like' a halcyon's nest. Covering the head and shoulders of the princess is 'a fine net made of those white shells retrieved from certain austral seas', where the almost scientific detail of the shells' geographical origin, unique in this passage, adds greatly to the reality effect. Mixed with pearls, in Parnassian vein no doubt, in the shade behind the princess, 'a human presence was revealed by the flashing mobility of the princess's eyes'. The detail of her lively eyes with 'motilité éclatante' and the emphasis on the 'human presence' in the back trace a portrait of the princess as altogether different in kind from all the other characters.

Furthermore, in what follows, we hear that it is her intrinsic beauty that places the princess 'far above all the other marvellous daughters of twilight', this beauty that is 'as the spectre of an ideal form projected onto darkness'. The particular phrase 'spectre d'une figure idéale' is reminiscent of the poem 'Le Spectre de la rose' by Théophile Gautier, which later became the lyric to one of Berlioz's arias in the cycle 'Nuits d'été' ['Summer Nights']. If my intuition is correct, Proust's allusion to the rose in the person of the princesse de Guermantes offers an oblique correspondence with his earlier version of the passage, where the group of women as a whole were represented as flowers rather than Nereids and the princesse de Guermantes would naturally assume the role of the rose, queen among flowers. The qualities of nobility, pride, passion and honour often associated with the symbolism of roses, the image of a 'thorny path of conquest', not incompatible with the princesses in many fairy tales that Proust mentions elsewhere in the novel (and more particularly that of Geneviève de Brabant, the scene on the magic lantern in his childhood bedroom), do have slightly more masculine undertones than the imagery of aquatic divinities that Proust finally favoured.[18]

> La beauté qui mettait celle-ci bien au-dessus des autres filles fabuleuses de la pénombre n'était pas tout entière matériellement et inclusivement inscrite dans sa nuque, dans ses épaules, dans ses bras, dans sa taille. Mais la ligne délicieuse et inachevée de celle-ci était l'exact point de départ, l'amorce inévitable de lignes invisibles en lesquelles l'œil ne pouvait s'empêcher de les prolonger, merveilleuses, engendrées autour de la femme comme le spectre d'une figure idéale projetée sur les ténèbres.[19]

> [The beauty, which set her far above all the other marvellous daughters of twilight, was not materially and completely inscribed on her neck, her shoulders, her arms, her waist. But the gracious and unfinished line of the last was the precise beginning, the inevitable starting point of invisible lines that no eye could refrain from prolonging, fantastic lines created around this woman like the spectre of an ideal shape projected onto darkness.]

After his homage to the natural beauty of the princesse de Guermantes, Proust turns his focus on the other members of the aristocracy to explain that, albeit in the appearance of nymphs, these women are not in themselves beautiful: 'ce qui permettait d'identifier leur visage, c'était la connexité d'un gros nez rouge avec un bec-de-lièvre, ou de deux joues ridées avec une fine moustache' ['their faces could be identified by the matching of a thick red nose and a hare lip, or of two wrinkled cheeks with a downy moustache']. The presence of Mme de Guermantes serves as a certificate of authenticity (here again, in a phrase reminiscent of jeweller's certificates, we have a quasi-technical reference) for the 'painting' that the box constitutes.

Mais comme certains artistes qui, au lieu des lettres de leur nom, mettent au bas de leur toile une forme belle par elle-même, un papillon, un lézard, une fleur, de même c'était la forme d'un corps et d'un visage délicieux que la princesse apposait à l'angle de sa loge, montrant par là que la beauté peut être la plus noble des signatures; car la présence de Mme de Guermantes, qui n'amenait au théâtre que des personnes qui le reste du temps faisaient partie de son intimité, était, aux yeux des amateurs d'aristocratie, le meilleur certificat d'authenticité du tableau que présentait sa baignoire, sorte d'évocation d'une scène de la vie familière et spéciale de la princesse dans ses palais de Munich et de Paris [...].[20]

[But, in the manner of certain artists who, instead of using the letters of their name, place at the bottom of their canvass a shape that is in itself beautiful, a butterfly, a lizard, or a flower, just so it was the form of an exquisite body and beautiful face that the princess placed in the corner of her box, thereby showing that beauty can be the noblest of signatures; for the presence of Mme de Guermantes, who brought to the theatre only such persons who otherwise were among her intimate friends, was in the eyes of lovers of the aristocracy the best authenticity certificate of the painting that was her box, almost summoning up scenes from the familiar and special life of the princess in her palaces in Munich and in Paris.]

Emerging as more beautiful, but also as more real than the others, the princess is human and at the same time divine, whilst the remaining Nereid-aristocrats are reduced to a grosser existence within their mythical context, a context which is, as the narrator indicates, inaccessible to humans, but in which they are themselves confined. Only the princesse de Guermantes has a double status. She offers sweets to those around her, including a real and far from perfect person:

Il me fallait l'en dépouiller maintenant que je la voyais, en train d'offrir des bonbons glacés à un gros monsieur en frac. Certes j'étais bien loin d'en conclure qu'elle et ses invités fussent des êtres pareils aux autres. Je comprenais bien que ce qu'ils faisaient là n'était qu'un jeu, et que pour préluder aux actes de leur vie véritable (dont sans doute ce n'est pas ici qu'ils vivaient la partie importante) ils convenaient en vertu des rites ignorés de moi, ils feignaient d'offrir et de refuser des bonbons, geste dépouillé de sa signification et réglé d'avance comme le pas d'une danseuse qui tour à tour s'élève sur sa pointe et tourne autour d'une écharpe. Qui sait? peut-être au moment où elle offrait ses bonbons, la Déesse disait-elle sur ce ton d'ironie (car je la voyais sourire): «Voulez-vous des bonbons?»[21]

[Now that I saw her, tendering frosted sweets to an overweight gentleman in dinner jacket, I needed to rid my imagination of these conceptions. To be sure, I was far from thinking that she and her guests were beings similar to others. I knew well that they were only playing a game, and that as a prelude to the activities of their real life (of which they doubtlessly weren't living the important part here) they were gathering by virtue of rites unknown to me, pretending to offer or decline sweets, a gesture void of meaning and agreed upon in advance as the step of a ballerina who rises in pointe turn after turn dancing around a shawl. Who knows, perhaps just as she was offering her sweets, the Goddess would say in a tone of irony (for I saw her smile) 'would you like some sweets?']

In Marcel's imaginative hypothesis, the ritual of offering sweets at the Opéra is a comic routine, intended to conceal the participants' 'true life', and there are pre-established rules of conduct for this routine. The all-pervading irony here infiltrates even the speech of the aristocracy itself. Aware of the artificiality of the situation, Mme de Guermantes speaks her lines in the role as goddess in the second degree, and the interlocutor answers, perhaps sounding perplexingly mundane after all the layers of meaning construed around her:

> Que m'importait? J'aurais trouvé d'un délicieux raffinement la sécheresse voulue, à la Mérimée ou à la Meilhac, de ces mots adressés par une déesse à un demi-dieu qui, lui, savait quelles étaient les pensées sublimes que tous deux résumaient, sans doute pour le moment où ils se remettraient à vivre leur vraie vie et qui, se prêtant à ce jeu, répondait avec la même mystérieuse malice: «Oui, je veux bien une cerise.» Et j'aurais écouté ce dialogue avec la même avidité que telle scène du *Mari de la Débutante*, où l'absence de poésie, de grandes pensées, choses si familières pour moi et que je suppose que Meilhac eût été mille fois capable d'y mettre, me semblait à elle seule une élégance, une élégance conventionnelle, et par là d'autant plus mystérieuse et plus instructive.[22]

> [What did it matter to me? I should have found deliciously refined the intentional dryness, in the style of Mérimée or Meilhac, of such words spoken by a goddess to a demi-god, who knew what sublime thoughts were in the mind of both, doubtless reserved for the moment when they would resume their true life, and who, going along with this game, was replying with the same mysterious mischievousness: 'Yes, I'd love a cherry'. And I would have listened to this conversation as avidly as to a scene from *Le Mari de la Débutante*, in which the lack of lyricism, of great thoughts, things so customary to me and that I suppose Meilhac would have been perfectly capable of adding, seemed to me an elegance in itself, elegance which was conventional and hence all the more mysterious, more instructive.]

Some have argued, in an attempt to locate the mythological scenario, that Mme de Guermantes in this constellation represents the goddess Thetis ('bien qu'allu-sivement'),[23] and that the other divinities participate in a 'vulgarised mythology'.[24] This again would give Mme de Guermantes a special, superior status. Laget does not cite convincing parallels for her identification with Thetis, and there is little profit in attempting to assign each of the remaining persons to a specific nymph named in classical texts; quite apart from the difficulties involved in such an exercise, any attempt to establish such direct links between Proust's work and classical precedents remains methodologically problematic since it ignores the fact that he was more interested in the imaginary Greece of the Parnassian poets than that of our ancient sources. The next figure that receives a close-up is the Marquis de Palancy, introduced to the reader by one of the 'common' people in the orchestra, who takes pride in having recognized someone important, though unfortunately getting it wrong.

> — Ce gros-là, c'est le marquis de Ganançay, dit d'un air renseigné mon voisin qui avait mal entendu le nom chuchoté derrière lui. Le marquis de Palancy, le cou tendu, la figure oblique, son gros œil rond collé contre le verre du monocle, se déplaçait lentement dans l'ombre transparente et paraissait ne pas plus voir le

public de l'orchestre qu'un poisson qui passe, ignorant de la foule des visiteurs curieux, derrière la cloison vitrée d'un aquarium. Par moment il s'arrêtait, vénérable, soufflant et moussu, et les spectateurs n'auraient pu dire s'il souffrait, dormait, nageait, était en train de pondre ou respirait seulement.[25]

['The fat man over there, that's the marquis de Ganançay', said with knowing air the gentleman next to me, who had misheard the name whispered behind him. The marquis of Palancy, neck outstretched, face turned sideways, his full, round eye stuck to the glass of his monocle, was moving slowly in the transparent shade and seemed no more aware of the audience in the orchestra than a large fish swimming by, unbothered by the crowd of intrigued guests, behind the glass wall of an aquarium. Time and again he stopped, venerable, gasping and mossy, and a spectator wouldn't have been able to say whether he was in pain, or sleeping, swimming, laying eggs, or simply breathing.]

Proust indulges in some humorous touches in describing the marquis's fish-like mannerisms. He too, once safely arrived in his box, has the princess offer him sweets, as she casts on him a gaze that seemed 'cut from a diamond' with 'mineral splendour' — congruent with the imagery discussed above:

Personne n'excitait en moi autant d'envie que lui, à cause de l'habitude qu'il avait l'air d'avoir de cette baignoire et de l'indifférence avec laquelle il laissait la princesse lui tendre des bonbons; elle jetait alors sur lui un regard de ses beaux yeux taillés dans un diamant que semblaient bien fluidifier, à ces moments-là, l'intelligence et l'amitié, mais qui, quand ils étaient au repos, réduits à leur pure beauté matérielle, à leur seul éclat minéralogique, si le moindre réflexe les déplaçait légèrement, incendiaient la profondeur du parterre de feux inhumains, horizontaux et splendides.[26]

[Nobody aroused my envy as much as he, for he seemed so accustomed to this box and so indifferently let the princess offer him sweets; and she threw him in such moments a glance from her beautiful eyes cut from a diamond, that intelligence and affection seemed to liquefy; but when they were still, reduced to their purest material beauty and merely mineral splendour, whenever the smallest reflex would slightly move their position, the eyes ignited the depth of the orchestra floor with their inhuman flames, horizontal and splendid.]

When, however, the light in the theatre changes, as the act is about to begin, a veritable metamorphosis occurs:

Cependant, parce que l'acte de Phèdre que jouait la Berma allait commencer, la princesse vint sur le devant de la baignoire; alors, comme si elle-même était une apparition de théâtre, dans la zone différente de lumière qu'elle traversa, je vis changer non seulement la couleur mais la matière de ses parures. Et dans la baignoire asséchée, émergée, qui n'appartenait plus au monde des eaux, la princesse cessant d'être une néréide apparut enturbannée de blanc et de bleu comme quelque merveilleuse tragédienne costumée en Zaïre ou peut-être en Orosmane; puis quand elle se fut assise au premier rang, je vis que le doux nid d'alcyon qui protégeait tendrement la nacre rose de ses joues était, douillet, éclatant et velouté, un immense oiseau de paradis.[27]

[But now, because the act of *Phaedra*, in which La Berma was playing, was about to begin, the princess came to the front of her box; and there, as if she herself were a theatrical fixture, in the different zone of light that she crossed,

I saw not only the colour, but also the material of her apparel change. And in this box now drained dry, no longer part of the world of water, the princess ceased being a Nereid and appeared turbaned in white and blue as a fabulous tragic lady dressed as Zaire or perhaps Orosmane; then once she had taken her seat in the front row, I saw that the halcyon's soft nest so tenderly guarding the iridescent rose of her cheeks was in fact a large bird of paradise, soft, resplendent and velvety.]

It is time to state the obvious, that there is a good deal of displaced theatricality in this theatre scene:[28] we have not heard anything at all yet about the Racine play which is the alleged chief reason for the gathering, but Marcel has paid ample attention to the costuming in the boxes and described the menagerie upstairs. Meanwhile, the individuals in the boxes are getting ready to view the 'spectacle of mortals', though it remains unclear whether the Racine act or the activity in the orchestra is meant by this. Conversely, from the orchestra, there are two aspects of classical tradition on display: the aristocracy, in Nereid garb or not, and the *Phèdre* act in the appropriate Opéra Garnier fixtures. There appears to be a certain competition between various spectacles, as well as between various traditions.

In Proust's description, the persons of the aristocracy are at the same time physically aloof and appear as socially unreachable, in their affinity with demi-gods. Although such a 'demi-deification' as a literary device at first seems to pay homage to the aristocracy, this is countervailed by the irony of the narrator's familiarity with these people, and his very low esteem of both their character and appearance.

> — C'est la princesse de Guermantes, dit ma voisine au monsieur qui était avec elle, en ayant soin de mettre devant le mot princesse plusieurs p indiquant que cette appellation était risible. Elle n'a pas économisé ses perles. Il me semble que si j'en avais autant, je n'en ferais pas un pareil étalage; je ne trouve pas que cela ait l'air comme il faut.'
>
> Et cependant, en reconnaissant la princesse, tous ceux qui cherchaient à savoir qui était dans la salle sentaient se relever dans leur cœur le trône légitime de la beauté. En effet, pour la duchesse de Luxembourg, pour Mme de Morienval, pour Mme de Saint-Euverte, pour tant d'autres, ce qui permettait d'identifier leur visage, c'était la connexité d'un gros nez rouge avec un bec de lièvre, ou de deux joues ridées avec une fine moustache. Ces traits étaient d'ailleurs suffisants pour charmer, puisque, n'ayant que la valeur conventionnelle d'une écriture, ils donnaient à lire un nom célèbre et qui imposait; mais aussi, ils finissaient par donner l'idée que la laideur a quelque chose d'aristocratique, et qu'il est indifférent que le visage d'une grande dame, s'il est distingué, soit beau.[29]

['That's the princesse de Guermantes', the lady sitting next to me was telling the man she was with, carefully uttering several 'p's at the start of the word 'princess', to indicate how laughable she thought this title. 'She hasn't economized on pearls. I fancy that if I had that many of them, I would not make such a display; I don't think it's appropriate'.

And yet, by identifying the princess, all those seeking to know who was in the house, felt rise in their hearts the legitimate throne of beauty. And indeed, for the duchess of Luxemburg, for Mme de Morienval, for Mme de Saint-Euverte, for so many others, their faces were identified by the matching of a thick red nose and a hare lip, or of two wrinkled cheeks with a downy moustache. These traits were nevertheless sufficient to confer charm, as, with

nothing more than the conventional value of a sort of calligraphy, they supplied
a famous and impressive name to be read; furthermore, they were able to give
the impression that ugliness had something aristocratic, and that it is irrelevant
whether the face of a lady, if it is illustrious, is pretty.]

The physical attributes of all but the princesse de Guermantes are, to say the least,
unappealing. In a slightly earlier paragraph, Proust even writes in aphoristic tone:
'c'était parce que les gens du monde étaient dans leurs loges [...] comme dans
des petits salons [...] que seuls ils auraient eu l'esprit libre pour écouter la pièce si
seulement ils avaient eu de l'esprit' ['it is because the people of high society were in
their boxes [...] as in their own living rooms [...] that they could have had their minds
free to attend to the piece, had they only had minds'].[30] The 'high society' who do
not care to be mindful of the theatre fixtures but 'posaient une main indifférente
sur les fûts dorés des colonnes qui soutenaient ce temple de l'art lyrique' ['rested an
indifferent hand on the gilded shafts of columns upholding this temple of lyrical
art'] are in the best position to hear and understand the piece, but unfortunately
lack the disposition for it. In Proust's reflection, these affluent theatre-goers are
so familiar with the décor that they are part of it, as opposed to the more modest
people who can only afford to visit the Palais Garnier occasionally and therefore
have not only the play of Racine to see, but also the opera-house architecture, and
the many evening dresses to admire. The firm line of division between aristocracy
and bourgeoisie that Proust draws here, with the help of the seat order and metamorphic musings on the evening dress of aristocratic ladies, is problematized,
however, by the disparaging irony that Proust injects into his layered description,
alternating between appearance, reality and imagination.

> Notre imagination étant comme un orgue de Barbarie détraqué qui joue
> toujours autre chose que l'air indiqué, chaque fois que j'avais entendu parler de
> la princesse de Guermantes-Bavière, le souvenir de certaines œuvres du XVIe
> siècle avait commencé à chanter en moi.[31]

> [Since our imagination, being like a derailed barrel organ, is continually
> playing something other than the tune we demand of it, each time I'd heard
> mention of the princess of Guermantes-Bavaria, the memory of certain works
> from the sixteenth century had begun to sing within me.]

On a larger scale, it has been argued that Proust's entire *Recherche* tells the story of
how an old order collapsed and how members of low society came to play the roles
formerly occupied by high members, and vice versa.[32] This can be pushed further.
I would argue that the seemingly effortless interchange of individuals acting
in various social roles that appear as so many fixed, predictable and rehearsable
parts as if it were all a play, suggests a view in Proust that all men are equal and
that the different social positions occupied by individuals, with their associated
fashions and manner, are nothing more than an act, a merely formal and entirely
dispensible arrangement. But to return to Proust's ironic and summary comment
on the aristocracy's intellectual vacuity and the description of persons of semi-
divine appearance: in this passage, he does not in fact offer psychological character
descriptions; instead he limits himself to remarks on external appearance. Both
this interest in the surface of things, and the approach to mythology here, are very

reminiscent of Parnassian poetry. In the next section, I shall explore the origins and workings of this mythological imagery a little further.

Parnassian Soundings

The Parnassians were a circle of mid-nineteenth-century poets whose most memorable motto was *l'art pour l'art* ('art for art's sake'), and who in this quest drew inspiration from the literature of Graeco-Roman antiquity. The naming of the group after Mount Parnassus is a prime indication of this aesthetic affiliation. Several members of the movement also produced contemporary translations of ancient texts, most notably Leconte de Lisle's *Iliad*, which Proust ridicules through the character Bloch in the *Recherche*: a man of no finesse, he speaks French using inelegant-sounding Homeric formulae, no doubt extracted from Leconte de Lisle's translation of the *Iliad*.[33] Proust himself was, of course, an avid reader of contemporary poetry and literary prose, as is Marcel in the narrative.[34] Along with a considerable degree of irony and self-awareness, Proust's writing betrays significant Parnassian influence.

There are several poems in which Parnassian poets offer descriptions of semi-divine creatures in an aesthetic manner that seems relevant to Proust's mythological imagery in our passage. Thus Théophile Gautier writes in his poem 'Les Néréides':

> Sur l'écume blanche qui frange
> le manteau glauque de la mer
> se groupent en bouquet étrange
> trois nymphes, fleurs du gouffre amer.[35]

> [Upon the white foam that fringes
> The glaucous cloak of the sea
> Are grouped, in strange bouquet,
> Three nymphs, flowers of the bitter abyss.]

In juxtaposition with a grotesque modern ship, Gautier's playful nymphs appear momentarily on the surface as a 'strange bouquet' over the 'bitter abyss'.[36] Today, these lines are perhaps not as well-remembered as other nineteenth-century poetry; however, readers of Baudelaire will recognize the expression 'gouffre amer', which is used in the poem 'L'Albatros', where it indicates the abyss of sin and moral decrepitude; here in Gautier, the image of flowers and the appeal to estrangement ('bouquet étrange') charge these lines with extra significance, especially if one keeps in mind that Baudelaire's *Flowers of Evil* bears a dedication to Théophile Gautier.

Furthermore, such close alliance of marine and floral imagery is particular to these nineteenth-century poets. It is thus significant that Proust's passage of aristocratic persons in the appearance of nymphs and Nereids had originally been drafted as an analogy between these ladies and flowers in a bouquet looming over an abyss and not as semi-divine mythological creatures of the sea. A Parnassian influence on Proust would therefore seem probable.[37] The connotations of the 'gouffre amer' of sinfulness and decrepitude as explored by Baudelaire and already, albeit only suggestively, present in Gautier's poem cited above, are also noticeable in Proust, who writes about the orchestra section as an abyss, wherein reside the 'monstres de l'orchestre', more markedly so in his earlier sketch than in the passage as it has been transmitted in the standard edition.

Proust's description of the jewelled evening gown of the aristocratic ladies, furthermore, has something in common with the fifth stanza of Gautier's same Nereid-poem, where he describes the pearls that decorate the nymphs:

> vidant sa nacre, l'huître à perle
> constelle de son blanc trésor
> Leur gorge, où le flot qui déferle
> Suspend d'autres perles encore.[38]

> [Emptying her nacre, the pearl oyster
> With her white treasure sprinkles stars
> On each breast, where the surging wave
> Affixes yet more pearls.]

In the sixth stanza, 'tritons' are mentioned:

> Et, jusqu'aux hanches soulevées
> par le bras des Tritons nerveux,
> elles luisent, d'azur lavées,
> Sous l'or vert de leurs longs cheveux.[39]

> [And, lifted to their hips
> By the sinewy arms of tritons,
> They shine, washed in azure,
> Under the green gold of their long hair.]

Proust's tritons may be 'barbus' rather than 'nerveux'; there is, nonetheless, a noticeable metric and sonoric similarity between 'tritons barbus' and 'tritons nerveux'. It seems significant that Proust, like Gautier, associates Nereids with tritons, as nymphs are common figures in much classical literature, whilst 'tritons' are somewhat rarer, so that it would have been hard for Proust to come across them in the classical corpus. Their presence is thus probably due to the influence of the Parnassians who had featured Tritons with more prominence in their writing.[40]

To return to pearls: in a different poem, 'Les Déesses posent', which does not feature a maritime setting, Gautier writes:

> Des perles à l'éclat tremblant
> ruissellent sur votre col blanc,
> comme des gouttes de lumière.[41]

> [Pearls, with trembling splendour,
> Glitter down your white neck,
> As drops of light.]

The whiteness of skin, a stereotype that Proust embraced in his own description, alongside the image of pearls trickling in the manner of dewdrops ('gouttes de lumière') and the fine tremor of light reflections, here suggests a still, sculpture-like, ideal of beauty, the very 'art pour l'art' aesthetic which Baudelaire was later so adamantly to deride. It implies detachment and a distance between the beautiful sight and the onlooker, creating a separation of spheres, similar to the effect in the Proust passage.

In *Fantaisies* V, Gautier writes of a

> jeune fée à l'aile de saphir
> sous une sombre et fraîche arcade,
> blanche comme un reflet de la perle d'Ophir.[42]

> [Young fairy with sapphire wing
> Under a cool and shaded arcade,
> White as a ray of the Ophir pearl.]

White as a pearl, this fairy scintillates from darkness, much like the sea-divinities in Proust's Opéra Garnier setting. The sapphire wing here leads us to the theme of precious stones and minerals, which Proust also employed in the description of aristocratic figures in our passage. In *Poésies diverses*, in the poem 'A deux beaux yeux', Gautier speaks of the eyes of his beloved in these terms:

> Ils semblent avoir pris ses feux au diamant
> ils sont de plus belle eau qu'une perle parfaite.[43]

> [They seem to have taken their fires from the diamond,
> They are of finer water than a perfect pearl.]

This has something in common with Proust's phrase 'éclat minéralogique' and the diamond imagery used in describing the eyes of the princess. Whilst Gautier's use of the diamond imagery inspires heat and desire, Proust's use of 'éclat mineralogique' leaves these eyes gleaming with inanimate fires. Gautier further connects his imagery with moonlight and deep waters:

> comme la lune au fond du lac qui la reflète
> votre prunelle où brille une humide paillette [44]

> [As the moon at the bottom of a lake that reflects it,
> Your pupil, where a moist sequin is glistening]

This is a near precursor to Baudelaire's lines in 'l'invitation au voyage':

> Les soleils mouillés
> De ces ciels brouillés
> Pour mon esprit ont les charmes
> Si mystérieux
> De tes traîtres yeux,
> Brillant à travers leurs larmes.[45]

> [The wet suns
> Of these overcast skies
> To my mind have the charms,
> So mysterious,
> Of your treacherous eyes
> Gleaming through their tears.]

Here the eyes, gleaming as 'wet suns', are 'treacherous', yet have an undeniable charm. The sombre undertone of 'overcast skies' and the notion of treason joined to the luminous image of suns and brilliance finds resonances in the writing of Proust, who certainly knew this poem.

Léon Dierx, also a Parnassian poet, writes in a poem titled 'L'Œil':

> Son regard fluide et phosphorescent
> fait trembler aux bords des corolles closes
> Les larmes des choses [46]
>
> [Her gaze, fluid and phosphorescent,
> Brings a tremble, by the edges of the closed petals,
> To the tears of things.]

Proust likewise uses the word 'phosphorescent', and here the gaze is also 'fluid', aligned with water imagery as well as the concept of trespassing limits, crossing lines ('aux bords des corolles closes'). The reminiscence of the *Aeneid* ('larmes des choses' — *lacrimae rerum*) inserts pathos into the situation, although here, unlike in Virgil, it appears that what is meant is that the natural world has the ability to shed tears, by way of dew drops, which the gaze of the eye in this poem can cause to quiver, whereas in Virgil the phrase refers to human tears of pity over affairs or events (the meaning of *res*) rather than the tears shed by things.[47] Dierx's use of such a blatant 'mistranslation' of Virgil, and his expansion of his model, while retaining the pathos in the situation, suggest an engagement with the classical heritage characteristic of the Parnassian poets, who frequently departed from a 'faithful' reading of ancient authors, and to a great extent the same is true of Proust.

Further Parnassian evocations in Proust may come from the poet José-Maria de Heredia; in a sketch entitled 'la mer', we read

> que frangent sur le bord de légères écumes
> tandis que palpitant au ciel immense et pur
> un grand nuage entr'ouvre en un frisson de plumes
> son éventail de cygne entremêlé d'azur [48]
>
> [Ruffled at its edges by light foam,
> Whilst, pulsing through the vast and clear sky,
> A great cloud opens up, in a shiver of down,
> its fan of swan feathers, inlaid with azure.]

The metaphoric reference to a fan here, the swan-feather fan belonging to a cloud is lexically (and visually) close to Proust's depiction of sea waves and their foam as forming a fan around the princess.

Heredia's 'Le Bain des nymphes' ('The Nymph-Bath'), in the collection *Trophées* has one stanza of particular interest here:

> Ses compagnes, d'un bond, à l'appel du buccin,
> dans l'onde jaillissante où s'ébat leur chair blanche
> plongent, et de l'écume émergent une hanche,
> de clairs cheveux, un torse ou la rose d'un sein.[49]
>
> [Her maids, with a leap at the call of the horn,
> Dive into the surging wave where their white flesh
> frolics, and from the foam rise a hip,
> Fair hair, a torso, or the rose of a breast.]

The expression of merriness, the white skin of the Nereids, the foam of the sea, even the half nakedness, together with the other examples, demonstrate that Proust, in his metamorphic description of sea-divinities, has in fact made extensive use of a well-established aesthetic topos in nineteenth-century poetry, with its peculiar spectrum of colours, moods, and ornamentation.

My final two examples come from the work of Leconte de Lisle. From our perspective, one poem, entitled 'Glaucé' after one of the Nereids, is of particular interest. It opens thus:

> Sous les grottes de nacre et les limons épais
> où la divine Mer sommeille et rêve en paix,
> vers l'heure où l'immortelle aux paupières dorées
> rougit le pâle azur de ses roses sacrées,
> Je suis née, et mes sœurs, qui nagent aux flots bleus,
> m'ont bercée en riant dans leurs bras onduleux
> et, sur la perle humide entrelaçant leurs danses,
> Instruit mes pieds aux divines cadences.[50]

> [In caves of nacre and thickest muds,
> Where the divine sea slumbers and dreams in peace,
> At the hour when the immortal one of gilded eyelids
> Reddens the pale azure with her sacred roses,
> I was born, and my sisters, who swim in blue waves,
> Lulled me with laughter in their flowing arms,
> And, entwining their dances on the humid pearl,
> Taught my feet the divine cadences.]

Again, the colours present here, nacre, gold, pale blue, rose, and pearl — all delicate and precious shades — are part of an aesthetic that reappears and informs Proust's description of sea-divinities, much more so than any direct reading of classical sources. The use of marine, fluid, pale and rainbow-coloured shades, so dear to the Parnassians and also to Proust in his depiction of sea creatures and décor, is more nineteenth-century French than ancient Greek or Roman in its development, not least in how it recalls the use of colour in impressionist art, with its pastel shades, inherent fluidity, and dissolving of silhouettes in soft and often mist-charged light. Proust of course, in the novel and his work more generally, has a great deal of time for the discussion of impressionist art. In fact, the *Recherche* notably features the painter-character Elstir, thought to be a hybrid of the historical Monet and Manet. Here it is pertinent to observe that Marcel's friend Bloch, who is ridiculed in the novel for his 'homerico-parnassian' way of speaking, is a close associate of the painter Elstir; at one point, the three meet by the seaside, where Bloch exclaims: 'Ils sont partis [...] hélas [...] l'héroique Hellas'. The full passage on the sea has Marcel attempting to

> me la représenter comme immémoriale, encore contemporaine des âges où elle avait été séparée de la terre, à tout le moins contemporaine des premiers siècles de la Grèce, ce qui me permettait de redire en toute vérité les vers du «père Leconte» chers à Bloch:

>> Ils sont partis, les rois des nefs éperonnées,
>> Entraînant sur la mer tempétueuse, hélas!
>> Les hommes chevelus de l'héroïque Hellas'.[51]

> [picture it to myself as immemorial, still contemporary with the age when it had been separate from the earth, or at least, contemporary with the first

centuries of Greece, which allowed me to repeat in all truth the verses of old Leconte, so dear to Bloch : 'They have left, the kings of the bronze-spurred ships, conveying over the tempestuous sea — alas! — the long-haired warriors of heroic Hellas.']

The irony is palpable: in an effort to conceive of the sea as more than just its material substance and to view it as a poetic topos of old, or, to put it differently, in order to transcend the moment and to see the very same sea that had inspired the Greeks, Marcel eventually resorts to the verse of Leconte de Lisle.

In the poem of Leconte de Lisle cited above, the beginning 'je suis née', together with the ensuing depiction, recalls the famous image of the Birth of Venus in Botticelli's painting 'La nascita di Venere' (*c.* 1485/86); and if we regard Venus as the Greek Aphrodite and consider the Greek etymology of her name ('the foam-born one'), suggestive correspondences emerge between this work and Proust's description of the princesse de Guermantes, in particular the foam-like, aqueous texture of her emergence and dress. It is, however, important to notice not only these convergences, but also a certain distance established by Proust from the tone in Homer or the Attic tragedians, in particular Sophocles, where the sea rarely is as joyous and innocent an image. For instance, the Homeric formula of πολυφλοίσβοιο θαλάσσης, ('the far-roaring sea') or Sophocles' unique formulation περιβρυχίοισιν οἴδμασιν ('the engulfing waves') in the *Antigone* (336–37) both carry connotations of danger, fright, and bitter fate more akin to the French 'gouffre amer' ('bitter abyss') discussed earlier, than the serene images of the Proust passage. Leconte de Lisle, known as the Parnassian movement's translator of the *Iliad*, offers this rendering of a passage featuring Thetis in Book XVIII:

> Et autour de la déesse étaient rassemblées toutes les Néréides qui sont au fond de la mer: Glauké [...] et les autres Néréides qui sont dans la profonde mer. Et elles emplissaient la grotte d'argent, et elles se frappaient la poitrine, et Thétis se lamentait ainsi: [...] ayant ainsi parlé, elle quitta la grotte, et toutes la suivaient pleurantes; et l'eau de la mer s'ouvrait devant elles.[52]

> [And around the goddess were gathered all the Nereids who are in the depth of the sea: Glauce [...] and the other Nereids who are in the deep sea. And they were filling the silver cave, and they were beating their chests, and Thetis thus lamented: [...] having thus spoken, she left the cave, and all followed her in tears; and the water of the sea opened before them.]

Leconte de Lisle's translation can be deemed a fairly faithful one.[53] Interestingly, there is a striking difference in tone and colour between the translation, which reflects the transmitted classical text itself, and the very similar, yet differently affiliated 'classicizing' setting of Leconte de Lisle's poem 'Glauce' (cited just above the *Iliad* passages): whereas Leconte's Homer translation had 'argent' ['silver'] for the Greek ἀργύρεον (a choice both straightforward and accurate), in his poem 'Glauce' he uses the word 'nacre' to describe the cave of the nymphs. Where the Homer translation had 'dans la profonde mer' ['in the deep sea'] corresponding to the Greek ἐν βένθεσσιν ἁλός ['in the depths of the sea'] Leconte has 'aux flots bleus' ['of blue waves'], a locution which, in contrast to the phrase in the translation, forgoes a number of the connotations resonating in the Greek ἐν βένθεσσιν, specifically the darkness, the frightfulness, the tears that in the Homeric passage are all congruent with the depiction of the sea and the mystery of its depth as perilous, rather than serene. The difference in mood is striking: what was originally a tearful scene in Homer, in Leconte de Lisle becomes a setting of laughter, much like Heredia's 'Bain des nymphes', to say nothing of other authors who may have influenced Proust's conception of sea nymphs as providing a literary occasion for passages of lightness and serenity and whose phrases, as we have seen, he often recapitulates virtually verbatim. But perhaps the best evidence of a specifically Parnassian aesthetic that mediates and supersedes the aesthetics of classical authors, is Leconte de Lisle's reworking of his *Iliad* translation through original poetry on kindred themes, not least because of his authoritative influence on the movement and, later on, Proust.

With respect to Proust, there is no need to go into further reviews of the Parnassian aesthetic in poetry, but some further comments on the passage quoted above are in order. As pointed out, Proust treats ironically the veneration of aristocratic figures as god-like, and the marine setting he is depicting in the theatre scene, for all the divinities he conjures up, is transitory rather than eternal. In the brief moments in which the light changes in the house, these characters change their status and, from indistinct and divine-seeming, become clearly recognizable and human. Proust's borrowing of the Parnassian aesthetic of eternity, grafted onto these bodies and faces, lasts only a brief moment. One of the great dilemmas throughout the *Recherche* is the quest for transcendence and the repeated discovery of entries to eternity which prove to be fleeting, connected to ephemeral changes of perception easier to miss than to grasp, so that Marcel passes them by and remains confined in materiality and the uninspiring present.

The forgoing analysis raises the question of genre distinctions and generic demarcations between poetry, prose, poetic prose, 'artless poetry', narrative, the novel, and so on, in nineteenth- and twentieth-century France (or, as some would say, 'the long nineteenth century', up to 1918), as well as how these relate to classical antiquity and the intervening tradition.

To begin with Racine: he is an author haunting the *Recherche* throughout, as one of the French neoclassical greats, for whom Marcel and his family and family friends have a special predilection alongside La Bruyère, Mme de Sévigné and Moliere. According to the narrator, his main accomplishment is perfect versification, a pure and noble rhythm of speech.[54] Marcel speaks of some 'monstrous' sentence which was the result of his attempting to remind himself of a Racine verse, not managing to do so, and instead creating a non-metrical arrangement which he then deems to sound awful. By 'monstrous', no doubt what is meant is something akin to 'vulgar', in the same way as he views the more common opera-goers in the orchestra as 'monsters' by comparison with the refined aristocracy and their manners. The opposition of noble purity and popular monstrosity, with Marcel placing his own language on the 'monstrous' side, reverberates with sharp irony and conveys a sense that past grandeur and nobility are being overturned by a violent and inelegant present, an idea that deserves further development. In our passage, the bright light cast on the aristocracy leaves an ambiguous impression. With their rehearsed and lifeless-looking mannerism in guise of meaningful acts, their oscillation between the inanimate world and the life of vanity, their lack of 'esprit' and their existence in Parnassian shades of the past, these people do seem to inhabit an extremely fragile realm of privilege; indeed, on a larger scale, the *Recherche* is very much the story of an old order overturned.[55]

In socio-historical terms, Proust's ekphrastic treatment of aristocratic patterns of behaviour, as well as names and wardrobe, records the perfected form and manners of an empire on the wane. We must not forget, after all, that the novel was written between 1916 and 1922, effectively after the destruction of most of the things spoken of in the *Recherche*. Proust thus aligns his perception of the aristocracy with an aesthetic of the century gone by. The effect is interesting: even though the recourse to a classical Greek tradition does at first give an impression of timelessness, the specific type of classical revival aimed for in the Parnassian aesthetic was, at the time of Proust's writing, already dated. The character Bloch says so in the novel, and indeed Baudelaire had already characterized the tradition as a 'siècle vaurien' ['a century good for nothing'] when speaking of the Parnassian ideal of 'art for art's sake', outlining his own call for deeper, more murder-reeking, intensely horrifying art works, as exemplified by his own poem 'Lady Macbeth', which is full of Aeschylean terror. Marcel himself is attracted to this type of aesthetic, which informs many scenes of the *Recherche*, such as the telephone scene, where his dying grandmother's voice begins to sound as a prophecy from a Dantesque underworld.[56]

'Proust's ambition was to awaken and free the dormant God in his reader, to urge him to partake in a new metamorphosis of himself and his world, to become a creator', writes Highet.[57] His insight finds support in one of the programmatic sentences in 'Combray': 'Chercher? pas seulement: créer' ['To search? Not just that: to create']. Combray and its way of life, Proust says, were 'mort pour moi' ['dead to me'], and the program of the *Recherche* was to re-create the past from memory. The narrator blames the death of memory on the distraction caused by aristocratic matinées and the intermittency of his heart and resolves to re-create the so-called primitive state — in a reaction similar to Baudelaire's hatred for Parnassian superficial decorousness. But with Proust, matters are more complex, insofar as the aristocratic milieu had also been all but erased by the time he was writing; and he extended his programme of recovery not only to Combray and the world of primal beliefs, but also to the lost world of precisely such aristocratic matinées, in an effort to rescue the past as a whole from oblivion.

Gérard Genette once wrote that 'Proust closes the history of genre and inaugurates [...] the limitless and, so to speak, undetermined space of modern literature.'[58] Proust was indeed writing in the wake of a historical watershed whereby the old aristocracy had lost its ethereal essence and place in society to a new group and the inaccessibly noble aquatic kingdom had disintegrated like a paradise lost. The concern with the passage of time is dramatically brought back into view in a late scene of the *Recherche* commonly referred to as the 'bal des têtes' ['the ball of faces'], where old age and ill health disfigure the aristocratic gathering despite pomp and fancy dress, introducing a poignant element into the idea of terminal disappearance as it touches not only the individuals under description, but the narrator himself, symbolizing the inevitable end of an epoch, and the impending loss of power. There is, in the 'ball of faces', the same idea of role play (or, as some critics would have it, 'marionette play' on the part of the author)[59] that was present in the Opéra scene, only now the ridicule and polemic are more bitter, the irony more poignant, as crimson gowns and other disguises can no longer mask the reality of time's ravages. The many medical conditions that continually receive allusive mention in Proust, and the apparent physical and mental ravages that time has worked on the persons described, make one wonder about the use of opium and other drugs in this society, though Proust says nothing about it.[60]

In Proust's treatment, these transformations occur by and large behind the concealment of appearances kept stable through the use of dress and make-up, and only become perceptible when they are already relatively far advanced.[61] Because these metamorphoses are resented both by the narrator and the characters, their narration is almost eclipsed, delayed until the last moment of one state, and then rushed through to the next state with as little ceremony as possible.

The narrator himself is aware of this quick lapse of time. In his report of a visit to the painter Elstir, he writes:

> j'avais devant moi les fragments de ce monde aux couleurs inconnues qui n'était que la projection, la manière de voir particulière à ce grand peintre et que ne traduisaient nullement ses paroles. [...] Parmi ces tableaux, quelques-uns de ceux qui semblaient le plus ridicules aux gens du monde m'intéressaient plus que les autres en ce qu'ils recréaient ces illusions d'optique qui nous prouvent que nous n'identifierions pas les objets si nous ne faisions pas intervenir le raisonnement.

> [I had, before me, fragments of this world of unknown colours that was only a projection, the special way of seeing particular to this great painter, and which his words did not render at all. [...] Among these paintings, some, that would have seemed ridiculous to high society, interested me more than others, in that they were recreating the sort of optical illusions that prove to us that we would not recognize objects if we did not make use of reasoning.]

Metamorphoses, Myths, and the Modern Mindset

As the editors note in the Introduction to Part III, the scope of the credibility of metamorphosis shrank with the onset of modernity, owing to such historical developments as the Enlightenment, changes to popular mindset effected by indust-rial revolution, advances in scientific method and the philosophy of science, and of course, the naturalist and the realist novel. Works such as the *Comédie humaine* by Balzac, Zola's *Rougon-Macquart* cycle (mainly concerned, as it is, with social contrasts and the conditions of factory workers), Flaubert's *L'Education sentimentale* (chronicling industrial and political activity before the days of Marx), Stendhal's *Le Rouge et le Noir* (a critique of the French social order), or, on the German side, the dramas of Georg Büchner, Frank Wedekind, or the novels of Heinrich Mann, all manifestly strive to chronicle, to record states of affairs, even to fuel public debates. Conversely, authors with a penchant for metamorphoses and an interest in the classical tradition became rarer after the seventeenth and eighteenth centuries, which witnessed the conflict between authors beholden to classicizing aesthetic norms and those who experimented with new, non-classical forms of expression, known as the *querelle des anciens et des modernes*. In certain genres, of course, the motif of metamorphosis certainly remains viable, as we see in the works of the celebrated seventeenth-century fabulist Jean de La Fontaine.[62]

The majority of metamorphoses in French literature of the nineteenth century are indeed not part of the novelistic, but of the poetic traditions, including authors such as Lautréamont, Baudelaire and Rimbaud, and some of the Parnassian writers mentioned above. Poets, it seems, had more scope for supernatural events — opting, if not always for metamorphosis, then at least for a kind of miraculous, allegorical, or deliberately unrealistic setting, which allowed for more imaginary developments than the generic protocols of the contemporary novel.[63] This raises the question of the generic appurtenances of Proust's *Recherche du temps perdu*, which many critics have already discussed.[64] One key consideration for our concerns is the fact that several poets of the late nineteenth and early twentieth centuries brought the notion of 'poème en prose' into vogue, most famously Baudelaire, who cast some of his own subject matter in both prose and verse (e.g. 'La Chevelure'), or, later, Apollinaire, who composed prose poetry. Proust's *Recherche du temps perdu* not only expresses an interest in poetry in many places, but also contains many passages which strike readers as poetic, rather than novelistic, in both their introspective quality and use of imagery; they tend to occur at isolated moments in which the capturing of a feeling becomes more important than the advancement of the narrative. Proust's work is at once a chronicle of social history and a poetic text which shares affiliations with poetic topoi derived from the literature of ancient Greece, the orient, the medieval saga, the *Aeneid*, and more.[65] It is, so to speak, both a lyrical and a narrative text, at once full of symbols and hybrid characters, and anchored in the reality of the day.

One interesting example of this complex layering, especially in the light of the theme of metamorphosis, is the naming of characters. As Roland Barthes has shown, the various names given to the different characters in the *Recherche* operate according to a system of both social and poetic connotations. To this discussion one might add that the pair of names, Swann and Odette (the names of an important couple in the novel), seem to evoke Tchaikovsky's ballet 'Swan Lake'. The story revolves around the daily metamorphosis of the young girl Odette into a white swan, and a deceit crafted against Siegfried, the lover of this young girl, by the magician Rothbart. The latter sends his daughter Odile, magically transformed into the likeness of Odette, to Siegfried, who is deceived and consequently swears eternal love and devotion to the wrong person. This error, as Rothbart had intended, leaves Odette eternally confined to the form of a swan. The magician's powers are ultimately broken by the joint suicide of Siegfried and Odette, who are at last united in death. Proust, I submit, had this storyline in mind when he named his characters Swann and Odette. This fits well with the mysterious social mobility of Proust's character Odette and the ever-looming dark mystery surrounding her past. As with the Nereid passage discussed earlier, Proust demonstrates a predilection for evoking the notion of metamorphosis as a figure of thought rather than a narrative event as such. This sublimation or troping of the notion is characteristic of the 'post-metamorphic' sensibility identified by the editors in the Introduction to Part III.

One early twentieth century movement that re-validated the theme of transformative flux on its own terms was surrealism, represented in French literature by the experiments of such writers as Louis Aragon, Robert Desnos and André Breton, who were very much enthused by the idea of breaking with the established traditions of realism,[66] and the 'vraisemblance' ['lifelikeness'] that French literary traditions reaching back beyond the nineteenth century had long endorsed, be it as a concern of enlightened prose, a convention in neoclassical drama, or an important compositional principle in the novel. Proust's figurative and finely nuanced handling of metamorphoses is rather different from the deliberately irrational depictions one finds in surrealist literature; he uses notions of metamorphosis for the representation of such intangible and internal processes as momentary changes in perception or the layering of subjective analepses of memory over variously construed present moments. In his depiction of transformative change, Proust makes use of various registers of language and thought, interspersing poetic with dramatic affiliations, rhetorical with novelistic conventions, and philosophical argument with psychological introspection.

Proust's device of lending certain persons the appearances of ancient divinities is bold and original. As pointed out above, in the wake of the industrial revolution, Marxist political thought, historical determinism and materialist-utilitarian philosophy, the representation of magic or the supernatural in literature (to which metamorphosis traditionally belonged, especially the transformation of humans into animals or features of the landscape) had seen a decline, in favour of the modern preoccupation with machines and mechanization, most conspicuous in films such as Lang's 'Metropolis', or Chaplin's 'Modern Times', but also visible in literature by Victor Hugo, Emile Zola, Gustave Flaubert, and, in the early twentieth century, the dada movement and its concern for a humanity lost amidst the machinery of modern warfare, or Franz Kafka's reflections on modern technological objects such as the telephone.[67] Proust engages with the 'incredible' process of metamorphosis is a discreet one. From the point of view of *Weltanschauung*, however, Proust's presentation of the state of affairs in the world and of the general spirit is a shattered and fragmented one, and in this his contents are kindred to those of his dadaist contemporaries.

He is also not very far in tone from ideas expressed in T. S. Eliot's *Waste Land*, famous for its cryptic and obfuscating handling of the classical tradition in brief fragments as a 'heap of broken images', adding to the fragments a brand-new, contemporary scholarly approach of anthropological analysis of myth. This leads us to what seems to me a third, equally important reason why nineteenth- and early twentieth-century writers were deterred from elaborating on supernatural topics. The anthropological scholarship that Eliot draws on, today mostly remembered through the work of J. G. Frazer's *The Golden Bough*, rests on theories of civilization developed in the context of colonial empires, in which a clear distinction is drawn between 'primitive' and 'civilized' cultures, the wild and the refined, the barbaric and the urbane, the uneducated and the enlightened; in this set of contrasts, naïve belief in metamorphoses was the stuff of primitive cultures valued as inferior. In *Totem und Tabu*, Sigmund Freud writes of the supernatural beliefs of 'wild' cultures and notices their similarities with supernatural beliefs — in particular the 'animism', the belief that fauna and flora are inhabited by souls of the dead — in the minds of some of his neuro-pathic patients.[68]

This unfavourable view of supernatural events, including metamorphoses, as either a sign of cultural primitiveness or as a mental pathology, could not but affect the representation of metamorphosis in literature; and in Proust's case, although he at times identifies himself with the ancient 'celtic beliefs' (as he calls them), he prefers to embrace the customary French predilection for analysis and the intellectual exercise in order to convince, with light play between real and imagined, metaphor and comparison, careful to insert the necessary 'it seemed to me', thus signalling affinity with philosophers, poets, novelists and social critics, who in the spirit of modern science seek empirical and coherent explanations for every phenomenon. Proust's thinking, excellently described by Anne Simon as a 'crisis of idealism',[69] full of slippage and oscillation, as she writes, between 'moi et monde' ['oneself and the world'], results in a self-conscious, shrewd and omniscient narration that wants nothing more than to be taken seriously in order to break the isolation of a writer wishing to share his *moi* with posterity. At the same time, the chemist Lavoisier was accredited with the remark that 'Dans la nature, rien ne se perd, rien ne se crée, tout se transforme' ['in nature, nothing is lost, nothing is created, all things transform themselves'] which at once gives room to believe the metamorphic character of certain processes, and points out the scientifically demonstrable model of molecular and atomic elements as a way of understanding these transformations. Proust's analysis of his own mental processes through tropes of metamorphosis may, then, be the result of the various zeitgeist pressures which I have alluded to, and these pressures in general can be surmised to have acted on many other (roughly) contemporary authors as well.

At the same time, authors could — and did — of course opt out of the 'realist paradigm'. A striking example is the 1964 play *Rhinocéros*, written in French by the Romanian playwright Eugène Ionesco. In this play, which is written in the 'absurdist' aesthetic, a small town is invaded by rhinoceroses, and as the characters of the play discuss this invasion, they come to understand that what is actually happening is that, one by one, the inhabitants of their town are being transformed into rhinoceroses; by the end of the play, only one character is left in human form. In *Rhinocéros*, concerns with and about logic, perception of reality, insanity and psychotic mental processes are so much in the foreground (for instance, one of the characters is identified as the resident 'logician', who spends his time teaching syllogism to passers-by, unfailingly finding impossible conclusions) that one might even speak of this piece as a parody of metamorphic literature. However, critique of any literary tradition of metamorphosis is not on Ionesco's agenda; rather, the absurdity of the situation is designed to criticize human affairs with the appropriate sarcasm.

With this, my discussion has nearly arrived at the twenty-first century. I wish for now to forego the grand turn towards political and sociological interpretations of literature so popular throughout the twentieth century, and in concluding to remain focused on the subject of poetic imagery, literary language, metamorphosis, and the classical tradition.

To a great extent, these are transhistorical elements of literary texts, timeless topics, so to speak. To inspect timeless topics is a theoretical exercise from which the impulse to find one true and final answer must be resisted. It strikes me that Proust's style and the Parnassian poetry I reviewed have something in common beyond the congruencies of mythical marine imagery and a shared aesthetic vocabulary. Both are also examples of literary writing that very much sets its own definitions and creates its own special setting before any developments can happen inside this setting, and as such, both present a world closed within itself, one that deliberately distances itself from generally accepted reality, a world that benefits from text-immanent analyses (analyses that seek to explain a text by the text itself) — which I hope to have provided. In both *corpora*, the Proustian and the Parnassian, the ease with which authors mirror, echo and borrow from one another elements such as imagery, myths of transformation and classical topoi, notwithstanding the apparent seclusion of their works, is so striking that it should help 'us' better understand what, in literature, is form and what is content, and instruct us on how and where we might find continuities that allow us to trace developments and follow the history of literature.

Notes to Chapter 9

1. Proust (1999), p. 776.
2. The topos of an imaginary voyage through a precious gem can be found for example in Henri Bosco, *L'Antiquaire*. Cf. also many titles of Parnassian collections e.g. *Emaux et Camées*, *Trophées*.
3. Proust (1999), p. 776.
4. In the English translation, it is impossible to reproduce the *double entendre* of the French *baignoire*, which means both theatre box and bathtub.
5. Proust (1964), II, 1080–1101.
6. Proust (1999), pp. 776–77.
7. Hassine (2001), p. 182.
8. Alcoloumbre (2004), p. 118; Benjamin (1961), p. 203.
9. Montenot (2002), p. 1530.
10. E. Guez explained this in his philosophy lessons at the Lycée Français de Berlin, in 2002.
11. Proust (1999), p. 2390.
12. Proust (1999), p. 777.
13. Proust (1999), p. 776.
14. My thanks to Professor Kirk Freudenburg who drew some enlightening analogies between cinematography, the use of close-up and panorama shots, and techniques of writing in Virgilian ekphrasis, in his lectures on Virgil's *Aeneid* at Yale University, in 2008.
15. Proust (1999), p. 777.
16. Proust (1999), p. 777.
17. Proust (1999), p. 777.
18. I agree with Carter (2006), pp. 13–15, that Proust's homosexual orientation, although it is concealed in the novel, should be taken into account for the added complexity it throws onto any reading of Proustian description of female characters. I will leave it to the reader to surmise in just what way a sexual orientation, concealed or suggested, informs literary character-making. My thanks to George Galfalvi for discussion of this point.
19. Proust (1999), pp. 777–78.
20. Proust (1999), p. 778.
21. Proust (1999), pp. 778–79.
22. Proust (1999), p. 779.

23. Thierry Laget in Proust (1964), II, 1549.
24. Miguet-Ollaigner (1982), p. 29.
25. Proust (1999), p. 779.
26. Proust (1999), p. 779.
27. Proust (1999), p. 779.
28. A few pages later we get : 'Et quand je portais mes yeux sur la baignoire, bien plus qu'au plafond du théâtre où étaient peintes de froides allégories, c'était comme si j'avais aperçu, grâce au déchirement miraculeux des nuées coutumières, l'assemblée des Dieux en train de contempler le spectacle des hommes' ['and as I brought my eyes upon the box, far more than on the theatre ceiling, which was painted with cold allegories, it was as if I had seen thanks to the miraculous breaking open of the customary clouds, the assembly of the gods contemplating the spectacle of mankind'] — a very Homeric image.
29. Proust (1999), p. 778.
30. Proust (1999), p. 776.
31. Proust (1999), p. 778.
32. Girard (1961), p. 226.
33. Kristeva (1996), p. 52.
34. Cf. Proust (1999), p. 16, or Proust's other, less-known books e.g. *On Reading*.
35. Gautier (1950).
36. The adjective 'glauque' is no doubt used to recall the Homeric epithet γλαυκῶπις used of Athena, conveying the depth and inscrutable nature of the sea, as opposed to the superficial and liminal 'white foam'.
37. Proust (1964), II, 1080–1101.
38. Gautier (1950), p. 87.
39. Gautier (1950), p. 87.
40. Granted, some nineteenth-century imperial naval design and architecture had also incorporated them, alongside fashioning Neptune, e.g. some iron works at Victoria Embankment in London and elsewhere probably. But that would again be a nineteenth-century tradition more than a classical one.
41. Gautier, Sonnet VIII ('Les Déesses posent'), 9–11.
42. Gautier (1870), p. 109.
43. Gautier (1870), p. 269.
44. Gautier (1870), p. 277.
45. Baudelaire (1961), p. 58.
46. Dierx (1980), p. 55.
47. Virgil, *Aeneid*, I. 462: *sunt lacrimae rerum et mentem mortalia tangunt*.
48. Heredia (1984 [1893])
49. Heredia (2005), p. 8.
50. De Lisle (1852), p. 18.
51. Proust (1999), p. 706. The verses come from the opening of the long poem 'Les Erinnyes' (1873).
52. De Lisle (1866), p. 337.
53. Compare the Greek original, *Iliad*, XVIII, 37–67: θεαὶ δέ μιν ἀμφαγέροντο | πᾶσαι ὅσαι κατὰ βένθος ἁλὸς Νηρηῖδες ἦσαν. | ἔνθ᾽ ἄρ᾽ ἔην Γλαύκη [...] | ἄλλαι θ᾽ αἳ κατὰ βένθος ἁλὸς Νηρηῖδες ἦσαν. | τῶν δὲ καὶ ἀργύρεον πλῆτο σπέος· αἳ δ᾽ ἅμα πᾶσαι | στήθεα πεπλήγοντο, Θέτις δ᾽ ἐξῆρχε γόοιο [...] | Ὣς ἄρα φωνήσασα λίπε σπέος· αἳ δὲ σὺν αὐτῇ | δακρυόεσσαι ἴσαν, περὶ δέ σφισι κῦμα θαλάσσης | ῥήγνυτο·
54. Proust (1999), p. 775.
55. Compagnon (1989), p. 294.
56. Squarzina (2004), p. 247.
57. Highet (1976), p. 194.
58. Genette (1972), p. 265 (translation mine).
59. Deleuze (1964), p. 218.
60. For historical documents, cf. the 2010–11 Wellcome Trust exhibition 'High Society: Drugs in Victorian Britain'.

61. In 'La Pharmacie de Platon', Derrida discusses the double meaning of the Greek word *pharmakon* (a slightly biased lexicographical discussion but interesting in its own right), as a cosmetic remedy to hide the brutal order of things, as the mask of death. 'Le *pharmakon*, he writes, introduit et abrite la mort. Il donne bonne figure au cadavre, le masque et le farde. Le parfume de son essence, comme il est dit dans Eschyle. Il transforme le cosmos en cosmétique. La mort, le masque, le fard, c'est la fête qui subvertit l'ordre de la cité, tel qu'il devrait être réglé par le dialecticien et par la science de l'être' (p. 177) ['The *pharmakon* introduces and shelters death. It gives good mien to a corpse, masks and powders it. It perfumes with its essence, as it says in Aeschylus. It transforms the cosmos into cosmetics. Death, masks, and make-up, here's the party that subverts order in the city, the way it should be ordered by the dialectician and the science of being']. What exactly is supposed to be in Aeschylus of these thoughts of Derrida's is difficult to divine. However, the core remark on the double meaning of *pharmakon*, that remedy can both bring recovery or death, and that in its capacity as a cosmetic 'to put something in order', it subverts the actual order of things in the manner of a mask, make-up or perfume to 'give a good air to a dead body', the idea that behind well-arranged facades, decay is happening, offers an interesting comparison with Proust's authorial vision.

62. Or at least its beginnings: 'la grenouille qui veut se faire aussi grosse que le Bœuf', J. De la Fontaine, *Fables* [1694].

63. For detailed analyses of the distinction between lyrical and narrative contents, their generic literary forms, cultural and cognitive explanations of the development, see e.g. Bakhtin, 'From the Prehistory of Novelistic Discourse' ed. by Holoquist (1981), or Walter Benjamin (1961) on motifs in Baudelaire.

64. See e.g. Roland Barthes's essay 'Proust et les noms', in Marty (1994), pp. 1368–77.

65. Hassine (2001), p. 187.

66. Breton, *Nadja*, pp. 19–24.

67. e.g. Kafka's tale 'Der Nachbar', Kafka (1970 [1935]), p. 300.

68. In line with Sigmund Freud, one could place the German poet and psychiatrist Gottfried Benn, best known perhaps for his expressionist poems but also a prolific essayist on the topic of racial anthropology and ranks of superiority and inferiority based on mentalities and types of minds (Gann, 2007). This is a belief that also deeply impressed Proust, who tentatively discusses his own sympathy for such beliefs at various points in the *Recherche*, for example in the episode of the three trees at Hudimesnil, connected in their imagery to the episode of his grandmother on the phone: see Spiegel (2011).

69. Simon (2000), p. 61.

CHAPTER 10

'Horror in a Covered Platter':
H. P. Lovecraft and the
Transformation of Petronius

Luke Pitcher

Sleep came quickly, but hideous dreams assailed me. There was a vision of a
Roman feast like that of Trimalchio, with a horror in a covered platter. Then
came that damnable, recurrent thing about the swineherd and his filthy drove
in the twilit grotto. Yet when I awoke it was full daylight, with normal sounds
in the house below. (H. P. Lovecraft, 'The Rats in the Walls')

Introduction

Scholarly approaches to Petronius's *Satyrica*[1] and its various literary receptions have
often enjoyed a close relationship with each other. A case in point is T. S. Eliot's
deployment of the novel in 'The Waste Land'. It is not hard to spot the subsequent
twentieth-century readings of the *Satyrica* which take their starting point from
endorsement or critique of the way in which Eliot visualizes Petronius.[2]

More recent Petronian criticism, however, has gone down avenues which are,
prima facie, harder to parallel in the way literary authors have used this novelist. In
particular, one notes a contemporary fascination with Petronius's ways of figuring
intertextuality, and the uses to which he puts the imagery of corporeality and
eating.[3] Indeed, influential recent readings have made much of the close linkage
between intertextuality and eating in the *Satyrica*. This seems to have taken us
some distance from the reading of Petronius as commentator on a spiritual desert
which Eliot and 'The Waste Land' helped to produce. It is tempting to think, then,
that the contemporary critic of Petronius has now left the emphases of his early-
twentieth-century reception behind.

Yet such is not the case. Eliot was not the only literary reader of Petronius in the
1920s, though he was, perhaps, the most celebrated. This essay examines allusion
to the *Satyrica* in a short story entitled 'The Rats in the Walls', published in the
periodical *Weird Tales* in March 1924.[4] The author of the story was Howard Phillips
Lovecraft (1890–1937), a writer almost unknown in his lifetime but one with
substantial posthumous influence.[5]

Lovecraft is an interesting figure for a collection such as this. It has been speculated
elsewhere in this volume that a shift in the status of metamorphosis occurs with the

onset of modernity, as belief in the possibility of 'actual' metamorphosis induced by supernatural forces such as the devil or demons fades away and the phenomenon becomes more and more a metaphor or narrative device; at the same time, however, discourses (the Gothic, horror, speculative fiction) emerge which, like pre-modern tales of transformation, might be seen (so the hypothesis goes) as breaking with the protocols of empiricism and rationality that inform the conception of the universe developed and endorsed by modern science.[6] Where does an individual like Lovecraft, the early-twentieth-century writer of 'weird tales' par excellence, fit in with such a hypothesis?

Rationality in the works of Lovecraft is certainly a problematic enterprise. It is misleading, however, to see his works as a denial of reason. Rationality in Lovecraft's *oeuvre* is not problematic because it does not work. If anything, a potential hazard is that it might work too well. The opening paragraph of 'The Call of Cthulhu', perhaps the most famous of his tales, is a case in point:

> The most merciful thing in the world, I think, is the inability of the human mind to correlate all its contents. We live on a placid island of ignorance in the midst of black seas of infinity, and it was not meant that we should voyage far. The sciences, each straining in its own direction, have hitherto harmed us little; but some day the piecing together of dissociated knowledge will open up such terrifying vistas of reality, and of our frightful position therein, that we shall either go mad from the revelation or flee from the deadly light into the peace and safety of a new dark age.[7]

Such matters go some way beyond the remit of the present endeavour. I propose to examine Lovecraft's reception of Petronius in his work, a process to which transformation is key on several levels. We shall see that Petronius's status as an early writer of stories of physical transformation makes him an important precursor for Lovecraft in the writing of 'weird tales'. But the use of the *Satyrica* in 'The Rats in the Walls' is also thematically linked to one very particular sort of transformation: carnal digestion, the process by which the meat of the devoured becomes the meat of the devourer, and what that entails. It will thereby become apparent that the contemporary reading of Petronius's novel as a text which delights in figuring its relationship to other texts as a form of physical consumption actually has a parallel in Lovecraft's deployment of the work in the 1920s.

Lovecraft and Petronius

Before Lovecraft wrote 'The Rats in the Walls', his interest in classical literature and its narratives of transformation was already well established. In his childhood, he wrote a translation of the first eighty-eight lines of Ovid's *Metamorphoses* into one hundred and sixteen pentameters, a work which still survives.[8] The *Metamorphoses* were evoked again in the title, 'Rudis Indigestaque Moles' [Shapeless, disorderly bulk], that he gave to his hostile review of 'The Waste Land', a matter to which we shall return.[9]

Lovecraft's classical erudition, then, can often be seen to inform his literary work. As a result, his deployment of the *Satyrica* at the climax of his short story 'The Rats in the Walls' is particularly interesting. It is an instance of Petronian reception in the 1920s which is often overlooked.[10]

'The Rats in the Walls' is narrated by Delapore,[11] a Virginian of English descent who at the beginning of the story returns to the seat of his forefathers at Exham Priory. Once there, he discovers that the edifice stands on the site of a prehistoric temple, and that his forefathers enjoyed an evil reputation in the area. Delapore promptly begins to experience recurring strange dreams, of 'a twilit grotto, knee-deep with filth, where a white-bearded daemon swineherd drove about with his staff a flock of fungous, flabby beasts whose appearance filled me with unutterable loathing. Then, as the swineherd paused and nodded over his task, a mighty swarm of rats rained down on the stinking abyss and fell to devouring beasts and man alike.'[12] He also notices a curious agitation in the behaviour of his pet cat. Thereafter, he repeatedly hears the sounds of enormous numbers of rats moving behind the walls of the Priory, which lead him to explore the prehistoric temple at the foundations of the house and discover a hidden trapdoor in it.

Delapore then assembles a team of experts to investigate what lies beneath the trapdoor. Just before the planned descent, he has a last night of hideous dreams: 'There was a vision of a Roman feast like that of Trimalchio, with a horror in a covered platter. Then came that damnable, recurrent thing about the swineherd and his filthy drove in the twilit grotto.' When the party descends beyond the trapdoor, they discover a 'twilit grotto of enormous height', containing innumerable bones of humans and semi-humans, as well as evidence that the de la Poers of old were members of an ancient, cannibalistic cult. The atmosphere and the sound of ghostly rats drive Delapore mad. At the end of the story, it becomes clear that he is telling the story from an asylum to which he has been confined after turning on and eating another member of the party.

Lovecraft's evocation of the *Satyrica* here is intriguing, simply because its relevance is not immediately obvious. The comparison with F. Scott Fitzgerald's use of the novel in *The Great Gatsby* is illuminating. In Fitzgerald, the analogy between Trimalchio and that rather different parvenu millionaire Gatsby is fairly obvious, as are the specific parallels and contrasts between them: Trimalchio's luxuriant emphasis on the grandeur of his own funeral arrangements, for example, stands in stark contrast to the wretched scene at Gatsby's under-attended obsequies.[13] Eliot's Petronian appropriations in 'The Waste Land' are more various and elusive, but they can still be teased out without too much difficulty: the Sibyl flows into the tired and ill prophets of the poem itself, while the fourth section, 'Death By Water', evokes the scene of Petronius's shipwreck.

The point of the reference in 'The Rats in the Walls' is a little more challenging. There is no mileage in trying to analogize Delapore himself to Trimalchio. After all, part of the point of the story is his ancient lineage, which Lovecraft spends several pages describing, and its ultimately unavoidable legacy.

It is also not altogether straightforward to determine what Delapore means when he speaks of a 'horror in a covered platter'. Trimalchio's feast does indeed contain several items which are originally covered or concealed, to be revealed with a later flourish. None of these dishes, however, obviously merits the description of a 'horror'. There is, for example, the wooden hen which conceals edible eggs,[14] the dish which symbolizes the Zodiac but turns out to have a hidden layer of 'fowls, sows' udders, and in the centre a hare equipped with wings',[15] the enormous pig which disgorges sausages and black puddings when cut,[16] and the fat goose 'surrounded by fish and every kind of bird', which are all ultimately discovered to be made from pork.[17] Many of these sound somewhat nauseous, and even the narrator Encolpius notes that the last was a 'preposterous dish which made even death by starvation preferable'.[18] None of it, however, sounds particularly 'horrific'. Wherein, then, does Lovecraft detect the 'horror' at Trimalchio's table?

For a solution to this problem, it is necessary to look at the image in its larger contexts within Lovecraft's work. In the first place, we must explore what part it plays within the larger thematic concerns of 'The Rats in the Walls'. These, in turn, are illuminated by the recurrent connexions between certain themes and preoccupations which emerge from Lovecraft's creative output.

Fare Exchange

As the story progresses, the true horror of Delapore's dreams, which goes beyond their repulsive iconography, slowly becomes evident. The swineherd's livestock are not loathsome pigs. They are, in fact, degenerate humans, raised by Delapore's ancestors as food animals.

The significance of the reference to the *Satyrica* now becomes clear. The relevance lies not in the actual foodstuffs on Trimalchio's table. Rather, it is to be found in the deceptive and transformational character of the dishes with which Encolpius is presented. The narrator of the *Satyrica* describes comestibles which turn out, upon closer inspection, to be something other than what they first appear: the Zodiac which conceals carnal abundance; the varied meats which are all revealed to have been made out of pork. In like vein, things which Delapore at first takes to be some form of revolting swine slowly resolve themselves into devolved humans treated as livestock. In fact, Lovecraft's image neatly inverts Petronius's. Encolpius mistakes pork for other foodstuffs; Delapore initially believes humans to be pigs.

The appropriation of Petronius, then, is more subtle than a simple one-to-one correspondence. Lovecraft has identified an element in the presentation of cuisine in the *Cena Trimalchionis*: the disguise of foodstuffs so that they lose or conceal their original characteristics. He has then transposed it into a horrific key. The horror is augmented because the image is part of a larger thematic preoccupation within the story. As we have seen, Delapore's subsequent investigations determine that his ancestors did indeed herd, and prey on, degenerate humans. Delapore himself finally descends into madness and emulates his forefathers in cannibalism. Petronius's text, which succinctly brings together themes of deception, change, and eating, is thus ideally fitted as a *comparandum*.

Moreover, a survey of Lovecraft's other creative works reveals further significant patterns in his interrelated treatments of transformation, consumption, and what it means to be human. Lovecraft thematizes the fragility of 'human nature' in stories where the human transforms into the monstrous, a transformation often stemming from or accompanied by the consumption of human flesh. This is clearest in his concept of 'ghouls', monstrous humanoids which eat the bodies of dead humans. The true horror of ghouls lies in Lovecraft's strong implication that humans who eat as they do can eventually forsake their humanity and transform into ghouls themselves.

The key text here is the story 'Pickman's Model', first published in 1927.[19] The narrator describes his friendship with the controversial and eponymous painter, Richard Upton Pickman, who specializes in the depiction of the supernatural in superbly naturalistic terms. In particular, Pickman's canvases detail a disturbingly symbiotic relationship between humans and ghouls, in which the possibility of the one turning into the other is made all too apparent:

> There was one thing called 'The Lesson' — Heaven pity me, that I ever saw it! Listen — can you fancy a squatting circle of nameless doglike things in a churchyard teaching a small child how to feed like themselves? The price of a changeling, I suppose — you know the old myth about how the weird people leave their spawn in cradles in exchange for the human babes they steal. Pickman was showing what happens to those stolen babes — how they grow up — and then I began to see a hideous relationship in the faces of the human and non-human figures. He was, in all his gradations of morbidity between the frankly non-human and the degradedly human, establishing a sardonic linkage and evolution. The dog-things were developed from mortals![20]

By this point in the story, Pickman's own disturbing characteristics have been established through the responses of others. Once again, the importance of diet in his deviation from the human norm is discreetly suggested: 'He said Pickman repelled him more and more every day, and almost frightened him towards the last — that the fellow's features and expression were slowly developing in a way he didn't like; in a way that wasn't human. He had a lot of talk about diet; and said Pickman must be abnormal and eccentric to the last degree.'[21] It comes as no surprise, then, when we learn at the end of the story that Pickman has disappeared. The dark suspicions to which this disappearance gives rise are confirmed in another story, 'The Dream-Quest of Unknown Kadath', where the hero is assisted by the ghoul which was once Pickman.

These other texts confirm Lovecraft's propensity to illustrate how fragile and vulnerable is the concept of 'humanity', by contriving situations where that human-ity, through choice, education, or hereditary tendency, transforms into something monstrous. Nor is the 'monstrous' a comfortingly stable category in Lovecraft: one of the key reversals in 'At the Mountains of Madness', a text to which we shall return, comes when the narrator perceives that the alien Old Ones whom he has been investigating actually manifested drives and concerns that were in many ways eminently human: 'Scientists to the last — what had they done that we would not have done in their place [...] Radiates, vegetables, monstrosities, star spawn — whatever they had been, they were men!'[22]

These texts likewise illustrate the symbolic importance of food in this nexus of concerns. Ghouls are defined by their appetite for human flesh, and such a diet is the doorway through which human can degenerate into ghoul. The motives behind the appropriation of Trimalchio's feast in 'The Rats in the Walls' are thus illuminated. Petronius serves up a meal where nothing is what it originally seems, where food has been nauseously switched from its original state into something else. The appeal of such imagery to Lovecraft as he plots Delapore's degradation should now be obvious.

Shaping the Past

In a collection focussed upon the relationship between tales of transformation and the notion of what it means to be human, what we have seen thus far of Lovecraft's strategies seems, perhaps, unsurprising. From Kafka downwards, writers have repeatedly used stories of physical transformation, often into a monstrous or repugnant form, as meditations on what it means to be human — and on how humanity can slip away. Lovecraft's use of Petronius appears a neat garnish (as it were) upon this theme, but nothing more.

Petronius, however, held more than one significance for Lovecraft. He was not simply a source for piquant similes; he was also an acknowledged predecessor in the writing of 'weird fiction'. Lovecraft's own critical overview of the history of 'weird tales', 'On Supernatural Horror in Literature', acknowledges both Petronius and Apuleius as standing at the fountain-head of the tradition in which he saw himself as writing. Also, Lovecraft's recurring obsession with themes of transformation, assimilation, and consumption was not geared simply towards exploring humanity and the ways in which it could become degraded; it also displays an interesting meta-textual emphasis. Throughout his fiction and critical work, Lovecraft uses these themes to structure his own theories on what makes for a successful work of art, and to define the position of his own creative output within the hierarchy of literary endeavour.

In this connection, an important document is Lovecraft's published response to a more famous instance of Petronian reception. This is his review of Eliot's 'The Waste Land', which we have already mentioned above. Lovecraft's reaction to the fragmentation characteristic of Eliot's poetic techniques was deeply hostile.[23] Particularly interesting for our purposes, however, is the Ovidian tag with which he chose to title his review: 'rudis indigestaque moles'.

The choice is an evocative one. Ovid, at the very beginning of the *Metamorphoses*, is describing the inchoate state of things before the first of the transformations which are his theme: the foundation of the cosmos itself. Lovecraft thus derisively compares 'The Waste Land' to the mere anarchy that obtains *before* the act of artistic creation. But he also implicitly associates successful literary composition with the act of transformation. 'The Waste Land' is 'rudis indigestaque moles'; the true work of art, by contrast, is what happens when such raw materials are shaped and transformed.

It may seem rash to read so much into an Ovidian locution. A survey of Lovecraft's own fiction, however, reveals the extent to which he uses stories of transformation, assimilation, and consumption to instantiate his own aesthetic theories. Lovecraft's stories contain a surprising number of individuals who could be viewed as successful artists. The disquieting thing is that most of them are also monsters.

Again, 'Pickman's Model' is a case in point. The narrator of this story is torn between his horror at the artist's deeds and reverence for his achievement: 'it takes profound art and profound insight into Nature to turn out stuff like Pickman's. Any magazine-cover hack can splash paint around wildly and call it a nightmare or a Witches' Sabbath or a portrait of the devil, but only a great painter can make such a thing really scare or ring true. That's because only a real artist knows the actual anatomy of the terrible or the physiology of fear'.[24] Numerous critics have noted the concinnity between the artistic philosophy attributed to the fictional Pickman and Lovecraft's own aesthetic pronouncements. Indeed, the story itself notably displays in prose the characteristics which it attributes to Pickman's art.[25] 'Pickman's Model', then, both instantiates an aesthetic doctrine and does so in a profoundly disturbing way. The story bears out Pickman's credo — but Pickman himself has become inhuman. This is the best-known case where Lovecraft plays out meta-textual reflection at the level of plot, as disquisitions within the narrative point up the nature of the story itself.[26]

It is, however, by no means the only such instance. Elsewhere, Lovecraft delights in collapsing the distinction between his activities as author and the machinations of figures within his narrative. The novella 'At the Mountains of Madness' affords an elegant example. The final challenge of this story is the nightmarish Shoggoths, entities created by an extinct alien civilization in the Antarctic as a slave race. The horror of Shoggoths is their adaptability; they gradually absorb and assimilate all the characteristics of their masters, until they rise in revolt and slay them. As they chase down the narrator at the climax of the story, they repeatedly call *Tekeli-li*, a cry that they have copied from their long-dead creators: 'the demoniac Shoggoths — given life, thought, and plastic organ patterns solely by the Old Ones [...] — had likewise no voice save the imitated accents of their bygone masters.'[27] The meta-textual irony lies in the fact that *Tekeli-li* is doubly copied. As the Shoggoths have taken it within the story from the Old Ones who created them, so Lovecraft has taken it from one of his predecessors in the writing of 'weird tales'. Indeed, he goes to some pains to advertise this fact: 'Danforth has hinted at queer notions about unsuspected and forbidden sources to which Poe may have had access when writing his *Arthur Gordon Pym* a century ago. It will be remembered that in that fantastic tale there is a word of unknown but terrible and prodigious significance connected with the Antarctic [...] "*Tekeli-li! Tekeli-li!*"'[28] The Shoggoths, then, echo the mimetic qualities of the text that contains them.

Once Lovecraft's propensity for such meta-textual echoing is recognized, one notices how often he figures a relationship to preceding texts in terms of meta-morphosis or consumption within his own narratives. Lovecraft's protagonists, like Lovecraft himself, are typically obsessed with making something new out of the past. Where the author operates upon the remains of earlier literature, his characters are more literal: they operate, again and again, upon the physical bodies of authors themselves. Lovecraft's transformation and assimilation of his predecessors is echoed in his stories by the necromantic practices of his protagonists.

In 'The Case of Charles Dexter Ward', for instance, the magician whose machinations drive the plot and his colleagues have mastered the art of rendering the corpses of great men into their essential salts, from which they can then raise them for interrogation: 'a hideous traffic was going on among these nightmare ghouls, whereby illustrious bones were bartered with the cold calculativeness of schoolboys swapping books'.[29] The simile here is significant. Through the practice of black magic, the physical remains of authors stand in for their literary works. Bodies become books, which the magicians consult at their leisure. 'Literary corpus' is a metaphor made flesh.

Lovecraft slyly adds another angle to this *mise en abyme*. The process by which the magicians raise the dead and make them speak is imperfect. Sometimes it botches. When it does, the failed result is a hideous and broken thing, which has only 'the liveliest awfulness'. At one point, the hero of the story finds himself trapped underground amongst the howling of these botched attempts to breathe life into the relics of the past. Remembering his discoveries, 'he tried to drive them out, and repeated the Lord's Prayer to himself; eventually trailing off into a mnemonic hodge-podge like the modernistic "Waste Land" of Mr. T. S. Eliot [...]'.[30] The irony of having this *bête noire* quoted in the midst of failed and fragmentary attempts to integrate the past with the present should now be obvious. Lovecraft sets what he sees as the aesthetic failures of Eliot's poem in the context of his own, different attempt to show his readers fear in a handful of dust.

Cannibalism and Cannibalization

'The Waste Land', then, had a continuing usefulness for Lovecraft in illustrating the failure of 'modernist' aesthetics. The backdrop of failed transformations in 'The Case of Charles Dexter Ward' was not, however, the only way in which he figured the poem's perceived inadequacies. The chaos before Ovid's creation is not just 'rudis'. It is also 'indigesta'. In its original context, 'indigesta' means no more than 'unarranged', 'disorderly', or 'confused'. The verb 'digero' *can* refer in classical Latin to what we would think of as 'digestion': the dispersal of assimilated food through a body. But it does not mean that at the beginning of the *Metamorphoses*.

For Lovecraft, however, the likening of the successful creative use of the past tradition to an act of physical digestion was an idea that proved tenacious. Again, 'Pickman's Model' has a relevant moment. One of Pickman's canvases of ghouls depicts 'a scene in an unknown vault, where scores of the beasts crowded about one who held a well-known Boston guidebook and was evidently reading aloud. All were pointing to a certain passage, and every face seemed so distorted with epileptic and reverberant laughter that I almost thought I heard the fiendish echoes. The title of the picture was, "Holmes, Lowell, and Longfellow Lie Buried in Mount Auburn".'[31] The implication, of course, is that the bodies of these famous writers have already been consumed and digested by ghouls.

Cannibalism in Lovecraft, then, is not just a marker of the fragility of 'human nature', as we have already observed. It also represents a very particular sort of meta-textual transformation. Cannibalism can, after all, serve as an analogue for an absolutely successful act of assimilating what already exists into something new: an act of perfect (and literal) incorporation of one thing, one body or corpus, into another.

The violation of societal norms which cannibalism represents, however, remains significant. Indeed, it is the *combination* of these two symbolic aspects of the act which makes it so useful as a meta-textual image for Lovecraft. Cannibalism is, at one and the same time, an act which brings a union between the consumer and the consumed, and also advertises a difference between them. A human that eats another human incorporates his meal into himself. But in his very willingness to perpetrate such an act, he forfeits his humanity. I would argue that it is this paradox which informs the meta-textual use of cannibalism in Lovecraft. Through such images as that of his ghouls devouring the famous names of American literature, Lovecraft announces both his own success in incorporating the prior literary tradition into his own texts and their element of irreducible strangeness. His 'Weird Tales' thus construct an interestingly ambiguous place for themselves within the canon: successfully absorbing what has gone before, but in so doing, becoming different from it.

Nor is Lovecraft alone in finding this trope appealing. Just as cannibalism is deployed to mark out the ambiguous status of his literary horror, so it has been pressed into service more recently to point up the like status of literary thrillers. The obvious examples here are the Hannibal Lecter novels of Thomas Harris, which, like Lovecraft, bring what might be seen as a distinctly 'highbrow' perspective to a genre which is not usually seen as harbouring such aspirations. In Harris's novels the link between the anti-hero's cannibalism and his aesthetic sense is repeatedly stressed. Lecter's most notorious instance of anthropophagy occurs when he serves 'the flautist Benjamin Raspail's sweetbreads to other members of the Baltimore Philharmonic Orchestra board'.[32] True enough, Harris does not explicitly use Lovecraft's trope of analogizing the way his charismatic but monstrous protagonist eats his victims to the way in which his erudite narrative assimilates preceding texts. Nonetheless, the entirely literal consumption of 'high culture' by an individual within his narrative is certainly a trick which he does play: in the first Lecter novel, *Red Dragon*, another serial killer, Francis Dolarhyde, attempts to control his own madness by physically stealing and eating a work of William Blake.[33]

These considerations throw another light on the use of the dinner of Trimalchio in 'The Rats in the Walls'. Lovecraft's text eats and digests Petronius's feast. In this story, Roman antiquity, like every other historical period, is subsumed and absorbed into the continuum that is Delapore's unavoidable inheritance. This is hinted in the opening paragraph, where Delapore is insistent upon the foundation of successive architectural traditions upon which Exham Priory is based ('much studied because of its peculiarly composite architecture [...] involving Gothic towers resting on a Saxon or Romanesque substructure, whose foundation in turn was of a still earlier order or blend of orders — Roman, and even Druidic or native Cymric').[34] At the end of the tale, Lovecraft's narrative makes it clear how thoroughly his hero has absorbed the entirety of the grisly tradition that is his birthright by having his delirious monologue regress first into archaic English and then into Latin. Once again, Lovecraft uses the imagery of consumption to point up the thoroughness with which both his hero and his text have assimilated what the past has to offer — however sinister that offering may be.

Conclusion

Lovecraft's appropriation of the *Satyrica* in 'The Rats in the Walls' reveals itself to be no idle allusion. Through it, the author focuses an impressive number of his characteristic preoccupations and techniques into a compact image. It is not just that Trimalchio's feast allows Lovecraft to play with the themes of illusion and how fragile and unstable 'human' nature can turn out to be. The allusion turns out to fit into a wider strategy, detectable throughout Lovecraft's creative work, of using the imagery of transformation and consumption to figure the characteristics of his own fiction and its place within the literary tradition.

Those familiar with the characteristic narrative manoeuvres of the *Satyrica* will note a further irony here. Recent scholarship has noted the extent to which Petronius's text, too, repeatedly figures its status as a work in terms of eating and consumption. The *Satyrica* is a glutton for other texts, which it assimilates into itself and, in doing so, both makes them a part of itself and flags up its own difference from them. It is no accident that we eventually discover the name of the cook at Trimalchio's banquet, who has fashioned these deceiving and meta-textual dishes, to be Daedalus, a figure deployed from Ovid to Joyce as a representative of the creative artist within a work of art. If the narrative strategy of 'The Rats in the Walls' turns Petronius into Lovecraft, it also turns Lovecraft into Petronius.

What wider conclusions can we draw, then, from this investigation? The more obvious one returns to the point made at the beginning of the study. The full richness of Petronius's reception remains an area much in need of investigation. An analysis of that reception in the 1920s which founds itself solely upon Fitzgerald and Eliot misses out on a response to the *Satyrica* which is arguably more in tune with the complexities of the original than anything in *The Great Gatsby* or 'The Waste Land'.

The other observation ties in more closely with the governing theme of this collection. Lovecraft's Petronian transformations illuminate several of the different uses to which metamorphosis can be put in a literary text. Apart from the ways in which transformation throws into relief what it means to be (or cease to be) human, it can also be used to highlight the meta-textual concerns of the author. In particular, it demonstrates how perilous it is to approach fiction with too rigid a set of categories. Lovecraft's transformations highlight the paradoxical generic position of his 'weird tales', both deeply indebted to what has gone before them and transforming that inheritance into something new and strange; moreover, we have seen how later texts which confuse a simplistic notion of the 'hierarchy of genres' can deploy a similar strategy. It is to be hoped that this investigation has whetted the appetite of others to approach such texts with an eye to further enquiry.

Notes to Chapter 10

1. I use this form of the novel's title throughout the present chapter. The traditional title *Satyricon* probably represents an original genitive plural dependent upon a word like *libri* ('the books of the *Satyrica*'). Cf. Walsh (1995), pp. xv–xvi. It is, of course, retained in quotations when the author has used that form.
2. See, for example, Walsh (1985), pp. xx–xxii.

3. Cf. Gowers (1993), pp. 109–219; Rimell (2002).

4. For the circumstances of publication, see Murray (1991), p. 107.

5. For Lovecraft's influence on subsequent popular culture, see Pomeroy (2008), p. 19, and Pitcher (2009), p. 33, with footnotes 54 and 55.

6. See the Introductions to Parts II and III.

7. 'The Call of Cthulhu', 61. See also the discussion at Burleson (1990), p. 156. In this article, all references to Lovecraft's creative works are numerated according to the text in the three volumes of the *H. P. Lovecraft Omnibus* (London: Grafton, 1985). All the stories quoted here are in Volume 3, unless otherwise stated.

8. See Joshi (2001), pp. 31–32, for more on the Ovid translation.

9. Ovid, *Met.* 1. 6. On the earlier fortunes of this phrase, see Velz (1985), pp. 46–47. Lovecraft's review originally appeared in *Conservative* (March, 1923).

10. For discussions of 'The Rats in the Walls', see in particular Armand (1977), Lévy (1985), pp. 95–96, and Joshi (2001), pp. 169–71.

11. In light of the story of hereditary tendencies and ancestral guilt which he tells, it is perhaps significant that the reader never learns Delapore's own given name(s). He notes too that once he arrived he adopted the earlier spelling of that name, 'de la Poer' (p. 26).

12. p. 30.

13. *The Great Gatsby*, Chapter 9.

14. Petronius 33.

15. Petronius 36.

16. Petronius 49.

17. Petronius 69–70.

18. Petronius 59.

19. For discussion, see, for example, Burleson (1990), pp. 86–93.

20. 'Pickman's Model', pp. 52–53.

21. 'Pickman's Model', p. 46.

22. 'At the Mountains of Madness' (*H. P. Lovecraft Omnibus, Vol. 1*), p. 126. See also Leiber (1965), p. 2.

23. For Lovecraft and Eliot, see in particular Cannon (1982) and Joshi (2001), pp. 178–80.

24. 'Pickman's Model', p. 45.

25. See in particular Joshi (1980) and (2001), pp. 174–82, 247.

26. Burleson (1990), pp. 86–93.

27. 'At the Mountains of Madness', p. 133.

28. 'At the Mountains of Madness', p. 128. See also Cerasini (1987).

29. 'The Case of Charles Dexter Ward', (*H. P. Lovecraft Omnibus, Vol. 1*), p. 251. See also Joshi (2001), pp. 253–55.

30. 'The Case of Charles Dexter Ward', p. 270.

31. 'Pickman's Model', p. 54.

32. Thomas Harris, *Hannibal*, p. 307.

33. In the 2002 film of this book (but not the novel itself), Lecter also quotes Horace, *Ep.* 1. 4. 15–16, to describe himself as 'a true hog of Epicurus' herd'.

34. 'The Rats in the Walls', p. 19.

CHAPTER 11

Transforming the Experience of War in the Fiction of Marcel Aymé, René Barjavel and Michel Tournier

Christopher Lloyd

One important cultural effect of the social and political upheavals caused by war in the twentieth century has been the production of thousands of literary texts which attempt to record and make sense of individuals' experiences of warfare. It is a reasonable generalization to assert that the vast majority of fictional works about the Second World War are grounded in documentary realism. Often they are based directly on their authors' personal memories of war, as witnesses or participants, or on painstaking research into historical sources, when an author is writing from the perspective of post-war generations.[1] Most twentieth-century French novelists implicitly adopt the realist aesthetic of their nineteenth-century forebears, who saw fiction as offering a carefully reconstructed chronicle of and commentary upon socio-political events and forces[2] (such as the Napoleonic wars in the case of Stendhal's *La Chartreuse de Parme* (1839), Balzac's *Le Colonel Chabert* (1832) and Tolstoy's *War and Peace* (1868–69), the 1848 revolutions in the case of Flaubert's *L'Éducation sentimentale* (1869), or the Franco-Prussian war in Zola's *La Débâcle* (1892)), even if they rarely follow their predecessors' epic ambitions.

Vercors's celebrated novella *Le Silence de la mer* (1942) thus presents the experience of occupation on the domestic level of one French household disrupted by the presence of a German officer, whose attempts at seduction are forestalled by his hosts' patriotic virtue and his own disillusionment with Nazism; in building his argument for passive resistance, the writer skilfully blends humdrum detail, plausible, low-key drama and understated didacticism. The crises brought by war seem to demand, for most fiction writers, clear linear narratives stressing the authenticity, veracity and referentiality of what they represent; stylistic experimentation or the disruption of narrative structure would be unwelcome distractions from the historical drama to the aesthetic domain. Yet there are exceptions, where authors seek to explore not only the transforming effect of war on people, but also how narrative may be transformed as part of the process. My topic here, however, is not so much authors who engage in formal experimentation (whether this involves emphasizing stylistic, rhetorical and poetic elements, or a solipsistic dissolution of inner and outer worlds and their conventional spatio-temporal boundaries, characteristics found in such well-known figures as Julien Gracq, Claude Simon or Marguerite Duras, all recently studied in this context by Yan Hamel),[3] but another minority, who use devices associated with the fantastic or science fiction, and specifically various types of metamorphosis, in order to offer a less predictable perspective on World War II.

War, by its massively destructive nature, inevitably causes radical transformations, to people and other sentient beings, societies, landscapes and objects, natural or man-made. Most chroniclers of warfare are aware of this phenomenon, though some strive to represent the effects of death, mutilation and desolation in memorable and unbearable detail. Such attempts to give aesthetic form to the horrific, alienating disturbance of normality (dismembered bodies, grotesque wounds, ravaged places) are what Samuel Hynes has called 'battlefield Gothic', because 'military service is a kind of exile from one's real life, a dislocation of the unfamiliar that the mind preserves as life in another world'.[4] In his *Poétique du récit de guerre*, Jean Kaempfer distinguishes the so-called classic war narrative, which adopts the rational, overarching perspective of the statesman or general, from the 'récit de guerre moderne [qui] entend se soustraire à tout modèle, parce que l'expérience extrême qu'il relate lui paraît se refuser à la raison' ['modern war narrative which aims to avoid all models, because the extreme experience which it relates seems to reject reason']. Typically, the modern (i.e. nineteenth-century and later) narrative adopts the perspective of low-ranking individuals in a dehumanized universe, for whom events and experience become unintelligible.[5] Such uncanny moments and defamiliarization suggest that any war narrative can at times verge on the fantastic. But when the fantastic becomes the defining characteristic of a narrative, this is because such perceptual distortions and transformations of normal reality have become systematic.

The fantastic invariably involves transformations that infringe the ontological categories and physical laws which govern the reader's universe (inanimate objects like statues or dolls come to life, people acquire novel characteristics like invisibility, are able to travel through time, lose vital attributes like their soul, shadow or reflection, find themselves fissured into doubles and replicas, turn into monstrous hybrids, and so on). At first sight, texts centred on such disturbances of normality seem to belong to myth or allegory rather than fiction based on socio-historical observation. Yet what distinguishes the fantastic as a narrative genre (as opposed to fantasy works presenting entirely imaginary worlds) is that it depends precisely on the *transformation* of consensual reality, on the crossing of a threshold that separates the everyday world from something unexpected or impossible. Thus Roger Caillois argues that, in terms of cultural evolution, the fantastic has replaced myth or fairy stories where magic may be an unremarkable norm, since the fantastic follows the triumph of scientific rationalism and causal determinism, but seeks to subvert them. 'Le fantastique suppose la solidité du monde réel, mais pour mieux la ravager' ['the fantastic presupposes the solidity of the real world, all the better to ravage it']. Indeed the fantastic 'manifeste un scandale, une déchirure, une irruption insolite, presque insupportable dans le monde réel' ['displays a scandal, a rupture, an unexpected, almost unbearable, eruption in the real world'].[6]

Though what lies beyond the threshold of normality may be purely imaginary, that is invented, its function is almost invariably to invite reflection on what we consider to be normal reality, its failures and shortcomings. To achieve both verisimilitude and allow disruption, a recognizable social world has to be depicted, a world which 'domesticates the impossible hypothesis', as H. G. Wells put it in 1933 in a preface to a collected edition of his novels.[7] In other words, the narrative is driven not so much by the fantastic phenomenon itself as by its transformational impact. Thus an adventure story with a satirical edge introduces a magical dimension, but invites interpretation as a philosophical fable: however different their cultural contexts, this is the pattern set by Apuleius, Swift or indeed Wells (who cites *The Golden Ass* and *Gulliver's Travels* as models which he aspired to update for a scientific age). At this point, it is worth noting that Tzvetan Todorov's celebrated study of the poetics of the fantastic does not deal very persuasively with Wells's successors in the twentieth century, particularly authors who have recourse to allegory or science fiction. This is because Todorov, in the interests of taxonomic tidiness, argues for a very narrow definition of the fantastic, as a form of perceptual dislocation caused by epistemological uncertainty: 'Le fantastique, c'est l'hésitation éprouvée par un être qui ne connaît que les lois naturelles, face à un événement en apparence surnaturel' ['the fantastic is the hesitation experienced by a being who knows only natural laws when confronted by an apparently supernatural event'].[8] An anguished confrontation with the supernatural, its causes and purpose (of the sort encountered in nineteenth-century writers like Mérimée, Maupassant, and Henry or M. R. James) is held to be a key defining feature of the fantastic, despite the fact that for many other authors, such as Gogol, Bulgakov and Kafka, the central issue is effect rather than cause, the adjustments needed to accommodate an inexplicable phenomenon, or the use of the fantastic as a pretext for delivering an ideological message.

As far as I know, relatively few fiction-writers have introduced fantastic elements into World War II novels (Grass's *The Tin Drum* (1959) and Vonnegut's *Slaughterhouse Five* (1969) are arguably the best-known examples). My aim here is to explore the use and effect of metamorphosis in three French writers' fictional accounts of the Second World War. They are Marcel Aymé (1902–1967), René Barjavel (1911–1985), and Michel Tournier (b. 1924). All three authors lived through the German occupation of France, although only Barjavel saw active military service (in 1939–40), as a supply-corps corporal. All three are more interested in the survival strategies adopted by civilians (who are sometimes reluctant conscripts) in the war than in depicting military combat, although in any case the traditional separation between combatants and civilians ceased to be meaningful during this period. Particularly in the final years of Nazi occupation and allied liberation, civilians fought in the Resistance, fell victim to bombing, or endured extreme hardship, conscription as slave workers, detention, summary execution as hostages, or deportation to concentration camps. While insisting on the material deprivation and moral and social collapse brought by defeat, all three novelists have recourse to forms of escapism, not in the sense of producing trivial entertainment, but rather of creating diverting narratives, which open up imaginary spaces apparently beyond the horrors of war. Ultimately, however, war proves inescapable, and the authors impose a moral reckoning which finally obliterates the refuge provisionally offered by the fantastic.

Taking the authors in order of age and dates of publication, Marcel Aymé characteristically uses the fantastic in a comic, subversive fashion, as a form of disorder which briefly disrupts the status quo, until unexpected consequences lead to the restoration of order. For example, his novel *La Belle Image* (1941) reverses the transformation of Kafka's justly celebrated fable 'Die Verwandlung' (1916); in it a dull family man is metamorphosed, not into a monstrous insect, but into a handsome stranger with a new-found seductive power over women. Is his new face merely a mask over the old one, or does a new face equate to a new soul? The first-person narrator's scruples and inhibitions prevent him from profiting from his new appearance, and he eventually reverts to his former nondescript state; given his very ordinariness, we may deduce that, for most people, mundane routine proves preferable to disruptive novelty.

Aymé's derisive and reductive reversal of Kafka's 'Metamorphosis' offers an amusing satire of petty-bourgeois morality, but has none of its existential terror and despair. It does however remind us how Kafka's novella resonates in so many twentieth-century texts that deal with monstrous transformations. Todorov notes that whereas classic fantastic stories move from the natural towards the super-natural, 'Metamorphosis' moves from the apparently supernatural (Gregor Samsa's transformation into a monstrous insect is famously presented without explanation in the opening sentence) towards the naturalization of the supernatural; the exceptional becomes the rule. For Todorov, this means that two supposedly incompatible genres (the marvellous and the uncanny) are made to coincide. An alternative conclusion would be that Todorov's generic categories are unduly rigid: his oppositional model is inadequate for a genre based on paradoxes.[9] Todorov notes too that 'Metamorphosis' invites allegorical readings (it can readily be seen as a parable about human animality, individual self-loathing and self-sacrifice, family betrayal, disease, and so forth), but apparently considers the literal nature of Kafka's text and the multivalent, indeterminate nature of such symbolic interpretations as somehow incompatible.[10] Todorov also acknowledges that metamorphosis is a useful term for categorizing certain thematic features which fall under his general heading of 'les thèmes du je' ['themes of the I'], that is, dealing with the relationship between self and world. No doubt Gregor Samsa's distressing transformation relates to a profoundly disturbed state of psychic and physical alienation, perhaps shared by his author. But one might again want to refine Todorov by suggesting that metamorphosis in fictional narratives is more an overarching structural device that determines a story's whole narration than a thematic category linked to the particular topics dealt with.

Aymé differed from Kafka in a more material sense, in that he was a full-time professional writer, entirely dependent on sales of his fiction and journalism and on regular production and publication for his livelihood. He therefore continued his industrious output during the Occupation; some of his novels and stories were serialized in the collaborationist journals *La Gerbe* and *Je suis partout* (notorious for their rabid anti-Semitism and pro-Nazi fervour). This association aside, Aymé was not ideologically engaged in favour of either collaboration or resistance; his neutrality and cautiousness, together with rigorous censorship, meant that there are few overt references to war and the increasingly intolerable conditions of Occupation in his wartime writings. The exception is found in a few stories contained in the collection *Le Passe-Muraille* (1943), which use the fantastic as a means of providing a more overt satirical commentary on the relations between individual citizens and the state. Adapting an earlier story ('Le Temps mort', 1938) to fit wartime shortages, 'La Carte' recounts how the government decides to ration time, with the number of days' existence granted to different categories of the population varying according to their perceived usefulness to the state (Jews are allowed half a day's life per month).

Unlike some later allegorical transformations of World War II phenomena (for example, Camus's *La Peste* (1947), or Amélie Nothomb's recent caustic fable about concentration camps being reinstated as an extreme form of television reality show in *Acide sulfurique* (2005)), Aymé's parable is intricately and persuasively embedded in detailed evocation and knowledge of the injustices and iniquities of commodity rationing and the black market. Amusing inventiveness is allied with an implicit condemnation of the Vichy government's economic and moral failures, indeed its complicity in the exclusion and extermination of unwanted citizens. While those exempted from time rationing remain callously indifferent to its effects, those subjected to it are treated with brutal contempt by the agents of the state, who consider them 'comme un rebut d'humanité' ['the dregs of humanity'].[11] The victims of rationing become phantoms who simply vanish on the days for which they do not have valid tickets. On the other hand, those wealthy enough to acquire black-market tickets are even able to add extra days to their existence, living for thirty-six, sixty-six days, or for years even, within a given month. Such trafficking eventually cancels out the savings in resources intended by the scheme and it is therefore withdrawn. The notion that time is a quantifiable commodity, along with the desperate anxiety that the war might never end, is further explored in 'Le Décret', when the authorities apply the solution of advancing time by seventeen years to a future date when the Second World War has finally ended. We discover that time is not merely relative and subjective, but physiological and compressible. For unexplained reasons, however, the narrator of this story falls back into the past and is thus obliged to live through the same seventeen years for a second time.

Aymé's *Le Passe-Muraille* (whose title story is about a clerk who discovers he can walk through walls) playfully transforms normal physical relations to space and time, thereby questioning both contemporary history and broader metaphysical issues. By using the fantastic as an allegorical device, the writer is able to challenge the oppressive power of the state and expose the callous and cowardly complicity of most citizens without himself incurring censure. The concluding story in the collection, 'En attendant', chronicles the privations suffered by people waiting in a queue during the war of '1939–72'. But apart from this reference to the interminable nature of the war, and the discovery that one person in the queue has expired, here Aymé remains within the boundaries of everyday reality, as he does in the debunking novels about the Occupation and Liberation which he published after the war finally ended. One senses that Aymé eschews the fantastic in these later works because, as a protective shield, it has become an unnecessary distraction.

It seems likely that my second author, René Barjavel, owed a great deal to *Le Passe-Muraille*, even if he acknowledged a more explicit debt to the late nineteenth-century pioneers of science fiction, Verne and Wells. Like Marcel Aymé, Barjavel's wartime career is loosely associated with collaboration (in that he worked for the publisher Denoël, whose other authors included some notorious anti-Semites). Neither Aymé nor Barjavel show any sympathy for the political forces associated with resistance (i.e. Gaullism and communism). Indeed, unlike Aymé, who rejected totalitarian systems of both right and left, Barjavel's early novels contain fascistic echoes that suggest a certain compliance with the Vichy government's or even National Socialism's hostility to democratic republicanism and its supposed cultural decadence. For instance, his first novel *Ravage* (1943) invites interpretation as an allegory about the fall of France in 1940 and its possible rebirth. Barjavel describes how the sudden disappearance of electricity in 2052 leads to the collapse of western civilization, which has become slavishly dependent on technology and an unjust social hierarchy. Most of the population perish rapidly from fire, famine, disease or strife amid apocalyptic scenes presented with grim relish. But Barjavel's hero, the aptly named François Deschamps, hitherto a peasant misfit in a world divorced from nature, makes his way to south-east Provence, where his physical strength and resourcefulness allow him to establish a self-sufficient, agricultural community. Over the next century, he becomes an authoritarian patriarch, fathering 228 children and ruthlessly suppressing any attempts to restore written culture and industrial technology, until he is killed by the inventor of a steam engine.

Ravage clearly echoes Marshal Pétain's celebration of alleged rustic virtues and his critique of perverted culture, although its environmentalist message is more immediately apparent and appealing to twenty-first-century readers. François warns that the immense transformative power given by technology to certain individuals and corporations is simply 'un progrès accéléré vers la mort' ['accelerated progress towards death'],[12] Perhaps the most extreme perversion of nature is the custom of preserving the bodies of the dead in transparent cold rooms built into their descendants' dwellings (allowing their families to maintain the illusion that their deceased ancestors are still among them, rather like the Victorians' fondness for keeping stuffed animals in glass cases). When electricity fails, these seventy million frozen corpses begin to thaw and putrefy, as they return to their natural state and threaten the living with infection. While *Ravage* anticipates the dystopian science fiction of the post-war period (and, most obviously, Orwell's *1984* (1949)), such examples of disastrous meddling with natural processes also recall classic nineteenth-century texts like Mary Shelley's *Frankenstein* (1821) and Villiers de l'Isle-Adam's *L'Ève future* (1886) that depict 'la tentation de la science et la récusation du scientisme' ['the temptation of science and the rejection of scientism'].[13]

As many commentators have objected, Todorov's theory of the fantastic deals inadequately with science fiction. He acknowledges SF's connection to the fantastic, but relegates it to the marvellous, a category where magical transformations are seen as the norm and which clearly better fits the archaic, folkloric world evoked by fairy stories. But as Jean Gattégno observes, science fiction needs science; it looks towards the future, and typically deals with the evolution of human society, individuals and knowledge in imagined times and places.[14] In Stanisław Lem's view, Todorov sees science fiction as 'irrationalism embodied in pseudoscience', whereas in practice it is 'nourished by scientific revelations'.[15] On the other hand, as Lem concedes, a common science fiction device like time travel 'implies a qualitative difference in the world's causal structure'; time, which seems to us to be irreversible, becomes reversible.[16] The paradoxical transformations which this permits evidently fascinated Aymé, Barjavel and many of their successors: not only can the time traveller reshape the course of his own existence, but that of the whole universe.[17] Whether any of this is scientifically grounded is highly doubtful. In a recent study of the physics and metaphysics of time, Michael Lockwood explains that 'Einstein has shown us that *forward* time travel is unquestionably allowed by the laws of physics'. Thus, assuming that one could travel at something approaching the speed of light, one could circumnavigate the entire universe in twenty-three years and arrive home in the distant future.[18] Whatever the theory, the practice remains in the realm of fiction. In this respect, Barjavel's second novel, *Le Voyageur imprudent* (1944), offers a more systematic account of the possibilities of time manipulation than Marcel Aymé, while again stressing the perils of unregulated technological and scientific discoveries.

Barjavel skilfully blends a naturalistic account of the miseries of war and occupation with characters and events that belong to fairy tales and science fiction. The grotesquely dehumanizing reality of war is demonstrated by a striking example of 'battlefield Gothic' in the first paragraph, when a soldier is discovered frozen to death in the latrines, his ears snapping off when his head is lifted. The following pages recount the struggle for survival of the mathematician Pierre Saint-Menoux, a reluctant conscript to a machine-gun company, who is himself on the point of freezing to death during the winter of 1940, when he literally stumbles through a doorway and encounters the physicist Noël Essaillon and his daughter Annette, 'belle comme une apparition' ['beautiful as an apparition'].[19] Thanks to Saint-Menoux's scientific papers, Essaillon has invented a substance that allows him to manipulate time; he invites Saint-Menoux to join him in his investigations. As in 'Le Décret', Saint-Menoux is permitted to escape the horrors of the debacle by fast-forwarding through two years until February 1942; this acceleration to a pleasanter future is teasingly called 'la guerre-éclair' (i.e. Blitzkrieg). His brief experience of time travel, he thinks, makes him 'léger et puissant comme un demi–dieu, aussi différent de ses conducteurs que ceux-ci de leurs mules' ['light and powerful as a demi-god, as different from his drivers as they are from their mules']. Yet he arrives in 1942 with 'les traits d'un homme qui avait durement appris à compter avec le réel' ['the look of a man who had learned the hard way to deal with reality'].[20] At this stage, at least, his supposed transformation is metaphorical and imaginary.

In the remainder of the novel, however, time travel does indeed transform Saint-Menoux more literally, as he becomes the imprudent voyager of the title and learns too of the future transformation of humanity. Unsurprisingly, perhaps, short-term gratification (power, adventure, love, knowledge) is eventually followed by more horrific metamorphoses. The ethical dilemmas and existential paradoxes generated by time travel are dealt with inventively and adroitly by Barjavel, whereas his hero gradually sheds most of his initial scruples, abetted by his rather sinister mentor Noël Essaillon. Essaillon's miraculous substance, 'noëlite', has various functions: for example, he is able to freeze time, thereby creating an eternal present, but only uses this in a food storage unit, a sort of temporal refrigerator. He has however also used the substance to manufacture a bomb, which was tested with devastating consequences (which Essaillon regards, characteristically, with callous indifference).

Travelling to the past allows the possibility of changing the direction of one's life; thus fatal accidents can be avoided and their victims resuscitated. Following the example of Wells's time traveller in *The Time Machine* (1895), Saint-Menoux visits the distant future, discovering in the year 100,000 that humanity has evolved, not into two hostile species à la Wells, but into innumerable specialized sub-species, which have lost all individual identity and autonomy and become cells in a perfect social body. To a twentieth-century observer, these are monstrous hybrids ('Les ventres hideux, les gueules de requin, les yeux baladeurs, les mains à crocs, les poitrines monstrueuses, les derrières soudés, dansaient dans sa mémoire une farandole de cauchemar' ['the hideous bellies, sharks' jaws, wandering eyes, hooked hands, monstrous chests, soldered behinds, danced in his memory in a nightmarish farandole'])[21] since their appearance and behaviour are determined entirely by their specialized function. Although Barjavel clearly borrows his entomological utopia from Wells's *The First Men in the Moon* (1901), this vision of a dehumanized yet functionally perfect mass of beings also suggests one possible evolutionary outcome of the totalitarian ideologies at war during the Occupation. As with Gregor Samsa's repellent metamorphosis, these creatures of the future arouse horror because they 'breach the norms of ontological propriety', at least when seen from our human, individualistic perspective. With their grotesquely over-developed, specialized parts, their atrophied non-functional organs, and bestial appearance, they illustrate the 'fusion, fission, magnification and horrific metonymy [which] are the major tropes of art-horror'[22] — and invite comparisons with earlier masters of the grotesque, from Ovid to Bosch.

Under Essaillon's nefarious influence, Saint-Menoux starts to lose his self-control and moral responsibility. He plays schoolboyish pranks in the past; after Essaillon is killed in a gruesome experiment, Saint-Menoux's interventions in the past become overtly criminal and indirectly cause two deaths. In fact, he discovers that his criminal ventures have been inscribed in history books and attributed to a mysterious 'diable vert' ['green devil'], named after the colour of his time-suit. From reluctant conscript and frustrated mathematician, Saint-Menoux has become both a gratified lover of Annette and a voyager who seeks to step outside the bounds of humanity. But when Saint-Menoux overweeningly attempts to change the course of past history by assassinating Napoleon, he succeeds only in causing his own destruction by accidentally eliminating his ancestor. As a direct result, Saint-Menoux himself is eliminated from existence, together with the possibility of time travel which he had helped invent. We return to the historical reality of the Second World War, as Barjavel closes and cancels out his fictional narrative in what seems like a deliberate assertion of conventional morality, a rejection of the changes caused by his voyager.

Michel Tournier's novel *Le Roi des aulnes* (1970) also depicts a central character who is a social misfit or deviant and imagines it is his destiny to change the course of history through a series of transformations that link myth to the events of the Second World War in France and Nazi Germany. Unlike Aymé or Barjavel, however, Tournier eschews magical or scientific devices that break normal physical laws, asserting in an essay on his novel that 'Il a toujours été hors de question pour moi de verser dans le genre fantastique. J'entends m'en tenir à un réalisme qui ne rejoint le fantastique que par un paroxysme de précision et de rationalisme, par hyperréalisme' ['It was always out of the question for me to use the fantastic genre. My intention was to limit myself to a type of realism that overlaps with the fantastic only through its paroxysmal precision and rationalism, through hyper-realism'].[23] In actual fact, *Le Roi des aulnes* fits the category of the fantastic defined by Todorov as the 'fantastique étrange' (the uncanny), where the supernatural is largely contained within the perspective of a deluded character whose judgements the reader is obliged to challenge. What for the character is a literal process of transformation, as destiny turns him into a mythic being, may be interpreted by the reader on the level of metaphor, as a symptom of megalomania or insanity.

Todorov in fact argues that the fantastic has to be grounded in a very literal interpretation of strange events (hence his reluctance to accept that it can coexist with allegorical or poetic readings which operate on a symbolic or figurative level). Indeed, he suggests that the process is reversed: 'Le surnaturel naît souvent de ce qu'on prend le sens figuré à la lettre' ['the supernatural often arises when a figurative sense is taken literally']. Further,

> Si le fantastique se sert sans cesse des figures rhétoriques, c'est qu'il y a trouvé son origine. Le surnaturel naît du langage, il en est à la fois la conséquence et la preuve: non seulement le diable et les vampires n'existent que dans les mots, mais aussi seul le langage permet de concevoir ce qui est toujours absent: le surnaturel.

> [If the fantastic constantly uses rhetorical figures, this is because that is where its origin lay. The supernatural is born in language, it is both its consequence and proof: not only do the devil and vampires exist only in words, but also language alone allows us to conceive what is always absent: the supernatural.][24]

Setting aside questions of religious belief, even from an anthropological, evolutionary point of view, this assertion is provocative rather than persuasive (it would be more plausible to imagine that awareness of the supernatural preceded the arrival of language in human evolution and was more probably a reaction to the mysterious metamorphoses observable in the natural world). But this insistence on linguistic over-determination (with its implicit rejection of an empirical reality knowable outside language) certainly illuminates the mental world inhabited by Tournier's hero in *Le Roi des aulnes*, and by countless other characters in fantastic narratives, where, as Todorov puts it, supernatural beings and events supplement a defective causality and chance is replaced by pan-determinism. That is, 'la limite entre le physique et le mental, entre la matière et l'esprit, entre la chose et le mot cesse d'être étanche' ['the boundary between physical and mental, between matter and mind, between thing and word gives way'].[25]

The title *Le Roi des aulnes* (variously translated into English as the Erl- or Alder-King or the Ogre) intentionally evokes Goethe's famous ballad 'Erlkönig' (1782), which describes how a rider carrying his child on horseback through the forest at night loses the child to the sinister King of the Alders (or Elves). Though the child's terror may be purely imaginary, he dies nonetheless. Defining myth in his intellectual autobiography *Le Vent Paraclet* as 'une histoire fondamentale' ['fundamental history or story'] which shapes the essence of humanity, Tournier attempts in his novel to blend the décor of German Romanticism with a realistic account of how a French prisoner of war called Abel Tiffauges witnesses the collapse of the Third Reich in East Prussia, as he rises to a position of power in an SS training school known as a Napola. As the majority of adult German males are transferred into combat zones, Tiffauges progresses from digging ditches to driving a lorry and transporting supplies, eventually becoming an active recruiting agent for the school. Delighting in the intimate company of pubescent boys and in the folkloric symbolism and rituals of the SS, only in the final pages does Tiffauges become aware of the full horrors of Nazi genocide, when he rescues a Jewish child and carries him into the marshes, while the advancing Russians destroy the castle housing the Napola and its juvenile defenders.

Tournier trained as a Germanist and philosopher, which partly explains why his novel is laden with intertextual references, symbolic parallels and inversions, as well as didactic judgements mostly delivered by Abel Tiffauges (whose first-person diary occupies about two-fifths of the text). Reviewers and critics have further deciphered Tiffauges's encodings and decodings, although few if any have devoted much attention to the process of metamorphosis in *Le Roi des aulnes*. The shifting boundaries between a metaphorical and literal interpretation of metamorphosis (a word which with its cognates occurs at least ten times in Tournier's text) thus merit more detailed exploration in the concluding section of this essay. Although Colin Davis begins his study of Tournier as philosopher and novelist by asserting that 'For Tournier, philosophical content has priority over literary form, and writing is the search for an adequate means of expression',[26] we should recall that Tournier actually abandoned his ambitions to become a professional philosopher after humiliatingly failing the *agrégation* (the postgraduate examination seen as a pathway to an academic career). Contrary to what some critics imply, his novels are not philosophical tracts, but engaging stories, full of dramatic episodes, and peopled with eccentric and memorable characters situated in a painstakingly detailed social reality. Contrasting metaphysics to the abstractions of mathematics (or much academic philosophy), Tournier takes the view that 'Le propre de la métaphysique au contraire, c'est toujours de plonger au cœur du concret' ['On the contrary, the distinctive feature of metaphysics is always to plunge into the heart of the concrete'].[27] Hence his fondness for 'hyper-realism' and his admiration for writers like Hans Christian Andersen who link 'la familiarité la plus quotidienne et le fantastique le plus grandiose' ['the most mundanely familiar with the most grandiosely fantastic'], as well as his own urge to write for children as well as adults.[28]

Colin Davis concedes that *Le Roi des aulnes* 'combines a self-regarding formalism with a closely documented realism',[29] although within the narrative economy, the 'formalism' is largely attributable to the characters' over-interpretative mania (caused by psychic instability or ideological fanaticism) rather than Tournier's personal obsessions. Unsurprisingly, Tournier's paroxysmal naturalism includes some horrific incidents of 'battlefield Gothic' during the concluding descriptions of the downfall of the Third Reich in East Prussia (such as the decapitation of a boy soldier caught by the back blast of a Panzerfaust, or the impalement of three boys on ceremonial swords, their blood forming a purple mantel on the immaculate snow).[30] Squeamish or prudish readers may well find Tournier's protracted, erotically charged descriptions of such extreme bodily mutilation and transformation disturbing, and his protagonist's preoccupation with his own and others' physiological functions and excretions repugnant or obscene. But, replying to complaints about the passages where Tiffauges inspects his stools (admiring 'ce beau poupon dodu de limon vivant que je viens d'enfanter' ['this fine, chubby infant of living earth to which I have just given birth'] (p. 144)), Tournier offers the following defence:

> J'ai dit que mes romans étaient autant de tentatives pour transcrire en images et en histoire un certain fonds métaphysique. Eh bien, c'est un fait, on dirait que jetée dans le creuset romanesque, l'ontologie se métamorphose en scatologie!

> [I've said that my novels were a series of attempts to transpose a certain meta-physical stock into images and stories. Well, it's a fact, it seems that when thrown into the fictional crucible, ontology is metamorphosed into scatology!][31]

Tiffauges's personal metamorphosis operates in at least three ways, literally, symbolically and linguistically, which sometimes overlap and sometimes remain distinct. On the mundane level of plot, he is transformed from being an ill-educated Parisian motor mechanic and reluctant conscript to become a sardonic philosopher and chronicler, and an enthralled and powerful acolyte of the Nazis in East Prussia. Tiffauges also imagines he is becoming an ogre, a mythic being destined to bear away children as part of a higher destiny (somehow linked both to figures of legend like the King of the Alders and Saint Christopher and to historical ogres like Göring and Hitler). In his own eyes, he is a saviour who discovers he is actually a malefactor capable of redemption. The reader may prefer to regard him as deluded (his insistence on his sanity from the opening pages invites a contrary diagnosis). But Tiffauges also possesses a transformative gaze and turn of mind, in his fondness for metaphors and analogies which reconfigure the world, if only in a figurative fashion.

Thus Tiffauges recalls how his boyhood mentor Nestor (to whom he attributes miraculous powers) was served by his schoolmates 'comme un dieu antique' ['like an ancient god'] (p. 40), although Nestor is later immolated when he sets fire to the school. A bleeding wound is compared explicitly to an 'œil de Cyclope' ['Cyclops eye'] (p. 172), and implicitly, as in an earlier episode when Tiffauges is forced by a bully to lick clean his gashed knee (p. 31), to a vulva. Fulfilling tedious and bureaucratic formalities, Tiffauges notes sarcastically that, for most people, 'vivre sans papiers, c'est vivre comme une bête' ['to live without papers is to live like a beast'] (p. 66). He imagines a parable about an anarchist who burns down all the records offices in the hope of liberating humanity, only to discover that, deprived of the arbitrary signs of identity imposed on them by the state, his fellow humans begin to turn into brute beasts, walking on all fours and uttering inarticulate noises, for 'l'âme humaine est en papier' ['the human soul is made of paper'] (p. 66). The new pope is compared to the mummy of Ramses II, 'en moins humain' ['only less human'] (p. 162), while the camera with which he captures his changing vision of the world is 'un sexe énorme, gaîné de cuir' ['an enormous penis, sheathed in leather'] (p. 167). While conventional values and figures of authority are derided and dehumanized (and will be swept away by the debacle of 1940), the tools and rites marking Tiffauges's transformation are positively charged and eroticized.

While some of these examples of imaginary metamorphoses faintly echo earlier writers and mythical sources (notably, Swift, Ovid, and Homer), the only extended reference to a literary predecessor relevant to this discussion (apart from Goethe) within the text of Le Roi des aulnes (as far as I am aware) is to Carlo Collodi's Pinocchio (1883). Reading this famous tale of a puppet (who finally becomes a boy when he abandons his wicked ways), Tiffauges recalls the episode when Pinocchio is transformed into an ass for not working at school. This is a revolting punishment, in his view, particularly as he interprets it as symbolizing the onslaught of puberty which inflicts 'les hideurs de la virilité' ['hideous virility'] and 'ce sexe d'âne démesuré, informe et puant' ['an enormous, shapeless, stinking donkey's penis'] on graceful youth (p. 154). Needless to say, this particular misfortune is not suffered by Pinocchio (unlike his classic predecessor in Apuleius's Golden Ass, who is not referenced directly). However, unlike Kafka or Barjavel, or earlier writers for whom transformation into an animal is a punishment for bestial behaviour, Tournier does not invariably present animalization in a negative fashion. Certain animals are perceived as symbols of power, strength and wisdom (in particular, the stag, horse and elk). Unlike Gregor Samsa, Tiffauges marks out his existential anguish by voluntarily inventing rituals that make him more rather than less like an animal. Thus he alternates his 'brame' (straining and bellowing like a rutting stag) with the 'shampooing-chiottes' (sluicing his head under the toilet), in the hope that his habitual human mask will have been replaced by the face of a roebuck when he looks in the mirror (pp. 73–74).

Even if we reject Tiffauges's belief that he is inscribed in destiny, there is little doubt that he is endowed with a vision that transforms his and the reader's perceptions of people, objects and events in disturbing and provocative ways. Some critics have claimed that Tournier has made Nazi iconography and anthropology too appealing[32] (although a satirical undertone can often be detected, for instance in the account of Göring's venery). On the other hand, Tournier's rejection of adult (or 'heterosexist') sexuality probably troubles twenty-first-century readers more, given the distinctly paedophiliac nature of Tiffauges's attraction to pubescent children (he narrowly escapes lengthy imprisonment for the alleged rape of a minor). Tiffauges's ultimate transformation into the 'cheval d'Israël' bearing the child Ephraïm remains metaphorical, even if Tournier has brilliantly portrayed what he calls 'la vocation ogresse du régime nazi' ['the ogreish vocation of the Nazi regime'].[33] Tournier's work, unlike Aymé's and Barjavel's, does offer a mythologized version of World War II which could be said to transform our perception of the Third Reich and its collaborators.

Although none of the three authors discussed cites classical mythology directly (their most obvious reference points are nineteenth- and twentieth-century predecessors, witness Tiffauges's discussion of *Pinocchio* and Barjavel's borrowing from Wells), perhaps one could argue, following Marina Warner, that in rejecting the Judaeo-Christian tradition of 'unique, individual integrity of identity',[34] they revitalize a pre-Christian type of metamorphosis, particularly in their insistence on transformation as a *collective* process affecting the nation at war rather than just exceptional individuals. Their protagonists are neither mythical heroes nor Romantic or fin-de-siècle anti-heroes, but distinctly ordinary men confronted by the extraordinary circumstances of industrialized warfare and the mass transformation of humanity which they bring.

Notes to Chapter 11

1. See Paris (1990), for an annotated bibliography of over 2,000 novels published in English (including translations) between 1939 and 1988. Taylor (1993), offers an analytical list of over 3,371 works. I am currently part of a research team based at Durham and Leeds Universities working on an AHRC-funded project on World War II narratives in French. Our aim is to produce an online analytical database of about 2,000 items, as well as four book-length studies. See <http://www.frame.leeds.ac.uk/>.

2. As David Lodge (1979), p. 25 writes: 'A working definition of realism in literature might be: *the representation of experience in a manner which approximates closely to descriptions of similar experience in nonliterary texts of the same culture.* Realistic fiction, being concerned with the action of individuals in time, approximates to history.'

3. Hamel (2006).

4. Hynes (1997), p. 8.

5. Kaempfer (1998), pp. 8–9.

6. Caillois (1966), p. 19, p. 15.

7. Reprinted in *H. G. Wells* (London: Book Club Associates, 1980), p. 14.

8. Todorov (1970), p. 29. This is not to deny that Todorov offers a lucid and influential introduction to the topic. For fuller discussion of theories of the fantastic, see Brooke-Rose (1983) and Cornwell (1990).

9. See Lem (1984).

10. Todorov (1970), pp. 177–83. For a counter-argument, see Sokel (1980). Citati (1989) insists on Kafka's obsession with animality: 'Il sentait, au-dedans de lui, un animal. Composant avec les figures de son inconscient un bestiaire tout aussi vaste que les bestiaires médiévaux [...]. Il avait en horreur de nombreux animaux [...]. Il les avait en horreur parce qu'il pressentait le fauve en puissance, encore inconnu, qui l'habitait' ['He felt within himself an animal. Composing with the figures of his unconscious a bestiary just as vast as medieval bestiaries [...]. He was horrified by numerous animals [...]. He was horrified by them because he had a presentment of the unknown, potentially wild beast that lived within him'] (p. 67).

11. Marcel Aymé, *Le Passe-Muraille* (Paris: Livre de Poche, 1958), p. 67.

12. René Barjavel, *Ravage*, ed. by Yves Ansel (Paris: Gallimard, Folio, 1996), p. 83. But what Ansel calls Deschamps's 'utopie régressive' (p. 323) is even less appealing.

13. Tritter (2001), p. 8.

14. Gattégno (1992).

15. Lem (1984), p. 219.

16. Lem (1984), p. 149.

17. As is shown parodically in Robert Heinlein's 'All You Zombies' (1959), a story about a time traveller who manages to be both his own father and (by a judicious sex change) mother, and by the episode of *The Simpsons* where Homer's time-travelling manages to eradicate the whole human race.

18. Lockwood (2005), p. 48. Moreover, 'If Einstein is right, the terms "past", "present", and "future" do not express objective differences between times, any more than "to the west", "here", and "to the east" express objective differences between places' (p. 53). And, according to Stephen Hawking, the 'idea that the universe has multiple histories may sound like science fiction, but it is now accepted as science fact (by cosmologists at least)' (quoted p. 329).

19. René Barjavel, *Le Voyageur imprudent* (Paris: Gallimard, Folio, 1996), p. 14.

20. *Le Voyageur imprudent*, p. 25, p. 33.

21. *Le Voyageur imprudent*, p.125.

22. Carroll (1990), p. 16, p. 52.

23. Michel Tournier, *Le Vent Paraclet* (Paris: Gallimard, Folio, 1977), p. 114.

24. Todorov (1970), p. 82, pp. 86–87. On the other hand, Massey (1976) argues that metamorphosis, which stresses the physical and the bodily, circumvents language (p. 51). Unlike the continuity or blending of separate forms in metamorphosis, 'metaphor provides a linguistic bridge between two terms which are understood to be physically different' (p. 187).

25. Todorov (1970), p. 116, p. 119.

26. Davis (1988), p. 10.

27. *Le Vent Paraclet*, p. 45.

28. *Le Vent Paraclet*, p. 52.

29. Davis (1988), p. 46.

30. Michel Tournier, *Le Roi des aulnes* (Paris: Gallimard, Folio, 1978), pp. 537–39, pp. 577–78. Such episodes combine extreme violence, pathos and the protagonist's ruminations on their symbolic import. Subsequent references to this edition are given in the text.

31. *Le Vent Paraclet*, p. 257.

32. Notably, Saul Friedländer. For a rebuttal, see Petit (1991), p. 38.

33. *Le Vent Paraclet*, p. 106.

34. Warner (2002), p. 2.

CHAPTER 12

The Parabola Paradox:
Transformation and Science Fiction[1]

Sarah Annes Brown

> What would humanity be had it no other care, no other ideal, no other aim in
> life than selfless giving and the happiness of others; if to work solely for one's
> neighbour, to sacrifice oneself permanently and wholly, were the only possible
> joy, the essential felicity, in a word, the supreme bliss, of which we perceive
> only a fugitive gleam in the arms of love?[2]

When considering the ways different kinds of metamorphoses from (or to) the
human have been represented in western culture, it is inviting to map such changes
of state onto a clearly defined spectrum or hierarchy. Thus if we are surveying the
range of transformations to be found in, say, Ovid's *Metamorphoses* we might divide
these into 'upwards' metamorphoses — from a human into some higher being,
generally a god — and 'downwards' metamorphoses — from a human into a plant,
animal or inanimate object of some kind.[3]

There are far more of the latter type in Ovid, and this is true of literature as a
whole. The concept of 'downwards' metamorphosis is a potent motif. However, such
transformations do not always have precisely the same resonance. Many Ovidian
examples, such as Arachne's metamorphosis into a spider or Actaeon's into a stag, are
framed as divine punishment, whether deserved or undeserved.[4] Sometimes a more
scientific explanation is supplied, as is the case in Robert Louis Stevenson's *Strange
Case of Dr Jekyll and Mr Hyde* (1886) in which Jekyll is transformed by a potion into
the degraded Hyde, who is untroubled by conscience or morality. A more dramatic
devolution is presented in Kurt Vonnegut's surreal science fictional novel, *Galápagos*
(1985). Here the entire human race undergoes a 'downwards' metamorphosis. The
same evolutionary imperative which gave humanity intelligence now operates in
reverse; the remnants of humanity who survive on Galápagos need to be excellent
swimmers in order to survive, and natural selection favours those with small,
streamlined heads. This process eventually leads to humankind's transformation
into a quite different species, a seal-like creature with a small brain:

> When my tale began, it appeared that the earthling part of the clockwork
> of the universe was in terrible danger, since many of its parts, which is to say
> people, no longer fitted in anywhere, and were damaging all the parts around
> them as well as themselves. I would have said back then that the damage was
> beyond repair.

> Not so!
> Thanks to certain modifications in the design of the human beings, I can see
> no reason why the earthling part of the clockwork can't go on ticking for ever
> the way it is ticking now.[5]

Thus devolution is, ironically, presented as an improvement, a development which saved rather than destroyed the human race.

Although there may be special circumstances which reconcile humans to such transformations — in Ovid they are often presented as the only alternative to death or dishonour[6] — in general any kind of 'downwards' metamorphosis is a fate to be feared and shunned. We might therefore expect 'upwards' metamorphoses, by contrast, to be welcomed and coveted. And although the apotheoses of Hercules and Julius Caesar don't seem to capture Ovid's imagination in the same way as 'downwards' metamorphoses, they are certainly seen as rare signs of special favour or merit.[7] But Ovid's (muted) celebration of apotheosis is perhaps atypical. It is easy to find examples of apparently positive transformations, either of humanity or of individual humans, into divine or otherwise posthuman forms which are treated with ambivalence or hostility. This trend seems particularly marked within modern Western culture. Thus, returning to the case of Hercules, it is interesting to note the ways in which the 1997 Disney film transformed the original myth. In one sense the film can be seen as a blandly child-friendly version which (not surprisingly) glosses over Hercules' murder of his wife and children in a fit of madness. However, another important change could be seen as negative. Hercules gives up his ambition for immortality in favour of a brief chance of human happiness with Megara. This example from popular culture is just one indication of a widespread human preference for staying human.[8]

Such reservations about human apotheosis or improvement might seem counter-intuitive. If it is almost universally thought to be bad to slip down the *scala naturae*, the great chain of being, towards the beastly, why should it not be considered admirable to strive to climb higher, to move nearer to God and His angels? One response might be that to attempt such an ascent might involve one in *hubris*, as is the case with figures from both classical and Judaeo-Christian culture.[9] But a fear of *hubris* alone does not, I think, account for the widespread aversion to 'upwards' metamorphosis in so many texts. Rather than seeing life as a kind of ladder with man in the middle trying to climb up rather than slide down, it may be more useful to think of created life as a kind of parabola, with man still in the middle perhaps, but also clearly on the summit, at the very top of the parabola's curve. Humanity is thus in the middle of creation (as it is, roughly, on the 'great chain of being') in one sense, but also, perhaps paradoxically, at its highest possible point. If we position man at the top of a parabola then a movement forwards is going to be just as much of a regression as a movement back. A possible illustration of this paradox can be identified within the *Metamorphoses*. We can view a human's metamorphosis into a star as a flattering reward, bestowing transcendence and immortality on beloved or deserving characters such as Ariadne and Callisto.[10] Yet a star, as an inanimate (though splendid) body, is in a sense lower down the hierarchy of being even than an insect.

A recurring theme in texts (particularly, though not exclusively, science fiction texts) which focus on humanity's improvement or perfection is a fear of loss of individuality, of what, in fact, makes us human. It is easy to find several examples of ambiguous fictional utopias where a precise correlation is implied between social improvement — characterized by increased rationality and selflessness and decreased aggression — and cultural decline. The association between social and political advance and cultural regression is explicit in Edward Bulwer-Lytton's Victorian science fiction novel *The Coming Race* (1871). Here the narrator happens upon a race of advanced humanoids, the Vril, living deep under the earth. At one point in the novel he is taken to an art gallery where he is surprised to see a gradual decline in Vril art from their earliest history, when they were flawed and closer to humans, to the present day, when their artists can only produce the most bland and generic portraits:

> The type of face began to evince a marked change about a thousand years after the vril revolution, becoming then, with each generation, more serene, and in that serenity more terribly distinct from the faces of labouring and sinful men; while in proportion as the beauty and the grandeur of the countenance itself became more fully developed, the art of the painter became more tame and monotonous.[11]

The Vril may be more socially advanced than us but they are still capable of interacting with humans and finding common ground. In other texts the possibility of still more radical 'improvements' to humanity is a source of fear, even horror. In *In Memoriam*, the prospect of Heaven fills Tennyson's narrator with anguish rather than joy; although he will in a sense be reunited with his friend Arthur Hallam, he will lose his particularity, merging with the rest of the saved in a blissful but un-individuated afterlife:

> And we shall sit at endless feast,
> Enjoying each the other's good:
> What vaster dream can hit the mood
> Of Love on earth? He seeks at least
>
> Upon the last and sharpest height,
> Before the spirits fade away,
> Some landing-place, to clasp and say,
> 'Farewell! We lose ourselves in light.'[12]

A similarly negative trajectory of 'improvement' is charted in Arthur C. Clarke's science fiction classic *Childhood's End* (1953).[13] The first stage of the journey is initiated by the arrival of the Overlords, a benevolent alien race who enforce peace and rationality on their (not altogether grateful) human protégés. As in *The Coming Race*, originality and genius in art decline rapidly once society becomes more peaceful and prosperous. After just a few generations of this inertia, the novel's final generation of humans realize with horror that their children are evolving into a new and different life form, eventually to be subsumed into an interstellar hive mind, the 'Overmind'. The Overlord Karellen tries to reassure the people of Earth that this metamorphosis represents an improvement, even a perfection, of humanity.

> What you have brought into the world may be utterly alien, it may share none of your desires or hopes, it may look upon your greatest achievements as childish toys — yet it is something wonderful, and you will have created it.[14]

However the novel's tone is elegiac, and the novel's final human characters regard the 'apotheosis' of their race with anguish.

If we think about the evolutionary trajectory traced within such science fiction texts, a trajectory whose starting point is human imperfection and which moves through intermediate states such as the Vril utopia before reaching its terminus in the more radically posthuman 'perfection' of Heaven or the hive mind, we can identify certain qualities becoming more pronounced over the course of this journey. Rationality, selflessness and cooperation are first of all greatly enhanced, leading to a more peaceful, if less dynamic, society where the will of the individual is subordinated without resentment to the good of the community. If such cooperation becomes absolute, with a complete loss of aggression or tension, then individuality — and eventually relationships — are lost. A recent fictional depiction of one such cooperative and single-minded society is the 'Borg', a cyborg collective which threatens humanity in the *Star Trek* universe.[15] The Borg — whose battle cry is 'resistance is futile' — assimilate all intelligent life forms in their quest for perfection, forcibly adding them to the collective in order to acquire their knowledge and technology. Although the Borg are presented as the Federation's most feared enemy, there is some ambiguity in their representation. They are too impersonal a force to register as 'evil', and they are incapable of understanding why anyone would not want to join them. It is possible to see the relationship between human individualism and Borg collectivism as something other than a morally clear-cut binary, for humans have their own problems with seeing another perspective. When 'Seven of Nine' (born human but assimilated into the Borg while still a child) is separated from the collective and obliged to join the Starship *Voyager*, the crew members are as anxious as the Borg, in their own way, to assimilate her.[16] This human pressure in favour of the individual affected the makers of *Star Trek* as well as its characters. In the film *Star Trek: First Contact* (1996) the Borg's status as a faceless collective is compromised by the introduction of the (decidedly individual) 'Hive Queen' played by Alice Krige, presumably because it was thought that an enemy with a more human face would enhance the film's box office appeal.[17] Rather similarly, in Bruce Sterling's 1982 short story 'Swarm', a frighteningly mindless collective entity reserves the power to achieve autonomous intelligent life on a purely temporary basis in order to deal with periodic problems (such as humanity) which threaten its existence. It is as though Sterling wanted to be able to depict a more 'human' adversary for his protagonist, even though it is precisely the swarm's complete lack of human qualities which makes it so implacable and so terrifying.[18] There is something deeply antipathetic to humanity, it would seem, about collective life forms, something which eludes our human impulse to love — and frustrates our equally human propensity to hate.

Yet despite its non-human qualities, collectivism is clearly central to many human visions of posthuman identity.[19] An important frame of reference for collectivism is the insect world, in particular the ant, even though the key term 'hive mind' suggests the bee.[20] If we think again of humanity representing the peak of a parabola then the ant may be associated both with the lowest early life forms from which humanity emerged, and with the higher posthuman state to which man might aspire.[21] This is partly because the things which characterize the pinnacle of human achievement — such as art, poetry and music — seem to be inseparable from the more destructive elements of human nature such as jealousy, religious conflict, nationalistic pride and competitive drive.[22] To move away from these negative emotions is thus to move away from genius and passion towards a peaceful yet bland existence on a human anthill. (A further more trivial sign of the insect's equivocal position is its apparent hairlessness. Hairlessness, within a posthuman context, could be seen as the result of humanity's drift away from the animal — or of its regression to the insect.)

It is of course important to acknowledge that the ant can also be perceived or depicted as a highly aggressive creature. This is the aspect of the ant which is to the fore in the cult science fiction film *Them!* (1954), in which the insects have mutated to gigantic size owing to the effects of atomic radiation.[23] Far from offering a blueprint for a more peaceful human society, the ants of *Them!* are represented as still more violent and bellicose than man. As the film's scientist hero Harold Medford explains:

> Ants are ruthless, savage and courageous fighters. Ants are the only other creatures on earth, other than man, who make war. They campaign. They are chronically aggressive. And they make slaves of the captives they don't kill. They have an instinct and a talent for the industry, social organization and savagery which makes man look feeble by contrast.[24]

However, the focus of the rest of this chapter will be on the ways in which science fiction has engaged with the ostensibly more attractive face of ant society, its capacity for cooperation and collectivism.

Although ant/human hybrids are the stuff of science fiction, an early example of an association between human and ant can be found in Ovid's *Metamorphoses*. Cephalus visits Aeacus, ruler of Aegina, to ask for men to help him in his war against Minos of Crete: He praises Aeacus on the prosperity of his people: 'In truth, as I came hither, I was rejoiced to meet youth so fair, so matched in age. And yet I miss many among the men whom I saw before when last I visited your city.'[25] Aeacus explains that Aegina has recently been afflicted by a devastating plague. Following the near extinction of his own people, Aeacus had begged the gods to restock his desolate island:

> It chanced there was an oak near by with branches unusually widespread, sacred to Jove and of Dodona's stock. Here we spied a swarm of grain-gathering ants in a long column, bearing heavy loads with their tiny mouths, and keeping their own path along the wrinkled bark. Wondering at their numbers, I said: 'O most excellent father, grant thou me just as many subjects, and fill my empty walls.'[26]

His wish is granted in a surprising fashion, for the ants themselves become the men who will populate his empty city, men whom he first sees in a dream, and who then become reality:

These seemed suddenly to grow larger and ever larger, to raise themselves from the ground and stand with form erect, to throw off their leanness, their many feet, their black colour, and to take on human limbs and a human form [...]. I went without, and there just such men as I had seen in my dream I now saw and recognized with my waking eyes. They approached and greeted me as king. I gave thanks to Jove, and to my new subjects I portioned out my city and my fields, forsaken by their former occupants; and I called them Myrmidons, nor did I cheat the name of its origin. You have seen their bodies; the habits which they had before they still keep, a thrifty race, inured to toil, keen in pursuit of gain and keeping what they get.[27]

Aeacus (and Ovid) seem unconcerned by the Myrmidons' insect origins. Their uniform youth and good looks are remarked on with apparent pleasure and approval. Even allowing for the fact that the Myrmidons are clearly a local phenomenon, rather than a blueprint for the entire human race, there does seem to be some cultural distance between Ovid's vision of useful, welcome antlike humans and more recent treatments of such hybrids, which tend to be more cautious.

Several modern science fiction narratives present us with posthumans who are becoming more antlike. Some of these respond explicitly to the dominance of females in the ant world. In John Wyndham's short story 'Consider Her Ways' (1956) men have become extinct, and an all-female society has developed which has adapted to the situation by borrowing from the ant world a highly eusocial caste system.[28] Women become intellectuals, servitors, workers or mothers and there are striking physical differences between these groups. The heroine, a twentieth-century woman called Jane, experiences mind transference (after testing a new drug) with one of the future world's Mothers, and reacts with horror to a world without men, denying the future women's claims that men exploited and victimized women. We are clearly meant to sympathize with the heroine's views, and in particular to share her distaste for the ant model which has been adopted. (Though readers may agree more with the future women's feminist analysis of mid-twentieth-century sexual politics than does Jane.) The first mention of ants comes when the heroine describes a woman attended by 'half a dozen small myrmidons', and we eventually learn that this world has turned to the Bible for inspiration: 'Go to the ant, thou sluggard; consider her ways.'[29]

A very different (and most unfeminine) vision of a meeting between ant life and humanity is offered by Wyndham's near contemporary Robert Heinlein. Heinlein's 1959 novel *Starship Troopers* is often characterized as a celebration of militarism with racist or fascist overtones. The narrative seems very simple, a kind of *Boy's Own* adventure story in space. Set during a future period of interplanetary war between Mankind and an alien arachnid race, it traces the fortunes of Johnnie Rico from a raw cadet to an experienced officer with the Terran Mobile Infantry. On the surface, neither Johnnie Rico nor Heinlein seems to feel any ethical qualms about attempting to obliterate an intelligent species. Yet *Starship Troopers* is a good deal more subtle than its reputation as an unpleasantly gung-ho celebration of war might suggest. Although Heinlein seems bent on reinforcing the differences between humans and bugs he silently invites the reader to make connections between the two species. Specifically, some of the advances made by society and technology make humans simultaneously stronger and more insect-like.[30]

Rico's post-democratic world is more stratified into groups or castes than modern western society. Only those who volunteer for military service become full citizens with the power to vote. Whereas Rico's infantry unit contains only men, piloting is a job for women because 'their reactions are faster and they can tolerate more gee'.[31] It thus more nearly approximates to the eusocial system of the insect world. In some ant species polymorphism results in a separate caste of soldier ants, dedicated to war by slightly larger mandibles. Personal choice, rather than physical characteristics, determines one's entry into the army in *Starship Troopers*, but once enlisted the technology of war begins to close up the divide between man and ant. The soldiers wear 'jump gear', complex personal armour which acts as an exoskeleton, protecting their bodies and enabling them to jump high up in the air, even 'fly' for short bursts:

> Our suits give us better eyes, better ears, stronger backs (to carry heavier weapons and more ammo), better legs, more intelligence ('intelligence' in the military meaning...), more firepower, greater endurance, less vulnerability.[32]

The suits also contain advanced communications technology which allows them, like ants, to act in apparent unison:

> The assortment of safe circuits we had available in the new model comm units certainly speeded things up; Jelly could talk to anybody or to his section leaders; a section leader could call his whole section, or his non-coms; and the platoon could muster twice as fast, when seconds matter.[33]

The soldiers are further dehumanized by the suits as they enable their wearers to be controlled remotely by a superior officer, and so lose their autonomy. This subjection to authority is also seen in the senior officers' use of remote hypnosis — at one point Rico is put to sleep against his will to ensure he is fresh for battle. Even when he wakes up he remains unaware of what has happened. This takes the human soldiers closer to the bugs who are controlled by the queen and by a caste of 'brains'. This analogy between soldiers and bugs is further reinforced by the way Rico describes the death of his senior officer: 'our family had had its head chopped off'.[34]

It could be argued that these advances are too generic and inevitable to trigger strong associations with insects. However Heinlein himself seems to invite the comparison when a civilian doctor tells Rico that 'military service is for ants'.[35] Although later in the novel a Major in the army dismisses as 'weird' the 'antlike communism urged by Plato',[36] the reader may feel by this stage that the world of *Starship Troopers* is quite as antlike as anything proposed in the *Republic*. The ant motif is continued when one of Rico's team mates is flogged after refusing an order to drop to the ground and freeze because he was right above an anthill. Later, immediately after a fairly detailed description of the Bugs' society, Rico again seems unwittingly to flag humanity's movement towards the insect by referring to his capsule as a cocoon. Also significant is the apparent emergence of a group of humans with massively enhanced sensory abilities, the 'sensers' who can detect the presence of bug tunnels under the ground with uncanny accuracy, a further example of antlike polymorphism.

Heinlein's description of the planet Sanctuary, an earth-like refuge which has been colonized by humans, also foregrounds the theme of evolution. Rico describes Sanctuary as 'like Earth, but retarded'.[37] He goes on to give a slightly more technical account of the planet's key difference from earth:

> You see, it's short on mutations; it does not enjoy Earth's high level of natural radiation [...] native life forms on Sanctuary just haven't had a decent chance to evolve and aren't fit to compete.[38]

Rico seems surprisingly negative about the fate of the humans who have colonized Sanctuary, as though assuming that fairly major changes in the human race are both inevitable and desirable:

> So what happens? Do they stay frozen at their present level while the rest of the human race moves on past them, until they are living fossils, as out of place as a pithecanthropus in a spaceship?[39]

These rather disparaging remarks invite the reader to wonder what Rico, and Heinlein, think humanity will become. The novel's internal evidence points (in defiance of scientific logic, admittedly) towards the insect. Another odd gesture towards 'becoming insect' involves Carmen, Rico's pilot friend. She takes off her hat revealing a completely bald head and we learn that most 'Navy girls' shave in this way.[40] The epigraph to the novel, 'Come on, you apes! You wanta live forever?' is credited to an 'Unknown platoon sergeant, 1918'. It is possible to see this apparently crude remark as a hint at the novel's evolutionary subtext. If humanity as a species wants to 'live forever' it will perhaps have to continue the journey started by evolution from the apes, rather as Vonnegut's humans, in *Galápagos*, had to become mindless seals in order to ensure the continuance of the race.

It is tempting to see Rico simply as Heinlein's mouthpiece. However Rico betrays some confusion and inconsistency in his characterization of the relationship between Bugs and humans. He is anxious to assert the superior empathy of humans, celebrating their noble, even foolish, efforts to save their comrades in defiance of logic. Yet he also lets slip remarks which suggest that humans are, or are becoming, just as ruthless in their willingness to sacrifice the individual as the Bugs. Thus on the top of page 153 Rico sneers: 'Bug commissars didn't care any more about expending soldiers than we cared about expending ammo'. Yet on the bottom of the same page he notes that 'Capsules are expendable (well, so were we)'. In the novel's climactic fight he asserts, yet again, the human army's greater care for its drones '*We* wouldn't send troopers out through a hole so radioactive that mere exit would kill them', even though he is clearly participating in a strategy which explicitly requires the tactical sacrifice of huge numbers of men.[41]

If we acknowledge that Heinlein's humans are not, after all, so very different from his bugs, we may see surprising affinities between *Starship Troopers* and later novels which have tended to be read as ripostes to Heinlein's vision of interstellar war. Joe Haldeman's *The Forever War* (1974) is a far more clearly relativist depiction of the relationship between human and alien life. After a gruelling campaign against the alien Taurans, it is finally revealed that the whole conflict was a terrible mistake, and that the war had been started by humanity rather than, as had previously been assumed, by the Taurans. By contrast with Heinlein, who depicts humans unconsciously aping insect characteristics in order to defeat their enemies, Haldeman presents a more positive vision of humans growing closer to the Taurans through evolution and thus acquiring the ability to communicate with their former enemies and eventually make peace. Humanity, in Haldeman's far future world, has become a clone species, just like the Taurans themselves. This development is treated with some equivocation by Haldeman. His hero (doomed by the effects of space travel to inhabit a far future earth which seems as remote to him as it does to us) rejects the clone society of earth to remain an 'old-style' human. Yet Haldeman is clearly willing to consider whether there might be some advantages in a more collective, more uniform humanity. Orson Scott Card's *Ender's Game* (1985) follows a rather similar pattern. Only at the end of what seems otherwise to be a gripping but rather conventional story of one brilliant youth's defeat of an alien enemy, the Formic race, is the truth revealed. The hero, 'Ender' Wiggins, discovers a single unborn Formic queen from whom he learns that her race had no idea humans were sentient, and were in fact anxious for peace. Ender's triumph is transformed into agonizing guilt for an act of genocide.

One of the most interesting recent examinations of 'becoming insect' is Stephen Baxter's *Coalescent* (2003), a novel with a double time line, set partly at the fall of the Roman Empire, partly in the present day. Like Wyndham, Baxter depicts a society which is both all-female and eusocial, and which he explicitly likens to an anthill.[42] But rather than depicting such a development as a fate to be viewed with horror by any 'normal' human, Baxter seems to reserve judgement on the matter. He relates how an underground society, composed almost entirely of women, was set up in order to safeguard a Roman family in the wake of barbarian invasions. The society, which is known as the Puissant Order of Holy Mary Queen of Virgins, keeps memories of the Roman Empire alive in a crypt reminiscent of a nuclear bunker, and has developed something approaching a hive mind whose members live together in a harmony and physical closeness which is simultaneously benign and disturbing. Most of the women are sterile and the main emotional bond is a sisterly one:

> At night, too, it wasn't uncommon for two, three or four to cluster together in each others' beds, whispering, kissing, at last sleeping in each other's arms. There was nothing sexual in any of this, for there was nothing sexual about the sisters. As slim as seven-year-olds, they huddled together innocently for companionship and warmth.[43]

Rather like Heinlein, although his relativism is closer to the surface of the text, Baxter destabilizes the divide between normative humanity and the new model offered by the Order. The swarm-like behaviour of human groups is repeatedly emphasized and the Roman Empire itself is likened to an anthill,[44] as is the US military industrial complex which enabled space flight to become a reality.[45] One character, Peter, is strongly alienated by the Order and endeavours to destroy it. Yet in a final twist it is suggested that he too is a member of a kind of 'hive mind', an online network of conspiracy theorists who call themselves the Slan(t)ers. The many tiny individual feedback decisions taken by online contributors to the Slan(t) ers' forum, perform, it is suggested, the same function as the pheromones emitted by ants — and by members of the Order.[46] However his friend George, who is himself part of the Order's wider family although he only discovers its secrets in middle age, is strongly attracted to the atmosphere of the hive, and feels drawn to its orderliness, to its warm, reassuringly tactile, culture. George is the opposite of the many heroes of science fiction who break away from the stifling conformity of some dystopian utopia in order to pursue a life of bracing individualism. Like Sterling, Baxter suggests that intelligence is a less desirable quality for the hive mind than it is for normal humanity. 'You didn't need a mind to create order', muses the Order's founder Regina. 'In fact, the last thing you wanted was a mind in control[.]'[47] One of the Order's three mottos is audaciously cast as an 'anticipation' of *1984*: 'ignorance is strength'. Given the extremely negative connotations of Orwell's dystopia, it is surprising that Baxter still contrives to elicit some sympathy and admiration for the Order.

It thus seems possible, tentatively, to trace in the science fiction of the last few decades a movement towards a greater readiness to accept that there may be other templates for life, even for humanity, than our preferred individualistic model. This posthuman stance is congruent with the work of recent thinkers such as Rosi Braidotti, but also chimes with an analysis of the respective qualities of ant and human life made by Henri Bergson back in 1911. He characterized the differences between them as ones of kind rather than (hierarchical) degree, identifying the ant as the pinnacle of instinctual development and human life as the corresponding pinnacle of another route, that of intelligence.[48] Within popular culture, the shift towards a greater receptivity to the insect Other is reflected in the gulf which separates *Them!* from a recent film for children, *The Ant Bully* (2006). Whereas *Them!* presented ants as terrifying monsters, *The Ant Bully* forces a little boy to see things (literally) from the ant's perspective as he shrinks to experience life in the ant world.[49] The young hero, Lucas, is criticized for his selfish and destructive individualism and must come to terms with (and adopt) the ants' contrasting impulse to work for the benefit of the whole colony. Perhaps confirming my hypothesis that the western world is beginning to look more kindly on the ant, this recent film's moderate formicophilia contrasts strongly with an earlier mid-twentieth-century account of a boy who shrinks and visits an anthill. This is an episode from T. H. White's *The Once and Future King* in which young Wart (King Arthur) is disgusted and alienated by the ants.[50] Here ant society is used to invoke a horror of authoritarian government and mindless conformity rather in the manner of Orwell or Huxley:

> 'How lucky we are born in the "A" nest, don't you think, and wouldn't it be hawful to be one of those orrid "B"s?'[51]

> 'Was it not awful about 310099/WD who refused to disgorge his syrup when he was asked? Of course he was executed at once by special order of our beloved leader.'[52]

Intriguingly, it is stated that long ago the ants, before they discovered communism, had been far more like men.[53] This idea is developed in the extended version of the episode included in *The Book of Merlyn*. Merlyn explains the ants' history to Arthur:

> The ants adopted the line of politics which man is flirting with at present, in the infinite past. They perfected it thirty million years ago, so that no further development was possible, and, since then, they have been stationary. Evolution ended with the ants some 30,000,000 years before the birth of Christ. They are the perfect Communist state.[54]

T. H. White's ants illustrate the fear latent in much science fiction, that any future perfection of human society will result in the destruction of humanity itself — the word 'perfect' is of course derived from the Latin *perficere*, to finish or complete.

Another episode from *The Once and Future King* also resonates suggestively with some of the material discussed in this essay. Bearing in mind the various artificial enhancements enabled by the jump armour depicted in *Starship Troopers*, enhancements which become in effect features of a new posthuman body, accessed as easily as natural human faculties, it is interesting to reflect on the striking creation fable which young Wart hears from a friendly badger. Embryonic versions of all living creatures are asked to choose one or two special gifts such as sharp claws or armoured skin. When Adam is asked to make his choice he decides to remain a naked embryo, to the delight of God:

> As for you, Man, you will be a naked tool all your life, though a user of tools. You will look like an embryo till they bury you, but all the others will be embryos before your might. Eternally undeveloped, you will always remain potential in Our image, able to see some of Our sorrows and to feel some of Our joys. We are partly sorry for you, Man, but partly hopeful.[55]

The rejection of this embryonic state in *Starship Troopers* goes hand in hand with a movement away from humanity towards the insect world. White's fable seems to draw on the well-known reflections on humanity in Pico della Mirandola's 1486 treatise *Oration on the Dignity of Man*, in which God asserts: 'We have given to thee, Adam, no fixed seat, no form of thy very own, no gift peculiarly thine.'[56] Although Pico does invoke the idea of a hierarchy, with angels at the top and beasts at the bottom, he problematizes the hierarchy by placing Man, not simply in the middle, but somehow orthogonal to this spectrum.

> Now the highest Father, God the master-builder, had, by the laws of His secret wisdom, fabricated this house, this world which we see, a very superb temple of divinity. He had adorned the super-celestial region with minds. He had animated the super-celestial globes with eternal souls; He had filled with a diverse throng of animals the cast-off and residual parts of the lower world. But, with the work finished, the Artisan desired that there be someone to reckon up the reason of such a big work, to love its beauty, and to wonder at its greatness. [...] *Everything was filled up; all things had been laid out in the highest, the lowest, and the middle orders.*[57]

Pico's musings on the unique place of man uphold my own tentative conclusion that humanity is located (or feels that it is located) on a special position on the evolutionary spectrum, and cannot rise further without compromising those enviably distinctive qualities such as passion and creativity which define what it means to be human:

Finally, it seemed to me that I understood why man is the animal that is most happy, and is therefore worthy of all wonder; and lastly, what the state is that is allotted to man in the succession of things, and that is capable of arousing envy not only in the brutes but also in the stars and even in the minds beyond the world. It is wonderful and beyond belief. For this is the reason why man is rightly said and thought to be a great marvel and the animal really worthy of wonder.[58]

Yet if Man cannot move (either backwards to the beast or forwards to the posthuman) without compromising his uniqueness, neither perhaps can he simply stay where he is. Rico's instinctive distaste for 'Sanctuary', for an environment in which humanity will effectively be fossilized in stasis, seems every bit as natural, as 'human', as the pervasive human anxiety generated by visions of a future in which we are, by contrast, very different beings. We are faced with a typically human tragic dilemma in which we can neither move forwards nor stay just where we are without forfeiting our humanity. Our propensity and attraction to metamorphosis is at the same time integral to what it means to be human and an indication that our species' defining qualities, and its position at the slippery summit of the parabola, may not be indefinitely sustained.

Notes to Chapter 12

1. I am grateful to the many useful suggestions made by Zoe Jaques, Patricia MacCormack and Jussi Parikka.
2. Maurice Maeterlinck, *The Life of the Ant*, trans. by Bernard Mall (London: Cassell and Company, Ltd, 1930), p. 43.
3. A great deal has been written on the topic of metamorphosis in literature and in culture more generally. Sustained studies of the topic include Asker (2001); Braidotti (2002); Bynum (2001); Clarke (1995); Massey (1976).
4. Ovid, *Metamorphoses*, VI. 1–145, III. 138–252.
5. Kurt Vonnegut, *Galápagos* (London: Flamingo, 1994), pp. 233–34.
6. Daphne's transformation into a laurel as a refuge from rape (*Metamorphoses*, I. 452–67) and the metamorphoses of Adonis and Narcissus into flowers after death (X. 708–39, III. 402–510) are among the best-known instances.
7. *Metamorphoses*, IX. 239–72; XV. 843–50.
8. *Hercules*, dir. by Ron Clements and John Musker (Walt Disney Pictures, 1997).
9. Marlowe's Dr Faustus and Ovid's Arachne are two familiar examples.
10. *Metamorphoses*, VIII. 152–82; II. 401–530.
11. Edward Bulwer-Lytton, *The Coming Race* (London: Hesperus Press, 2007), p. 61.
12. Alfred Lord Tennyson, *The Poems*, ed. by Christopher Ricks, 3 vols (London: Longman, 1969), II, 365.2.
13. A similar discussion of *In Memoriam* and *Childhood's End*, within the context of 'upwards' tragedy, is included in Brown (2007), pp. 11–12.
14. Arthur C. Clarke, *Childhood's End* (London: Pan, 1990), p. 169.
15. The Borg do not feature in the original series of *Star Trek*, but play a major role in the later *Next Generation* and *Voyager* series.
16. 'Seven of Nine' has some affinities with two other *Star Trek* characters: Mr Spock, half rational Vulcan, half emotional human, and Mr Data, the android who yearns to be human and often demonstrates more 'humanity' than his colleagues.
17. *Star Trek: First Contact*, dir. by Jonathan Frakes (Paramount Pictures, 1996).
18. *The Oxford Book of Science Fiction Stories*, ed. by Tom Shippey (Oxford: Oxford Paperbacks, 2003), pp. 472–95.

19. For a useful recent account of the cultural significance of the swarm see Parikka (2008), 112–24.

20. Kropotkin (1998) saw the ant as a model for a harmonious anarchist society, noting that 'mutual aid within the community, self-devotion grown into a habit, and very often self-sacrifice for the common welfare, are the rule' (p. 24).

21. For a discussion of the place of ants and other insects within discourses of posthumanism see Braidotti (2002), pp. 148–71. See also Shaviro (1995). Two more general studies of the cultural significance of the ant are King (2006) and Sleigh (2003).

22. The bee society described by Virgil (*Georgics* IV) represents a civil ideal, in many respects, but lacks art, poetry or passion.

23. A useful survey of responses to the film is given by Tsutsui (2007).

24. *Them!*, dir. by Gordon Douglas (Warner Bros Pictures Inc., 1954).

25. *Metamorphoses*, VII. 512–16.

26. Ibid., 622–28.

27. Ibid., 639–42; 649–57.

28. A brief analysis of the story is offered in Clareson and Clareson (1990).

29. John Wyndham, *Infinite Moment* (New York: Ballantine Books, 1961), p. 28. The reference is to Proverbs 6. 6.

30. Smith (1978) offers a useful account of the influence of Darwinian thinking on Heinlein's work.

31. Robert Heinlein, *Starship Troopers* (New York: Ace, 1987), p. 5.

32. Ibid., p. 99.

33. Ibid., p. 17.

34. Ibid., p. 145.

35. Ibid., p. 32.

36. Ibid., p. 181.

37. Ibid., p. 155.

38. Ibid., p. 155.

39. Ibid., p. 156.

40. Ibid., p. 175.

41. Ibid., p. 230.

42. Stephen Baxter, *Coalescent* (London: Gollancz, 2004), p. 477.

43. Ibid., p. 292.

44. Ibid., p. 89.

45. Ibid., p. 167.

46. This aspect of the novel chimes with the observation by Shaviro (1995–97): 'Cybernetic regulation is the human equivalent of the pheromone systems that regulate all activity in an ant colony.'

47. Baxter, *Coalescent*, p. 365.

48. Bergson (1944), p. 112.

49. *Ant Bully*, dir. by John A. Davis (Warner Bros, 2006). For a brief discussion of the film see King (2006), p. 63.

50. The episode exists in slightly different versions. It has been included in some versions of *The Sword in the Stone*, and thus takes place during the boyhood of Arthur, but also published separately in *The Book of Merlyn*, an account of the very end of Arthur's life.

51. T. H. White, *The Once and Future King* (London: Harper Collins, 2001), p. 132.

52. T. H. White, *The Book of Merlyn* (London: Shaftesbury, 2000), p. 56.

53. White, *The Once and Future King*, p. 135.

54. White, *The Book of Merlyn*, p. 64.

55. White, *The Once and Future King*, p. 205.

56. Giovanni Pico della Mirandola, *Oration on the Dignity of Man*, trans. by Charles Glenn Wallis, Paul J. W. Miller, Douglas Carmichael (Indianapolis: Hackett Publishing, 1996), p. 4.

57. Ibid., p. 4 (italics mine).

58. Ibid., pp. 3–4.

Epilogue

Ingo Gildenhard & Andrew Zissos

Our volume has traced the shifting presence and plausibility of various modes of transformative change from archaic Greece to the cusp of the third millennium, covering just about three thousand years of cultural history. In terms of chronology, our journey began with consideration of myths of transformation and their precarious referential value in Homer (and the tradition of epic song that he represents); and it ended with various species of humanoid and human-made creatures (cyborgs, androids, robots) that have begun to populate our imaginary and to infiltrate and inflect our lives, arguably heralding the dawn of a trans- or posthuman age. As our history unfolded, three defining forces in Western cultural experience came gradually into view: the literary record left behind by Graeco-Roman antiquity; Judeo-Christian religion as codified in the Bible and attending discourses of theology; and the scientific revolution, in particular the ensuing insights into the building blocks of nature and the evolution of life-forms.

This 'sequential' presentation ought not to obscure the fact that long before the rise of modern science critical discourses invoked proto-scientific standards of empiricism and rationality to question and circumscribe the domain of the metamorphic: scepticism and restraint are already apparent in Homer and remain a constant down the centuries; conversely, also after the rise of modern science, empirically inexplicable instances of miraculous transformation (and miracles more generally) have continued to command belief within significant social groups or institutional settings. Few other themes bring out the inherent dialogicity in Western culture better than transformative change, and our volume has tried not just to chronicle the meaning and value of metamorphosis in successive 'reality-paradigms', but also to explore the co-presence of classical, biblical, and scientific conceptions of the miraculous and metamorphic in our cultural memory, both in terms of productive tussles and less sensational but equally formative dynamics of sedimentation and reactivation. The limits and possibilities of transformative change have given rise to the free play of the imagination as well as critical strictures, and it is, not least, the dialectic between imagination and critique that has enabled humanity to turn — *mutatis mutandis* — (science) fiction into fact, myth into reality, or the statue of Pygmalion into a cyborg.

The story of transformative change in Western thought includes divine polymorphism as well as the transformation undergone by animals and inanimate objects; but its undisputed protagonist is the human being. And again, there are few other notions better suited to explore what it means — and has meant — to be human than metamorphosis, in part because it suggestively addresses what one tradition of anthropological thought has called our 'world openness', i.e. our infinite cultural plasticity, which has recently resulted, among other things, in our ability to alter our natural constitution as well, via technologies of bio-engineering. From a bird's-eye view, we may indeed observe two countervailing tendencies in the time-span under investigation: the gradual deracination of supernatural forces (of whatever kind) as privileged motors of transformative change; and the concomitant empowerment of the human species to reconfigure itself and transform its natural environment. From victims, we have become agents of transformative change, characterized by a metamorphic creativity that manifests itself in Promethean modes of self-transformation and the creative transformation of other creatures (including fellow humans).

★   ★   ★   ★   ★

Authors, thinkers, and artists throughout the centuries have resorted to the theme of metamorphosis, frequently with gestures to classical and biblical precedents, in an effort to capture the elusive essence of humanity. Our volume could only sample very selectively from the rich artistic record, not least since our main focus was on metamorphosis as a phenomenon, concept, or figure of thought, rather than its representation in various media. But the challenge of how to visualize change more generally and transformative change in particular is an abiding concern in the history of metamorphosis — from Greek vase paintings to contemporary cinema. In our choice of illustrations, we have tried to convey a sense of the range of possibilities, and we would like to conclude by situating this material within a wider frame of reference.

Our surviving evidence of efforts to represent metamorphosis in the pre-modern era is limited to static media (vase paintings, mosaics, various genres of sculpture, manuscript illustrations, and woodcuts in particular). But it bears stressing that dramatic genres existed which allowed the enactment of transformative change in 'real time' before the advent of moving images. The representation of metamorphosis in tragedy was rather limited (see Introduction to Part I) and occurred (if it featured at all) before or after the action of the play, or else took place off-stage. In comedy it was a matter of costume mainly, but the most popular performance genre in the imperial period, that is, pantomime, considered the display of metamorphosis a special challenge, indeed the epitome of what one could call the 'pantomime aesthetics'.[1] In static media, the representation of metamorphosis is a particular challenge: 'Metamorphosis is necessarily anti-static: it is by definition diachronic, and so shares in the general problem of the visual representation of narrative, which requires the con-fusion of diachronicity and synchronicity.'[2] Here again the modern period constitutes a genuine watershed: with the invention of analogic and digital media, the realistic representation of 'quick change' has gradually ceased to be a problem. The emergence of new technologies has enabled the visual depiction of motion (and hence also metamorphosis) by means of special effects and morphing, cinematography and computer animation.[3] Some of these advances took place fairly recently. Animation technology began to be employed in the early 1980s and started to have a significant impact a decade later, with the life-like portrayal of pre-historical predators (*Jurassic Park* in 1993), historical collage (*Forrest Gump* in 1994), or metamorphosis (*Terminator 2* in 1991, with its notoriously protean villain).[4]

These new means of visualization raise philosophical and sociological questions, to do with the realistic ('life-like') representation of the impossible and how cinema communicates with its viewers. Thus the ontological status of film sequences created by digital imaging can upset traditional notions of photographic indexicality: 'a digitally designed or created image can be subject to infinite manipulation. Its reality is a function of complex algorithms stored in computer memory rather than a necessary mechanical resemblance to a referent.'[5] Still, even the realistic representation of a phenomenon does not make it 'real' — that depends on the reality paradigm applied by (members of) the audience; yet any representation of metamorphosis (whether realistic or not) constitutes a reality to be reckoned with: it is an index, at the very least, of the conceivability of transformative change that underlies human cultural achievements and evinces our potential for imaginary world-making. Indeed, according to Baudrillard, we are currently experiencing the rise of a new world, virtual reality, defined by constant change without becoming — a kind of eternal and infinite morphism that sharply contrasts with metamorphosis, insofar as metamorphosis implies a restabilized identity after a moment of radical change.[6] It appears, then, that we end where it all started, at least according to Ovid: chaos.

Notes to the Epilogue

1. See e.g. Webb (2005), Lada-Richards (2007), Zanobi (2008).
2. Sharrock (1996), p. 107. She identifies 'three main ways of dealing with this problem ... (i) by panels, (ii) by suggestion, and (iii) by incomplete metamorphosis.'
3. For discussions from various angles, see the papers collected in Sobchak (2000).
4. Prince (1996), p. 27. See also Haworth-Booth (1994), p. 7: 'Electronic images no longer legitimate the photographic. In fact, they usurp and reconstitute the analog as algorithmic; visual order is formulated by a mathematical order. And once the image is digital, it has little to do with photographic systems except by implication. It is in this sense that these images can be called postphotographic, as they no longer rely on the character of the photograph to verify something in the world.'
5. Prince (1996), p. 29.
6. See the discussion by Maciocco (2008), p. 4.

BIBLIOGRAPHY: PRIMARY SOURCES

Note: anonymous works or those penned by multiple authors (such as the Anthologia Palatina) are listed by their title. Falsely attributed works (such as the pseudo-Ovidian de Vetula) are listed immediately after the genuine entries for the author in question.

Authors and texts

AELIAN (*c.* 175–*c.* 235)
——*De Natura Animalium/On Animals*: ed. and trans. by A. F. Scholfield (Cambridge, MA: Loeb Classical Library, 1959)

AESCHYLUS (*c.* 525/524–*c.* 456/455 BC)
——*Plays and Fragments*: ed. and trans. by A. H. Sommerstein, 3 vols (Cambridge, MA: Loeb Classical Library, 2009)

AESOP (*c.* 620–564 BC)
——*Corpus fabularum Aesopicarum*: ed. by A. Hausrath (Leipzig: Teubner, 1957)
——*Fables*: translated with an introduction and notes by Laura Gibbs (Oxford: Oxford University Press, 2002)

ALAIN DE LILLE (*c.* 1116/1117–1202/1203)
——*Anticlaudianus*, ed. by Robert Bossuat (Paris: Vrin, 1955)

ALAMANNI, LUDOVICO (1495–1556) and RUCELLAI, GIOVANNI (1475–1525)
——*La coltivazione e Le api* (Padua: Comino, 1718)

ALLESTREE, RICHARD (1619–1681)
—— *The Government of the Tongue* (Oxford: At the Theater in Oxford, 1674)

AMMIANUS MARCELLINUS (325/330–after 391)
——*History*: ed. and trans. by J. C. Rolfe, 3 vols (Cambridge, MA: Loeb Classical Library, 1939–50)

ANDERSEN, HANS CHRISTIAN (1805–1875)
—— *The Complete Fairy Tales* (London: Wordsworth, 1998)

ANTHOLOGIA PALATINA (material from the 7th century BC to 6th century AD)
——Greek text and German translation by H. Beckby, 4 vols, 2nd edn (Munich: Heimeran, 1957–58)

ANTONINUS LIBERALIS (active between 100 and 300)
——*Metamorphoses*: F. Celoria, *The Metamorphoses of Antoninus Liberalis: A Translation With Commentary* (London and New York: Routledge, 1992)
——*Les Métamorphoses*: Greek text and French translation by M. Papathomopoulos (Paris: Les Belles Lettres, 1968)

APOLLONIUS RHODIUS (active first half of third century BC)
——*Argonautica*: ed. and trans. by W. H. Race (Cambridge, MA: Loeb Classical Library, 2009)

APPENDIX PROVERBIORUM: ed. by E. L. von Leutsch and F. G. Schneidewin, *Corpus paroemiographorum Graecorum*, vol. 1 (Göttingen: Vandenhoeck & Ruprecht, 1839; repr. Hildesheim: Olms, 1965)

PSEUDO-APOLLODORUS
——*Bibliotheca/The Library*: ed. and trans. by J. G. Frazer, 2 vols (Cambridge, MA: Loeb Classical Library, 1921)

——*The Library of Greek Mythology*: trans. with an introduction and notes by R. Hard (Oxford: Oxford University Press, 1997)

APULEIUS (*c.* 125–*c.* 180)

——*Metamorphoses* [a.k.a. *Asinus Aureus/The Golden Ass*]: ed. and trans. by J. A. Hanson, 2 vols (Cambridge, MA: Loeb Classical Library, 1989)

——*De deo Socratis*: ed. and trans. by J. Beaujeu (Paris: Les Belles Lettres, 1973)

ARISTOPHANES (*c.* 446–*c.* 386 BC)

——*Plays and Fragments*: ed. and trans. by J. Henderson, 5 vols (Cambridge, MA: Loeb Classical Library, 1998–2008)

——*Scholia Vetera in Aristophanis Aves*: ed. by D. Holwerda (Groningen: Bouma, 1991)

ARISTOTLE (384–322 BC)

——*De Anima/On the Soul*: ed. and trans. by W. S. Hett (Cambridge, MA: Loeb Classical Library, 1957)

——*Historia Animalium/History of Animals*: ed. and trans. by A. L. Peck, 2 vols (Cambridge, MA: Loeb Classical Library, 1965–70)

——*Metaphysics*: ed. and trans. by H. Tredennick and G. C. Armstrong, 2 vols (Cambridge, MA: Loeb Classical Library, 1933–35)

——*Meteorologica*, ed. by H. D. P. Lee (Cambridge, MA: Loeb Classical Library, 1952)

——*Poetics*: ed. and trans. by S. Halliwell (Cambridge, MA: Loeb Classical Library, 1995)

PSEUDO-ARISTOTLE

——*Mirabilium Auscultationes*: ed. by A. Westermann, in *Paradoxographoi. Scriptores rerum mirabilium Graeci* (Braunschweig, 1839; repr. Amsterdam: A. M. Hakkert, 1963)

ARNULF OF ORLÉANS (active in 1170s)

——*Allegorie super Ovidii Metamorphosin*: ed. by Fausto Ghisalberti, in 'Arnolfo d'Orléans: Un Cultore di Ovidio nel secolo XII', *Memorie del Reale Istituto Lombardo di Scienze e Lettere* 24, 4, 1932: 155–234

ARRIAN (*c.* 86–160)

——*Cynegeticus*: edited with an introduction, translation and commentary by A. A. Phillips and M. M. Willcock, in *Xenophon & Arrian, On Hunting* (Warminster: Aris & Phillips, 1999)

ARTEMIDORUS (2nd century AD)

——*Onirocriticon Libri V*, ed. by R. A. Pack (Leipzig: Teubner, 1963); *The Interpretation of Dreams: Oneirocritica by Artemidorus*, trans. by R. J. White (Torrance, CA: Original Books, 1990)

ASIMOV, ISAAC (1920–1992)

——*I, Robot* (Garden City, NY: Doubleday, 1950)

ATHANASIUS (*c.* 296/298–373)

——*De Incarnatione Verbi*: Einleitung, Übersetzung, Kommentar by E. P. Meijering (Amsterdam: J. C. Gieben, 1989)

ATHENAEUS (active at the end of the 2nd/beginning of the 3rd century)

——*Deipnosophistae/The Learned Banqueters*: ed. and trans. by D. Olson, 8 vols (Cambridge, MA: Loeb Classical Library, 2007–12)

AUGUSTINE (354–430)

——*Confessions*: ed. and trans. by W. Watts, 2 vols (Cambridge, MA: Loeb Classical Library, 1912)

——*De Civitate Dei/The City of God*: ed. and trans. by G. E. McCracken et al., 7 vols (Cambridge, MA: Loeb Classical Library, 1957–72)

——*De Doctrina Christiana/On Christian teaching*: *Patrologia Latina*, XXXIV; trans. with an introduction and notes by R. P. H. Green (Oxford: Oxford University Press, 1997)

——*De Musica*: *Patrologia Latina*, XXXII

——*Sermo* XLVII: *Patrologia Latina*, XXXVIII

Pseudo-Augustine
—— *De spiritu et anima*: *Patrologia Latina*, xl
'Augustinus Hibernicus' or 'Irish Augustine' (mid 7th century)
—— *De mirabilibus sacrae scripturae libri tres*: *Patrologia Latina* xxxv
Aymé, Marcel (1902–1967)
—— *Le Passe-Muraille* (Paris: Livre de Poche, 1958)
Balzac, Honoré de (1799–1850)
—— *La Peau de Chagrin* (1831)
Barbaro, Ermolao (1453/1454–1493)
—— *Castigationes Plinianae et in Pomponium Melam*: 4 vols, ed. by G. Pozzi (Padua: Antenore, 1973–79)
Barjavel, René (1911–1985)
—— *Ravage*: ed. by Yves Ansel (Paris: Gallimard, Folio, 1996 [1943])
—— *Le Voyageur imprudent* (Paris: Gallimard, Folio, 1996 [1944])
Baudelaire, Charles (1821–1867)
—— *Les Fleurs du mal*, ed. by A. Adam (Paris: Garnier 1961 [1857])
Baxter, Stephen (1957–)
—— *Coalescent* (London: Gollancz, 2004)
Bede (673–735)
—— *On the nature of things and On times*: trans. with introduction, notes and commentary by Calvin B. Kendall and Faith Wallis (Liverpool: Liverpool University Press, 2010)
—— *In Marci Evangelium Expositio*: *Patrologia Latina*, XCII.
The Bible. Cited variously in English, Latin, and Greek from the following editions:
—— *The Bible: Authorized King James Version*, ed. by R. Carroll and S. Prickett (Oxford: Oxford University Press, 1997)
—— *Biblia sacra iuxta Vulgatam versionem*, ed. by B. Fischer et al. (Stuttgart: Deutsche Bibelgesellschaft, 1994)
—— *Septuaginta*, ed. by A. Rahlfs (Stuttgart: Württemberg Bible Society, 1935)
—— *The Greek New Testament*, ed. by K. Aland et al. (Stuttgart: Württemberg Bible Society, 1968)
Boccaccio, Giovanni (1313–1375)
—— *Decameron*: ed. by V. Branca (Turin: Einaudi, 1985)
—— *Genealogie deorum Gentilium*: ed. by V. Zaccaria, 2 vols (Milan: Mondadori, 1998–99)
Bodin, Jean (1530–1590)
—— *De magorum daemonomania, seu de testando lamiarum ac magorum cum Satana commercio, libri IV. Recens recogniti, et ... repurgati. Accessit eiusdem opinionum Ioannis Wieri confutatio ...* (Frankfurt: Wolffgang Richter, impensis omnium haeredum Nicolai Bassaei, 1603), trans. *De la Démonomanie des sorciers* (Paris: Iacques du Puys, 1582); *On the Demon-Mania of Witches*, trans. by Randy A. Scott (Toronto: Centre for Reformation and Renaissance Studies, 1995)
Breton, André (1896–1966)
—— *Nadja*: (Paris: Gallimard 1964 [1924])
Bucolici Graeci: ed. by A. S. F. Gow (Oxford: Clarendon Press, 1952)
Bulfinch, Thomas (1796–1867)
—— *Bulfinch's Mythology* (London: Spring Hill, 1967 [1881])
Bulwer-Lytton, Edward (1803–1873)
—— *The Coming Race* [reprinted as: *Vril, the Power of the Coming Race*] (London: Hesperus Press, 2007 [1871])
Calcagnini, Celio (1479–1541)
—— *Opera aliquot* (Basel: Froben, 1544)
Čapek, Karel (1890-1938)
—— *R. U. R. (Rossum's Universal Robots)*: trans. by Claudia Novack (London and New York: Penguin 2004 [1926])

CARDANO, GIROLAMO (1501–1576)

——*De varietate rerum*, in *Opera omnia*: ed. by C. Spon, 10 vols (Lyon: Jean Antoine Huguetan and Marc Antoine Ravaud, 1663; repr. Stuttgart and Bad Cannstatt: Frommann, 1966)

CHEMNITZ, MARTIN (1522–1586)

——*De duabus naturis in Christo*: (Leipzig 1578) [English translation: *The Two Natures in Christ*, trans. by J. A. O. Preus, St. Louis: Concordia Publishing House, 1971]

CICERO, MARCUS TULLIUS (106–43 BC)

——*de Haruspicum Responso*: ed. and trans. by N. H. Watts (Cambridge, MA: Loeb Classical Library, 1923)

——*de Natura Deorum*: ed. and trans. by H. Rackham (Cambridge, MA: Loeb Classical Library, 1933)

——*Philippics*: ed. and trans. by D. R. Shackleton Bailey, revised by J. T. Ramsey and G. Manuwald, 2 vols (Cambridge, MA: Loeb Classical Library, 2010)

CICERONIAN CONTROVERSIES, ed. by J. DellaNeva, tr. B. Duvick (Cambridge, MA: Harvard University Press, 2007)

CLARKE, ARTHUR C. (1917–2008)

——*Childhood's End* (London: Pan, 1990 [1953])

COLLODI, CARLO (1826–1890)

——*Le avventure di Pinocchio: Storia di un burattino*: trans. by Ann Lawson Lucas (Oxford: Oxford University Press, 2004)

COLONNA, FRANCESCO (*c.* 1433–1527)

——*Hypnerotomachia Poliphili*: ed. by L. A. Ciapponi and G. Pozzi, 2 vols (Padua: Antenore, 1980)

COLUMELLA, LUCIUS JUNIUS MODERATUS (4–*c.* 70)

——*De re rustica*: ed. by R. H. Rodgers (Oxford: Clarendon Press, 2010)

CONRAD OF HIRSAU (*c.* 1070–1150)

——*Dialogus super auctores*: ed. with Italian translation, introduction, and notes by R. Marchionni (Pisa and Roma: Fabrizio Serra, 2008)

COTTA, JOHN (1575–1650)

——*The triall of vvitch-craft shewing the true and right methode of the discouery: with a confutation of erroneous wayes* (London: George Purslowe for Samuel Rand, 1616)

CRESCENZI (DE'), PIETRO (*c.* 1230/35–*c.* 1320)

——*Ruralia commoda*: ed. by W. Richter and R. Richter-Bergmeier, 2 vols (Heidelberg: Universitätsverlag C. Winter, 1995–98)

CYRANIDES, ed. by D. V. Kaimakes, *Die Kyraniden* (Meisenheim am Glan: Hain, 1976)

CRICHTON, MICHAEL (1942-2008)

——*Jurassic Park* (New York: Ballantine 1990)

DAMIGERON-EVAX (active sometime between the 1st and 5th centuries)

——*De Lapidibus*: ed. by R. Halleux and J. Schamp, in *Les Lapidaires Grecs* (Paris: Les Belles Lettres, 1985), pp. 230–90

DANTE ALIGHIERI (1265–1321)

——*Divina Commedia/Divine Comedy*: trans. by R. and J. Hollander (New York: Doubleday/Anchor, 2000 (*Inferno*), 2003 (*Purgatorio*), 2007 (*Paradiso*)

DARWIN, CHARLES (1809–1882)

——*The Origin of Species* (1859)

DICK, PHILIP K. (1928-1982)

——*Do Androids Dream of Electric Sheep?* (New York: Del Rey 1996 [1968])

DIERX, LÉON (1838–1912)

——*Œuvres complètes I–III* (Geneva: Slatkine Reprints, 1980)

DIODORUS SICULUS (active 60–30 BC)

——*Bibliotheca Historica/Library of History*: ed. and trans. by C. H. Oldfather et al., 12 vols (Cambridge, MA: Loeb Classical Library, 1933–67)

DIOSCORIDES PEDANIUS (*c.* 40–90)
——*De Materia Medica*: ed. by M. Wellmann, 3 vols (Berlin: Weidmann, 1:1907; 2:1906, 3:1914; repr. 1958); *De Materia Medica: Being an Herbal with many other medicinal materials*, translated by Tess Anne Osbaldeston (Johannesburg: Ibidis Press, 2000)

ECLOGA THEODULI (sometime between the 8th and 10th centuries)
——*Carolingian Pastoral: Seven Versions of Carolingian Pastoral*, ed. by R. P. H. Green (Bristol: Bristol University Press, 1980); *Il Canto della Verità e della Menzogna*, ed. by F. Mosetti Casaretto (Florence: Sismel, 1997); *An English translation of Auctores Octo, A Medieval Reader*, by R. E. Pepin (Lewiston, NY, Queenston, and Lampeter: Edwin Mellen Press, 1999)

EMPEDOCLES (*c.* 495–435 BC)
——*Fragments*: ed. by H. Diels and W. Kranz, *Die Fragmente der Vorsokratiker*, 3 vols (Berlin: Weidmannsche Verlagsbuchhandlung, 1960); ed. and trans. by A. Fairbanks, *The First Philosophers of Greece* (London: K. Paul, Trench, Trubner, 1898), 157–234

ENNIUS (*c.* 239–*c.* 169 BC)
——*Annals*: ed. with introduction and commentary by O. Skutsch (Oxford: Clarendon Press, 1985); translation in: *Remains of Old Latin, Volume I: Ennius. Caecilius*, by E. H. Warmington (Cambridge, MA: Loeb Classical Library, 1935)

ERASMUS, DESIDERIUS (1466–1536)
——*Opera omnia*: 10 vols (Leiden: Petrus van der Aa, 1703–06)

EURIPIDES (*c.* 480–406 BC)
——*Plays*: ed. and trans. by D. Kovacs, 6 vols (Cambridge, MA: Loeb Classical Library, 1994–2003)

EUSTATHIUS OF THESSALONIKA (*c.* 1115–1195/6)
——*Commentary on Dionysius the Periegete*: ed. by C. Müller, in *Geographici Graeci minores 2* (Paris: Didot, 1861)

FICINO, MARSILIO (1433–1499)
——*Opera omnia*: 2 vols (Basel: Heinrich Petri, 1576; repr. Turin: Bottega d'Erasmo, 1962)

FONTAINE, JEAN DE LA (1621–1695)
——*Fables* (Paris: Le Livre de poche, 2009 [1694])

FRACASTORO, GIROLAMO (1478–1553)
——*Syphilis sive De morbo gallico*: 2 vols, in G. Fracastoro (et al.), *Carminum editio II* (Padua: Comino, 1739)

GALLUS, AEGIDIUS (active around 1500)
——*De Viridario Augustini Chisii Vera Libellus*, in Quinlan McGrath, M. 'Blasius Pallidius Agustini Chigii Suburbanum. Introduction, Latin Text and English Translation', *Humanistica Lovaniensia*, 39 (1990), 93–157

GARCÍA MÁRQUEZ, GABRIEL (1927–)
——*Cien años de soledad*: trans. as *One Hundred Years of Solitude* (Harper & Rowe, 1970 [1967])

GARLAND, JOHN OF (GIOVANNI DI GARLANDIA) (active *c.* 1205–1255)
——*Integumenta Ovidii*: ed. by F. Ghisalberti, *Testi e documenti inediti o rari*, no. 2 (Messina and Milan: Giuseppe Principato, 1933)

GARRICK, DAVID [?] (1717–1779)
——*Adam's tail; or, the first metamorphosis* (London: John Bell, 4th edn, 1774)

GAUTIER, THÉOPHILE (1811–1872)
——*Arria Marcella* (Paris: Charpentier, 1881 [1852])
——*Emaux et Camées* (Geneva: Librairie Droz, 1950 [1852]).
——*Le Capitaine Fracasse* (Paris: Larousse, 1929 [1863])
——*Premières Poésies* (Paris: Charpentier, 1870 [1852]).
——*Le Roman de la momie* (Paris: Larousse, 1929 [1858])

GIFFORD, GEORGE (*c.* 1548–1600)
——*A dialogue concerning witches and witchcraftes* (London: John Windet for Tobie Cooke and Mihil Hart, 1593)
GOETHE, JOHANN WOLFGANG VON (1742–1832)
——*Versuch die Metamorphose der Pflanzen zu erklären* (1790)
——*Die Metamorphose der Pflanzen* (1798)
——*Die Metamorphose der Tiere* (1799)
GRIMM, JACOB (1785–1863) and Grimm, Wilhelm (1786–1859)
——*The Complete Fairy Tales of the Brothers Grimm*: trans. by Padraic Colum (London: Wordsworth, 1997)
GUAZZO, FRANCESCO MARIA
——*Compendium maleficarum ... per Fratrem Franciscum Mariam Guaccium ... compilatum* [1608], 2nd edn. (Milan: Ex collegii Ambrosiani Typographia, 1626)
HAECKEL, ERNST (1834–1919)
——*Natürliche Schöpfungsgeschichte* (1868; translated into English as *The History of Creation*, 1876)
——*Kunstformen der Natur* (1899–1903)
HARRIS, THOMAS (1940–)
——*Hannibal* (New York: Delacorte Press, 1999)
HECATAEUS OF MILETUS (*c.* 550–*c.* 490)
——*Fragmente der Griechischen Historiker*: ed. by F. Jacoby, vol. 1.1 (Leiden: Brill, 1957)
HEINLEIN, ROBERT (1907–1988)
——*Starship Troopers* (New York: Ace, 1987)
HEREDIA, JOSÉ-MARIA DE (1842–1905)
——*Œuvres poétiques complètes: Autres sonnets et poésies diverses* (Paris: Les Belles Lettres, 1984 [1893])
——*Les Trophées* (Project Gutenberg, 2005 [1893])
HERODOTUS (*c.* 484–425 BC)
——*The Persian Wars*: ed. and trans. by A. D. Godley, 4 vols (Cambridge, MA: Loeb Classical Library, 1920–25)
HESIOD (active between 750 and 650 BC)
——*Theogony. Works & Days. Testimonia*: ed. and trans. by G. W. Most (Cambridge, MA: Loeb Classical Library, 2007)
——*The Shield. Catalogue of Women. Other Fragments*: ed. and trans. by G. W. Most (Cambridge, MA: Loeb Classical Library, 2007)
HOFFMANN, E. T. A. (1776–1822)
——*Der Sandmann* (1816)
HOMER (*c.* 8th century BC)
——*Iliad*: ed. and trans. by A. T. Murray, 2 vols (Cambridge, MA: Loeb Classical Library, 1924–25)
——*Odyssey*: ed. and trans. by A. T. Murray, 2 vols (Cambridge, MA: Loeb Classical Library, 1919)
——*Scholia Graeca in Homeri Odysseam*: ed. by W. Dindorf (Oxford: Oxford University Press, 1855; repr. Amsterdam: Hakkert, 1962)
——*The Homeric Hymns, and Homerica*: trans. by Hugh G. Evelyn White (London: Heinemann, 1964)
HORACE (65–8 BC)
——*Satires. Epistles. Ars Poetica/The Art of Poetry*: ed. and trans. by H. R. Fairclough (Cambridge, MA: Loeb Classical Library, 1926)
HYGINUS (*c.* 64 BC–AD 17)
——*Fabulae*: ed. by P. K. Marshall (Stuttgart: Teubner, 1993)
ISIDORE OF SEVILLE (*c.* 560–636)

——*Etymologiae*: ed. by W. M. Lindsay (Oxford: Clarendon Press, 1911); translation by S. A. Barney et al. (Cambridge: Cambridge University Press, 2006)

JEROME (*c.* 347–420)

——*Commentariorum in Ezechielem Prophetam libri quatuordecim*: *Patrologia Latina*, XXV

——*Epistulae*: *Patrologia Latina* XXII

JONSON, BEN (1572–1637)

——*The Devil is an Ass*: in *The Complete Plays of Ben Jonson*, ed. by G. A. Wilkes, vol. IX (Oxford: Clarendon Press, 1982), pp. 123–241

JOYCE, JAMES (1882–1941)

——*Ulysses* (Paris: Shakespeare and Company, 1922)

KAFKA, FRANZ (1883–1924)

——*Sämtliche Erzählungen* (Frankfurt: Fischer, 1970 [1935])

KRAMER, HEINRICH (*c.* 1430–1505) and Sprenger, Jacob (1436/1438–1495)

——Henricus Institoris and Jacobus Sprenger, *Malleus Maleficarum*: ed. and trans. by Christopher S. Mackay, 2 vols (Cambridge: Cambridge University Press, 2006)

——*Malleus maleficarum in tres divisus partes* (Frankfurt on Meine: Nicolaus Bassaeus, 1580)

LACTANTIUS (*c.* 240–*c.* 320)

——*Divinae Institutiones/Divine Institutes*: ed. by S. Brandt (Vienna, 1890); translation with an introduction and notes by A. Bowen and P. Garnsey (Liverpool: Liverpool University Press, 2003)

LAMARCK, JEAN-BAPTISTE (1744–1829)

——*Philosophie zoologique* (1809)

LAMBERTUS DANÆUS (*c.* 1535–*c.* 1590)

——*A Dialogue of Witches, in foretime named Lot-tellers, and novv commonly called Sorcerers. VVherein is declared breefely and effectually, vvhat soeuer may be required, touching that argument. A treatise very profitable, by reason of the diuerse and sundry opinions of men in their question, and right necessary for Judges to vnderstand, which sit vpon lyfe and death,* [trans. by Tho: Twyne] ([London]: [T. East? for] R. W[atkins], 1575)

LAPIDAIRE ORPHIQUE: ed. and trans. by R. Halleux and J. Schamp, in *Les Lapidaires Grecs* (Paris: Les Belles Lettres), pp. 1–123

LA METTRIE, JULIEN OFFRAY DE (1709-1751)

——*L'Homme-Machine* (Paris: Galerie D'Orléans 1865 [1748])

LA PRIMAUDAYE, PIERRE DE (*c.* 1545–1619)

——*The second part of the French academie*: trans. by T. B. (London. G. B[ishop] R[alph] N[ewbery] R. B[arker], 1594)

LECONTE DE LISLE, CHARLES MARIE RENÉ (1818–1894)

——*Poèmes barbares* (Paris: Lemerre, 1889 [1866])

——*Poèmes antiques* (Paris: Librairie de Marc Dulcoux, Editeur, 1857)

——*Homère: Iliade. Traduction nouvelle* (Paris: Lemerre, 1866)

LES LAPIDAIRES GRECS, ed. and trans. by R. Halleux and J. Schamp (Paris: Les Belles Lettres, 1985)

LEM, STANISLAW (1921-2006)

——*Cyberiad*: trans. by Michael Kandel (London: Secker and Warburg 1974 [1965])

LEWIS, C. S. (1898–1963)

——*The Chronicles of Narnia: The Last Battle* (London: HarperCollins, 1998 [1956])

LINNAEUS, CARL (1707–1778)

——*Systema Naturae* (1st edn 1735, 12th edn 1766–68)

LONGINUS (active in the 1st century)

——*On the Sublime*: ed. and trans. by W. H. Fyfe (Cambridge, MA: Loeb Classical Library, 1995)

LOVECRAFT, H. P. (1890–1937)

—— *Omnibus* (London: Grafton, 1985)

LUCIAN (*c*. 125–*c*. 180)

—— *De dea Syria/On the Syrian Goddess*: ed. with introduction, translation, and commentary by J. L. Lightfoot (Oxford: Oxford University Press, 2003)

LUCRETIUS (*c*. 99–55 BC)

—— *De Rerum Natura/On the Nature of the Universe*: ed. and trans. by W. H. D. Rouse (Cambridge, MA: Loeb Classical Library, 1924); trans. by R. Melville (Oxford: Clarendon Press, 1997)

LYLY, JOHN (1553/54–1606)

—— *Euphues, the Anatomy of Wit* (London: T. East for Gabriel Cawood, 1578)

—— *Loues metamorphosis. A vvittie and courtly pastorall ... . First playd by the Children of Paules, and now by the Children of the Chappel* (London: [S. Stafford] for William Wood, 1601)

—— *Midas Plaied before the Queenes Maiestie vpon Tvvelfe day at night, by the Children of Paules* (London: Thomas Scarlet for I[ohn] B[roome], 1592)

MAETERLINCK, MAURICE (1862–1949)

—— *La Vie des termites/The Life of Termites*: trans. by Bernard Mall (London: Cassell and Company, Ltd, 1930)

MACROBIUS (active during the early fifth century)

—— *Commentarii in Somnium Scipionis*: ed. and trans. by M. Armisen-Marchetti (Paris: Les Belles Lettres, 2003)

—— *Saturnalia*: ed. and trans. by R. A. Kaster, 3 vols (Cambridge, MA: Loeb Classical Library, 2011)

MANILIUS (1st century AD)

—— *Astronomica*: ed. and trans. by G. P. Goold (Cambridge, MA: Loeb Classical Library, 1977)

MANUZIO, ALDO (1449–1515)

—— *Aldo Manuzio editore. Dediche, prefazioni, note ai testi*: ed. by G. Orlandi, introduction by C. Dionisotti, 2 vols (Milan: Il Polifilo, 1975)

MARLOWE, CHRISTOPHER (1564–1593)

—— *Tamburlaine, Parts I and II*; *Doctor Faustus, A- and B-Texts*; *The Jew of Malta*; *Edward II*, ed. by David Bevington and Eric Rasmussen (Oxford: Oxford University Press, 1995)

MARTIANUS CAPELLA (5th century)

—— *De nuptiis Philologiae et Mercurii/On the Marriage of Philology and Mercury*: ed. by J. Willis (Leipzig: B. G. Teubner Verlagsgesellschaft, 1983); translation by W. H. Stahl and R. Johnson, with E. L. Burge (New York: Columbia University Press, 1977)

MATTIOLI, PIETRO ANDREA (1501–1578)

—— *I discorsi [...] nelli sei libri di Pedacio Dioscoride Anazarbeo della materia Medicinale*: 5 vols (Venice: Vincenzo Valgrisi, 1568)

MILTON, JOHN (1608–1674)

—— *Paradise Lost*, ed. by A. Fowler (London: Longman, 1968)

MOLZA, FRANCESCO MARIA (1489–1544)

—— *Elegiae et alia*: ed. by M. Scorsone and R. Sodano (Turin: RES, 1999)

NAUDÉ, GABRIEL (1600–1653)

—— *The history of magick by way of apology, for all the wise men who have unjustly been reputed magicians, from the Creation, to the present age. /Written in French, by G. Naudaeus late library-keeper to Cardinal Mazarin. Englished by J. Davies* (London: John Streater, 1657)

NICANDER OF COLOPHON (2nd century BC)

—— *The Poems and Poetical Fragments*: ed. with introduction, translation, and notes by A. S. F. Gow and A. F. Scholfield (Cambridge: Cambridge University Press, 1953)

NIETZSCHE, FRIEDRICH (1844–1900)

—— *Also sprach Zarathustra: Ein Buch für Alle und Keinen*: trans. by R. J. Hollingdale (Harmondsworth: Penguin Books, 1974)

Nonnos (active end of the 4th/beginning of the 5th century)
——*Dionysiaka*: ed. and trans. by W. H. D. Rouse, 3 vols (Cambridge, MA: Harvard University Press, 1940)
Oppian (early 3rd century)
——*Cynegetica*: ed. and trans. by A. W. Mair (Cambridge, MA: Harvard University Press, 1928)
Origen (184/185–253/254)
——*Selecta in Ezechielem*: *Patrologia Graeca*, xiii
Orphei Lithica Kerygmata: ed. and trans. by R. Halleux and J. Schamp, in *Les Lapidaires Grecs* (Paris: Les Belles Lettres, 1985)
Ovid (43 bc–ad 17/18)
——*Amores*: ed. and trans. by G. Showerman (Cambridge, MA: Harvard University Press, 1914)
——*Epistulae ex Ponto*: ed. and trans. by A. L. Wheeler (Cambridge, MA: Harvard University Press, 1924)
——*Heroides*: ed. and trans. by G. Showerman (Cambridge, MA: Harvard University Press, 1914)
——*Metamorphoses*: ed. by R. Tarrant (Oxford: Oxford University Press, 2004); ed. and trans. by F. J. Miller, 2 vols (Cambridge, MA: Harvard University Press, 1984)
——*Tristia*: ed. and trans. by A. L. Wheeler (Cambridge, MA: Harvard University Press, 1924)
[Pseudo-Ovid] (12th century)
——*de vetula*: *Pseudo-Ovidius De vetula: Untersuchungen und Text*, by P. Klopsch (Leiden: Brill, 1967)
Palaephatus (late 4th century bc?)
——Περὶ ἀπίστων/*On Unbelievable Tales*: translation, introduction and commentary (with notes and Greek text from the 1902 B. G. Teubner edition), by J. Stern (Wauconda, IL: Bolchazy-Carducci Publishers, 1996)
Palladius (4th century ad)
——*Opus agriculturae*: ed. by R. H. Rodgers (Leipzig: Teubner, 1975)
Paschasius Radbertus, Saint (785–865)
——*De corpore et sanguine Domini; cum appendice Epistola ad Fredugardum*: ed. by B. Paulus (= CCCM 16) (Turnholti: Brepols, 1969)
Passavanti, Jacopo (*c.* 1302–1357)
——*Lo specchio della vera penitenzia*: trans. by A. Charles and E. K. Peters, 'Jacopo Passavanti', in *Witchcraft in Europe 400–1700: A Documentary History*, ed. by Alan Charles and Edward Kors Peters (Philadelphia: University of Pennsylvania Press, 2001), pp. 106–11
Pausanias (2nd century ad)
——*Description of Greece*: ed. and trans. by W. H. S. Jones et al., 5 vols (Cambridge, MA: Loeb Classical Library, 1918–35)
Petrarch, Francesco (1304–1374)
——*Canzoniere*: *Petrarch's Lyric Poems: The Rime Sparse and Other Lyrics*, trans. and ed. by R. M. Durling (Cambridge, MA: Harvard University Press, 1976)
——*Epistolae Familiares*: *Petrarca, Prose*, ed. by G. Martellotti et al. (Milan: R. Ricciardi, 1955)
——*Secretum/The Secret*, ed. and trans. by Carol E. Quillen (Boston: Bedford/St Martin's 2003)
Petronius (*c.* 27–66)
——*The Satyricon*: ed. and trans. by M. Heseltine and W. H. D. Rouse (Cambridge, MA: Loeb Classical Library, 1913); translated with introduction and explanatory notes by P. G. Walsh (Oxford: Clarendon Press 1995)

PICO DELLA MIRANDOLA, GIOVANNI (1463–1494)
——*De hominis dignitate/Oration on the Dignity of Man*: trans. by Charles Glenn Wallis, Paul J. W. Miller, Douglas Carmichael (Indianapolis: Hackett Publishing, 1996)
PLATO (424/423–348/347 BC)
——*Phaedrus*: ed. and trans. by H. N. Fowler (Cambridge, MA: Loeb Classical Library, 1914)
——*Republic*: ed. and trans. by P. Shorey (Cambridge, MA: Loeb Classical Library, 1930–35)
——*Timaeus*: ed. and trans. by R. G. Bury (Cambridge, MA: Loeb Classical Library, 1929)
PLINY THE ELDER (23–79)
——*Natural History*: ed. and trans. by H. Rackham et al., 10 vols (Cambridge, MA: Loeb Classical Library, 1938–63)
PLUTARCH (*c*. 46–120)
——*Bruta animalia ratione uti, siue Gryllus*: ed. and trans. by H. Cherniss and W. C. Helmbold, *Moralia*, vol. 12 (Cambridge, MA: Loeb Classical Library, 1957)
——*De Iside et Osiride*: ed. and trans. by F. C. Babbitt, *Moralia*, vol. 5 (Cambridge, MA: Loeb Classical Library, 1936)
——*De Sollertia Animalium/On the Intelligence of Animals*: ed. and trans. by H. Cherniss and W. C. Helmbold, *Moralia*, vol. 12 (Cambridge, MA: Loeb Classical Library, 1957)
PSEUDO-PLUTARCH
——*De Vita Homeri*: ed. and trans. by M. L. West (Cambridge, MA: Loeb Classical Library, 2003)
——*On Rivers*: ed. and trans. by A. De Lazzer et al. (Naples: D'Auria, 2003)
POLIZIANO, ANGELO (1454–1494)
——*Commento inedito alle Georgiche di Virgilio*: ed. by L. Castano Musicò (Florence: Olschki, 1990)
POLLUX, JULIUS (2nd century)
——*Onomasticon*: ed. by E. Bethe, 3 vols (Leipzig: Teubner, 1900–37)
PONTANO, GIOVANNI (1426–1503)
——*Carmina*: 2 vols, ed. by B. Soldati (Florence: Barbèra, 1902–05)
——*Carmina*: ed. by J. Oeschger (Bari: Laterza, 1948)
——*Dialoghi*: ed. by C. Privitera. Edizione critica (Florence: Sansoni, 1943)
PROUST, MARCEL (1871–1922)
——*A la recherche du temps perdu*, ed. by J.-Y. Tadié (Paris: Quarto Gallimard, 1999 [1922])
——*A la recherche du temps perdu*, ed. by J.-Y. Tadié (Paris: Editions de la Pléiade, 1964 [1922]) (with T. Laget, 'Esquisses, notes et variantes: Esquisse XII: La Soirée a l'opéra')
PRYNNE, WILLIAM (1600–1669)
——*Histrio-mastix. The players scourge, or, actors tragœdie, divided into two parts* (London: E[dward] A[llde] et al. for Michael Sparke, 1633)
PULLMAN, PHILIP (1946–)
—— *The Amber Spyglass* (London: Scholastic, 2001)
REMY, NICHOLAS (1530–1616)
——*Daemonolatreiae Libri Tres Ex Iudicijs capitalibus nongentorum plus minus hominum; qui sortilegij crimen intra annos quindecim in Lotharingia capite luerunt* (Lyon, 1595), trans. as *Demonolatry: An Account of the Historical Practice of Witchcraft* by E. A. Ashwin, ed. by Montague Summers (London: John Rodker, 1930; repr. Mineola, NY: Dover Books, 2008)
RIORDAN, RICK (1964–)
——*Percy Jackson and the Lightning Thief* (London: Puffin Books, 2006)
——*Percy Jackson and the Titan's Curse* (London: Puffin Books, 2007)
—— *The Last Olympian* (London: Puffin Books, 2009)
ROGER OF WENDOVER (active *c*. 1215)
——*Chronica sive Flores Historiarum*: ed. by H. O. Coxe (London: English Historical Society, 1841)

ROWLING, J. K. (1965–)
—— *Harry Potter and the Philosopher's Stone* (London: Bloomsbury, 1997)
—— *Harry Potter and the Chamber of Secrets* (London: Bloomsbury, 1998)
—— *Harry Potter and the Prisoner of Azkaban* (London: Bloomsbury, 1999)
—— *Harry Potter and the Goblet of Fire* (London: Bloomsbury, 2000)
—— *Harry Potter and the Order of the Phoenix* (London: Bloomsbury, 2003)
—— *Harry Potter and the Half-Blood Prince* (London: Bloomsbury, 2005)
—— *Harry Potter and the Deathly Hallows* (London: Bloomsbury, 2007)
RUSHDIE, SALMAN (1947–)
—— *The Satanic Verses* (Viking Press, 1988)
SAINT-EXUPÉRY, ANTOINE (1900–1944)
—— *Le Petit Prince/The Little Prince*: trans. by I. Testot-Ferry (London: Wordsworth, 1995)
SANNAZARO, IACOPO (1458–1530)
—— *Opere*: ed. by A. Mauro (Bari: Laterza, 1961)
—— *Arcadia*: ed. by F. Erspamer (Milan: Mursia, 1990)
—— *The Major Latin Poems*: trans. by R. Nash (Detroit, MI: Wayne State University Press, 1996)
—— *Latin Poetry*: trans. by M. C. J. Putnam (Cambridge, MA, and London: Harvard University Press, 2009)
SAPPHO (*c.* 630–*c.* 570 BC)
—— *Fragments*: ed. and trans. by D. A. Campbell (Cambridge, MA: Loeb Classical Library, 1982)
SCHILLER, FRIEDRICH (1759–1805)
—— 'Die Götter Griechenlands': in *Werke und Briefe*, vol. 1, ed. by G. Kurscheidt (Frankfurt a. M.: Deutscher Klassiker Verlag, 1992), first version: pp. 285–91; second version: pp. 162–65
SCOTT FITZGERALD, F. (1896–1940)
—— *The Great Gatsby* (Charles Scribner's Sons, 1925)
SENECA THE YOUNGER (*c.* 4 BC–AD 65)
—— *Apocolocyntosis (divi) Claudii/The Gourdification of (the Divine) Claudius*: ed. and trans. by W. H. D. Rouse (Cambridge, MA: Loeb Classical Library, 1913)
—— *Epistulae ad Lucilium*: ed. and trans. by R. M. Gummere, 3 vols (Cambridge, MA: Loeb Classical Library, 1917–1925)
—— *Natural Questions*: ed. by T. H. Corcoran (Cambridge, MA: Loeb Classical Library, 1971)
SERVIUS (late 4th century)
—— *Commentary on Virgil*: ed. by T. and H. Hagen, 3 vols (Leipzig: Teubner, 1881–1902; repr. Olms: Hildesheim, 1961)
SEXTUS EMPIRICUS (*c.* 160–210)
—— *Pyrrhoniae Hypotyposes/Outlines of Pyrrhonism*: ed. and trans. by R. G. Bury (Cambridge, MA: Loeb Classical Library, 1933)
SHAKESPEARE, WILLIAM (1564–1616)
—— *The Complete Works*, ed. by Stanley Wells et al., 2nd edn (Oxford: Clarendon Press, 2005)
SHELLEY, M. (1797–1851)
—— *Frankenstein; or, The Modern Prometheus*
SIEDER, JOHANN
—— *Ain schön lieblich auch kurtzweylig Gedichte Lutij Apuleij von ainem gulden Esel* (Augsburg: Alexander Weissenborn, 1538)
SOLINUS, JULIUS (active in the early 3rd century?)
—— *Epitome/Collectanea rerum memorabilium*: ed. by T. Mommsen (Berlin: Weidmann, 1895)

SOPHOCLES (*c.* 496–406 BC)
——*Plays*: ed. and trans. by H. Lloyd-Jones, 2 vols (Cambridge, MA: Loeb Classical Library, 1994)
——*Fragments*: *Tragicorum Graecorum Fragmenta, Vol. 4: Sophocles*, edited by S. Radt (Göttingen: Vandenhoeck & Ruprecht, 1977); ed. and trans. by H. Lloyd-Jones (Cambridge, MA: Loeb Classical Library, 1996)
SPENSER, EDMUND (*c.* 1552–1599)
—— *The Faerie Queene* (1590–96)
STERLING, BRUCE (1954–)
——*Swarm*: in *The Oxford Book of Science Fiction Stories*, ed. by Tom Shippey (Oxford: Oxford Paperbacks, 2003 [1982]), pp. 472–95
STEVENSON, ROBERT LOUIS BALFOUR (1850–1894)
—— *The Strange Case of Dr Jekyll and Mr Hyde* (London: Longmans, Green & co., 1886)
STOCKTON, FRANK (1834–1902)
—— *Old Pipes and the Dryad* (London: Franklin Watts, 1969 [1885])
STOKER, BRAM (1847–1912)
——*Dracula* (London: Archibald Constable and Company, 1897)
STRABO (64/63 BC–*c.* 24 AD)
——*Geography*, ed. and trans. by H. L. Jones, 8 vols (Cambridge, MA: Loeb Classical Library, 1917–32)
TACITUS (56–117)
——*Histories*: ed. and trans. by C. H. Moore and J. Jackson, 2 vols (Cambridge, MA: Loeb Classical Library, 1925–31)
TENNYSON, ALFRED LORD (1809–1892)
—— *The Poems*: 3 vols, ed. by C. Ricks (London: Longman, 1969)
TERTULLIAN (*c.* 160–*c.* 225)
——*Adversus Praxean/Against Praxeas*: edited, with an introduction, translation, and commentary by Ernest Evans (London: Society for Promoting Christian Knowledge, 1948)
——*de Carne Christi*: E. Evans, *Tertullian's Treatise on the Incarnation. The text edited with introduction, translation, and commentary* (London: Society for Promoting Christian Knowledge, 1956)
THEOCRITUS (active in the third century BC)
——*Poems*: edited with a translation and commentary by A. S. F. Gow (Cambridge: Cambridge University Press, 1950)
THEODULF OF ORLÉANS (750/760–821)
——*Carmina*: *Monumenta Germaniae Historica: Poetae Latini Medii Aevi* I
THEOPHRASTUS (*c.* 371–*c.* 287 BC)
——*De causis plantarum*: ed. and trans. by B. Einarson and G. K. K. Link, 3 vols (Cambridge, MA: Loeb Classical Library, 1976–90)
——*Enquiry into Plants*: ed. and trans. by A. F. Hort, 2 vols (Cambridge, MA: Loeb Classical Library, 1916); *Recherches sur les plantes I–V*, ed. by S. Amigues (Paris: Les Belles Lettres, 1988–2006)
—— *On Stones/De Lapidibus*: Introduction, Greek Text, English Translation, and Commentary by E. R. Caley and J. F. C. Richards (Columbus: Ohio State University Press, 1956)
THUCYDIDES (*c.* 460–395 BC)
——*History of the Peloponnesian War*: ed. and trans. by C. F. Smith, 4 vols (Cambridge, MA: Loeb Classical Library, 1919–23)
TOLKIEN, J. R. R. (1892–1973)
—— *The Lord of the Rings* (London: HarperCollins, 1999 [1954–1955])
TOURNIER, MICHEL (1924–)

—— *Le Roi des aulnes* (Paris: Gallimard, Folio, 1978 [1970])

—— *Le Vent Paraclet* (Paris: Gallimard, Folio, 1977)

VALERIUS FLACCUS (active in 70s/80s)

——*Argonautica*: ed. and trans. by J. H. Mozley (Cambridge, MA: Loeb Classical Library, 1934)

VARRO (116–27 BC)

——*Antiquitates rerum divinarum*: ed. with commentary by B. Cardauns (Mainz: Akademie der Wissenschaften und der Literatur, 1976)

——*De lingua latina*: ed. and trans. by R. G. Kent, 2 vols (Cambridge, MA: Loeb Classical Library, 1938)

VILLIERS DE L'ISLE-ADAM, AUGUSTE (1838-1889)

——*L'Ève future* (Paris: Monnier 1886)

VIRGIL (70–19 BC)

——*Eclogues, Georgics, Aeneid*: ed. by R. A. B. Mynors (Oxford: Clarendon Press, 1969); ed. and trans. by H. R. Fairclough, rev. by G. P. Goold, 2 vols (Cambridge, MA: Loeb Classical Library, 1999–2001)

VIRGILIO, GIOVANNI DEL (active at the beginning of the 14th century)

——*Allegorie librorum Ovidii Metamorphoseos a magistro Johanne de Virgilio prosaice ac metrice compilate*: ed. F. Ghisalberti, in 'Giovanni del Virgilio espositore delle "Metamorfosi"', *Il giornale dantesco* n.s. 4, no. 34, 1933, 3–110

VONNEGUT, KURT (1922–2007)

—— *Galápagos* (London: Flamingo, 1994)

WALPOLE, HORACE (1717–1797)

——*Castle of Otranto* (London, 1764)

WELLS, H. G. (1866–1946)

—— *The Food of the Gods* (London: Macmillan, 1904)

—— *The Invisible Man* (London: C. Arthur Pearson, 1897)

—— *The Island of Dr Moreau* (London: Heinemann, Stone & Kimball, 1896)

—— *The Time Machine* (London: William Heinemann, 1895)

WEYER, JOHANN (1515–1588)

—— *Opera omnia* (Amsterdam: Peter van den Berge, 1660)

WHITE, TERENCE HANBURY (1906–1964)

—— *The Book of Merlyn* (London: Shaftesbury, 2000)

—— *The Once and Future King* (London: Harper Collins, 2001)

WILDE, OSCAR (1854–1900)

—— *The Picture of Dorian Gray* (Lippincott's Monthly Magazine, 1890)

WILLIAM OF MALMESBURY (b. c. 1090, d. in or after 1142)

——*Gesta regum anglorum*: ed. and trans. R. A. B. Mynors, R. M. Thompson, and M. Winterbottom, 2 vols (Oxford: Clarendon, 1998–99)

WYNDHAM, JOHN (1903–1969)

——*Infinite Moment* (New York: Ballantine Books, 1961)

XENOPHANES OF COLOPHON (late 6th–early 5th century BC)

——*Fragments*: ed. by J. H. Lesher (*Xenophanes of Colophon: Fragments: A Text and Translation with Commentary*, Toronto: University of Toronto Press, 1992)

BIBLIOGRAPHY: SECONDARY LITERATURE

ABBAMONTE, G. (2004), 'Esegesi virgiliana nella Roma del Secondo Quattrocento: osservazioni sulle fonti del commento di G. Pomponio Leto alle *Georgiche*', in *Societas studiorum: Per Salvatore D'Elia*, ed. by U. Criscuolo, Naples: Dipartimento di Filologia classica dell'Università di Napoli, pp. 545–83

——(2008), 'Gli studi lessicografici negli ambienti accademici di Roma e Napoli nella seconda metà del Quattrocento', in *Les Académies dans l'Europe humaniste: Idéaux et pratiques. Actes du Colloque international de Paris (10–13 juin 2003)*, ed. by M. Deramaix, Geneva: Droz, pp. 339–67

ALCOLOUMBRE, T. (2004), 'Aristote lecteur de Proust', *Revue des lettres modernes: Marcel Proust*, 4, 118–33

ALESSIO, G. C. (ed.) (2005), *Il mito nella letteratura italiana*. General Editor P. Gibellini. I. *Dal Medioevo al Rinascimento*, Brescia: Morcelliana

ALLEN, D. C. (1970), *Mysteriously Meant: The Rediscovery of Pagan Symbolism and Allegorical Interpretation in the Renaissance*, Baltimore, MD, and London: Johns Hopkins University Press

ALLESCH, C., and M. SCHWARZBAUER (eds) (2007), *Die Kultur und die Künste*, Heidelberg: Winter

ALTER, R. (1981), 'Sacred History and the Beginnings of Prose Fiction', in *The Art of Biblical Narrative*, Basic Books, pp. 23–46

ANDERSON, J. A. (2005), *Translating Investments: Metaphor and the Dynamic of Cultural Change in Tudor-Stuart England*, New York: Fordham University Press

ANDERSON, M. M. (1992), *Kafka's Clothes: Ornament and Aestheticism in the Habsburg Fin de Siècle*, Oxford: Oxford University Press

ANDERSON, W. (ed.) (1972), *Ovid's Metamorphoses. Books 6–10*, Norman: University of Oklahoma Press

ANDERSON, W. S. (1963), 'Multiple Change in the *Metamorphoses*', *Transactions of the American Philological Association*, 94, 1–27

——(1989), 'Lycaon: Ovid's Deceptive Paradigm in *Metamorphoses* 1', *ICS*, 14, 91–101

ANDREOPOULOS, A. (2005), *Metamorphosis: The Transfiguration in Byzantine Theology and Iconography*, Crestwood, NY: St. Vladimir's Seminary Press

ANGLO, S. (1976), 'Melancholia und Witchcraft: The Debate between Wier, Bodin and Scot', in *Folie et déraison à la Renaissance*, Brussels: Éditions de l'Université de Bruxelles, pp. 209–28

ANOLIK, R. B. (2007), 'Introduction: Sexual Horror: Fears of the Sexual Other', in *Horrifying Sex: Essays on Sexual Difference in Gothic Literature*, ed. by R. B. Anolik, Jefferson, NC, and London: McFarland & Company, Inc., pp. 1–24

ARENDT, H. (1961/2006a), 'Preface: The Gap between Past and Future', in *Between Past and Future: Eight Exercises in Political Thought*, introduction by Jerome Kohn, London: Penguin, pp. 3–15

——(1961/2006b), 'What is Authority?', in *Between Past and Future: Eight Exercises in Political Thought*, introduction by Jerome Kohn, London: Penguin, pp. 91–141

ARMAND, B. L. ST. (1977), *The Roots of Horror in the Fiction of H. P. Lovecraft*, Elizabethtown, NY: Dragon Press

ARNALDI, F., L. MONTI SABIA, and L. GUALDO ROSA (eds) (1964), *Poeti latini del Quattrocento*, Milan and Naples: Ricciardi

ASKER, D. B. D. (2001), *Aspects of Metamorphosis: Fictional Representations of the Becoming Human*, Amsterdam: Rodopi

ASQUITH, H. (2005). 'From Genealogy to Catalogue: The Hellenistic Adaptation of the Hesiodic Catalogue Form', in *The Hesiodic Catalogue of Women: Constructions and Reconstructions*, ed. by R. Hunter, Cambridge: Cambridge University Press, pp. 266–86

ASSMANN, A., and J. (2006), 'Einleitung', in *Verwandlungen: Archäologie der literarischen Kommunikation IX*, ed. by A. and J. Assmann, Munich: Wilhelm Fink Verlag, pp. 9–24

ASSMANN, J. (2003), *Die Mosaische Unterscheidung, oder der Preis des Monotheismus*, Munich and Vienna: Carl Hanser Verlag

ATALLAH, W. (1966), *Adonis dans la littérature et l'art grecs*, Paris: Klincksieck

AUERBACH, E. (1959), 'Figura', in *Scenes from the Drama of European Literature: Six Essays*, New York: Meridian Books

AUHAGEN, U. (1999), *Der Monolog bei Ovid*, Tübingen: Gunter Narr Verlag

AVERY-PECK, A. J., and J. NEUSNER (eds) (2000), *Judaism in Late Antiquity, Part Four: Death, Life-After-Death, Resurrection and the World-To-Come in the Judaisms of Antiquity*, Leiden: Brill

BACHELARD, G. (1939), *Lautréamont*, Paris: Librairie Jose Corti

BACHMANN, V. (2009), *Die Welt im Ausnahmezustand: Eine Untersuchung zu Aussagegehalt und Theologie des Wächterbuches (1 Hen 1–36)* (= Beihefte zur Zeitschrift für die alttestamentliche Wissenschaft, 409), Berlin: de Gruyter

BACK, F. (2002), *Verwandlung durch Offenbarung bei Paulus*, Tübingen: Mohr

BAILEY, C. (1949), *Titi Lucreti Cari De Rerum Natura Libri Sex, edited with Prolegomena, Critical Apparatus, Translation and Commentary, Volume II: Commentary, Books I–III*, Oxford: Clarendon Press

BAKHTIN, M. M. (1981), *The Dialogic Imagination: Four Essays*, ed. by Michael Holquist; trans. by Caryl Emerson and Michael Holquist, Austin: University of Texas Press

BÄR, S. (2007), 'Quintus Smyrnaeus und die Tradition des epischen Musenanrufs', in *Quintus Smyrnaeus: Transforming Homer in Second Sophistic Epic*, ed. by M. Baumbach and S. Bär, in collaboration with N. Dümmler, Berlin and New York: de Gruyter, 29–64

—— *Quintus Smyrnaeus. 'Posthomerica' 1. Die Wiedergeburt des Epos aus dem Geiste der Amazonomachie. Mit einem Kommentar zu den Versen 1–219*, Göttingen: Vandenhoeck & Ruprecht

BARASCH, M. (2000), *Theories of Art: 3. From Impressionism to Kandinsky*, New York: Routledge

BARCHIESI, A. (2001), 'The Crossing', in *Texts, Ideas, and the Classics*, ed. by S. J. Harrison, Oxford: Oxford, University Press, pp. 142–63

—— (2005), *Ovidio, Metamorfosi. Testo latino a fronte, vol. 1 (Libri I–II), con un saggio introduttivo di Charles Segal; testo critico basato sull'edizione oxoniense di Richard Tarrant; traduzione di Ludovica Koch*, Rome: Fondazione Lorenzo Valla; Milan: A. Mondadori

BARCHIESI, A., and G. ROSATI (2007), *Ovidio, Metamorfosi. Testo latino a fronte, vol. 2 (Libri III–IV); testo critico basato sull'edizione oxoniense di Richard Tarrant; traduzione di Ludovica Koch*, Rome: Fondazione Lorenzo Valla; Milan: A. Mondadori

BARDON, H. (1958), 'Ovide et le baroque', in *Ovidiana: Recherches sur Ovide publiées à l'occasion du bimillénaire de la naissance du poète*, ed. by N. Herescu, Paris: Les Belles Lettres, pp. 75–100

BARKAN, L. (1975), *Nature's Work of Art: The Human Body as Image of the World*, New Haven, CT, and London: Yale University Press

—— (1986), *The Gods Made Flesh: Metamorphosis and the Pursuit of Paganism*, New Haven, CT: Yale University Press

BARNARD, M. E. (1987), *The Myth of Apollo and Daphne from Ovid to Quevedo: Love, Agon, and the Grotesque*, Durham, NC: Duke University Press

BAROLINI, T. (1987/1989), 'Arachne, Argus, and St. John: Transgressive Art in Dante and Ovid', *Mediaevalia*, 13, 207–26

BAROLSKY, P. (2010), *A Brief History of the Artist from God to Picasso*, University Park: The Pennsylvania State University Press

BARTEL, H., and A. SIMON (eds) (2010), *Unbinding Medea: Interdisciplinary Approaches to a Classical Myth from Antiquity to the 21st Century*, London: Legenda

BARTHES, R. (1994 [1973]), 'Proust et les noms', in *Roland Barthes, œuvres complètes*, ed. by E. Marty, Paris: Le Seuil, pp. 1368–77

BARTKOWSKI, F. (2008), *Kissing Cousins: A New Kinship Bestiary*, New York: Columbia University Press

——(2009), 'Emilie Clark, Beth Cavener Stichter, Kate Clark: Engaging the Wild', *Antennae Review*, Autumn 2009

BATE, C. (1997), 'No Sin but Irony: Kierkegaard and Milton's Satan', *Literature and Theology*, 11. 1, 1–26

BATE, J. (1994), *Shakespeare and Ovid*, Oxford: Clarendon Press

BAUDRILLARD, J. (1999), *L'Échange impossible*, Paris: Édition Galilée

BAUMBACH, M. (2012), 'Quae mox ventura trahantur. Der Meergott Proteus und die Poetologie der Metamorphose in Vergils Georgica,' in Innovation aus Tradition: Literaturwissenschaftliche Perspektiven der Vergilforschung, ed. by M. Baumbach and W. Polleichtner, Trier: Wissenschaftlicher Verlag Trier, pp. 1–21

BEAGON, M. (1992), *Roman Nature: The Thought of Pliny the Elder*, Oxford: Clarendon Press

——(2009), 'Ordering Wonderland: Ovid's Pythagoras and the Augustan Vision', in *Paradox and the Marvellous in Augustan Literature and Culture*, ed. by P. Hardie, Oxford: Oxford University Press, pp. 288–309

BENDLIN, A. (2000), 'Looking Beyond the Civic Compromise: Religious Pluralism in Late Republican Rome', in *Religion in Archaic and Republican Rome and Italy: Evidence and Experience*, ed. by E. Bispham and C. Smith, Edinburgh: Edinburgh University Press, pp. 115–35 and 167–71

BERGER, P., and T. LUCKMANN (1967), *The Social Construction of Reality*, London: Penguin

BERGHAHN, K. (1985), 'Schillers mythologische Symbolik: Erläutert am Beispiel der *Götter Griechenlands*', *Weimarer Beiträge*, 31, 1803–22

BERGSON, H. (1944), *Creative Evolution*, trans. by Arthur Mitchell, New York: Random House

BERNAL, M. (1987), *Black Athena: The Afroasiatic Roots of Classical Civilization*, New Brunswick: Rutgers University Press

BERNHEIMER, R. (1952), *Wild Men in the Middle Ages*, Cambridge, MA: Harvard University Press

BERNSDORFF, H. (2007), 'P. Oxy. 4711 and the Poetry of Parthenius', *Journal of Hellenic Studies*, 127, 1–18

BETHE, E. (1904), 'Ovid und Nikander', *Hermes*, 39, 1–14

BETTELHEIM, B. (1975), *The Uses of Enchantment: The Meaning and Importance of Fairy Tales*, New York: Alfred A. Knopf

BETTINI, M. (1986), *Antropologia e Cultura Romana*, Rome: La Nuova Italia Scientifica

——(1998), *Nascere. Storie di Donne, Donnole, Madri ed Eroi*, Turin: Einaudi

BINDER, H. (2004), *Kafkas 'Verwandlung'. Entstehung, Deutung, Wirkung*, Frankfurt a. M.: Stroemfeld Verlag

BING, P. (1988), *The Well-Read Muse: Present and Past in Callimachus and the Hellenistic Poets*, Göttingen: Vandenhoeck & Ruprecht

BINROTH-BANK, C. (1994), *Medea in den Metamorphosen Ovids: Untersuchungen zur ovidischen Erzähl- und Darstellungsweise*, Frankfurt am Main: P. Lang

BIOW, J. (1996), *Mirabile dictu: Representations of the Marvelous in Medieval and Renaissance Epic*, Ann Arbor: University of Michigan Press

BLOOM, H. (2004), *Frankenstein*, Infobase Publishing

BLUMENBERG, H. (1979), *Arbeit am Mythos*, Frankfurt a. M: Suhrkamp

BOCKMUEHL, M. (2001), 'Resurrection', in *The Cambridge Companion to Jesus*, ed. by id., Cambridge: Cambridge University Press

BOEDEKER, D. (1997), 'Becoming Medea: Assimilation in Euripides', in *Medea: Essays on Medea in Myth, Literature, Philosophy and Art*, ed. by J. J. Clauss and S. I. Johnston, Princeton, NJ: Princeton University Press, pp. 127–48

BÖMER, F. (1969–86), *P. Ovidius Naso: Metamorphosen: Kommentar*, 6 vols, Heidelberg: C. Winter

BONNER, G. (1999), 'Deification, Divinization', in *Augustine through the Ages: An Encyclopedia*, ed. by A. D. Fitzgerald, Grand Rapids, MI: Eerdmans, pp. 265–66

BORCHARDT, F. L. (1990), 'The *Magus* as Renaissance Man', *Sixteenth Century Journal*, 21, 57–76

BORUTTA, M. (2010), 'Genealogie der Säkularisierungstheorie: Zur Historisierung einer großen Erzählung der Moderne', *Geschichte und Gesellschaft*, 36.3, 347–76

BOSWORTH, B. (1999), 'Augustus, the *Res Gestae* and Hellenistic Theories of Apotheosis', *Journal of Roman Studies*, 89, 1–18

BOTTIGHEIMER, R. (1987), *Grimms' Bad Girls and Bold Boys*, New Haven, CT: Yale University Press

BOTTING, F. (1995), *The Gothic*, London: Routledge

BOWIE, A. M. (1993), *Aristophanes: Myth, Ritual, Comedy*, Cambridge: Cambridge University Press

BOWIE, E. L. (1996), 'Past and Present in Pausanias', in *Pausanias Historien* (Fondation Hardt Entretiens Tome XLI), ed. by O. Reverdin and B. Grange, Geneva: Fondation Hardt, pp. 207–30

——(2001), 'Inspiration and Aspiration: Date, Genre, and Readership', in *Pausanias: Travel and Memory in Roman Greece*, ed. by S. E. Alcock, J. F. Cherry, and J. Elsner, Oxford: Oxford University Press, pp. 21–32

BOYLE, N. (1999), *Goethe. Der Dichter in seiner Zeit*, vol. 2, Munich: C. H. Beck Verlag

BOYS-STONES, G. R. (ed.) (2003), *Metaphor, Allegory, and the Classical Tradition: Ancient Thought and Modern Revisions*, Oxford: Oxford University Press

BRAIDOTTI, R. (2002), *Metamorphoses: Towards a Materialist Theory of Becoming*, Cambridge: Polity Press

BREIDBACH, O. (2006), *Goethes Metamorphosenlehre*, Munich: Wilhelm Fink

——(2011), *Goethes Naturverständnis*, Munich: Wilhelm Fink

BREMMER, J. N., and J. R. VEENSTRA (eds) (2002), *The Metamorphosis of Magic from Late Antiquity to the Early Modern Period*, Leuven, Paris, and Dudley, MA: Peeters

BRENKMANN, J. (1974), 'Writing, Desire, Dialectic in Petrarch's *Rime 23*', *Pacific Coast Philology*, 9, 12–19

BRODERSEN, K. (2005), '"Das aber ist eine Lüge": Zur rationalistischen Mythenkritik des Palaiphatos', in *Griechische Mythologie und frühes Christentum*, ed. by R. von Haehling (Darmstadt: Wissenschaftliche Buchgesellschaft, 2005), pp. 44–57

BROOKE-ROSE, C. (1983), *A Rhetoric of the Unreal*, Cambridge: Cambridge University Press

BROWN, A. (2010), *De rerum natura: The Return of Lucretius to Renaissance Florence*, Cambridge, MA: Harvard University Press

BROWN, M. (2008), 'Solved: Mystery of The Ugly Duchess — and the Da Vinci connection. Subject was suffering from rare disease, say experts, and painting is not a copy', *The Guardian*, Saturday 11 October 2008

BROWN, S. A. (1999), *The Metamorphosis of Ovid: From Chaucer to Ted Hughes*, London: Duckworth

——(2005), *Ovid: Myth and Metamorphosis*, London: Bristol Classical Press

——(2007), 'Introduction: Tragedy in Transition', in *Tragedy in Transition*, ed. by Sarah Annes Brown and Catherine Silverstone, London: Blackwell, 1–15

BROWN, V. (1976), 'Columella', *Catalogus translationum et commentariorum. Mediaeval and Renaissance Latin Translations and Commentaries: Annotated Lists and Guides*, ed. by P. O. Kristeller et al., Washington, DC: Catholic University of America Press, 1960–, III, 173–93

BROWNLEE, K. (1978), 'Dante and Narcissus (Purg. XXX, 76–99)', *Dante Studies, with the Annual Report of the Dante Society*, 96, 201–06

——(1984a), 'Phaeton's Fall and Dante's Ascent' in *Dante Studies, with the Annual Report of the Dante Society*, 102, 135–44

——(1984b), 'Why the Angels Speak Italian: Dante as Vernacular *Poeta* in Paradiso XXV', *Poetics Today*, 5, 597–610

——(1985), 'Dante's Poetics of Transfiguration: The Case of Ovid', *Literature and Belief*, 5, 13–29

——(1986), 'Ovid's Semele and Dante's Metamorphosis: *Paradiso* XXI–XXIII', *Modern Language Notes*, 101, 147–56

——(1993), 'Dante and the Classical Poets', in *The Cambridge Companion to Dante*, ed. by R. Jacoff, Cambridge: Cambridge University Press, pp. 100–19

BRUCE, I. (1987), 'Kafka's *Metamorphosis*: Folklore, Hasidism, and the Jewish Tradition', *Journal of the Kafka Society of America*, 11, 9–27

BRUNNER UNGRICHT, G. (1988), *Die Mensch-Tier-Verwandlung: Eine Motivgeschichte unter besonderer Berücksichtigung des deutschen Märchens in der ersten Hälfte des 19. Jahrhunderts*, Bern: P. Lang

BÜHLER, P. (2008), 'Tertullian: The Teacher of *Credo Quia Absurdum*', in *Kierkegaard and the Patristic and Medieval Traditions*, ed. by J. B. Stewart, Ashgate Publishing, pp. 131–42

BUNTFUSS, M. (2006), 'Mythos und Metapher bei Vico, Cassirer und Blumenberg', in *Moderne und Mythos*, ed. by S. Vietta and H. Uerlings, Munich: Wilhelm Fink Verlag, pp. 67–78

BURCKHARDT, J. (1956), *Griechische Kulturgeschichte II* (= Gesammelte Werke VI), Darmstadt: Wissenschaftliche Buchgesellschaft

BURKERT, W. (2005), 'Vergöttlichung von Menschen in der griechisch-römischen Antike', in *Grenzen des Menschseins: Probleme einer Definition des Menschlichen*, ed. by J. Stagl and W. Reinhard, Vienna: Böhlau Verlag, pp. 401–20

BURLESON, D. R. (1990), *Lovecraft: Disturbing the Universe*, Lexington: University Press of Kentucky

BURNETT, C., and W. F. RYAN (eds) (2006), *Magic and the Classical Tradition*, Warburg Institute Colloquia 7, London & Turin: The Warburg Institute/Nino Aragno Editore

BURNHAM, D., and E. GIACCHERINI (eds) (2005), *The Poetics Of Transubstantiation: From Theology To Metaphor*, Aldershot: Ashgate

BURROW, C. (1988), 'Original Fictions: Metamorphoses in *The Faerie Queene*', in *Ovid Renewed*, ed. by C. Martindale, Cambridge: Cambridge University Press, pp. 99–119

BUTLER, E. (2010), *Metamorphoses of the Vampire in Literature and Film: Cultural Transformations in Europe, 1732–1933*, Rochester, NY: Camden House

BUXTON, R. (ed.) (2002), *From Myth to Reason? Studies in the Development of Greek Thought*, Oxford: Oxford University Press

BUXTON, R. (2009), *Forms of Astonishment: Greek Myths of Metamorphosis*, Oxford: Oxford University Press

——(2010), 'How Medea Moves: Versions of a Myth in Apollonius and Elsewhere', in *Unbinding Medea. Interdisciplinary Approaches to a Classical Myth from Antiquity to the 21st Century*, ed. by H. Bartel and A. Simon, London: The Modern Humanities Research Association and Maney Publishing, pp. 25–38

BYNUM, C. W. (1995), *The Resurrection of the Body in Western Christianity, 200–1336*, New York: Columbia University Press

——(1998), 'Metamorphosis, or Gerald and the Werewolf', *Speculum*, 73, 987–1013

——(2001), *Metamorphosis and Identity*, New York: Zone Books

——(2011), *Christian Materiality: An Essay on Religion in Late Medieval Europe*, New York: Zone Books

CADILI, L. (2001), *'Viamque adfectat Olympo': Memoria ellenistica nelle 'Georgiche' di Virgilio*, Milan: LED

CAILLOIS, R. (1966), *Images, images: Essais sur le rôle et les pouvoirs de l'imagination*, Paris: Corti

CALABRESE, F. (2004), *La favolosa storia degli agrumi*, Palermo: L'Epos (1st edn 1998)

CALBOLI MONTEFUSCO, L. (1994), 'Aristotle and Cicero on the *officia oratoris*', in *Peripatetic Rhetoric after Aristotle*, ed. by W. W. Fortenbaugh and D. C. Mirhady, Brunswick, NJ: Rutgers University Press, pp. 66–94

CALEY, E. R., and J. F. C. RICHARDS (1956), *Theophrastus, On Stones, Introduction, Greek Text, English Translation, and Commentary*, Columbus: Ohio State University Press

CAMERON, A. (2004), *Greek Mythography in the Roman World*, Oxford: Oxford University Press

——(2011), *The Last Pagans of Rome*, Oxford and New York: Oxford University Press

CAMERON, E. (2010), *Enchanted Europe: Superstition, Reason, and Religion, 1250–1750*, Oxford: Oxford University Press

——(2010), *The Psychopathology of the Gothic Romance: Perversion, Neuroses and Psychosis in Early Works of the Genre*, Jefferson, NC, and London: McFarland & Company

CAMPANA, A. (1962), 'Atti, Isotta degli', in *Dizionario biografico degli Italiani*, Rome: Istituto della Enciclopedia Italiana, 1960–, 4, 547–56

——(1965), 'Basinio da Parma', in *Dizionario biografico degli Italiani*, Rome: Istituto della Enciclopedia Italiana, 1960–, 7, 89–98

CAMPBELL, M. B. (1999), *Wonder and Science: Imagining Worlds in Early Modern Europe*, Ithaca, NY: Cornell University Press

CANGUILHEM, G. (1966), *Le Normal et le Pathologique*, Paris: Presses Universitaires de France

CANNON, P. (1982), 'Lovecraft and the Mainstream Literature of His Day', *Lovecraft Studies*, 7, 25–29

CARDAUNS, B. (1976) *M. Terentius Varro, Antiquitates rerum divinarum, 1: Die Fragmente. 2: Kommentar* (= Akademie der Wissenschaften und der Literatur, Mainz, Abhandlungen der Geistes- und sozialwissenschaftlichen Klasse 1), Wiesbaden

——(1978), 'Varro und die römische Religion: Zur Theologie, Wirkungsgeschichte und Leistung der *Antiquitates Rerum Divinarum*', *Aufstieg und Niedergang der Römischen Welt* 2.16.1, 80–103

CARRAI, S. (ed.) (1998), *La poesia pastorale del Rinascimento italiano*, Padua: Antenore

CARRARA, E. (1936), *La poesia pastorale*, Milan: Vallardi (1st edn 1909)

CARROLL, N. (1990), *The Philosophy of Horror or Paradoxes of the Heart*, London: Routledge

CARSPECKEN, J. F. (1952), 'Apollonius Rhodius and the Homeric Epic', *Yale Classical Studies*, 13, 33–143

CARTER, W. C. (2006), *Proust in Love*, London and New Haven, CT: Yale University Press

CARUSO, C. (1997), 'Poesia umanistica di villa', in *'Feconde venner le carte'. Studi in onore di Ottavio Besomi*, ed. by T. Crivelli, 2 vols, Bellinzona: Casagrande, II, 272–94

CARVER, R. H. F. (1991), 'The Protean Ass: The *Metamorphoses* of Apuleius from Antiquity to the English Renaissance', unpublished DPhil thesis, University of Oxford

——(1998a), '"Transformed in Show": The Rhetoric of Transvestism in Sidney's *Arcadia*', *English Literary Renaissance*, 28, 323–52

——(1998b), 'A New Source for Sidney's *Arcadia*: Pierio Valeriano's *Leucippus* (Text, Translation, and Commentary)', *English Literary Renaissance*, 28, 353–71

——(2001), '*Quis ille?* The Role of the Prologue in Apuleius' *Nachleben*', in *A Companion to the Prologue of Apuleius' 'Metamorphoses'*, ed. by A. Kahane and A. Laird, Oxford: Oxford University Press, pp. 163–74

——(2007), *The Protean Ass: The Metamorphoses of Apuleius from Antiquity to the Renaissance*, Oxford: Oxford University Press

——(2010), 'Apuleius, *Metamorphoses*', in *Die Rezeption der antiken Literatur: Kulturhistorisches Werklexikon*, ed. by Christine Walde (Stuttgart: Verlag J. B. Metzler), Supplemente Band 7 of *Der Neue Pauly* (*Realencyclopädie der classischen Altertumswissenschaft*), pp. 45–62

——(2013a), 'Bologna as Hypata: Annotation, Transformation, and Transl(oc)ation in the Circles of Filippo Beroaldo and Francesco Colonna', in Proceedings of the International Conference on the Ancient Novel IV (Lisbon, 21–26 July 2008), ed. by Marília Futre Pinheiro et al., *Ancient Narrative Supplementum*, Groningen: Barkhuis Publishing & The University Library Groningen

——(2013b), 'Between Photis and Isis: Fiction, Reality, and the Ideal in *The Golden Ass* of Apuleius', in *The Ideal and the Real in the Ancient Novel* (*Ancient Narrative Supplementum*), ed. by Michael Paschalis and Stelios Panayotakis, Groningen: Barkhuis Publishing & The University Library

CASANOVA-ROBIN, H. (ed.) (2009), *Ovide. Figures de l'hybride: Illustrations littéraires et figurées de l'esthétique ovidienne à travers les âges*, Paris: Honoré Champion

CASTIGLIONI, L. (1906), *Studi intorno alle fonti e alla composizione delle Metamorfosi di Ovidio*, Pisa: Ff. Nistri

CERASINI, M. A. (1987), 'Thematic Links in *Arthur Gordon Pym*, "At the Mountains of Madness", and *Moby Dick*', *Crypt of Cthulhu*, 49, 3–20

CHAMBERAS, P. A. (1970), 'The Transfiguration of Christ: A Study in Patristic Exegesis of Scripture', *Saint Vladimir's Theological Quarterly*, 14, 48–65

CHAMBERS, E. K. (1923), *The Elizabethan Stage*, Oxford: Clarendon Press

CHAPIN, D. D. (1971), *Metamorphosis as Punishment and Reward: Pagan and Christian Perspectives*, unpublished doctoral thesis: Cornell University, NY

CHARLES, A., and PETERS, E. K. (2001), *Witchcraft in Europe, 400–1700: A Documentary History*, Philadelphia: University of Pennsylvania Press

CHAUDHURI, S. (1990), 'Metamorphosis', in *The Spenser Encyclopedia*, ed. by A. C. Hamilton, Toronto: University of Toronto Press, pp. 471–72

CHAZELLE, C. (1992), 'Figure, Character, and the Glorified Body in the Carolingian Eucharistic Controversy', *Traditio*, 47, 1–36

CINGANO, E. (ed.) (2010), *Tra panellenismo e tradizioni locali: Generi poetici e storiografia* (Hellenica 34), Alessandria: Edizioni dell'Orso

CIOFFI, C. A. (1994), 'The Anxieties of Ovidian Influence: Theft in Inferno XXIV and XXV', *Dante Studies, with the Annual Report of the Dante Society*, 112, 77–100

CIPOLLONE, A. (1998), '"Né per nova figura il primo alloro...". La chiusa di *Rerum vulgarium fragmenta* XXIII, il *Canzoniere* e Dante', *Rassegna Europea di Letteratura Italiana*, 11, 29–46

——(2009), 'Ovidio nel Petrarca volgare', *Per leggere*, 16, 157–74

CITATI, P. (1989), *Kafka*, trans. by B. Pérol, Paris: Gallimard

CLAIR, J. (1989), *Méduse. Contribution à une anthropologie des arts du visuel*, Gallimard

CLARE, R. J. (2002), *The Path of the Argo: Language, Imagery and Narrative in the Argonautica of Apollonius Rhodius*, Cambridge: Cambridge University Press

CLARK, S. (1991), 'The Rational Witchfinder: Conscience, Demonological Naturalism and Popular Superstition', in *Science, Culture and Popular Belief in Renaissance Europe*, ed. by S. Pumfrey, P. L. Rossi, and M. Slawinski, Manchester: Manchester University Press, pp. 222–48

——(1997), *Thinking with Demons: The Idea of Witchcraft in Early Modern Europe*, Oxford: Oxford University Press

——(2007), *Vanities of the Eye: Vision in Early Modern European Culture*, Oxford: Oxford University Press

CLARK, W., and M. MCMUNN (1989), *Beasts and Birds of the Middle Ages: The Bestiary and its Legacy*, Philadelphia: University of Pennsylvania Press

CLARESON, T. D., and A. S. CLARESON (1990), 'The Neglected Fiction of John Wyndham: "Consider Her Ways", *Trouble with Lichen and Web*', in *Science Fiction Roots and Branches: Contemporary Critical Approaches*, ed. by R. Garnett and R. J. Ellis, London: Macmillan, pp. 88–103

CLARKE, B. (1995), *Allegories of Writing: The Subject of Metamorphosis*, New York: State University of New York Press

——(2008), *Posthuman Metamorphosis: Narrative and Systems*, New York: Fordham University Press

CLASSEN, C. J. (1962), 'Romulus in der römischen Republik', *Philologus*, 106, 174–204

——(1963), 'Gottmenschentum in der römischen Republik', *Gymnasium*, 70, 312–38

CLAUSS, J. J., and ISLE JOHNSTON, S. (eds) (1997), *Medea: Essays on Medea in Myth, Literature, Philosophy and Art*, Princeton, NJ: Princeton University Press

CLAUSS, M. (2011), *Der Kaiser und sein wahrer Gott: Der spätantike Streit um die Natur Christi*, Darmstadt: Primus Verlag

COELSCH-FOISNER, S. (ed.) (2006), *Fantastic Body Transformations in English Literature*, Heidelberg: Winter

COELSCH-FOISNER, S., and W. GÖRTSCHACHER (eds) (2009), *Ovid's Metamorphoses in English Poetry*, Heidelberg: Winter

COELSCH-FOISNER, S., and M. SCHWARZBAUER (eds) (2005), *Metamorphosen*, Heidelberg: Winter

COLE, T. (2008), *Ovidius Mythistoricus: Legendary Time in the Metamorphoses*, Frankfurt a. M.: Peter Lang

COLISH, M. L. (2004), 'Authority and Interpretation in Scholastic Theology', in *Religious Identity and the Problem of Historical Foundation: The Foundational Character of Authoritative Sources in the History of Christianity and Judaism*, ed. by J. Frishman, W. Otten, and G. Rouwhorst, Leiden and Boston, MA: Brill, pp. 369–86

COMPAGNON, A. (1989), *Proust entre deux siècles*, Paris: Le Seuil

COMPARETTI, D. (1966), *Vergil in the Middle Ages*, trans. by E. F. M. Benecke, with an introduction by R. Ellis, London: Allen & Unwin

CONTE, G. B. (1982), 'L'Inventario del Mondo. Ordine e Linguaggio della Natura nell'Opera di Plinio il Vecchio', in *Plinio. Storia Naturale*, I, Turin: Einaudi

——(1996), *The Rhetoric of Imitation*, Ithaca NY: Cornell University Press (1st Ital. edn 1974)

COOPER, H. (1988), 'Chaucer and Ovid', in *Ovid Renewed*, ed. by C. Martindale, Cambridge: Cambridge University Press, pp. 71–81

COPELAND, R., and S. MELVILLE (1991), 'Allegory and Allegoresis, Rhetoric and Hermeneutics', *Exemplaria*, 3.1, 159–87

COPELAND, R., and P. T. STRUCK (eds) (2010), *The Cambridge Companion to Allegory*, Cambridge: Cambridge University Press

COPPER, B. (1977), *The Werewolf in Legend, Fact, and Art*, London: St Martins Press

CORBYN, Z. (2011), 'How the Penis Lost Its Spikes: Humans Ditched DNA to Evolve Smooth Penises and Bigger Brains', *NatureNews*, 9 March 2011 <http://www.nature.com/news/2011/110309/full/news.2011.148.html>

CORNGOLD, S. (1973), *The Commentators' Despair: The Interpretation of Kafka's Metamorphosis*, New York and London: Kennikat Press

——(ed. and tr.) (1996), *Franz Kafka, The Metamorphosis*, New York and London: W. W. Norton and Company

CORNWELL, N. (1990), *The Literary Fantastic*, London: Harvester Wheatsheaf

COULSON, F. T. (1987), 'The Vulgate Commentary on Ovid's *Metamorphoses*', in *Ovid in Medieval Culture [= Mediaevalia 13]*, ed. by M. Desmond, pp. 29–61

——(1991), *The 'Vulgate' Commentary on Ovid's Metamorphoses: The Creation Myth and the Story of Orpheus*, Toronto: Toronto Medieval Latin Texts

——(2007), 'Ovid's Transformations in Medieval France (ca. 1100–ca. 1350)', in *Metamorphosis: The Changing Face of Ovid in Medieval and Early Modern Europe*, ed. by A. Keith and S. Rupp, Toronto: Centre for Reformation and Renaissance Studies, pp. 33–60

COUSAR, C. B. (1990), *A Theology of the Cross: The Death of Jesus in the Pauline Letters*, Minneapolis: Fortress

COWAN, R. (2010), 'A Stranger in a Strange Land: Medea in Roman Republican Tragedy', in *Unbinding Medea: Interdisciplinary Approaches to a Classical Myth from Antiquity to the 21st Century*, ed. by H. Bartel and A. Simon, London: The Modern Humanities Research Association and Maney Publishing, pp. 39–52

CRABBE, A. (1981), 'Structure and Content in Ovid's *Metamorphoses*', *Aufstieg und Niedergang der Römischen Welt*, II. 31.4, 2288–90

CRANE, W. (1907), *An Artist's Reminiscences*, London: The Macmillan Company

CRAVEN, W. G. (1981), *Giovanni Pico Della Mirandola, Symbol of His Age: Modern Interpretations of a Renaissance Philosopher*, Geneva: Droz

DAHAN, G., and R. GOULET (eds) (2005), *Allégorie des Poètes, Allégorie des Philosophes: Études sur la poétique et l'herméneutique de l'allégorie de l'Antiquité à la Réforme*, Paris: J. Vrin

DAHNKE, H.-D. (1989), 'Die Debatte um "Die Götter Griechenlandes"', in *Debatten und Kontroversen: Literarische Auseinandersetzungen in Deutschland am Ende des 18. Jahrhunderts*, ed. by H.-D. Dahnke et al. vol. 1, Berlin: Aufbau Verlag, pp. 193–269

DALLEY, S. (ed. and trans.) (1998), *Myths from Mesopotamia: Creation, The Flood, Gilgamesh, and Others*, Oxford: Oxford University Press

DANTINI, M. (2008), *Modern and Contemporary Art*, New York: Sterling Publishing

DASTON, L., and E. LUNBECK (eds) (2011), *Histories of Scientific Observation*, Chicago, IL, and London: University of Chicago Press

DASTON, L., and PARK, K. (1998), *Wonder and the Order of Nature, 1150–1750*, New York: Zone Books

DAVIS, C. (1988), *Michel Tournier: Philosophy and Fiction*, Oxford: Clarendon Press

DAVIS, S. T. (1997), '"Seeing" the Risen Jesus', in *The Resurrection: An Interdisciplinary Symposium on the Resurrection of Jesus*, ed. by S. T. Davis et al., Oxford: Oxford University Press, pp. 126–47

DAY, J. (1997), 'Resurrection Imagery from Baal to the Book of Daniel', in *Congress Volume, Cambridge 1995*, ed. by J. A. Emerton, Leiden, New York, Cologne: Brill, pp. 125–34

DE BEAUVOIR, S. (1997), *The Second Sex*, trans. by H. M. Parshley, London: Vintage

DE JONG, I. J. F. (2001), *A Narratological Commentary on the Odyssey*, Cambridge: Cambridge University Press

DELEUZE, G. (1964), *Proust et les signes*, Paris: Presses Universitaires de France

DE LUBAC, H. (1959–64), *Exégèse médiéval: Les Quatre Sens de l'Écriture*, 4 vols, Paris: Édition Montaigne

DE MELY, F. (1890), 'Les Reliques du Lait de la Vierge et la Galactite', *Revue Archéologique*, 15, 103–16

DE NICHILO, M. (1975), *I poemi astrologici di Giovanni Pontano: Storia del testo. Con un saggio di edizione critica del 'Meteororum liber'*, Bari: Dedalo

——(1977), 'Lo sconosciuto apografo avellinese del *De hortis Hesperidum* di Giovanni Pontano', *Filologia e critica*, 2, 217–46

DENTE, C., G. FERZOCO, M. GILL and M. SPUNTA (eds) (2005), *Proteus: The Language Of Metamorphosis* (Aldershot: Ashgate, 2005)

DERRIDA, J. (1972), *La Dissémination*, Paris: Editions du Seuil

DETIENNE, M. (1977), *Dionysos Mis à Mort*, Paris: Gallimard

——(2001), *Les Jardins d'Adonis: La Mythologie des aromates en Grèce*, Paris: Gallimard (1st edn 1972)

DEVUN, L. (2008), 'The Jesus Hermaphrodite: Science and Sex Difference in Premodern Europe', *Journal of the History of Ideas*, 69, 193–218

DICKENSON, M., and J. EVANS (2006), *Ents, Elves and Eriador: The Environmental Vision of J. R. R. Tolkien*, Lexington: University of Kentucky Press

DIETE, J. (1905), *Komposition und Quellenbenutzung in Ovids Metamorphosen*, Hamburg: Lütcke & Wulff

DI LELLO-FINUOLI, A. L. (2000), 'Per la storia del testo di Ateneo', in *Miscellanea Bibliothecae Apostolicae Vaticanae VII*, Vatican City: Biblioteca Apostolica Vaticana, 129–82

DILLON, M. P. J. (2006), '"Woe for Adonis": But in Spring, not Summer', *Hermes*, 131, 1–16

DIONISOTTI, A. C. (1982), 'From Ausonius' Schooldays? A Schoolbook and its Relatives', *Journal of Roman Studies*, 72, 83–125

DIONISOTTI, C. (2009a), 'Appunti sulle *Rime* del Sannazaro' (1963), in *Scritti di storia della letteratura italiana*, ed. by T. Basile, V. Fera, S. Villari, 4 vols, Rome: Edizioni di Storia e Letteratura, 2009, II, 1–37

——(2009b), '*Juvenilia* del Pontano' (1964), in *Scritti di storia della letteratura italiana*, II, 73–94

DOBRIN, S., and K. KIDD (eds) (2004), *Wild Things: Children's Culture and Ecocriticism*, Detroit, MI: Wayne State University Press

DOBROV, G. (1997), *The City as Comedy: Society and Representation in Athenian Drama*, Chapel Hill: University of North Carolina Press

DODDS, E. R. (1960), *Euripides, Bacchae, edited with introduction and commentary*, Oxford: Clarendon Press

DOLLIMORE, J. (2003), *Death, Desire and Loss in Western Culture*, London: Routledge

——(2004), *Radical Tragedy: Religion, Ideology and Power in the Drama of Shakespeare and His Contemporaries*, 3rd edn, Durham, NC: Duke University Press

DOUGHERTY, M. V. (2008), *Pico della Mirandola: New Essays*, Cambridge: Cambridge University Press, 2008

DOUGLAS, A. (1994), *The Beast Within: A History of the Werewolf*, New York: Avon Books

DOWDEN, K. (2000), *European Paganism: The Realities of Cult from Antiquity to the Middle Ages*, Routledge: London and New York

DRONKE, P. (1974), *Fabula: Explorations into the Uses of Myth in Medieval Platonism*, Leiden and Köln: Brill

DUE, O. T. (1974), *Changing Forms: Studies in the Metamorphoses of Ovid*, Copenhagen: Gyldendale

DUFFIN, C. J. (2005), 'The Western Lapidary Tradition in Early Geological Literature: Medicinal and Magical Minerals', *Geology Today*, 21, 58–63

DUNN, J. D. G. (1989), *Christology in the Making: A New Testament Inquiry into the Origins of the Doctrine of the Incarnation*, London: SCM (prev. edn. 1980)

——(2001), 'The Ascension of Jesus: A Test Case for Hermeneutics', in *Auferstehung — Resurrection. The Fourth Durham–Tübingen Research Symposium Resurrection, Transfiguration and Exaltation in Old Testament, Ancient Judaism and Early Christianity (Tübingen, September, 1999)*, ed. by F. Avemarie and H. Lichtenberger, Tübingen: Mohr Siebeck, pp. 301–22

DUPLESSIS, N. M. (2004), 'ecoLewis: Conservationism and Anticolonialism in *The Chronicles of Narnia*', in *Wild Things: Children's Culture and Ecocriticism*, ed. by S. Dobrin and K. Kidd, Detroit, MI: Wayne State University Press, pp. 115–27

Eagleton, T. (2003), *Sweet Violence: The Idea of the Tragic*, Oxford: Blackwell

Edwards, A. (1985), *Odysseus against Achilles: The Role of Allusion in the Homeric Epic*, Königstein im Taunus: Hain

Eichholz, D. E. (1949), 'Aristotle's Theory of the Formation of Metals and Minerals', *Classical Quarterly*, 43, 141–46

——(1967), 'Some Mineralogical Problems in Theophrastus' *De Lapidibus*', *Classical Quarterly*, 17, 103–09

Elsner, J. (1992), 'Pausanias: A Greek Pilgrim in the Roman World', *Past & Present*, 135, 3–29

Empson, W. (1981), *Milton's God*, Cambridge: Cambridge University Press

Ernst, G. (2006), 'Cardano e le streghe', *Bruniana et Campanelliana*, 12, 395–410

Erskine, A. (2001), *Troy between Greece and Rome: Local Tradition and Imperial Power*, Oxford: Oxford University Press

Evans, G. R. (1990), *Augustine on Evil*, Cambridge: Cambridge University Press

Evans, R. J. W., and A. Marr (2006), *Curiosity and Wonder from the Renaissance to the Enlightenment*, London: Ashgate Publishing

Fabre-Serris, J. (2009), 'Constructing a Narrative of *mira deum*: The Story of Philemon and Baucis (Ovid, *Metamorphoses* 8), in *Paradox and the Marvellous in Augustan Literature and Culture*, ed. by P. Hardie, Oxford: Oxford University Press, pp. 231–47

Fambach, O. (1957), *Schiller und sein Kreis*, Berlin: Akademie-Verlag (= *Ein Jahrhundert deutscher Literaturkritik. 1750 — 1850*, vol. 2)

Fantham, E. (1990), '*Nymphas ... e navibus esse*: Decorum and Poetic Fiction in *Aeneid* 9. 77–122 and 10. 215–59', *Classical Philology*, 85.2, 102–19

Fattori, M., and M. Bianchi (eds) (1998), *Phantasia~Imaginatio*, Rome: Edizioni dell'Ateneo

Fauth, W. (1975), 'Zur Typologie mythischer Metamorphosen in der homerischen Dichtung', *Poetica*, 7, 235–68

Feeney, D. C. (1991), *The Gods in Epic: Poets and Critics of the Classical Tradition*, Oxford: Oxford University Press

——(1993), 'Epilogue', in *Lies and Fiction in the Ancient World*, ed. by T. P. Wiseman and C. Gill, Exeter: Exeter University Press, pp. 151–55

——(1998), *Literature and Religion at Rome: Cultures, Context, and Beliefs*, Cambridge: Cambridge University Press

——(1999), '*Mea Tempora*: Patterning of Time in the *Metamorphoses*', in *Ovidian Transformations: Essays on Ovid's Metamorphoses and its Reception*, ed. by P. Hardie, A. Barchiesi, and S. Hinds, Cambridge: Cambridge Philological Society, pp. 13–30

——(2005), 'Review Article: The Beginnings of a Literature in Latin', *Journal of Roman Studies*, 95, 226–40

Feldherr, A. (2002), 'Metamorphosis in the *Metamorphoses*', in *The Cambridge Companion to Ovid*, ed. by P. Hardie, Cambridge: Cambridge University Press, pp. 163–79

——(2010), *Playing Gods: Ovid's Metamorphoses and the Politics of Fiction*, Princeton, NJ, and Oxford: Princeton University Press

Ferber, M. (1999), *Dictionary of Literary Symbols*, Cambridge: Cambridge University Press

Ferzoco, G., and M. Gill (2005), 'Introduction. *De hereditate Protei*: Ways of Metamorphoses', *Proteus: The Language of Metamorphosis*, ed. by C. Dente, G. Ferzoco, M. Gill, and M. Spunta, Aldershot: Ashgate, pp. 1–9

Fiedrowicz, M. (2000), *Apologie im frühen Christentum: Die Kontroverse um den christlichen Wahrheitsanspruch in den ersten Jahrhunderten*, 3rd updated and expanded edition, Paderborn: Schöningh

Finkelpearl, E. D. (1998), *Metamorphosis of Language in Apuleius: A Study of Allusion in the Novel*, Ann Arbor: Michigan University Press

FLAIG, E. (1993), 'Politisierte Lebensführung und ästhetische Kultur: eine semiotische Untersuchung am römischen Adel', *Historische Anthropologie*, 1, 193–217

——(1995), 'Die *pompa funebris*: Adlige Konkurrenz und annalistische Erinnerung in der Römischen Republik', in *Memoria als Kultur*, ed. by O. G. Oexle, Göttingen: Vandenhoeck & Ruprecht, pp. 115–48

——(1999), 'Über die Grenzen der Akkulturation: Wider die Verdinglichung des Kulturbegriffs', in *Rezeption und Identität: Die kulturelle Auseinandersetzung Roms mit Griechenland als europäisches Paradigma*, ed. by G. Vogt-Spira and B. Rommel, Stuttgart: Franz Steiner Verlag, 81–112

——(2003), *Ritualisierte Politik: Zeichen, Gesten und Herrschaft im Alten Rom*, Göttingen: Vandenhoeck & Ruprecht

FLETCHER, R. (2005), 'Or Such as Ovid's *Metamorphoses*...', in *The Hesiodic Catalogue of Women: Constructions and Reconstructions*, ed. by R. Hunter, Cambridge: Cambridge University Press, pp. 299–319

FLETCHER-LOUIS, C. H. T. (1997), *Luke-Acts: Angels, Christology and Soteriology*, Tübingen: Mohr Siebeck

——(2001), 'The Revelation of the Sacral Son of Man. The Genre, History of Religions Context and the Meaning of the Transfiguration', in *Auferstehung — Resurrection. The Fourth Durham-Tübingen Research Symposium Resurrection, Transfiguration and Exaltation in Old Testament, Ancient Judaism and Early Christianity (Tübingen, September, 1999)*, ed. by F. Avemarie and H. Lichtenberger, Tübingen: Mohr Siebeck, pp. 247–98

FLORIDIA, S. (1936), *Gli agrumi*, Catania: Muglia

FLOWER, H. I. (1996), *Ancestor Masks and Aristocratic Power in Roman Culture*, Oxford: Oxford University Press

FORBES IRVING, P. M. C. (1990), *Metamorphosis in Greek Myths*, Oxford: Oxford University Press

FOSSUM, J. E. (1995), *The Image of the Invisible God: Essays on the Influence of Jewish Mysticism on Early Christianity*, Göttingen: Vandenhoeck & Ruprecht

FOWLER, R. (2006), ' "This tart fable": Daphne and Apollo in Modern Women's Poetry', in *Laughing with Medusa: Classical Myth and Feminist Thought*, ed. by V. Zajko and M. Leonard, Oxford: Oxford University Press, pp. 381–98

FOX, C. (2007), 'Authorising the Metamorphic Witch: Ovid in Reginald Scot's Discoverie of Witchcraft', in *Metamorphosis: The Changing Face of Ovid in Medieval and Early Modern Europe*, ed. by A. Keith and S. Rupp, Toronto: Centre for Reformation and Renaissance Studies, pp. 165–78

FRÄNKEL, H. (1945), *Ovid: A Poet between Two Worlds*, Berkeley: University of California Press

FRANKFURTER, D. (2001), 'The Perils of Love: Magic and Countermagic in Coptic Egypt', in *Sexuality in Late Antiquity*, ed. by Daniel Boyarin and Elizabeth A. Castelli, special issue of *Journal of the History of Sexuality*, 10.3/4, pp. 480–500

FRAZER, J. G. (1914), *The Dying God*, London: Macmillan

——(1919), *Adonis Attis Osiris: Studies in the History of Oriental Religion*. 3rd edn, revised and enlarged, 2 vols, London: Macmillan

FRÉCAUT, J. M. (1985), 'Un thème particulier dans les Métamorphoses d'Ovide: Le Personnage métamorphosé gardant la conscience de soi (*Mens antiqua manet*: II, 485)', *Journées ovidiennes de Parménie. Actes du Colloque sur Ovide 24–26 juin 1983*, ed. by J. M. Frécaut and D. Porte, Bruxelles: Société d'études latines, pp. 115–43

FRECCERO, J. (1975), 'The Fig Tree and the Laurel: Petrarch's Poetics', *Diacritics*, 5, 34–40

FRICK, W. (1998), 'Schiller und die Antike', *Schiller-Handbuch*, ed. by H. Koopmann, Stuttgart: Kröner, pp. 91–116

FRONTISI-DUCROUX, F. (1996), 'Andromède et la Naissance du Corail', in *Mythes Grecs au*

Figuré de l'Antiquité au Baroque, ed. by S. Georgoudi and J. P. Vernant, Paris: Gallimard, pp. 135–65

FRÜHWALD, W. (1969), 'Die Auseinandersetzung um Schillers Gedicht "Die Götter Griechenlandes"', *Jahrbuch der Deutschen Schillergesellschaft*, 13, 251–71

FUCECCHI, M. (2009), 'Encountering the Fantastic: Expectations, Forms of Communication, Reactions', in *Paradox and the Marvellous in Augustan Literature and Culture*, ed. by P. Hardie, Oxford: Oxford University Press, pp. 213–30

FUHRMANN, M. (1990), 'Die antiken Mythen im christlich-heidnischen Weltanschauungskampf der Spätantike', *Antike & Abendland*, 36, 138–51

FUKUYAMA, F. (2002), *Our Posthuman Future: Consequences of the Biotechnology Revolution*, New York: Farrar Straus & Giroux

FULLER, S. (2011), *Humanity 2.0: What It Means to be Human Past, Present and Future*, Basingstoke: Palgrave Macmillan

FUNKENSTEIN, A. (1986), *Theology and the Scientific Imagination from the Middle Ages to the Seventeenth Century*, Princeton, NJ: Princeton University Press

FURNISH, V. P. (1984), *The Anchor Bible: II Corinthians. Translated with introduction, notes and commentary*, New York: Doubleday

GAISSER, J. H. (2008), *The Fortunes of Apuleius and the Golden Ass. A Study in Transmission and Reception*, Princeton, NJ: Princeton University Press

GALASSO, L. (2000), *Ovidio, Opere II: Le metamorfosi*, edizione con testo a fronte, traduzione di Guido Paduano, introduzione di Alessandro Perutelli, commento di Luigi Galasso, Turin: Giulio Einaudi

GALINSKY, K. (1975), *Ovid's Metamorphoses: An Introduction to the Basic Aspects*, Oxford: Blackwell

GALLESIO, G. (1811), *Traité du Citrus*, Paris: L. Fantin

GANN, T. (2007), *Gehirn und Züchtung: Gottfried Benns psychiatrische Poetik, 1910– 1933/34*, Bielefeld: Transcript Verlag

GANTZ, T. (1993), *Early Greek Myth: A Guide to Literary and Artistic Sources*, Baltimore, MD: Johns Hopkins University Press

GÄRTNER, T. (2007), 'Die Geschlechtsmetamorphose der ovidischen Caenis und ihr hellenistischer Hintergrund', *Latomus*, 66, 891–99

GATTÉGNO, J. (1992), *La Science-Fiction*, 5th edition, Paris: Presses Universitaires de France

GENETTE, G. (1972), *Figures III*, Paris: Seuil

GEORGOUDI, S. (1988), 'La Mer, la mort et le discours des épigrammes funéraires', *Annali. Sezione di Archeologia e Storia Antica*, 10, 53–61

GEPPERT, A., and T. KÖSSLER (2011), *Wunder: Poetik und Politik des Staunens im 20. Jahrhundert* (Berlin: Suhrkamp Verlag, 2011)

GERHARD, E. S. (1942), 'Schiller's "Die Götter Griechenlands"', *The German Quarterly*, 15, 86–92

GERKEN, M. (2007), *The Picture of Dorian Gray and Gothicism*, GRIN Verlag

GERTZ, S. K. (2003), *Echoes and Reflections: Memory and Memorials in Ovid and Marie de France*, New York: Rodopi

GHISALBERTI, F. (1933), *Giovanni del Virgilio espositore delle 'Metamorfosi'*, Florence: Olschki

GIANNINI, A. (1963), 'Studi sulla paradossografia greca, I. Da Omero a Callimaco: Motivi e forme del meraviglioso', *RIL*, 97, 247–66

——(1964), 'Studi sulla paradossografia greca, II. Da Callimaco all'età imperiale: La letteratura paradossografica', *Acme*, 17, 99–140

GIANNINI, A. (ed. and trans.) (1966), *Paradoxographorum Graecorum reliquiae*, Milan: Istituto Editoriale Italiano

GIGLIONI, G. (2010), 'Fantasy Islands: *Utopia, The Tempest* and *New Atlantis* as Places of Controlled Credulousness', in *World-Building in Early Modern Natural Philosophy*, ed. by Allison Kavey, New York: Palgrave Macmillan, 91–117

——(2012), 'Coping with Inner and Outer Demons: Marsilio Ficino's Theory of the Imagination', in *Diseases of the Imagination and Imaginary Diseases: Disease in the Early Modern Period*, ed. by Yasmin Haskell, Turnhout: Brepols, pp. 19–50

GILDENHARD, I. (2003), 'Review of Suerbaum (2002)', *Bryn Mawr Classical Review*, 2003.09.39

——(2009a), 'Gelegenheitsmetaphysik: Religiöse Semantik in Reden Ciceros', in *Römische Religion im historischen Wandel: Diskursentwicklung von Plautus bis Ovid*, ed. by A. Bendlin and J. Rüpke, Stuttgart: Franz Steiner Verlag, pp. 87–112

——(2009b), 'Ontological Fluidity', in *Jane Alexander: On Being Human*, ed. P. Subirós, Durham: Institute of Advanced Study, pp. 28–31

——(2010), 'Buskins and SPQR: The Roman Reception of Greek Tragedy', in *Beyond the Fifth Century: Interactions with Greek Tragedy from the Fourth Century BCE to the Middle Ages*, ed. by I. Gildenhard and M. Revermann, Berlin and New York: de Gruyter, pp. 153–85

——(2011), *Creative Eloquence: The Construction of Reality in Cicero's Speeches*, Oxford: Oxford University Press

GILDENHARD, I., and A. ZISSOS (1999a), 'Problems of Time in *Metamorphoses 2*', in *Ovidian Transformations: Essays on Ovid's Metamorphoses and its Reception*, ed. by P. Hardie, A. Barchiesi, and S. Hinds, Cambridge: Cambridge Philological Society, pp. 31–47

——(1999b), 'Somatic Economies: Tragic Bodies and Poetic Design in Ovid's *Metamorphoses*', in *Ovidian Transformations: Essays on Ovid's Metamorphoses and its Reception*, ed. by P. Hardie, A. Barchiesi, and S. Hinds, Cambridge: Cambridge Philological Society, pp. 162–81

——(2004), 'Ovid's "Hecale": Deconstructing Athens in the *Metamorphoses*', *Journal of Roman Studies*, 94, 47–72

——(2007), 'Barbarian Variations: Tereus, Procne and Philomela in Ovid (*Met.* 6.412–674) and Beyond', *Dictynna*, 4, 1–25

——(2010), 'Metamorphosis: Angles of Approach', *Insights*, 3.12, 1–14 <http://www.dur.ac.uk/ias/insights/>

GINSBERG, W. (1989), 'Ovid's *Metamorphoses* and the Politics of Interpretation' *Classical Journal*, 84, 222–31

——(1991), 'Dante, Ovid, and the Transformation of Metamorphosis', *Traditio*, 46, 205–33

GIRARD, R. (1961), 'Les Mondes proustiens', in *Mensonge romantique et vérité*, Paris: Grasset, pp. 197–230

GLEASON, M. W. (1995), *Making Men: Sophists and Self-Presentation in Ancient Rome*, Princeton, NJ: Princeton University Press

GNILKA, C. (1984), *Chrêsis: Die Methode der Kirchenväter im Umgang mit der antiken Kultur 1: Der Begriff des 'rechten Gebrauchs'*, Basel: Schwabe

——(1988), *Das Matthäusevangelium II. Teil: Kommentar zu Kap. 14, 1–28, 20 und Einleitungsfragen*, Freiburg, Basel, and Vienna: Herder

——(1993), *Chrêsis: Die Methode der Kirchenväter im Umgang mit der antiken Kultur 2: Kultur und Conversion*, Basel: Schwabe

GODWIN, W. (1834), *Lives of the Necromancers*, London: Frederick J. Mason

GOERING, J. W. (1991), 'The Invention of Transubstantiation', *Traditio. Studies in Ancient and Medieval History, Thought and Religion*, 46, 147–70

GÖTZ, I. L. (2002), *Faith, Humor, and Paradox*, Westport, CT: Praeger

GOLDBERG, S. M. (2005), *Constructing Literature in the Roman Republic: Poetry and its Reception*, Cambridge: Cambridge University Press

GOLDHILL, S. (ed.) (2001), *Being Greek under Rome: Cultural Identity, the Second Sophistic and the Development of Empire*, Cambridge: Cambridge University Press

——(2011), *Victorian Culture and Classical Antiquity: Art, Opera, Fiction, and the Proclamation of Modernity*, Princeton, NJ: Princeton University Press

GOMME, A. W. (1956), *A Historical Commentary on Thucydides, Volume II: The Ten Years' War, Books II–III*, Oxford: Clarendon Press

GOTTER, U. (2000), 'Akkulturation als Methodenproblem der historischen Wissenschaften', in *wir/ihr/sie. Identität und Alterität in Theorie und Methode*, ed. by W. Eßbach, Würzburg: Ergon Verlag, pp. 373–406

——(2008), 'Cultural Differences and Cross-Cultural Contact: Greek and Roman Concepts of "Power"', *Harvard Studies in Classical Philology*, 104, 179–230

GOTTWALD, H. (2005), 'Die Metamorphose aus mythostheoretischer und literaturwissenschaftlicher Sicht', in *Konzepte der Metamorphose in den Geisteswissenschaften*, ed. by H. Gottwald and H. Klein, Heidelberg: Winter, pp. 81–102

GOTTWALD, H., and H. KLEIN (eds) (2005), *Konzepte der Metamorphose in den Geisteswissenschaften*, Heidelberg: Winter

GOW, A. S. F. (1952), 'Introduction', in *Bucolici Graeci* recensuit A. S. F. Gow, Oxford: Clarendon Press, pp. i–xxiii

GOW, A. S. F., and A. F. SCHOLFIELD (1953), *Nicander: The Poems and Poetical Fragments*, ed. with introduction, translation, and notes, Cambridge: Cambridge University Press

GOWERS, E. (1993), *The Loaded Table: Representations of Food in Roman Literature*, Oxford: Oxford University Press

GRAF, F. (1988), 'Ovide, les *Métamorphoses* et la véracité du mythe', in *Métamorphoses du Mythe en Grèce*, ed. by C. Calame, Geneva, pp. 57–70

GRAFTON, A., and N. SIRAISI (1992), *New Worlds, Ancient Texts: The Power of Tradition and the Shock of Discovery*, Cambridge, MA: Harvard University Press

GRAHAM, E. L. (2002), *Representations of the Post/Human: Monsters, Aliens and Others in Popular Culture*, Manchester: Manchester University Press

GRANT, W. L. (1965), *Neo-Latin Literature and the Pastoral*, Chapel Hill: University of North Carolina Press

GRAVERINI, L. (2004–05), 'A Booklike Self: Ovid and Apuleius', *Hermathena*, 177/178, 225–50

GRAYSON, C. (1970), 'Bonincontri, Lorenzo', in *Dizionario biografico degli Italiani*, Rome: Istituto della Enciclopedia Italiana, 1960–, 12, 209–11

GREEN, M. (2009), *Milton's Ovidian Eve*, Farnham, Surrey: Ashgate

GREEN, R. P. H. (1982), 'The Genesis of a Medieval Textbook: The Models and Sources of the *Ecloga Theoduli*', *Viator*, 13, 49–106

GREENBLATT, S. (1980), *Renaissance Self-Fashioning: From More to Shakespeare*, Chicago, IL: Chicago University Press

——(1991), *Marvelous Possessions: The Wonder of the New World*, Chicago, IL: University of Chicago Press

——(2011), *The Swerve: How the World Became Modern*, New York: W. W. Norton & Co.

GREG, W. W. (1946), 'The Damnation of Faustus', *Modern Language Review*, 41, 106–07

GRIFFIN, J. (1977), 'The Epic Cycle and the Uniqueness of Homer', *Journal of Hellenic Studies*, 97, 39–53

——(1980), *Homer on Life and Death*, Oxford: Oxford University Press

——(1986), 'Homeric Words and Speakers', *Journal of Hellenic Studies*, 106, 36–57

GRIFFITH, M. (ed.) (1983), *Aeschylus, Prometheus Bound*, Cambridge: Cambridge University Press

GRIFFITH, D. R. (1987), 'The Hoopoe's Name (A Note on *Birds* 48)', *Quaderni Urbinati di Cultura Classica*, New Series, 26.2, 59–63

GRIFFITHS, J. G. (1975), *The Isis-Book (Metamorphoses, Book XI)*, Leiden: E. J. Brill

GROSS, K. (1985), 'Infernal Metamorphoses: An Interpretation of Dante's "Counterpass"', *Modern Language Notes*, 100, 42–69

GRUEN, E. S. (1992), *Culture and National Identity in Republican Rome*, Ithaca, NY: Cornell University Press

Gruppe, O. (1921), *Geschichte der klassischen Mythologie und Religionsgeschichte während des Mittelalters im Abendland und während der Neuzeit*, in *Ausführliches Lexikon der griechischen und römischen Mythologie*, ed. by W. H. Roscher, vol. 10 (Supplement), Leipzig: Teubner

Gualdo Rosa, L., and P. Osmond (2009), 'Piero Tamira', *Repertorium Pomponianum*, <www.repertoriumpomponianum.it/pomponiani/tamira_piero.htm> (consulted 16 June 2010)

Guidorizzi, G. (2000), *Igino, Miti*, Milan: Adelphi

Habicht, C. (1985), 'An Ancient Baedeker and his Critics: Pausanias' *Guide to Greece*', *Proceedings of the American Philosophical Society*, 129, 220–24

Habinek, T. (1998), *The Politics of Latin Literature: Writing, Identity, and Empire in Ancient Rome*, Princeton, NJ: Princeton University Press

——(2005), *The World of Roman Song: From Ritualized Speech to Social Order*, Baltimore, MD: Johns Hopkins University Press

Haehling, R. von (ed.) (2005), *Griechische Mythologie und frühes Christentum*, Darmstadt: Wissenschaftliche Buchgesellschaft

Hagedorn, A. C. (ed.) (2005), *Perspectives on the Song of Songs — Perspektiven der Hoheliedauslegung*, Berlin and New York: Walter de Gruyter

Hagendahl, H. (1958), *Latin Fathers and the Classics*, Stockholm: Almqvist & Wiksell

——(1967), *Augustine and the Latin Classics*, 2 vols, Guteborg: Acta Universitatis Cothoburgensis

Hahn, A. (2006), 'Verwandlungszwänge: Identitätsbrüche zwischen natürlichen und juristischen Personen (oder der aristophanische Fehlschluß)', in *Verwandlungen. Archäologie der literarischen Kommunikation IX*, ed. by A. and J. Assmann, Munich: Wilhelm Fink Verlag, pp. 47–65

Halacy, D. S. (1965), *Cyborg: Evolution of the Superman*, New York: Harper and Row

Hall, E. (1996), 'When Is a Myth Not a Myth? Bernal's Ancient Model', in *Black Athena Revisited*, ed. by M. R. Lefkowitz and G. M. Rogers, Chapel Hill: University of North Carolina Press, pp. 333–48

——(2008), *The Return of Ulysses: A Cultural History of Homer's Odyssey*, London: I. B. Tauris

Hall, E., F. Macintosh, and O. Taplin (eds) (2000), *Medea in Performance, 1500–2000*, Oxford: Legenda

Halleux, R. (1970), 'Fécondité des mines et sexualité des pierres dans l'antiquité gréco-romaine', *Revue Belge de Philologie et d'Histoire*, 48, 16–25

Halleux, R., and J. Schamp (1985), *Les Lapidaires Grecs*, Paris: Les Belles Lettres

Halna-Klein, E. (1995), 'Sur les traces du lynx', *Médiévales*, 28, 119–28

Hamel, Y. (2006), *La Bataille des mémoires: La Seconde Guerre mondiale et le roman français*, Presses de l'Université de Montréal

Hankey, T. (1998), 'La *Genealogia deorum* di Paolo da Perugia', in *Gli Zibaldoni di Boccaccio: Memoria, scrittura, riscrittura. Atti del Seminario internazionale di Firenze-Certaldo (26–28 aprile 1996)*, ed. by M. Picone and C. Cazalé Bérard, Florence: Cesati, pp. 81–94

Haraway, D. (1991), *Simians, Cyborgs, and Women: The Reinvention of Nature*, New York: Routledge

Hardie, P. R. (1986), *Virgil's Aeneid: Cosmos and Imperium*, Oxford: Clarendon Press

——(1992), 'Augustan Poets and the Mutability of Rome', in *Roman Poetry and Propaganda in the Age of Augustus*, ed. by A. Powell, London: Bristol Classical Press, pp. 59–82

——(2002a), *Ovid's Poetics of Illusion*, Cambridge: Cambridge University Press

——(ed.) (2002b), *The Cambridge Companion to Ovid*, Cambridge: Cambridge University Press

——(2002c), 'The Historian in Ovid. The Roman History of *Metamorphoses* 14–15', in *Clio and the Poets: Augustan Poetry and the Traditions of Ancient Historiography*, ed. by D. S. Levene and D. Nelis, Leiden: Brill, pp. 191–210

——(2005), 'The Hesiodic *Catalogue of Women* and Latin Poetry' in *The Hesiodic Catalogue of Women: Constructions and Reconstructions*, ed. by R. Hunter, Cambridge: Cambridge University Press, pp. 287–98

——(2008), 'Review of C. Zgoll, *Phänomenologie der Metamorphose*', *Gnomon*, 80, 175–77

——(2009), 'The Speech of Pythagoras in Ovid *Metamorphoses* 15: Empedoclean Epos', in *Lucretian Receptions: History, The Sublime, Knowledge*, Cambridge: Cambridge University Press, pp. 136–52

HARRIES, B. (1990), 'The Spinner and the Poet: Arachne in Ovid's *Metamorphoses*', *Proceedings of the Cambridge Philological Society*, 36, 64–82

HARRISON, R. P. (1992), *Wälder: Ursprung und Spiegel der Kultur*, Munich and Vienna: Carl Hanser Verlag

HARRISON, S. J. (1998), 'The Milesian Tales and the Roman Novel', *Groningen Colloquia on the Novel*, 9, 61–73

——(2000), *Apuleius: A Latin Sophist*, Oxford: Oxford University Press

HARRISON, S. J. and M. WINTERBOTTOM (2001), 'The Prologue to Apuleius' Metamorphoses: Text, Translation, and Commentary', in *A Companion to the Prologue of Apuleius' Metamorphoses*, ed. by A. Kahane and A. Laird, Oxford: Oxford University Press, pp. 9–15

HARVEY, A. E. (1994), '"They discussed among themselves what this 'rising from the dead' could mean" (Mark 9. 10)', in *Resurrection: Essays in Honour of Leslie Houlden*, ed. by S. C. Barton and G. Stanton, London: Society for Promoting Christian Knowledge, pp. 69–78

HARVEY, E. R. (1975), *The Inward Wits: Psychological Theory in the Middle Ages and the Renaissance*, London: Warburg

HASSIG, D. (1995), *Medieval Bestiaries: Text, Image, Ideology*, Cambridge: Cambridge University Press

HASSINE, J. (2001), 'Biblisme et intertextualité dans l'œuvre proustienne', *Revue des lettres modernes: Marcel Proust*, 3, 179–97

HAUBOLD, J. (2002), 'Greek Epic: A Near Eastern Genre?', *Proceedings of the Cambridge Philological Society*, 48, 1–19

——(2005), 'Heracles in the Hesiodic Catalogue of Women', in *The Hesiodic Catalogue of Women: Constructions and Reconstructions*, ed. by R. Hunter, Cambridge: Cambridge University Press, pp. 85–98

HAUG, W. (ed.) (1979), *Formen und Funktionen der Allegorie. Symposium Wolfenbüttel 1978*, Stuttgart: DVJS Schriftenreihe

HAWORTH-BOOTH, M. (1994), 'Introduction', in *Metamorphoses: Photography in the Electronic Age*, New York: Aperture

HAYLES, N. K. (1999), *How We Became Posthuman: Virtual Bodies in Cybernetics, Literature, and Informatics*, Chicago, IL, and London: University of Chicago Press

HEALY, J. F. (1999), *Pliny the Elder on Science and Technology*, Oxford: Oxford University Press

HEGERFELDT, A. (2005), *Lies that Tell the Truth: Magical Realism Seen through Contemporary Fiction*, Amsterdam: Editions Rodopi

HEHN, V. (1911/1885), *Kulturpflanzen und Haustiere in ihrem Übergang aus Asien nach Griechenland und Italien sowie in das übrige Europa. 8. Auflage*, Berlin: Borntraeger (abridged English translation: *The Wanderings of Plants and Animals from their First Home*, trans. J. S. Stallybrass, London: Swan Sonnenschein and Co., 1885)

HEIL, J. P. (2000), *The Transfiguration of Jesus: Narrative Meaning and Function of Mark 9:2–8, Matt 17:1–8 and Luke 9:28–36*, Rome: Editrice Pontificio Istituto Biblico

HENDERSON, J. (1992), 'The *dēmos* and the Comic Competition', in *Nothing To Do With Dionysos? Athenian Drama in Its Social Context*, ed. by J. J. Winkler and F. I. Zeitlin, Princeton, NJ: Princeton University Press, pp. 271–313

HENRY, E. (1988), 'Seneca's Hecuba', *Bulletin of the Institute of Classical Studies*, 35, Supplement 51, 44–52

HERREN, M. (2007), 'Reflections on the Meaning of the *Ecloga Theoduli*: Where is the Authorial Voice?', in *Poetry and Exegesis in Premodern Latin Christianity: The Encounter between Classical and Christian Strategies of Interpretation*, ed. by W. Otten & K. Pollmann, Leiden and Boston: Brill, pp. 199–230

HESELHAUS, C. (1953), 'Metamorphose-Dichtungen und Metamorphose-Anschauungen', *Euphorion*, 47, 121–46

HIGHET, G. (1976), *The Classical Tradition*, Oxford and New York: Oxford University Press [1949]

HILDBURGH, W. L. (1951), 'Some Spanish Amulets Connected with Lactation', *Folklore*, 62.4, 43–48

HINDS, S. (1987), *Metamorphosis of Persephone: Ovid and the Self-Conscious Muse*, Cambridge: Cambridge University Press

——(1994), 'Medea in Ovid: Scenes from the Life of an Intertextual Heroine', *Materiali e discussioni per l'analisi dei testi classici*, 30, 9–47

HIRSCH, B. D. (2005), 'An Italian Werewolf in London: Lycanthropy and *The Duchess of Malfi*', *Early Modern Literary Studies*, 11.2, 1–43

HOFMANN, M., and J. LASDUN (ed.) (1994), *After Ovid: New Metamorphoses*, London: Faber and Faber

HÖLKESKAMP, K.-J. (1999), 'Römische *gentes* und griechische Genealogien', in *Rezeption und Identität: Die kulturelle Auseinandersetzung Roms mit Griechenland als europäisches Paradigma*, ed. by G. Vogt-Spira and B. Rommel, Stuttgart: Franz Steiner Verlag, 3–21. [Reprinted, with bibliographical update, in: *Senatus Populusque Romanus: Die politische Kultur der Republik — Dimensionen und Deutungen*, Stuttgart 2004, pp. 199–217.]

HOLLAND, J. (2009), *German Romanticism and Science: The Procreative Poetics of Goethe, Novalis, and Ritter*, London and New York: Routledge)

HOLLAND, N. N. (1958), 'Kafka's *Metamorphosis*: Realism and Unrealism', *Modern Fiction Studies*, 4, 143–50

HOORENS, V. (2011), *Een ketterse arts voor de heksen: Jan Wier (1515–1588)*, Amsterdam: Bert Bakker

HOPKINSON, N. (1994), 'Nonnos and Homer', in *Studies in the Dionysiaca of Nonnos*, Cambridge: Cambridge Philological Society, 9–42

HORN, H.-J., and H. WALTER (eds) (1997), *Die Allegorese des antiken Mythos*, Wiesbaden: HAB Wolfenbüttel

HORSFALL, N. (1994), 'The Prehistory of Latin Poetry: Some Problems of Method', *Rivista di Filologia e d'Istruzione Classica*, 122, 50–75

HORSTMANN, A. (1979), 'Der Mythosbegriff vom frühen Christentum bis zur Gegenwart', *Archiv für Begriffsgeschichte*, 23, 7–54 and 197–245

HOUSMAN, A. E. (1937), M. Manilius, *Astronomicon libri quinque*, recensuit et enarrauit A. E. Housman, 5 vols, Cantabrigiae: Typis Academiae

HUGHES, T. (1997), *Tales from Ovid*, Faber and Faber

HUNINK, V. (2003), '*Apuleius, qui nobis afris afer est notior*: Augustine's Polemic against Apuleius in *De Civitate Dei*', *Scholia*, ns 12, 82–95

HUNTER, R. (1987), 'Medea's Flight', *Classical Quarterly*, 37, 129–39

——(ed.) (1989), *Apollonius of Rhodes. Argonautica Book III*, Cambridge: Cambridge University Press

——(1993), *The Argonautica of Apollonius Rhodius: Literary Studies*, Cambridge: Cambridge University Press

——(ed.) (2005a), *The Hesiodic Catalogue of Women: Constructions and Reconstructions*, Cambridge: Cambridge University Press

——(2005b), 'Introduction', in *The Hesiodic Catalogue of Women: Constructions and Reconstructions*, ed. by R. Hunter, Cambridge: Cambridge University Press, pp. 1–4

——(2005c), 'The Hesiodic *Catalogue* and Hellenistic Poetry', in *The Hesiodic Catalogue of Women: Constructions and Reconstructions*, ed. by R. Hunter, Cambridge: Cambridge University Press, pp. 239–65

HUTCHINSON, G. O. (2008), 'The Metamorphosis of Metamorphosis: P. Oxy. 4711 and Ovid', in *Talking Books: Readings in Hellenistic and Roman Books of Poetry*, Oxford: Oxford University Press, pp. 200–27

HUTTON, W. (2005), *Describing Greece: Landscape and Literature in the Periegesis of Pausanias*, Cambridge: Cambridge University Press

HYNES, S. (1997), *The Soldier's Tale: Bearing Witness to Modern War*, London: Allen Lane, The Penguin Press

INGLEHEART, J. (2010), *A Commentary on Ovid, Tristia, Book 2*, Oxford: Oxford University Press

JAEGER, M. (2007), 'Kontemplation und Kolonisation der Natur. Klassische Überlieferung und moderne Negation von Goethes Metamorphosendenken', *Goethe Jahrbuch*, 124, 60–73

JARDINE, N. (2011), 'Chalk to Cheese: Progress, Power, Cooperation and Topography: Stages towards Understanding How Science Happened', *TLS*, December 16 2011, pp. 3–4

JENSEN, R. C. (1968), 'Coluccio Salutati's *Lament of Phyllis*', *Studies in Philology*, 65, 109–23

JOHNSON, W. R. (2000), *Lucretius and the Modern World*, London: Duckworth

JONES, C. P. (2010), *New Heroes in Antiquity: From Achilles to Antinoos*, Cambridge, MA, and London: Harvard University Press

JORISSEN, H. (1965), *Die Entfaltung der Transsubstantiationslehre bis zum Beginn der Hochscholastik*, Münster: Aschendorffsche Verlagsbuchhandlung

JOSHI, S. T. (1980), '"Reality" and Knowledge: Some Notes on the Aesthetic Thought of H. P. Lovecraft', *Lovecraft Studies*, 1, 17–27

——(2001), *A Dreamer and a Visionary: H. P. Lovecraft in his Time*, Liverpool: Liverpool University Press

JOST, M. (1994), 'The Distribution of Sanctuaries in Civic Space in Arcadia', in *Placing the Gods: Sanctuaries and Sacred Space in Ancient Greece*, ed. by S. E. Alcock and R. Osborne, Oxford: Oxford University Press, pp. 217–30

——(1998), 'Versions locales et versions "panhelléniques" des myths arcadiens chez Pausanias', in *Les Panthéons des cités: Des origines à la Périégèse de Pausanias*, ed. by V. Pirenne-Delforge, Liège, pp. 209–26

KABLITZ, A. (2003), 'Inkarnation: Überlegungen zur Konstitution eines Kulturmusters (*Novum Testamentum* — Dante: *Vita nova, Commedia*)', in *Transgressionen: Literatur als Ethnographie*, ed. by G. Neumann and R. Warning, Freiburg i. Br.: Rombach, pp. 3–79

KAEMPFER, J. (1998), *Poétique du récit de guerre*, Paris: Corti

KAIMAKIS, D. (1976), *Die Kyraniden*, Meisenheim am Glan: Anton Hain

KASTER, R. A. (1988), *Guardians of Language: The Grammarian and Society in Late Antiquity*, Berkeley: University of California Press

KAUFFMAN, S. A. (1993), *The Origins of Order: Self-Organization and Selection in Evolution*, New York: Oxford University Press

KEE, H. C. (1972), 'The Transfiguration in Mark: Epiphany or Apocalyptic Vision?', in *Understanding the Sacred Text*, ed. by J. Reumann, Valley Forge: Judson, pp. 137–52

KEITH, A., and S. RUPP (eds.) (2007), *Metamorphosis: The Changing Face of Ovid in Medieval and Early Modern Europe*, Toronto: Centre for Reformation and Renaissance Studies

KELLER, O. (ed.) (1877), *Rerum naturalium scriptores Graeci minores, 1 (Paradoxographi: Antigonus, Apollonius, Phlegon, Anonymus Vaticanus)*, Leipzig: Teubner

KENNEDY, D. F. (2002), *Rethinking Reality: Lucretius and the Textualization of Nature*, Ann Arbor: University of Michigan Press

KENNEY, E. J. (1982), 'Ovid', in *The Cambridge History of Classical Literature*, ed. by P. E. Easterling and E. J. Kenney, Cambridge: Cambridge University Press, 420–57

——(1986), 'Notes to A. D. Melville (tr.), *Ovid: Metamorphoses*', Oxford: Oxford University Press

——(2001), '*Est deus in nobis...*; Medea Meets her Maker', in *A Companion to Apollonius Rhodius*, ed. by T. Papanghelis and A Rengakos, Brill: Leiden, pp. 261–83

——(2011), *Ovidio, Metamorfosi. Testo latino a fronte, vol. 4 (Libri VII–IX); testo critico basato sull'edizione oxoniense di Richard Tarrant; traduzione di Gioachino Koch*, Rome: Fondazione Lorenzo Valla; Milan: A. Mondadori

KENSETH, J. (ed.) (1991), *The Age of the Marvellous*, Hanover, NH: Hood Museum of Art

KIDWELL, C. (1991), *Pontano: Poet & Prime Minister*, London: Duckworth

KIENZLE (1903), *Ovidius. Qua ratione compendium mythologicum ad Metamorphoseis componendas adhibuerit*, Basel: Basler Berichthaus

KIESSLING, N. (1975), 'Doctor Faustus and the Sin of Demoniality', *Studies in English Literature, 1500–1900*, 15. 2, 205–11

KILGOUR, M. (2012), *Milton and the Metamorphosis of Ovid*, New York: Oxford University Press

KINCAID, J. (1992), *Child Loving: The Erotic Child and Victorian Culture*, London: Routledge

KING, S. (2006), *Insect Nations: Visions of the Ant World from Kropotkin to Bergson*, Ashby-de-la-Zouch: Inkerman

KINLAW, P. E. (2005), *The Christ is Jesus: Metamorphosis, Possession, and Johannine Christology*, Leiden and Boston: Brill

KIRK, G. S. (1970), *Myth: Its Meaning and Function in Ancient and Other Cultures*, Sather Classical Lectures, Berkeley: University of California Press

KLAUCK, H.-J. (1982), *Herrenmahl und Hellenistischer Kult: Eine religionsgeschichtliche Untersuchung zum ersten Korintherbrief*, Münster: Aschendorf

——(2008), *Die apokryphe Bibel: Ein anderer Zugang zum frühen Christentum*, Tübingen: Mohr Siebeck

KLAWANS, J. (2002), 'Interpreting the Last Supper: Sacrifice, Spiritualization, and Anti-Sacrifice', *New Testament Studies*, 48, 1–17

KLEIN, F. (2009), '*Prodigiosa mendacia uatum*: Responses to the Marvellous in Ovid's Narrative of Perseus (*Metamorphoses* 4–5), in *Paradox and the Marvellous in Augustan Literature and Culture*, ed. by P. Hardie, Oxford: Oxford University Press, pp. 189–212

KLOPSCH, P. (1967), *Pseudo-Ovidius De vetula: Untersuchungen und Text*, Leiden: Brill

KNOEPFLMACHER, U. C. (1998), *Ventures into Childland: Victorians, Fairytales, and Femininity*, Chicago, IL: Chicago University Press

KNOEPFLMACHER, U. C., and N. AUERBACH (1992), *Forbidden Journeys: Fairy Tales and Fantasies by Victorian Women Writers*, Chicago, IL: Chicago University Press

KNOX, P. (1986), 'Ovid's Medea and the Authenticity of *Heroides* 12', *Harvard Studies of Classical Philology*, 90, 207–23

KOLB, C. (2010), *Kafka: A Guide for the Perplexed*, London and New York: Continuum

KÖNIG, R. (1976), C. *Plinius Secundus d. Ä., Naturalis Historiae Liber VIII. Naturkunde, Lateinisch-deutsch Buch VIII*, ed. and trans. by R. König, in collaboration with G. Winkler, Munich: Heimeran

——(1994), C. *Plinius Secundus d. Ä., Naturalis Historiae Liber XXXVII. Naturkunde, Lateinisch-deutsch Buch XXXVII*, ed. and trans. by R. König, in collaboration with J. Hopp, Zurich: Artemis

KOOPMANN, H. (1996), 'Poetischer Rückruf: Zu Schillers "Die Götter Griechenlands"', in *Interpretationen: Gedichte von Friedrich Schiller*, ed. by N. Oellers, Stuttgart: Reclam, pp. 64–83

KOOPMANS, R. (2011), *Wonderful to Relate: Miracle Stories and Miracle Collecting in High Medieval England*, Philadelphia: University of Pennsylvania Press

KRABBE, J. K. (1989), *The 'Metamorphoses' of Apuleius*, New York: Peter Lang

KREVANS, N. (1997), 'Medea as Foundation-Heroine', in *Medea: Essays on Medea in Myth, Literature, Philosophy, and Art*, ed. by J. J. Clauss and S. I. Johnston, Princeton, NJ: Princeton University Press, pp. 71–82

KRISTEVA, J. (1996), *Le Temps sensible*, Paris: Gallimard

KROPOTKIN, P. (1998), *Mutual Aid: A Factor in Evolution*, London: Freedom Press

KULLMANN, W. (1985), 'Gods and Men in the *Iliad* and the *Odyssey*', *Harvard Studies of Classical Philology*, 89, 1–23

KUNTZE, P. (1912), *The Grand Olympe, eine alchemistische Deutung von Ovids Metamorphosen* (doctoral dissertation, Halle/Saale)

KUON, P. (2005), 'Metamorphose als geisteswissenschaftlicher Begriff', in *Konzepte der Metamorphose in den Geisteswissenschaften*, ed. by H. Gottwald and H. Klein, Heidelberg: Winter, pp. 1–16

KUSCHEL, K.-J. (1990), *Geboren vor aller Zeit? Der Streit um Christi Ursprung*, Munich and Zurich: Piper

LAARMANN, M. (1999), 'Transsubstantiation: Begriffsgeschichtliche Materialien und bibliographische Notizen', *Archiv für Begriffsgeschichte*, 41, 119–50

LACHMANN, R. (1990), *Gedächtnis und Literatur: Intertextualität in der russischen Moderne*, Frankfurt a. M.: Suhrkamp

LADA-RICHARDS, I. (2007), *Silent Eloquence: Lucian and Pantomime Dancing*, London: Duckworth

LAFAYE, G. (1904), *Les Métamorphoses d'Ovide et leurs modèles grecs*, Paris: F. Alcan

LANGTON, C. G. (1992), 'Computation at the Edge of Chaos: Phase Transition and Emergent Computation', *Physica D*, 42, 12–37

LANZA, D. (1930), 'Agrumi', *Enciclopedia italiana di scienze, lettere ed arti*, Milan and Rome: Treves Tumminelli Treccani-Istituto dell'Enciclopedia Italiana, 1929–39, II, 6–10

LAFOND, Y. (2001), 'Lire Pausanias à l'époque des Antonins: Réflexions sur la place de la *Périégèse* dans l'histoire culturelle, religieuse et sociale de la Grèce romaine', in *éditer, traduire, commenter Pausanias en l'an 2000. Actes du colloque de Neuchâtel et de Fribourg (18–22 septembre 1998)*, ed. by D. Knoepfler and M. Piérart, Geneva: Droz S. A., pp. 387–406

LAPIDE, P. (1983), *The Resurrection of Jesus: A Jewish Perspective*, London: Society for Promoting Christian Knowledge

LARMOUR, D. (1990), 'Tragic Contaminatio in Ovid's *Metamorphoses*: Procne and Medea; Philomela and Iphigeneia (6. 424–674); Scylla and Phaedra (8. 19–151)', *Illinois Classical Studies*, 15, 131–41

LAURENT, J. (1993), 'C. S. Lewis and Animal Rights', *Mythlore*, 19.1, 46–51

LAWALL, G. (1966), 'Apollonius' *Argonautica*: Jason as Anti-Hero', *Yale Classical Studies*, 19, 119–69

LE GUERN, M. (1981), 'La Métamorphose poétique: Essai de définition', in *Poétiques de la métamorphose: De Pétrarque à John Donne*, ed. by G. Demerson, Saint-Etienne: Publications de l'Université de Saint-Etienne, pp. 27–36

LEE, M. M. (2009), 'Body-Modification in Classical Greece', in *Bodies and Boundaries in Graeco-Roman Antiquity*, ed. by T. Fögen and M. M. Lee, Berlin and New York: de Gruyter, pp. 155–80

LEIBER, F. (1965), *ap.* Los Angeles Science Fantasy Society, *H. P. Lovecraft: A Symposium*, Los Angeles

LEM, S. (1984), *Microworlds: Writings on Science Fiction and Fantasy*, ed. by Franz Rottensteiner, San Diego: Harcourt Brace Jovanovich

LENOIR, G. (1982), 'La Fuite de Médée (Ovide, *Métamorphose* VII, 350392)', in *Colloque Présence d'Ovide*, ed. by R. Chevalier, Paris: Les Belles Lettres, pp. 51–56

LESHER, J. H. (1992), *Xenophanes of Colophon: Fragments. A Text and Translation with a Commentary*, Phoenix Supplementary Volume XXX, Presocratics Volume IV, Toronto: University of Toronto Press

Letteratura di villa (2004), *La letteratura di villa e di villeggiatura. Atti del Convegno di Parma, 29 settembre–1 ottobre 2003*, Rome: Salerno

LEVENSTEIN, J. (1996), 'The Pilgrim, the Poet, and the Cowgirl: Dante's Alter-"Io" in Purgatorio XXX–XXXI', *Dante Studies, with the Annual Report of the Dante Society*, 114, 189–208

LÉVY, M. (1985), *Lovecraft, ou, Du fantastique*, Paris : Christian Bourgois

LEWIS, C. S. (1960), *A Preface to Paradise Lost*, London: Oxford University Press

LICHTENSTERN, C. (1990), *Metamorphose in der Kunst des 19. und 20. Jahrhunderts, vol. 1: Die Wirkungsgeschichte der Metamorphosenlehre Goethes*, Weinheim: Acta humaniora

——(1992), *Metamorphose: Vom Mythos zum Prozeßdenken. Ovid-Rezeption, Surrealistische Ästhetik, Verwandlungsthematik der Nachkriegskunst*, Weinheim: Weinheim VCH

LIDDELL, H. G., and R. SCOTT (1968), *A Greek–English Lexicon*, Oxford: Clarendon Press

LINDENLAUF, A. (2003), 'The Sea as a Place of No Return in Ancient Greece', *World Archaeology*, 35, 416–33

LITTLE, D. (1970), 'The Speech of Pythagoras in *Metamorphoses* 15 and the Structure of the *Metamorphoses*', *Hermes*, 98, 340–60

LIVELEY, G. (2006), 'Science Fictions and Cyber Myths; or, Do Cyborgs Dream of Dolly the Sheep?', in *Laughing with Medusa: Classical Myth and Feminist Thought*, ed. by V. Zajko and M. Leonard, Oxford: Oxford University Press, 275–94

——(2011), *Ovid's Metamorphoses: A Reader's Guide*, London: Continuum

LIVINGSTONE, D. N., and C. W. J. WITHERS (eds) (2011), *Geographies of Nineteenth-Century Science*, Chicago, IL: University of Chicago Press

LLEWELLYN, N. (1988), 'Illustrating Ovid', in *Ovid Renewed: Ovidian Influences on Literature and Art from the Middle Ages to the Twentieth Century*, ed. by Charles Martindale, Cambridge: Cambridge University Press, pp. 151–66

LLOYD, G. R. E. (1966), *Polarity and Analogy: Two Types of Argumentation in Early Greek Thought*, Cambridge: Cambridge University Press

LLOYD-JONES, H. (ed. and trans.) (1996), *Sophocles III: Fragments*, Cambridge, MA: Loeb Classical Library

LOCKWOOD, M. (2005), *The Labyrinth of Time: Introducing the Universe*, Oxford: Oxford University Press

LODGE, D. (1979), *The Modes of Modern Writing: Metaphor, Metonymy, and the Typology of Modern Literature*, London: Arnold

LONG, A. A. (1992), 'Stoic Readings of Homer', in *Homer's Ancient Readers: The Hermeneutics of Greek Epic's Earliest Exegetes*, ed. by R. Lamberton and J. J. Keaney, Princeton, NJ: Princeton University Press, pp. 41–66

LONSDALE, S. H. (1988), 'Protean Forms and Disguise in *Odyssey* 4', *Lexis*, 2, 165–78

LOUTH, A. (2007), *Greek East and Latin West: The Church, AD 681–1071*, Crestwood, NY: St Vladimir's Press

LOVEJOY, A. O. (1936), *The Great Chain of Being: A Study of the History of an Idea*, Cambridge, MA: Harvard University Press

LUDWIG, W. (1965), *Struktur und Einheit der Metamorphosen Ovids*, Berlin: De Gruyter

——(1982), 'Neulateinische Lehrgedichte und Vergils *Georgica*', in *From Wolfram and Petrarch to Goethe and Grass. Studies in Honour of L. Forster*, ed. by D. H. Green, L. P. Johnson and D. Wuttke, Baden-Baden: Verlag V. Koerner, 151–80

LUNELLI, A. (1983), 'Il commento virgiliano di Pomponio Leto', in *Atti del convegno virgiliano di Brindisi nel bimillenario della morte*, Perugia: Istituto di Filologia Latina dell'Università, 309–22

——(1997), 'Leto, Giulio Pomponio', in *Enciclopedia virgiliana*, Rome: Istituto dell'Enciclopedia Italiana, III, 192–95

LUHMANN, N. (1997), *Die Gesellschaft der Gesellschaft*, Frankfurt a. M.: Suhrkamp

LUZZATTO, M. J. (2012), 'Aesop', in *Brill's New Pauly*, Antiquity Volumes, edited by H. Cancik and H. Schneider, Brill Online, 2012

LYNE, R. (2001), *Ovid's Changing Worlds: English Metamorphoses, 1567–1632*, Oxford: Oxford University Press

MACH, M. (1992), '*Christus Mutans*: Zur Bedeutung der "Verklärung Jesu" im Wechsel von jüdischer Messianität zur neutestamentlichen Christologie', in *Messiah and Christos: Studies in the Jewish Origins of Christianity, presented to David Flusser on the Occasion of His Seventy-Fifth Birthday*, ed. by I. Gruenwald, S. Shaked and G. G. Stroumsa, Tübingen: Mohr Siebeck, pp. 177–98

MACIOCCO, G. (2008), 'Urban Landscape Perspectives: Landscape Project, City Project', in *Urban Landscape Perspectives*, ed. by G. Maciocco, Berlin: Springer, pp. 1–26

MACK, P. (2004), 'Early Modern Ideas of Imagination: The Rhetorical Tradition', in *Imagination in the Later Middle Ages and Early Modern Times*, ed. by Lodi Nauta and Detlev Pätzold, Leuven: Peeters, pp. 59–76

MACRÌ, S. (2009), *Pietre Viventi: I Minerali nell'Immaginario del Mondo Antico*, UTET Libreria: Turin

MACY, G. (1984), *Theologies of the Eucharist in the Early Scholastic Period: A Study of the Salvific Function of the Sacrament according to the Theologians, ca. 1180–ca. 1220*, Oxford: Clarendon Press

——(1991), 'Of Mice and Manna: *Quid Mus Sumit* as a Pastoral Question', *Recherches de Théologie Ancienne et Médiévale*, 58, 157–66

——(1994), 'The Dogma of Transubstantiation in the Middle Ages', *The Journal of Ecclesiastical History*, 45, 11–41 [= *Treasures from the Storehouse: Medieval Religion and the Eucharist*, Collegeville, MN, 1999, 81–120]

MAGDELAINE, C. (2000), 'Le Corail dans la Littérature Médicale de l'Antiquité Gréco-Romaine au Moyen-Age', in *Corallo di Ieri, Corallo di Oggi. Atti del Convegno, Ravello 1996*, ed. by J. P. Morel, C. Rondi-Costanzo, and D. Ugolini, Bari: Edipuglia, pp. 239–53

MAGRATH, W. T. (1982), 'The Progression of the Lion Simile in the *Odyssey*', *Classical Journal*, 77, 205–12

MANTELLO, F. A. C., and A. G. RIGG (1996), *Medieval Latin: An Introduction and Bibliographical Guide*, Washington, DC: Catholic University of America Press

MARCOZZI, L. (2001), 'Petrarca lettore di Ovidio', in *Testimoni del vero: Su alcuni libri in biblioteche d'autore*, ed. by Emilio Russo, Rome: Bulzoni, pp. 57–106

MARGULIS, L., and D. SAGAN (1997), *Microcosmos: Four Billion Years of Evolution from Our Microbial Ancestors* 2nd edn, Berkeley: University of California Press

MARTIN, J. (1979), 'Two Ancient Histories: A Comparative Study of Greece and Rome', *Social History*, 4, 285–98

——(1994), 'Der Wandel des Beständigen: Überlegungen zu einer historischen Anthropologie', *Freiburger Universitätsblätter*, 126.4, 35–46

——(1997), 'Zwei alte Geschichten: Vergleichende historisch-anthropologische Betrachtungen zu Griechenland und Rom', *Saeculum*, 48, 1–20

MARTINDALE, C. (ed.) (1988), *Ovid Renewed: Ovidian Influences on Literature and Art from the Middle Ages to the Twentieth Century*, Cambridge: Cambridge University Press

MARTINDALE, C., and M. (1990), *Shakespeare and the Uses of Antiquity: An Introductory Essay*, London: Routledge

MASSEY, I. (1976), *The Gaping Pig: Literature and Metamorphosis*, Berkeley, Los Angeles and London: University of California Press

MATZ, W. (1994), 'Der Schlaf der Vernunft gebiert Ungeheuer: Motive zu einer Lektüre von Kafkas *Verwandlung*', *Text und Kritik*, 7, 73–85

MAXWELL-STUART, P. (2007), 'The Contemporary Historical Debate', in *Witchcraft Historiography*, ed. by Jonathan Barry and Owen Davies, New York: Palgrave, pp. 11–32

MAYER, M., and G. NEUMANN (eds) (1997), *Pygmalion: Die Geschichte des Mythos in der abendländischen Kultur*, Freiburg im Breisgau: Rombach

MAZZA, A. (1966), 'L'inventario della *parva libraria* di Santo Spirito e la biblioteca di Boccaccio', *Italia medioevale e umanistica*, 9, 1–74

McLAUGHLIN, M. (1995), *Literary Imitation in the Italian Renaissance: The Theory and Practice of Literary Imitation in Italy from Dante to Bembo*, Oxford: Clarendon Press

MELLIDI, C. (2007), 'Mancinelli, Antonio', in *Dizionario biografico degli Italiani*, Rome: Istituto della Enciclopedia Italiana, 1960–, 68, 450–53

MENDIETA, E. (2010), 'Political Bestiary: On the Uses of Violence', *Insights*, 3.2, 1–14

METTINGER, T. N. D. (2001), *The Riddle of Resurrection: Dying and Rising Gods in the Ancient Near East*, Stockholm: Almqvist & Wiksell International

MEYERS, J. (2004), 'L'Églogue de Théodule: "Démonisation" ou "Sacralisation" de la mythologie?', in *L'Allégorie de l'antiquité à la Renaissance*, ed. by B. Pérez-Jean and P. Eichel-Lojkine, Paris: Champion, pp. 335–47

MICHALOPOULOS, A. (2001), *Ancient Etymologies in Ovid's Metamorphoses: A Commented Lexicon*, Leeds: ARCA

MICHEL, G. (1992), '*Die Verwandlung* von Franz Kafka — psychopathologisch gelesen: Aspekte eines schizophren-psychologischen Zusammenbruchs', *Jahrbuch für Internationale Germanistik*, 23, 69–92

MIDELFORT, H. C. E. (1999), *A History of Madness in Sixteenth-Century Germany*, Stanford, CA: Stanford University Press

MIGHALL, R. (1999), *A Geography of Victorian Gothic Fiction: Mapping History's Nightmares*, Oxford: Oxford University Press

MIGUET-OLLAIGNER, M. (1982), *La Mythologie de Marcel Proust*, Paris: Les Belles Lettres

MIKKONEN, K. (1996), 'Theories of Metamorphosis: From Metatrope to Textual Revision', *Style*, 30.2, 309–40

MILLER, J. H. (1990), *Versions of Pygmalion*, Cambridge, MA, and London: Harvard University Press

MILOWICKI, E. J., and R. R. WILSON (1995), 'Ovid through Shakespeare: The Divided Self', *Poetics Today*, 16, 217–52

MILTON, E. (1987), 'The Track of the Mutant', *Boston Review* (Dec. 1987), 11–13

MITHEN, S. (2008), 'Is Religion Inevitable? An Archaeologist's View from the Past', in *The Edge of Reason? Science and Religion in Modern Society*, ed. by A. Bentley, London: Continuum, pp. 82–94

MOMIGLIANO, A. (1963), 'Pagan and Christian Historiography in the Fourth Century A D', in *The Conflict Between Paganism and Christianity in the Fourth Century* (Oxford: Clarendon Press, 1963), pp. 79–99

MONTENOT, J. (ed.) (2002), *Encyclopédie de la philosophie*, Paris: Librairie Générale Française

MONTER, E. W. (2007), *A Bewitched Duchy: Lorraine and Its Dukes, 1477–1736*, Travaux d'Humanisme et Renaissance 432, Geneva: Librairie Droz S. A.

MONTI SABIA, L. (1969), 'Una schermaglia editoriale tra Napoli e Venezia agli albori del secolo XVI', *Vichiana*, 6, 319–36

——(1996), 'Tra realtà e poesia: per una nuova cronologia di alcuni carmi del *De amore coniugali* di Giovanni Pontano (I 5–8)', in *Classicità, Medioevo e Umanesimo. Studi in onore di Salvatore Monti*, ed. by G. Germano, Naples: Dipartimento di Filologia classica dell'Università degli studi di Napoli Federico II, pp. 351–70

MORALES, H. (2007), *Classical Mythology: A Very Short Introduction*, Oxford: Oxford University Press

MORAVEC, H. (1988), *Mind Children: The Future of Robot and Human Intelligence*, Cambridge, MA: Harvard University Press

MOSS, A. (1997), 'Allegory in a Rhetorical Mode', in *Die Allegorese des antiken Mythos*, ed. by H.-J. Horn and J. Walter, Wiesbaden: HAB Wolfenbüttel, pp. 395–406

MOSSMAN, J. (1995), *Wild Justice: A Study of Euripides' Hecuba*, Oxford: Oxford University Press

MOST, G. W. (2005), *Doubting Thomas*, Cambridge, MA: Harvard University Press

MÜLLER-SIEVERS, H. (1997), *Self-Generation: Biology, Philosophy, and Literature around 1800*, Stanford, CA: Stanford University Press

MURRAY, P. (1998), 'Bodies in Flux: Ovid's *Metamorphoses*', in *Changing Bodies, Changing Meanings: Studies on the Human Body in Antiquity*, ed. by D. Montserrat, London and New York: Routledge, pp. 80–98

MURRAY, R. D. (1958), *The Motif of Io in Aeschylus' Suppliants*, Princeton, NJ: Princeton University Press

MURRAY, W. (1991), 'Lovecraft and the Pulp Magazine Tradition', in *An Epicure in the Terrible: A Centennial Anthology of Essays in Honor of H. P. Lovecraft*, ed. by D. E. Schultz and S. T. Joshi, London: Fairleigh Dickinson University Press, pp. 101–31

MUSTARD, W. P. (1909), 'Later Echoes of the Greek Bucolic Poets', *American Journal of Philology*, 30, 245–83

——(1918), 'Later Echoes of the Greek Bucolic Poets', *American Journal of Philology*, 39, 193–98

MYERS, K. S. (1994), *Ovid's Causes: Cosmogony and Aetiology in the Metamorphoses*, Ann Arbor: The University of Michigan Press

MYNORS, R. A. B. (ed.) (1994), Virgil, *Georgics*, Oxford: Clarendon Press (1st edn 1990)

NAGY, G. (1990), *Greek Mythology and Poetics*, Ithaca, NY: Cornell University Press

NAGY, G. (1996), *Poetry and Performance: Homer and Beyond*, Cambridge and New York: Cambridge University Press

NELIS, D. (2009), 'Ovid, *Metamorphoses* 1.416–51: *noua monstra* and the *foedera naturae*', in *Paradox and the Marvellous in Augustan Literature and Culture*, ed. by P. Hardie, Oxford: Oxford University Press, pp. 248–67

NEUMANN, G. (2006), 'Kafkas Verwandlungen', in *Verwandlungen. Archäologie der literarischen Kommunikation IX*, ed. by A. and J. Assmann, Munich: Wilhelm Fink Verlag, pp. 245–66

NEVO, R. (1980), *Comic Transformations in Shakespeare* (London: Methuen)

NEWLANDS, C. (1997), 'The Metamorphosis of Ovid's Medea', in *Medea: Essays on Medea in Myth, Literature, Philosophy and Art*, ed. by J. J. Clauss and S. I. Johnston, Princeton, NJ: Princeton University Press, pp. 178–208

NICKLAS, P. (2002) *Die Beständigkeit des Wandels: Metamorphosen in Literatur und Wissenschaft*, Hildesheim, Zurich and New York: Olms

NICKLAS, T., F. V. REITERER and J. VERHEYDEN (eds) (2009), *The Human Body in Death and Resurrection*, Berlin: de Gruyter

NICOLINI, F. (1925), *L'arte napoletana del Rinascimento e la lettera di Pietro Summonte a Marcantonio Michiel*, Naples: Ricciardi

OELLERS, N. (2002), 'Stolberg, das Christentum und die Antike: Der Streit mit Schiller', in *Friedrich Leopold Graf zu Stolberg (1750–1819). Beiträge zum Eutiner Symposium im September 1997*, ed. by Frank Baudach et al., Eutin: Struve, pp. 109–26

——(2006), 'Schiller und die Religion', in *Friedrich Schiller und der Weg in die Moderne*, ed. by W. Hinderer, Würzburg: Königshausen & Neumann, pp. 165–86

OGDEN, D. (2001), *Greek and Roman Necromancy*, Princeton, NJ: Princeton University Press

O'HARA, J. H. (1996), 'History and Elegy in Hellenistic Greece. Sostratus *Suppl. Hell.* 733: A Lost, Possibly Catullan-Era Elegy on the Six Sex Changes of Tiresias', *Transactions of the American Philological Association*, 126, 173–219

OHLY, F. (1979), 'Typologische Figuren aus Natur und Mythos', in *Formen und Funktionen der Allegorie. Symposium Wolfenbüttel 1978*, ed. by W. Haug, Stuttgart: Metzler, pp. 126–66

ØISTEIN ENDSJØ, D. (2009), *Greek Resurrection Beliefs and the Success of Christianity*, New York: Palgrave Macmillan

OLCK, F. (1899), 'Citrone', in *Paulys Real-Encyclopädie der classischen Altertumswissenschaft*, ed. by A. F. von Pauly and G. Wissowa (Stuttgart: Metzler, 1893–1972), 3.2, cols 2612–24

O'LEARY, J. S. (1992), 'Rethinking the Incarnation', *Hermathena* 152, 59–69

OLIVIERI, R. (1998), 'Ligorio è pietra preziosa', in *ΛΑΘΗ ΒΙΩΣΑΣ. Ricordando Ennio S. Burioni*, ed. by R. Gendre (Alessandria: Ed. dell'Orso), pp. 257–69

O'NOLAN, K. (1960), 'The Proteus Legend', *Hermes*, 88, 129–38

OTIS, B. (1970), *Ovid as an Epic Poet*, Cambridge: Cambridge University Press

OTTEN, C. F. (ed.) (1986), *A Lycanthropy Reader: Werewolves in Western Culture*, Syracuse, NY: Syracuse University Press

PACKER, S. (2010), Superheroes and Superegos: Analyzing the Minds behind the Masks, Santa Barbara, CA: Greenwood Publishing Group

PAGE, D. L. (ed.) (1990), *Euripides: Medea*, Oxford: Oxford University Press

PAGLIA, C. (1990), *Sexual Personae: Art and Decadence from Nefertiti to Emily Dickinson*, Vintage Books

PAPAIOANNOU, S. (2007), *Redesigning Achilles*, Berlin: Walter de Gruyter

PARENTI, G. (1985), *Poëta Proteus alter: Forma e storia di tre libri di Pontano*, Florence: Olschki

PARIKKA, J. (2008), 'Politics of Swarms: Translations between Entomology and Politics', *Parallax*, 14.3, 112–24

PARIS, M. (1990), *The Novels of World War Two*, London: Library Association

PASQUALI, G. (1985), 'Mutamenti nel paesaggio italiano' (1942), in *Lingua nuova e antica*, ed. by G. Folena, Florence: Le Monnier, pp. 315–43

——(1994), 'Arte allusiva', in *Pagine stravaganti di un filologo*, ed. by C. F. Russo, 2 vols, Florence: Le Lettere, 275–82

PASSANNANTE, G. (2011), *The Lucretian Renaissance: Philology and the Afterlife of Tradition*, Chicago, IL, and London: University of Chicago Press

PATTERSON, L. E. (2010), *Kinship Myth in Ancient Greece*, Austin: University of Texas Press

PATTERSON, N.-L. (1994), 'The Green Lewis: Inklings of Environmentalism in the Writings of C. S. Lewis', *Lamp-Post of the Southern California C. S. Lewis Society*, 18, 4–14

PAVLOCK, B. (2009), *The Image of the Poet in Ovid's Metamorphoses*, Madison: University of Wisconsin Press

PÉPIN, J. (1976), *Mythe et allégorie: Les Origines grecques et les contestations judéo–chrétiennes*, Paris: Etudes augustiniennes

PÈRCOPO, E. (1936–37), 'La vita di Giovanni Pontano', ed. by Michele Manfredi, *Archivio storico delle province napoletane*, 61 (1936), 116–250; 62 (1937), 57–237

PÉREZ-JEAN, B., and EICHEL-LOJKINE, P. (eds) (2004), *L'Allégorie de l'Antiquité à la Renaissance*, Paris: Champion

PERKINS, J. (2009), 'Early Christian and Judicial Bodies', in *Bodies and Boundaries in Graeco-Roman Antiquity*, ed. by T. Fögen and M. M. Lee, Berlin and New York: de Gruyter, pp. 237–60

PERKINS, R. (1985), 'Metamorphosis in Nietzsche and Its Sources in Satiric Fable', *Comparative Literature Studies*, 22.4, 472–96

PERRY, K. A. (1990), *Another Reality: Metamorphosis and the Imagination in the Poetry of Ovid, Petrarch, and Ronsard*, New York: Lang

PESIC, P. (1999), 'Wrestling with Proteus: Francis Bacon and the "Torture" of Nature', *Isis*, 90: 81–94

——(2008), 'Proteus Rebound: Reconsidering the 'Torture of Nature'', *Isis*, 99, 304–17

——(2010), 'Shapes of Proteus in Renaissance Art', *Huntington Library Quarterly*, 73, 57–82

PETIT, S. (1991), *Michel Tournier's Metaphysical Fictions*, Amsterdam and Philadelphia, John Benjamins

PFEIFFER, R. (1976), *History of Classical Scholarship from 1300 to 1850*, Oxford: Clarendon Press

PIANEZZOLA, E. (1979), 'La metamorfosi ovidiana come metafora narrativa', in *Retorica e Poetica: Atti del III convegno italiano-tedesco (Brixen 1975)*, Padova, 77–91

PICKERAL, T. (2010), *Chris Gollon: Humanity in Art*, Headcorn, Kent: Hyde and Hughes Publishing

PINOTTI, P. (1989), 'Aristotele, Platone e la meraviglia del filosofo', in *Il Meraviglioso e il Verosimile fra Antichità e Medioevo*, ed. by D. Lanza and O. Longo, Florence: Olschki, pp. 29–55

PITCHER, L. V. (2009), 'Saying "Shazam": The Magic of Antiquity in Superhero Comics', in *New Voices in Classical Reception Studies*, 4, 27–43

PITCHERS, A. L. M. (2004), 'The Eucharist: Concepts in the Western Church from the Ninth Century to the Twelfth Century and their Present Relevance', *Studia Historiae Ecclesiasticae*, 30, 140–50

PLAEHN, G. (1882), *De Nicandro aliisque poetis graecis ab Ovidio in Metamorphosibus conscribendis adhibitis*, Halle

PLATT, P. G. (1999), *Wonders, Marvels, and Monsters in Early Modern Culture*, Newark and London: University of Delaware Press

POMEROY, A. (2008), *Then It Was Destroyed by the Volcano: The Ancient World in Film and Television*, London: Duckworth

POTTER, K. R. (trans.) (1955), *The Historia Novella by William of Malmesbury*, London: Thomas Nelson

PRINCE, S. (1996), 'True Lies: Perceptual Realism, Digital Images, and Film Theory', *Film Quarterly*, 49.3, 27–37

PROPP, V. (1968), *The Morphology of the Folktale* [1928], trans. by Laurence Scott. Austin: University of Texas Press

PULLMAN, P. (1998), 'The Dark Side of Narnia', *The Guardian*. 1 October 1998

QUINLAN-MCGRATH, M. (1990), 'Blosius Pallardius: *Agustini Chigii: Suburbanum*. Introduction, Latin Text and English Translation', *Humanistica Lovaniensia*, 39, 93–157

QUINN, B. N. (1971), 'Ps. Theodulus', in *Catalogus translationum et commentariorum: vol. 2, Medieval and Renaissance Latin Translations and Commentaries*, ed. by P. O. Kristeller, Washington, DC: CUA Press, 383–408

RÄDLE, F. (1997), 'Zur Begründung des literarischen Allegorese bei Kommentatoren des 11. und 12. Jahrhunderts', in *Die Allegorese des antiken Mythos*, ed. by H.-J. Horn and H. Walter, Wiesbaden: Harrassowitz, pp. 147–67

RADULET, C. M. (1994), *Vasco da Gama: La prima circumnavigazione dell'Africa, 1497–1499*, Reggio Emilia: Edizioni Diabasis

RAQUEJO, T. (2004), *Dalí: Metamorphoses*, Madrid: Edilupa Ediciones

RATZINGER, J. (1967), 'Das Problem der Transsubstantiation und die Frage nach dem Sinn der Eucharistie', *Theological Quarterly*, 147, 129–58

READ, J. (1957), *Through Alchemy to Chemistry: A Procession of Ideas & Personalities*, London: G. Bell

REED, A. Y. (2005), *Fallen Angels and the History of Judaism and Christianity: The Reception of Enochic Literature*, Cambridge: Cambridge University Press

REED, JOSEPH D. (1995), 'The Sexuality of Adonis', *Classical Antiquity*, 14, 317–47

REEVE, M. D. (1977), 'Statius' *Silvae* in the Fifteenth Century', *Classical Quarterly*, 27, 202–25

REITZENSTEIN, R. (1927), *Die hellenistischen Mysterienreligionen nach ihren Grundgedanken und Wirkungen*, 3rd, expanded edition, Leipzig: B. G. Teubner

REVERMANN, M. (2010), 'Situating the Gaze of the Recipient(s): Theatre-Related Vase Paintings and their Contexts of Reception', in *Beyond the Fifth Century: Interactions with*

Greek Tragedy from the Fourth Century BCE to the Middle Ages, ed. by I. Gildenhard and M. Revermann, Berlin and New York: de Gruyter, 69–97

RIBICHINI, S. (1981), *Adonis: Aspetti orientali di un mito greco*, Rome: Consiglio nazionale delle ricerche

RICE, E. F. JR. (1976), 'The *De Magia Naturali* of Jacques Lefèvre d'Etaples', in *Philosophy and Humanism: Renaissance Essays in Honor of Paul Oskar Kristeller*, ed. by Edward P. Mahoney, Leiden: Brill, 1976, pp. 19–49

RICHARDS, R. J. (2002), *The Romantic Conception of Life: Science and Philosophy in the Age of Goethe*, Chicago, IL, and London: University of Chicago Press

RICHARDSON, N. (1993), *The Iliad: A Commentary, Volume VI: Books 21–24*, Cambridge: Cambridge University Press

RIDDEHOUGH, G. B. (1959), 'Man-into-Beast Changes in Ovid', *Phoenix*, 13, 201–09

RIMELL, V. (2002), *Petronius and the Anatomy of Fiction*, Cambridge: Cambridge University Press

RINALDI, M. (2002),'*Sic itur ad astra': Giovanni Pontano e la sua opera astrologica nel quadro della tradizione manoscritta della Mathesis di Giulio Firmico Materno*, Naples: Loffredo

——(2003), 'Pontano e le tradizioni astrologiche latine medioevali: le postille dell'umanista nel codice Clm 234 della Bayerische Staatsbibliothek di Monaco e nel Barberiniano Latino 172 della Biblioteca Apostolica Vaticana', *Atti dell'Accademia Pontaniana*, 52, 295–324

RIVERO, A. J. (1979), 'Petrarch's "Nel dolce tempo de la prima etade"', *Modern Language Notes*, 94, 92–112

ROBATHAN, D. M. (1968), *The Pseudo-Ovidian De vetula: text, introduction and notes*, Amsterdam: Hakkert

RODGERS, R. (2002), '*Κηποποιΐα*: Garden Making and Garden Culture in the *Geoponika*', in *Byzantine Garden Culture*, ed. by A. Littlewood, H. Maguire, and J. Wolschke-Bulmahn, Dumbarton Oaks, Washington, DC: Dumbarton Oaks Research Library and Collection, pp. 159–75

ROLET, A. (ed.) (2009), *Protée en trompe-l'œil: Genèse et survivances d'un mythe, d'Homère à Bouchardon. Interférences*, Rennes: Presses universitaires de Rennes

ROLOFF, V. (2006), 'Anmerkungen zur neuen Mythologie der Surrealisten', in *Alte Mythen – Neue Medie*, ed. by Y. Hoffmann, W. Hülk, V. Roloff, Heidelberg: Winter, pp. 11–18

ROLING, B. (2006), 'Glaube, Imagination und leibliche Auferstehung: Pietro Pomponazzi zwischen Avicenna, Averroes und jüdische Averroismus', in *Wissen über Grenzen: Arabisches Wissen und lateinisches Mittelalter*, ed. by Andreas Speer und Lydia Wegener, Berlin and New York: de Gruyter, 677–99

ROSATI, G. (2009), *Ovidio, Metamorfosi: Testo latino a fronte, vol. 3 (Libri V–VI); testo critico basato sull'edizione oxoniense di Richard Tarrant; traduzione di Gioachino Koch*, Rome: Fondazione Lorenzo Valla; Milan: A. Mondadori

ROSCHER, W. H. (1884–86), 'Adonis', in *Ausführliches Lexikon der griechischen und römischen Mythologie*, 10 vols, ed. by W. H. Roscher, Leipzig: Teubner, 1884–1921, 1.1, cols 69–77

ROSCOE, W. (1805), *The Life and Pontificate of Leo the Tenth*, 4 vols, Liverpool: J. McCreery

ROSENBERGER, V. (2001), 'Der alte Mann und das Meer: Das Meer und seine Bewohner als Träger prophetischen Wissens', in *Prognosis: Studien zur Funktion von Zukunftsvorhersagen in Literatur und Geschichte seit der Antike*, ed. by K. Brodersen, Munster: LIT Verlag, pp. 61–72

ROSENTHAL, T. (2004), 'Warm Beds are Good: Sex and Libido in Tolkien's Writing', *Mallorn*, 42, 35–42

RÖSLER, W. (1980), 'Die Entdeckung der Fiktionalität in der Antike', *Poetica*, 12, 283–319

ROSNER-SIEGEL, J. A. (1982), 'Amor, Metamorphosis and Magic: Ovid's Medea (*Met.* 7.1–424)', *Classical Journal*, 77, 231–43

ROSSI, P. (1974), *Francesco Bacone: Dalla magia alla scienza*, Turin: Giulio Einaudi

Rossi, V. (1938), *Il Quattrocento*, Milan: Vallardi

Rothwell, K. S. (2007), *Nature, Culture and the Origins of Greek Comedy: A Study of Animal Choruses*, Cambridge: Cambridge University Press

Rubin, M. (1991), *Corpus Christi: The Eucharist in Late Medieval Culture*, Cambridge: Cambridge University Press

Rudloff, H. (1988), 'Zu Kafkas Erzählung *Die Verwandlung*: Metamorphose-Dichtung zwischen Degradation und Emanzipation', *Wirkendes Wort*, 38, 321–37

Rüpke, J. (2000), 'Räume literarischer Kommunikation in der Formierungsphase römischer Literatur', in *Moribus antiquis res stat Romana. Römische Werte und römische Literatur im 3. und 2. Jh. v. Chr.*, ed. by M. Braun et al., Munich and Leipzig: K. G. Saur, pp. 31–52

Russo et al. (1993), *A Commentary on Homer's Odyssey, Volume III*, Oxford: Clarendon Press

Ryan, M. T. (1981), 'Assimilating New Worlds in the Sixteenth and Seventeenth Centuries', *Comparative Studies in Society and History*, 23, 519–38

Sabbadini, R. (1877), *Antonio Mancinelli: Saggio storico-letterario*, Velletri: Tip. Sartori

——(1899), 'Notizie storico-critiche di alcuni codici latini', *Studi italiani di filologia classica*, 7, 99–136

Santoni, A. (2000), *Palefato: Storie incredibili*, Pisa: Edizioni ETS

Sargeaunt, J. (1920), *The Trees, Shrubs and Plants of Virgil*, Oxford: Blackwell

Sassi, M. M. (1986), *La Scienza dell'Uomo nell'Antica Grecia*, Turin: Bollati-Boringhieri

Saunders, C. (2010), 'Magic and Christianity', in *Christianity and Romance in Medieval England*, ed. by R. Field, P. Hardman & M. Sweeney, Cambridge: D. S. Brewer, pp. 84–101

Scarborough, J. (1991), 'The Pharmacology of Sacred Plants, Herbs, and Roots', in *Magika Hiera: Ancient Greek Magic and Religion*, ed. by C. A. Faraone and D. Obbink, New York and Oxford: Oxford University Press, pp. 138–74

Scharold, I. (2000), *Epiphanie, Tierbild, Metamorphose, Passion und Eucharistie. Zur Kodierung des 'Anderen' in den Werken von Robert Musil, Clarice Lispector und J. M. G. Le Clézio*, Heidelberg: Winter

Schepens, G., and K. Delcroix (1996), 'Ancient Paradoxography: Origin, Evolution, Production and Reception', in *La Letteratura di Consumo nel Mondo Greco-Latino*, ed. by O. Pecere and A. Stramaglia, Cassino: Università degli studi di Cassino, pp. 375–460

Scheib, A. (ed.) (2008), *'Dies ist mein Leib': Philosophische Texte zur Eucharistie-Debatte im 17. Jahrhundert*, Darmstadt: Wissenschaftliche Buchgesellschaft

Schildkrout, E. (2004), 'Inscribing the Body', *Annual Review of Anthropology*, 33, 319–44

Schmidt, E. A. (1991), *Ovids poetische Menschenwelt: Die Metamorphosen als Metapher und Symphonie*, Heidelberg: Sitzungsberichte der Heidelberger Akademie der Wissenschaften

——(2006), 'Verwandlung und Identität in Ovids *Metamorphosen*', in *Verwandlungen: Archäologie der literarischen Kommunikation IX*, ed. by A. and J. Assmann, Munich: Wilhelm Fink Verlag, 225–44

Schmidt, J. (2007), *Melancholy and the Care of the Soul: Religion, Moral Philosophy and Madness in Early Modern England*, Aldershot: Ashgate

Schmidt, L. E. (1998), 'From Demon Possession to Magic Show: Ventriloquism, Religion, and the Enlightenment', *Church History*, 67, 274–304

Schmitz, C. (2001), '"Denn auch Niobe ...": Die Bedeutung der Niobe-Erzählung in Achills Rede (Ω 599–620)', *Hermes*, 129, 145–57

Schmitz, C., and A. Bettenworth (eds) (2009), *Menschen — Heros — Gott: Weltentwürfe und Lebensmodelle im Mythos der Vormoderne*, Stuttgart: Franz Steiner Verlag

Schmitz, T. A. (2005), 'Nonnos und seine Tradition', in *Die Bibel im Dialog der Schriften, Konzepte intertextueller Bibellektüre*, ed. by S. Alkier and R. B. Hays, Tübingen and Basel: Francke, pp. 195–216

SCHMITZ-EMANS, M. (2006), 'Metamorphose und Metempsychose: Zwei konkurrierende Modelle von Verwandlung im Spiegel der Gegenwartsliteratur', *Arcadia*, 40, 390–413

SCHNAPP, J. T. (1986), *The Transfiguration of History at the Center of Dante's Paradise*, Princeton, NJ: Princeton University Press

SCHULTE, L. R., and T. J. SCHNEIDER (2009), 'The Absence of the Deity in Rape Scenes of the Hebrew Bible', in *The Presence and Absence of God*, ed. by I. U. Dalferth, Tübingen: Mohr Siebeck, pp. 21–33

SCOBIE, A. (1983), *Apuleius and Folklore*, London: Folklore Society

SCOTTI, M. T. (1982), 'Il proemio delle *Metamorfosi* tra Ovidio ed Apuleio', *Giornale italiano di filologia*, 34, 43–65

SCRIBANO, E. (1988), *Da Descartes a Spinoza: Percorsi della teologia razionale nel Seicento*, Milan: Angeli

SCRIBNER, R. W. (1993), 'The Reformation, Popular Magic, and the "Disenchantment of the World"', *Journal of Interdisciplinary History*, 23, 475–94

SEELIGER, K. (1886–90), 'Hesperiden', in *Ausführliches Lexikon der griechischen und römischen Mythologie*, ed. by W. H. Roscher, 10 vols, Leipzig: Teubner, 1884–1921, I.2, cols 2594–2603

SEGAL, C. (1968), 'Circean Temptations: Homer, Virgil, Ovid', *Transactions of the American Philological Association*, 99, 419–42

——(2002), 'Black and White Magic in Ovid's *Metamorphoses*', *Arion*, 8, 1–34

——(2005), 'Il corpo e l'io', in *Ovidio, Metamorfosi: Testo latino a fronte, vol. 1 (Libri I–II)*, con un saggio introduttivo di Charles Segal; testo critico basato sull'edizione oxoniense di Richard Tarrant; traduzione di Ludovica Koch, ed. by A. Barchiesi, Rome: Fondazione Lorenzo Valla; Milan: A. Mondadori, pp. xix–ci

SEZNEC, J. (1953), *The Survival of the Pagan Gods*, Princeton, NJ: Princeton University Press (1st French edn 1940)

SHARROCK, A. (1996), 'Representing Metamorphosis', in *Art and Text in Roman Culture*, ed. by J. Elsner, Cambridge: Cambridge University Press, pp. 103–30 and 300–04

SHAVIRO, S. (1995), 'Two Lessons from Burroughs', in *Posthuman Bodies*, ed. by Judith Halberstam and Ira Livingstone, Bloomington: Indiana University Press, pp. 38–56

——(1995–97) '11. David Cronenberg', in *Doom Patrols*, http://www.dhalgren.com/Doom/ch11.html [accessed 10 October 2011]

SHOHET, L. (2005), 'Reading Dark Materials', in *His Dark Materials Illuminated: Critical Essays on Pullman's Trilogy*, ed. by Millicent Lenz and Carole Scott, Detroit, MI: Wayne State University Press, pp. 75–94

SHORROCK, R. (2001), *The Challenge of Epic: Allusive Engagement in the Dionysiaka of Nonnus*, Leiden and Boston: Brill

——(2011), *The Myth of Paganism: Nonnus, Dionysus and the World of Late Antiquity*, Bristol: Bristol Classical Press

SILK, M. S. (2000), *Aristophanes and the Definition of Comedy*, Oxford: Oxford University Press

SIMCOX, G. A. (1883), *A History of Latin Literature from Ennius to Boethius*, London: Longmans, Green

SIMON, A. (2000), 'Proust ou la crise de l'idéalisme', *Revue des lettres modernes: Marcel Proust*, 2, 61–75

SKULSKY, H. (1981), *Metamorphosis: The Mind in Exile*, Cambridge, MA: Harvard University Press

SLEIGH, C. (2003), *Ant*, London: Reaktion Books

SMITH, A. (2010), *The Ghost Story, 1840–1920: A Cultural History*, Manchester and New York: Manchester University Press

SMITH, N. (ed.) (1982), *Philosophers Look at Science Fiction*, Chicago, IL: Nelson-Hall

SMITH, P. E. II (1978), 'The Evolution of Politics and the Politics of Evolution: Social Darwinism in Heinlein's Fiction', in *Robert A. Heinlein*, ed. by Joseph D. Olander and Martin Harry Greenbert, Edinburgh: Paul Harris Publishing, pp. 137–71

SMOL, A. (2004), '"Oh... oh... Frodo!": Readings of Male Intimacy in *The Lord of the Rings*', *Modern Fiction Studies*, 50, 949–79

SOBCHAK, V. (ed.) (2000), *Meta-Morphing: Visual Transformation and the Culture of Quick-Change*, Minneapolis and London: University of Minnesota Press

SOKEL, W. H. (1980), 'Freud and the Magic of Kafka's Writing', in *The World of Franz Kafka*, ed. by J. P. Stern, London: Weidenfeld and Nicolson, 145–58

SOLDATI, B. (1986), *La poesia astrologica nel Quattrocento: Ricerche e studi*, Florence: Le Lettere (1st edn 1906)

SOLODOW, J. B. (1988), *The World of Ovid's Metamorphoses*, Chapel Hill: University of North Carolina Press

SOLOMON, J. (1998), 'Our Decentered Culture', in *The Postmodern Presence: Readings on Postmodernism in American Culture and Society*, ed. by A. A. Berger, Walnut Creek CA: AltaMira Press

SPIEGEL, F. (2011), 'In Search of Lost Time and Pompeii', in *Pompeii in the Public Imagination*, ed. by S. Hales & J. Paul, Oxford: Oxford University Press, pp. 232–45

SPOONER, C., and E. MCEVOY (eds) (2007), *The Routledge Companion to Gothic*, London and New York: Routledge

SQUARZINA, A. I. (2004), '"Bis nigra videre tartara": Proust et la catabase virgilienne', *Marcel Proust aujourd'hui*, 2, 45–63

STABLEFORD, B. (2004), *Historical Dictionary of Science Fiction Literature*, Lanham MD: Scarecrow Press

STAGL, J. (ed.) (2007), *Sozio-kulturelle Metamorphosen*, Heidelberg: Winter

——(2008), 'Thesen zur europäischen Fremd- und Selbsterkundung in der Frühen Neuzeit', in *Information in der Frühen Neuzeit: Status, Bestände, Strategien*, ed. by A. Brendecke, M. Friedrich, and S. Friedrich Berlin: Lit Verlag, pp. 65–79

STANFORD, W. B. (1945), 'That Circe's ῥάβδος was not a Wand', *Hermathena*, 66, 69–71

STANTON, G. (1994), 'Early Objections to the Resurrection of Jesus', in *Resurrection: Essays in Honour of Leslie Houlden*, ed. by S. C. Barton and G. Stanton, London: Society for Promoting Christian Knowledge, pp. 79–94

STEINERT, H. (2010), *Max Webers unwiderlegbare Fehlkonstruktionen: Die protestantische Ethik und der Geist des Kapitalismus*, Frankfurt a. M.: Campus

STEINRÜCK, M. (1992), 'Der Bericht des Proteus', *Quaderni Urbinati di Cultura Classica*, 71: 47–60

STEINTRAGER, J. (2012), 'Oscillate and Reflect: La Mettrie, Materialist Physiology and the Revival of the Epicurean Canon' in *Dynamic Reading: Studies in the Reception of Epicureanism*, ed. by B. Holmes, Oxford: Oxford University Press, pp. 162–98

STERN, J. (1996), Περὶ ἀπίστων. *On Unbelievable Tales: Translation, Introduction and Commentary* (with notes and Greek text from the 1902 B. G. Teubner edition), Wauconda, IL: Bolchazy-Carducci Publishers

STERN, J. (2002), 'Rationalizing Myth: Methods and Motives in Palaephatus', in *From Myth to Reason? Studies in the Development of Greek Thought*, ed. by R. Buxton (Oxford: Oxford University Press), pp. 215–22

——(2003), 'Heraclitus the Paradoxographer: Περὶ Ἀπίστων, *On Unbelievable Tales*', *Transactions of the American Philological Association*, 133, 51–97

STIERLE, K. (1991), 'Metamorphosen des Mythos: Petrarcas Kanzone "Nel dolce tempo" (*Rime XXIII*)', in *Traditionswandel und Traditionverhalten*, ed. by W. Haug and B. Wachinger, Tübingen: Max Niemeyer, pp. 24–45

——(2003), *Francesco Petrarca: Ein Intellektueller im Europa des 14. Jahrhunderts*, Munich and Vienna: Carl Hanser Verlag

STOICHITA, V. I. (2008), *The Pygmalion Effect: From Ovid to Hitchcock*, trans. by A. Anderson, Chicago, IL: University of Chicago Press

STRAUSS-CLAY, J. (1997), *The Wrath of Athena: Gods and Men in the Odyssey*, Lanham: Rowman & Littlefield

STURM-MADDOX, S. (1985), *Petrarch's Metamorphoses: Text and Subtext in the 'Rime Sparse'*, Columbia: University of Missouri Press

SUBIRÓS, P. (ed.) (2009), *Jane Alexander on Being Human*, Durham: Institute of Advanced Study and Durham University

SUBIRÓS, P. (ed.) (2011), *Jane Alexander Surveys (from the Cape of Good Hope)*, New York: Museum for African Art; Barcelona: Actar

SUERBAUM, W. (ed.) (2002), *Handbuch der lateinischen Literatur der Antike, vol. 1: die archaische Literatur. Von den Anfängen bis Sullas Tod. Die vorliterarische Periode und die Zeit von 240 bis 78 v. Chr.* (= Handbuch der Altertumswissenschaften, VIII.1), Munich: C. H. Beck

SUMMERS, M. (1926), *The History of Witchcraft and Demonology*, London: K. Paul, Trench, Trubner & Co.

SUTTON, D. F. (1979), *Sophocles' Inachus*, Meisenheim am Glan: Hain

SUVIN, D. (1979), *Metamorphoses of Science Fiction: On the Poetics and History of a Literary Genre*, New Haven, CT, and London: Yale University Press

SWEENEY, K. W. (1990), 'Competing Theories of Identity in Kafka's *The Metamorphosis*', *Mosaic*, 23, 23–35

SWINBURNE, R. (1994), *The Christian God*, Oxford: Oxford University Press

TATAR, M. (1987), *The Hard Facts of Grimms' Fairy-tales*, Princeton, NJ: Princeton University Press

TATEO, F. (1995), 'Ovidio nell'*Urania* di Pontano', in *Aetates Ovidianae: Lettori di Ovidio dall'antichità al Rinascimento. Atti del Convegno di Salerno e Fisciano, 25–27 gennaio 1992*, ed. by I. Gallo and L. Nicastri, Naples: Edizioni scientifiche italiane, pp. 279–91

TAYLOR, D. (1993), *The Novels of World War Two*, New York and London: Garland

TELLE, J. (1980), 'Mythologie und Alchemie: Zum Fortleben der antiken Götter in der frühneuzeitlichen Alchemieliteratur', *Humanismus und Naturwissenschaften* (= Beiträge zur Humanismusforschung, VI), ed. by R. Schmitz and F. Krafft, Boldt, pp. 135–54

TEUFFEL, W. S. (1870), *Geschichte der römischen Literatur*, Leipzig: B. G. Teubner

THOMAS, K. (1971), *Religion and the Decline of Magic*, New York: Scribner's

THOMAS, R. F. (ed.) (1988), Virgil, *Georgics*, 2 vols Cambridge: Cambridge University Press

THOMPSON, D. W. (1947), *A Glossary of Greek Fishes*, London: Oxford University Press

THORNDIKE, L. (1923–58), *History of Magic and Experimental Science*, 8 vols, New York: Macmillan

TISSOL, G. (1997), *The Face of Nature: Wit, Narrative, and Cosmic Origins in Ovid's Metamorphoses*, Princeton, NJ: Princeton University Press

TISSONI BENVENUTI, A. (1979), 'Schede per una storia della poesia pastorale nel secolo XV: La scuola Guariniana a Ferrara', in *In ricordo di Cesare Angelini. Studi di letteratura e filologia*, ed. by F. Alessio and A. Stella, Milan: Il saggiatore, pp. 96–131

——(2000), *L'Orfeo del Poliziano. Con il testo critico dell'originale e delle successive forme teatrali*, Rome: Antenore (1st edn 1986)

TODOROV, T. (1970), *Introduction à la littérature fantastique*, Paris: Seuil

TOLKOWSKY, S. (1938), *Hesperides: A History of the Culture and Use of Citrus Fruits*, London: J. Bale & Co

TOMLINSON, C. (1983), *Poetry and Metamorphosis*, Cambridge: Cambridge University Press

TORNAU, C. (2008), '*Mens antiqua manet* oder Wie es ist, eine Bärin zu sein', in *Mensch und Tier in der Antike: Grenzziehung und Grenzüberschreitung. Symposion vom 7. bis 9. April 2005 in Rostock*, ed. by A. Alexandridis, M. Wild and L. Winkler-Horacek, Wiesbaden: Reichert, pp. 243–61

TORTZEN, C. G. (1991), 'Male and Female in Peripatetic Botany', *Classica et Mediaevalia*, 42, 81–110

TRAPP, M. B. (2001), 'On Tickling the Ears: Apuleius' Prologue and the Anxieties of Philosophers', in *A Companion to the Prologue of Apuleius' Metamorphoses*, ed. by A. Kahane and A. Laird, Oxford: Oxford University Press, pp. 39–63

TREGUNNA, D., and T. PICKERAL (eds) (2009), *Being Human: Paintings by Chris Gollon*, Durham and London: The Institute of Advanced Study and IAP Fine Art

TRITTER, V. (2001), *Le Fantastique*, Paris: Ellipses

TSUTSUI, W. (2007), 'Looking Straight at *Them!*: Understanding the Big Bug Movies of the 1950s', *Environmental History*, 12.2, 237–53

TUMLISON, R. (1987), '*Felix lynx*', *Mammalian Species*, 269, 1–8

TUNBERG, T. O. (1987), 'Conrad of Hirsau and his Approach to the "Auctores"', *Medievalia et Humanistica*, 15, 65–94

TUPET, A.-M. (1986), 'Rites magiques dans l'Antiquité romaine', *Aufstieg und Niedergang der Römischen Welt*, 2.16.3, pp. 2591–2675

TUZET, H. (1987), *Mort et résurrection d'Adonis: Étude de l'évolution d'un mythe*, Paris: Corti

ULRICH, J., A.-C. JACOBSEN and M. KAHLOS (eds) (2009), *Continuity and Discontinuity in Early Christian Apologetics* (= Early Christianity in the Context of Antiquity 5), Frankfurt am Main: Peter Lang

VALENTE, M. (2003), *Johann Wier*, Florence: Olschki

VAN DER PAARDT, R. TH. (1981), 'The Unmasked "I": *Met.* XI 27', *Mnemosyne*, 34, 96–106

VANOTTI, G. (2007), Aristotele, *Racconti Meravigliosi*, with introduction, translation, notes and apparati, Milan: Bompiani

VEENSTRA, J. R. (2002), 'The Ever-Changing Nature of the Beast: Cultural Change, Lycanthropy and the Question of Substantial Transformation (From Petronius to Del Rio)', in *The Metamorphosis of Magic from Late Antiquity to the Early Modern Period*, ed. by J. N. Bremmer & J. R. Veenstra, Leuven, Paris, Dudley, MA: Peeters, pp. 133–66

VELZ, J. W. (1985), 'Topoi in Edward Ravenscroft's Indictment of Shakespeare's *Titus Andronicus*', *Modern Philology*, 83.1, 45–50

VERDUCCI, F. (1985), *Ovid's Toyshop of the Heart: Epistulae Heroidum*, Princeton, NJ: Princeton University Press

VERMES, G. (2008), *The Resurrection*, London: Penguin Books

VERMEULE, E. (1979), *Aspects of Death in Early Greek Art and Poetry*, Berkeley and Los Angeles: University of California Press

VERNANT, J. P. (1965), 'Figuration de l'invisible et catégorie psychologique du double: Le Kolossos', in *Mythe et Pensée chez les Grecs: Études de psychologie historique*, Paris: Maspero, pp. 165–78

——(1985), *La Mort dans les yeux: Figures de l'Autre dans la Grèce ancienne*, Paris: Hachette

——(1991), 'La Mort dans les yeux', *Métis: Anthropologie des mondes grecs anciens*, 6, 283–99

VERNER, L. (2005), *The Epistemology of the Monstrous in the Middle Ages*, New York and London: Routledge

VEYNE, P. (1983), *Did the Greeks Believe in Their Myths?*, trans. by P. Wissing, Chicago, IL, and London: University of Chicago Press

VIAL, H. (2010), *La Métamorphose dans les Métamorphoses d'Ovide: Études sur l'art de la variation*, Paris: Belles Lettres

VICKERS, B. (1988), *In Defence of Rhetoric*, Oxford: Clarendon Press

VOELKE-VISCARDI, G. (2001), 'Les Gemmes dans l' *Histoire Naturelle* de Pline l'Ancien: Discours et Modes de Fonctionnement de l'Univers', *Museum Helveticum*, 58.2, 99–122

VOLKMANN, R. (1852), *De Nicandri Colophonii vita et scriptis*, Halle

WAEGEMAN, M. (1987), *Amulet and Alphabet: Magical Amulets in the First Book of Cyranides*, Amsterdam: J. C. Gieben

WALKER, D. P. (1958), *Spiritual and Demonic Magic from Ficino to Campanella*, London: Warburg Institute, University of London

WALL, K. (1988), *The Callisto Myth from Ovid to Atwood: Initiation and Rape in Literature*, Kingston, Ont.: McGill-Queen's University Press

WALSH, P. G. (1995), *The Satyricon; Translated with Introduction and Explanatory Notes*, Oxford: Clarendon Press

WALSHAM, A. (2008), 'The Reformation and the "Disenchantment of the World" Reassessed', *The Historical Journal*, 51, 497–528

WALTON, S. A. (2001), 'Theophrastus on Lyngurium: Medieval and Early Modern Lore from the Classical Lapidary Tradition', *Annals of Science*, 58, 357–79

WARNER, M. (1994), *From the Beast to the Blonde*, New York: Farrar, Straus and Giroux

——(2002), *Fantastic Metamorphoses, Other Worlds: Ways of Telling the Self*, Oxford: Oxford University Press

WATSON, W. (1759–60), 'Some Observations Relating to the Lyncurium of the Ancients', *Philosophical Transactions*, 51, 394–98

WEBB, R. (2005), 'The Protean Performer: Mimesis and Identity in Late Antique Discussions of the Theater', in *Performing Ecstasies: Music, Dance, and Ritual in the Mediterranean*, ed. by L. Del Guidice and N. Van Deusen, Ottawa: Institute of Medieval Music, pp. 3–11

WEISS, G. (1999), *Body Images: Embodiment as Intercorporality*, London: Routledge

WELTECKE, D. (2010), *'Der Narr spricht: Es ist kein Gott'. Atheismus, Unglauben und Glaubenszweifel vom 12. Jahrhundert bis zur Neuzeit*, Frankfurt a. M.: Campus Verlag

WEST, M. L. (1966), *Hesiod, Theogony, edited with prolegomena and commentary*, Oxford: Clarendon Press

——(1985), *The Hesiodic Catalogue of Women: Its Nature, Structure, and Origins*, Oxford: Oxford University Press

——(1997), *The East Face of Helicon: West Asiatic Elements in Early Poetry and Myth*, Oxford: Oxford University Press

WESTERMANN, A. (ed.) (1839), *Paradoxographoi: Scriptores rerum mirabilium Graeci*, London

WETHERBEE, W. (2008), *The Ancient Flame: Dante and the Poets*, Notre Dame, IN: University of Notre Dame Press

WHEELER, S. M. (1999), *A Discourse of Wonders: Audience and Performance in Ovid's Metamorphoses*, Philadelphia: University of Pennsylvania Press

——(2002), 'Ovid's *Metamorphoses* and Universal History', in *Clio and the Poets: Augustan Poetry and the Traditions of Ancient Historiography*, ed. by D. S. Levene and D. Nelis, Leiden: Brill, pp. 163–90

WHITBREAD, L. G. (1972), 'Conrad of Hirsau as Literary Critic', *Speculum*, 47, 234–45

WHITLEY, D. (2008), *The Idea of Nature in Disney Animation*, Aldershot: Ashgate

WHITMAN, J. (1987), *Allegory: The Dynamics of an Ancient and Medieval Technique*, Oxford and Cambridge, MA: Clarendon Press and Oxford University Press

WHITMAN, J. (2003), *Interpretation and Allegory: Antiquity to the Modern Period*, Leiden: Brill

WHITMARSH, T. (2005), *The Second Sophistic*, Cambridge: Cambridge University Press

WHITTAKER, C. R. (2004), *Rome and its Frontiers: The Dynamics of Empire*, London and New York: Routledge

WILKINSON, L. P. (1955), *Ovid Recalled*, Cambridge: Cambridge University Press

WILLARD, T. (2007), 'The Metamorphoses of Metals: Ovid and the Alchemists', in *Metamorphosis: The Changing Face of Ovid in Medieval and Early Modern Europe*, ed. by A. Keith and S. Rupp, Toronto: Centre for Reformation and Renaissance Studies, pp. 151–63

WILLIAMS, K. (2007), *H. G. Wells, Modernity and the Movies*, Liverpool: Liverpool University Press

WINIARCZYK, M. (1994), 'Ennius' *Euhemerus sive Sacra historia*', *Rheinisches Museum*, 137, 274–91

——(2002), *Euhemeros von Messene: Leben, Werk und Nachwirkung*, Munich and Leipzig: K. G. Saur Verlag

WINKLER, J. J. (1985), *Auctor & Actor: A Narratological Reading of Apuleius's Golden Ass*, Berkeley: University of California Press

WISE, V. (1982), 'Ovid's Medea and the Magic of Language', *Ramus*, 11, 16–25

WISEMAN, T. P. (1998), *Roman Drama and Roman History*, Exeter: Exeter University Press

——(2004), *The Myths of Rome*, Exeter: Exeter University Press

WISKER, G. (2005), *Horror Fiction: An Introduction*, New York and London: Continuum

WOHLMUTH, J. (2002), 'Eucharistie als liturgische Feier der Gegenwart Jesu Christi: Realpräsenz und Transsubstantiation im Verständnis katholischer Theologie', in *Eucharistie. Positionen katholischer Theologie*, ed. by T. Söding, Regensburg: Pustet, pp. 87–119

WOLFE, C. (2010), *What is Posthumanism?*, Minneapolis: University of Minnesota Press

WOOWARD, I. (1979), *The Werewolf Delusion*, New York and London: Paddington Press

YARNALL, J. (1994), *The Transformations of Circe: The History of an Enchantress*, Urbana: University of Illinois Press

YATES, F. A. (1992), *The Art of Memory*, London: Pimlico

ZABUGHIN, V. (2000), *Vergilio nel Rinascimento italiano da Dante a Torquato Tasso* (1st edn 1921–23), ed. by S. Carrai and A. Cavarzere, introduction by A. Campana, 2 vols, Trento: Università degli Studi

ZACCARIA, V. (2001), *Boccaccio narratore, storico, moralista e mitografo*, Florence: Olschki

ZAMBELLI, P. (1991), 'L'immaginazione e il suo potere: Desiderio e fantasia psicosomatica o transitiva', in ead., *L'ambigua natura della magia*, Milan: Il Saggiatore, pp. 53–75

——(2007), *White Magic, Black Magic in the European Renaissance: From Ficino, Pico, Della Porta to Trithemius, Agrippa, Bruno*, Leiden and Boston: Brill

ZANOBI, A. (2008), *Seneca's Tragedies and the Aesthetics of Pantomime* (doctoral dissertation, University of Durham); available online at <http://etheses.dur.ac.uk/2158/>

ZATTA, C. (1997), *Incontri con Proteo*, Venice: Istituto Veneto di Scienze, Lettere e Arti

ZIEGLER, K. (1949), 'Paradoxographoi', in *Realencyclopädie*, XVIII. 3, 1137–66

ZIKA, C. (2002), 'Images of Circe and Discourses of Witchcraft, 1480–1580', *zeitenblicke*, 1.1, <http://www.zeitenblicke.historicum.net/2002/01/zika/zika.html>

ZIMMERMAN, M. (2000), *Apuleius Madaurensis: Metamorphoses, Book X: Text, Introduction and Commentary*, Groningen Commentaries on Apuleius, Groningen: Egbert Forsten

ZIMMERMANN, H. D. (2008), '"Die Götter Griechenlands". Zu Friedrich Schiller und Friedrich Hölderlin', in *Schiller und die Antike*, ed. by P. Chiarini and W. Hinderer, Würzburg: Königshausen & Neumann, pp. 75–89

ZIOLKOWSKI, T. (2005), *Ovid and the Moderns*, Ithaca, NY: Cornell University Press

ZIOGAS, I. (2011), 'Ovid as a Hesiodic Poet: Atalanta in the *Catalogue of Women* (fr. 72–6 M–W) and the *Metamorphoses* (10.560–707)', *Mnemosyne*, 64, 249–70

ZIRKEL, P. M. (1994), 'The Ninth Century Eucharistic Controversy: A Context for the Beginnings of the Eucharistic Doctrine in the West', *Worship*, 68 (January), 2–23

ZIPES, J. (1979), *Breaking the Magic Spell: Radical Theories of Folk and Fairy Tales*, London: Heinemann

——(1991), *Fairy Tales and the Art of Subversion*, London: Heinemann

ZISSOS, A. (1999), 'The Rape of Proserpina in Ovid *Met.* 5.341–661: Internal Audience and Narrative Distortion', *Phoenix*, 53, 97–113

——(2008), *Valerius Flaccus: Argonautica Book 1. A Commentary*, Oxford: Oxford University Press

ZGOLL, C. (2004), *Phänomenologie der Metamorphose: Verwandlungen und Verwandtes in der augusteischen Dichtung*, Tübingen: G. Narr

ZUFFI, S. (2008), *Love and the Erotic in Art*, Los Angeles: Getty Publications

Index 1
Names, Concepts and Themes

*Note: writers and artists who are discussed principally
in terms of their writing or artwork are listed in more detail
in* INDEX II, *as are directors and their films.*

Index II
Authors, Artists, Directors and their Works

Note: works of uncertain attribution are listed by title, unless they are associated with a particular author (such as the Prometheus Bound, *traditionally credited to Aeschylus). Pseudonymous works are listed after the regular entries of the author with whom they are associated. Films are listed under the director's name, but are also searchable by title.*